MASSACHUSETTS
RULES OF COURT

VOLUME II – FEDERAL

2012

WEST®

A Thomson Reuters business

Mat#41130385

ISBN: 978–0–314–94296–8

PREFACE

This edition of the *Massachusetts Rules of Court, Volume II – Federal, 2012*, replaces the 2011 edition and any accompanying supplement(s). This volume provides in convenient form court rules governing federal practice in Massachusetts and is current with amendments received through January 1, 2012.

THE PUBLISHER

February 2012

ADDITIONAL INFORMATION OR RESEARCH ASSISTANCE

For additional information or research assistance call the West reference attorneys at 1-800-REF-ATTY (1-800-733-2889). Contact West's editorial department directly with your questions and suggestions by e-mail at west.editor@thomson.com.

Visit West's home page at west.thomson.com.

WestlawNext™

THE NEXT GENERATION OF ONLINE RESEARCH

WestlawNext is the world's most advanced legal research system. By leveraging more than a century of information and legal analysis from Westlaw, this easy-to-use system not only helps you find the information you need quickly, but offers time-saving tools to organize and annotate your research online. As with Westlaw.com, WestlawNext includes the editorial enhancements (e.g., case headnotes, topics, key numbers) that make it a perfect complement to West print resources.

- FIND ANYTHING by entering citations, descriptive terms, or Boolean terms and connectors into the WestSearch™ box at the top of every page.

- USE KEYCITE® to determine whether a case, statute, regulation, or administrative decision is good law.

- BROWSE DATABASES right from the home page.

- SAVE DOCUMENTS to folders and add notes and highlighting online.

SIGN ON: next.westlaw.com
LEARN MORE: West.Thomson.com/WestlawNext
FOR HELP: 1–800–WESTLAW (1–800–937–8529)

*

TABLE OF CONTENTS

*

FEDERAL
RULES OF CIVIL PROCEDURE
FOR THE
UNITED STATES DISTRICT COURTS

Effective September 16, 1938

Including Amendments Effective December 1, 2010

Research Note

These rules may be searched electronically on Westlaw in the US-RULES database; updates to these rules may be found on Westlaw in US-RULESPDATES. For search tips, and a detailed summary of database content, consult the Westlaw Scope Screen of each database.

TITLE I. SCOPE OF RULES; FORM OF ACTION

RULE 1. SCOPE AND PURPOSE

These rules govern the procedure in all civil actions and proceedings in the United States district courts, except as stated in Rule 81. They should be construed and administered to secure the just, speedy, and inexpensive determination of every action and proceeding.

(Amended December 29, 1948, effective October 20, 1949; February 28, 1966, effective July 1, 1966; April 22, 1993, effective December 1, 1993; April 30, 2007, effective December 1, 2007.)

RULE 2. ONE FORM OF ACTION

There is one form of action—the civil action.

(Amended April 30, 2007, effective December 1, 2007.)

TITLE II. COMMENCING AN ACTION; SERVICE OF PROCESS, PLEADINGS, MOTIONS, AND ORDERS

RULE 3. COMMENCING AN ACTION

A civil action is commenced by filing a complaint with the court.

(Amended April 30, 2007, effective December 1, 2007.)

RULE 4. SUMMONS

(a) Contents; Amendments.

  (1) *Contents.* A summons must:

    (A) name the court and the parties;

    (B) be directed to the defendant;

    (C) state the name and address of the plaintiff's attorney or—if unrepresented—of the plaintiff;

    (D) state the time within which the defendant must appear and defend;

    (E) notify the defendant that a failure to appear and defend will result in a default judgment against the defendant for the relief demanded in the complaint;

    (F) be signed by the clerk; and

    (G) bear the court's seal.

  (2) *Amendments.* The court may permit a summons to be amended.

(b) Issuance. On or after filing the complaint, the plaintiff may present a summons to the clerk for signature and seal. If the summons is properly completed, the clerk must sign, seal, and issue it to the plaintiff for service on the defendant. A summons—or a copy of a summons that is addressed to multiple defendants—must be issued for each defendant to be served.

(c) Service.

  (1) *In General.* A summons must be served with a copy of the complaint. The plaintiff is responsible for having the summons and complaint served within the time allowed by Rule 4(m) and must furnish the necessary copies to the person who makes service.

  (2) *By Whom.* Any person who is at least 18 years old and not a party may serve a summons and complaint.

  (3) *By a Marshal or Someone Specially Appointed.* At the plaintiff's request, the court may order that service be made by a United States marshal or deputy marshal or by a person specially appointed by the court. The court must so order if the plaintiff is authorized to proceed in forma pauperis under 28 U.S.C. § 1915 or as a seaman under 28 U.S.C. § 1916.

(d) Waiving Service.

  (1) *Requesting a Waiver.* An individual, corporation, or association that is subject to service under Rule 4(e), (f), or (h) has a duty to avoid unnecessary expenses of serving the summons. The plaintiff may notify such a defendant that an action has been commenced and request that the defendant waive service of a summons. The notice and request must:

(A) be in writing and be addressed:

 (i) to the individual defendant; or

 (ii) for a defendant subject to service under Rule 4(h), to an officer, a managing or general agent, or any other agent authorized by appointment or by law to receive service of process;

(B) name the court where the complaint was filed;

(C) be accompanied by a copy of the complaint, two copies of a waiver form, and a prepaid means for returning the form;

(D) inform the defendant, using text prescribed in Form 5, of the consequences of waiving and not waiving service;

(E) state the date when the request is sent;

(F) give the defendant a reasonable time of at least 30 days after the request was sent—or at least 60 days if sent to the defendant outside any judicial district of the United States—to return the waiver; and

(G) be sent by first-class mail or other reliable means.

(2) *Failure to Waive.* If a defendant located within the United States fails, without good cause, to sign and return a waiver requested by a plaintiff located within the United States, the court must impose on the defendant:

(A) the expenses later incurred in making service; and

(B) the reasonable expenses, including attorney's fees, of any motion required to collect those service expenses.

(3) *Time to Answer After a Waiver.* A defendant who, before being served with process, timely returns a waiver need not serve an answer to the complaint until 60 days after the request was sent—or until 90 days after it was sent to the defendant outside any judicial district of the United States.

(4) *Results of Filing a Waiver.* When the plaintiff files a waiver, proof of service is not required and these rules apply as if a summons and complaint had been served at the time of filing the waiver.

(5) *Jurisdiction and Venue Not Waived.* Waiving service of a summons does not waive any objection to personal jurisdiction or to venue.

(e) Serving an Individual Within a Judicial District of the United States. Unless federal law provides otherwise, an individual—other than a minor, an incompetent person, or a person whose waiver has been filed—may be served in a judicial district of the United States by:

(1) following state law for serving a summons in an action brought in courts of general jurisdiction in the state where the district court is located or where service is made; or

(2) doing any of the following:

 (A) delivering a copy of the summons and of the complaint to the individual personally;

 (B) leaving a copy of each at the individual's dwelling or usual place of abode with someone of suitable age and discretion who resides there; or

 (C) delivering a copy of each to an agent authorized by appointment or by law to receive service of process.

(f) Serving an Individual in a Foreign Country. Unless federal law provides otherwise, an individual—other than a minor, an incompetent person, or a person whose waiver has been filed—may be served at a place not within any judicial district of the United States:

(1) by any internationally agreed means of service that is reasonably calculated to give notice, such as those authorized by the Hague Convention on the Service Abroad of Judicial and Extrajudicial Documents;

(2) if there is no internationally agreed means, or if an international agreement allows but does not specify other means, by a method that is reasonably calculated to give notice:

 (A) as prescribed by the foreign country's law for service in that country in an action in its courts of general jurisdiction;

 (B) as the foreign authority directs in response to a letter rogatory or letter of request; or

 (C) unless prohibited by the foreign country's law, by:

  (i) delivering a copy of the summons and of the complaint to the individual personally; or

  (ii) using any form of mail that the clerk addresses and sends to the individual and that requires a signed receipt; or

(3) by other means not prohibited by international agreement, as the court orders.

(g) Serving a Minor or an Incompetent Person. A minor or an incompetent person in a judicial district of the United States must be served by following state law for serving a summons or like process on such a defendant in an action brought in the courts of general jurisdiction of the state where service is made. A minor or an incompetent person who is not within any judicial district of the United States must be served in the manner prescribed by Rule 4(f)(2)(A), (f)(2)(B), or (f)(3).

(h) Serving a Corporation, Partnership, or Association. Unless federal law provides otherwise or the defendant's waiver has been filed, a domestic or foreign corporation, or a partnership or other unincorporated association that is subject to suit under a common name, must be served:

  (1) in a judicial district of the United States:

    (A) in the manner prescribed by Rule 4(e)(1) for serving an individual; or

    (B) by delivering a copy of the summons and of the complaint to an officer, a managing or general agent, or any other agent authorized by appointment or by law to receive service of process and—if the agent is one authorized by statute and the statute so requires—by also mailing a copy of each to the defendant; or

  (2) at a place not within any judicial district of the United States, in any manner prescribed by Rule 4(f) for serving an individual, except personal delivery under (f)(2)(C)(i).

(i) Serving the United States and Its Agencies, Corporations, Officers, or Employees.

  (1) *United States.* To serve the United States, a party must:

    (A)(i) deliver a copy of the summons and of the complaint to the United States attorney for the district where the action is brought—or to an assistant United States attorney or clerical employee whom the United States attorney designates in a writing filed with the court clerk—or

      (ii) send a copy of each by registered or certified mail to the civil-process clerk at the United States attorney's office;

    (B) send a copy of each by registered or certified mail to the Attorney General of the United States at Washington, D.C.; and

    (C) if the action challenges an order of a nonparty agency or officer of the United States, send a copy of each by registered or certified mail to the agency or officer.

  (2) *Agency; Corporation; Officer or Employee Sued in an Official Capacity.* To serve a United States agency or corporation, or a United States officer or employee sued only in an official capacity, a party must serve the United States and also send a copy of the summons and of the complaint by registered or certified mail to the agency, corporation, officer, or employee.

  (3) *Officer or Employee Sued Individually.* To serve a United States officer or employee sued in an individual capacity for an act or omission occurring in connection with duties performed on the United States' behalf (whether or not the officer or employee is also sued in an official capacity), a party must serve the United States and also serve the officer or employee under Rule 4(e), (f), or (g).

  (4) *Extending Time.* The court must allow a party a reasonable time to cure its failure to:

    (A) serve a person required to be served under Rule 4(i)(2), if the party has served either the United States attorney or the Attorney General of the United States; or

    (B) serve the United States under Rule 4(i)(3), if the party has served the United States officer or employee.

(j) Serving a Foreign, State, or Local Government.

  (1) *Foreign State.* A foreign state or its political subdivision, agency, or instrumentality must be served in accordance with 28 U.S.C. § 1608.

  (2) *State or Local Government.* A state, a municipal corporation, or any other state-created governmental organization that is subject to suit must be served by:

    (A) delivering a copy of the summons and of the complaint to its chief executive officer; or

    (B) serving a copy of each in the manner prescribed by that state's law for serving a summons or like process on such a defendant.

(k) Territorial Limits of Effective Service.

  (1) *In General.* Serving a summons or filing a waiver of service establishes personal jurisdiction over a defendant:

    (A) who is subject to the jurisdiction of a court of general jurisdiction in the state where the district court is located;

    (B) who is a party joined under Rule 14 or 19 and is served within a judicial district of the United States and not more than 100 miles from where the summons was issued; or

    (C) when authorized by a federal statute.

  (2) *Federal Claim Outside State–Court Jurisdiction.* For a claim that arises under federal law, serving a summons or filing a waiver of service establishes personal jurisdiction over a defendant if:

    (A) the defendant is not subject to jurisdiction in any state's courts of general jurisdiction; and

    (B) exercising jurisdiction is consistent with the United States Constitution and laws.

(l) Proving Service.

  (1) *Affidavit Required.* Unless service is waived, proof of service must be made to the court. Except for service by a United States marshal or deputy marshal, proof must be by the server's affidavit.

   (2) *Service Outside the United States.* Service not within any judicial district of the United States must be proved as follows:

     (A) if made under Rule 4(f)(1), as provided in the applicable treaty or convention; or

     (B) if made under Rule 4(f)(2) or (f)(3), by a receipt signed by the addressee, or by other evidence satisfying the court that the summons and complaint were delivered to the addressee.

   (3) *Validity of Service; Amending Proof.* Failure to prove service does not affect the validity of service. The court may permit proof of service to be amended.

(m) Time Limit for Service. If a defendant is not served within 120 days after the complaint is filed, the court—on motion or on its own after notice to the plaintiff—must dismiss the action without prejudice against that defendant or order that service be made within a specified time. But if the plaintiff shows good cause for the failure, the court must extend the time for service for an appropriate period. This subdivision (m) does not apply to service in a foreign country under Rule 4(f) or 4(j)(1).

(n) Asserting Jurisdiction over Property or Assets.

   (1) *Federal Law.* The court may assert jurisdiction over property if authorized by a federal statute. Notice to claimants of the property must be given as provided in the statute or by serving a summons under this rule.

   (2) *State Law.* On a showing that personal jurisdiction over a defendant cannot be obtained in the district where the action is brought by reasonable efforts to serve a summons under this rule, the court may assert jurisdiction over the defendant's assets found in the district. Jurisdiction is acquired by seizing the assets under the circumstances and in the manner provided by state law in that district.

(Amended January 21, 1963, effective July 1, 1963; February 28, 1966, effective July 1, 1966; April 29, 1980, effective August 1, 1980; amended by Pub.L. 97-462, § 2, January 12, 1983, 96 Stat. 2527, effective 45 days after January 12, 1983; amended March 2, 1987, effective August 1, 1987; April 22, 1993, effective December 1, 1993; April 17, 2000, effective December 1, 2000; April 30, 2007, effective December 1, 2007.)

RULE 4.1. SERVING OTHER PROCESS

(a) In General. Process—other than a summons under Rule 4 or a subpoena under Rule 45—must be served by a United States marshal or deputy marshal or by a person specially appointed for that purpose. It may be served anywhere within the territorial limits of the state where the district court is located and, if authorized by a federal statute, beyond those limits. Proof of service must be made under Rule 4(*l*).

(b) Enforcing Orders: Committing for Civil Contempt. An order committing a person for civil contempt of a decree or injunction issued to enforce federal law may be served and enforced in any district. Any other order in a civil-contempt proceeding may be served only in the state where the issuing court is located or elsewhere in the United States within 100 miles from where the order was issued.

(Adopted April 22, 1993, effective December 1, 1993; amended April 30, 2007, effective December 1, 2007.)

RULE 5. SERVING AND FILING PLEADINGS AND OTHER PAPERS

(a) Service: When Required.

   (1) *In General.* Unless these rules provide otherwise, each of the following papers must be served on every party:

     (A) an order stating that service is required;

     (B) a pleading filed after the original complaint, unless the court orders otherwise under Rule 5(c) because there are numerous defendants;

     (C) a discovery paper required to be served on a party, unless the court orders otherwise;

     (D) a written motion, except one that may be heard ex parte; and

     (E) a written notice, appearance, demand, or offer of judgment, or any similar paper.

   (2) *If a Party Fails to Appear.* No service is required on a party who is in default for failing to appear. But a pleading that asserts a new claim for relief against such a party must be served on that party under Rule 4.

   (3) *Seizing Property.* If an action is begun by seizing property and no person is or need be named as a defendant, any service required before the filing of an appearance, answer, or claim must be made on the person who had custody or possession of the property when it was seized.

(b) Service: How Made.

   (1) *Serving an Attorney.* If a party is represented by an attorney, service under this rule must be made on the attorney unless the court orders service on the party.

   (2) *Service in General.* A paper is served under this rule by:

     (A) handing it to the person;

(B) leaving it:

    (i) at the person's office with a clerk or other person in charge or, if no one is in charge, in a conspicuous place in the office; or

    (ii) if the person has no office or the office is closed, at the person's dwelling or usual place of abode with someone of suitable age and discretion who resides there;

(C) mailing it to the person's last known address—in which event service is complete upon mailing;

(D) leaving it with the court clerk if the person has no known address;

(E) sending it by electronic means if the person consented in writing—in which event service is complete upon transmission, but is not effective if the serving party learns that it did not reach the person to be served; or

(F) delivering it by any other means that the person consented to in writing—in which event service is complete when the person making service delivers it to the agency designated to make delivery.

(3) *Using Court Facilities.* If a local rule so authorizes, a party may use the court's transmission facilities to make service under Rule 5(b)(2)(E).

(c) Serving Numerous Defendants.

(1) *In General.* If an action involves an unusually large number of defendants, the court may, on motion or on its own, order that:

(A) defendants' pleadings and replies to them need not be served on other defendants;

(B) any crossclaim, counterclaim, avoidance, or affirmative defense in those pleadings and replies to them will be treated as denied or avoided by all other parties; and

(C) filing any such pleading and serving it on the plaintiff constitutes notice of the pleading to all parties.

(2) *Notifying Parties.* A copy of every such order must be served on the parties as the court directs.

(d) Filing.

(1) *Required Filings; Certificate of Service.* Any paper after the complaint that is required to be served—together with a certificate of service—must be filed within a reasonable time after service. But disclosures under Rule 26(a)(1) or (2) and the following discovery requests and responses must not be filed until they are used in the proceeding or the court orders filing: depositions, interrogatories, requests for documents or tangible things or to permit entry onto land, and requests for admission.

(2) *How Filing Is Made—In General.* A paper is filed by delivering it:

(A) to the clerk; or

(B) to a judge who agrees to accept it for filing, and who must then note the filing date on the paper and promptly send it to the clerk.

(3) *Electronic Filing, Signing, or Verification.* A court may, by local rule, allow papers to be filed, signed, or verified by electronic means that are consistent with any technical standards established by the Judicial Conference of the United States. A local rule may require electronic filing only if reasonable exceptions are allowed. A paper filed electronically in compliance with a local rule is a written paper for purposes of these rules.

(4) *Acceptance by the Clerk.* The clerk must not refuse to file a paper solely because it is not in the form prescribed by these rules or by a local rule or practice.

(Amended January 21, 1963, effective July 1, 1963; March 30, 1970, effective July 1, 1970; April 29, 1980, effective August 1, 1980; March 2, 1987, effective August 1, 1987; April 30, 1991, effective December 1, 1991; April 22, 1993, effective December 1, 1993; April 23, 1996, effective December 1, 1996; April 17, 2000, effective December 1, 2000; April 23, 2001, effective December 1, 2001; April 12, 2006, effective December 1, 2006; April 30, 2007, effective December 1, 2007.)

RULE 5.1. CONSTITUTIONAL CHALLENGE TO A STATUTE—NOTICE, CERTIFICATION, AND INTERVENTION

(a) Notice by a Party. A party that files a pleading, written motion, or other paper drawing into question the constitutionality of a federal or state statute must promptly:

(1) file a notice of constitutional question stating the question and identifying the paper that raises it, if:

(A) a federal statute is questioned and the parties do not include the United States, one of its agencies, or one of its officers or employees in an official capacity; or

(B) a state statute is questioned and the parties do not include the state, one of its agencies, or one of its officers or employees in an official capacity; and

(2) serve the notice and paper on the Attorney General of the United States if a federal statute is questioned—or on the state attorney general if a state statute is questioned—either by certified or registered mail or by sending it to an electronic address designated by the attorney general for this purpose.

(b) Certification by the Court. The court must, under 28 U.S.C. § 2403, certify to the appropriate attorney general that a statute has been questioned.

(c) Intervention; Final Decision on the Merits. Unless the court sets a later time, the attorney general may intervene within 60 days after the notice is filed or after the court certifies the challenge, whichever is earlier. Before the time to intervene expires, the court may reject the constitutional challenge, but may not enter a final judgment holding the statute unconstitutional.

(d) No Forfeiture. A party's failure to file and serve the notice, or the court's failure to certify, does not forfeit a constitutional claim or defense that is otherwise timely asserted.

(Adopted April 12, 2006, effective December 1, 2006; amended April 30, 2007, effective December 1, 2007.)

RULE 5.2. PRIVACY PROTECTION FOR FILINGS MADE WITH THE COURT

(a) Redacted Filings. Unless the court orders otherwise, in an electronic or paper filing with the court that contains an individual's social-security number, taxpayer-identification number, or birth date, the name of an individual known to be a minor, or a financial-account number, a party or nonparty making the filing may include only:

(1) the last four digits of the social-security number and taxpayer-identification number;

(2) the year of the individual's birth;

(3) the minor's initials; and

(4) the last four digits of the financial-account number.

(b) Exemptions from the Redaction Requirement. The redaction requirement does not apply to the following:

(1) a financial-account number that identifies the property allegedly subject to forfeiture in a forfeiture proceeding;

(2) the record of an administrative or agency proceeding;

(3) the official record of a state-court proceeding;

(4) the record of a court or tribunal, if that record was not subject to the redaction requirement when originally filed;

(5) a filing covered by Rule 5.2(c) or (d); and

(6) a pro se filing in an action brought under 28 U.S.C. §§ 2241, 2254, or 2255.

(c) Limitations on Remote Access to Electronic Files; Social–Security Appeals and Immigration Cases. Unless the court orders otherwise, in an action for benefits under the Social Security Act, and in an action or proceeding relating to an order of removal, to relief from removal, or to immigration benefits or detention, access to an electronic file is authorized as follows:

(1) the parties and their attorneys may have remote electronic access to any part of the case file, including the administrative record;

(2) any other person may have electronic access to the full record at the courthouse, but may have remote electronic access only to:

(A) the docket maintained by the court; and

(B) an opinion, order, judgment, or other disposition of the court, but not any other part of the case file or the administrative record.

(d) Filings Made Under Seal. The court may order that a filing be made under seal without redaction. The court may later unseal the filing or order the person who made the filing to file a redacted version for the public record.

(e) Protective Orders. For good cause, the court may by order in a case:

(1) require redaction of additional information; or

(2) limit or prohibit a nonparty's remote electronic access to a document filed with the court.

(f) Option for Additional Unredacted Filing Under Seal. A person making a redacted filing may also file an unredacted copy under seal. The court must retain the unredacted copy as part of the record.

(g) Option for Filing a Reference List. A filing that contains redacted information may be filed together with a reference list that identifies each item of redacted information and specifies an appropriate identifier that uniquely corresponds to each item listed. The list must be filed under seal and may be amended as of right. Any reference in the case to a listed identifier will be construed to refer to the corresponding item of information.

(h) Waiver of Protection of Identifiers. A person waives the protection of Rule 5.2(a) as to the person's own information by filing it without redaction and not under seal.

(Adopted April 30, 2007, effective December 1, 2007.)

RULE 6. COMPUTING AND EXTENDING TIME; TIME FOR MOTION PAPERS

(a) Computing Time. The following rules apply in computing any time period specified in these rules, in any local rule or court order, or in any statute that does not specify a method of computing time.

(1) *Period Stated in Days or a Longer Unit.* When the period is stated in days or a longer unit of time:

(A) exclude the day of the event that triggers the period;

(B) count every day, including intermediate Saturdays, Sundays, and legal holidays; and

(C) include the last day of the period, but if the last day is a Saturday, Sunday, or legal holiday, the period continues to run until the end of the next day that is not a Saturday, Sunday, or legal holiday.

(2) *Period Stated in Hours.* When the period is stated in hours:

(A) begin counting immediately on the occurrence of the event that triggers the period;

(B) count every hour, including hours during intermediate Saturdays, Sundays, and legal holidays; and

(C) if the period would end on a Saturday, Sunday, or legal holiday, the period continues to run until the same time on the next day that is not a Saturday, Sunday, or legal holiday.

(3) *Inaccessibility of the Clerk's Office.* Unless the court orders otherwise, if the clerk's office is inaccessible:

(A) on the last day for filing under Rule 6(a)(1), then the time for filing is extended to the first accessible day that is not a Saturday, Sunday, or legal holiday; or

(B) during the last hour for filing under Rule 6(a)(2), then the time for filing is extended to the same time on the first accessible day that is not a Saturday, Sunday, or legal holiday.

(4) *"Last Day" Defined.* Unless a different time is set by a statute, local rule, or court order, the last day ends:

(A) for electronic filing, at midnight in the court's time zone; and

(B) for filing by other means, when the clerk's office is scheduled to close.

(5) *"Next Day" Defined.* The "next day" is determined by continuing to count forward when the period is measured after an event and backward when measured before an event.

(6) *"Legal Holiday" Defined.* "Legal holiday" means:

(A) the day set aside by statute for observing New Year's Day, Martin Luther King Jr.'s Birthday, Washington's Birthday, Memorial Day, Independence Day, Labor Day, Columbus Day, Veterans' Day, Thanksgiving Day, or Christmas Day;

(B) any day declared a holiday by the President or Congress; and

(C) for periods that are measured after an event, any other day declared a holiday by the state where the district court is located.

(b) **Extending Time.**

(1) *In General.* When an act may or must be done within a specified time, the court may, for good cause, extend the time:

(A) with or without motion or notice if the court acts, or if a request is made, before the original time or its extension expires; or

(B) on motion made after the time has expired if the party failed to act because of excusable neglect.

(2) *Exceptions.* A court must not extend the time to act under Rules 50(b) and (d), 52(b), 59(b), (d), and (e), and 60(b).

(c) **Motions, Notices of Hearing, and Affidavits.**

(1) *In General.* A written motion and notice of the hearing must be served at least 14 days before the time specified for the hearing, with the following exceptions:

(A) when the motion may be heard ex parte;

(B) when these rules set a different time; or

(C) when a court order—which a party may, for good cause, apply for ex parte—sets a different time.

(2) *Supporting Affidavit.* Any affidavit supporting a motion must be served with the motion. Except as Rule 59(c) provides otherwise, any opposing affidavit must be served at least 7 days before the hearing, unless the court permits service at another time.

(d) **Additional Time After Certain Kinds of Service.** When a party may or must act within a specified time after service and service is made under Rule 5(b)(2)(C), (D), (E), or (F), 3 days are added after the period would otherwise expire under Rule 6(a).

(Amended December 27, 1946, effective March 19, 1948; January 21, 1963, effective July 1, 1963; February 28, 1966, effective July 1, 1966; December 4, 1967, effective July 1, 1968; March 1, 1971, effective July 1, 1971; April 28, 1983, effective August 1, 1983; April 29, 1985, effective August 1, 1985; March 2, 1987, effective August 1, 1987; April 29, 1999, effective December 1, 1999; April 23, 2001, effective December 1, 2001; April 25, 2005, effective December 1, 2005; April 30, 2007, effective December 1, 2007; March 26, 2009, effective December 1, 2009.)

TITLE III. PLEADINGS AND MOTIONS

RULE 7. PLEADINGS ALLOWED; FORM OF MOTIONS AND OTHER PAPERS

(a) Pleadings. Only these pleadings are allowed:

(1) a complaint;

(2) an answer to a complaint;

(3) an answer to a counterclaim designated as a counterclaim;

(4) an answer to a crossclaim;

(5) a third-party complaint;

(6) an answer to a third-party complaint; and

(7) if the court orders one, a reply to an answer.

(b) Motions and Other Papers.

(1) *In General.* A request for a court order must be made by motion. The motion must:

    (A) be in writing unless made during a hearing or trial;

    (B) state with particularity the grounds for seeking the order; and

    (C) state the relief sought.

(2) *Form.* The rules governing captions and other matters of form in pleadings apply to motions and other papers.

(Amended December 27, 1946, effective March 19, 1948; January 21, 1963, effective July 1, 1963; April 28, 1983, effective August 1, 1983; April 30, 2007, effective December 1, 2007.)

RULE 7.1. DISCLOSURE STATEMENT

(a) Who Must File; Contents. A nongovernmental corporate party must file two copies of a disclosure statement that:

(1) identifies any parent corporation and any publicly held corporation owning 10% or more of its stock; or

(2) states that there is no such corporation.

(b) Time to File; Supplemental Filing. A party must:

(1) file the disclosure statement with its first appearance, pleading, petition, motion, response, or other request addressed to the court; and

(2) promptly file a supplemental statement if any required information changes.

(Adopted April 29, 2002, effective December 1, 2002; April 30, 2007, effective December 1, 2007.)

RULE 8. GENERAL RULES OF PLEADING

(a) Claim for Relief. A pleading that states a claim for relief must contain:

(1) a short and plain statement of the grounds for the court's jurisdiction, unless the court already has jurisdiction and the claim needs no new jurisdictional support;

(2) a short and plain statement of the claim showing that the pleader is entitled to relief; and

(3) a demand for the relief sought, which may include relief in the alternative or different types of relief.

(b) Defenses; Admissions and Denials.

(1) *In General.* In responding to a pleading, a party must:

    (A) state in short and plain terms its defenses to each claim asserted against it; and

    (B) admit or deny the allegations asserted against it by an opposing party.

(2) *Denials—Responding to the Substance.* A denial must fairly respond to the substance of the allegation.

(3) *General and Specific Denials.* A party that intends in good faith to deny all the allegations of a pleading—including the jurisdictional grounds—may do so by a general denial. A party that does not intend to deny all the allegations must either specifically deny designated allegations or generally deny all except those specifically admitted.

(4) *Denying Part of an Allegation.* A party that intends in good faith to deny only part of an allegation must admit the part that is true and deny the rest.

(5) *Lacking Knowledge or Information.* A party that lacks knowledge or information sufficient to form a belief about the truth of an allegation must so state, and the statement has the effect of a denial.

(6) *Effect of Failing to Deny.* An allegation—other than one relating to the amount of damages—is admitted if a responsive pleading is required and the allegation is not denied. If a responsive pleading is not required, an allegation is considered denied or avoided.

(c) Affirmative Defenses.

(1) *In General.* In responding to a pleading, a party must affirmatively state any avoidance or affirmative defense, including:

- accord and satisfaction;
- arbitration and award;
- assumption of risk;
- contributory negligence;
- duress;
- estoppel;

- failure of consideration;
- fraud;
- illegality;
- injury by fellow servant;
- laches;
- license;
- payment;
- release;
- res judicata;
- statute of frauds;
- statute of limitations; and
- waiver.

(2) *Mistaken Designation.* If a party mistakenly designates a defense as a counterclaim, or a counterclaim as a defense, the court must, if justice requires, treat the pleading as though it were correctly designated, and may impose terms for doing so.

(d) **Pleading to Be Concise and Direct; Alternative Statements; Inconsistency.**

(1) *In General.* Each allegation must be simple, concise, and direct. No technical form is required.

(2) *Alternative Statements of a Claim or Defense.* A party may set out 2 or more statements of a claim or defense alternatively or hypothetically, either in a single count or defense or in separate ones. If a party makes alternative statements, the pleading is sufficient if any one of them is sufficient.

(3) *Inconsistent Claims or Defenses.* A party may state as many separate claims or defenses as it has, regardless of consistency.

(e) **Construing Pleadings.** Pleadings must be construed so as to do justice.

(Amended February 28, 1966, effective July 1, 1966; March 2, 1987, effective August 1, 1987; April 30, 2007, effective December 1, 2007; April 28, 2010, effective December 1, 2010.)

RULE 9.   PLEADING SPECIAL MATTERS

(a) **Capacity or Authority to Sue; Legal Existence.**

(1) *In General.* Except when required to show that the court has jurisdiction, a pleading need not allege:

(A) a party's capacity to sue or be sued;

(B) a party's authority to sue or be sued in a representative capacity; or

(C) the legal existence of an organized association of persons that is made a party.

(2) *Raising Those Issues.* To raise any of those issues, a party must do so by a specific denial,

which must state any supporting facts that are peculiarly within the party's knowledge.

(b) **Fraud or Mistake; Conditions of Mind.** In alleging fraud or mistake, a party must state with particularity the circumstances constituting fraud or mistake. Malice, intent, knowledge, and other conditions of a person's mind may be alleged generally.

(c) **Conditions Precedent.** In pleading conditions precedent, it suffices to allege generally that all conditions precedent have occurred or been performed. But when denying that a condition precedent has occurred or been performed, a party must do so with particularity.

(d) **Official Document or Act.** In pleading an official document or official act, it suffices to allege that the document was legally issued or the act legally done.

(e) **Judgment.** In pleading a judgment or decision of a domestic or foreign court, a judicial or quasi-judicial tribunal, or a board or officer, it suffices to plead the judgment or decision without showing jurisdiction to render it.

(f) **Time and Place.** An allegation of time or place is material when testing the sufficiency of a pleading.

(g) **Special Damages.** If an item of special damage is claimed, it must be specifically stated.

(h) **Admiralty or Maritime Claim.**

(1) *How Designated.* If a claim for relief is within the admiralty or maritime jurisdiction and also within the court's subject-matter jurisdiction on some other ground, the pleading may designate the claim as an admiralty or maritime claim for purposes of Rules 14(c), 38(e), and 82 and the Supplemental Rules for Admiralty or Maritime Claims and Asset Forfeiture Actions. A claim cognizable only in the admiralty or maritime jurisdiction is an admiralty or maritime claim for those purposes, whether or not so designated.

(2) *Designation for Appeal.* A case that includes an admiralty or maritime claim within this subdivision (h) is an admiralty case within 28 U.S.C. § 1292(a)(3).

(Amended February 28, 1966, effective July 1, 1966; December 4, 1967, effective July 1, 1968; March 30, 1970, effective July 1, 1970; March 2, 1987, effective August 1, 1987; April 11, 1997, effective December 1, 1997; April 12, 2006, effective December 1, 2006; April 30, 2007, effective December 1, 2007.)

RULE 10.   FORM OF PLEADINGS

(a) **Caption; Names of Parties.** Every pleading must have a caption with the court's name, a title, a file number, and a Rule 7(a) designation. The title of the complaint must name all the parties; the title of other pleadings, after naming the first party on each side, may refer generally to other parties.

(b) Paragraphs; Separate Statements. A party must state its claims or defenses in numbered paragraphs, each limited as far as practicable to a single set of circumstances. A later pleading may refer by number to a paragraph in an earlier pleading. If doing so would promote clarity, each claim founded on a separate transaction or occurrence—and each defense other than a denial—must be stated in a separate count or defense.

(c) Adoption by Reference; Exhibits. A statement in a pleading may be adopted by reference elsewhere in the same pleading or in any other pleading or motion. A copy of a written instrument that is an exhibit to a pleading is a part of the pleading for all purposes.

(Amended April 30, 2007, effective December 1, 2007.)

RULE 11. SIGNING PLEADINGS, MOTIONS, AND OTHER PAPERS; REPRESENTATIONS TO THE COURT; SANCTIONS

(a) Signature. Every pleading, written motion, and other paper must be signed by at least one attorney of record in the attorney's name—or by a party personally if the party is unrepresented. The paper must state the signer's address, e-mail address, and telephone number. Unless a rule or statute specifically states otherwise, a pleading need not be verified or accompanied by an affidavit. The court must strike an unsigned paper unless the omission is promptly corrected after being called to the attorney's or party's attention.

(b) Representations to the Court. By presenting to the court a pleading, written motion, or other paper—whether by signing, filing, submitting, or later advocating it—an attorney or unrepresented party certifies that to the best of the person's knowledge, information, and belief, formed after an inquiry reasonable under the circumstances:

(1) it is not being presented for any improper purpose, such as to harass, cause unnecessary delay, or needlessly increase the cost of litigation;

(2) the claims, defenses, and other legal contentions are warranted by existing law or by a nonfrivolous argument for extending, modifying, or reversing existing law or for establishing new law;

(3) the factual contentions have evidentiary support or, if specifically so identified, will likely have evidentiary support after a reasonable opportunity for further investigation or discovery; and

(4) the denials of factual contentions are warranted on the evidence or, if specifically so identified,

are reasonably based on belief or a lack of information.

(c) Sanctions.

(1) *In General.* If, after notice and a reasonable opportunity to respond, the court determines that Rule 11(b) has been violated, the court may impose an appropriate sanction on any attorney, law firm, or party that violated the rule or is responsible for the violation. Absent exceptional circumstances, a law firm must be held jointly responsible for a violation committed by its partner, associate, or employee.

(2) *Motion for Sanctions.* A motion for sanctions must be made separately from any other motion and must describe the specific conduct that allegedly violates Rule 11(b). The motion must be served under Rule 5, but it must not be filed or be presented to the court if the challenged paper, claim, defense, contention, or denial is withdrawn or appropriately corrected within 21 days after service or within another time the court sets. If warranted, the court may award to the prevailing party the reasonable expenses, including attorney's fees, incurred for the motion.

(3) *On the Court's Initiative.* On its own, the court may order an attorney, law firm, or party to show cause why conduct specifically described in the order has not violated Rule 11(b).

(4) *Nature of a Sanction.* A sanction imposed under this rule must be limited to what suffices to deter repetition of the conduct or comparable conduct by others similarly situated. The sanction may include nonmonetary directives; an order to pay a penalty into court; or, if imposed on motion and warranted for effective deterrence, an order directing payment to the movant of part or all of the reasonable attorney's fees and other expenses directly resulting from the violation.

(5) *Limitations on Monetary Sanctions.* The court must not impose a monetary sanction:

(A) against a represented party for violating Rule 11(b)(2); or

(B) on its own, unless it issued the show-cause order under Rule 11(c)(3) before voluntary dismissal or settlement of the claims made by or against the party that is, or whose attorneys are, to be sanctioned.

(6) *Requirements for an Order.* An order imposing a sanction must describe the sanctioned conduct and explain the basis for the sanction.

(d) Inapplicability to Discovery. This rule does not apply to disclosures and discovery requests, responses, objections, and motions under Rules 26 through 37.

(Amended April 28, 1983, effective August 1, 1983; March 2, 1987, effective August 1, 1987; April 22, 1993, effective December 1, 1993; April 30, 2007, effective December 1, 2007.)

RULE 12. DEFENSES AND OBJECTIONS: WHEN AND HOW PRESENTED; MOTION FOR JUDGMENT ON THE PLEADINGS; CONSOLIDATING MOTIONS; WAIVING DEFENSES; PRETRIAL HEARING

(a) **Time to Serve a Responsive Pleading.**

(1) *In General.* Unless another time is specified by this rule or a federal statute, the time for serving a responsive pleading is as follows:

(A) A defendant must serve an answer:

(i) within 21 days after being served with the summons and complaint; or

(ii) if it has timely waived service under Rule 4(d), within 60 days after the request for a waiver was sent, or within 90 days after it was sent to the defendant outside any judicial district of the United States.

(B) A party must serve an answer to a counterclaim or crossclaim within 21 days after being served with the pleading that states the counterclaim or crossclaim.

(C) A party must serve a reply to an answer within 21 days after being served with an order to reply, unless the order specifies a different time.

(2) *United States and Its Agencies, Officers, or Employees Sued in an Official Capacity.* The United States, a United States agency, or a United States officer or employee sued only in an official capacity must serve an answer to a complaint, counterclaim, or crossclaim within 60 days after service on the United States attorney.

(3) *United States Officers or Employees Sued in an Individual Capacity.* A United States officer or employee sued in an individual capacity for an act or omission occurring in connection with duties performed on the United States' behalf must serve an answer to a complaint, counterclaim, or crossclaim within 60 days after service on the officer or employee or service on the United States attorney, whichever is later.

(4) *Effect of a Motion.* Unless the court sets a different time, serving a motion under this rule alters these periods as follows:

(A) if the court denies the motion or postpones its disposition until trial, the responsive pleading must be served within 14 days after notice of the court's action; or

(B) if the court grants a motion for a more definite statement, the responsive pleading must be served within 14 days after the more definite statement is served.

(b) **How to Present Defenses.** Every defense to a claim for relief in any pleading must be asserted in the responsive pleading if one is required. But a party may assert the following defenses by motion:

(1) lack of subject-matter jurisdiction;

(2) lack of personal jurisdiction;

(3) improper venue;

(4) insufficient process;

(5) insufficient service of process;

(6) failure to state a claim upon which relief can be granted; and

(7) failure to join a party under Rule 19.

A motion asserting any of these defenses must be made before pleading if a responsive pleading is allowed. If a pleading sets out a claim for relief that does not require a responsive pleading, an opposing party may assert at trial any defense to that claim. No defense or objection is waived by joining it with one or more other defenses or objections in a responsive pleading or in a motion.

(c) **Motion for Judgment on the Pleadings.** After the pleadings are closed—but early enough not to delay trial—a party may move for judgment on the pleadings.

(d) **Result of Presenting Matters Outside the Pleadings.** If, on a motion under Rule 12(b)(6) or 12(c), matters outside the pleadings are presented to and not excluded by the court, the motion must be treated as one for summary judgment under Rule 56. All parties must be given a reasonable opportunity to present all the material that is pertinent to the motion.

(e) **Motion for a More Definite Statement.** A party may move for a more definite statement of a pleading to which a responsive pleading is allowed but which is so vague or ambiguous that the party cannot reasonably prepare a response. The motion must be made before filing a responsive pleading and must point out the defects complained of and the details desired. If the court orders a more definite statement and the order is not obeyed within 14 days after notice of the order or within the time the court sets, the court may strike the pleading or issue any other appropriate order.

(f) Motion to Strike. The court may strike from a pleading an insufficient defense or any redundant, immaterial, impertinent, or scandalous matter. The court may act:

(1) on its own; or

(2) on motion made by a party either before responding to the pleading or, if a response is not allowed, within 21 days after being served with the pleading.

(g) Joining Motions.

(1) *Right to Join.* A motion under this rule may be joined with any other motion allowed by this rule.

(2) *Limitation on Further Motions.* Except as provided in Rule 12(h)(2) or (3), a party that makes a motion under this rule must not make another motion under this rule raising a defense or objection that was available to the party but omitted from its earlier motion.

(h) Waiving and Preserving Certain Defenses.

(1) *When Some Are Waived.* A party waives any defense listed in Rule 12(b)(2)-(5) by:

(A) omitting it from a motion in the circumstances described in Rule 12(g)(2); or

(B) failing to either:

(i) make it by motion under this rule; or

(ii) include it in a responsive pleading or in an amendment allowed by Rule 15(a)(1) as a matter of course.

(2) *When to Raise Others.* Failure to state a claim upon which relief can be granted, to join a person required by Rule 19(b), or to state a legal defense to a claim may be raised:

(A) in any pleading allowed or ordered under Rule 7(a);

(B) by a motion under Rule 12(c); or

(C) at trial.

(3) *Lack of Subject–Matter Jurisdiction.* If the court determines at any time that it lacks subject-matter jurisdiction, the court must dismiss the action.

(i) Hearing Before Trial. If a party so moves, any defense listed in Rule 12(b)(1)-(7)—whether made in a pleading or by motion—and a motion under Rule 12(c) must be heard and decided before trial unless the court orders a deferral until trial.

(Amended December 27, 1946, effective March 19, 1948; January 21, 1963, effective July 1, 1963; February 28, 1966, effective July 1, 1966; March 2, 1987, effective August 1, 1987; April 22, 1993, effective December 1, 1993; April 17, 2000, effective December 1, 2000; April 30, 2007, effective December 1, 2007; March 26, 2009, effective December 1, 2009.)

RULE 13. COUNTERCLAIM AND CROSSCLAIM

(a) Compulsory Counterclaim.

(1) *In General.* A pleading must state as a counterclaim any claim that—at the time of its service—the pleader has against an opposing party if the claim:

(A) arises out of the transaction or occurrence that is the subject matter of the opposing party's claim; and

(B) does not require adding another party over whom the court cannot acquire jurisdiction.

(2) *Exceptions.* The pleader need not state the claim if:

(A) when the action was commenced, the claim was the subject of another pending action; or

(B) the opposing party sued on its claim by attachment or other process that did not establish personal jurisdiction over the pleader on that claim, and the pleader does not assert any counterclaim under this rule.

(b) Permissive Counterclaim. A pleading may state as a counterclaim against an opposing party any claim that is not compulsory.

(c) Relief Sought in a Counterclaim. A counterclaim need not diminish or defeat the recovery sought by the opposing party. It may request relief that exceeds in amount or differs in kind from the relief sought by the opposing party.

(d) Counterclaim Against the United States. These rules do not expand the right to assert a counterclaim—or to claim a credit—against the United States or a United States officer or agency.

(e) Counterclaim Maturing or Acquired After Pleading. The court may permit a party to file a supplemental pleading asserting a counterclaim that matured or was acquired by the party after serving an earlier pleading.

(f) [Abrogated]

(g) Crossclaim Against a Coparty. A pleading may state as a crossclaim any claim by one party against a coparty if the claim arises out of the transaction or occurrence that is the subject matter of the original action or of a counterclaim, or if the claim relates to any property that is the subject matter of the original action. The crossclaim may include a claim that the coparty is or may be liable to the cross-claimant for all or part of a claim asserted in the action against the crossclaimant.

(h) Joining Additional Parties. Rules 19 and 20 govern the addition of a person as a party to a counterclaim or crossclaim.

(i) Separate Trials; Separate Judgments. If the court orders separate trials under Rule 42(b), it may enter judgment on a counterclaim or cross-claim under Rule 54(b) when it has jurisdiction to do so, even if the opposing party's claims have been dismissed or otherwise resolved.

(Amended December 27, 1946, effective March 19, 1948; January 21, 1963, effective July 1, 1963; February 28, 1966, effective July 1, 1966; March 2, 1987, effective August 1, 1987; April 30, 2007, effective December 1, 2007; March 26, 2009, effective December 1, 2009.)

RULE 14. THIRD–PARTY PRACTICE

(a) When a Defending Party May Bring in a Third Party.

(1) *Timing of the Summons and Complaint.* A defending party may, as third-party plaintiff, serve a summons and complaint on a nonparty who is or may be liable to it for all or part of the claim against it. But the third-party plaintiff must, by motion, obtain the court's leave if it files the third-party complaint more than 14 days after serving its original answer.

(2) *Third–Party Defendant's Claims and Defenses.* The person served with the summons and third-party complaint—the "third-party defendant":

(A) must assert any defense against the third-party plaintiff's claim under Rule 12;

(B) must assert any counterclaim against the third-party plaintiff under Rule 13(a), and may assert any counterclaim against the third-party plaintiff under Rule 13(b) or any crossclaim against another third-party defendant under Rule 13(g);

(C) may assert against the plaintiff any defense that the third-party plaintiff has to the plaintiff's claim; and

(D) may also assert against the plaintiff any claim arising out of the transaction or occurrence that is the subject matter of the plaintiff's claim against the third-party plaintiff.

(3) *Plaintiff's Claims Against a Third–Party Defendant.* The plaintiff may assert against the third-party defendant any claim arising out of the transaction or occurrence that is the subject matter of the plaintiff's claim against the third-party plaintiff. The third-party defendant must then assert any defense under Rule 12 and any counterclaim under Rule 13(a), and may assert any counterclaim under Rule 13(b) or any crossclaim under Rule 13(g).

(4) *Motion to Strike, Sever, or Try Separately.* Any party may move to strike the third-party claim, to sever it, or to try it separately.

(5) *Third–Party Defendant's Claim Against a Nonparty.* A third-party defendant may proceed under this rule against a nonparty who is or may be liable to the third-party defendant for all or part of any claim against it.

(6) *Third–Party Complaint In Rem.* If it is within the admiralty or maritime jurisdiction, a third-party complaint may be in rem. In that event, a reference in this rule to the "summons" includes the warrant of arrest, and a reference to the defendant or third-party plaintiff includes, when appropriate, a person who asserts a right under Supplemental Rule C(6)(a)(i) in the property arrested.

(b) When a Plaintiff May Bring in a Third Party. When a claim is asserted against a plaintiff, the plaintiff may bring in a third party if this rule would allow a defendant to do so.

(c) Admiralty or Maritime Claim.

(1) *Scope of Impleader.* If a plaintiff asserts an admiralty or maritime claim under Rule 9(h), the defendant or a person who asserts a right under Supplemental Rule C(6)(a)(i) may, as a third-party plaintiff, bring in a third-party defendant who may be wholly or partly liable—either to the plaintiff or to the third-party plaintiff—for remedy over, contribution, or otherwise on account of the same transaction, occurrence, or series of transactions or occurrences.

(2) *Defending Against a Demand for Judgment for the Plaintiff.* The third-party plaintiff may demand judgment in the plaintiff's favor against the third-party defendant. In that event, the third-party defendant must defend under Rule 12 against the plaintiff's claim as well as the third-party plaintiff's claim; and the action proceeds as if the plaintiff had sued both the third-party defendant and the third-party plaintiff.

(Amended December 27, 1946, effective March 19, 1948; January 21, 1963, effective July 1, 1963; February 28, 1966, effective July 1, 1966; March 2, 1987, effective August 1, 1987; April 17, 2000, effective December 1, 2000; April 12, 2006, effective December 1, 2006; April 30, 2007, effective December 1, 2007; March 26, 2009, effective December 1, 2009.)

RULE 15. AMENDED AND SUPPLEMENTAL PLEADINGS

(a) Amendments Before Trial.

(1) *Amending as a Matter of Course.* A party may amend its pleading once as a matter of course within:

(A) 21 days after serving it, or

(B) if the pleading is one to which a responsive pleading is required, 21 days after service of a responsive pleading or 21 days after service of a motion under Rule 12(b), (e), or (f), whichever is earlier.

(2) *Other Amendments.* In all other cases, a party may amend its pleading only with the opposing party's written consent or the court's leave. The court should freely give leave when justice so requires.

(3) *Time to Respond.* Unless the court orders otherwise, any required response to an amended pleading must be made within the time remaining to respond to the original pleading or within 14 days after service of the amended pleading, whichever is later.

(b) Amendments During and After Trial.

(1) *Based on an Objection at Trial.* If, at trial, a party objects that evidence is not within the issues raised in the pleadings, the court may permit the pleadings to be amended. The court should freely permit an amendment when doing so will aid in presenting the merits and the objecting party fails to satisfy the court that the evidence would prejudice that party's action or defense on the merits. The court may grant a continuance to enable the objecting party to meet the evidence.

(2) *For Issues Tried by Consent.* When an issue not raised by the pleadings is tried by the parties' express or implied consent, it must be treated in all respects as if raised in the pleadings. A party may move—at any time, even after judgment—to amend the pleadings to conform them to the evidence and to raise an unpleaded issue. But failure to amend does not affect the result of the trial of that issue.

(c) Relation Back of Amendments.

(1) *When an Amendment Relates Back.* An amendment to a pleading relates back to the date of the original pleading when:

(A) the law that provides the applicable statute of limitations allows relation back;

(B) the amendment asserts a claim or defense that arose out of the conduct, transaction, or occurrence set out—or attempted to be set out—in the original pleading; or

(C) the amendment changes the party or the naming of the party against whom a claim is asserted, if Rule 15(c)(1)(B) is satisfied and if, within the period provided by Rule 4(m) for serving the summons and complaint, the party to be brought in by amendment:

(i) received such notice of the action that it will not be prejudiced in defending on the merits; and

(ii) knew or should have known that the action would have been brought against it, but for a mistake concerning the proper party's identity.

(2) *Notice to the United States.* When the United States or a United States officer or agency is added as a defendant by amendment, the notice requirements of Rule 15(c)(1)(C)(i) and (ii) are satisfied if, during the stated period, process was delivered or mailed to the United States attorney or the United States attorney's designee, to the Attorney General of the United States, or to the officer or agency.

(d) Supplemental Pleadings. On motion and reasonable notice, the court may, on just terms, permit a party to serve a supplemental pleading setting out any transaction, occurrence, or event that happened after the date of the pleading to be supplemented. The court may permit supplementation even though the original pleading is defective in stating a claim or defense. The court may order that the opposing party plead to the supplemental pleading within a specified time.

(Amended January 21, 1963, effective July 1, 1963; February 28, 1966, effective July 1, 1966; March 2, 1987, effective August 1, 1987; April 30, 1991, effective December 1, 1991; amended by Pub.L. 102–198, § 11, December 9, 1991, 105 Stat. 1626; amended April 22, 1993, effective December 1, 1993; April 30, 2007, effective December 1, 2007; March 26, 2009, effective December 1, 2009.)

RULE 16. PRETRIAL CONFERENCES; SCHEDULING; MANAGEMENT

(a) Purposes of a Pretrial Conference. In any action, the court may order the attorneys and any unrepresented parties to appear for one or more pretrial conferences for such purposes as:

(1) expediting disposition of the action;

(2) establishing early and continuing control so that the case will not be protracted because of lack of management;

(3) discouraging wasteful pretrial activities;

(4) improving the quality of the trial through more thorough preparation; and

(5) facilitating settlement.

(b) Scheduling.

(1) *Scheduling Order.* Except in categories of actions exempted by local rule, the district judge—or a magistrate judge when authorized by local rule—must issue a scheduling order:

(A) after receiving the parties' report under Rule 26(f); or

(B) after consulting with the parties' attorneys and any unrepresented parties at a scheduling conference or by telephone, mail, or other means.

(2) *Time to Issue.* The judge must issue the scheduling order as soon as practicable, but in any event within the earlier of 120 days after any defendant has been served with the complaint or 90 days after any defendant has appeared.

(3) *Contents of the Order.*

  (A) *Required Contents.* The scheduling order must limit the time to join other parties, amend the pleadings, complete discovery, and file motions.

  (B) *Permitted Contents.* The scheduling order may:

    (i) modify the timing of disclosures under Rules 26(a) and 26(e)(1);

    (ii) modify the extent of discovery;

    (iii) provide for disclosure or discovery of electronically stored information;

    (iv) include any agreements the parties reach for asserting claims of privilege or of protection as trial-preparation material after information is produced;

    (v) set dates for pretrial conferences and for trial; and

    (vi) include other appropriate matters.

(4) *Modifying a Schedule.* A schedule may be modified only for good cause and with the judge's consent.

(c) **Attendance and Matters for Consideration at a Pretrial Conference.**

(1) *Attendance.* A represented party must authorize at least one of its attorneys to make stipulations and admissions about all matters that can reasonably be anticipated for discussion at a pretrial conference. If appropriate, the court may require that a party or its representative be present or reasonably available by other means to consider possible settlement.

(2) *Matters for Consideration.* At any pretrial conference, the court may consider and take appropriate action on the following matters:

  (A) formulating and simplifying the issues, and eliminating frivolous claims or defenses;

  (B) amending the pleadings if necessary or desirable;

  (C) obtaining admissions and stipulations about facts and documents to avoid unnecessary proof, and ruling in advance on the admissibility of evidence;

  (D) avoiding unnecessary proof and cumulative evidence, and limiting the use of testimony under Federal Rule of Evidence 702;

  (E) determining the appropriateness and timing of summary adjudication under Rule 56;

  (F) controlling and scheduling discovery, including orders affecting disclosures and discovery under Rule 26 and Rules 29 through 37;

  (G) identifying witnesses and documents, scheduling the filing and exchange of any pretrial briefs, and setting dates for further conferences and for trial;

  (H) referring matters to a magistrate judge or a master;

  (I) settling the case and using special procedures to assist in resolving the dispute when authorized by statute or local rule;

  (J) determining the form and content of the pretrial order;

  (K) disposing of pending motions;

  (L) adopting special procedures for managing potentially difficult or protracted actions that may involve complex issues, multiple parties, difficult legal questions, or unusual proof problems;

  (M) ordering a separate trial under Rule 42(b) of a claim, counterclaim, crossclaim, third-party claim, or particular issue;

  (N) ordering the presentation of evidence early in the trial on a manageable issue that might, on the evidence, be the basis for a judgment as a matter of law under Rule 50(a) or a judgment on partial findings under Rule 52(c);

  (O) establishing a reasonable limit on the time allowed to present evidence; and

  (P) facilitating in other ways the just, speedy, and inexpensive disposition of the action.

(d) **Pretrial Orders.** After any conference under this rule, the court should issue an order reciting the action taken. This order controls the course of the action unless the court modifies it.

(e) **Final Pretrial Conference and Orders.** The court may hold a final pretrial conference to formulate a trial plan, including a plan to facilitate the admission of evidence. The conference must be held as close to the start of trial as is reasonable, and must be attended by at least one attorney who will conduct the trial for each party and by any unrepresented party. The court may modify the order issued after a final pretrial conference only to prevent manifest injustice.

(f) **Sanctions.**

(1) *In General.* On motion or on its own, the court may issue any just orders, including those authorized by Rule 37(b)(2)(A)(ii)-(vii), if a party or its attorney:

(A) fails to appear at a scheduling or other pretrial conference;

(B) is substantially unprepared to participate—or does not participate in good faith—in the conference; or

(C) fails to obey a scheduling or other pretrial order.

(2) *Imposing Fees and Costs.* Instead of or in addition to any other sanction, the court must order the party, its attorney, or both to pay the reasonable expenses—including attorney's fees—incurred because of any noncompliance with this rule, unless the noncompliance was substantially justified or other circumstances make an award of expenses unjust.

(Amended April 28, 1983, effective August 1, 1983; March 2, 1987, effective August 1, 1987; April 22, 1993, effective December 1, 1993; April 12, 2006, effective December 1, 2006; April 30, 2007, effective December 1, 2007.)

TITLE IV. PARTIES

RULE 17. PLAINTIFF AND DEFENDANT; CAPACITY; PUBLIC OFFICERS

(a) Real Party in Interest.

(1) *Designation in General.* An action must be prosecuted in the name of the real party in interest. The following may sue in their own names without joining the person for whose benefit the action is brought:

(A) an executor;

(B) an administrator;

(C) a guardian;

(D) a bailee;

(E) a trustee of an express trust;

(F) a party with whom or in whose name a contract has been made for another's benefit; and

(G) a party authorized by statute.

(2) *Action in the Name of the United States for Another's Use or Benefit.* When a federal statute so provides, an action for another's use or benefit must be brought in the name of the United States.

(3) *Joinder of the Real Party in Interest.* The court may not dismiss an action for failure to prosecute in the name of the real party in interest until, after an objection, a reasonable time has been allowed for the real party in interest to ratify, join, or be substituted into the action. After ratification, joinder, or substitution, the action proceeds as if it had been originally commenced by the real party in interest.

(b) Capacity to Sue or Be Sued. Capacity to sue or be sued is determined as follows:

(1) for an individual who is not acting in a representative capacity, by the law of the individual's domicile;

(2) for a corporation, by the law under which it was organized; and

(3) for all other parties, by the law of the state where the court is located, except that:

(A) a partnership or other unincorporated association with no such capacity under that state's law may sue or be sued in its common name to enforce a substantive right existing under the United States Constitution or laws; and

(B) 28 U.S.C. §§ 754 and 959(a) govern the capacity of a receiver appointed by a United States court to sue or be sued in a United States court.

(c) Minor or Incompetent Person.

(1) *With a Representative.* The following representatives may sue or defend on behalf of a minor or an incompetent person:

(A) a general guardian;

(B) a committee;

(C) a conservator; or

(D) a like fiduciary.

(2) *Without a Representative.* A minor or an incompetent person who does not have a duly appointed representative may sue by a next friend or by a guardian ad litem. The court must appoint a guardian ad litem—or issue another appropriate order—to protect a minor or incompetent person who is unrepresented in an action.

(d) Public Officer's Title and Name. A public officer who sues or is sued in an official capacity may be designated by official title rather than by name, but the court may order that the officer's name be added.

(Amended December 27, 1946, effective March 19, 1948; December 29, 1948, effective October 20, 1949; February 28, 1966, effective July 1, 1966; March 2, 1987, effective August 1, 1987; April 25, 1988, effective August 1, 1988; amended by Pub.L. 100–690, Title VII, § 7049, November 18, 1988, 102 Stat. 4401 (although amendment by Pub.L. 100–690 could not be executed due to prior amendment by Court order which made the same change effective August 1, 1988); April 30, 2007, effective December 1, 2007.)

RULE 18. JOINDER OF CLAIMS

(a) In General. A party asserting a claim, counterclaim, crossclaim, or third-party claim may join, as independent or alternative claims, as many claims as it has against an opposing party.

(b) Joinder of Contingent Claims. A party may join two claims even though one of them is contingent on the disposition of the other; but the court may grant relief only in accordance with the parties' relative substantive rights. In particular, a plaintiff may state a claim for money and a claim to set aside a conveyance that is fraudulent as to that plaintiff, without first obtaining a judgment for the money.

(Amended February 28, 1966, effective July 1, 1966; March 2, 1987, effective August 1, 1987; April 30, 2007, effective December 1, 2007.)

RULE 19. REQUIRED JOINDER OF PARTIES

(a) Persons Required to Be Joined if Feasible.

 (1) *Required Party.* A person who is subject to service of process and whose joinder will not deprive the court of subject-matter jurisdiction must be joined as a party if:

 (A) in that person's absence, the court cannot accord complete relief among existing parties; or

 (B) that person claims an interest relating to the subject of the action and is so situated that disposing of the action in the person's absence may:

 (i) as a practical matter impair or impede the person's ability to protect the interest; or

 (ii) leave an existing party subject to a substantial risk of incurring double, multiple, or otherwise inconsistent obligations because of the interest.

 (2) *Joinder by Court Order.* If a person has not been joined as required, the court must order that the person be made a party. A person who refuses to join as a plaintiff may be made either a defendant or, in a proper case, an involuntary plaintiff.

 (3) *Venue.* If a joined party objects to venue and the joinder would make venue improper, the court must dismiss that party.

(b) When Joinder Is Not Feasible. If a person who is required to be joined if feasible cannot be joined, the court must determine whether, in equity and good conscience, the action should proceed among the existing parties or should be dismissed. The factors for the court to consider include:

 (1) the extent to which a judgment rendered in the person's absence might prejudice that person or the existing parties;

 (2) the extent to which any prejudice could be lessened or avoided by:

 (A) protective provisions in the judgment;

 (B) shaping the relief; or

 (C) other measures;

 (3) whether a judgment rendered in the person's absence would be adequate; and

 (4) whether the plaintiff would have an adequate remedy if the action were dismissed for nonjoinder.

(c) Pleading the Reasons for Nonjoinder. When asserting a claim for relief, a party must state:

 (1) the name, if known, of any person who is required to be joined if feasible but is not joined; and

 (2) the reasons for not joining that person.

(d) Exception for Class Actions. This rule is subject to Rule 23.

(Amended February 28, 1966, effective July 1, 1966; March 2, 1987, effective August 1, 1987; April 30, 2007, effective December 1, 2007.)

RULE 20. PERMISSIVE JOINDER OF PARTIES

(a) Persons Who May Join or Be Joined.

 (1) *Plaintiffs.* Persons may join in one action as plaintiffs if:

 (A) they assert any right to relief jointly, severally, or in the alternative with respect to or arising out of the same transaction, occurrence, or series of transactions or occurrences; and

 (B) any question of law or fact common to all plaintiffs will arise in the action.

 (2) *Defendants.* Persons—as well as a vessel, cargo, or other property subject to admiralty process in rem—may be joined in one action as defendants if:

 (A) any right to relief is asserted against them jointly, severally, or in the alternative with respect to or arising out of the same transaction, occurrence, or series of transactions or occurrences; and

 (B) any question of law or fact common to all defendants will arise in the action.

 (3) *Extent of Relief.* Neither a plaintiff nor a defendant need be interested in obtaining or defending against all the relief demanded. The court may grant judgment to one or more plaintiffs according to their rights, and against one or more defendants according to their liabilities.

(b) Protective Measures. The court may issue orders—including an order for separate trials—to protect a party against embarrassment, delay, expense, or other prejudice that arises from including a person against whom the party asserts no claim and who asserts no claim against the party.

(Amended February 28, 1966, effective July 1, 1966; March 2, 1987, effective August 1, 1987; April 30, 2007, effective December 1, 2007.)

RULE 21.   MISJOINDER AND NONJOINDER OF PARTIES

Misjoinder of parties is not a ground for dismissing an action. On motion or on its own, the court may at any time, on just terms, add or drop a party. The court may also sever any claim against a party.

(Amended April 30, 2007, effective December 1, 2007.)

RULE 22.   INTERPLEADER

(a) Grounds.

(1) *By a Plaintiff.* Persons with claims that may expose a plaintiff to double or multiple liability may be joined as defendants and required to interplead. Joinder for interpleader is proper even though:

   (A) the claims of the several claimants, or the titles on which their claims depend, lack a common origin or are adverse and independent rather than identical; or

   (B) the plaintiff denies liability in whole or in part to any or all of the claimants.

(2) *By a Defendant.* A defendant exposed to similar liability may seek interpleader through a crossclaim or counterclaim.

(b) Relation to Other Rules and Statutes. This rule supplements—and does not limit—the joinder of parties allowed by Rule 20. The remedy this rule provides is in addition to—and does not supersede or limit—the remedy provided by 28 U.S.C. §§ 1335, 1397, and 2361. An action under those statutes must be conducted under these rules.

(Amended December 29, 1948, effective October 20, 1949; March 2, 1987, effective August 1, 1987; April 30, 2007, effective December 1, 2007.)

RULE 23.   CLASS ACTIONS

(a) Prerequisites. One or more members of a class may sue or be sued as representative parties on behalf of all members only if:

(1) the class is so numerous that joinder of all members is impracticable;

(2) there are questions of law or fact common to the class;

(3) the claims or defenses of the representative parties are typical of the claims or defenses of the class; and

(4) the representative parties will fairly and adequately protect the interests of the class.

(b) Types of Class Actions. A class action may be maintained if Rule 23(a) is satisfied and if:

(1) prosecuting separate actions by or against individual class members would create a risk of:

   (A) inconsistent or varying adjudications with respect to individual class members that would establish incompatible standards of conduct for the party opposing the class; or

   (B) adjudications with respect to individual class members that, as a practical matter, would be dispositive of the interests of the other members not parties to the individual adjudications or would substantially impair or impede their ability to protect their interests;

(2) the party opposing the class has acted or refused to act on grounds that apply generally to the class, so that final injunctive relief or corresponding declaratory relief is appropriate respecting the class as a whole; or

(3) the court finds that the questions of law or fact common to class members predominate over any questions affecting only individual members, and that a class action is superior to other available methods for fairly and efficiently adjudicating the controversy. The matters pertinent to these findings include:

   (A) the class members' interests in individually controlling the prosecution or defense of separate actions;

   (B) the extent and nature of any litigation concerning the controversy already begun by or against class members;

   (C) the desirability or undesirability of concentrating the litigation of the claims in the particular forum; and

   (D) the likely difficulties in managing a class action.

(c) Certification Order; Notice to Class Members; Judgment; Issues Classes; Subclasses.

(1) *Certification Order.*

   (A) *Time to Issue.* At an early practicable time after a person sues or is sued as a class representative, the court must determine by order whether to certify the action as a class action.

   (B) *Defining the Class; Appointing Class Counsel.* An order that certifies a class action must define the class and the class claims, issues, or defenses, and must appoint class counsel under Rule 23(g).

  (C) *Altering or Amending the Order.* An order that grants or denies class certification may be altered or amended before final judgment.

(2) *Notice.*

  (A) *For (b)(1) or (b)(2) Classes.* For any class certified under Rule 23(b)(1) or (b)(2), the court may direct appropriate notice to the class.

  (B) *For (b)(3) Classes.* For any class certified under Rule 23(b)(3), the court must direct to class members the best notice that is practicable under the circumstances, including individual notice to all members who can be identified through reasonable effort. The notice must clearly and concisely state in plain, easily understood language:

    (i) the nature of the action;

    (ii) the definition of the class certified;

    (iii) the class claims, issues, or defenses;

    (iv) that a class member may enter an appearance through an attorney if the member so desires;

    (v) that the court will exclude from the class any member who requests exclusion;

    (vi) the time and manner for requesting exclusion; and

    (vii) the binding effect of a class judgment on members under Rule 23(c)(3).

(3) *Judgment.* Whether or not favorable to the class, the judgment in a class action must:

  (A) for any class certified under Rule 23(b)(1) or (b)(2), include and describe those whom the court finds to be class members; and

  (B) for any class certified under Rule 23(b)(3), include and specify or describe those to whom the Rule 23(c)(2) notice was directed, who have not requested exclusion, and whom the court finds to be class members.

(4) *Particular Issues.* When appropriate, an action may be brought or maintained as a class action with respect to particular issues.

(5) *Subclasses.* When appropriate, a class may be divided into subclasses that are each treated as a class under this rule.

(d) Conducting the Action.

(1) *In General.* In conducting an action under this rule, the court may issue orders that:

  (A) determine the course of proceedings or prescribe measures to prevent undue repetition or complication in presenting evidence or argument;

  (B) require—to protect class members and fairly conduct the action—giving appropriate notice to some or all class members of:

    (i) any step in the action;

    (ii) the proposed extent of the judgment; or

    (iii) the members' opportunity to signify whether they consider the representation fair and adequate, to intervene and present claims or defenses, or to otherwise come into the action;

  (C) impose conditions on the representative parties or on intervenors;

  (D) require that the pleadings be amended to eliminate allegations about representation of absent persons and that the action proceed accordingly; or

  (E) deal with similar procedural matters.

(2) *Combining and Amending Orders.* An order under Rule 23(d)(1) may be altered or amended from time to time and may be combined with an order under Rule 16.

(e) Settlement, Voluntary Dismissal, or Compromise. The claims, issues, or defenses of a certified class may be settled, voluntarily dismissed, or compromised only with the court's approval. The following procedures apply to a proposed settlement, voluntary dismissal, or compromise:

(1) The court must direct notice in a reasonable manner to all class members who would be bound by the proposal.

(2) If the proposal would bind class members, the court may approve it only after a hearing and on finding that it is fair, reasonable, and adequate.

(3) The parties seeking approval must file a statement identifying any agreement made in connection with the proposal.

(4) If the class action was previously certified under Rule 23(b)(3), the court may refuse to approve a settlement unless it affords a new opportunity to request exclusion to individual class members who had an earlier opportunity to request exclusion but did not do so.

(5) Any class member may object to the proposal if it requires court approval under this subdivision (e); the objection may be withdrawn only with the court's approval.

(f) Appeals. A court of appeals may permit an appeal from an order granting or denying class-action certification under this rule if a petition for permission to appeal is filed with the circuit clerk within 14 days after the order is entered. An appeal does not stay proceedings in the district court unless the district judge or the court of appeals so orders.

(g) Class Counsel.

(1) *Appointing Class Counsel.* Unless a statute provides otherwise, a court that certifies a class must appoint class counsel. In appointing class counsel, the court:

(A) must consider:

(i) the work counsel has done in identifying or investigating potential claims in the action;

(ii) counsel's experience in handling class actions, other complex litigation, and the types of claims asserted in the action;

(iii) counsel's knowledge of the applicable law; and

(iv) the resources that counsel will commit to representing the class;

(B) may consider any other matter pertinent to counsel's ability to fairly and adequately represent the interests of the class;

(C) may order potential class counsel to provide information on any subject pertinent to the appointment and to propose terms for attorney's fees and nontaxable costs;

(D) may include in the appointing order provisions about the award of attorney's fees or nontaxable costs under Rule 23(h); and

(E) may make further orders in connection with the appointment.

(2) *Standard for Appointing Class Counsel.* When one applicant seeks appointment as class counsel, the court may appoint that applicant only if the applicant is adequate under Rule 23(g)(1) and (4). If more than one adequate applicant seeks appointment, the court must appoint the applicant best able to represent the interests of the class.

(3) *Interim Counsel.* The court may designate interim counsel to act on behalf of a putative class before determining whether to certify the action as a class action.

(4) *Duty of Class Counsel.* Class counsel must fairly and adequately represent the interests of the class.

(h) Attorney's Fees and Nontaxable Costs. In a certified class action, the court may award reasonable attorney's fees and nontaxable costs that are authorized by law or by the parties' agreement. The following procedures apply:

(1) A claim for an award must be made by motion under Rule 54(d)(2), subject to the provisions of this subdivision (h), at a time the court sets. Notice of the motion must be served on all parties and, for motions by class counsel, directed to class members in a reasonable manner.

(2) A class member, or a party from whom payment is sought, may object to the motion.

(3) The court may hold a hearing and must find the facts and state its legal conclusions under Rule 52(a).

(4) The court may refer issues related to the amount of the award to a special master or a magistrate judge, as provided in Rule 54(d)(2)(D).

(Amended February 28, 1966, effective July 1, 1966; March 2, 1987, effective August 1, 1987; April 24, 1998, effective December 1, 1998; March 27, 2003, effective December 1, 2003; April 30, 2007, effective December 1, 2007; March 26, 2009, effective December 1, 2009.)

RULE 23.1. DERIVATIVE ACTIONS

(a) Prerequisites. This rule applies when one or more shareholders or members of a corporation or an unincorporated association bring a derivative action to enforce a right that the corporation or association may properly assert but has failed to enforce. The derivative action may not be maintained if it appears that the plaintiff does not fairly and adequately represent the interests of shareholders or members who are similarly situated in enforcing the right of the corporation or association.

(b) Pleading Requirements. The complaint must be verified and must:

(1) allege that the plaintiff was a shareholder or member at the time of the transaction complained of, or that the plaintiff's share or membership later devolved on it by operation of law;

(2) allege that the action is not a collusive one to confer jurisdiction that the court would otherwise lack; and

(3) state with particularity:

(A) any effort by the plaintiff to obtain the desired action from the directors or comparable authority and, if necessary, from the shareholders or members; and

(B) the reasons for not obtaining the action or not making the effort.

(c) Settlement, Dismissal, and Compromise. A derivative action may be settled, voluntarily dismissed, or compromised only with the court's approval. Notice of a proposed settlement, voluntary dismissal, or compromise must be given to shareholders or members in the manner that the court orders.

(Adopted February 28, 1966, effective July 1, 1966; amended March 2, 1987, effective August 1, 1987; April 30, 2007, effective December 1, 2007.)

RULE 23.2. ACTIONS RELATING TO UNINCORPORATED ASSOCIATIONS

This rule applies to an action brought by or against the members of an unincorporated association as a class by naming certain members as representative parties. The action may be maintained only if it appears that those parties will fairly and adequately protect the interests of the association and its members. In conducting the action, the court may issue any appropriate orders corresponding with those in Rule 23(d), and the procedure for settlement, voluntary dismissal, or compromise must correspond with the procedure in Rule 23(e).

(Adopted February 28, 1966, effective July 1, 1966; amended April 30, 2007, effective December 1, 2007.)

RULE 24. INTERVENTION

(a) Intervention of Right. On timely motion, the court must permit anyone to intervene who:

(1) is given an unconditional right to intervene by a federal statute; or

(2) claims an interest relating to the property or transaction that is the subject of the action, and is so situated that disposing of the action may as a practical matter impair or impede the movant's ability to protect its interest, unless existing parties adequately represent that interest.

(b) Permissive Intervention.

(1) *In General.* On timely motion, the court may permit anyone to intervene who:

(A) is given a conditional right to intervene by a federal statute; or

(B) has a claim or defense that shares with the main action a common question of law or fact.

(2) *By a Government Officer or Agency.* On timely motion, the court may permit a federal or state governmental officer or agency to intervene if a party's claim or defense is based on:

(A) a statute or executive order administered by the officer or agency; or

(B) any regulation, order, requirement, or agreement issued or made under the statute or executive order.

(3) *Delay or Prejudice.* In exercising its discretion, the court must consider whether the intervention will unduly delay or prejudice the adjudication of the original parties' rights.

(c) Notice and Pleading Required. A motion to intervene must be served on the parties as provided in Rule 5. The motion must state the grounds for intervention and be accompanied by a pleading that sets out the claim or defense for which intervention is sought.

(Amended December 27, 1946, effective March 19, 1948; December 29, 1948, effective October 20, 1949; January 21, 1963, effective July 1, 1963; February 28, 1966, effective July 1, 1966; March 2, 1987, effective August 1, 1987; April 30, 1991, effective December 1, 1991; April 12, 2006, effective December 1, 2006; April 30, 2007, effective December 1, 2007.)

RULE 25. SUBSTITUTION OF PARTIES

(a) Death.

(1) *Substitution if the Claim Is Not Extinguished.* If a party dies and the claim is not extinguished, the court may order substitution of the proper party. A motion for substitution may be made by any party or by the decedent's successor or representative. If the motion is not made within 90 days after service of a statement noting the death, the action by or against the decedent must be dismissed.

(2) *Continuation Among the Remaining Parties.* After a party's death, if the right sought to be enforced survives only to or against the remaining parties, the action does not abate, but proceeds in favor of or against the remaining parties. The death should be noted on the record.

(3) *Service.* A motion to substitute, together with a notice of hearing, must be served on the parties as provided in Rule 5 and on nonparties as provided in Rule 4. A statement noting death must be served in the same manner. Service may be made in any judicial district.

(b) Incompetency. If a party becomes incompetent, the court may, on motion, permit the action to be continued by or against the party's representative. The motion must be served as provided in Rule 25(a)(3).

(c) Transfer of Interest. If an interest is transferred, the action may be continued by or against the original party unless the court, on motion, orders the transferee to be substituted in the action or joined with the original party. The motion must be served as provided in Rule 25(a)(3).

(d) Public Officers; Death or Separation from Office. An action does not abate when a public officer who is a party in an official capacity dies, resigns, or otherwise ceases to hold office while the action is pending. The officer's successor is automatically substituted as a party. Later proceedings should be in the substituted party's name, but any misnomer not affecting the parties' substantial rights must be disregarded. The court may order substitution at any time, but the absence of such an order does not affect the substitution.

(Amended December 29, 1948, effective October 20, 1949; April 17, 1961, effective July 19, 1961; January 21, 1963, effective July 1, 1963; March 2, 1987, effective August 1, 1987; April 30, 2007, effective December 1, 2007.)

TITLE V. DISCLOSURES AND DISCOVERY

RULE 26. DUTY TO DISCLOSE; GENERAL PROVISIONS GOVERNING DISCOVERY

(a) Required Disclosures.

(1) *Initial Disclosure.*

(A) *In General.* Except as exempted by Rule 26(a)(1)(B) or as otherwise stipulated or ordered by the court, a party must, without awaiting a discovery request, provide to the other parties:

(i) the name and, if known, the address and telephone number of each individual likely to have discoverable information—along with the subjects of that information—that the disclosing party may use to support its claims or defenses, unless the use would be solely for impeachment;

(ii) a copy—or a description by category and location—of all documents, electronically stored information, and tangible things that the disclosing party has in its possession, custody, or control and may use to support its claims or defenses, unless the use would be solely for impeachment;

(iii) a computation of each category of damages claimed by the disclosing party—who must also make available for inspection and copying as under Rule 34 the documents or other evidentiary material, unless privileged or protected from disclosure, on which each computation is based, including materials bearing on the nature and extent of injuries suffered; and

(iv) for inspection and copying as under Rule 34, any insurance agreement under which an insurance business may be liable to satisfy all or part of a possible judgment in the action or to indemnify or reimburse for payments made to satisfy the judgment.

(B) *Proceedings Exempt from Initial Disclosure.* The following proceedings are exempt from initial disclosure:

(i) an action for review on an administrative record;

(ii) a forfeiture action in rem arising from a federal statute;

(iii) a petition for habeas corpus or any other proceeding to challenge a criminal conviction or sentence;

(iv) an action brought without an attorney by a person in the custody of the United States, a state, or a state subdivision;

(v) an action to enforce or quash an administrative summons or subpoena;

(vi) an action by the United States to recover benefit payments;

(vii) an action by the United States to collect on a student loan guaranteed by the United States;

(viii) a proceeding ancillary to a proceeding in another court; and

(ix) an action to enforce an arbitration award.

(C) *Time for Initial Disclosures—In General.* A party must make the initial disclosures at or within 14 days after the parties' Rule 26(f) conference unless a different time is set by stipulation or court order, or unless a party objects during the conference that initial disclosures are not appropriate in this action and states the objection in the proposed discovery plan. In ruling on the objection, the court must determine what disclosures, if any, are to be made and must set the time for disclosure.

(D) *Time for Initial Disclosures—For Parties Served or Joined Later.* A party that is first served or otherwise joined after the Rule 26(f) conference must make the initial disclosures within 30 days after being served or joined, unless a different time is set by stipulation or court order.

(E) *Basis for Initial Disclosure; Unacceptable Excuses.* A party must make its initial disclosures based on the information then reasonably available to it. A party is not excused from making its disclosures because it has not fully investigated the case or because it challenges the sufficiency of another party's disclosures or because another party has not made its disclosures.

(2) *Disclosure of Expert Testimony.*

(A) *In General.* In addition to the disclosures required by Rule 26(a)(1), a party must disclose to the other parties the identity of any witness it may use at trial to present evidence under Federal Rule of Evidence 702, 703, or 705.

(B) *Witnesses Who Must Provide a Written Report.* Unless otherwise stipulated or ordered by the court, this disclosure must be accompanied by a written report—prepared and signed by the witness—if the witness is one retained or specially employed to provide expert testimony in the case or one whose duties as the party's employee regularly involve giving expert testimony. The report must contain:

(i) a complete statement of all opinions the witness will express and the basis and reasons for them;

(ii) the facts or data considered by the witness in forming them;

(iii) any exhibits that will be used to summarize or support them;

(iv) the witness's qualifications, including a list of all publications authored in the previous 10 years;

(v) a list of all other cases in which, during the previous 4 years, the witness testified as an expert at trial or by deposition; and

(vi) a statement of the compensation to be paid for the study and testimony in the case.

(C) *Witnesses Who Do Not Provide a Written Report.* Unless otherwise stipulated or ordered by the court, if the witness is not required to provide a written report, this disclosure must state:

(i) the subject matter on which the witness is expected to present evidence under Federal Rule of Evidence 702, 703, or 705; and

(ii) a summary of the facts and opinions to which the witness is expected to testify.

(D) *Time to Disclose Expert Testimony.* A party must make these disclosures at the times and in the sequence that the court orders. Absent a stipulation or a court order, the disclosures must be made:

(i) at least 90 days before the date set for trial or for the case to be ready for trial; or

(ii) if the evidence is intended solely to contradict or rebut evidence on the same subject matter identified by another party under Rule 26(a)(2)(B) or (C), within 30 days after the other party's disclosure.

(E) *Supplementing the Disclosure.* The parties must supplement these disclosures when required under Rule 26(e).

(3) *Pretrial Disclosures.*

(A) *In General.* In addition to the disclosures required by Rule 26(a)(1) and (2), a party must provide to the other parties and promptly file the following information about the evidence that it may present at trial other than solely for impeachment:

(i) the name and, if not previously provided, the address and telephone number of each witness—separately identifying those the party expects to present and those it may call if the need arises;

(ii) the designation of those witnesses whose testimony the party expects to present by deposition and, if not taken stenographically, a transcript of the pertinent parts of the deposition; and

(iii) an identification of each document or other exhibit, including summaries of other evidence—separately identifying those items the party expects to offer and those it may offer if the need arises.

(B) *Time for Pretrial Disclosures; Objections.* Unless the court orders otherwise, these disclosures must be made at least 30 days before trial. Within 14 days after they are made, unless the court sets a different time, a party may serve and promptly file a list of the following objections: any objections to the use under Rule 32(a) of a deposition designated by another party under Rule 26(a)(3)(A)(ii); and any objection, together with the grounds for it, that may be made to the admissibility of materials identified under Rule 26(a)(3)(A)(iii). An objection not so made—except for one under Federal Rule of Evidence 402 or 403—is waived unless excused by the court for good cause.

(4) *Form of Disclosures.* Unless the court orders otherwise, all disclosures under Rule 26(a) must be in writing, signed, and served.

(b) Discovery Scope and Limits.

(1) *Scope in General.* Unless otherwise limited by court order, the scope of discovery is as follows: Parties may obtain discovery regarding any nonprivileged matter that is relevant to any party's claim or defense—including the existence, description, nature, custody, condition, and location of any documents or other tangible things and the identity and location of persons who know of any discoverable matter. For good cause, the court may order discovery of any matter relevant to the subject matter involved in the action. Relevant information need not be admissible at the trial if the discovery appears reasonably calculated to lead to the discovery of admissible evidence. All discovery is subject to the limitations imposed by Rule 26(b)(2)(C).

(2) *Limitations on Frequency and Extent.*

(A) *When Permitted.* By order, the court may alter the limits in these rules on the number of depositions and interrogatories or on the length of depositions under Rule 30. By order or local rule, the court may also limit the number of requests under Rule 36.

(B) *Specific Limitations on Electronically Stored Information.* A party need not provide discovery of electronically stored information from sources that the party identifies as not reasonably accessible because of undue burden or cost. On motion to compel discovery or for a protective order, the party from whom discovery is sought must show that the information is not reasonably accessible because of undue burden or cost. If that showing is made, the court may nonetheless order discovery from such sources if the requesting party shows good cause, considering the limitations of Rule 26(b)(2)(C). The court may specify conditions for the discovery.

(C) *When Required.* On motion or on its own, the court must limit the frequency or extent of discovery otherwise allowed by these rules or by local rule if it determines that:

(i) the discovery sought is unreasonably cumulative or duplicative, or can be obtained from some other source that is more convenient, less burdensome, or less expensive;

(ii) the party seeking discovery has had ample opportunity to obtain the information by discovery in the action; or

(iii) the burden or expense of the proposed discovery outweighs its likely benefit, considering the needs of the case, the amount in controversy, the parties' resources, the importance of the issues at stake in the action, and the importance of the discovery in resolving the issues.

(3) *Trial Preparation: Materials.*

(A) *Documents and Tangible Things.* Ordinarily, a party may not discover documents and tangible things that are prepared in anticipation of litigation or for trial by or for another party or its representative (including the other party's attorney, consultant, surety, indemnitor, insurer, or agent). But, subject to Rule 26(b)(4), those materials may be discovered if:

(i) they are otherwise discoverable under Rule 26(b)(1); and

(ii) the party shows that it has substantial need for the materials to prepare its case and cannot, without undue hardship, obtain their substantial equivalent by other means.

(B) *Protection Against Disclosure.* If the court orders discovery of those materials, it must protect against disclosure of the mental impressions, conclusions, opinions, or legal theories of a party's attorney or other representative concerning the litigation.

(C) *Previous Statement.* Any party or other person may, on request and without the required showing, obtain the person's own previous statement about the action or its subject matter. If the request is refused, the person may move for a court order, and Rule 37(a)(5) applies to the award of expenses. A previous statement is either:

(i) a written statement that the person has signed or otherwise adopted or approved; or

(ii) a contemporaneous stenographic, mechanical, electrical, or other recording—or a transcription of it—that recites substantially verbatim the person's oral statement.

(4) *Trial Preparation: Experts.*

(A) *Deposition of an Expert Who May Testify.* A party may depose any person who has been identified as an expert whose opinions may be presented at trial. If Rule 26(a)(2)(B) requires a report from the expert, the deposition may be conducted only after the report is provided.

(B) *Trial–Preparation Protection for Draft Reports or Disclosures.* Rules 26(b)(3)(A) and (B) protect drafts of any report or disclosure required under Rule 26(a)(2), regardless of the form in which the draft is recorded.

(C) *Trial–Preparation Protection for Communications Between a Party's Attorney and Expert Witnesses.* Rules 26(b)(3)(A) and (B) protect communications between the party's attorney and any witness required to provide a report under Rule 26(a)(2)(B), regardless of the form of the communications, except to the extent that the communications:

(i) relate to compensation for the expert's study or testimony;

(ii) identify facts or data that the party's attorney provided and that the expert considered in forming the opinions to be expressed; or

(iii) identify assumptions that the party's attorney provided and that the expert relied on in forming the opinions to be expressed.

(D) *Expert Employed Only for Trial Preparation.* Ordinarily, a party may not, by interrogatories or deposition, discover facts known or opinions held by an expert who has been retained or specially employed by another party in anticipation of litigation or to prepare for trial and who is not expected to be called as a witness at trial. But a party may do so only:

(i) as provided in Rule 35(b); or

(ii) on showing exceptional circumstances under which it is impracticable for the party to obtain facts or opinions on the same subject by other means.

(E) *Payment.* Unless manifest injustice would result, the court must require that the party seeking discovery:

(i) pay the expert a reasonable fee for time spent in responding to discovery under Rule 26(b)(4)(A) or (D); and

(ii) for discovery under (D), also pay the other party a fair portion of the fees and expenses it reasonably incurred in obtaining the expert's facts and opinions.

(5) *Claiming Privilege or Protecting Trial-Preparation Materials.*

(A) *Information Withheld.* When a party withholds information otherwise discoverable by claiming that the information is privileged or subject to protection as trial-preparation material, the party must:

(i) expressly make the claim; and

(ii) describe the nature of the documents, communications, or tangible things not produced or disclosed—and do so in a manner that, without revealing information itself privileged or protected, will enable other parties to assess the claim.

(B) *Information Produced.* If information produced in discovery is subject to a claim of privilege or of protection as trial-preparation material, the party making the claim may notify any party that received the information of the claim and the basis for it. After being notified, a party must promptly return, sequester, or destroy the specified information and any copies it has; must not use or disclose the information until the claim is resolved; must take reasonable steps to retrieve the information if the party disclosed it before being notified; and may promptly present the information to the court under seal for a determination of the claim. The

producing party must preserve the information until the claim is resolved.

(c) **Protective Orders.**

(1) *In General.* A party or any person from whom discovery is sought may move for a protective order in the court where the action is pending—or as an alternative on matters relating to a deposition, in the court for the district where the deposition will be taken. The motion must include a certification that the movant has in good faith conferred or attempted to confer with other affected parties in an effort to resolve the dispute without court action. The court may, for good cause, issue an order to protect a party or person from annoyance, embarrassment, oppression, or undue burden or expense, including one or more of the following:

(A) forbidding the disclosure or discovery;

(B) specifying terms, including time and place, for the disclosure or discovery;

(C) prescribing a discovery method other than the one selected by the party seeking discovery;

(D) forbidding inquiry into certain matters, or limiting the scope of disclosure or discovery to certain matters;

(E) designating the persons who may be present while the discovery is conducted;

(F) requiring that a deposition be sealed and opened only on court order;

(G) requiring that a trade secret or other confidential research, development, or commercial information not be revealed or be revealed only in a specified way; and

(H) requiring that the parties simultaneously file specified documents or information in sealed envelopes, to be opened as the court directs.

(2) *Ordering Discovery.* If a motion for a protective order is wholly or partly denied, the court may, on just terms, order that any party or person provide or permit discovery.

(3) *Awarding Expenses.* Rule 37(a)(5) applies to the award of expenses.

(d) **Timing and Sequence of Discovery.**

(1) *Timing.* A party may not seek discovery from any source before the parties have conferred as required by Rule 26(f), except in a proceeding exempted from initial disclosure under Rule 26(a)(1)(B), or when authorized by these rules, by stipulation, or by court order.

(2) *Sequence.* Unless, on motion, the court orders otherwise for the parties' and witnesses' convenience and in the interests of justice:

(A) methods of discovery may be used in any sequence; and

(B) discovery by one party does not require any other party to delay its discovery.

(e) Supplementing Disclosures and Responses.

(1) *In General.* A party who has made a disclosure under Rule 26(a)—or who has responded to an interrogatory, request for production, or request for admission—must supplement or correct its disclosure or response:

(A) in a timely manner if the party learns that in some material respect the disclosure or response is incomplete or incorrect, and if the additional or corrective information has not otherwise been made known to the other parties during the discovery process or in writing; or

(B) as ordered by the court.

(2) *Expert Witness.* For an expert whose report must be disclosed under Rule 26(a)(2)(B), the party's duty to supplement extends both to information included in the report and to information given during the expert's deposition. Any additions or changes to this information must be disclosed by the time the party's pretrial disclosures under Rule 26(a)(3) are due.

(f) Conference of the Parties; Planning for Discovery.

(1) *Conference Timing.* Except in a proceeding exempted from initial disclosure under Rule 26(a)(1)(B) or when the court orders otherwise, the parties must confer as soon as practicable— and in any event at least 21 days before a scheduling conference is to be held or a scheduling order is due under Rule 16(b).

(2) *Conference Content; Parties' Responsibilities.* In conferring, the parties must consider the nature and basis of their claims and defenses and the possibilities for promptly settling or resolving the case; make or arrange for the disclosures required by Rule 26(a)(1); discuss any issues about preserving discoverable information; and develop a proposed discovery plan. The attorneys of record and all unrepresented parties that have appeared in the case are jointly responsible for arranging the conference, for attempting in good faith to agree on the proposed discovery plan, and for submitting to the court within 14 days after the conference a written report outlining the plan. The court may order the parties or attorneys to attend the conference in person.

(3) *Discovery Plan.* A discovery plan must state the parties' views and proposals on:

(A) what changes should be made in the timing, form, or requirement for disclosures under Rule 26(a), including a statement of when initial disclosures were made or will be made;

(B) the subjects on which discovery may be needed, when discovery should be completed, and whether discovery should be conducted in phases or be limited to or focused on particular issues;

(C) any issues about disclosure or discovery of electronically stored information, including the form or forms in which it should be produced;

(D) any issues about claims of privilege or of protection as trial-preparation materials, including—if the parties agree on a procedure to assert these claims after production— whether to ask the court to include their agreement in an order;

(E) what changes should be made in the limitations on discovery imposed under these rules or by local rule, and what other limitations should be imposed; and

(F) any other orders that the court should issue under Rule 26(c) or under Rule 16(b) and (c).

(4) *Expedited Schedule.* If necessary to comply with its expedited schedule for Rule 16(b) conferences, a court may by local rule:

(A) require the parties' conference to occur less than 21 days before the scheduling conference is held or a scheduling order is due under Rule 16(b); and

(B) require the written report outlining the discovery plan to be filed less than 14 days after the parties' conference, or excuse the parties from submitting a written report and permit them to report orally on their discovery plan at the Rule 16(b) conference.

(g) Signing Disclosures and Discovery Requests, Responses, and Objections.

(1) *Signature Required; Effect of Signature.* Every disclosure under Rule 26(a)(1) or (a)(3) and every discovery request, response, or objection must be signed by at least one attorney of record in the attorney's own name—or by the party personally, if unrepresented—and must state the signer's address, e-mail address, and telephone number. By signing, an attorney or party certifies that to the best of the person's knowledge, information, and belief formed after a reasonable inquiry:

(A) with respect to a disclosure, it is complete and correct as of the time it is made; and

(B) with respect to a discovery request, response, or objection, it is:

(i) consistent with these rules and warranted by existing law or by a nonfrivolous argument for extending, modifying, or reversing existing law, or for establishing new law;

(ii) not interposed for any improper purpose, such as to harass, cause unnecessary delay, or needlessly increase the cost of litigation; and

(iii) neither unreasonable nor unduly burdensome or expensive, considering the needs of the case, prior discovery in the case, the amount in controversy, and the importance of the issues at stake in the action.

(2) *Failure to Sign.* Other parties have no duty to act on an unsigned disclosure, request, response, or objection until it is signed, and the court must strike it unless a signature is promptly supplied after the omission is called to the attorney's or party's attention.

(3) *Sanction for Improper Certification.* If a certification violates this rule without substantial justification, the court, on motion or on its own, must impose an appropriate sanction on the signer, the party on whose behalf the signer was acting, or both. The sanction may include an order to pay the reasonable expenses, including attorney's fees, caused by the violation.

(Amended December 27, 1946, effective March 19, 1948; January 21, 1963, effective July 1, 1963; February 28, 1966, effective July 1, 1966; March 30, 1970, effective July 1, 1970; April 29, 1980, effective August 1, 1980; April 28, 1983, effective August 1, 1983; March 2, 1987, effective August 1, 1987; April 22, 1993, effective December 1, 1993; April 17, 2000, effective December 1, 2000; April 12, 2006, effective December 1, 2006; April 30, 2007, effective December 1, 2007; April 28, 2010, effective December 1, 2010.)

RULE 27. DEPOSITIONS TO PERPETUATE TESTIMONY

(a) **Before an Action Is Filed.**

(1) *Petition.* A person who wants to perpetuate testimony about any matter cognizable in a United States court may file a verified petition in the district court for the district where any expected adverse party resides. The petition must ask for an order authorizing the petitioner to depose the named persons in order to perpetuate their testimony. The petition must be titled in the petitioner's name and must show:

(A) that the petitioner expects to be a party to an action cognizable in a United States court but cannot presently bring it or cause it to be brought;

(B) the subject matter of the expected action and the petitioner's interest;

(C) the facts that the petitioner wants to establish by the proposed testimony and the reasons to perpetuate it;

(D) the names or a description of the persons whom the petitioner expects to be adverse parties and their addresses, so far as known; and

(E) the name, address, and expected substance of the testimony of each deponent.

(2) *Notice and Service.* At least 21 days before the hearing date, the petitioner must serve each expected adverse party with a copy of the petition and a notice stating the time and place of the hearing. The notice may be served either inside or outside the district or state in the manner provided in Rule 4. If that service cannot be made with reasonable diligence on an expected adverse party, the court may order service by publication or otherwise. The court must appoint an attorney to represent persons not served in the manner provided in Rule 4 and to cross-examine the deponent if an unserved person is not otherwise represented. If any expected adverse party is a minor or is incompetent, Rule 17(c) applies.

(3) *Order and Examination.* If satisfied that perpetuating the testimony may prevent a failure or delay of justice, the court must issue an order that designates or describes the persons whose depositions may be taken, specifies the subject matter of the examinations, and states whether the depositions will be taken orally or by written interrogatories. The depositions may then be taken under these rules, and the court may issue orders like those authorized by Rules 34 and 35. A reference in these rules to the court where an action is pending means, for purposes of this rule, the court where the petition for the deposition was filed.

(4) *Using the Deposition.* A deposition to perpetuate testimony may be used under Rule 32(a) in any later-filed district-court action involving the same subject matter if the deposition either was taken under these rules or, although not so taken, would be admissible in evidence in the courts of the state where it was taken.

(b) **Pending Appeal.**

(1) *In General.* The court where a judgment has been rendered may, if an appeal has been taken or may still be taken, permit a party to depose witnesses to perpetuate their testimony for use in the event of further proceedings in that court.

(2) *Motion.* The party who wants to perpetuate testimony may move for leave to take the depositions, on the same notice and service as if the action were pending in the district court. The motion must show:

(A) the name, address, and expected substance of the testimony of each deponent; and

(B) the reasons for perpetuating the testimony.

(3) *Court Order.* If the court finds that perpetuating the testimony may prevent a failure or delay of justice, the court may permit the depositions to be taken and may issue orders like those authorized by Rules 34 and 35. The depositions may be taken and used as any other deposition taken in a pending district-court action.

(c) Perpetuation by an Action. This rule does not limit a court's power to entertain an action to perpetuate testimony.

(Amended December 27, 1946, effective March 19, 1948; December 29, 1948, effective October 20, 1949; March 1, 1971, effective July 1, 1971; March 2, 1987, effective August 1, 1987; April 25, 2005, effective December 1, 2005; April 30, 2007, effective December 1, 2007; March 26, 2009, effective December 1, 2009.)

RULE 28. PERSONS BEFORE WHOM DEPOSITIONS MAY BE TAKEN

(a) Within the United States.

(1) *In General.* Within the United States or a territory or insular possession subject to United States jurisdiction, a deposition must be taken before:

(A) an officer authorized to administer oaths either by federal law or by the law in the place of examination; or

(B) a person appointed by the court where the action is pending to administer oaths and take testimony.

(2) *Definition of "Officer".* The term "officer" in Rules 30, 31, and 32 includes a person appointed by the court under this rule or designated by the parties under Rule 29(a).

(b) In a Foreign Country.

(1) *In General.* A deposition may be taken in a foreign country:

(A) under an applicable treaty or convention;

(B) under a letter of request, whether or not captioned a "letter rogatory";

(C) on notice, before a person authorized to administer oaths either by federal law or by the law in the place of examination; or

(D) before a person commissioned by the court to administer any necessary oath and take testimony.

(2) *Issuing a Letter of Request or a Commission.* A letter of request, a commission, or both may be issued:

(A) on appropriate terms after an application and notice of it; and

(B) without a showing that taking the deposition in another manner is impracticable or inconvenient.

(3) *Form of a Request, Notice, or Commission.* When a letter of request or any other device is used according to a treaty or convention, it must be captioned in the form prescribed by that treaty or convention. A letter of request may be addressed "To the Appropriate Authority in [name of country]." A deposition notice or a commission must designate by name or descriptive title the person before whom the deposition is to be taken.

(4) *Letter of Request—Admitting Evidence.* Evidence obtained in response to a letter of request need not be excluded merely because it is not a verbatim transcript, because the testimony was not taken under oath, or because of any similar departure from the requirements for depositions taken within the United States.

(c) Disqualification. A deposition must not be taken before a person who is any party's relative, employee, or attorney; who is related to or employed by any party's attorney; or who is financially interested in the action.

(Amended December 27, 1946, effective March 19, 1948; January 21, 1963, effective July 1, 1963; April 29, 1980, effective August 1, 1980; March 2, 1987, effective August 1, 1987; April 22, 1993, effective December 1, 1993; April 30, 2007, effective December 1, 2007.)

RULE 29. STIPULATIONS ABOUT DISCOVERY PROCEDURE

Unless the court orders otherwise, the parties may stipulate that:

(a) a deposition may be taken before any person, at any time or place, on any notice, and in the manner specified—in which event it may be used in the same way as any other deposition; and

(b) other procedures governing or limiting discovery be modified—but a stipulation extending the time for any form of discovery must have court approval if it would interfere with the time set for completing discovery, for hearing a motion, or for trial.

(Amended March 30, 1970, effective July 1, 1970; April 22, 1993, effective December 1, 1993; April 30, 2007, effective December 1, 2007.)

RULE 30. DEPOSITIONS BY ORAL EXAMINATION

(a) When a Deposition May Be Taken.

(1) *Without Leave.* A party may, by oral questions, depose any person, including a party, without leave of court except as provided in Rule 30(a)(2). The deponent's attendance may be compelled by subpoena under Rule 45.

(2) *With Leave.* A party must obtain leave of court, and the court must grant leave to the extent consistent with Rule 26(b)(2):

  (A) if the parties have not stipulated to the deposition and:

    (i) the deposition would result in more than 10 depositions being taken under this rule or Rule 31 by the plaintiffs, or by the defendants, or by the third-party defendants;

    (ii) the deponent has already been deposed in the case; or

    (iii) the party seeks to take the deposition before the time specified in Rule 26(d), unless the party certifies in the notice, with supporting facts, that the deponent is expected to leave the United States and be unavailable for examination in this country after that time; or

  (B) if the deponent is confined in prison.

(b) Notice of the Deposition; Other Formal Requirements.

(1) *Notice in General.* A party who wants to depose a person by oral questions must give reasonable written notice to every other party. The notice must state the time and place of the deposition and, if known, the deponent's name and address. If the name is unknown, the notice must provide a general description sufficient to identify the person or the particular class or group to which the person belongs.

(2) *Producing Documents.* If a subpoena duces tecum is to be served on the deponent, the materials designated for production, as set out in the subpoena, must be listed in the notice or in an attachment. The notice to a party deponent may be accompanied by a request under Rule 34 to produce documents and tangible things at the deposition.

(3) *Method of Recording.*

  (A) *Method Stated in the Notice.* The party who notices the deposition must state in the notice the method for recording the testimony. Unless the court orders otherwise, testimony may be recorded by audio, audiovisual, or stenographic means. The noticing party bears the recording costs. Any party may arrange to transcribe a deposition.

  (B) *Additional Method.* With prior notice to the deponent and other parties, any party may designate another method for recording the testimony in addition to that specified in the original notice. That party bears the expense of the additional record or transcript unless the court orders otherwise.

(4) *By Remote Means.* The parties may stipulate— or the court may on motion order—that a deposition be taken by telephone or other remote means. For the purpose of this rule and Rules 28(a), 37(a)(2), and 37(b)(1), the deposition takes place where the deponent answers the questions.

(5) *Officer's Duties.*

  (A) *Before the Deposition.* Unless the parties stipulate otherwise, a deposition must be conducted before an officer appointed or designated under Rule 28. The officer must begin the deposition with an on-the-record statement that includes:

    (i) the officer's name and business address;

    (ii) the date, time, and place of the deposition;

    (iii) the deponent's name;

    (iv) the officer's administration of the oath or affirmation to the deponent; and

    (v) the identity of all persons present.

  (B) *Conducting the Deposition; Avoiding Distortion.* If the deposition is recorded non-stenographically, the officer must repeat the items in Rule 30(b)(5)(A)(i)-(iii) at the beginning of each unit of the recording medium. The deponent's and attorneys' appearance or demeanor must not be distorted through recording techniques.

  (C) *After the Deposition.* At the end of a deposition, the officer must state on the record that the deposition is complete and must set out any stipulations made by the attorneys about custody of the transcript or recording and of the exhibits, or about any other pertinent matters.

(6) *Notice or Subpoena Directed to an Organization.* In its notice or subpoena, a party may name as the deponent a public or private corporation, a partnership, an association, a governmental agency, or other entity and must describe with reasonable particularity the matters for examination. The named organization must then designate one or more officers, directors, or managing agents, or designate other persons who consent to testify on its behalf; and it may set out the matters on which each person designated will testify. A subpoena must advise a nonparty organization of its duty to make this designation. The persons designated must testify about information known or reasonably available to the organization. This paragraph (6) does not preclude a deposition by any other procedure allowed by these rules.

(c) **Examination and Cross–Examination; Record of the Examination; Objections; Written Questions.**

(1) *Examination and Cross–Examination.* The examination and cross-examination of a deponent proceed as they would at trial under the Federal Rules of Evidence, except Rules 103 and 615. After putting the deponent under oath or affirmation, the officer must record the testimony by the method designated under Rule 30(b)(3)(A). The testimony must be recorded by the officer personally or by a person acting in the presence and under the direction of the officer.

(2) *Objections.* An objection at the time of the examination—whether to evidence, to a party's conduct, to the officer's qualifications, to the manner of taking the deposition, or to any other aspect of the deposition—must be noted on the record, but the examination still proceeds; the testimony is taken subject to any objection. An objection must be stated concisely in a nonargumentative and nonsuggestive manner. A person may instruct a deponent not to answer only when necessary to preserve a privilege, to enforce a limitation ordered by the court, or to present a motion under Rule 30(d)(3).

(3) *Participating Through Written Questions.* Instead of participating in the oral examination, a party may serve written questions in a sealed envelope on the party noticing the deposition, who must deliver them to the officer. The officer must ask the deponent those questions and record the answers verbatim.

(d) **Duration; Sanction; Motion to Terminate or Limit.**

(1) *Duration.* Unless otherwise stipulated or ordered by the court, a deposition is limited to 1 day of 7 hours. The court must allow additional time consistent with Rule 26(b)(2) if needed to fairly examine the deponent or if the deponent, another person, or any other circumstance impedes or delays the examination.

(2) *Sanction.* The court may impose an appropriate sanction—including the reasonable expenses and attorney's fees incurred by any party—on a person who impedes, delays, or frustrates the fair examination of the deponent.

(3) *Motion to Terminate or Limit.*

(A) *Grounds.* At any time during a deposition, the deponent or a party may move to terminate or limit it on the ground that it is being conducted in bad faith or in a manner that unreasonably annoys, embarrasses, or oppresses the deponent or party. The motion may be filed in the court where the action is pending or the deposition is being taken. If the objecting deponent or party so demands, the deposition must be suspended for the time necessary to obtain an order.

(B) *Order.* The court may order that the deposition be terminated or may limit its scope and manner as provided in Rule 26(c). If terminated, the deposition may be resumed only by order of the court where the action is pending.

(C) *Award of Expenses.* Rule 37(a)(5) applies to the award of expenses.

(e) **Review by the Witness; Changes.**

(1) *Review; Statement of Changes.* On request by the deponent or a party before the deposition is completed, the deponent must be allowed 30 days after being notified by the officer that the transcript or recording is available in which:

(A) to review the transcript or recording; and

(B) if there are changes in form or substance, to sign a statement listing the changes and the reasons for making them.

(2) *Changes Indicated in the Officer's Certificate.* The officer must note in the certificate prescribed by Rule 30(f)(1) whether a review was requested and, if so, must attach any changes the deponent makes during the 30–day period.

(f) **Certification and Delivery; Exhibits; Copies of the Transcript or Recording; Filing.**

(1) *Certification and Delivery.* The officer must certify in writing that the witness was duly sworn and that the deposition accurately records the witness's testimony. The certificate must accompany the record of the deposition. Unless the court orders otherwise, the officer must seal the deposition in an envelope or package bearing the title of the action and marked "Deposition of [witness's name]" and must promptly send it to the attorney who arranged for the transcript or recording. The attorney must store it under conditions that will protect it against loss, destruction, tampering, or deterioration.

(2) *Documents and Tangible Things.*

(A) *Originals and Copies.* Documents and tangible things produced for inspection during a deposition must, on a party's request, be marked for identification and attached to the deposition. Any party may inspect and copy them. But if the person who produced them wants to keep the originals, the person may:

(i) offer copies to be marked, attached to the deposition, and then used as originals—after giving all parties a fair opportunity to verify the copies by comparing them with the originals; or

(ii) give all parties a fair opportunity to inspect and copy the originals after they are marked—in which event the originals may be used as if attached to the deposition.

(B) *Order Regarding the Originals.* Any party may move for an order that the originals be attached to the deposition pending final disposition of the case.

(3) *Copies of the Transcript or Recording.* Unless otherwise stipulated or ordered by the court, the officer must retain the stenographic notes of a deposition taken stenographically or a copy of the recording of a deposition taken by another method. When paid reasonable charges, the officer must furnish a copy of the transcript or recording to any party or the deponent.

(4) *Notice of Filing.* A party who files the deposition must promptly notify all other parties of the filing.

(g) **Failure to Attend a Deposition or Serve a Subpoena; Expenses.** A party who, expecting a deposition to be taken, attends in person or by an attorney may recover reasonable expenses for attending, including attorney's fees, if the noticing party failed to:

(1) attend and proceed with the deposition; or

(2) serve a subpoena on a nonparty deponent, who consequently did not attend.

(Amended January 21, 1963, effective July 1, 1963; March 30, 1970, effective July 1, 1970; March 1, 1971, effective July 1, 1971; November 20, 1972, effective July 1, 1975; April 29, 1980, effective August 1, 1980; March 2, 1987, effective August 1, 1987; April 22, 1993, effective December 1, 1993; April 17, 2000, effective December 1, 2000; April 30, 2007, effective December 1, 2007.)

RULE 31. DEPOSITIONS BY WRITTEN QUESTIONS

(a) **When a Deposition May Be Taken.**

(1) *Without Leave.* A party may, by written questions, depose any person, including a party, without leave of court except as provided in Rule 31(a)(2). The deponent's attendance may be compelled by subpoena under Rule 45.

(2) *With Leave.* A party must obtain leave of court, and the court must grant leave to the extent consistent with Rule 26(b)(2):

(A) if the parties have not stipulated to the deposition and:

(i) the deposition would result in more than 10 depositions being taken under this rule or Rule 30 by the plaintiffs, or by the defendants, or by the third-party defendants;

(ii) the deponent has already been deposed in the case; or

(iii) the party seeks to take a deposition before the time specified in Rule 26(d); or

(B) if the deponent is confined in prison.

(3) *Service; Required Notice.* A party who wants to depose a person by written questions must serve them on every other party, with a notice stating, if known, the deponent's name and address. If the name is unknown, the notice must provide a general description sufficient to identify the person or the particular class or group to which the person belongs. The notice must also state the name or descriptive title and the address of the officer before whom the deposition will be taken.

(4) *Questions Directed to an Organization.* A public or private corporation, a partnership, an association, or a governmental agency may be deposed by written questions in accordance with Rule 30(b)(6).

(5) *Questions from Other Parties.* Any questions to the deponent from other parties must be served on all parties as follows: cross-questions, within 14 days after being served with the notice and direct questions; redirect questions, within 7 days after being served with cross-questions; and recross-questions, within 7 days after being served with redirect questions. The court may, for good cause, extend or shorten these times.

(b) **Delivery to the Officer; Officer's Duties.** The party who noticed the deposition must deliver to the officer a copy of all the questions served and of the notice. The officer must promptly proceed in the manner provided in Rule 30(c), (e), and (f) to:

(1) take the deponent's testimony in response to the questions;

(2) prepare and certify the deposition; and

(3) send it to the party, attaching a copy of the questions and of the notice.

(c) **Notice of Completion or Filing.**

(1) *Completion.* The party who noticed the deposition must notify all other parties when it is completed.

(2) *Filing.* A party who files the deposition must promptly notify all other parties of the filing.

(Amended March 30, 1970, effective July 1, 1970; March 2, 1987, effective August 1, 1987; April 22, 1993, effective December 1, 1993; April 30, 2007, effective December 1, 2007.)

RULE 32. USING DEPOSITIONS IN COURT PROCEEDINGS

(a) **Using Depositions.**

(1) *In General.* At a hearing or trial, all or part of a deposition may be used against a party on these conditions:

(A) the party was present or represented at the taking of the deposition or had reasonable notice of it;

(B) it is used to the extent it would be admissible under the Federal Rules of Evidence if the deponent were present and testifying; and

(C) the use is allowed by Rule 32(a)(2) through (8).

(2) *Impeachment and Other Uses.* Any party may use a deposition to contradict or impeach the testimony given by the deponent as a witness, or for any other purpose allowed by the Federal Rules of Evidence.

(3) *Deposition of Party, Agent, or Designee.* An adverse party may use for any purpose the deposition of a party or anyone who, when deposed, was the party's officer, director, managing agent, or designee under Rule 30(b)(6) or 31(a)(4).

(4) *Unavailable Witness.* A party may use for any purpose the deposition of a witness, whether or not a party, if the court finds:

(A) that the witness is dead;

(B) that the witness is more than 100 miles from the place of hearing or trial or is outside the United States, unless it appears that the witness's absence was procured by the party offering the deposition;

(C) that the witness cannot attend or testify because of age, illness, infirmity, or imprisonment;

(D) that the party offering the deposition could not procure the witness's attendance by subpoena; or

(E) on motion and notice, that exceptional circumstances make it desirable—in the interest of justice and with due regard to the importance of live testimony in open court—to permit the deposition to be used.

(5) *Limitations on Use.*

(A) *Deposition Taken on Short Notice.* A deposition must not be used against a party who, having received less than 14 days' notice of the deposition, promptly moved for a protective order under Rule 26(c)(1)(B) requesting that it not be taken or be taken at a different time or place—and this motion was still pending when the deposition was taken.

(B) *Unavailable Deponent; Party Could Not Obtain an Attorney.* A deposition taken without leave of court under the unavailability provision of Rule 30(a)(2)(A)(iii) must not be used against a party who shows that, when served with the notice, it could not, despite diligent efforts, obtain an attorney to represent it at the deposition.

(6) *Using Part of a Deposition.* If a party offers in evidence only part of a deposition, an adverse party may require the offeror to introduce other parts that in fairness should be considered with the part introduced, and any party may itself introduce any other parts.

(7) *Substituting a Party.* Substituting a party under Rule 25 does not affect the right to use a deposition previously taken.

(8) *Deposition Taken in an Earlier Action.* A deposition lawfully taken and, if required, filed in any federal- or state-court action may be used in a later action involving the same subject matter between the same parties, or their representatives or successors in interest, to the same extent as if taken in the later action. A deposition previously taken may also be used as allowed by the Federal Rules of Evidence.

(b) **Objections to Admissibility.** Subject to Rules 28(b) and 32(d)(3), an objection may be made at a hearing or trial to the admission of any deposition testimony that would be inadmissible if the witness were present and testifying.

(c) **Form of Presentation.** Unless the court orders otherwise, a party must provide a transcript of any deposition testimony the party offers, but may provide the court with the testimony in nontranscript form as well. On any party's request, deposition testimony offered in a jury trial for any purpose other than impeachment must be presented in nontranscript form, if available, unless the court for good cause orders otherwise.

(d) **Waiver of Objections.**

(1) *To the Notice.* An objection to an error or irregularity in a deposition notice is waived unless promptly served in writing on the party giving the notice.

(2) *To the Officer's Qualification.* An objection based on disqualification of the officer before whom a deposition is to be taken is waived if not made:

(A) before the deposition begins; or

(B) promptly after the basis for disqualification becomes known or, with reasonable diligence, could have been known.

(3) *To the Taking of the Deposition.*

(A) *Objection to Competence, Relevance, or Materiality.* An objection to a deponent's competence—or to the competence, relevance, or materiality of testimony—is not waived by a failure to make the objection before or during the deposition, unless the ground for it might have been corrected at that time.

(B) *Objection to an Error or Irregularity.* An objection to an error or irregularity at an oral examination is waived if:

   (i) it relates to the manner of taking the deposition, the form of a question or answer, the oath or affirmation, a party's conduct, or other matters that might have been corrected at that time; and

   (ii) it is not timely made during the deposition.

(C) *Objection to a Written Question.* An objection to the form of a written question under Rule 31 is waived if not served in writing on the party submitting the question within the time for serving responsive questions or, if the question is a recross-question, within 7 days after being served with it.

(4) ***To Completing and Returning the Deposition.*** An objection to how the officer transcribed the testimony—or prepared, signed, certified, sealed, endorsed, sent, or otherwise dealt with the deposition—is waived unless a motion to suppress is made promptly after the error or irregularity becomes known or, with reasonable diligence, could have been known.

(Amended March 30, 1970, effective July 1, 1970; November 20, 1972, effective July 1, 1975; April 29, 1980, effective August 1, 1980; March 2, 1987, effective August 1, 1987; April 22, 1993, effective December 1, 1993; April 30, 2007, effective December 1, 2007; March 26, 2009, effective December 1, 2009.)

RULE 33. INTERROGATORIES TO PARTIES

(a) In General.

(1) *Number.* Unless otherwise stipulated or ordered by the court, a party may serve on any other party no more than 25 written interrogatories, including all discrete subparts. Leave to serve additional interrogatories may be granted to the extent consistent with Rule 26(b)(2).

(2) *Scope.* An interrogatory may relate to any matter that may be inquired into under Rule 26(b). An interrogatory is not objectionable merely because it asks for an opinion or contention that relates to fact or the application of law to fact, but the court may order that the interrogatory need not be answered until designated discovery is complete, or until a pretrial conference or some other time.

(b) Answers and Objections.

(1) ***Responding Party.*** The interrogatories must be answered:

   (A) by the party to whom they are directed; or

   (B) if that party is a public or private corporation, a partnership, an association, or a governmental agency, by any officer or agent, who must furnish the information available to the party.

(2) ***Time to Respond.*** The responding party must serve its answers and any objections within 30 days after being served with the interrogatories. A shorter or longer time may be stipulated to under Rule 29 or be ordered by the court.

(3) ***Answering Each Interrogatory.*** Each interrogatory must, to the extent it is not objected to, be answered separately and fully in writing under oath.

(4) ***Objections.*** The grounds for objecting to an interrogatory must be stated with specificity. Any ground not stated in a timely objection is waived unless the court, for good cause, excuses the failure.

(5) ***Signature.*** The person who makes the answers must sign them, and the attorney who objects must sign any objections.

(c) Use. An answer to an interrogatory may be used to the extent allowed by the Federal Rules of Evidence.

(d) Option to Produce Business Records. If the answer to an interrogatory may be determined by examining, auditing, compiling, abstracting, or summarizing a party's business records (including electronically stored information), and if the burden of deriving or ascertaining the answer will be substantially the same for either party, the responding party may answer by:

(1) specifying the records that must be reviewed, in sufficient detail to enable the interrogating party to locate and identify them as readily as the responding party could; and

(2) giving the interrogating party a reasonable opportunity to examine and audit the records and to make copies, compilations, abstracts, or summaries.

(Amended December 27, 1946, effective March 19, 1948; March 30, 1970, effective July 1, 1970; April 29, 1980, effective August 1, 1980; April 22, 1993, effective December 1, 1993; April 12, 2006, effective December 1, 2006; April 30, 2007, effective December 1, 2007.)

RULE 34. PRODUCING DOCUMENTS, ELECTRONICALLY STORED INFORMATION, AND TANGIBLE THINGS, OR ENTERING ONTO LAND, FOR INSPECTION AND OTHER PURPOSES

(a) In General. A party may serve on any other party a request within the scope of Rule 26(b):

(1) to produce and permit the requesting party or its representative to inspect, copy, test, or sample the following items in the responding party's possession, custody, or control:

(A) any designated documents or electronically stored information—including writings, drawings, graphs, charts, photographs, sound recordings, images, and other data or data compilations—stored in any medium from which information can be obtained either directly or, if necessary, after translation by the responding party into a reasonably usable form; or

(B) any designated tangible things; or

(2) to permit entry onto designated land or other property possessed or controlled by the responding party, so that the requesting party may inspect, measure, survey, photograph, test, or sample the property or any designated object or operation on it.

(b) Procedure.

(1) *Contents of the Request.* The request:

(A) must describe with reasonable particularity each item or category of items to be inspected;

(B) must specify a reasonable time, place, and manner for the inspection and for performing the related acts; and

(C) may specify the form or forms in which electronically stored information is to be produced.

(2) *Responses and Objections.*

(A) *Time to Respond.* The party to whom the request is directed must respond in writing within 30 days after being served. A shorter or longer time may be stipulated to under Rule 29 or be ordered by the court.

(B) *Responding to Each Item.* For each item or category, the response must either state that inspection and related activities will be permitted as requested or state an objection to the request, including the reasons.

(C) *Objections.* An objection to part of a request must specify the part and permit inspection of the rest.

(D) *Responding to a Request for Production of Electronically Stored Information.* The response may state an objection to a requested form for producing electronically stored information. If the responding party objects to a requested form—or if no form was specified in the request—the party must state the form or forms it intends to use.

(E) *Producing the Documents or Electronically Stored Information.* Unless otherwise stipulated or ordered by the court, these procedures apply to producing documents or electronically stored information:

(i) A party must produce documents as they are kept in the usual course of business or must organize and label them to correspond to the categories in the request;

(ii) If a request does not specify a form for producing electronically stored information, a party must produce it in a form or forms in which it is ordinarily maintained or in a reasonably usable form or forms; and

(iii) A party need not produce the same electronically stored information in more than one form.

(c) Nonparties. As provided in Rule 45, a nonparty may be compelled to produce documents and tangible things or to permit an inspection.

(Amended December 27, 1946, effective March 19, 1948; March 30, 1970, effective July 1, 1970; April 29, 1980, effective August 1, 1980; March 2, 1987, effective August 1, 1987; April 30, 1991, effective December 1, 1991; April 22, 1993, effective December 1, 1993; April 12, 2006, effective December 1, 2006; April 30, 2007, effective December 1, 2007.)

RULE 35.   PHYSICAL AND MENTAL EXAMINATIONS

(a) Order for an Examination.

(1) *In General.* The court where the action is pending may order a party whose mental or physical condition—including blood group—is in controversy to submit to a physical or mental examination by a suitably licensed or certified examiner. The court has the same authority to order a party to produce for examination a person who is in its custody or under its legal control.

(2) *Motion and Notice; Contents of the Order.* The order:

(A) may be made only on motion for good cause and on notice to all parties and the person to be examined; and

(B) must specify the time, place, manner, conditions, and scope of the examination, as well as the person or persons who will perform it.

(b) Examiner's Report.

(1) *Request by the Party or Person Examined.* The party who moved for the examination must, on request, deliver to the requester a copy of the examiner's report, together with like reports of all earlier examinations of the same condition. The request may be made by the party against whom the examination order was issued or by the person examined.

(2) *Contents.* The examiner's report must be in writing and must set out in detail the examiner's findings, including diagnoses, conclusions, and the results of any tests.

(3) *Request by the Moving Party.* After delivering the reports, the party who moved for the examination may request—and is entitled to receive—from the party against whom the examination order was issued like reports of all earlier or later examinations of the same condition. But those reports need not be delivered by the party with custody or control of the person examined if the party shows that it could not obtain them.

(4) *Waiver of Privilege.* By requesting and obtaining the examiner's report, or by deposing the examiner, the party examined waives any privilege it may have—in that action or any other action involving the same controversy—concerning testimony about all examinations of the same condition.

(5) *Failure to Deliver a Report.* The court on motion may order—on just terms—that a party deliver the report of an examination. If the report is not provided, the court may exclude the examiner's testimony at trial.

(6) *Scope.* This subdivision (b) applies also to an examination made by the parties' agreement, unless the agreement states otherwise. This subdivision does not preclude obtaining an examiner's report or deposing an examiner under other rules.

(Amended March 30, 1970, effective July 1, 1970; March 2, 1987, effective August 1, 1987; amended by Pub.L. 100–690, Title VII, § 7047(b), November 18, 1988, 102 Stat. 4401; amended April 30, 1991, effective December 1, 1991; April 30, 2007, effective December 1, 2007.)

RULE 36. REQUESTS FOR ADMISSION

(a) Scope and Procedure.

(1) *Scope.* A party may serve on any other party a written request to admit, for purposes of the pending action only, the truth of any matters within the scope of Rule 26(b)(1) relating to:

(A) facts, the application of law to fact, or opinions about either; and

(B) the genuineness of any described documents.

(2) *Form; Copy of a Document.* Each matter must be separately stated. A request to admit the genuineness of a document must be accompanied by a copy of the document unless it is, or has been, otherwise furnished or made available for inspection and copying.

(3) *Time to Respond; Effect of Not Responding.* A matter is admitted unless, within 30 days after being served, the party to whom the request is directed serves on the requesting party a written answer or objection addressed to the matter

and signed by the party or its attorney. A shorter or longer time for responding may be stipulated to under Rule 29 or be ordered by the court.

(4) *Answer.* If a matter is not admitted, the answer must specifically deny it or state in detail why the answering party cannot truthfully admit or deny it. A denial must fairly respond to the substance of the matter; and when good faith requires that a party qualify an answer or deny only a part of a matter, the answer must specify the part admitted and qualify or deny the rest. The answering party may assert lack of knowledge or information as a reason for failing to admit or deny only if the party states that it has made reasonable inquiry and that the information it knows or can readily obtain is insufficient to enable it to admit or deny.

(5) *Objections.* The grounds for objecting to a request must be stated. A party must not object solely on the ground that the request presents a genuine issue for trial.

(6) *Motion Regarding the Sufficiency of an Answer or Objection.* The requesting party may move to determine the sufficiency of an answer or objection. Unless the court finds an objection justified, it must order that an answer be served. On finding that an answer does not comply with this rule, the court may order either that the matter is admitted or that an amended answer be served. The court may defer its final decision until a pretrial conference or a specified time before trial. Rule 37(a)(5) applies to an award of expenses.

(b) Effect of an Admission; Withdrawing or Amending It. A matter admitted under this rule is conclusively established unless the court, on motion, permits the admission to be withdrawn or amended. Subject to Rule 16(e), the court may permit withdrawal or amendment if it would promote the presentation of the merits of the action and if the court is not persuaded that it would prejudice the requesting party in maintaining or defending the action on the merits. An admission under this rule is not an admission for any other purpose and cannot be used against the party in any other proceeding.

(Amended December 27, 1946, effective March 19, 1948; March 30, 1970, effective July 1, 1970; March 2, 1987, effective August 1, 1987; April 22, 1993, effective December 1, 1993; April 30, 2007, effective December 1, 2007.)

RULE 37. FAILURE TO MAKE DISCLOSURES OR TO COOPERATE IN DISCOVERY; SANCTIONS

(a) Motion for an Order Compelling Disclosure or Discovery.

(1) *In General.* On notice to other parties and all affected persons, a party may move for an order compelling disclosure or discovery. The motion must include a certification that the movant has in good faith conferred or attempted to confer with the person or party failing to make disclosure or discovery in an effort to obtain it without court action.

(2) *Appropriate Court.* A motion for an order to a party must be made in the court where the action is pending. A motion for an order to a nonparty must be made in the court where the discovery is or will be taken.

(3) *Specific Motions.*

(A) *To Compel Disclosure.* If a party fails to make a disclosure required by Rule 26(a), any other party may move to compel disclosure and for appropriate sanctions.

(B) *To Compel a Discovery Response.* A party seeking discovery may move for an order compelling an answer, designation, production, or inspection. This motion may be made if:

(i) a deponent fails to answer a question asked under Rule 30 or 31;

(ii) a corporation or other entity fails to make a designation under Rule 30(b)(6) or 31(a)(4);

(iii) a party fails to answer an interrogatory submitted under Rule 33; or

(iv) a party fails to respond that inspection will be permitted—or fails to permit inspection—as requested under Rule 34.

(C) *Related to a Deposition.* When taking an oral deposition, the party asking a question may complete or adjourn the examination before moving for an order.

(4) *Evasive or Incomplete Disclosure, Answer, or Response.* For purposes of this subdivision (a), an evasive or incomplete disclosure, answer, or response must be treated as a failure to disclose, answer, or respond.

(5) *Payment of Expenses; Protective Orders.*

(A) *If the Motion Is Granted (or Disclosure or Discovery Is Provided After Filing).* If the motion is granted—or if the disclosure or requested discovery is provided after the motion was filed—the court must, after giving an opportunity to be heard, require the party or deponent whose conduct necessitated the motion, the party or attorney advising that conduct, or both to pay the movant's reasonable expenses incurred in making the motion, including attorney's fees. But the court must not order this payment if:

(i) the movant filed the motion before attempting in good faith to obtain the disclosure or discovery without court action;

(ii) the opposing party's nondisclosure, response, or objection was substantially justified; or

(iii) other circumstances make an award of expenses unjust.

(B) *If the Motion Is Denied.* If the motion is denied, the court may issue any protective order authorized under Rule 26(c) and must, after giving an opportunity to be heard, require the movant, the attorney filing the motion, or both to pay the party or deponent who opposed the motion its reasonable expenses incurred in opposing the motion, including attorney's fees. But the court must not order this payment if the motion was substantially justified or other circumstances make an award of expenses unjust.

(C) *If the Motion Is Granted in Part and Denied in Part.* If the motion is granted in part and denied in part, the court may issue any protective order authorized under Rule 26(c) and may, after giving an opportunity to be heard, apportion the reasonable expenses for the motion.

(b) **Failure to Comply with a Court Order.**

(1) *Sanctions in the District Where the Deposition Is Taken.* If the court where the discovery is taken orders a deponent to be sworn or to answer a question and the deponent fails to obey, the failure may be treated as contempt of court.

(2) *Sanctions in the District Where the Action Is Pending.*

(A) *For Not Obeying a Discovery Order.* If a party or a party's officer, director, or managing agent—or a witness designated under Rule 30(b)(6) or 31(a)(4)—fails to obey an order to provide or permit discovery, including an order under Rule 26(f), 35, or 37(a), the court where the action is pending may issue further just orders. They may include the following:

(i) directing that the matters embraced in the order or other designated facts be taken as established for purposes of the action, as the prevailing party claims;

(ii) prohibiting the disobedient party from supporting or opposing designated claims or defenses, or from introducing designated matters in evidence;

(iii) striking pleadings in whole or in part;

    (iv) staying further proceedings until the order is obeyed;

    (v) dismissing the action or proceeding in whole or in part;

    (vi) rendering a default judgment against the disobedient party; or

    (vii) treating as contempt of court the failure to obey any order except an order to submit to a physical or mental examination.

  (B) *For Not Producing a Person for Examination.* If a party fails to comply with an order under Rule 35(a) requiring it to produce another person for examination, the court may issue any of the orders listed in Rule 37(b)(2)(A)(i)-(vi), unless the disobedient party shows that it cannot produce the other person.

  (C) *Payment of Expenses.* Instead of or in addition to the orders above, the court must order the disobedient party, the attorney advising that party, or both to pay the reasonable expenses, including attorney's fees, caused by the failure, unless the failure was substantially justified or other circumstances make an award of expenses unjust.

(c) Failure to Disclose, to Supplement an Earlier Response, or to Admit.

  (1) *Failure to Disclose or Supplement.* If a party fails to provide information or identify a witness as required by Rule 26(a) or (e), the party is not allowed to use that information or witness to supply evidence on a motion, at a hearing, or at a trial, unless the failure was substantially justified or is harmless. In addition to or instead of this sanction, the court, on motion and after giving an opportunity to be heard:

    (A) may order payment of the reasonable expenses, including attorney's fees, caused by the failure;

    (B) may inform the jury of the party's failure; and

    (C) may impose other appropriate sanctions, including any of the orders listed in Rule 37(b)(2)(A)(i)-(vi).

  (2) *Failure to Admit.* If a party fails to admit what is requested under Rule 36 and if the requesting party later proves a document to be genuine or the matter true, the requesting party may move that the party who failed to admit pay the reasonable expenses, including attorney's fees, incurred in making that proof. The court must so order unless:

    (A) the request was held objectionable under Rule 36(a);

    (B) the admission sought was of no substantial importance;

    (C) the party failing to admit had a reasonable ground to believe that it might prevail on the matter; or

    (D) there was other good reason for the failure to admit.

(d) Party's Failure to Attend Its Own Deposition, Serve Answers to Interrogatories, or Respond to a Request for Inspection.

  (1) *In General.*

    (A) *Motion; Grounds for Sanctions.* The court where the action is pending may, on motion, order sanctions if:

      (i) a party or a party's officer, director, or managing agent—or a person designated under Rule 30(b)(6) or 31(a)(4)—fails, after being served with proper notice, to appear for that person's deposition; or

      (ii) a party, after being properly served with interrogatories under Rule 33 or a request for inspection under Rule 34, fails to serve its answers, objections, or written response.

    (B) *Certification.* A motion for sanctions for failing to answer or respond must include a certification that the movant has in good faith conferred or attempted to confer with the party failing to act in an effort to obtain the answer or response without court action.

  (2) *Unacceptable Excuse for Failing to Act.* A failure described in Rule 37(d)(1)(A) is not excused on the ground that the discovery sought was objectionable, unless the party failing to act has a pending motion for a protective order under Rule 26(c).

  (3) *Types of Sanctions.* Sanctions may include any of the orders listed in Rule 37(b)(2)(A)(i)-(vi). Instead of or in addition to these sanctions, the court must require the party failing to act, the attorney advising that party, or both to pay the reasonable expenses, including attorney's fees, caused by the failure, unless the failure was substantially justified or other circumstances make an award of expenses unjust.

(e) Failure to Provide Electronically Stored Information. Absent exceptional circumstances, a court may not impose sanctions under these rules on a party for failing to provide electronically stored information lost as a result of the routine, good-faith operation of an electronic information system.

(f) Failure to Participate in Framing a Discovery Plan. If a party or its attorney fails to participate in good faith in developing and submitting a proposed discovery plan as required by Rule 26(f), the court may, after giving an opportunity to be heard, require that party or attorney to pay to any other party the reasonable expenses, including attorney's fees, caused by the failure.

(Amended December 29, 1948, effective October 20, 1949; March 30, 1970, effective July 1, 1970; April 29, 1980, effective August 1, 1980; amended by Pub.L. 96–481, Title II, § 205(a), October 21, 1980, 94 Stat. 2330, effective October 1, 1981; amended March 2, 1987, effective August 1, 1987; April 22, 1993, effective December 1, 1993; April 17, 2000, effective December 1, 2000; April 12, 2006, effective December 1, 2006; April 30, 2007, effective December 1, 2007.)

TITLE VI. TRIALS

RULE 38. RIGHT TO A JURY TRIAL; DEMAND

(a) Right Preserved. The right of trial by jury as declared by the Seventh Amendment to the Constitution—or as provided by a federal statute—is preserved to the parties inviolate.

(b) Demand. On any issue triable of right by a jury, a party may demand a jury trial by:

  (1) serving the other parties with a written demand—which may be included in a pleading—no later than 14 days after the last pleading directed to the issue is served; and

  (2) filing the demand in accordance with Rule 5(d).

(c) Specifying Issues. In its demand, a party may specify the issues that it wishes to have tried by a jury; otherwise, it is considered to have demanded a jury trial on all the issues so triable. If the party has demanded a jury trial on only some issues, any other party may—within 14 days after being served with the demand or within a shorter time ordered by the court—serve a demand for a jury trial on any other or all factual issues triable by jury.

(d) Waiver; Withdrawal. A party waives a jury trial unless its demand is properly served and filed. A proper demand may be withdrawn only if the parties consent.

(e) Admiralty and Maritime Claims. These rules do not create a right to a jury trial on issues in a claim that is an admiralty or maritime claim under Rule 9(h).

(Amended February 28, 1966, effective July 1, 1966; March 2, 1987, effective August 1, 1987; April 22, 1993, effective December 1, 1993; April 30, 2007, effective December 1, 2007; March 26, 2009, effective December 1, 2009.)

RULE 39. TRIAL BY JURY OR BY THE COURT

(a) When a Demand Is Made. When a jury trial has been demanded under Rule 38, the action must be designated on the docket as a jury action. The trial on all issues so demanded must be by jury unless:

  (1) the parties or their attorneys file a stipulation to a nonjury trial or so stipulate on the record; or

  (2) the court, on motion or on its own, finds that on some or all of those issues there is no federal right to a jury trial.

(b) When No Demand Is Made. Issues on which a jury trial is not properly demanded are to be tried by the court. But the court may, on motion, order a jury trial on any issue for which a jury might have been demanded.

(c) Advisory Jury; Jury Trial by Consent. In an action not triable of right by a jury, the court, on motion or on its own:

  (1) may try any issue with an advisory jury; or

  (2) may, with the parties' consent, try any issue by a jury whose verdict has the same effect as if a jury trial had been a matter of right, unless the action is against the United States and a federal statute provides for a nonjury trial.

(Amended April 30, 2007, effective December 1, 2007.)

RULE 40. SCHEDULING CASES FOR TRIAL

Each court must provide by rule for scheduling trials. The court must give priority to actions entitled to priority by a federal statute.

(Amended April 30, 2007, effective December 1, 2007.)

RULE 41. DISMISSAL OF ACTIONS

(a) Voluntary Dismissal.

  (1) *By the Plaintiff.*

    (A) *Without a Court Order.* Subject to Rules 23(e), 23.1(c), 23.2, and 66 and any applicable federal statute, the plaintiff may dismiss an action without a court order by filing:

      (i) a notice of dismissal before the opposing party serves either an answer or a motion for summary judgment; or

      (ii) a stipulation of dismissal signed by all parties who have appeared.

(B) *Effect.* Unless the notice or stipulation states otherwise, the dismissal is without prejudice. But if the plaintiff previously dismissed any federal- or state-court action based on or including the same claim, a notice of dismissal operates as an adjudication on the merits.

(2) ***By Court Order; Effect.*** Except as provided in Rule 41(a)(1), an action may be dismissed at the plaintiff's request only by court order, on terms that the court considers proper. If a defendant has pleaded a counterclaim before being served with the plaintiff's motion to dismiss, the action may be dismissed over the defendant's objection only if the counterclaim can remain pending for independent adjudication. Unless the order states otherwise, a dismissal under this paragraph (2) is without prejudice.

(b) Involuntary Dismissal; Effect. If the plaintiff fails to prosecute or to comply with these rules or a court order, a defendant may move to dismiss the action or any claim against it. Unless the dismissal order states otherwise, a dismissal under this subdivision (b) and any dismissal not under this rule—except one for lack of jurisdiction, improper venue, or failure to join a party under Rule 19—operates as an adjudication on the merits.

(c) Dismissing a Counterclaim, Crossclaim, or Third–Party Claim. This rule applies to a dismissal of any counterclaim, crossclaim, or third-party claim. A claimant's voluntary dismissal under Rule 41(a)(1)(A)(i) must be made:

(1) before a responsive pleading is served; or

(2) if there is no responsive pleading, before evidence is introduced at a hearing or trial.

(d) Costs of a Previously Dismissed Action. If a plaintiff who previously dismissed an action in any court files an action based on or including the same claim against the same defendant, the court:

(1) may order the plaintiff to pay all or part of the costs of that previous action; and

(2) may stay the proceedings until the plaintiff has complied.

(Amended December 27, 1946, effective March 19, 1948; January 21, 1963, effective July 1, 1963; February 28, 1966, effective July 1, 1966; December 4, 1967, effective July 1, 1968; March 2, 1987, effective August 1, 1987; April 30, 1991, effective December 1, 1991; April 30, 2007, effective December 1, 2007.)

RULE 42. CONSOLIDATION; SEPARATE TRIALS

(a) Consolidation. If actions before the court involve a common question of law or fact, the court may:

(1) join for hearing or trial any or all matters at issue in the actions;

(2) consolidate the actions; or

(3) issue any other orders to avoid unnecessary cost or delay.

(b) Separate Trials. For convenience, to avoid prejudice, or to expedite and economize, the court may order a separate trial of one or more separate issues, claims, crossclaims, counterclaims, or third-party claims. When ordering a separate trial, the court must preserve any federal right to a jury trial.

(Amended February 28, 1966, effective July 1, 1966; April 30, 2007, effective December 1, 2007.)

RULE 43. TAKING TESTIMONY

(a) In Open Court. At trial, the witnesses' testimony must be taken in open court unless a federal statute, the Federal Rules of Evidence, these rules, or other rules adopted by the Supreme Court provide otherwise. For good cause in compelling circumstances and with appropriate safeguards, the court may permit testimony in open court by contemporaneous transmission from a different location.

(b) Affirmation Instead of an Oath. When these rules require an oath, a solemn affirmation suffices.

(c) Evidence on a Motion. When a motion relies on facts outside the record, the court may hear the matter on affidavits or may hear it wholly or partly on oral testimony or on depositions.

(d) Interpreter. The court may appoint an interpreter of its choosing; fix reasonable compensation to be paid from funds provided by law or by one or more parties; and tax the compensation as costs.

(Amended February 28, 1966, effective July 1, 1966; November 20, 1972, and December 18, 1972, effective July 1, 1975; March 2, 1987, effective August 1, 1987; April 23, 1996, effective December 1, 1996; April 30, 2007, effective December 1, 2007.)

RULE 44. PROVING AN OFFICIAL RECORD

(a) Means of Proving.

(1) ***Domestic Record.*** Each of the following evidences an official record—or an entry in it—that is otherwise admissible and is kept within the United States, any state, district, or commonwealth, or any territory subject to the administrative or judicial jurisdiction of the United States:

(A) an official publication of the record; or

(B) a copy attested by the officer with legal custody of the record—or by the officer's deputy—and accompanied by a certificate that the officer has custody. The certificate must be made under seal:

  (i) by a judge of a court of record in the district or political subdivision where the record is kept; or

  (ii) by any public officer with a seal of office and with official duties in the district or political subdivision where the record is kept.

(2) *Foreign Record.*

  (A) *In General.* Each of the following evidences a foreign official record—or an entry in it—that is otherwise admissible:

    (i) an official publication of the record; or

    (ii) the record—or a copy—that is attested by an authorized person and is accompanied either by a final certification of genuineness or by a certification under a treaty or convention to which the United States and the country where the record is located are parties.

  (B) *Final Certification of Genuineness.* A final certification must certify the genuineness of the signature and official position of the attester or of any foreign official whose certificate of genuineness relates to the attestation or is in a chain of certificates of genuineness relating to the attestation. A final certification may be made by a secretary of a United States embassy or legation; by a consul general, vice consul, or consular agent of the United States; or by a diplomatic or consular official of the foreign country assigned or accredited to the United States.

  (C) *Other Means of Proof.* If all parties have had a reasonable opportunity to investigate a foreign record's authenticity and accuracy, the court may, for good cause, either:

    (i) admit an attested copy without final certification; or

    (ii) permit the record to be evidenced by an attested summary with or without a final certification.

(b) Lack of a Record. A written statement that a diligent search of designated records revealed no record or entry of a specified tenor is admissible as evidence that the records contain no such record or entry. For domestic records, the statement must be authenticated under Rule 44(a)(1). For foreign records, the statement must comply with (a)(2)(C)(ii).

(c) Other Proof. A party may prove an official record—or an entry or lack of an entry in it—by any other method authorized by law.

(Amended February 28, 1966, effective July 1, 1966; March 2, 1987, effective August 1, 1987; April 30, 1991, effective December 1, 1991; April 30, 2007, effective December 1, 2007.)

RULE 44.1. DETERMINING FOREIGN LAW

A party who intends to raise an issue about a foreign country's law must give notice by a pleading or other writing. In determining foreign law, the court may consider any relevant material or source, including testimony, whether or not submitted by a party or admissible under the Federal Rules of Evidence. The court's determination must be treated as a ruling on a question of law.

(Adopted February 28, 1966, effective July 1, 1966; amended November 20, 1972, effective July 1, 1975; March 2, 1987, effective August 1, 1987; April 30, 2007, effective December 1, 2007.)

RULE 45. SUBPOENA

(a) In General.

(1) *Form and Contents.*

  (A) *Requirements—In General.* Every subpoena must:

    (i) state the court from which it issued;

    (ii) state the title of the action, the court in which it is pending, and its civil-action number;

    (iii) command each person to whom it is directed to do the following at a specified time and place: attend and testify; produce designated documents, electronically stored information, or tangible things in that person's possession, custody, or control; or permit the inspection of premises; and

    (iv) set out the text of Rule 45(c) and (d).

  (B) *Command to Attend a Deposition—Notice of the Recording Method.* A subpoena commanding attendance at a deposition must state the method for recording the testimony.

  (C) *Combining or Separating a Command to Produce or to Permit Inspection; Specifying the Form for Electronically Stored Information.* A command to produce documents, electronically stored information, or tangible things or to permit the inspection of premises may be included in a subpoena commanding attendance at a deposition, hearing, or trial, or may be set out in a separate subpoena. A subpoena may specify the form or forms in which electronically stored information is to be produced.

(D) *Command to Produce; Included Obligations.* A command in a subpoena to produce documents, electronically stored information, or tangible things requires the responding party to permit inspection, copying, testing, or sampling of the materials.

(2) *Issued from Which Court.* A subpoena must issue as follows:

(A) for attendance at a hearing or trial, from the court for the district where the hearing or trial is to be held;

(B) for attendance at a deposition, from the court for the district where the deposition is to be taken; and

(C) for production or inspection, if separate from a subpoena commanding a person's attendance, from the court for the district where the production or inspection is to be made.

(3) *Issued by Whom.* The clerk must issue a subpoena, signed but otherwise in blank, to a party who requests it. That party must complete it before service. An attorney also may issue and sign a subpoena as an officer of:

(A) a court in which the attorney is authorized to practice; or

(B) a court for a district where a deposition is to be taken or production is to be made, if the attorney is authorized to practice in the court where the action is pending.

(b) **Service.**

(1) *By Whom; Tendering Fees; Serving a Copy of Certain Subpoenas.* Any person who is at least 18 years old and not a party may serve a subpoena. Serving a subpoena requires delivering a copy to the named person and, if the subpoena requires that person's attendance, tendering the fees for 1 day's attendance and the mileage allowed by law. Fees and mileage need not be tendered when the subpoena issues on behalf of the United States or any of its officers or agencies. If the subpoena commands the production of documents, electronically stored information, or tangible things or the inspection of premises before trial, then before it is served, a notice must be served on each party.

(2) *Service in the United States.* Subject to Rule 45(c)(3)(A)(ii), a subpoena may be served at any place:

(A) within the district of the issuing court;

(B) outside that district but within 100 miles of the place specified for the deposition, hearing, trial, production, or inspection;

(C) within the state of the issuing court if a state statute or court rule allows service at that place of a subpoena issued by a state court of general jurisdiction sitting in the place specified for the deposition, hearing, trial, production, or inspection; or

(D) that the court authorizes on motion and for good cause, if a federal statute so provides.

(3) *Service in a Foreign Country.* 28 U.S.C. § 1783 governs issuing and serving a subpoena directed to a United States national or resident who is in a foreign country.

(4) *Proof of Service.* Proving service, when necessary, requires filing with the issuing court a statement showing the date and manner of service and the names of the persons served. The statement must be certified by the server.

(c) **Protecting a Person Subject to a Subpoena.**

(1) *Avoiding Undue Burden or Expense; Sanctions.* A party or attorney responsible for issuing and serving a subpoena must take reasonable steps to avoid imposing undue burden or expense on a person subject to the subpoena. The issuing court must enforce this duty and impose an appropriate sanction—which may include lost earnings and reasonable attorney's fees—on a party or attorney who fails to comply.

(2) *Command to Produce Materials or Permit Inspection.*

(A) *Appearance Not Required.* A person commanded to produce documents, electronically stored information, or tangible things, or to permit the inspection of premises, need not appear in person at the place of production or inspection unless also commanded to appear for a deposition, hearing, or trial.

(B) *Objections.* A person commanded to produce documents or tangible things or to permit inspection may serve on the party or attorney designated in the subpoena a written objection to inspecting, copying, testing or sampling any or all of the materials or to inspecting the premises—or to producing electronically stored information in the form or forms requested. The objection must be served before the earlier of the time specified for compliance or 14 days after the subpoena is served. If an objection is made, the following rules apply:

(i) At any time, on notice to the commanded person, the serving party may move the issuing court for an order compelling production or inspection.

(ii) These acts may be required only as directed in the order, and the order must protect a person who is neither a party nor a party's officer from significant expense resulting from compliance.

(3) *Quashing or Modifying a Subpoena.*

(A) *When Required.* On timely motion, the issuing court must quash or modify a subpoena that:

(i) fails to allow a reasonable time to comply;

(ii) requires a person who is neither a party nor a party's officer to travel more than 100 miles from where that person resides, is employed, or regularly transacts business in person—except that, subject to Rule 45(c)(3)(B)(iii), the person may be commanded to attend a trial by traveling from any such place within the state where the trial is held;

(iii) requires disclosure of privileged or other protected matter, if no exception or waiver applies; or

(iv) subjects a person to undue burden.

(B) *When Permitted.* To protect a person subject to or affected by a subpoena, the issuing court may, on motion, quash or modify the subpoena if it requires:

(i) disclosing a trade secret or other confidential research, development, or commercial information;

(ii) disclosing an unretained expert's opinion or information that does not describe specific occurrences in dispute and results from the expert's study that was not requested by a party; or

(iii) a person who is neither a party nor a party's officer to incur substantial expense to travel more than 100 miles to attend trial.

(C) *Specifying Conditions as an Alternative.* In the circumstances described in Rule 45(c)(3)(B), the court may, instead of quashing or modifying a subpoena, order appearance or production under specified conditions if the serving party:

(i) shows a substantial need for the testimony or material that cannot be otherwise met without undue hardship; and

(ii) ensures that the subpoenaed person will be reasonably compensated.

(d) **Duties in Responding to a Subpoena.**

(1) *Producing Documents or Electronically Stored Information.* These procedures apply to producing documents or electronically stored information:

(A) *Documents.* A person responding to a subpoena to produce documents must produce them as they are kept in the ordinary course of business or must organize and label them to correspond to the categories in the demand.

(B) *Form for Producing Electronically Stored Information Not Specified.* If a subpoena does not specify a form for producing electronically stored information, the person responding must produce it in a form or forms in which it is ordinarily maintained or in a reasonably usable form or forms.

(C) *Electronically Stored Information Produced in Only One Form.* The person responding need not produce the same electronically stored information in more than one form.

(D) *Inaccessible Electronically Stored Information.* The person responding need not provide discovery of electronically stored information from sources that the person identifies as not reasonably accessible because of undue burden or cost. On motion to compel discovery or for a protective order, the person responding must show that the information is not reasonably accessible because of undue burden or cost. If that showing is made, the court may nonetheless order discovery from such sources if the requesting party shows good cause, considering the limitations of Rule 26(b)(2)(C). The court may specify conditions for the discovery.

(2) *Claiming Privilege or Protection.*

(A) *Information Withheld.* A person withholding subpoenaed information under a claim that it is privileged or subject to protection as trial-preparation material must:

(i) expressly make the claim; and

(ii) describe the nature of the withheld documents, communications, or tangible things in a manner that, without revealing information itself privileged or protected, will enable the parties to assess the claim.

(B) *Information Produced.* If information produced in response to a subpoena is subject to a claim of privilege or of protection as trial-preparation material, the person making the claim may notify any party that received the information of the claim and the basis for it. After being notified, a party must promptly return, sequester, or destroy the specified information and any copies it has; must not use or disclose the information until the claim is resolved; must take reasonable steps to retrieve the information if the party disclosed it before being notified; and may promptly present the information to the court under seal for a determination of the claim. The person who produced the information must preserve the information until the claim is resolved.

(e) Contempt. The issuing court may hold in contempt a person who, having been served, fails without adequate excuse to obey the subpoena. A nonparty's failure to obey must be excused if the subpoena purports to require the nonparty to attend or produce at a place outside the limits of Rule 45(c)(3)(A)(ii).

(Amended December 27, 1946, effective March 19, 1948; December 29, 1948, effective October 20, 1949; March 30, 1970, effective July 1, 1970; April 29, 1980, effective August 1, 1980; April 29, 1985, effective August 1, 1985; March 2, 1987, effective August 1, 1987; April 30, 1991, effective December 1, 1991; April 25, 2005, effective December 1, 2005; April 12, 2006, effective December 1, 2006; April 30, 2007, effective December 1, 2007.)

RULE 46. OBJECTING TO A RULING OR ORDER

A formal exception to a ruling or order is unnecessary. When the ruling or order is requested or made, a party need only state the action that it wants the court to take or objects to, along with the grounds for the request or objection. Failing to object does not prejudice a party who had no opportunity to do so when the ruling or order was made.

(Amended March 2, 1987, effective August 1, 1987; April 30, 2007, effective December 1, 2007.)

RULE 47. SELECTING JURORS

(a) Examining Jurors. The court may permit the parties or their attorneys to examine prospective jurors or may itself do so. If the court examines the jurors, it must permit the parties or their attorneys to make any further inquiry it considers proper, or must itself ask any of their additional questions it considers proper.

(b) Peremptory Challenges. The court must allow the number of peremptory challenges provided by 28 U.S.C. § 1870.

(c) Excusing a Juror. During trial or deliberation, the court may excuse a juror for good cause.

(Amended February 28, 1966, effective July 1, 1966; April 30, 1991, effective December 1, 1991; April 30, 2007, effective December 1, 2007.)

RULE 48. NUMBER OF JURORS; VERDICT; POLLING

(a) Number of Jurors. A jury must begin with at least 6 and no more than 12 members, and each juror must participate in the verdict unless excused under Rule 47(c).

(b) Verdict. Unless the parties stipulate otherwise, the verdict must be unanimous and must be returned by a jury of at least 6 members.

(c) Polling. After a verdict is returned but before the jury is discharged, the court must on a party's request, or may on its own, poll the jurors individually. If the poll reveals a lack of unanimity or lack of assent by the number of jurors that the parties stipulated to, the court may direct the jury to deliberate further or may order a new trial.

(Amended April 30, 1991, effective December 1, 1991; April 30, 2007, effective December 1, 2007; March 26, 2009, effective December 1, 2009.)

RULE 49. SPECIAL VERDICT; GENERAL VERDICT AND QUESTIONS

(a) Special Verdict.

(1) *In General.* The court may require a jury to return only a special verdict in the form of a special written finding on each issue of fact. The court may do so by:

   (A) submitting written questions susceptible of a categorical or other brief answer;

   (B) submitting written forms of the special findings that might properly be made under the pleadings and evidence; or

   (C) using any other method that the court considers appropriate.

(2) *Instructions.* The court must give the instructions and explanations necessary to enable the jury to make its findings on each submitted issue.

(3) *Issues Not Submitted.* A party waives the right to a jury trial on any issue of fact raised by the pleadings or evidence but not submitted to the jury unless, before the jury retires, the party demands its submission to the jury. If the party does not demand submission, the court may make a finding on the issue. If the court makes no finding, it is considered to have made a finding consistent with its judgment on the special verdict.

(b) General Verdict with Answers to Written Questions.

(1) *In General.* The court may submit to the jury forms for a general verdict, together with written questions on one or more issues of fact that the jury must decide. The court must give the

instructions and explanations necessary to enable the jury to render a general verdict and answer the questions in writing, and must direct the jury to do both.

  (2) *Verdict and Answers Consistent.* When the general verdict and the answers are consistent, the court must approve, for entry under Rule 58, an appropriate judgment on the verdict and answers.

  (3) *Answers Inconsistent with the Verdict.* When the answers are consistent with each other but one or more is inconsistent with the general verdict, the court may:

    (A) approve, for entry under Rule 58, an appropriate judgment according to the answers, notwithstanding the general verdict;

    (B) direct the jury to further consider its answers and verdict; or

    (C) order a new trial.

  (4) *Answers Inconsistent with Each Other and the Verdict.* When the answers are inconsistent with each other and one or more is also inconsistent with the general verdict, judgment must not be entered; instead, the court must direct the jury to further consider its answers and verdict, or must order a new trial.

(Amended January 21, 1963, effective July 1, 1963; March 2, 1987, effective August 1, 1987; April 30, 2007, effective December 1, 2007.)

RULE 50. JUDGMENT AS A MATTER OF LAW IN A JURY TRIAL; RELATED MOTION FOR A NEW TRIAL; CONDITIONAL RULING

(a) **Judgment as a Matter of Law.**

  (1) *In General.* If a party has been fully heard on an issue during a jury trial and the court finds that a reasonable jury would not have a legally sufficient evidentiary basis to find for the party on that issue, the court may:

    (A) resolve the issue against the party; and

    (B) grant a motion for judgment as a matter of law against the party on a claim or defense that, under the controlling law, can be maintained or defeated only with a favorable finding on that issue.

  (2) *Motion.* A motion for judgment as a matter of law may be made at any time before the case is submitted to the jury. The motion must specify the judgment sought and the law and facts that entitle the movant to the judgment.

(b) **Renewing the Motion After Trial; Alternative Motion for a New Trial.** If the court does not grant a motion for judgment as a matter of law made under Rule 50(a), the court is considered to have submitted the action to the jury subject to the court's later deciding the legal questions raised by the motion. No later than 28 days after the entry of judgment—or if the motion addresses a jury issue not decided by a verdict, no later than 28 days after the jury was discharged—the movant may file a renewed motion for judgment as a matter of law and may include an alternative or joint request for a new trial under Rule 59. In ruling on the renewed motion, the court may:

  (1) allow judgment on the verdict, if the jury returned a verdict;

  (2) order a new trial; or

  (3) direct the entry of judgment as a matter of law.

(c) **Granting the Renewed Motion; Conditional Ruling on a Motion for a New Trial.**

  (1) *In General.* If the court grants a renewed motion for judgment as a matter of law, it must also conditionally rule on any motion for a new trial by determining whether a new trial should be granted if the judgment is later vacated or reversed. The court must state the grounds for conditionally granting or denying the motion for a new trial.

  (2) *Effect of a Conditional Ruling.* Conditionally granting the motion for a new trial does not affect the judgment's finality; if the judgment is reversed, the new trial must proceed unless the appellate court orders otherwise. If the motion for a new trial is conditionally denied, the appellee may assert error in that denial; if the judgment is reversed, the case must proceed as the appellate court orders.

(d) **Time for a Losing Party's New–Trial Motion.** Any motion for a new trial under Rule 59 by a party against whom judgment as a matter of law is rendered must be filed no later than 28 days after the entry of the judgment.

(e) **Denying the Motion for Judgment as a Matter of Law; Reversal on Appeal.** If the court denies the motion for judgment as a matter of law, the prevailing party may, as appellee, assert grounds entitling it to a new trial should the appellate court conclude that the trial court erred in denying the motion. If the appellate court reverses the judgment, it may order a new trial, direct the trial court to determine whether a new trial should be granted, or direct the entry of judgment.

(Amended January 21, 1963, effective July 1, 1963; March 2, 1987, effective August 1, 1987; April 30, 1991, effective December 1, 1991; April 22, 1993, effective December 1, 1993; April 27, 1995, effective December 1, 1995; April 12, 2006, effective December 1, 2006; April 30, 2007, effective December 1, 2007; March 26, 2009, effective December 1, 2009.)

RULE 51. INSTRUCTIONS TO THE JURY; OBJECTIONS; PRESERVING A CLAIM OF ERROR

(a) Requests.

  (1) *Before or at the Close of the Evidence.* At the close of the evidence or at any earlier reasonable time that the court orders, a party may file and furnish to every other party written requests for the jury instructions it wants the court to give.

  (2) *After the Close of the Evidence.* After the close of the evidence, a party may:

    (A) file requests for instructions on issues that could not reasonably have been anticipated by an earlier time that the court set for requests; and

    (B) with the court's permission, file untimely requests for instructions on any issue.

(b) Instructions. The court:

  (1) must inform the parties of its proposed instructions and proposed action on the requests before instructing the jury and before final jury arguments;

  (2) must give the parties an opportunity to object on the record and out of the jury's hearing before the instructions and arguments are delivered; and

  (3) may instruct the jury at any time before the jury is discharged.

(c) Objections.

  (1) *How to Make.* A party who objects to an instruction or the failure to give an instruction must do so on the record, stating distinctly the matter objected to and the grounds for the objection.

  (2) *When to Make.* An objection is timely if:

    (A) a party objects at the opportunity provided under Rule 51(b)(2); or

    (B) a party was not informed of an instruction or action on a request before that opportunity to object, and the party objects promptly after learning that the instruction or request will be, or has been, given or refused.

(d) Assigning Error; Plain Error.

  (1) *Assigning Error.* A party may assign as error:

    (A) an error in an instruction actually given, if that party properly objected; or

    (B) a failure to give an instruction, if that party properly requested it and—unless the court rejected the request in a definitive ruling on the record—also properly objected.

  (2) *Plain Error.* A court may consider a plain error in the instructions that has not been preserved

as required by Rule 51(d)(1) if the error affects substantial rights.

(Amended March 2, 1987, effective August 1, 1987; March 27, 2003, effective December 1, 2003; April 30, 2007, effective December 1, 2007.)

RULE 52. FINDINGS AND CONCLUSIONS BY THE COURT; JUDGMENT ON PARTIAL FINDINGS

(a) Findings and Conclusions.

  (1) *In General.* In an action tried on the facts without a jury or with an advisory jury, the court must find the facts specially and state its conclusions of law separately. The findings and conclusions may be stated on the record after the close of the evidence or may appear in an opinion or a memorandum of decision filed by the court. Judgment must be entered under Rule 58.

  (2) *For an Interlocutory Injunction.* In granting or refusing an interlocutory injunction, the court must similarly state the findings and conclusions that support its action.

  (3) *For a Motion.* The court is not required to state findings or conclusions when ruling on a motion under Rule 12 or 56 or, unless these rules provide otherwise, on any other motion.

  (4) *Effect of a Master's Findings.* A master's findings, to the extent adopted by the court, must be considered the court's findings.

  (5) *Questioning the Evidentiary Support.* A party may later question the sufficiency of the evidence supporting the findings, whether or not the party requested findings, objected to them, moved to amend them, or moved for partial findings.

  (6) *Setting Aside the Findings.* Findings of fact, whether based on oral or other evidence, must not be set aside unless clearly erroneous, and the reviewing court must give due regard to the trial court's opportunity to judge the witnesses' credibility.

(b) Amended or Additional Findings. On a party's motion filed no later than 28 days after the entry of judgment, the court may amend its findings—or make additional findings—and may amend the judgment accordingly. The motion may accompany a motion for a new trial under Rule 59.

(c) Judgment on Partial Findings. If a party has been fully heard on an issue during a nonjury trial and the court finds against the party on that issue, the court may enter judgment against the party on a claim or defense that, under the controlling law, can be maintained or defeated only with a favorable finding on that issue. The court may, however, decline to render any judgment until the close of the evidence. A judgment on partial findings must be supported by findings of fact and conclusions of law as required by Rule 52(a).

(Amended December 27, 1946, effective March 19, 1948; January 21, 1963, effective July 1, 1963; April 28, 1983, effective August 1, 1983; April 29, 1985, effective August 1, 1985; April 30, 1991, effective December 1, 1991; April 22, 1993, effective December 1, 1993; April 27, 1995, effective December 1, 1995; April 30, 2007, effective December 1, 2007; March 26, 2009, effective December 1, 2009.)

RULE 53.   MASTERS

(a) Appointment.

(1) *Scope.* Unless a statute provides otherwise, a court may appoint a master only to:

  (A) perform duties consented to by the parties;

  (B) hold trial proceedings and make or recommend findings of fact on issues to be decided without a jury if appointment is warranted by:

    (i) some exceptional condition; or

    (ii) the need to perform an accounting or resolve a difficult computation of damages; or

  (C) address pretrial and posttrial matters that cannot be effectively and timely addressed by an available district judge or magistrate judge of the district.

(2) *Disqualification.* A master must not have a relationship to the parties, attorneys, action, or court that would require disqualification of a judge under 28 U.S.C. § 455, unless the parties, with the court's approval, consent to the appointment after the master discloses any potential grounds for disqualification.

(3) *Possible Expense or Delay.* In appointing a master, the court must consider the fairness of imposing the likely expenses on the parties and must protect against unreasonable expense or delay.

(b) Order Appointing a Master.

(1) *Notice.* Before appointing a master, the court must give the parties notice and an opportunity to be heard. Any party may suggest candidates for appointment.

(2) *Contents.* The appointing order must direct the master to proceed with all reasonable diligence and must state:

  (A) the master's duties, including any investigation or enforcement duties, and any limits on the master's authority under Rule 53(c);

  (B) the circumstances, if any, in which the master may communicate ex parte with the court or a party;

  (C) the nature of the materials to be preserved and filed as the record of the master's activities;

  (D) the time limits, method of filing the record, other procedures, and standards for reviewing the master's orders, findings, and recommendations; and

  (E) the basis, terms, and procedure for fixing the master's compensation under Rule 53(g).

(3) *Issuing.* The court may issue the order only after:

  (A) the master files an affidavit disclosing whether there is any ground for disqualification under 28 U.S.C. § 455; and

  (B) if a ground is disclosed, the parties, with the court's approval, waive the disqualification.

(4) *Amending.* The order may be amended at any time after notice to the parties and an opportunity to be heard.

(c) Master's Authority.

(1) *In General.* Unless the appointing order directs otherwise, a master may:

  (A) regulate all proceedings;

  (B) take all appropriate measures to perform the assigned duties fairly and efficiently; and

  (C) if conducting an evidentiary hearing, exercise the appointing court's power to compel, take, and record evidence.

(2) *Sanctions.* The master may by order impose on a party any noncontempt sanction provided by Rule 37 or 45, and may recommend a contempt sanction against a party and sanctions against a nonparty.

(d) Master's Orders. A master who issues an order must file it and promptly serve a copy on each party. The clerk must enter the order on the docket.

(e) Master's Reports. A master must report to the court as required by the appointing order. The master must file the report and promptly serve a copy on each party, unless the court orders otherwise.

(f) Action on the Master's Order, Report, or Recommendations.

(1) *Opportunity for a Hearing; Action in General.* In acting on a master's order, report, or recommendations, the court must give the parties notice and an opportunity to be heard; may receive evidence; and may adopt or affirm, modify, wholly or partly reject or reverse, or resubmit to the master with instructions.

(2) *Time to Object or Move to Adopt or Modify.* A party may file objections to—or a motion to adopt or modify—the master's order, report, or

recommendations no later than 21 days after a copy is served, unless the court sets a different time.

(3) *Reviewing Factual Findings.* The court must decide de novo all objections to findings of fact made or recommended by a master, unless the parties, with the court's approval, stipulate that:

(A) the findings will be reviewed for clear error; or

(B) the findings of a master appointed under Rule 53(a)(1)(A) or (C) will be final.

(4) *Reviewing Legal Conclusions.* The court must decide de novo all objections to conclusions of law made or recommended by a master.

(5) *Reviewing Procedural Matters.* Unless the appointing order establishes a different standard of review, the court may set aside a master's ruling on a procedural matter only for an abuse of discretion.

(g) **Compensation.**

(1) *Fixing Compensation.* Before or after judgment, the court must fix the master's compensation on the basis and terms stated in the appointing order, but the court may set a new basis and terms after giving notice and an opportunity to be heard.

(2) *Payment.* The compensation must be paid either:

(A) by a party or parties; or

(B) from a fund or subject matter of the action within the court's control.

(3) *Allocating Payment.* The court must allocate payment among the parties after considering the nature and amount of the controversy, the parties' means, and the extent to which any party is more responsible than other parties for the reference to a master. An interim allocation may be amended to reflect a decision on the merits.

(h) **Appointing a Magistrate Judge.** A magistrate judge is subject to this rule only when the order referring a matter to the magistrate judge states that the reference is made under this rule.

(Amended February 28, 1966, effective July 1, 1966; April 28, 1983, effective August 1, 1983; March 2, 1987, effective August 1, 1987; April 30, 1991, effective December 1, 1991; April 22, 1993, effective December 1, 1993; March 27, 2003, effective December 1, 2003; April 30, 2007, effective December 1, 2007; March 26, 2009, effective December 1, 2009.)

TITLE VII. JUDGMENT

RULE 54. JUDGMENT; COSTS

(a) **Definition; Form.** "Judgment" as used in these rules includes a decree and any order from which an appeal lies. A judgment should not include recitals of pleadings, a master's report, or a record of prior proceedings.

(b) **Judgment on Multiple Claims or Involving Multiple Parties.** When an action presents more than one claim for relief—whether as a claim, counterclaim, crossclaim, or third-party claim—or when multiple parties are involved, the court may direct entry of a final judgment as to one or more, but fewer than all, claims or parties only if the court expressly determines that there is no just reason for delay. Otherwise, any order or other decision, however designated, that adjudicates fewer than all the claims or the rights and liabilities of fewer than all the parties does not end the action as to any of the claims or parties and may be revised at any time before the entry of a judgment adjudicating all the claims and all the parties' rights and liabilities.

(c) **Demand for Judgment; Relief to Be Granted.** A default judgment must not differ in kind from, or exceed in amount, what is demanded in the pleadings. Every other final judgment should grant the relief to which each party is entitled, even if the party has not demanded that relief in its pleadings.

(d) **Costs; Attorney's Fees.**

(1) *Costs Other Than Attorney's Fees.* Unless a federal statute, these rules, or a court order provides otherwise, costs—other than attorney's fees—should be allowed to the prevailing party. But costs against the United States, its officers, and its agencies may be imposed only to the extent allowed by law. The clerk may tax costs on 14 days' notice. On motion served within the next 7 days, the court may review the clerk's action.

(2) *Attorney's Fees.*

(A) *Claim to Be by Motion.* A claim for attorney's fees and related nontaxable expenses must be made by motion unless the substantive law requires those fees to be proved at trial as an element of damages.

(B) *Timing and Contents of the Motion.* Unless a statute or a court order provides otherwise, the motion must:

(i) be filed no later than 14 days after the entry of judgment;

(ii) specify the judgment and the statute, rule, or other grounds entitling the movant to the award;

(iii) state the amount sought or provide a fair estimate of it; and

(iv) disclose, if the court so orders, the terms of any agreement about fees for the services for which the claim is made.

(C) *Proceedings.* Subject to Rule 23(h), the court must, on a party's request, give an opportunity for adversary submissions on the motion in accordance with Rule 43(c) or 78. The court may decide issues of liability for fees before receiving submissions on the value of services. The court must find the facts and state its conclusions of law as provided in Rule 52(a).

(D) *Special Procedures by Local Rule; Reference to a Master or a Magistrate Judge.* By local rule, the court may establish special procedures to resolve fee-related issues without extensive evidentiary hearings. Also, the court may refer issues concerning the value of services to a special master under Rule 53 without regard to the limitations of Rule 53(a)(1), and may refer a motion for attorney's fees to a magistrate judge under Rule 72(b) as if it were a dispositive pretrial matter.

(E) *Exceptions.* Subparagraphs (A)-(D) do not apply to claims for fees and expenses as sanctions for violating these rules or as sanctions under 28 U.S.C. § 1927.

(Amended December 27, 1946, effective March 19, 1948; April 17, 1961, effective July 19, 1961; March 2, 1987, effective August 1, 1987; April 22, 1993, effective December 1, 1993; April 29, 2002, effective December 1, 2002; March 27, 2003, effective December 1, 2003; April 30, 2007, effective December 1, 2007; March 26, 2009, effective December 1, 2009.)

RULE 55. DEFAULT; DEFAULT JUDGMENT

(a) Entering a Default. When a party against whom a judgment for affirmative relief is sought has failed to plead or otherwise defend, and that failure is shown by affidavit or otherwise, the clerk must enter the party's default.

(b) Entering a Default Judgment.

(1) *By the Clerk.* If the plaintiff's claim is for a sum certain or a sum that can be made certain by computation, the clerk—on the plaintiff's request, with an affidavit showing the amount due—must enter judgment for that amount and costs against a defendant who has been default-ed for not appearing and who is neither a minor nor an incompetent person.

(2) *By the Court.* In all other cases, the party must apply to the court for a default judgment. A default judgment may be entered against a minor or incompetent person only if represented by a general guardian, conservator, or other like fiduciary who has appeared. If the party against whom a default judgment is sought has appeared personally or by a representative, that party or its representative must be served with written notice of the application at least 7 days before the hearing. The court may conduct hearings or make referrals—preserving any federal statutory right to a jury trial—when, to enter or effectuate judgment, it needs to:

(A) conduct an accounting;

(B) determine the amount of damages;

(C) establish the truth of any allegation by evidence; or

(D) investigate any other matter.

(c) Setting Aside a Default or a Default Judgment. The court may set aside an entry of default for good cause, and it may set aside a default judgment under Rule 60(b).

(d) Judgment Against the United States. A default judgment may be entered against the United States, its officers, or its agencies only if the claimant establishes a claim or right to relief by evidence that satisfies the court.

(Amended March 2, 1987, effective August 1, 1987; April 30, 2007, effective December 1, 2007; March 26, 2009, effective December 1, 2009.)

RULE 56. SUMMARY JUDGMENT

(a) Motion for Summary Judgment or Partial Summary Judgment. A party may move for summary judgment, identifying each claim or defense—or the part of each claim or defense—on which summary judgment is sought. The court shall grant summary judgment if the movant shows that there is no genuine dispute as to any material fact and the movant is entitled to judgment as a matter of law. The court should state on the record the reasons for granting or denying the motion.

(b) Time to File a Motion. Unless a different time is set by local rule or the court orders otherwise, a party may file a motion for summary judgment at any time until 30 days after the close of all discovery.

(c) Procedures.

(1) *Supporting Factual Positions.* A party asserting that a fact cannot be or is genuinely disputed must support the assertion by:

(A) citing to particular parts of materials in the record, including depositions, documents, electronically stored information, affidavits or declarations, stipulations (including those made for purposes of the motion only), admissions, interrogatory answers, or other materials; or

(B) showing that the materials cited do not establish the absence or presence of a genuine dispute, or that an adverse party cannot produce admissible evidence to support the fact.

(2) *Objection That a Fact Is Not Supported by Admissible Evidence.* A party may object that the material cited to support or dispute a fact cannot be presented in a form that would be admissible in evidence.

(3) *Materials Not Cited.* The court need consider only the cited materials, but it may consider other materials in the record.

(4) *Affidavits or Declarations.* An affidavit or declaration used to support or oppose a motion must be made on personal knowledge, set out facts that would be admissible in evidence, and show that the affiant or declarant is competent to testify on the matters stated.

(d) **When Facts Are Unavailable to the Nonmovant.** If a nonmovant shows by affidavit or declaration that, for specified reasons, it cannot present facts essential to justify its opposition, the court may:

(1) defer considering the motion or deny it;

(2) allow time to obtain affidavits or declarations or to take discovery; or

(3) issue any other appropriate order.

(e) **Failing to Properly Support or Address a Fact.** If a party fails to properly support an assertion of fact or fails to properly address another party's assertion of fact as required by Rule 56(c), the court may:

(1) give an opportunity to properly support or address the fact;

(2) consider the fact undisputed for purposes of the motion;

(3) grant summary judgment if the motion and supporting materials—including the facts considered undisputed—show that the movant is entitled to it; or

(4) issue any other appropriate order.

(f) **Judgment Independent of the Motion.** After giving notice and a reasonable time to respond, the court may:

(1) grant summary judgment for a nonmovant;

(2) grant the motion on grounds not raised by a party; or

(3) consider summary judgment on its own after identifying for the parties material facts that may not be genuinely in dispute.

(g) **Failing to Grant All the Requested Relief.** If the court does not grant all the relief requested by the motion, it may enter an order stating any material fact—including an item of damages or other relief—that is not genuinely in dispute and treating the fact as established in the case.

(h) **Affidavit or Declaration Submitted in Bad Faith.** If satisfied that an affidavit or declaration under this rule is submitted in bad faith or solely for delay, the court—after notice and a reasonable time to respond—may order the submitting party to pay the other party the reasonable expenses, including attorney's fees, it incurred as a result. An offending party or attorney may also be held in contempt or subjected to other appropriate sanctions.

(Amended December 27, 1946, effective March 19, 1948; January 21, 1963, effective July 1, 1963; March 2, 1987, effective August 1, 1987; April 30, 2007, effective December 1, 2007; March 26, 2009, effective December 1, 2009; April 28, 2010, effective December 1, 2010.)

RULE 57. DECLARATORY JUDGMENT

These rules govern the procedure for obtaining a declaratory judgment under 28 U.S.C. § 2201. Rules 38 and 39 govern a demand for a jury trial. The existence of another adequate remedy does not preclude a declaratory judgment that is otherwise appropriate. The court may order a speedy hearing of a declaratory-judgment action.

(Amended December 29, 1948, effective October 20, 1949; April 30, 2007, effective December 1, 2007.)

RULE 58. ENTERING JUDGMENT

(a) **Separate Document.** Every judgment and amended judgment must be set out in a separate document, but a separate document is not required for an order disposing of a motion:

(1) for judgment under Rule 50(b);

(2) to amend or make additional findings under Rule 52(b);

(3) for attorney's fees under Rule 54;

(4) for a new trial, or to alter or amend the judgment, under Rule 59; or

(5) for relief under Rule 60.

(b) **Entering Judgment.**

(1) *Without the Court's Direction.* Subject to Rule 54(b) and unless the court orders otherwise, the clerk must, without awaiting the court's direction, promptly prepare, sign, and enter the judgment when:

(A) the jury returns a general verdict;

(B) the court awards only costs or a sum certain; or

(C) the court denies all relief.

(2) *Court's Approval Required.* Subject to Rule 54(b), the court must promptly approve the form of the judgment, which the clerk must promptly enter, when:

(A) the jury returns a special verdict or a general verdict with answers to written questions; or

(B) the court grants other relief not described in this subdivision (b).

(c) **Time of Entry.** For purposes of these rules, judgment is entered at the following times:

(1) if a separate document is not required, when the judgment is entered in the civil docket under Rule 79(a); or

(2) if a separate document is required, when the judgment is entered in the civil docket under Rule 79(a) and the earlier of these events occurs:

(A) it is set out in a separate document; or

(B) 150 days have run from the entry in the civil docket.

(d) **Request for Entry.** A party may request that judgment be set out in a separate document as required by Rule 58(a).

(e) **Cost or Fee Awards.** Ordinarily, the entry of judgment may not be delayed, nor the time for appeal extended, in order to tax costs or award fees. But if a timely motion for attorney's fees is made under Rule 54(d)(2), the court may act before a notice of appeal has been filed and become effective to order that the motion have the same effect under Federal Rule of Appellate Procedure 4(a)(4) as a timely motion under Rule 59.

(Amended December 27, 1946, effective March 19, 1948; January 21, 1963, effective July 1, 1963; April 22, 1993, effective December 1, 1993; April 29, 2002, effective December 1, 2002; April 30, 2007, effective December 1, 2007.)

RULE 59. NEW TRIAL; ALTERING OR AMENDING A JUDGMENT

(a) **In General.**

(1) *Grounds for New Trial.* The court may, on motion, grant a new trial on all or some of the issues—and to any party—as follows:

(A) after a jury trial, for any reason for which a new trial has heretofore been granted in an action at law in federal court; or

(B) after a nonjury trial, for any reason for which a rehearing has heretofore been granted in a suit in equity in federal court.

(2) *Further Action After a Nonjury Trial.* After a nonjury trial, the court may, on motion for a new trial, open the judgment if one has been entered, take additional testimony, amend findings of fact and conclusions of law or make new ones, and direct the entry of a new judgment.

(b) **Time to File a Motion for a New Trial.** A motion for a new trial must be filed no later than 28 days after the entry of judgment.

(c) **Time to Serve Affidavits.** When a motion for a new trial is based on affidavits, they must be filed with the motion. The opposing party has 14 days after being served to file opposing affidavits. The court may permit reply affidavits.

(d) **New Trial on the Court's Initiative or for Reasons Not in the Motion.** No later than 28 days after the entry of judgment, the court, on its own, may order a new trial for any reason that would justify granting one on a party's motion. After giving the parties notice and an opportunity to be heard, the court may grant a timely motion for a new trial for a reason not stated in the motion. In either event, the court must specify the reasons in its order.

(e) **Motion to Alter or Amend a Judgment.** A motion to alter or amend a judgment must be filed no later than 28 days after the entry of the judgment.

(Amended December 27, 1946, effective March 19, 1948; February 28, 1966, effective July 1, 1966; April 27, 1995, effective December 1, 1995; April 30, 2007, effective December 1, 2007; March 26, 2009, effective December 1, 2009.)

RULE 60. RELIEF FROM A JUDGMENT OR ORDER

(a) **Corrections Based on Clerical Mistakes; Oversights and Omissions.** The court may correct a clerical mistake or a mistake arising from oversight or omission whenever one is found in a judgment, order, or other part of the record. The court may do so on motion or on its own, with or without notice. But after an appeal has been docketed in the appellate court and while it is pending, such a mistake may be corrected only with the appellate court's leave.

(b) **Grounds for Relief from a Final Judgment, Order, or Proceeding.** On motion and just terms, the court may relieve a party or its legal representative from a final judgment, order, or proceeding for the following reasons:

(1) mistake, inadvertence, surprise, or excusable neglect;

(2) newly discovered evidence that, with reasonable diligence, could not have been discovered in time to move for a new trial under Rule 59(b);

(3) fraud (whether previously called intrinsic or extrinsic), misrepresentation, or misconduct by an opposing party;

(4) the judgment is void;

(5) the judgment has been satisfied, released or discharged; it is based on an earlier judgment that has been reversed or vacated; or applying it prospectively is no longer equitable; or

(6) any other reason that justifies relief.

(c) **Timing and Effect of the Motion.**

(1) *Timing.* A motion under Rule 60(b) must be made within a reasonable time—and for reasons (1), (2), and (3) no more than a year after the entry of the judgment or order or the date of the proceeding.

(2) *Effect on Finality.* The motion does not affect the judgment's finality or suspend its operation.

(d) **Other Powers to Grant Relief.** This rule does not limit a court's power to:

(1) entertain an independent action to relieve a party from a judgment, order, or proceeding;

(2) grant relief under 28 U.S.C. § 1655 to a defendant who was not personally notified of the action; or

(3) set aside a judgment for fraud on the court.

(e) **Bills and Writs Abolished.** The following are abolished: bills of review, bills in the nature of bills of review, and writs of coram nobis, coram vobis, and audita querela.

(Amended December 27, 1946, effective March 19, 1948; December 29, 1948, effective October 20, 1949; March 2, 1987, effective August 1, 1987; April 30, 2007, effective December 1, 2007.)

RULE 61. HARMLESS ERROR

Unless justice requires otherwise, no error in admitting or excluding evidence—or any other error by the court or a party—is ground for granting a new trial, for setting aside a verdict, or for vacating, modifying, or otherwise disturbing a judgment or order. At every stage of the proceeding, the court must disregard all errors and defects that do not affect any party's substantial rights.

(Amended April 30, 2007, effective December 1, 2007.)

RULE 62. STAY OF PROCEEDINGS TO ENFORCE A JUDGMENT

(a) **Automatic Stay; Exceptions for Injunctions, Receiverships, and Patent Accountings.** Except as stated in this rule, no execution may issue on a judgment, nor may proceedings be taken to enforce it, until 14 days have passed after its entry. But unless the court orders otherwise, the following are not stayed after being entered, even if an appeal is taken:

(1) an interlocutory or final judgment in an action for an injunction or a receivership; or

(2) a judgment or order that directs an accounting in an action for patent infringement.

(b) **Stay Pending the Disposition of a Motion.** On appropriate terms for the opposing party's security, the court may stay the execution of a judgment—or any proceedings to enforce it—pending disposition of any of the following motions:

(1) under Rule 50, for judgment as a matter of law;

(2) under Rule 52(b), to amend the findings or for additional findings;

(3) under Rule 59, for a new trial or to alter or amend a judgment; or

(4) under Rule 60, for relief from a judgment or order.

(c) **Injunction Pending an Appeal.** While an appeal is pending from an interlocutory order or final judgment that grants, dissolves, or denies an injunction, the court may suspend, modify, restore, or grant an injunction on terms for bond or other terms that secure the opposing party's rights. If the judgment appealed from is rendered by a statutory three-judge district court, the order must be made either:

(1) by that court sitting in open session; or

(2) by the assent of all its judges, as evidenced by their signatures.

(d) **Stay with Bond on Appeal.** If an appeal is taken, the appellant may obtain a stay by supersedeas bond, except in an action described in Rule 62(a)(1) or (2). The bond may be given upon or after filing the notice of appeal or after obtaining the order allowing the appeal. The stay takes effect when the court approves the bond.

(e) **Stay Without Bond on an Appeal by the United States, Its Officers, or Its Agencies.** The court must not require a bond, obligation, or other security from the appellant when granting a stay on an appeal by the United States, its officers, or its agencies or on an appeal directed by a department of the federal government.

(f) **Stay in Favor of a Judgment Debtor Under State Law.** If a judgment is a lien on the judgment debtor's property under the law of the state where the court is located, the judgment debtor is entitled to the same stay of execution the state court would give.

(g) **Appellate Court's Power Not Limited.** This rule does not limit the power of the appellate court or one of its judges or justices:

(1) to stay proceedings—or suspend, modify, restore, or grant an injunction—while an appeal is pending; or

(2) to issue an order to preserve the status quo or the effectiveness of the judgment to be entered.

(h) Stay with Multiple Claims or Parties. A court may stay the enforcement of a final judgment entered under Rule 54(b) until it enters a later judgment or judgments, and may prescribe terms necessary to secure the benefit of the stayed judgment for the party in whose favor it was entered.

(Amended December 27, 1946, effective March 19, 1948; December 29, 1948, effective October 20, 1949; April 17, 1961, effective July 19, 1961; March 2, 1987, effective August 1, 1987; April 30, 2007, effective December 1, 2007; March 26, 2009, effective December 1, 2009.)

RULE 62.1. INDICATIVE RULING ON A MOTION FOR RELIEF THAT IS BARRED BY A PENDING APPEAL

(a) Relief Pending Appeal. If a timely motion is made for relief that the court lacks authority to grant because of an appeal that has been docketed and is pending, the court may:

(1) defer considering the motion;

(2) deny the motion; or

(3) state either that it would grant the motion if the court of appeals remands for that purpose or that the motion raises a substantial issue.

(b) Notice to the Court of Appeals. The movant must promptly notify the circuit clerk under Federal Rule of Appellate Procedure 12.1 if the district court states that it would grant the motion or that the motion raises a substantial issue.

(c) Remand. The district court may decide the motion if the court of appeals remands for that purpose.

(Added March 26, 2009, effective December 1, 2009.)

RULE 63. JUDGE'S INABILITY TO PROCEED

If a judge conducting a hearing or trial is unable to proceed, any other judge may proceed upon certifying familiarity with the record and determining that the case may be completed without prejudice to the parties. In a hearing or a nonjury trial, the successor judge must, at a party's request, recall any witness whose testimony is material and disputed and who is available to testify again without undue burden. The successor judge may also recall any other witness.

(Amended March 2, 1987, effective August 1, 1987; April 30, 1991, effective December 1, 1991; April 30, 2007, effective December 1, 2007.)

TITLE VIII. PROVISIONAL AND FINAL REMEDIES

RULE 64. SEIZING A PERSON OR PROPERTY

(a) Remedies Under State Law—In General. At the commencement of and throughout an action, every remedy is available that, under the law of the state where the court is located, provides for seizing a person or property to secure satisfaction of the potential judgment. But a federal statute governs to the extent it applies.

(b) Specific Kinds of Remedies. The remedies available under this rule include the following—however designated and regardless of whether state procedure requires an independent action:

- arrest;
- attachment;
- garnishment;
- replevin;
- sequestration; and
- other corresponding or equivalent remedies.

(Amended April 30, 2007, effective December 1, 2007.)

RULE 65. INJUNCTIONS AND RESTRAINING ORDERS

(a) Preliminary Injunction.

(1) *Notice.* The court may issue a preliminary injunction only on notice to the adverse party.

(2) *Consolidating the Hearing with the Trial on the Merits.* Before or after beginning the hearing on a motion for a preliminary injunction, the court may advance the trial on the merits and consolidate it with the hearing. Even when consolidation is not ordered, evidence that is received on the motion and that would be admissible at trial becomes part of the trial record and need not be repeated at trial. But the court must preserve any party's right to a jury trial.

(b) Temporary Restraining Order.

(1) *Issuing Without Notice.* The court may issue a temporary restraining order without written or oral notice to the adverse party or its attorney only if:

(A) specific facts in an affidavit or a verified complaint clearly show that immediate and irreparable injury, loss, or damage will result to the movant before the adverse party can be heard in opposition; and

  (B) the movant's attorney certifies in writing any efforts made to give notice and the reasons why it should not be required.

(2) *Contents; Expiration.* Every temporary restraining order issued without notice must state the date and hour it was issued; describe the injury and state why it is irreparable; state why the order was issued without notice; and be promptly filed in the clerk's office and entered in the record. The order expires at the time after entry—not to exceed 14 days—that the court sets, unless before that time the court, for good cause, extends it for a like period or the adverse party consents to a longer extension. The reasons for an extension must be entered in the record.

(3) *Expediting the Preliminary–Injunction Hearing.* If the order is issued without notice, the motion for a preliminary injunction must be set for hearing at the earliest possible time, taking precedence over all other matters except hearings on older matters of the same character. At the hearing, the party who obtained the order must proceed with the motion; if the party does not, the court must dissolve the order.

(4) *Motion to Dissolve.* On 2 days' notice to the party who obtained the order without notice—or on shorter notice set by the court—the adverse party may appear and move to dissolve or modify the order. The court must then hear and decide the motion as promptly as justice requires.

(c) Security. The court may issue a preliminary injunction or a temporary restraining order only if the movant gives security in an amount that the court considers proper to pay the costs and damages sustained by any party found to have been wrongfully enjoined or restrained. The United States, its officers, and its agencies are not required to give security.

(d) Contents and Scope of Every Injunction and Restraining Order.

(1) *Contents.* Every order granting an injunction and every restraining order must:

  (A) state the reasons why it issued;

  (B) state its terms specifically; and

  (C) describe in reasonable detail—and not by referring to the complaint or other document—the act or acts restrained or required.

(2) *Persons Bound.* The order binds only the following who receive actual notice of it by personal service or otherwise:

  (A) the parties;

  (B) the parties' officers, agents, servants, employees, and attorneys; and

  (C) other persons who are in active concert or participation with anyone described in Rule 65(d)(2)(A) or (B).

(e) Other Laws Not Modified. These rules do not modify the following:

  (1) any federal statute relating to temporary restraining orders or preliminary injunctions in actions affecting employer and employee;

  (2) 28 U.S.C. § 2361, which relates to preliminary injunctions in actions of interpleader or in the nature of interpleader; or

  (3) 28 U.S.C. § 2284, which relates to actions that must be heard and decided by a three-judge district court.

(f) Copyright Impoundment. This rule applies to copyright-impoundment proceedings.

(Amended December 27, 1946, effective March 19, 1948; December 29, 1948, effective October 20, 1949; February 28, 1966, effective July 1, 1966; March 2, 1987, effective August 1, 1987; April 23, 2001, effective December 1, 2001; April 30, 2007, effective December 1, 2007; March 26, 2009, effective December 1, 2009.)

RULE 65.1. PROCEEDINGS AGAINST A SURETY

Whenever these rules (including the Supplemental Rules for Admiralty or Maritime Claims and Asset Forfeiture Actions) require or allow a party to give security, and security is given through a bond or other undertaking with one or more sureties, each surety submits to the court's jurisdiction and irrevocably appoints the court clerk as its agent for receiving service of any papers that affect its liability on the bond or undertaking. The surety's liability may be enforced on motion without an independent action. The motion and any notice that the court orders may be served on the court clerk, who must promptly mail a copy of each to every surety whose address is known.

(Adopted February 28, 1966, effective July 1, 1966; amended March 2, 1987, effective August 1, 1987; April 12, 2006, effective December 1, 2006; April 30, 2007, effective December 1, 2007.)

RULE 66. RECEIVERS

These rules govern an action in which the appointment of a receiver is sought or a receiver sues or is sued. But the practice in administering an estate by a receiver or a similar court-appointed officer must accord with the historical practice in federal courts or with a local rule. An action in which a receiver has been appointed may be dismissed only by court order.

(Amended December 27, 1946, effective March 19, 1948; December 29, 1948, effective October 20, 1949; April 30, 2007, effective December 1, 2007.)

RULE 67.　DEPOSIT INTO COURT

(a) Depositing Property. If any part of the relief sought is a money judgment or the disposition of a sum of money or some other deliverable thing, a party—on notice to every other party and by leave of court—may deposit with the court all or part of the money or thing, whether or not that party claims any of it. The depositing party must deliver to the clerk a copy of the order permitting deposit.

(b) Investing and Withdrawing Funds. Money paid into court under this rule must be deposited and withdrawn in accordance with 28 U.S.C. §§ 2041 and 2042 and any like statute. The money must be deposited in an interest-bearing account or invested in a court-approved, interest-bearing instrument.

(Amended December 29, 1948, effective October 20, 1949; April 28, 1983, effective August 1, 1983; April 30, 2007, effective December 1, 2007.)

RULE 68.　OFFER OF JUDGMENT

(a) Making an Offer; Judgment on an Accepted Offer. At least 14 days before the date set for trial, a party defending against a claim may serve on an opposing party an offer to allow judgment on specified terms, with the costs then accrued. If, within 14 days after being served, the opposing party serves written notice accepting the offer, either party may then file the offer and notice of acceptance, plus proof of service. The clerk must then enter judgment.

(b) Unaccepted Offer. An unaccepted offer is considered withdrawn, but it does not preclude a later offer. Evidence of an unaccepted offer is not admissible except in a proceeding to determine costs.

(c) Offer After Liability is Determined. When one party's liability to another has been determined but the extent of liability remains to be determined by further proceedings, the party held liable may make an offer of judgment. It must be served within a reasonable time—but at least 14 days—before the date set for a hearing to determine the extent of liability.

(d) Paying Costs After an Unaccepted Offer. If the judgment that the offeree finally obtains is not more favorable than the unaccepted offer, the offeree must pay the costs incurred after the offer was made.

(Amended December 27, 1946, effective March 19, 1948; February 28, 1966, effective July 1, 1966; March 2, 1987, effective August 1, 1987; April 30, 2007, effective December 1, 2007; March 26, 2009, effective December 1, 2009.)

RULE 69.　EXECUTION

(a) In General.

(1) Money Judgment; Applicable Procedure. A money judgment is enforced by a writ of execution, unless the court directs otherwise. The procedure on execution—and in proceedings supplementary to and in aid of judgment or execution—must accord with the procedure of the state where the court is located, but a federal statute governs to the extent it applies.

(2) Obtaining Discovery. In aid of the judgment or execution, the judgment creditor or a successor in interest whose interest appears of record may obtain discovery from any person—including the judgment debtor—as provided in these rules or by the procedure of the state where the court is located.

(b) Against Certain Public Officers. When a judgment has been entered against a revenue officer in the circumstances stated in 28 U.S.C. § 2006, or against an officer of Congress in the circumstances stated in 2 U.S.C. § 118, the judgment must be satisfied as those statutes provide.

(Amended December 29, 1948, effective October 20, 1949; March 30, 1970, effective July 1, 1970; March 2, 1987 effective August 1, 1987; April 30, 2007, effective December 1, 2007.)

RULE 70.　ENFORCING A JUDGMENT FOR A SPECIFIC ACT

(a) Party's Failure to Act; Ordering Another to Act. If a judgment requires a party to convey land, to deliver a deed or other document, or to perform any other specific act and the party fails to comply within the time specified, the court may order the act to be done—at the disobedient party's expense—by another person appointed by the court. When done, the act has the same effect as if done by the party.

(b) Vesting Title. If the real or personal property is within the district, the court—instead of ordering a conveyance—may enter a judgment divesting any party's title and vesting it in others. That judgment has the effect of a legally executed conveyance.

(c) Obtaining a Writ of Attachment or Sequestration. On application by a party entitled to performance of an act, the clerk must issue a writ of attachment or sequestration against the disobedient party's property to compel obedience.

(d) Obtaining a Writ of Execution or Assistance. On application by a party who obtains a judgment or order for possession, the clerk must issue a writ of execution or assistance.

(e) Holding in Contempt. The court may also hold the disobedient party in contempt.

(Amended April 30, 2007, effective December 1, 2007.)

RULE 71. ENFORCING RELIEF FOR OR AGAINST A NONPARTY

When an order grants relief for a nonparty or may be enforced against a nonparty, the procedure for enforcing the order is the same as for a party.

(Amended March 2, 1987, effective August 1, 1987; April 30, 2007, effective December 1, 2007.)

TITLE IX. SPECIAL PROCEEDINGS

RULE 71.1. CONDEMNING REAL OR PERSONAL PROPERTY

(a) Applicability of Other Rules. These rules govern proceedings to condemn real and personal property by eminent domain, except as this rule provides otherwise.

(b) Joinder of Properties. The plaintiff may join separate pieces of property in a single action, no matter whether they are owned by the same persons or sought for the same use.

(c) Complaint.

(1) *Caption.* The complaint must contain a caption as provided in Rule 10(a). The plaintiff must, however, name as defendants both the property—designated generally by kind, quantity, and location—and at least one owner of some part of or interest in the property.

(2) *Contents.* The complaint must contain a short and plain statement of the following:

(A) the authority for the taking;

(B) the uses for which the property is to be taken;

(C) a description sufficient to identify the property;

(D) the interests to be acquired; and

(E) for each piece of property, a designation of each defendant who has been joined as an owner or owner of an interest in it.

(3) *Parties.* When the action commences, the plaintiff need join as defendants only those persons who have or claim an interest in the property and whose names are then known. But before any hearing on compensation, the plaintiff must add as defendants all those persons who have or claim an interest and whose names have become known or can be found by a reasonably diligent search of the records, considering both the property's character and value and the interests to be acquired. All others may be made defendants under the designation "Unknown Owners."

(4) *Procedure.* Notice must be served on all defendants as provided in Rule 71.1(d), whether they were named as defendants when the action commenced or were added later. A defendant may answer as provided in Rule 71.1(e). The court, meanwhile, may order any distribution of a deposit that the facts warrant.

(5) *Filing; Additional Copies.* In addition to filing the complaint, the plaintiff must give the clerk at least one copy for the defendants' use and additional copies at the request of the clerk or a defendant.

(d) Process.

(1) *Delivering Notice to the Clerk.* On filing a complaint, the plaintiff must promptly deliver to the clerk joint or several notices directed to the named defendants. When adding defendants, the plaintiff must deliver to the clerk additional notices directed to the new defendants.

(2) *Contents of the Notice.*

(A) *Main Contents.* Each notice must name the court, the title of the action, and the defendant to whom it is directed. It must describe the property sufficiently to identify it, but need not describe any property other than that to be taken from the named defendant. The notice must also state:

(i) that the action is to condemn property;

(ii) the interest to be taken;

(iii) the authority for the taking;

(iv) the uses for which the property is to be taken;

(v) that the defendant may serve an answer on the plaintiff's attorney within 21 days after being served with the notice;

(vi) that the failure to so serve an answer constitutes consent to the taking and to the court's authority to proceed with the action and fix the compensation; and

(vii) that a defendant who does not serve an answer may file a notice of appearance.

(B) *Conclusion.* The notice must conclude with the name, telephone number, and e-mail address of the plaintiff's attorney and an address within the district in which the action is brought where the attorney may be served.

(3) *Serving the Notice.*

(A) *Personal Service.* When a defendant whose address is known resides within the United States or a territory subject to the administrative or judicial jurisdiction of the United States, personal service of the notice (without a copy of the complaint) must be made in accordance with Rule 4.

(B) *Service by Publication.*

(i) A defendant may be served by publication only when the plaintiff's attorney files a certificate stating that the attorney believes the defendant cannot be personally served, because after diligent inquiry within the state where the complaint is filed, the defendant's place of residence is still unknown or, if known, that it is beyond the territorial limits of personal service. Service is then made by publishing the notice—once a week for at least 3 successive weeks—in a newspaper published in the county where the property is located or, if there is no such newspaper, in a newspaper with general circulation where the property is located. Before the last publication, a copy of the notice must also be mailed to every defendant who cannot be personally served but whose place of residence is then known. Unknown owners may be served by publication in the same manner by a notice addressed to "Unknown Owners."

(ii) Service by publication is complete on the date of the last publication. The plaintiff's attorney must prove publication and mailing by a certificate, attach a printed copy of the published notice, and mark on the copy the newspaper's name and the dates of publication.

(4) *Effect of Delivery and Service.* Delivering the notice to the clerk and serving it have the same effect as serving a summons under Rule 4.

(5) *Amending the Notice; Proof of Service and Amending the Proof.* Rule 4(a)(2) governs amending the notice. Rule 4(*l*) governs proof of service and amending it.

(e) **Appearance or Answer.**

(1) *Notice of Appearance.* A defendant that has no objection or defense to the taking of its property may serve a notice of appearance designating the property in which it claims an interest. The defendant must then be given notice of all later proceedings affecting the defendant.

(2) *Answer.* A defendant that has an objection or defense to the taking must serve an answer within 21 days after being served with the notice. The answer must:

(A) identify the property in which the defendant claims an interest;

(B) state the nature and extent of the interest; and

(C) state all the defendant's objections and defenses to the taking.

(3) *Waiver of Other Objections and Defenses; Evidence on Compensation.* A defendant waives all objections and defenses not stated in its answer. No other pleading or motion asserting an additional objection or defense is allowed. But at the trial on compensation, a defendant—whether or not it has previously appeared or answered—may present evidence on the amount of compensation to be paid and may share in the award.

(f) **Amending Pleadings.** Without leave of court, the plaintiff may—as often as it wants—amend the complaint at any time before the trial on compensation. But no amendment may be made if it would result in a dismissal inconsistent with Rule 71.1(i)(1) or (2). The plaintiff need not serve a copy of an amendment, but must serve notice of the filing, as provided in Rule 5(b), on every affected party who has appeared and, as provided in Rule 71.1(d), on every affected party who has not appeared. In addition, the plaintiff must give the clerk at least one copy of each amendment for the defendants' use, and additional copies at the request of the clerk or a defendant. A defendant may appear or answer in the time and manner and with the same effect as provided in Rule 71.1(e).

(g) **Substituting Parties.** If a defendant dies, becomes incompetent, or transfers an interest after being joined, the court may, on motion and notice of hearing, order that the proper party be substituted. Service of the motion and notice on a nonparty must be made as provided in Rule 71.1(d)(3).

(h) **Trial of the Issues.**

(1) *Issues Other Than Compensation; Compensation.* In an action involving eminent domain under federal law, the court tries all issues, including compensation, except when compensation must be determined:

(A) by any tribunal specially constituted by a federal statute to determine compensation; or

(B) if there is no such tribunal, by a jury when a party demands one within the time to answer or within any additional time the court sets, unless the court appoints a commission.

(2) Appointing a Commission; Commission's Powers and Report.

(A) Reasons for Appointing. If a party has demanded a jury, the court may instead appoint a three-person commission to determine compensation because of the character, location, or quantity of the property to be condemned or for other just reasons.

(B) Alternate Commissioners. The court may appoint up to two additional persons to serve as alternate commissioners to hear the case and replace commissioners who, before a decision is filed, the court finds unable or disqualified to perform their duties. Once the commission renders its final decision, the court must discharge any alternate who has not replaced a commissioner.

(C) Examining the Prospective Commissioners. Before making its appointments, the court must advise the parties of the identity and qualifications of each prospective commissioner and alternate, and may permit the parties to examine them. The parties may not suggest appointees, but for good cause may object to a prospective commissioner or alternate.

(D) Commission's Powers and Report. A commission has the powers of a master under Rule 53(c). Its action and report are determined by a majority. Rule 53(d), (e), and (f) apply to its action and report.

(i) Dismissal of the Action or a Defendant.

(1) Dismissing the Action.

(A) By the Plaintiff. If no compensation hearing on a piece of property has begun, and if the plaintiff has not acquired title or a lesser interest or taken possession, the plaintiff may, without a court order, dismiss the action as to that property by filing a notice of dismissal briefly describing the property.

(B) By Stipulation. Before a judgment is entered vesting the plaintiff with title or a lesser interest in or possession of property, the plaintiff and affected defendants may, without a court order, dismiss the action in whole or in part by filing a stipulation of dismissal. And if the parties so stipulate, the court may vacate a judgment already entered.

(C) By Court Order. At any time before compensation has been determined and paid, the court may, after a motion and hearing, dismiss the action as to a piece of property. But if the plaintiff has already taken title, a lesser interest, or possession as to any part of it,

the court must award compensation for the title, lesser interest, or possession taken.

(2) Dismissing a Defendant. The court may at any time dismiss a defendant who was unnecessarily or improperly joined.

(3) Effect. A dismissal is without prejudice unless otherwise stated in the notice, stipulation, or court order.

(j) Deposit and Its Distribution.

(1) Deposit. The plaintiff must deposit with the court any money required by law as a condition to the exercise of eminent domain and may make a deposit when allowed by statute.

(2) Distribution; Adjusting Distribution. After a deposit, the court and attorneys must expedite the proceedings so as to distribute the deposit and to determine and pay compensation. If the compensation finally awarded to a defendant exceeds the amount distributed to that defendant, the court must enter judgment against the plaintiff for the deficiency. If the compensation awarded to a defendant is less than the amount distributed to that defendant, the court must enter judgment against that defendant for the overpayment.

(k) Condemnation Under a State's Power of Eminent Domain. This rule governs an action involving eminent domain under state law. But if state law provides for trying an issue by jury—or for trying the issue of compensation by jury or commission or both—that law governs.

(l) Costs. Costs are not subject to Rule 54(d).

(Adopted April 30, 1951, effective August 1, 1951; amended January 21, 1963, effective July 1, 1963; April 29, 1985, effective August 1, 1985; March 2, 1987, effective August 1, 1987; April 25, 1988, effective August 1, 1988; amended by Pub.L. 100–690, Title VII, § 7050, November 18, 1988, 102 Stat. 4401 (although amendment by Pub.L. 100–690 could not be executed due to prior amendment by Court order which made the same change effective August 1, 1988); amended April 22, 1993, effective December 1, 1993; March 27, 2003, effective December 1, 2003; April 30, 2007, effective December 1, 2007; March 26, 2009, effective December 1, 2009.)

RULE 72. MAGISTRATE JUDGES: PRETRIAL ORDER

(a) Nondispositive Matters. When a pretrial matter not dispositive of a party's claim or defense is referred to a magistrate judge to hear and decide, the magistrate judge must promptly conduct the required proceedings and, when appropriate, issue a written order stating the decision. A party may serve and file objections to the order within 14 days after being served with a copy. A party may not assign as error a defect in the order not timely objected to. The district judge in the case must consider timely objections and modify or set aside any part of the order that is clearly erroneous or is contrary to law.

(b) Dispositive Motions and Prisoner Petitions.

  (1) *Findings and Recommendations.* A magistrate judge must promptly conduct the required proceedings when assigned, without the parties' consent, to hear a pretrial matter dispositive of a claim or defense or a prisoner petition challenging the conditions of confinement. A record must be made of all evidentiary proceedings and may, at the magistrate judge's discretion, be made of any other proceedings. The magistrate judge must enter a recommended disposition, including, if appropriate, proposed findings of fact. The clerk must promptly mail a copy to each party.

  (2) *Objections.* Within 14 days after being served with a copy of the recommended disposition, a party may serve and file specific written objections to the proposed findings and recommendations. A party may respond to another party's objections within 14 days after being served with a copy. Unless the district judge orders otherwise, the objecting party must promptly arrange for transcribing the record, or whatever portions of it the parties agree to or the magistrate judge considers sufficient.

  (3) *Resolving Objections.* The district judge must determine de novo any part of the magistrate judge's disposition that has been properly objected to. The district judge may accept, reject, or modify the recommended disposition; receive further evidence; or return the matter to the magistrate judge with instructions.

(Former Rule 72 abrogated December 4, 1967, effective July 1, 1968; new Rule 72 adopted April 28, 1983, effective August 1, 1983; amended April 30, 1991, effective December 1, 1991; April 22, 1993, effective December 1, 1993; April 30, 2007, effective December 1, 2007; March 26, 2009, effective December 1, 2009.)

RULE 73. MAGISTRATE JUDGES: TRIAL BY CONSENT; APPEAL

(a) Trial by Consent. When authorized under 28 U.S.C. § 636(c), a magistrate judge may, if all parties consent, conduct a civil action or proceeding, including a jury or nonjury trial. A record must be made in accordance with 28 U.S.C. § 636(c)(5).

(b) Consent Procedure.

  (1) *In General.* When a magistrate judge has been designated to conduct civil actions or proceedings, the clerk must give the parties written notice of their opportunity to consent under 28 U.S.C. § 636(c). To signify their consent, the

parties must jointly or separately file a statement consenting to the referral. A district judge or magistrate judge may be informed of a party's response to the clerk's notice only if all parties have consented to the referral.

  (2) *Reminding the Parties About Consenting.* A district judge, magistrate judge, or other court official may remind the parties of the magistrate judge's availability, but must also advise them that they are free to withhold consent without adverse substantive consequences.

  (3) *Vacating a Referral.* On its own for good cause—or when a party shows extraordinary circumstances—the district judge may vacate a referral to a magistrate judge under this rule.

(c) Appealing a Judgment. In accordance with 28 U.S.C. § 636(c)(3), an appeal from a judgment entered at a magistrate judge's direction may be taken to the court of appeals as would any other appeal from a district-court judgment.

(Former Rule 73 abrogated December 4, 1967, effective July 1, 1968; new Rule 73 adopted April 28, 1983, effective August 1, 1983; amended March 2, 1987, effective August 1, 1987; April 22, 1993, effective December 1, 1993; April 11, 1997, effective December 1, 1997; April 30, 2007, effective December 1, 2007.)

RULE 74. METHOD OF APPEAL FROM MAGISTRATE JUDGE TO DISTRICT JUDGE UNDER TITLE 28, U.S.C. § 636(c)(4) AND RULE 73(d) [ABROGATED]

(Former Rule 74 abrogated December 4, 1967, effective July 1, 1968; new Rule 74 adopted April 28, 1983, effective August 1, 1983; amended April 22, 1993, effective December 1, 1993; abrogated April 11, 1997, effective December 1, 1997; April 30, 2007, effective December 1, 2007.)

RULE 75. PROCEEDINGS ON APPEAL FROM MAGISTRATE JUDGE TO DISTRICT JUDGE UNDER RULE 73(d) [ABROGATED]

(Former Rule 75 abrogated December 4, 1967, effective July 1, 1968; new Rule 75 adopted April 28, 1983, effective August 1, 1983; amended March 2, 1987, effective August 1, 1987; April 22, 1993, effective December 1, 1993; abrogated April 11, 1997, effective December 1, 1997; April 30, 2007, effective December 1, 2007.)

RULE 76. JUDGMENT OF THE DISTRICT JUDGE ON THE APPEAL UNDER RULE 73(d) AND COSTS [ABROGATED]

(Former Rule 76 abrogated December 4, 1967, effective July 1, 1968; new Rule 76 adopted April 28, 1983, effective August 1, 1983; amended April 22, 1993, effective December 1, 1993;

abrogated April 11, 1997, effective December 1, 1997; April 30, 2007, effective December 1, 2007.)

TITLE X. DISTRICT COURTS AND CLERKS: CONDUCTING BUSINESS; ISSUING ORDERS

RULE 77. CONDUCTING BUSINESS; CLERK'S AUTHORITY; NOTICE OF AN ORDER OR JUDGMENT

(a) When Court Is Open. Every district court is considered always open for filing any paper, issuing and returning process, making a motion, or entering an order.

(b) Place for Trial and Other Proceedings. Every trial on the merits must be conducted in open court and, so far as convenient, in a regular courtroom. Any other act or proceeding may be done or conducted by a judge in chambers, without the attendance of the clerk or other court official, and anywhere inside or outside the district. But no hearing—other than one ex parte—may be conducted outside the district unless all the affected parties consent.

(c) Clerk's Office Hours; Clerk's Orders.

    (1) *Hours.* The clerk's office—with a clerk or deputy on duty—must be open during business hours every day except Saturdays, Sundays, and legal holidays. But a court may, by local rule or order, require that the office be open for specified hours on Saturday or a particular legal holiday other than one listed in Rule 6(a)(4)(A).

    (2) *Orders.* Subject to the court's power to suspend, alter, or rescind the clerk's action for good cause, the clerk may:

        (A) issue process;

        (B) enter a default;

        (C) enter a default judgment under Rule 55(b)(1); and

        (D) act on any other matter that does not require the court's action.

(d) Serving Notice of an Order or Judgment.

    (1) *Service.* Immediately after entering an order or judgment, the clerk must serve notice of the entry, as provided in Rule 5(b), on each party who is not in default for failing to appear. The clerk must record the service on the docket. A party also may serve notice of the entry as provided in Rule 5(b).

    (2) *Time to Appeal Not Affected by Lack of Notice.* Lack of notice of the entry does not affect the time for appeal or relieve—or authorize the court to relieve—a party for failing to appeal within the time allowed, except as allowed by Federal Rule of Appellate Procedure (4)(a).

(Amended December 27, 1946, effective March 19, 1948; January 21, 1963, effective July 1, 1963; December 4, 1967, effective July 1, 1968; March 1, 1971, effective July 1, 1971; March 2, 1987, effective August 1, 1987; April 30, 1991, effective December 1, 1991; April 23, 2001, effective December 1, 2001; April 30, 2007, effective December 1, 2007.)

RULE 78. HEARING MOTIONS; SUBMISSION ON BRIEFS

(a) Providing a Regular Schedule for Oral Hearings. A court may establish regular times and places for oral hearings on motions.

(b) Providing for Submission on Briefs. By rule or order, the court may provide for submitting and determining motions on briefs, without oral hearings.

(Amended March 2, 1987, effective August 1, 1987; April 30, 2007, effective December 1, 2007.)

RULE 79. RECORDS KEPT BY THE CLERK

(a) Civil Docket.

    (1) *In General.* The clerk must keep a record known as the "civil docket" in the form and manner prescribed by the Director of the Administrative Office of the United States Courts with the approval of the Judicial Conference of the United States. The clerk must enter each civil action in the docket. Actions must be assigned consecutive file numbers, which must be noted in the docket where the first entry of the action is made.

    (2) *Items to be Entered.* The following items must be marked with the file number and entered chronologically in the docket:

        (A) papers filed with the clerk;

        (B) process issued, and proofs of service or other returns showing execution; and

        (C) appearances, orders, verdicts, and judgments.

    (3) *Contents of Entries; Jury Trial Demanded.* Each entry must briefly show the nature of the paper filed or writ issued, the substance of each proof of service or other return, and the substance and date of entry of each order and judgment. When a jury trial has been properly demanded or ordered, the clerk must enter the word "jury" in the docket.

(b) Civil Judgments and Orders. The clerk must keep a copy of every final judgment and appealable order; of every order affecting title to or a lien on real or personal property; and of any other order that the court directs to be kept. The clerk must keep these in the form and manner prescribed by the Director of the Administrative Office of the United States Courts with the approval of the Judicial Conference of the United States.

(c) Indexes; Calendars. Under the court's direction, the clerk must:

(1) keep indexes of the docket and of the judgments and orders described in Rule 79(b); and

(2) prepare calendars of all actions ready for trial, distinguishing jury trials from nonjury trials.

(d) Other Records. The clerk must keep any other records required by the Director of the Administrative Office of the United States Courts with the approval of the Judicial Conference of the United States.

(Amended December 27, 1946, effective March 19, 1948; December 29, 1948, effective October 20, 1949; January 21, 1963, effective July 1, 1963; April 30, 2007, effective December 1, 2007.)

RULE 80. STENOGRAPHIC TRANSCRIPT AS EVIDENCE

If stenographically reported testimony at a hearing or trial is admissible in evidence at a later trial, the testimony may be proved by a transcript certified by the person who reported it.

(Amended December 27, 1946, effective March 19, 1948; April 30, 2007, effective December 1, 2007.)

TITLE XI. GENERAL PROVISIONS

RULE 81. APPLICABILITY OF THE RULES IN GENERAL; REMOVED ACTIONS

(a) Applicability to Particular Proceedings.

(1) *Prize Proceedings.* These rules do not apply to prize proceedings in admiralty governed by 10 U.S.C. §§ 7651–7681.

(2) *Bankruptcy.* These rules apply to bankruptcy proceedings to the extent provided by the Federal Rules of Bankruptcy Procedure.

(3) *Citizenship.* These rules apply to proceedings for admission to citizenship to the extent that the practice in those proceedings is not specified in federal statutes and has previously conformed to the practice in civil actions. The provisions of 8 U.S.C. § 1451 for service by publication and for answer apply in proceedings to cancel citizenship certificates.

(4) *Special Writs.* These rules apply to proceedings for habeas corpus and for quo warranto to the extent that the practice in those proceedings:

(A) is not specified in a federal statute, the Rules Governing Section 2254 Cases, or the Rules Governing Section 2255 Cases; and

(B) has previously conformed to the practice in civil actions.

(5) *Proceedings Involving a Subpoena.* These rules apply to proceedings to compel testimony or the production of documents through a subpoena issued by a United States officer or agency under a federal statute, except as otherwise

provided by statute, by local rule, or by court order in the proceedings.

(6) *Other Proceedings.* These rules, to the extent applicable, govern proceedings under the following laws, except as these laws provide other procedures:

(A) 7 U.S.C. §§ 292, 499g(c), for reviewing an order of the Secretary of Agriculture;

(B) 9 U.S.C., relating to arbitration;

(C) 15 U.S.C. § 522, for reviewing an order of the Secretary of the Interior;

(D) 15 U.S.C. § 715d(c), for reviewing an order denying a certificate of clearance;

(E) 29 U.S.C. §§ 159, 160, for enforcing an order of the National Labor Relations Board;

(F) 33 U.S.C. §§ 918, 921, for enforcing or reviewing a compensation order under the Longshore and Harbor Workers' Compensation Act; and

(G) 45 U.S.C. § 159, for reviewing an arbitration award in a railway-labor dispute.

(b) Scire Facias and Mandamus. The writs of scire facias and mandamus are abolished. Relief previously available through them may be obtained by appropriate action or motion under these rules.

(c) Removed Actions.

(1) *Applicability.* These rules apply to a civil action after it is removed from a state court.

(2) *Further Pleading.* After removal, repleading is unnecessary unless the court orders it. A defendant who did not answer before removal must answer or present other defenses or objections under these rules within the longest of these periods:

    (A) 21 days after receiving—through service or otherwise—a copy of the initial pleading stating the claim for relief;

    (B) 21 days after being served with the summons for an initial pleading on file at the time of service; or

    (C) 7 days after the notice of removal is filed.

  (3) *Demand for a Jury Trial.*

    (A) *As Affected by State Law.* A party who, before removal, expressly demanded a jury trial in accordance with state law need not renew the demand after removal. If the state law did not require an express demand for a jury trial, a party need not make one after removal unless the court orders the parties to do so within a specified time. The court must so order at a party's request and may so order on its own. A party who fails to make a demand when so ordered waives a jury trial.

    (B) *Under Rule 38.* If all necessary pleadings have been served at the time of removal, a party entitled to a jury trial under Rule 38 must be given one if the party serves a demand within 14 days after:

      (i) it files a notice of removal; or

      (ii) it is served with a notice of removal filed by another party.

(d) Law Applicable.

  (1) *"State Law" Defined.* When these rules refer to state law, the term "law" includes the state's statutes and the state's judicial decisions.

  (2) *"State" Defined.* The term "state" includes, where appropriate, the District of Columbia and any United States commonwealth or territory.

  (3) *"Federal Statute" Defined in the District of Columbia.* In the United States District Court for the District of Columbia, the term "federal statute" includes any Act of Congress that applies locally to the District.

(Amended December 28, 1939, effective April 3, 1941; December 27, 1946, effective March 19, 1948; December 29, 1948, effective October 20, 1949; April 30, 1951, effective August 1, 1951; January 21, 1963, effective July 1, 1963; February 28, 1966, effective July 1, 1966; December 4, 1967, effective July 1, 1968; March 1, 1971, effective July 1, 1971; March 2, 1987, effective August 1, 1987; April 23, 2001, effective December 1, 2001; April 29, 2002, effective December 1, 2002; April 30, 2007, effective December 1, 2007; March 26, 2009, effective December 1, 2009.)

RULE 82. JURISDICTION AND VENUE UNAFFECTED

These rules do not extend or limit the jurisdiction of the district courts or the venue of actions in those courts. An admiralty or maritime claim under Rule 9(h) is not a civil action for purposes of 28 U.S.C. §§ 1391–1392.

(Amended December 29, 1948, effective October 20, 1949; February 28, 1966, effective July 1, 1966; April 23, 2001, effective December 1, 2001; April 30, 2007, effective December 1, 2007.)

RULE 83. RULES BY DISTRICT COURTS; JUDGE'S DIRECTIVES

(a) Local Rules.

  (1) *In General.* After giving public notice and an opportunity for comment, a district court, acting by a majority of its district judges, may adopt and amend rules governing its practice. A local rule must be consistent with—but not duplicate—federal statutes and rules adopted under 28 U.S.C. §§ 2072 and 2075, and must conform to any uniform numbering system prescribed by the Judicial Conference of the United States. A local rule takes effect on the date specified by the district court and remains in effect unless amended by the court or abrogated by the judicial council of the circuit. Copies of rules and amendments must, on their adoption, be furnished to the judicial council and the Administrative Office of the United States Courts and be made available to the public.

  (2) *Requirement of Form.* A local rule imposing a requirement of form must not be enforced in a way that causes a party to lose any right because of a nonwillful failure to comply.

(b) Procedure When There Is No Controlling Law. A judge may regulate practice in any manner consistent with federal law, rules adopted under 28 U.S.C. §§ 2072 and 2075, and the district's local rules. No sanction or other disadvantage may be imposed for noncompliance with any requirement not in federal law, federal rules, or the local rules unless the alleged violator has been furnished in the particular case with actual notice of the requirement.

(Amended April 29, 1985, effective August 1, 1985; April 27, 1995, effective December 1, 1995; April 30, 2007, effective December 1, 2007.)

RULE 84. FORMS

The forms in the Appendix suffice under these rules and illustrate the simplicity and brevity that these rules contemplate.

(Amended December 27, 1946, effective March 19, 1948; April 30, 2007, effective December 1, 2007.)

RULE 85. TITLE

These rules may be cited as the Federal Rules of Civil Procedure.

(Amended April 30, 2007, effective December 1, 2007.)

RULE 86. EFFECTIVE DATES

(a) In General. These rules and any amendments take effect at the time specified by the Supreme Court, subject to 28 U.S.C. § 2074. They govern:

(1) proceedings in an action commenced after their effective date; and

(2) proceedings after that date in an action then pending unless:

(A) the Supreme Court specifies otherwise; or

(B) the court determines that applying them in a particular action would be infeasible or work an injustice.

(b) December 1, 2007 Amendments. If any provision in Rules 1–5.1, 6–73, or 77–86 conflicts with another law, priority in time for the purpose of 28 U.S.C. § 2072(b) is not affected by the amendments taking effect on December 1, 2007.

(Amended December 27, 1946, effective March 19, 1948; December 29, 1948, effective October 20, 1949; April 17, 1961, effective July 19, 1961; January 21, 1963, and March 18, 1963, effective July 1, 1963; April 30, 2007, effective December 1, 2007.)

APPENDIX OF FORMS

(See Rule 84)

FORM 1.   CAPTION

(Use on every summons, complaint, answer, motion, or other document.)

United States District Court
for the
_____ District of _____

A B, Plaintiff	)	
	)	
v.	)	
	)	Civil Action No. _____
C D, Defendant	)	
	)	
v.	)	
	)	
E F, Third–Party Defendant	)	
(Use if needed.)	)	

(Name of Document)

(Added Apr. 30, 2007, eff. Dec. 1, 2007.)

FORM 2.   DATE, SIGNATURE, ADDRESS, E–MAIL ADDRESS, AND TELEPHONE NUMBER

(Use at the conclusion of pleadings and other papers that require a signature.)

Date _____

_____
(Signature of the attorney or unrepresented party)

_____
(Printed name)

_____
(Address)

_____
(E-mail address)

_____
(Telephone number)

(Added Apr. 30, 2007, eff. Dec. 1, 2007.)

FORM 3. SUMMONS
(Caption—See Form 1.)

To *name the defendant*:

A lawsuit has been filed against you.

Within 21 days after service of this summons on you (not counting the day you received it), you must serve on the plaintiff an answer to the attached complaint or a motion under Rule 12 of the Federal Rules of Civil Procedure. The answer or motion must be served on the plaintiff's attorney, _____, whose address is _____. If you fail to do so, judgment by default will be entered against you for the relief demanded in the complaint. You also must file your answer or motion with the court.

Date _____

_____
Clerk of Court

(Court Seal)

(Use 60 days if the defendant is the United States or a United States agency, or is an officer or employee of the United States allowed 60 days by Rule 12(a)(3).)

(Added Apr. 30, 2007, eff. Dec. 1, 2007, and amended Mar. 26, 2009, eff. Dec. 1, 2009.)

FORM 4. SUMMONS ON A THIRD-PARTY COMPLAINT
(Caption—See Form 1.)

To *name the third-party defendant*:

A lawsuit has been filed against defendant _____, who as third-party plaintiff is making this claim against you to pay part or all of what [he] may owe to the plaintiff _____.

Within 21 days after service of this summons on you (not counting the day you received it), you must serve on the plaintiff and on the defendant an answer to the attached third-party complaint or a motion under Rule 12 of the Federal Rules of Civil Procedure. The answer or motion must be served on the defendant's attorney, _____, whose address is, _____, and also on the plaintiff's attorney, _____, whose address is, _____. If you fail to do so, judgment by default will be entered against you for the relief demanded in the third-party complaint. You also must file the answer or motion with the court and serve it on any other parties.

A copy of the plaintiff's complaint is also attached. You may—but are not required to—respond to it.

Date _____

_____
Clerk of Court

(Court Seal)

(Added Apr. 30, 2007, eff. Dec. 1, 2007, and amended Mar. 26, 2009, eff. Dec. 1, 2009.)

FORM 5. NOTICE OF A LAWSUIT AND REQUEST
TO WAIVE SERVICE OF A SUMMONS

(Caption—See Form 1.)

To *(name the defendant—or if the defendant is a corporation, partnership, or association name an officer or agent authorized to receive service)*:

Why are you getting this?

A lawsuit has been filed against you, or the entity you represent, in this court under the number shown above. A copy of the complaint is attached.

This is not a summons, or an official notice from the court. It is a request that, to avoid expenses, you waive formal service of a summons by signing and returning the enclosed waiver. To avoid these expenses, you must return the signed waiver within *(give at least 30 days or at least 60 days if the defendant is outside any judicial district of the United States)* from the date shown below, which is the date this notice was sent. Two copies of the waiver form are enclosed, along with a stamped, self-addressed envelope or other prepaid means for returning one copy. You may keep the other copy.

What happens next?

If you return the signed waiver, I will file it with the court. The action will then proceed as if you had been served on the date the waiver is filed, but no summons will be served on you and you will have 60 days from the date this notice is sent (see the date below) to answer the complaint (or 90 days if this notice is sent to you outside any judicial district of the United States).

If you do not return the signed waiver within the time indicated, I will arrange to have the summons and complaint served on you. And I will ask the court to require you, or the entity you represent, to pay the expenses of making service.

Please read the enclosed statement about the duty to avoid unnecessary expenses.

I certify that this request is being sent to you on the date below.

(Date and sign—See Form 2.)

(Added Apr. 30, 2007, eff. Dec. 1, 2007.)

FORM 6. WAIVER OF THE SERVICE OF SUMMONS

(Caption—See Form 1.)

To *name the plaintiff's attorney or the unrepresented plaintiff*:

I have received your request to waive service of a summons in this action along with a copy of the complaint, two copies of this waiver form, and a prepaid means of returning one signed copy of the form to you.

I, or the entity I represent, agree to save the expense of serving a summons and complaint in this case.

I understand that I, or the entity I represent, will keep all defenses or objections to the lawsuit, the court's jurisdiction, and the venue of the action, but that I waive any objections to the absence of a summons or of service.

I also understand that I, or the entity I represent, must file and serve an answer or a motion under Rule 12 within 60 days from _____, the date when this request was sent (or 90 days if it was sent outside the United States). If I fail to do so, a default judgment will be entered against me or the entity I represent.

(Date and sign—See Form 2.)

(Attach the following to Form 6.)

Duty to Avoid Unnecessary Expenses of Serving a Summons

Rule 4 of the Federal Rules of Civil Procedure requires certain defendants to cooperate in saving unnecessary expenses of serving a summons and complaint. A defendant who is located in the United States and who fails to return a signed waiver of service requested by a plaintiff located in the United States will be required to pay the expenses of service, unless the defendant shows good cause for the failure.

"Good cause" does *not* include a belief that the lawsuit is groundless, or that it has been brought in an improper venue, or that the court has no jurisdiction over this matter or over the defendant or the defendant's property.

If the waiver is signed and returned, you can still make these and all other defenses and objections, but you cannot object to the absence of a summons or of service.

If you waive service, then you must, within the time specified on the waiver form, serve an answer or a motion under Rule 12 on the plaintiff and file a copy with the court. By signing and returning the waiver form, you are allowed more time to respond than if a summons had been served.

(Added Apr. 30, 2007, eff. Dec. 1, 2007.)

FORM 7. STATEMENT OF JURISDICTION

a. (*For diversity-of-citizenship jurisdiction.*) The plaintiff is [a citizen of *Michigan*] [a corporation incorporated under the laws of *Michigan* with its principal place of business in *Michigan*]. The defendant is [a citizen of *New York*] [a corporation incorporated under the laws of *New York* with its principal place of business in *New York*]. The amount in controversy, without interest and costs, exceeds the sum or value specified by 28 U.S.C. § 1332.

b. (*For federal-question jurisdiction.*) This action arises under [the United States Constitution, *specify the article or amendment and the section*] [a United States treaty *specify*] [a federal statute, ___ U.S.C. § ___].

c. (*For a claim in the admiralty or maritime jurisdiction.*) This is a case of admiralty or maritime jurisdiction. (*To invoke admiralty status under Rule 9(h) use the following:* This is an admiralty or maritime claim within the meaning of Rule 9(h).)

(Added Apr. 30, 2007, eff. Dec. 1, 2007.)

FORM 8. STATEMENT OF REASONS FOR OMITTING A PARTY

(*If a person who ought to be made a party under Rule 19(a) is not named, include this statement in accordance with Rule 19(c).*)

This complaint does not join as a party *name* who [is not subject to this court's personal jurisdiction] [cannot be made a party without depriving this court of subject-matter jurisdiction] because *state the reason.*

(Added Apr. 30, 2007, eff. Dec. 1, 2007.)

FORM 9. STATEMENT NOTING A PARTY'S DEATH
(Caption—See Form 1.)

In accordance with Rule 25(a) *name the person,* who is [a party to this action] [a representative of or successor to the deceased party] notes the death during the pendency of this action of *name*, [*describe as party* in this action].

(Date and sign—See Form 2.)

(Added Apr. 30, 2007, eff. Dec. 1, 2007.)

FORM 10. COMPLAINT TO RECOVER A SUM CERTAIN

(Caption—See Form 1.)

1. (Statement of Jurisdiction—See Form 7.)

(Use one or more of the following as appropriate and include a demand for judgment.)

(a) On a Promissory Note

2. On *date,* the defendant executed and delivered a note promising to pay the plaintiff on *date* the sum of $_____ with interest at the rate of ___ percent. A copy of the note [is attached as Exhibit A] [is summarized as follows: _____.]

3. The defendant has not paid the amount owed.

(b) On an Account

2. The defendant owes the plaintiff $_____ according to the account set out in Exhibit A.

(c) For Goods Sold and Delivered

2. The defendant owes the plaintiff $_____ for goods sold and delivered by the plaintiff to the defendant from *date* to *date.*

(d) For Money Lent

2. The defendant owes the plaintiff $_____ for money lent by the plaintiff to the defendant on *date.*

(e) For Money Paid by Mistake

2. The defendant owes the plaintiff $_____ for money paid by mistake to the defendant on *date* under these circumstances: *describe with particularity in accordance with Rule 9(b).*

(f) For Money Had and Received

2. The defendant owes the plaintiff $_____ for money that was received from *name* on *date* to be paid by the defendant to the plaintiff.

Demand for Judgment

Therefore, the plaintiff demands judgment against the defendant for $_____, plus interest and costs.

(Date and sign—See Form 2.)

(Added Apr. 30, 2007, eff. Dec. 1, 2007.)

FORM 11.   COMPLAINT FOR NEGLIGENCE

(Caption—See Form 1.)

1. (Statement of Jurisdiction—See Form 7.)
2. On *date*, at *place*, the defendant negligently drove a motor vehicle against the plaintiff.
3. As a result, the plaintiff was physically injured, lost wages or income, suffered physical and mental pain, and incurred medical expenses of $_____.

Therefore, the plaintiff demands judgment against the defendant for $_____, plus costs.

(Date and sign—See Form 2).

(Added Apr. 30, 2007, eff. Dec. 1, 2007.)

FORM 12.   COMPLAINT FOR NEGLIGENCE WHEN THE PLAINTIFF DOES NOT KNOW WHO IS RESPONSIBLE

(Caption—See Form 1.)

1. (Statement of Jurisdiction—See Form 7.)
2. On *date*, at *place*, defendant *name* or defendant *name* or both of them willfully or recklessly or negligently drove, or caused to be driven, a motor vehicle against the plaintiff.
3. As a result, the plaintiff was physically injured, lost wages or income, suffered mental and physical pain, and incurred medical expenses of $_____.

Therefore, the plaintiff demands judgment against one or both defendants for $_____, plus costs.

(Date and sign—See Form 2.)

(Added Apr. 30, 2007, eff. Dec. 1, 2007.)

FORM 13.   COMPLAINT FOR NEGLIGENCE UNDER THE FEDERAL EMPLOYERS' LIABILITY ACT

(Caption—See Form 1.)

1.   (Statement of Jurisdiction—See Form 7.)

2.   At the times below, the defendant owned and operated in interstate commerce a railroad line that passed through a tunnel located at _____.

3.   On *date*, the plaintiff was working to repair and enlarge the tunnel to make it convenient and safe for use in interstate commerce.

4.   During this work, the defendant, as the employer, negligently put the plaintiff to work in a section of the tunnel that the defendant had left unprotected and unsupported.

5.   The defendant's negligence caused the plaintiff to be injured by a rock that fell from an unsupported portion of the tunnel.

6.   As a result, the plaintiff was physically injured, lost wages or income, suffered mental and physical pain, and incurred medical expenses of $_____.

Therefore, the plaintiff demands judgment against the defendant for $_____, and costs.

(Date and sign—See Form 2.)

(Added Apr. 30, 2007, eff. Dec. 1, 2007.)

FORM 14.   COMPLAINT FOR DAMAGES UNDER THE MERCHANT MARINE ACT

(Caption—See Form 1.)

1.   (Statement of Jurisdiction—See Form 7.)

2.   At the times below, the defendant owned and operated the vessel *name* and used it to transport cargo for hire by water in interstate and foreign commerce.

3.   On *date*, at *place*, the defendant hired the plaintiff under seamen's articles of customary form for a voyage from _____ to _____ and return at a wage of $_____ a month and found, which is equal to a shore worker's wage of $_____ a month.

4.   On *date*, the vessel was at sea on the return voyage. (*Describe the weather and the condition of the vessel.*)

5.   (*Describe as in Form 11 the defendant's negligent conduct.*)

6.   As a result of the defendant's negligent conduct and the unseaworthiness of the vessel, the plaintiff was physically injured, has been incapable of any gainful activity, suffered mental and physical pain, and has incurred medical expenses of $_____.

Therefore, the plaintiff demands judgment against the defendant for $_____, plus costs.

(Date and sign—See Form 2.)

(Added Apr. 30, 2007, eff. Dec. 1, 2007.)

FORM 15. COMPLAINT FOR THE CONVERSION OF PROPERTY

(Caption—See Form 1.)

1. (Statement of Jurisdiction—See Form 7.)

2. On *date*, at *place*, the defendant converted to the defendant's own use property owned by the plaintiff. The property converted consists of *describe*.

3. The property is worth $_____.

Therefore, the plaintiff demands judgment against the defendant for $_____, plus costs.

(Date and sign—See Form 2.)

(Added Apr. 30, 2007, eff. Dec. 1, 2007.)

FORM 16. THIRD–PARTY COMPLAINT

(Caption—See Form 1.)

1. Plaintiff *name* has filed against defendant *name* a complaint, a copy of which is attached.

2. (*State grounds entitling defendant's name to recover from third-party defendant's name for (all or an identified share) of any judgment for plaintiff's name against defendant's name.*)

Therefore, the defendant demands judgment against *third-party defendant's name* for *all or an identified share* of sums that may be adjudged against the defendant in the plaintiff's favor.

(Date and sign—See Form 2.)

(Added Apr. 30, 2007, eff. Dec. 1, 2007.)

FORM 17.   COMPLAINT FOR SPECIFIC PERFORMANCE
OF A CONTRACT TO CONVEY LAND

(Caption—See Form 1.)

1. (Statement of Jurisdiction—See Form 7.)

2. On *date*, the parties agreed to the contract [attached as Exhibit A][summarize the contract].

3. As agreed, the plaintiff tendered the purchase price and requested a conveyance of the land, but the defendant refused to accept the money or make a conveyance.

4. The plaintiff now offers to pay the purchase price.

Therefore, the plaintiff demands that:

(a) the defendant be required to specifically perform the agreement and pay damages of $_____, plus interest and costs, or

(b) if specific performance is not ordered, the defendant be required to pay damages of $_____, plus interest and costs.

(Date and sign—See Form 2.)

(Added Apr. 30, 2007, eff. Dec. 1, 2007.)

FORM 18.   COMPLAINT FOR PATENT INFRINGEMENT

(Caption—See Form 1.)

1. (Statement of Jurisdiction—See Form 7.)

2. On *date*, United States Letters Patent No. _____ were issued to the plaintiff for an invention in an *electric motor*. The plaintiff owned the patent throughout the period of the defendant's infringing acts and still owns the patent.

3. The defendant has infringed and is still infringing the Letters Patent by making, selling, and using *electric motors* that embody the patented invention, and the defendant will continue to do so unless enjoined by this court.

4. The plaintiff has complied with the statutory requirement of placing a notice of the Letters Patent on all *electric motors* it manufactures and sells and has given the defendant written notice of the infringement.

Therefore, the plaintiff demands:

(a) a preliminary and final injunction against the continuing infringement;

(b) an accounting for damages; and

(c) interest and costs.

(Date and sign—See Form 2.)

(Added Apr. 30, 2007, eff. Dec. 1, 2007.)

FORM 19. COMPLAINT FOR COPYRIGHT INFRINGEMENT AND UNFAIR COMPETITION

(Caption—See Form 1.)

1. (Statement of Jurisdiction—See Form 7.)

2. Before _date_, the plaintiff, a United States citizen, wrote a book entitled _____.

3. The book is an original work that may be copyrighted under United States law. A copy of the book is attached as Exhibit A.

4. Between _date_ and _date_, the plaintiff applied to the copyright office and received a certificate of registration dated _____ and identified as _date, class, number_.

5. Since _date_, the plaintiff has either published or licensed for publication all copies of the book in compliance with the copyright laws and has remained the sole owner of the copyright.

6. After the copyright was issued, the defendant infringed the copyright by publishing and selling a book entitled _____, which was copied largely from the plaintiff's book. A copy of the defendant's book is attached as Exhibit B.

7. The plaintiff has notified the defendant in writing of the infringement.

8. The defendant continues to infringe the copyright by continuing to publish and sell the infringing book in violation of the copyright, and further has engaged in unfair trade practices and unfair competition in connection with its publication and sale of the infringing book, thus causing irreparable damage.

Therefore, the plaintiff demands that:

(a) until this case is decided the defendant and the defendant's agents be enjoined from disposing of any copies of the defendant's book by sale or otherwise;

(b) the defendant account for and pay as damages to the plaintiff all profits and advantages gained from unfair trade practices and unfair competition in selling the defendant's book, and all profits and advantages gained from infringing the plaintiff's copyright (but no less than the statutory minimum);

(c) the defendant deliver for impoundment all copies of the book in the defendant's possession or control and deliver for destruction all infringing copies and all plates, molds, and other materials for making infringing copies;

(d) the defendant pay the plaintiff interest, costs, and reasonable attorney's fees; and

(e) the plaintiff be awarded any other just relief.

(Date and sign—See Form 2.)

(Added Apr. 30, 2007, eff. Dec. 1, 2007.)

FORM 20. COMPLAINT FOR INTERPLEADER
AND DECLARATORY RELIEF

(Caption—See Form 1.)

1. (Statement of Jurisdiction—See Form 7.)

2. On *date*, the plaintiff issued a life insurance policy on the life of *name* with *name* as the named beneficiary.

3. As a condition for keeping the policy in force, the policy required payment of a premium during the first year and then annually.

4. The premium due on *date* was never paid, and the policy lapsed after that date.

5. On *date*, after the policy had lapsed, both the insured and the named beneficiary died in an automobile collision.

6. Defendant *name* claims to be the beneficiary in place of *name* and has filed a claim to be paid the policy's full amount.

7. The other two defendants are representatives of the deceased persons' estates. Each defendant has filed a claim on behalf of each estate to receive payment of the policy's full amount.

8. If the policy was in force at the time of death, the plaintiff is in doubt about who should be paid.

Therefore, the plaintiff demands that:

(a) each defendant be restrained from commencing any action against the plaintiff on the policy;

(b) a judgment be entered that no defendant is entitled to the proceeds of the policy or any part of it, but if the court determines that the policy was in effect at the time of the insured's death, that the defendants be required to interplead and settle among themselves their rights to the proceeds, and that the plaintiff be discharged from all liability except to the defendant determined to be entitled to the proceeds; and

(c) the plaintiff recover its costs.

(Date and sign—See Form 2.)

(Added Apr. 30, 2007, eff. Dec. 1, 2007.)

FORM 21. COMPLAINT ON A CLAIM FOR A DEBT AND TO SET ASIDE A FRAUDULENT CONVEYANCE UNDER RULE 18(b)

(Caption—See Form 1.)

1. (Statement of Jurisdiction—See Form 7.)

2. On *date*, defendant *name* signed a note promising to pay to the plaintiff on *date* the sum of $_____ with interest at the rate of ___ percent. [The pleader may, but need not, attach a copy or plead the note verbatim.]

3. Defendant *name* owes the plaintiff the amount of the note and interest.

4. On *date*, defendant *name* conveyed all defendant's real and personal property *if less than all, describe it fully* to defendant *name* for the purpose of defrauding the plaintiff and hindering or delaying the collection of the debt.

Therefore, the plaintiff demands that:

 (a) judgment for $_____, plus costs, be entered against defendant(s) *name(s)*; and

 (b) the conveyance to defendant *name* be declared void and any judgment granted be made a lien on the property.

(Date and sign—See Form 2.)

(Added Apr. 30, 2007, eff. Dec. 1, 2007.)

FORM 30.   ANSWER PRESENTING DEFENSES UNDER RULE 12(b)

(Caption—See Form 1.)

Responding to Allegations in the Complaint

1. Defendant admits the allegations in paragraphs _____.

2. Defendant lacks knowledge or information sufficient to form a belief about the truth of the allegations in paragraphs _____.

3. Defendant admits *identify part of the allegation* in paragraph _____ and denies or lacks knowledge or information sufficient to form a belief about the truth of the rest of the paragraph.

Failure to State a Claim

4. The complaint fails to state a claim upon which relief can be granted.

Failure to Join a Required Party

5. If there is a debt, it is owed jointly by the defendant and *name* who is a citizen of _____. This person can be made a party without depriving this court of jurisdiction over the existing parties.

Affirmative Defense—Statute of Limitations

6. The plaintiff's claim is barred by the statute of limitations because it arose more than _____ years before this action was commenced.

Counterclaim

7. (*Set forth any counterclaim in the same way a claim is pleaded in a complaint. Include a further statement of jurisdiction if needed.*)

Crossclaim

8. (*Set forth a crossclaim against a coparty in the same way a claim is pleaded in a complaint. Include a further statement of jurisdiction if needed.*)

(Date and sign—See Form 2.)

(Added Apr. 30, 2007, eff. Dec. 1, 2007.)

FORM 31.   ANSWER TO A COMPLAINT FOR MONEY HAD AND RECEIVED WITH A COUNTERCLAIM FOR INTERPLEADER

(Caption—See Form 1.)

Response to the Allegations in the Complaint
(See Form 30.)

Counterclaim for Interpleader

1. The defendant received from *name* a deposit of $_____.

2. The plaintiff demands payment of the deposit because of a purported assignment from *name*, who has notified the defendant that the assignment is not valid and who continues to hold the defendant responsible for the deposit.

Therefore, the defendant demands that:

(a) *name* be made a party to this action;

(b) the plaintiff and *name* be required to interplead their respective claims;

(c) the court decide whether the plaintiff or *name* or either of them is entitled to the deposit and discharge the defendant of any liability except to the person entitled to the deposit; and

(d) the defendant recover costs and attorney's fees.

(Date and sign—See Form 2.)

(Added Apr. 30, 2007, eff. Dec. 1, 2007.)

FORM 40.   MOTION TO DISMISS UNDER RULE 12(B) FOR LACK OF JURISDICTION, IMPROPER VENUE, INSUFFICIENT SERVICE OF PROCESS, OR FAILURE TO STATE A CLAIM

(Caption—See Form 1.)

The defendant moves to dismiss the action because:

1. the amount in controversy is less than the sum or value specified by 28 U.S.C. § 1332;

2. the defendant is not subject to the personal jurisdiction of this court;

3. venue is improper (this defendant does not reside in this district and no part of the events or omissions giving rise to the claim occurred in the district);

4. the defendant has not been properly served, as shown by the attached affidavits of _____; or

5. the complaint fails to state a claim upon which relief can be granted.

(Date and sign—See Form 2.)

(Added Apr. 30, 2007, eff. Dec. 1, 2007.)

FORM 41.   MOTION TO BRING IN A THIRD–PARTY DEFENDANT

(Caption—See Form 1.)

The defendant, as third-party plaintiff, moves for leave to serve on *name* a summons and third-party complaint, copies of which are attached.

(Date and sign—See Form 2.)

(Added Apr. 30, 2007, eff. Dec. 1, 2007.)

FORM 42.   MOTION TO INTERVENE AS A DEFENDANT UNDER RULE 24

(Caption—See Form 1.)

1. *name* moves for leave to intervene as a defendant in this action and to file the attached answer.

(State grounds under Rule 24(a) or (b).)

2. The plaintiff alleges patent infringement. We manufacture and sell to the defendant the articles involved, and we have a defense to the plaintiff's claim.

3. Our defense presents questions of law and fact that are common to this action.

(Date and sign—See Form 2.)

[An Intervener's Answer must be attached. See Form 30.]

(Added Apr. 30, 2007, eff. Dec. 1, 2007.)

FORM 50.   REQUEST TO PRODUCE DOCUMENTS AND TANGIBLE THINGS, OR TO ENTER ONTO LAND UNDER RULE 34

(Caption—See Form 1.)

The plaintiff *name* requests that the defendant *name* respond within ＿＿ days to the following requests:

1.   To produce and permit the plaintiff to inspect and copy and to test or sample the following documents, including electronically stored information:

(Describe each document and the electronically stored information, either individually or by category.)

(State the time, place, and manner of the inspection and any related acts.)

2.   To produce and permit the plaintiff to inspect and copy—and to test or sample—the following tangible things:

(Describe each thing, either individually or by category.)

(State the time, place, and manner of the inspection and any related acts.)

3.   To permit the plaintiff to enter onto the following land to inspect, photograph, test, or sample the property or an object or operation on the property.

(Describe the property and each object or operation.)

(State the time and manner of the inspection and any related acts.)

(Date and sign—See Form 2.)

(Added Apr. 30, 2007, eff. Dec. 1, 2007.)

FORM 51.   REQUEST FOR ADMISSIONS UNDER RULE 36

(Caption—See Form 1.)

The plaintiff *name* asks the defendant *name* to respond within 30 days to these requests by admitting, for purposes of this action only and subject to objections to admissibility at trial:

1.   The genuineness of the following documents, copies of which [are attached] [are or have been furnished or made available for inspection and copying].

(List each document.)

2.   The truth of each of the following statements:

(List each statement.)

(Date and sign—See Form 2.)

(Added Apr. 30, 2007, eff. Dec. 1, 2007.)

FORM 52. REPORT OF THE PARTIES' PLANNING MEETING

(Caption—See Form 1.)

1. The following persons participated in a Rule 26(f) conference on _____date_____ by _state the method of conferring_____:

2. Initial Disclosures. The parties [have completed] [will complete by _____date___] the initial disclosures required by Rule 26(a)(1).

3. Discovery Plan. The parties propose this discovery plan:

   (Use separate paragraphs or subparagraphs if the parties disagree.)

   (a) Discovery will be needed on these subjects: (*describe*)

   (b) Disclosure or discovery of electronically stored information should be handled as follows: (*briefly describe the parties' proposals, including the form or forms for production.*)

   (c) The parties have agreed to an order regarding claims of privilege or of protection as trial-preparation material asserted after production, as follows: (*briefly describe the provisions of the proposed order.*)

   (d) (Dates for commencing and completing discovery, including discovery to be commenced or completed before other discovery.)

   (e) (Maximum number of interrogatories by each party to another party, along with dates the answers are due.)

   (f) (Maximum number of requests for admission, along with the dates responses are due.)

   (g) (Maximum number of depositions for each party.)

   (h) (Limits on the length of depositions, in hours.)

   (i) (Dates for exchanging reports of expert witnesses.)

   (j) (Dates for supplementations under Rule 26(e).)

4. Other Items:

   (a) (A date if the parties ask to meet with the court before a scheduling order.)

   (b) (Requested dates for pretrial conferences.)

   (c) (Final dates for the plaintiff to amend pleadings or to join parties.)

   (d) (Final dates for the defendant to amend pleadings or to join parties.)

   (e) (Final dates to file dispositive motions.)

   (f) (State the prospects for settlement.)

   (g) (Identify any alternative dispute resolution procedure that may enhance settlement prospects.)

   (h) (Final dates for submitting Rule 26(a)(3) witness lists, designations of witnesses whose testimony will be presented by deposition, and exhibit lists.)

   (i) (Final dates to file objections under Rule 26(a)(3).)

   (j) (Suggested trial date and estimate of trial length.)

   (k) (Other matters.)

(Date and sign—see Form 2.)

(Added Apr. 30, 2007, eff. Dec. 1, 2007. As amended Apr. 28, 2010, eff. Dec. 1, 2010.)

FORM 60. NOTICE OF CONDEMNATION

(Caption—See Form 1.)

To *name the defendant*.

1. A complaint in condemnation has been filed in the United States District Court for the _____District of _____, to take property to use for *purpose*. The interest to be taken is *describe*. The court is located in the United States courthouse at this address: _____.

2. The property to be taken is described below. You have or claim an interest in it.

(*Describe the property.*)

3. The authority for taking this property is *cite*.

4. If you want to object or present any defense to the taking you must serve an answer on the plaintiff's attorney within 21 days [after being served with this notice][from *(insert the date of the last publication of notice)*]. Send your answer to this address: _____.

5. Your answer must identify the property in which you claim an interest, state the nature and extent of that interest, and state all your objections and defenses to the taking. Objections and defenses not presented are waived.

6. If you fail to answer you consent to the taking and the court will enter a judgment that takes your described property interest.

7. Instead of answering, you may serve on the plaintiff's attorney a notice of appearance that designates the property in which you claim an interest. After you do that, you will receive a notice of any proceedings that affect you. Whether or not you have previously appeared or answered, you may present evidence at a trial to determine compensation for the property and share in the overall award.

(Date and sign—See Form 2.)

(Added Apr. 30, 2007, eff. Dec. 1, 2007, and amended Mar. 26, 2009, eff. Dec. 1, 2009.)

FORM 61. COMPLAINT FOR CONDEMNATION

(Caption—See Form 1; name as defendants the property and at least one owner.)

1. (Statement of Jurisdiction—See Form 7.)
2. This is an action to take property under the power of eminent domain and to determine just compensation to be paid to the owners and parties in interest.
3. The authority for the taking is _____.
4. The property is to be used for _____.
5. The property to be taken is (*describe in enough detail for identification—or attach the description and state "is described in Exhibit A, attached."*)
6. The interest to be acquired is _____.
7. The persons known to the plaintiff to have or claim an interest in the property are: _____. (*For each person include the interest claimed.*)
8. There may be other persons who have or claim an interest in the property and whose names could not be found after a reasonably diligent search. They are made parties under the designation "Unknown Owners."

Therefore, the plaintiff demands judgment:

(a) condemning the property;

(b) determining and awarding just compensation; and

(c) granting any other lawful and proper relief.

(Date and sign—See Form 2.)

(Added Apr. 30, 2007, eff. Dec. 1, 2007.)

FORM 70. JUDGMENT ON A JURY VERDICT

(Caption—See Form 1.)

This action was tried by a jury with Judge _____ presiding, and the jury has rendered a verdict.

It is ordered that:

[the plaintiff *name* recover from the defendant *name* the amount of $_____ with interest at the rate of ___%, along with costs.]

[the plaintiff recover nothing, the action be dismissed on the merits, and the defendant *name* recover costs from the plaintiff *name.*]

Date _____

_____

Clerk of Court

(Added Apr. 30, 2007, eff. Dec. 1, 2007.)

FORM 71. JUDGMENT BY THE COURT WITHOUT A JURY

(Caption—See Form 1.)

This action was tried by Judge _____ without a jury and the following decision was reached:

It is ordered that [the plaintiff *name* recover from the defendant *name* the amount of $_____, with prejudgment interest at the rate of __%, postjudgment interest at the rate of __%, along with costs.] [the plaintiff recover nothing, the action be dismissed on the merits, and the defendant *name* recover costs from the plaintiff *name*.]

Date_____

_____
Clerk of Court

(Added Apr. 30, 2007, eff. Dec. 1, 2007.)

FORM 80. NOTICE OF A MAGISTRATE JUDGE'S AVAILABILITY

1. A magistrate judge is available under title 28 U.S.C. § 636(c) to conduct the proceedings in this case, including a jury or nonjury trial and the entry of final judgment. But a magistrate judge can be assigned only if all parties voluntarily consent.

2. You may withhold your consent without adverse substantive consequences. The identity of any party consenting or withholding consent will not be disclosed to the judge to whom the case is assigned or to any magistrate judge.

3. If a magistrate judge does hear your case, you may appeal directly to a United States court of appeals as you would if a district judge heard it.

A form called *Consent to an Assignment to a United States Magistrate Judge* is available from the court clerk's office.

(Added Apr. 30, 2007, eff. Dec. 1, 2007.)

FORM 81.   CONSENT TO AN ASSIGNMENT
TO A MAGISTRATE JUDGE

(Caption—See Form 1.)

I voluntarily consent to have a United States magistrate judge conduct all further proceedings in this case, including a trial, and order the entry of final judgment. (Return this form to the court clerk—not to a judge or magistrate judge.)

Date_____

_____
Signature of the Party

(Added Apr. 30, 2007, eff. Dec. 1, 2007.)

FORM 82.   ORDER OF ASSIGNMENT TO A MAGISTRATE JUDGE

(Caption—See Form 1.)

With the parties' consent it is ordered that this case be assigned to United States Magistrate Judge _____ of this district to conduct all proceedings and enter final judgment in accordance with 28 U.S.C. § 636(c).

Date _____

_____
United States District Judge

(Added Apr. 30, 2007, eff. Dec. 1, 2007.)

SUPPLEMENTAL RULES FOR ADMIRALTY OR MARITIME CLAIMS AND ASSET FORFEITURE ACTIONS

RULE A. SCOPE OF RULES

(1) These Supplemental Rules apply to:

(A) the procedure in admiralty and maritime claims within the meaning of Rule 9(h) with respect to the following remedies:

(i) maritime attachment and garnishment,

(ii) actions in rem,

(iii) possessory, petitory, and partition actions, and

(iv) actions for exoneration from or limitation of liability;

(B) forfeiture actions in rem arising from a federal statute; and

(C) the procedure in statutory condemnation proceedings analogous to maritime actions in rem, whether within the admiralty and maritime jurisdiction or not. Except as otherwise provided, references in these Supplemental Rules to actions in rem include such analogous statutory condemnation proceedings.

(2) The Federal Rules of Civil Procedure also apply to the foregoing proceedings except to the extent that they are inconsistent with these Supplemental Rules.

(Added Feb. 28, 1966, eff. July 1, 1966, and amended Apr. 12, 2006, eff. Dec. 1, 2006.)

RULE B. IN PERSONAM ACTIONS: ATTACHMENT AND GARNISHMENT

(1) **When Available; Complaint, Affidavit, Judicial Authorization, and Process.** In an in personam action:

(a) If a defendant is not found within the district when a verified complaint praying for attachment and the affidavit required by Rule B(1)(b) are filed, a verified complaint may contain a prayer for process to attach the defendant's tangible or intangible personal property—up to the amount sued for—in the hands of garnishees named in the process.

(b) The plaintiff or the plaintiff's attorney must sign and file with the complaint an affidavit stating that, to the affiant's knowledge, or on information and belief, the defendant cannot be found within the district. The court must review the complaint and affidavit and, if the conditions of this Rule B appear to exist, enter an order so stating and authorizing process of attachment and garnishment. The clerk

may issue supplemental process enforcing the court's order upon application without further court order.

(c) If the plaintiff or the plaintiff's attorney certifies that exigent circumstances make court review impracticable, the clerk must issue the summons and process of attachment and garnishment. The plaintiff has the burden in any post-attachment hearing under Rule E(4)(f) to show that exigent circumstances existed.

(d)(i) If the property is a vessel or tangible property on board a vessel, the summons, process, and any supplemental process must be delivered to the marshal for service.

(ii) If the property is other tangible or intangible property, the summons, process, and any supplemental process must be delivered to a person or organization authorized to serve it, who may be (A) a marshal; (B) someone under contract with the United States; (C) someone specially appointed by the court for that purpose; or, (D) in an action brought by the United States, any officer or employee of the United States.

(e) The plaintiff may invoke state-law remedies under Rule 64 for seizure of person or property for the purpose of securing satisfaction of the judgment.

(2) **Notice to Defendant.** No default judgment may be entered except upon proof—which may be by affidavit—that:

(a) the complaint, summons, and process of attachment or garnishment have been served on the defendant in a manner authorized by Rule 4;

(b) the plaintiff or the garnishee has mailed to the defendant the complaint, summons, and process of attachment or garnishment, using any form of mail requiring a return receipt; or

(c) the plaintiff or the garnishee has tried diligently to give notice of the action to the defendant but could not do so.

(3) **Answer.**

(a) **By Garnishee.** The garnishee shall serve an answer, together with answers to any interrogatories served with the complaint, within 21 days after service of process upon the garnishee. Interrogatories to the garnishee may be served with the complaint without leave of court. If the garnishee refuses or neglects to answer on oath as to the debts, credits, or effects of the defendant in the garnishee's hands, or any interrogatories concerning such debts, credits, and effects that may be propounded by the plaintiff, the court may award compulsory process against the garnishee. If the garnishee admits any debts, credits, or effects, they shall be held in the garnishee's hands or paid into the registry of the court, and shall be held in either case subject to the further order of the court.

(b) By Defendant. The defendant shall serve an answer within 30 days after process has been executed, whether by attachment of property or service on the garnishee.

(Added Feb. 28, 1966, eff. July 1, 1966, and amended Apr. 29, 1985, eff. Aug. 1, 1985; Mar. 2, 1987, eff. Aug. 1, 1987; Apr. 17, 2000, eff. Dec. 1, 2000; Apr. 25, 2005, eff. Dec. 1, 2005; Mar. 26, 2009, eff. Dec. 1, 2009.)

RULE C. IN REM ACTIONS: SPECIAL PROVISIONS

(1) When Available. An action in rem may be brought:

    (a) To enforce any maritime lien;

    (b) Whenever a statute of the United States provides for a maritime action in rem or a proceeding analogous thereto.

Except as otherwise provided by law a party who may proceed in rem may also, or in the alternative, proceed in personam against any person who may be liable.

Statutory provisions exempting vessels or other property owned or possessed by or operated by or for the United States from arrest or seizure are not affected by this rule. When a statute so provides, an action against the United States or an instrumentality thereof may proceed on in rem principles.

(2) Complaint. In an action in rem the complaint must:

    (a) be verified;

    (b) describe with reasonable particularity the property that is the subject of the action; and

    (c) state that the property is within the district or will be within the district while the action is pending.

(3) Judicial Authorization and Process.

    (a) Arrest Warrant.

      (i) The court must review the complaint and any supporting papers. If the conditions for an in rem action appear to exist, the court must issue an order directing the clerk to issue a warrant for the arrest of the vessel or other property that is the subject of the action.

      (ii) If the plaintiff or the plaintiff's attorney certifies that exigent circumstances make court review impracticable, the clerk must promptly issue a summons and a warrant for the arrest of the vessel or other property that is the subject of the action. The plaintiff has the burden in any post-arrest hearing under Rule E(4)(f) to show that exigent circumstances existed.

    (b) Service.

      (i) If the property that is the subject of the action is a vessel or tangible property on board a vessel, the warrant and any supplemental process must be delivered to the marshal for service.

      (ii) If the property that is the subject of the action is other property, tangible or intangible, the warrant and any supplemental process must be delivered to a person or organization authorized to enforce it, who may be: (A) a marshal; (B) someone under contract with the United States; (C) someone specially appointed by the court for that purpose; or, (D) in an action brought by the United States, any officer or employee of the United States.

    (c) Deposit in Court. If the property that is the subject of the action consists in whole or in part of freight, the proceeds of property sold, or other intangible property, the clerk must issue—in addition to the warrant—a summons directing any person controlling the property to show cause why it should not be deposited in court to abide the judgment.

    (d) Supplemental Process. The clerk may upon application issue supplemental process to enforce the court's order without further court order.

(4) Notice. No notice other than execution of process is required when the property that is the subject of the action has been released under Rule E(5). If the property is not released within 14 days after execution, the plaintiff must promptly—or within the time that the court allows—give public notice of the action and arrest in a newspaper designated by court order and having general circulation in the district, but publication may be terminated if the property is released before publication is completed. The notice must specify the time under Rule C(6) to file a statement of interest in or right against the seized property and to answer. This rule does not affect the notice requirements in an action to foreclose a preferred ship mortgage under 46 U.S.C. §§ 31301 et seq., as amended.

(5) Ancillary Process. In any action in rem in which process has been served as provided by this rule, if any part of the property that is the subject of the action has not been brought within the control of the court because it has been removed or sold, or because it is intangible property in the hands of a person who has not been served with process, the court may, on motion, order any person having possession or control of such property or its proceeds to show cause why it should not be delivered into the custody of the marshal or other person or organization having a warrant for the arrest of the property, or paid into court to abide the judgment; and, after hearing, the court may enter such judgment as law and justice may require.

(6) Responsive Pleading; Interrogatories.

(a) Statement of Interest; Answer. In an action in rem:

(i) a person who asserts a right of possession or any ownership interest in the property that is the subject of the action must file a verified statement of right or interest:

(A) within 14 days after the execution of process, or

(B) within the time that the court allows;

(ii) the statement of right or interest must describe the interest in the property that supports the person's demand for its restitution or right to defend the action;

(iii) an agent, bailee, or attorney must state the authority to file a statement of right or interest on behalf of another; and

(iv) a person who asserts a right of possession or any ownership interest must serve an answer within 21 days after filing the statement of interest or right.

(b) Interrogatories. Interrogatories may be served with the complaint in an in rem action without leave of court. Answers to the interrogatories must be served with the answer to the complaint.

(Added Feb. 28, 1966, eff. July 1, 1966, and amended Apr. 29, 1985, eff. Aug. 1, 1985; Mar. 2, 1987, eff. Aug. 1, 1987; Apr. 30, 1991, eff. Dec. 1, 1991; Apr. 17, 2000, eff. Dec. 1, 2000; Apr. 29, 2002, eff. Dec. 1, 2002; Apr. 25, 2005, eff. Dec. 1, 2005; Apr. 12, 2006, eff. Dec. 1, 2006; Apr. 23, 2008, eff. Dec. 1, 2008; Mar. 26, 2009, eff. Dec. 1, 2009.)

RULE D. POSSESSORY, PETITORY, AND PARTITION ACTIONS

In all actions for possession, partition, and to try title maintainable according to the course of the admiralty practice with respect to a vessel, in all actions so maintainable with respect to the possession of cargo or other maritime property, and in all actions by one or more part owners against the others to obtain security for the return of the vessel from any voyage undertaken without their consent, or by one or more part owners against the others to obtain possession of the vessel for any voyage on giving security for its safe return, the process shall be by a warrant of arrest of the vessel, cargo, or other property, and by

notice in the manner provided by Rule B(2) to the adverse party or parties.

(Added Feb. 28, 1966, eff. July 1, 1966.)

RULE E. ACTIONS IN REM AND QUASI IN REM: GENERAL PROVISIONS

(1) Applicability. Except as otherwise provided, this rule applies to actions in personam with process of maritime attachment and garnishment, actions in rem, and petitory, possessory, and partition actions, supplementing Rules B, C, and D.

(2) Complaint; Security.

(a) Complaint. In actions to which this rule is applicable the complaint shall state the circumstances from which the claim arises with such particularity that the defendant or claimant will be able, without moving for a more definite statement, to commence an investigation of the facts and to frame a responsive pleading.

(b) Security for Costs. Subject to the provisions of Rule 54(d) and of relevant statutes, the court may, on the filing of the complaint or on the appearance of any defendant, claimant, or any other party, or at any later time, require the plaintiff, defendant, claimant, or other party to give security, or additional security, in such sum as the court shall direct to pay all costs and expenses that shall be awarded against the party by any interlocutory order or by the final judgment, or on appeal by any appellate court.

(3) Process.

(a) In admiralty and maritime proceedings process in rem or of maritime attachment and garnishment may be served only within the district.

(b) Issuance and Delivery. Issuance and delivery of process in rem, or of maritime attachment and garnishment, shall be held in abeyance if the plaintiff so requests.

(4) Execution of Process; Marshal's Return; Custody of Property; Procedures for Release.

(a) In General. Upon issuance and delivery of the process, or, in the case of summons with process of attachment and garnishment, when it appears that the defendant cannot be found within the district, the marshal or other person or organization having a warrant shall forthwith execute the process in accordance with this subdivision (4), making due and prompt return.

(b) Tangible Property. If tangible property is to be attached or arrested, the marshal or other person or organization having the warrant shall take it into the marshal's possession for safe custody. If the character or situation of the property is such that the taking of actual possession is impracticable, the marshal or other person executing the process shall affix a copy thereof to the property in a conspicuous place and leave a copy of the complaint and process with the person having possession or the person's agent. In furtherance of the marshal's custody of any vessel the marshal is authorized to make a written request to the collector of customs not to grant clearance to such vessel until notified by the marshal or deputy marshal or by the clerk that the vessel has been released in accordance with these rules.

(c) Intangible Property. If intangible property is to be attached or arrested the marshal or other person or organization having the warrant shall execute the process by leaving with the garnishee or other obligor a copy of the complaint and process requiring the garnishee or other obligor to answer as provided in Rules B(3)(a) and C(6); or the marshal may accept for payment into the registry of the court the amount owed to the extent of the amount claimed by the plaintiff with interest and costs, in which event the garnishee or other obligor shall not be required to answer unless alias process shall be served.

(d) Directions With Respect to Property in Custody. The marshal or other person or organization having the warrant may at any time apply to the court for directions with respect to property that has been attached or arrested, and shall give notice of such application to any or all of the parties as the court may direct.

(e) Expenses of Seizing and Keeping Property; Deposit. These rules do not alter the provisions of Title 28, U.S.C., § 1921, as amended, relative to the expenses of seizing and keeping property attached or arrested and to the requirement of deposits to cover such expenses.

(f) Procedure for Release From Arrest or Attachment. Whenever property is arrested or attached, any person claiming an interest in it shall be entitled to a prompt hearing at which the plaintiff shall be required to show why the arrest or attachment should not be vacated or other relief granted consistent with these rules. This subdivision shall have no application to suits for seamen's wages when process is issued upon a certification of sufficient cause filed pursuant to Title 46, U.S.C. §§ 603 and 604 or to actions by the United States for forfeitures for violation of any statute of the United States.

(5) Release of Property.

(a) Special Bond. Whenever process of maritime attachment and garnishment or process in rem is issued the execution of such process shall be stayed, or the property released, on the giving of security, to be approved by the court or clerk, or by stipulation of the parties, conditioned to answer the judgment of the court or of any appellate court.

The parties may stipulate the amount and nature of such security. In the event of the inability or refusal of the parties so to stipulate the court shall fix the principal sum of the bond or stipulation at an amount sufficient to cover the amount of the plaintiff's claim fairly stated with accrued interest and costs; but the principal sum shall in no event exceed (i) twice the amount of the plaintiff's claim or (ii) the value of the property on due appraisement, whichever is smaller. The bond or stipulation shall be conditioned for the payment of the principal sum and interest thereon at 6 per cent per annum.

(b) General Bond. The owner of any vessel may file a general bond or stipulation, with sufficient surety, to be approved by the court, conditioned to answer the judgment of such court in all or any actions that may be brought thereafter in such court in which the vessel is attached or arrested. Thereupon the execution of all such process against such vessel shall be stayed so long as the amount secured by such bond or stipulation is at least double the aggregate amount claimed by plaintiffs in all actions begun and pending in which such vessel has been attached or arrested. Judgments and remedies may be had on such bond or stipulation as if a special bond or stipulation had been filed in each of such actions. The district court may make necessary orders to carry this rule into effect, particularly as to the giving of proper notice of any action against or attachment of a vessel for which a general bond has been filed. Such bond or stipulation shall be indorsed by the clerk with a minute of the actions wherein process is so stayed. Further security may be required by the court at any time.

If a special bond or stipulation is given in a particular case, the liability on the general bond or stipulation shall cease as to that case.

(c) Release by Consent or Stipulation; Order of Court or Clerk; Costs. Any vessel, cargo, or other property in the custody of the marshal or other person or organization having the warrant may be released forthwith upon the marshal's acceptance and approval of a stipulation, bond, or other security, signed by the party on whose behalf the property is detained or the party's attorney and expressly authorizing such release, if all costs and charges of the court and its officers shall have first been paid. Otherwise no property in the custody of the marshal, other person or organization having the warrant, or other officer of the court shall be released without an order of the court; but such order may be entered as of course by the clerk, upon the giving of approved security as provided by law and these rules, or upon the dismissal or discontinuance of the action; but the marshal or other person or organization having the warrant shall not deliver any property so released until the costs and charges of the officers of the court shall first have been paid.

(d) Possessory, Petitory, and Partition Actions. The foregoing provisions of this subdivision (5) do not apply to petitory, possessory, and partition actions. In such cases the property arrested shall be released only by order of the court, on such terms and conditions and on the giving of such security as the court may require.

(6) Reduction or Impairment of Security. Whenever security is taken the court may, on motion and hearing, for good cause shown, reduce the amount of security given; and if the surety shall be or become insufficient, new or additional sureties may be required on motion and hearing.

(7) Security on Counterclaim.

(a) When a person who has given security for damages in the original action asserts a counterclaim that arises from the transaction or occurrence that is the subject of the original action, a plaintiff for whose benefit the security has been given must give security for damages demanded in the counterclaim unless the court for cause shown, directs otherwise. Proceedings on the original claim must be stayed until this security is given unless the court directs otherwise.

(b) The plaintiff is required to give security under Rule E(7)(a) when the United States or its corporate instrumentality counterclaims and would have been required to give security to respond in damages if a private party but is relieved by law from giving security.

(8) Restricted Appearance. An appearance to defend against an admiralty and maritime claim with respect to which there has issued process in rem, or process of attachment and garnishment, may be expressly restricted to the defense of such claim, and in that event is not an appearance for the purposes of any other claim with respect to which such process is not available or has not been served.

(9) Disposition of Property; Sales.

(a) Interlocutory Sales; Delivery.

(i) On application of a party, the marshal, or other person having custody of the property, the court may order all or part of the property sold—with the sales proceeds, or as much of them as will satisfy the judgment, paid into court to await further orders of the court—if:

(A) the attached or arrested property is perishable, or liable to deterioration, decay, or injury by being detained in custody pending the action;

(B) the expense of keeping the property is excessive or disproportionate; or

(C) there is an unreasonable delay in securing release of the property.

(ii) In the circumstances described in Rule E(9)(a)(i), the court, on motion by a defendant or a person filing a statement of interest or right under Rule C(6), may order that the property, rather than being sold, be delivered to the movant upon giving security under these rules.

(b) Sales; Proceeds. All sales of property shall be made by the marshal or a deputy marshal, or by other person or organization having the warrant, or by any other person assigned by the court where the marshal or other person or organization having the warrant is a party in interest; and the proceeds of sale shall be forthwith paid into the registry of the court to be disposed of according to law.

(10) Preservation of Property. When the owner or another person remains in possession of property attached or arrested under the provisions of Rule E(4)(b) that permit execution of process without taking actual possession, the court, on a party's motion or on its own, may enter any order necessary to preserve the property and to prevent its removal.

(Added Feb. 28, 1966, eff. July 1, 1966, and amended Apr. 29, 1985, eff. Aug. 1, 1985; Mar. 2, 1987, eff. Aug. 1, 1987; Apr. 30, 1991, eff. Dec. 1, 1991; Apr. 17, 2000, eff. Dec. 1, 2000; Apr. 12, 2006, eff. Dec. 1, 2006.)

RULE F. LIMITATION OF LIABILITY

(1) Time for Filing Complaint; Security. Not later than six months after receipt of a claim in writing, any vessel owner may file a complaint in the appropriate district court, as provided in subdivision (9) of this rule, for limitation of liability pursuant to statute. The owner (a) shall deposit with the court, for the benefit of claimants, a sum equal to the amount or value of the owner's interest in the vessel and pending freight, or approved security therefor, and in addition such sums, or approved security therefor, as the court may from time to time fix as necessary to carry out the provisions of the statutes as amended; or (b) at the owner's option shall transfer to a trustee to be appointed by the court, for the benefit of claimants, the owner's interest in the vessel and pending freight, together with such sums, or approved security therefor, as the court may from time to time fix as necessary to carry out the provisions of the statutes as amended. The plaintiff shall also give security for costs and, if the plaintiff elects to give security, for interest at the rate of 6 percent per annum from the date of the security.

(2) Complaint. The complaint shall set forth the facts on the basis of which the right to limit liability is asserted and all facts necessary to enable the court to determine the amount to which the owner's liability shall be limited. The complaint may demand exoneration from as well as limitation of liability. It shall state the voyage if any, on which the demands sought to be limited arose, with the date and place of its termination; the amount of all demands including all unsatisfied liens or claims of lien, in contract or in tort or otherwise, arising on that voyage, so far as known to the plaintiff, and what actions and proceedings, if any, are pending thereon; whether the vessel was damaged, lost, or abandoned, and, if so, when and where; the value of the vessel at the close of the voyage or, in case of wreck, the value of her wreckage, strippings, or proceeds, if any, and where and in whose possession they are; and the amount of any pending freight recovered or recoverable. If the plaintiff elects to transfer the plaintiff's interest in the vessel to a trustee, the complaint must further show any prior paramount liens thereon, and what voyages or trips, if any, she has made since the voyage or trip on which the claims sought to be limited arose, and any existing liens arising upon any such subsequent voyage or trip, with the amounts and causes thereof, and the names and addresses of the lienors, so far as known; and whether the vessel sustained any injury upon or by reason of such subsequent voyage or trip.

(3) Claims Against Owner; Injunction. Upon compliance by the owner with the requirements of subdivision (1) of this rule all claims and proceedings against the owner or the owner's property with respect to the matter in question shall cease. On application of the plaintiff the court shall enjoin the further prosecution of any action or proceeding against the plaintiff or the plaintiff's property with respect to any claim subject to limitation in the action.

(4) Notice to Claimants. Upon the owner's compliance with subdivision (1) of this rule the court shall issue a notice to all persons asserting claims with respect to which the complaint seeks limitation, admonishing them to file their respective claims with the clerk of the court and to serve on the attorneys for the plaintiff a copy thereof on or before a date to be named in the notice. The date so fixed shall not be less than 30 days after issuance of the notice. For cause shown, the court may enlarge the time within which claims may be filed. The notice shall be published in such newspaper or newspapers as the court may direct once a week for four successive weeks prior to the date fixed for the filing of claims. The plaintiff not later than the day of second publication shall also mail a copy of the notice to every person known to have made any claim against the vessel or the plaintiff arising out of the voyage or trip on which the claims sought to be limited arose. In cases involving death a copy of such notice shall be mailed to the decedent at the decedent's last known address, and also to any person who shall be known to have made any claim on account of such death.

(5) Claims and Answer. Claims shall be filed and served on or before the date specified in the notice provided for in subdivision (4) of this rule. Each claim shall specify the facts upon which the claimant relies in support of the claim, the items thereof, and the dates on which the same accrued. If a claimant desires to contest either the right to exoneration from or the right to limitation of liability the claimant shall file and serve an answer to the complaint unless the claim has included an answer.

(6) Information to be Given Claimants. Within 30 days after the date specified in the notice for filing claims, or within such time as the court thereafter may allow, the plaintiff shall mail to the attorney for each claimant (or if the claimant has no attorney to the claimant) a list setting forth (a) the name of each claimant, (b) the name and address of the claimant's attorney (if the claimant is known to have one), (c) the nature of the claim, i.e., whether property loss, property damage, death, personal injury etc., and (d) the amount thereof.

(7) Insufficiency of Fund or Security. Any claimant may by motion demand that the funds deposited in court or the security given by the plaintiff be increased on the ground that they are less than the value of the plaintiff's interest in the vessel and pending freight. Thereupon the court shall cause due appraisement to be made of the value of the plaintiff's interest in the vessel and pending freight; and if the court finds that the deposit or security is either insufficient or excessive it shall order its increase or reduction. In like manner any claimant may demand that the deposit or security be increased on the ground that it is insufficient to carry out the provisions of the statutes relating to claims in respect of loss of life or bodily injury; and, after notice and hearing, the court may similarly order that the deposit or security be increased or reduced.

(8) Objections to Claims: Distribution of Fund. Any interested party may question or controvert any claim without filing an objection thereto. Upon determination of liability the fund deposited or secured, or the proceeds of the vessel and pending freight, shall be divided pro rata, subject to all relevant provisions of law, among the several claimants in proportion to the amounts of their respective claims, duly proved, saving, however, to all parties any priority to which they may be legally entitled.

(9) Venue; Transfer. The complaint shall be filed in any district in which the vessel has been attached or arrested to answer for any claim with respect to which the plaintiff seeks to limit liability; or, if the vessel has not been attached or arrested, then in any district in which the owner has been sued with respect to any such claim. When the vessel has not been attached or arrested to answer the matters aforesaid, and suit has not been commenced against the owner, the proceedings may be had in the district in which the vessel may be, but if the vessel is not within any district and no suit has been commenced in any district, then the complaint may be filed in any district. For the convenience of parties and witnesses, in the interest of justice, the court may transfer the action to any district; if venue is wrongly laid the court shall dismiss or, if it be in the interest of justice, transfer the action to any district in which it could have been brought. If the vessel shall have been sold, the proceeds shall represent the vessel for the purposes of these rules.

(Added Feb. 28, 1966, eff. July 1, 1966, and amended Mar. 2, 1987, eff. Aug. 1, 1987.)

RULE G. FORFEITURE ACTIONS IN REM

(1) Scope. This rule governs a forfeiture action in rem arising from a federal statute. To the extent that this rule does not address an issue, Supplemental Rules C and E and the Federal Rules of Civil Procedure also apply.

(2) Complaint. The complaint must:

(a) be verified;

(b) state the grounds for subject-matter jurisdiction, in rem jurisdiction over the defendant property, and venue;

(c) describe the property with reasonable particularity;

(d) if the property is tangible, state its location when any seizure occurred and — if different — its location when the action is filed;

(e) identify the statute under which the forfeiture action is brought; and

(f) state sufficiently detailed facts to support a reasonable belief that the government will be able to meet its burden of proof at trial.

(3) Judicial Authorization and Process.

(a) Real Property. If the defendant is real property, the government must proceed under 18 U.S.C. § 985.

(b) Other Property; Arrest Warrant. If the defendant is not real property:

(i) the clerk must issue a warrant to arrest the property if it is in the government's possession, custody, or control;

(ii) the court—on finding probable cause—must issue a warrant to arrest the property if it is not in the government's possession, custody, or control and is not subject to a judicial restraining order; and

(iii) a warrant is not necessary if the property is subject to a judicial restraining order.

(c) Execution of Process.

(i) The warrant and any supplemental process must be delivered to a person or organization authorized to execute it, who may be: (A) a marshal or any other United States officer or employee; (B) someone under contract with the United States; or (C) someone specially appointed by the court for that purpose.

(ii) The authorized person or organization must execute the warrant and any supplemental process on property in the United States as soon as practicable unless:

(A) the property is in the government's possession, custody, or control; or

(B) the court orders a different time when the complaint is under seal, the action is stayed before the warrant and supplemental process are executed, or the court finds other good cause.

(iii) The warrant and any supplemental process may be executed within the district or, when authorized by statute, outside the district.

(iv) If executing a warrant on property outside the United States is required, the warrant may be transmitted to an appropriate authority for serving process where the property is located.

(4) Notice.

(a) Notice by Publication.

(i) When Publication Is Required. A judgment of forfeiture may be entered only if the government has published notice of the action within a reasonable time after filing the complaint or at a time the court orders. But notice need not be published if:

(A) the defendant property is worth less than $1,000 and direct notice is sent under Rule G(4)(b) to every person the government can reasonably identify as a potential claimant; or

(B) the court finds that the cost of publication exceeds the property's value and that other means of notice would satisfy due process.

(ii) Content of the Notice. Unless the court orders otherwise, the notice must:

(A) describe the property with reasonable particularity;

(B) state the times under Rule G(5) to file a claim and to answer; and

(C) name the government attorney to be served with the claim and answer.

(iii) Frequency of Publication. Published notice must appear:

(A) once a week for three consecutive weeks; or

(B) only once if, before the action was filed, notice of nonjudicial forfeiture of the same property was published on an official internet government forfeiture site for at least 30 consecutive days, or in a newspaper of general circulation for three consecutive weeks in a district where publication is authorized under Rule G(4)(a)(iv).

(iv) Means of Publication. The government should select from the following options a means of publication reasonably calculated to notify potential claimants of the action:

(A) if the property is in the United States, publication in a newspaper generally circulated in the district where the action is filed, where the property was seized, or where property that was not seized is located;

(B) if the property is outside the United States, publication in a newspaper generally circulated in a district where the action is filed, in a newspaper generally circulated in the country where the property is located, or in legal notices published and generally circulated in the country where the property is located; or

(C) instead of (A) or (B), posting a notice on an official internet government forfeiture site for at least 30 consecutive days.

(b) Notice to Known Potential Claimants.

(i) Direct Notice Required. The government must send notice of the action and a copy of the complaint to any person who reasonably appears to be a potential claimant on the facts known to the government before the end of the time for filing a claim under Rule G(5)(a)(ii)(B).

(ii) Content of the Notice. The notice must state:

(A) the date when the notice is sent;

(B) a deadline for filing a claim, at least 35 days after the notice is sent;

(C) that an answer or a motion under Rule 12 must be filed no later than 21 days after filing the claim; and

(D) the name of the government attorney to be served with the claim and answer.

(iii) Sending Notice.

(A) The notice must be sent by means reasonably calculated to reach the potential claimant.

(B) Notice may be sent to the potential claimant or to the attorney representing the potential claimant with respect to the seizure of the property or in a related investigation, administrative forfeiture proceeding, or criminal case.

(C) Notice sent to a potential claimant who is incarcerated must be sent to the place of incarceration.

(D) Notice to a person arrested in connection with an offense giving rise to the forfeiture who is not incarcerated when notice is sent may be sent to the address that person last gave to the agency that arrested or released the person.

(E) Notice to a person from whom the property was seized who is not incarcerated when notice is sent may be sent to the last address that person gave to the agency that seized the property.

(iv) When Notice Is Sent. Notice by the following means is sent on the date when it is placed in the mail, delivered to a commercial carrier, or sent by electronic mail.

(v) Actual Notice. A potential claimant who had actual notice of a forfeiture action may not oppose or seek relief from forfeiture because of the government's failure to send the required notice.

(5) Responsive Pleadings.

(a) Filing a Claim.

(i) A person who asserts an interest in the defendant property may contest the forfeiture by filing a claim in the court where the action is pending. The claim must:

(A) identify the specific property claimed;

(B) identify the claimant and state the claimant's interest in the property;

(C) be signed by the claimant under penalty of perjury; and

(D) be served on the government attorney designated under Rule G(4)(a)(ii)(C) or (b)(ii)(D).

(ii) Unless the court for good cause sets a different time, the claim must be filed:

(A) by the time stated in a direct notice sent under Rule G(4)(b);

(B) if notice was published but direct notice was not sent to the claimant or the claimant's attorney, no later than 30 days after final publication of newspaper notice or legal notice under Rule G(4)(a) or no later than 60 days after the first day of publication on an official internet government forfeiture site; or

(C) if notice was not published and direct notice was not sent to the claimant or the claimant's attorney:

(1) if the property was in the government's possession, custody, or control when the complaint was filed, no later than 60 days after the filing, not counting any time when the complaint was under seal or when the action was stayed before execution of a warrant issued under Rule G(3)(b); or

(2) if the property was not in the government's possession, custody, or control when the complaint was filed, no later than 60 days after the government complied with 18 U.S.C. § 985(c) as to real property, or 60 days after process was executed on the property under Rule G(3).

(iii) A claim filed by a person asserting an interest as a bailee must identify the bailor, and if filed on the bailor's behalf must state the authority to do so.

(b) Answer. A claimant must serve and file an answer to the complaint or a motion under Rule 12 within 21 days after filing the claim. A claimant waives an objection to in rem jurisdiction or to venue if the objection is not made by motion or stated in the answer.

(6) Special Interrogatories.

(a) Time and Scope. The government may serve special interrogatories limited to the claimant's identity and relationship to the defendant property without the court's leave at any time after the claim is filed and before discovery is closed. But if the claimant serves a motion to dismiss the action, the government must serve the interrogatories within 21 days after the motion is served.

(b) Answers or Objections. Answers or objections to these interrogatories must be served within 21 days after the interrogatories are served.

(c) Government's Response Deferred. The government need not respond to a claimant's motion to dismiss the action under Rule G(8)(b) until 21 days after the claimant has answered these interrogatories.

(7) Preserving, Preventing Criminal Use, and Disposing of Property; Sales.

(a) Preserving and Preventing Criminal Use of Property. When the government does not have actual possession of the defendant property the court, on motion or on its own, may enter any order necessary to preserve the property, to prevent its removal or encumbrance, or to prevent its use in a criminal offense.

(b) Interlocutory Sale or Delivery.

(i) Order to Sell. On motion by a party or a person having custody of the property, the court may order all or part of the property sold if:

(A) the property is perishable or at risk of deterioration, decay, or injury by being detained in custody pending the action;

(B) the expense of keeping the property is excessive or is disproportionate to its fair market value;

(C) the property is subject to a mortgage or to taxes on which the owner is in default; or

(D) the court finds other good cause.

(ii) Who Makes the Sale. A sale must be made by a United States agency that has authority to sell the property, by the agency's contractor, or by any person the court designates.

(iii) Sale Procedures. The sale is governed by 28 U.S.C. §§ 2001, 2002, and 2004, unless all parties, with the court's approval, agree to the sale, aspects of the sale, or different procedures.

(iv) Sale Proceeds. Sale proceeds are a substitute res subject to forfeiture in place of the property that was sold. The proceeds must be held in an interest-bearing account maintained by the United States pending the conclusion of the forfeiture action.

(v) Delivery on a Claimant's Motion. The court may order that the property be delivered to the claimant pending the conclusion of the action if the claimant shows circumstances that would permit sale under Rule G(7)(b)(i) and gives security under these rules.

(c) Disposing of Forfeited Property. Upon entry of a forfeiture judgment, the property or proceeds from selling the property must be disposed of as provided by law.

(8) Motions.

(a) Motion To Suppress Use of the Property as Evidence. If the defendant property was seized, a party with standing to contest the lawfulness of the seizure may move to suppress use of the property as evidence. Suppression does not affect forfeiture of the property based on independently derived evidence.

(b) Motion To Dismiss the Action.

(i) A claimant who establishes standing to contest forfeiture may move to dismiss the action under Rule 12(b).

(ii) In an action governed by 18 U.S.C. § 983(a)(3)(D) the complaint may not be dismissed on the ground that the government did not have adequate evidence at the time the complaint was filed to establish the forfeitability of the property. The sufficiency of the complaint is governed by Rule G(2).

(c) Motion To Strike a Claim or Answer.

(i) At any time before trial, the government may move to strike a claim or answer:

(A) for failing to comply with Rule G(5) or (6), or

(B) because the claimant lacks standing.

(ii) The motion:

(A) must be decided before any motion by the claimant to dismiss the action; and

(B) may be presented as a motion for judgment on the pleadings or as a motion to determine after a hearing or by summary judgment whether the claimant can carry the burden of establishing standing by a preponderance of the evidence.

(d) Petition To Release Property.

(i) If a United States agency or an agency's contractor holds property for judicial or nonjudicial forfeiture under a statute governed by 18 U.S.C. § 983(f), a person who has filed a claim to the property may petition for its release under § 983(f).

(ii) If a petition for release is filed before a judicial forfeiture action is filed against the property, the petition may be filed either in the district where the property was seized or in the district where a warrant to seize the property issued. If a judicial forfeiture action against the property is later filed in another district — or if the government shows that the action will be filed in another district — the petition may be transferred to that district under 28 U.S.C. § 1404.

(e) Excessive Fines. A claimant may seek to mitigate a forfeiture under the Excessive Fines Clause of the Eighth Amendment by motion for summary judgment or by motion made after entry of a forfeiture judgment if:

(i) the claimant has pleaded the defense under Rule 8; and

(ii) the parties have had the opportunity to conduct civil discovery on the defense.

(9) Trial. Trial is to the court unless any party demands trial by jury under Rule 38.

(Added Apr. 12, 2006, eff. Dec. 1, 2006, and amended Mar. 26, 2009, eff. Dec. 1, 2009.)

INDEX TO FEDERAL RULES OF CIVIL PROCEDURE

*

FEDERAL RULES OF EVIDENCE

Including Amendments Effective December 1, 2011

Research Note

These rules may be searched electronically on Westlaw in the US-RULES database; updates to these rules may be found on Westlaw in US-RULESPDATES. For search tips, and a detailed summary of database content, consult the Westlaw Scope Screen of each database.

ARTICLE I. GENERAL PROVISIONS

RULE 101. SCOPE; DEFINITIONS

(a) Scope. These rules apply to proceedings in United States courts. The specific courts and proceedings to which the rules apply, along with exceptions, are set out in Rule 1101.

(b) Definitions. In these rules:

(1) "civil case" means a civil action or proceeding;

(2) "criminal case" includes a criminal proceeding;

(3) "public office" includes a public agency;

(4) "record" includes a memorandum, report, or data compilation;

(5) a "rule prescribed by the Supreme Court" means a rule adopted by the Supreme Court under statutory authority; and

(6) a reference to any kind of written material or any other medium includes electronically stored information.

(Pub.L. 93–595, § 1, Jan. 2, 1975, 88 Stat. 1929; Mar. 2, 1987, eff. Oct. 1, 1987; Apr. 25, 1988, eff. Nov. 1, 1988; Apr. 22, 1993, eff. Dec. 1, 1993; Apr. 26, 2011, eff. Dec. 1, 2011.)

RULE 102. PURPOSE

These rules should be construed so as to administer every proceeding fairly, eliminate unjustifiable expense and delay, and promote the development of evidence law, to the end of ascertaining the truth and securing a just determination.

(Pub.L. 93–595, § 1, Jan. 2, 1975, 88 Stat.1929; Apr. 26, 2011, eff. Dec. 1, 2011.)

RULE 103. RULINGS ON EVIDENCE

(a) Preserving a Claim of Error. A party may claim error in a ruling to admit or exclude evidence only if the error affects a substantial right of the party and:

(1) if the ruling admits evidence, a party, on the record:

  (A) timely objects or moves to strike; and

  (B) states the specific ground, unless it was apparent from the context; or

(2) if the ruling excludes evidence, a party informs the court of its substance by an offer of proof, unless the substance was apparent from the context.

(b) Not Needing to Renew an Objection or Offer of Proof. Once the court rules definitively on the record—either before or at trial—a party need not renew an objection or offer of proof to preserve a claim of error for appeal.

(c) Court's Statement About the Ruling; Directing an Offer of Proof. The court may make any statement about the character or form of the evidence, the objection made, and the ruling. The court may direct that an offer of proof be made in question-and-answer form.

(d) Preventing the Jury from Hearing Inadmissible Evidence. To the extent practicable, the court must conduct a jury trial so that inadmissible evidence is not suggested to the jury by any means.

(e) Taking Notice of Plain Error. A court may take notice of a plain error affecting a substantial right, even if the claim of error was not properly preserved.

(Pub.L. 93–595, § 1, Jan. 2, 1975, 88 Stat. 1929; Apr. 17, 2000, eff. Dec. 1, 2000; Apr. 26, 2011, eff. Dec. 1, 2011.)

RULE 104. PRELIMINARY QUESTIONS

(a) In General. The court must decide any preliminary question about whether a witness is qualified, a privilege exists, or evidence is admissible. In so deciding, the court is not bound by evidence rules, except those on privilege.

(b) Relevance That Depends on a Fact. When the relevance of evidence depends on whether a fact exists, proof must be introduced sufficient to support a finding that the fact does exist. The court may admit the proposed evidence on the condition that the proof be introduced later.

(c) Conducting a Hearing So That the Jury Cannot Hear It. The court must conduct any hearing on a preliminary question so that the jury cannot hear it if:

(1) the hearing involves the admissibility of a confession;

(2) a defendant in a criminal case is a witness and so requests; or

(3) justice so requires.

(d) Cross–Examining a Defendant in a Criminal Case. By testifying on a preliminary question, a defendant in a criminal case does not become subject to cross-examination on other issues in the case.

(e) Evidence Relevant to Weight and Credibility. This rule does not limit a party's right to introduce before the jury evidence that is relevant to the weight or credibility of other evidence.

(Pub.L. 93–595, § 1, Jan. 2, 1975, 88 Stat.1930; Mar. 2, 1987, eff. Oct. 1, 1987; Apr. 26, 2011, eff. Dec. 1, 2011.)

RULE 105. LIMITING EVIDENCE THAT IS NOT ADMISSIBLE AGAINST OTHER PARTIES OR FOR OTHER PURPOSES

If the court admits evidence that is admissible against a party or for a purpose—but not against another party or for another purpose—the court, on timely request, must restrict the evidence to its proper scope and instruct the jury accordingly.

(Pub.L. 93–595, § 1, Jan. 2, 1975, 88 Stat. 1930; Apr. 26, 2011, eff. Dec. 1, 2011.)

RULE 106. REMAINDER OF OR RELATED WRITINGS OR RECORDED STATEMENTS

If a party introduces all or part of a writing or recorded statement, an adverse party may require the introduction, at that time, of any other part—or any other writing or recorded statement—that in fairness ought to be considered at the same time.

(Pub.L. 93–595, § 1, Jan. 2, 1975, 88 Stat. 1930; Mar. 2, 1987, eff. Oct. 1, 1987; Apr. 26, 2011, eff. Dec. 1, 2011.)

ARTICLE II. JUDICIAL NOTICE

RULE 201. JUDICIAL NOTICE OF ADJUDICATIVE FACTS

(a) Scope. This rule governs judicial notice of an adjudicative fact only, not a legislative fact.

(b) Kinds of Facts That May Be Judicially Noticed. The court may judicially notice a fact that is not subject to reasonable dispute because it:

(1) is generally known within the trial court's territorial jurisdiction; or

(2) can be accurately and readily determined from sources whose accuracy cannot reasonably be questioned.

(c) Taking Notice. The court:

(1) may take judicial notice on its own; or

(2) must take judicial notice if a party requests it and the court is supplied with the necessary information.

(d) Timing. The court may take judicial notice at any stage of the proceeding.

(e) Opportunity to Be Heard. On timely request, a party is entitled to be heard on the propriety of taking judicial notice and the nature of the fact to be noticed. If the court takes judicial notice before notifying a party, the party, on request, is still entitled to be heard.

(f) Instructing the Jury. In a civil case, the court must instruct the jury to accept the noticed fact as conclusive. In a criminal case, the court must instruct the jury that it may or may not accept the noticed fact as conclusive.

(Pub.L. 93–595, § 1, Jan. 2, 1975, 88 Stat. 1930; Apr. 26, 2011, eff. Dec. 1, 2011.)

ARTICLE III. PRESUMPTIONS IN CIVIL CASES

RULE 301. PRESUMPTIONS IN CIVIL CASES GENERALLY

In a civil case, unless a federal statute or these rules provide otherwise, the party against whom a presumption is directed has the burden of producing evidence to rebut the presumption. But this rule does not shift the burden of persuasion, which remains on the party who had it originally.

(Pub.L. 93–595, § 1, Jan. 2, 1975, 88 Stat. 1931; Apr. 26, 2011, eff. Dec. 1, 2011.)

RULE 302. APPLYING STATE LAW TO PRESUMPTIONS IN CIVIL CASES

In a civil case, state law governs the effect of a presumption regarding a claim or defense for which state law supplies the rule of decision.

(Pub.L. 93–595, § 1, Jan. 2, 1975, 88 Stat. 1931; Apr. 26, 2011, eff. Dec. 1, 2011.)

ARTICLE IV. RELEVANCE AND ITS LIMITS

RULE 401. TEST FOR RELEVANT EVIDENCE

Evidence is relevant if:

(a) it has any tendency to make a fact more or less probable than it would be without the evidence; and

(b) the fact is of consequence in determining the action.

(Pub.L. 93–595, § 1, Jan. 2, 1975, 88 Stat.1931; Apr. 26, 2011, eff. Dec. 1, 2011.)

RULE 402. GENERAL ADMISSIBILITY OF RELEVANT EVIDENCE

Relevant evidence is admissible unless any of the following provides otherwise:

- the United States Constitution;
- a federal statute;
- these rules; or
- other rules prescribed by the Supreme Court.

Irrelevant evidence is not admissible.

(Pub.L. 93–595, § 1, Jan. 2, 1975, 88 Stat. 1931; Apr. 26, 2011, eff. Dec. 1, 2011.)

RULE 403. EXCLUDING RELEVANT EVIDENCE FOR PREJUDICE, CONFUSION, WASTE OF TIME, OR OTHER REASONS

The court may exclude relevant evidence if its probative value is substantially outweighed by a danger of one or more of the following: unfair prejudice, confusing the issues, misleading the jury, undue delay, wasting time, or needlessly presenting cumulative evidence.

(Pub.L. 93–595, § 1, Jan. 2, 1975, 88 Stat. 1932; Apr. 26, 2011, eff. Dec. 1, 2011.)

RULE 404. CHARACTER EVIDENCE; CRIMES OR OTHER ACTS

(a) Character Evidence.

(1) *Prohibited Uses.* Evidence of a person's character or character trait is not admissible to prove that on a particular occasion the person acted in accordance with the character or trait.

(2) *Exceptions for a Defendant or Victim in a Criminal Case.* The following exceptions apply in a criminal case:

(A) a defendant may offer evidence of the defendant's pertinent trait, and if the evidence is admitted, the prosecutor may offer evidence to rebut it;

(B) subject to the limitations in Rule 412, a defendant may offer evidence of an alleged victim's pertinent trait, and if the evidence is admitted, the prosecutor may:

    (i) offer evidence to rebut it; and

    (ii) offer evidence of the defendant's same trait; and

(C) in a homicide case, the prosecutor may offer evidence of the alleged victim's trait of peacefulness to rebut evidence that the victim was the first aggressor.

(3) *Exceptions for a Witness.* Evidence of a witness's character may be admitted under Rules 607, 608, and 609.

(b) Crimes, Wrongs, or Other Acts.

(1) *Prohibited Uses.* Evidence of a crime, wrong, or other act is not admissible to prove a person's character in order to show that on a particular occasion the person acted in accordance with the character.

(2) *Permitted Uses; Notice in a Criminal Case.* This evidence may be admissible for another purpose, such as proving motive, opportunity, intent, preparation, plan, knowledge, identity, absence of mistake, or lack of accident. On request by a defendant in a criminal case, the prosecutor must:

(A) provide reasonable notice of the general nature of any such evidence that the prosecutor intends to offer at trial; and

(B) do so before trial—or during trial if the court, for good cause, excuses lack of pretrial notice.

(Pub.L. 93–595, § 1, Jan. 2, 1975, 88 Stat.1932; Mar. 2, 1987, eff. Oct. 1, 1987; Apr. 30, 1991, eff. Dec. 1, 1991; Apr. 17, 2000, eff. Dec. 1, 2000; Apr. 12, 2006, eff. Dec. 1, 2006; Apr. 26, 2011, eff. Dec. 1, 2011.)

RULE 405. METHODS OF PROVING CHARACTER

(a) **By Reputation or Opinion.** When evidence of a person's character or character trait is admissible, it may be proved by testimony about the person's reputation or by testimony in the form of an opinion. On cross-examination of the character witness, the court may allow an inquiry into relevant specific instances of the person's conduct.

(b) **By Specific Instances of Conduct.** When a person's character or character trait is an essential element of a charge, claim, or defense, the character or trait may also be proved by relevant specific instances of the person's conduct.

(Pub.L. 93–595, § 1, Jan. 2, 1975, 88 Stat. 1932; Mar. 2, 1987, eff. Oct. 1, 1987; Apr. 26, 2011, eff. Dec. 1, 2011.)

RULE 406. HABIT; ROUTINE PRACTICE

Evidence of a person's habit or an organization's routine practice may be admitted to prove that on a particular occasion the person or organization acted in accordance with the habit or routine practice. The court may admit this evidence regardless of whether it is corroborated or whether there was an eyewitness.

(Pub.L. 93–595, § 1, Jan. 2, 1975, 88 Stat. 1932; Apr. 26, 2011, eff. Dec. 1, 2011.)

RULE 407. SUBSEQUENT REMEDIAL MEASURES

When measures are taken that would have made an earlier injury or harm less likely to occur, evidence of the subsequent measures is not admissible to prove:

- negligence;
- culpable conduct;
- a defect in a product or its design; or
- a need for a warning or instruction.

But the court may admit this evidence for another purpose, such as impeachment or—if disputed—prov-

ing ownership, control, or the feasibility of precautionary measures.

(Pub.L. 93–595, § 1, Jan. 2, 1975, 88 Stat. 1932; Apr. 11, 1997, eff. Dec. 1, 1997; Apr. 26, 2011, eff. Dec. 1, 2011.)

RULE 408. COMPROMISE OFFERS AND NEGOTIATIONS

(a) **Prohibited Uses.** Evidence of the following is not admissible—on behalf of any party—either to prove or disprove the validity or amount of a disputed claim or to impeach by a prior inconsistent statement or a contradiction:

(1) furnishing, promising, or offering—or accepting, promising to accept, or offering to accept—a valuable consideration in compromising or attempting to compromise the claim; and

(2) conduct or a statement made during compromise negotiations about the claim—except when offered in a criminal case and when the negotiations related to a claim by a public office in the exercise of its regulatory, investigative, or enforcement authority.

(b) **Exceptions.** The court may admit this evidence for another purpose, such as proving a witness's bias or prejudice, negating a contention of undue delay, or proving an effort to obstruct a criminal investigation or prosecution.

(Pub.L. 93–595, § 1, Jan. 2, 1975, 88 Stat. 1933; Apr. 12, 2006, eff. Dec. 1, 2006; Apr. 26, 2011, eff. Dec. 1, 2011.)

RULE 409. OFFERS TO PAY MEDICAL AND SIMILAR EXPENSES

Evidence of furnishing, promising to pay, or offering to pay medical, hospital, or similar expenses resulting from an injury is not admissible to prove liability for the injury.

(Pub.L. 93–595, § 1, Jan. 2, 1975, 88 Stat.1933; Apr. 26, 2011, eff. Dec. 1, 2011.)

RULE 410. PLEAS, PLEA DISCUSSIONS, AND RELATED STATEMENTS

(a) **Prohibited Uses.** In a civil or criminal case, evidence of the following is not admissible against the defendant who made the plea or participated in the plea discussions:

(1) a guilty plea that was later withdrawn;

(2) a nolo contendere plea;

(3) a statement made during a proceeding on either of those pleas under Federal Rule of Criminal Procedure 11 or a comparable state procedure; or

(4) a statement made during plea discussions with an attorney for the prosecuting authority if the

discussions did not result in a guilty plea or they resulted in a later-withdrawn guilty plea.

(b) Exceptions. The court may admit a statement described in Rule 410(a)(3) or (4):

(1) in any proceeding in which another statement made during the same plea or plea discussions has been introduced, if in fairness the statements ought to be considered together; or

(2) in a criminal proceeding for perjury or false statement, if the defendant made the statement under oath, on the record, and with counsel present.

(Pub.L. 93–595, § 1, Jan. 2, 1975, 88 Stat. 1933; Pub.L. 94–149, § 1(9), Dec. 12, 1975, 89 Stat. 805; Apr. 30, 1979, eff. Dec. 1, 1980; Apr. 26, 2011, eff. Dec. 1, 2011.)

RULE 411. LIABILITY INSURANCE

Evidence that a person was or was not insured against liability is not admissible to prove whether the person acted negligently or otherwise wrongfully. But the court may admit this evidence for another purpose, such as proving a witness's bias or prejudice or proving agency, ownership, or control.

(Pub.L. 93–595, § 1, Jan. 2, 1975, 88 Stat.1933; Mar. 2, 1987, eff. Oct. 1, 1987; Apr. 26, 2011, eff. Dec. 1, 2011.)

RULE 412. SEX–OFFENSE CASES: THE VICTIM'S SEXUAL BEHAVIOR OR PREDISPOSITION

(a) Prohibited Uses. The following evidence is not admissible in a civil or criminal proceeding involving alleged sexual misconduct:

(1) evidence offered to prove that a victim engaged in other sexual behavior; or

(2) evidence offered to prove a victim's sexual predisposition.

(b) Exceptions.

(1) *Criminal Cases*. The court may admit the following evidence in a criminal case:

(A) evidence of specific instances of a victim's sexual behavior, if offered to prove that someone other than the defendant was the source of semen, injury, or other physical evidence;

(B) evidence of specific instances of a victim's sexual behavior with respect to the person accused of the sexual misconduct, if offered by the defendant to prove consent or if offered by the prosecutor; and

(C) evidence whose exclusion would violate the defendant's constitutional rights.

(2) *Civil Cases*. In a civil case, the court may admit evidence offered to prove a victim's sexu-

al behavior or sexual predisposition if its probative value substantially outweighs the danger of harm to any victim and of unfair prejudice to any party. The court may admit evidence of a victim's reputation only if the victim has placed it in controversy.

(c) Procedure to Determine Admissibility.

(1) *Motion*. If a party intends to offer evidence under Rule 412(b), the party must:

(A) file a motion that specifically describes the evidence and states the purpose for which it is to be offered;

(B) do so at least 14 days before trial unless the court, for good cause, sets a different time;

(C) serve the motion on all parties; and

(D) notify the victim or, when appropriate, the victim's guardian or representative.

(2) *Hearing*. Before admitting evidence under this rule, the court must conduct an in camera hearing and give the victim and parties a right to attend and be heard. Unless the court orders otherwise, the motion, related materials, and the record of the hearing must be and remain sealed.

(d) Definition of "Victim." In this rule, "victim" includes an alleged victim.

(Added Pub.L. 95–540, § 2(a), Oct. 28, 1978, 92 Stat. 2046, and amended Pub.L. 100–690, Title VII, § 7046(a), Nov. 18, 1988, 102 Stat. 4400; Apr. 29, 1994, eff. Dec. 1, 1994; Pub.L. 103–322, Title IV, § 40141(b), Sept. 13, 1994, 108 Stat. 1919; Apr. 26, 2011, eff. Dec. 1, 2011.)

RULE 413. SIMILAR CRIMES IN SEXUAL–ASSAULT CASES

(a) Permitted Uses. In a criminal case in which a defendant is accused of a sexual assault, the court may admit evidence that the defendant committed any other sexual assault. The evidence may be considered on any matter to which it is relevant.

(b) Disclosure to the Defendant. If the prosecutor intends to offer this evidence, the prosecutor must disclose it to the defendant, including witnesses' statements or a summary of the expected testimony. The prosecutor must do so at least 15 days before trial or at a later time that the court allows for good cause.

(c) Effect on Other Rules. This rule does not limit the admission or consideration of evidence under any other rule.

(d) Definition of "Sexual Assault." In this rule and Rule 415, "sexual assault" means a crime under federal law or under state law (as "state" is defined in 18 U.S.C. § 513) involving:

(1) any conduct prohibited by 18 U.S.C. chapter 109A;

(2) contact, without consent, between any part of the defendant's body—or an object—and another person's genitals or anus;

(3) contact, without consent, between the defendant's genitals or anus and any part of another person's body;

(4) deriving sexual pleasure or gratification from inflicting death, bodily injury, or physical pain on another person; or

(5) an attempt or conspiracy to engage in conduct described in subparagraphs (1)–(4).

(Added Pub.L. 103–322, Title XXXII, § 320935(a), Sept. 13, 1994, 108 Stat. 2136; Apr. 26, 2011, eff. Dec. 1, 2011.)

RULE 414. SIMILAR CRIMES IN CHILD–MOLESTATION CASES

(a) **Permitted Uses.** In a criminal case in which a defendant is accused of child molestation, the court may admit evidence that the defendant committed any other child molestation. The evidence may be considered on any matter to which it is relevant.

(b) **Disclosure to the Defendant.** If the prosecutor intends to offer this evidence, the prosecutor must disclose it to the defendant, including witnesses' statements or a summary of the expected testimony. The prosecutor must do so at least 15 days before trial or at a later time that the court allows for good cause.

(c) **Effect on Other Rules.** This rule does not limit the admission or consideration of evidence under any other rule.

(d) **Definition of "Child" and "Child Molestation."** In this rule and Rule 415:

(1) "child" means a person below the age of 14; and

(2) "child molestation" means a crime under federal law or under state law (as "state" is defined in 18 U.S.C. § 513) involving:

(A) any conduct prohibited by 18 U.S.C. chapter 109A and committed with a child;

(B) any conduct prohibited by 18 U.S.C. chapter 110;

(C) contact between any part of the defendant's body—or an object—and a child's genitals or anus;

(D) contact between the defendant's genitals or anus and any part of a child's body;

(E) deriving sexual pleasure or gratification from inflicting death, bodily injury, or physical pain on a child; or

(F) an attempt or conspiracy to engage in conduct described in subparagraphs (A)–(E).

(Added Pub.L. 103–322, Title XXXII, § 320935(a), Sept. 13, 1994, 108 Stat. 2135; Apr. 26, 2011, eff. Dec. 1, 2011.)

RULE 415. SIMILAR ACTS IN CIVIL CASES INVOLVING SEXUAL ASSAULT OR CHILD MOLESTATION

(a) **Permitted Uses.** In a civil case involving a claim for relief based on a party's alleged sexual assault or child molestation, the court may admit evidence that the party committed any other sexual assault or child molestation. The evidence may be considered as provided in Rules 413 and 414.

(b) **Disclosure to the Opponent.** If a party intends to offer this evidence, the party must disclose it to the party against whom it will be offered, including witnesses' statements or a summary of the expected testimony. The party must do so at least 15 days before trial or at a later time that the court allows for good cause.

(c) **Effect on Other Rules.** This rule does not limit the admission or consideration of evidence under any other rule.

(Added Pub.L. 103–322, Title XXXII, § 320935(a), Sept. 13, 1994, 108 Stat. 2137; Apr. 26, 2011, eff. Dec. 1, 2011.)

ARTICLE V. PRIVILEGES

RULE 501. PRIVILEGE IN GENERAL

The common law—as interpreted by United States courts in the light of reason and experience—governs a claim of privilege unless any of the following provides otherwise:

• the United States Constitution;

• a federal statute; or

• rules prescribed by the Supreme Court.

But in a civil case, state law governs privilege regarding a claim or defense for which state law supplies the rule of decision.

(Pub.L. 93–595, § 1, Jan. 2, 1975, 88 Stat. 1933; Apr. 26, 2011, eff. Dec. 1, 2011.)

RULE 502. ATTORNEY–CLIENT PRIVILEGE AND WORK PRODUCT; LIMITATIONS ON WAIVER

The following provisions apply, in the circumstances set out, to disclosure of a communication or information covered by the attorney-client privilege or work-product protection.

(a) Disclosure Made in a Federal Proceeding or to a Federal Office or Agency; Scope of a Waiver. When the disclosure is made in a federal proceeding or to a federal office or agency and waives the attorney-client privilege or work-product protection, the waiver extends to an undisclosed communication or information in a federal or state proceeding only if:

(1) the waiver is intentional;

(2) the disclosed and undisclosed communications or information concern the same subject matter; and

(3) they ought in fairness to be considered together.

(b) Inadvertent Disclosure. When made in a federal proceeding or to a federal office or agency, the disclosure does not operate as a waiver in a federal or state proceeding if:

(1) the disclosure is inadvertent;

(2) the holder of the privilege or protection took reasonable steps to prevent disclosure; and

(3) the holder promptly took reasonable steps to rectify the error, including (if applicable) following Federal Rule of Civil Procedure 26(b)(5)(B).

(c) Disclosure Made in a State Proceeding. When the disclosure is made in a state proceeding and is not the subject of a state-court order concerning waiver, the disclosure does not operate as a waiver in a federal proceeding if the disclosure:

(1) would not be a waiver under this rule if it had been made in a federal proceeding; or

(2) is not a waiver under the law of the state where the disclosure occurred.

(d) Controlling Effect of a Court Order. A federal court may order that the privilege or protection is not waived by disclosure connected with the litigation pending before the court—in which event the disclosure is also not a waiver in any other federal or state proceeding.

(e) Controlling Effect of a Party Agreement. An agreement on the effect of disclosure in a federal proceeding is binding only on the parties to the agreement, unless it is incorporated into a court order.

(f) Controlling Effect of This Rule. Notwithstanding Rules 101 and 1101, this rule applies to state proceedings and to federal court-annexed and federal court-mandated arbitration proceedings, in the circumstances set out in the rule. And notwithstanding Rule 501, this rule applies even if state law provides the rule of decision.

(g) Definitions. In this rule:

(1) "attorney-client privilege" means the protection that applicable law provides for confidential attorney-client communications; and

(2) "work-product protection" means the protection that applicable law provides for tangible material (or its intangible equivalent) prepared in anticipation of litigation or for trial.

(Pub.L. 110–322, § 1(a), Sept. 19, 2008, 122 Stat. 3537; Apr. 26, 2011, eff. Dec. 1, 2011.)

ARTICLE VI. WITNESSES

RULE 601. COMPETENCY TO TESTIFY IN GENERAL

Every person is competent to be a witness unless these rules provide otherwise. But in a civil case, state law governs the witness's competency regarding a claim or defense for which state law supplies the rule of decision.

(Pub.L. 93–595, § 1, Jan. 2, 1975, 88 Stat.1934; Apr. 26, 2011, eff. Dec. 1, 2011.)

RULE 602. NEED FOR PERSONAL KNOWLEDGE

A witness may testify to a matter only if evidence is introduced sufficient to support a finding that the witness has personal knowledge of the matter. Evidence to prove personal knowledge may consist of the witness's own testimony. This rule does not apply to a witness's expert testimony under Rule 703.

(Pub.L. 93–595, § 1, Jan. 2, 1975, 88 Stat. 1934; Mar. 2, 1987, eff. Oct. 1, 1987; Apr. 25, 1988, eff. Nov. 1, 1988; Apr. 26, 2011, eff. Dec. 1, 2011.)

RULE 603. OATH OR AFFIRMATION TO TESTIFY TRUTHFULLY

Before testifying, a witness must give an oath or affirmation to testify truthfully. It must be in a form designed to impress that duty on the witness's conscience.

(Pub.L. 93–595, § 1, Jan. 2, 1975, 88 Stat. 1934; Mar. 2, 1987, eff. Oct. 1, 1987; Apr. 26, 2011, eff. Dec. 1, 2011.)

RULE 604. INTERPRETER

An interpreter must be qualified and must give an oath or affirmation to make a true translation.

(Pub.L. 93–595, § 1, Jan. 2, 1975, 88 Stat. 1934; Mar. 2, 1987, eff. Oct. 1, 1987; Apr. 26, 2011, eff. Dec. 1, 2011.)

RULE 605. JUDGE'S COMPETENCY AS A WITNESS

The presiding judge may not testify as a witness at the trial. A party need not object to preserve the issue.

(Pub.L. 93–595, § 1, Jan. 2, 1975, 88 Stat. 1934; Apr. 26, 2011, eff. Dec. 1, 2011.)

RULE 606. JUROR'S COMPETENCY AS A WITNESS

(a) **At the Trial.** A juror may not testify as a witness before the other jurors at the trial. If a juror is called to testify, the court must give a party an opportunity to object outside the jury's presence.

(b) **During an Inquiry Into the Validity of a Verdict or Indictment.**

(1) **Prohibited Testimony or Other Evidence.** During an inquiry into the validity of a verdict or indictment, a juror may not testify about any statement made or incident that occurred during the jury's deliberations; the effect of anything on that juror's or another juror's vote; or any juror's mental processes concerning the verdict or indictment. The court may not receive a juror's affidavit or evidence of a juror's statement on these matters.

(2) **Exceptions.** A juror may testify about whether:

(A) extraneous prejudicial information was improperly brought to the jury's attention;

(B) an outside influence was improperly brought to bear on any juror; or

(C) a mistake was made in entering the verdict on the verdict form.

(Pub.L. 93–595, § 1, Jan. 2, 1975, 88 Stat. 1934; Pub.L. 94–149, § 1(10), Dec. 12, 1975, 89 Stat. 805; Mar. 2, 1987, eff. Oct. 1, 1987; Apr. 12, 2006, eff. Dec. 1, 2006; Apr. 26, 2011, eff. Dec. 1, 2011.)

RULE 607. WHO MAY IMPEACH A WITNESS

Any party, including the party that called the witness, may attack the witness's credibility.

(Pub.L. 93–595, § 1, Jan. 2, 1975, 88 Stat.1934; Mar. 2, 1987, eff. Oct. 1, 1987; Apr. 26, 2011, eff. Dec. 1, 2011.)

RULE 608. A WITNESS'S CHARACTER FOR TRUTHFULNESS OR UNTRUTHFULNESS

(a) **Reputation or Opinion Evidence.** A witness's credibility may be attacked or supported by testimony about the witness's reputation for having a character for truthfulness or untruthfulness, or by testimony in the form of an opinion about that character. But evidence of truthful character is admissible only after the witness's character for truthfulness has been attacked.

(b) **Specific Instances of Conduct.** Except for a criminal conviction under Rule 609, extrinsic evidence is not admissible to prove specific instances of a witness's conduct in order to attack or support the witness's character for truthfulness. But the court may, on cross-examination, allow them to be inquired into if they are probative of the character for truthfulness or untruthfulness of:

(1) the witness; or

(2) another witness whose character the witness being cross-examined has testified about.

By testifying on another matter, a witness does not waive any privilege against self-incrimination for testimony that relates only to the witness's character for truthfulness.

(Pub.L. 93–595, § 1, Jan. 2, 1975, 88 Stat.1935; Mar. 2, 1987, eff. Oct. 1, 1987; Apr. 25, 1988, eff. Nov. 1, 1988; Mar. 27, 2003, eff. Dec. 1, 2003; Apr. 26, 2011, eff. Dec. 1, 2011.)

RULE 609. IMPEACHMENT BY EVIDENCE OF A CRIMINAL CONVICTION

(a) **In General.** The following rules apply to attacking a witness's character for truthfulness by evidence of a criminal conviction:

(1) for a crime that, in the convicting jurisdiction, was punishable by death or by imprisonment for more than one year, the evidence:

(A) must be admitted, subject to Rule 403, in a civil case or in a criminal case in which the witness is not a defendant; and

(B) must be admitted in a criminal case in which the witness is a defendant, if the probative value of the evidence outweighs its prejudicial effect to that defendant; and

(2) for any crime regardless of the punishment, the evidence must be admitted if the court can readily determine that establishing the elements of the crime required proving—or the witness's admitting—a dishonest act or false statement.

(b) **Limit on Using the Evidence After 10 Years.** This subdivision (b) applies if more than 10 years have passed since the witness's conviction or release from confinement for it, whichever is later. Evidence of the conviction is admissible only if:

(1) its probative value, supported by specific facts and circumstances, substantially outweighs its prejudicial effect; and

(2) the proponent gives an adverse party reasonable written notice of the intent to use it so that the party has a fair opportunity to contest its use.

(c) **Effect of a Pardon, Annulment, or Certificate of Rehabilitation.** Evidence of a conviction is not admissible if:

(1) the conviction has been the subject of a pardon, annulment, certificate of rehabilitation, or other equivalent procedure based on a finding that the person has been rehabilitated, and the person has not been convicted of a later crime punishable by death or by imprisonment for more than one year; or

(2) the conviction has been the subject of a pardon, annulment, or other equivalent procedure based on a finding of innocence.

(d) **Juvenile Adjudications.** Evidence of a juvenile adjudication is admissible under this rule only if:

(1) it is offered in a criminal case;

(2) the adjudication was of a witness other than the defendant;

(3) an adult's conviction for that offense would be admissible to attack the adult's credibility; and

(4) admitting the evidence is necessary to fairly determine guilt or innocence.

(e) **Pendency of an Appeal.** A conviction that satisfies this rule is admissible even if an appeal is pending. Evidence of the pendency is also admissible.

(Pub.L. 93–595, § 1, Jan. 2, 1975, 88 Stat.1935; Mar. 2, 1987, eff. Oct. 1, 1987; Jan. 26, 1990, eff. Dec. 1, 1990; Apr. 12, 2006, eff. Dec. 1, 2006; Apr. 26, 2011, eff. Dec. 1, 2011.)

RULE 610. RELIGIOUS BELIEFS OR OPINIONS

Evidence of a witness's religious beliefs or opinions is not admissible to attack or support the witness's credibility.

(Pub.L. 93–595, § 1, Jan. 2, 1975, 88 Stat.1936; Mar. 2, 1987, eff. Oct. 1, 1987; Apr. 26, 2011, eff. Dec. 1, 2011.)

RULE 611. MODE AND ORDER OF EXAMINING WITNESSES AND PRESENTING EVIDENCE

(a) **Control by the Court; Purposes.** The court should exercise reasonable control over the mode and order of examining witnesses and presenting evidence so as to:

(1) make those procedures effective for determining the truth;

(2) avoid wasting time; and

(3) protect witnesses from harassment or undue embarrassment.

(b) **Scope of Cross–Examination.** Cross-examination should not go beyond the subject matter of the direct examination and matters affecting the witness's credibility. The court may allow inquiry into additional matters as if on direct examination.

(c) **Leading Questions.** Leading questions should not be used on direct examination except as necessary to develop the witness's testimony. Ordinarily, the court should allow leading questions:

(1) on cross-examination; and

(2) when a party calls a hostile witness, an adverse party, or a witness identified with an adverse party.

(Pub.L. 93–595, § 1, Jan. 2, 1975, 88 Stat. 1936; Mar. 2, 1987, eff. Oct. 1, 1987; Apr. 26, 2011, eff. Dec. 1, 2011.)

RULE 612. WRITING USED TO REFRESH A WITNESS'S MEMORY

(a) **Scope.** This rule gives an adverse party certain options when a witness uses a writing to refresh memory:

(1) while testifying; or

(2) before testifying, if the court decides that justice requires the party to have those options.

(b) **Adverse Party's Options; Deleting Unrelated Matter.** Unless 18 U.S.C. § 3500 provides otherwise in a criminal case, an adverse party is entitled to have the writing produced at the hearing, to inspect it, to cross-examine the witness about it, and to introduce in evidence any portion that relates to the witness's testimony. If the producing party claims that the writing includes unrelated matter, the court must examine the writing in camera, delete any unrelated portion, and order that the rest be delivered to the adverse party. Any portion deleted over objection must be preserved for the record.

(c) **Failure to Produce or Deliver the Writing.** If a writing is not produced or is not delivered as ordered, the court may issue any appropriate order. But if the prosecution does not comply in a criminal case, the court must strike the witness's testimony or—if justice so requires—declare a mistrial.

(Pub.L. 93–595, § 1, Jan. 2, 1975, 88 Stat. 1936; Mar. 2, 1987, eff. Oct. 1, 1987; Apr. 26, 2011, eff. Dec. 1, 2011.)

RULE 613. WITNESS'S PRIOR STATEMENT

(a) Showing or Disclosing the Statement During Examination. When examining a witness about the witness's prior statement, a party need not show it or disclose its contents to the witness. But the party must, on request, show it or disclose its contents to an adverse party's attorney.

(b) Extrinsic Evidence of a Prior Inconsistent Statement. Extrinsic evidence of a witness's prior inconsistent statement is admissible only if the witness is given an opportunity to explain or deny the statement and an adverse party is given an opportunity to examine the witness about it, or if justice so requires. This subdivision (b) does not apply to an opposing party's statement under Rule 801(d)(2).

(Pub.L. 93–595, § 1, Jan. 2, 1975, 88 Stat.1936; Mar. 2, 1987, eff. Oct. 1, 1987; Apr. 25, 1988, eff. Nov. 1, 1988; Apr. 26, 2011, eff. Dec. 1, 2011.)

RULE 614. COURT'S CALLING OR EXAMINING A WITNESS

(a) Calling. The court may call a witness on its own or at a party's request. Each party is entitled to cross-examine the witness.

(b) Examining. The court may examine a witness regardless of who calls the witness.

(c) Objections. A party may object to the court's calling or examining a witness either at that time or at the next opportunity when the jury is not present.

(Pub.L. 93–595, § 1, Jan. 2, 1975, 88 Stat.1937; Apr. 26, 2011, eff. Dec. 1, 2011.)

RULE 615. EXCLUDING WITNESSES

At a party's request, the court must order witnesses excluded so that they cannot hear other witnesses' testimony. Or the court may do so on its own. But this rule does not authorize excluding:

(a) a party who is a natural person;

(b) an officer or employee of a party that is not a natural person, after being designated as the party's representative by its attorney;

(c) a person whose presence a party shows to be essential to presenting the party's claim or defense; or

(d) a person authorized by statute to be present.

(Pub.L. 93–595, § 1, Jan. 2, 1975, 88 Stat.1937; Mar. 2, 1987, eff. Oct. 1, 1987; Apr. 25, 1988, eff. Nov. 1, 1988; Pub.L. 100–690, Nov. 18, 1988, Title VII, § 7075(a), 102 Stat. 4405; Apr. 24, 1998, eff. Dec. 1, 1998; Apr. 26, 2011, eff. Dec. 1, 2011.)

ARTICLE VII. OPINIONS AND EXPERT TESTIMONY

RULE 701. OPINION TESTIMONY BY LAY WITNESSES

If a witness is not testifying as an expert, testimony in the form of an opinion is limited to one that is:

(a) rationally based on the witness's perception;

(b) helpful to clearly understanding the witness's testimony or to determining a fact in issue; and

(c) not based on scientific, technical, or other specialized knowledge within the scope of Rule 702.

(Pub.L. 93–595, § 1, Jan. 2, 1975, 88 Stat.1937; Mar. 2, 1987, eff. Oct. 1, 1987; Apr. 17, 2000, eff. Dec. 1, 2000; Apr. 26, 2011, eff. Dec. 1, 2011.)

RULE 702. TESTIMONY BY EXPERT WITNESSES

A witness who is qualified as an expert by knowledge, skill, experience, training, or education may testify in the form of an opinion or otherwise if:

(a) the expert's scientific, technical, or other specialized knowledge will help the trier of fact to understand the evidence or to determine a fact in issue;

(b) the testimony is based on sufficient facts or data;

(c) the testimony is the product of reliable principles and methods; and

(d) the expert has reliably applied the principles and methods to the facts of the case.

(Pub.L. 93–595, § 1, Jan. 2, 1975, 88 Stat. 1937; Apr. 17, 2000, eff. Dec. 1, 2000; Apr. 26, 2011, eff. Dec. 1, 2011.)

RULE 703. BASES OF AN EXPERT'S OPINION TESTIMONY

An expert may base an opinion on facts or data in the case that the expert has been made aware of or personally observed. If experts in the particular field would reasonably rely on those kinds of facts or data in forming an opinion on the subject, they need not be admissible for the opinion to be admitted. But if the facts or data would otherwise be inadmissible, the proponent of the opinion may disclose them to the jury only if their probative value in helping the jury evaluate the opinion substantially outweighs their prejudicial effect.

(Pub.L. 93–595, § 1, Jan. 2, 1975, 88 Stat.1937; Mar. 2, 1987, eff. Oct. 1, 1987; Apr. 17, 2000, eff. Dec. 1, 2000; Apr. 26, 2011, eff. Dec. 1, 2011.)

RULE 704. OPINION ON AN ULTIMATE ISSUE

(a) In General—Not Automatically Objectionable. An opinion is not objectionable just because it embraces an ultimate issue.

(b) Exception. In a criminal case, an expert witness must not state an opinion about whether the defendant did or did not have a mental state or condition that constitutes an element of the crime charged or of a defense. Those matters are for the trier of fact alone.

(Pub.L. 93–595, § 1, Jan. 2, 1975, 88 Stat. 1937; Pub.L. 98–473, Title IV, § 406, Oct. 12, 1984, 98 Stat. 2067; Apr. 26, 2011, eff. Dec. 1, 2011.)

RULE 705. DISCLOSING THE FACTS OR DATA UNDERLYING AN EXPERT'S OPINION

Unless the court orders otherwise, an expert may state an opinion—and give the reasons for it—without first testifying to the underlying facts or data. But the expert may be required to disclose those facts or data on cross-examination.

(Pub.L. 93–595, § 1, Jan. 2, 1975, 88 Stat. 1938; Mar. 2, 1987, eff. Oct. 1, 1987; Apr. 22, 1993, eff. Dec. 1, 1993; Apr. 26, 2011, eff. Dec. 1, 2011.)

RULE 706. COURT–APPOINTED EXPERT WITNESSES

(a) Appointment Process. On a party's motion or on its own, the court may order the parties to show cause why expert witnesses should not be appointed and may ask the parties to submit nominations. The court may appoint any expert that the parties agree on and any of its own choosing. But the court may only appoint someone who consents to act.

(b) Expert's Role. The court must inform the expert of the expert's duties. The court may do so in writing and have a copy filed with the clerk or may do so orally at a conference in which the parties have an opportunity to participate. The expert:

(1) must advise the parties of any findings the expert makes;

(2) may be deposed by any party;

(3) may be called to testify by the court or any party; and

(4) may be cross-examined by any party, including the party that called the expert.

(c) Compensation. The expert is entitled to a reasonable compensation, as set by the court. The compensation is payable as follows:

(1) in a criminal case or in a civil case involving just compensation under the Fifth Amendment, from any funds that are provided by law; and

(2) in any other civil case, by the parties in the proportion and at the time that the court directs—and the compensation is then charged like other costs.

(d) Disclosing the Appointment to the Jury. The court may authorize disclosure to the jury that the court appointed the expert.

(e) Parties' Choice of Their Own Experts. This rule does not limit a party in calling its own experts.

(Pub.L. 93–595, § 1, Jan. 2, 1975, 88 Stat.1938; Mar. 2, 1987, eff. Oct. 1, 1987; Apr. 26, 2011, eff. Dec. 1, 2011.)

ARTICLE VIII. HEARSAY

RULE 801. DEFINITIONS THAT APPLY TO THIS ARTICLE; EXCLUSIONS FROM HEARSAY

(a) Statement. "Statement" means a person's oral assertion, written assertion, or nonverbal conduct, if the person intended it as an assertion.

(b) Declarant. "Declarant" means the person who made the statement.

(c) Hearsay. "Hearsay" means a statement that:

(1) the declarant does not make while testifying at the current trial or hearing; and

(2) a party offers in evidence to prove the truth of the matter asserted in the statement.

(d) Statements That Are Not Hearsay. A statement that meets the following conditions is not hearsay:

(1) **A Declarant–Witness's Prior Statement.** The declarant testifies and is subject to cross-examination about a prior statement, and the statement:

(A) is inconsistent with the declarant's testimony and was given under penalty of perjury at a trial, hearing, or other proceeding or in a deposition;

(B) is consistent with the declarant's testimony and is offered to rebut an express or implied charge that the declarant recently fabricated it or acted from a recent improper influence or motive in so testifying; or

(C) identifies a person as someone the declarant perceived earlier.

(2) An Opposing Party's Statement. The statement is offered against an opposing party and:

(A) was made by the party in an individual or representative capacity;

(B) is one the party manifested that it adopted or believed to be true;

(C) was made by a person whom the party authorized to make a statement on the subject;

(D) was made by the party's agent or employee on a matter within the scope of that relationship and while it existed; or

(E) was made by the party's coconspirator during and in furtherance of the conspiracy.

The statement must be considered but does not by itself establish the declarant's authority under (C); the existence or scope of the relationship under (D); or the existence of the conspiracy or participation in it under (E).

(Pub.L. 93–595, § 1, Jan. 2, 1975, 88 Stat.1938; Pub.L. 94–113, § 1, Oct. 16, 1975, 89 Stat. 576; Mar. 2, 1987, eff. Oct. 1, 1987; Apr. 11, 1997, eff. Dec. 1, 1997; Apr. 26, 2011, eff. Dec. 1, 2011.)

RULE 802. THE RULE AGAINST HEARSAY

Hearsay is not admissible unless any of the following provides otherwise:

- a federal statute;
- these rules; or
- other rules prescribed by the Supreme Court.

(Pub.L. 93–595, § 1, Jan. 2, 1975, 88 Stat. 1939; Apr. 26, 2011, eff. Dec. 1, 2011.)

RULE 803. EXCEPTIONS TO THE RULE AGAINST HEARSAY—REGARDLESS OF WHETHER THE DECLARANT IS AVAILABLE AS A WITNESS

The following are not excluded by the rule against hearsay, regardless of whether the declarant is available as a witness:

(1) Present Sense Impression. A statement describing or explaining an event or condition, made while or immediately after the declarant perceived it.

(2) Excited Utterance. A statement relating to a startling event or condition, made while the declarant was under the stress of excitement that it caused.

(3) Then–Existing Mental, Emotional, or Physical Condition. A statement of the declarant's then-existing state of mind (such as motive, intent, or plan) or emotional, sensory, or physical condition (such as mental feeling, pain, or bodily health), but not including a statement of memory or belief to prove the fact remembered or believed unless it relates to the validity or terms of the declarant's will.

(4) Statement Made for Medical Diagnosis or Treatment. A statement that:

(A) is made for—and is reasonably pertinent to—medical diagnosis or treatment; and

(B) describes medical history; past or present symptoms or sensations; their inception; or their general cause.

(5) Recorded Recollection. A record that:

(A) is on a matter the witness once knew about but now cannot recall well enough to testify fully and accurately;

(B) was made or adopted by the witness when the matter was fresh in the witness's memory; and

(C) accurately reflects the witness's knowledge.

If admitted, the record may be read into evidence but may be received as an exhibit only if offered by an adverse party.

(6) Records of a Regularly Conducted Activity. A record of an act, event, condition, opinion, or diagnosis if:

(A) the record was made at or near the time by—or from information transmitted by—someone with knowledge;

(B) the record was kept in the course of a regularly conducted activity of a business, organization, occupation, or calling, whether or not for profit;

(C) making the record was a regular practice of that activity;

(D) all these conditions are shown by the testimony of the custodian or another qualified witness, or by a certification that complies with Rule 902(11) or (12) or with a statute permitting certification; and

(E) neither the source of information nor the method or circumstances of preparation indicate a lack of trustworthiness.

(7) Absence of a Record of a Regularly Conducted Activity. Evidence that a matter is not included in a record described in paragraph (6) if:

(A) the evidence is admitted to prove that the matter did not occur or exist;

(B) a record was regularly kept for a matter of that kind; and

(C) neither the possible source of the information nor other circumstances indicate a lack of trustworthiness.

(8) Public Records. A record or statement of a public office if:

(A) it sets out:

(i) the office's activities;

(ii) a matter observed while under a legal duty to report, but not including, in a criminal case, a matter observed by law-enforcement personnel; or

(iii) in a civil case or against the government in a criminal case, factual findings from a legally authorized investigation; and

(B) neither the source of information nor other circumstances indicate a lack of trustworthiness.

(9) Public Records of Vital Statistics. A record of a birth, death, or marriage, if reported to a public office in accordance with a legal duty.

(10) Absence of a Public Record. Testimony—or a certification under Rule 902—that a diligent search failed to disclose a public record or statement if the testimony or certification is admitted to prove that:

(A) the record or statement does not exist; or

(B) a matter did not occur or exist, if a public office regularly kept a record or statement for a matter of that kind.

(11) Records of Religious Organizations Concerning Personal or Family History. A statement of birth, legitimacy, ancestry, marriage, divorce, death, relationship by blood or marriage, or similar facts of personal or family history, contained in a regularly kept record of a religious organization.

(12) Certificates of Marriage, Baptism, and Similar Ceremonies. A statement of fact contained in a certificate:

(A) made by a person who is authorized by a religious organization or by law to perform the act certified;

(B) attesting that the person performed a marriage or similar ceremony or administered a sacrament; and

(C) purporting to have been issued at the time of the act or within a reasonable time after it.

(13) Family Records. A statement of fact about personal or family history contained in a family record, such as a Bible, genealogy, chart, engraving on a ring, inscription on a portrait, or engraving on an urn or burial marker.

(14) Records of Documents That Affect an Interest in Property. The record of a document that purports to establish or affect an interest in property if:

(A) the record is admitted to prove the content of the original recorded document, along with its signing and its delivery by each person who purports to have signed it;

(B) the record is kept in a public office; and

(C) a statute authorizes recording documents of that kind in that office.

(15) Statements in Documents That Affect an Interest in Property. A statement contained in a document that purports to establish or affect an interest in property if the matter stated was relevant to the document's purpose—unless later dealings with the property are inconsistent with the truth of the statement or the purport of the document.

(16) Statements in Ancient Documents. A statement in a document that is at least 20 years old and whose authenticity is established.

(17) Market Reports and Similar Commercial Publications. Market quotations, lists, directories, or other compilations that are generally relied on by the public or by persons in particular occupations.

(18) Statements in Learned Treatises, Periodicals, or Pamphlets. A statement contained in a treatise, periodical, or pamphlet if:

(A) the statement is called to the attention of an expert witness on cross-examination or relied on by the expert on direct examination; and

(B) the publication is established as a reliable authority by the expert's admission or testimony, by another expert's testimony, or by judicial notice.

If admitted, the statement may be read into evidence but not received as an exhibit.

(19) Reputation Concerning Personal or Family History. A reputation among a person's family by blood, adoption, or marriage—or among a person's associates or in the community—concerning the person's birth, adoption, legitimacy, ancestry, marriage, divorce, death, relationship by blood, adoption, or marriage, or similar facts of personal or family history.

(20) Reputation Concerning Boundaries or General History. A reputation in a community—arising before the controversy—concerning boundaries of land in the community or customs that affect the land, or concerning general historical events important to that community, state, or nation.

(21) Reputation Concerning Character. A reputation among a person's associates or in the community concerning the person's character.

(22) Judgment of a Previous Conviction. Evidence of a final judgment of conviction if:

(A) the judgment was entered after a trial or guilty plea, but not a nolo contendere plea;

(B) the conviction was for a crime punishable by death or by imprisonment for more than a year;

(C) the evidence is admitted to prove any fact essential to the judgment; and

(D) when offered by the prosecutor in a criminal case for a purpose other than impeachment, the judgment was against the defendant.

The pendency of an appeal may be shown but does not affect admissibility.

(23) Judgments Involving Personal, Family, or General History, or a Boundary. A judgment that is admitted to prove a matter of personal, family, or general history, or boundaries, if the matter:

(A) was essential to the judgment; and

(B) could be proved by evidence of reputation.

(24) [Other Exceptions.] [Transferred to Rule 807.]

(Pub.L. 93–595, § 1, Jan. 2, 1975, 88 Stat. 1939; Pub.L. 94–149, § 1(11), Dec. 12, 1975, 89 Stat. 805; Mar. 2, 1987, eff. Oct. 1, 1987; Apr. 11, 1997, eff. Dec. 1, 1997; Apr. 17, 2000, eff. Dec. 1, 2000; Apr. 26, 2011, eff. Dec. 1, 2011.)

RULE 804. EXCEPTIONS TO THE RULE AGAINST HEARSAY—WHEN THE DECLARANT IS UNAVAILABLE AS A WITNESS

(a) Criteria for Being Unavailable. A declarant is considered to be unavailable as a witness if the declarant:

(1) is exempted from testifying about the subject matter of the declarant's statement because the court rules that a privilege applies;

(2) refuses to testify about the subject matter despite a court order to do so;

(3) testifies to not remembering the subject matter;

(4) cannot be present or testify at the trial or hearing because of death or a then-existing infirmity, physical illness, or mental illness; or

(5) is absent from the trial or hearing and the statement's proponent has not been able, by process or other reasonable means, to procure:

(A) the declarant's attendance, in the case of a hearsay exception under Rule 804(b)(1) or (6); or

(B) the declarant's attendance or testimony, in the case of a hearsay exception under Rule 804(b)(2), (3), or (4).

But this subdivision (a) does not apply if the statement's proponent procured or wrongfully caused the declarant's unavailability as a witness in order to prevent the declarant from attending or testifying.

(b) The Exceptions. The following are not excluded by the rule against hearsay if the declarant is unavailable as a witness:

(1) Former Testimony. Testimony that:

(A) was given as a witness at a trial, hearing, or lawful deposition, whether given during the current proceeding or a different one; and

(B) is now offered against a party who had—or, in a civil case, whose predecessor in interest had—an opportunity and similar motive to develop it by direct, cross-, or redirect examination.

(2) Statement Under the Belief of Imminent Death. In a prosecution for homicide or in a civil case, a statement that the declarant, while believing the declarant's death to be imminent, made about its cause or circumstances.

(3) Statement Against Interest. A statement that:

(A) a reasonable person in the declarant's position would have made only if the person believed it to be true because, when made, it was so contrary to the declarant's proprietary or pecuniary interest or had so great a tendency to invalidate the declarant's claim against someone else or to expose the declarant to civil or criminal liability; and

(B) is supported by corroborating circumstances that clearly indicate its trustworthiness, if it is offered in a criminal case as one that tends to expose the declarant to criminal liability.

(4) Statement of Personal or Family History. A statement about:

(A) the declarant's own birth, adoption, legitimacy, ancestry, marriage, divorce, relationship by blood, adoption, or marriage, or similar facts of personal or family history, even though the declarant had no way of acquiring personal knowledge about that fact; or

(B) another person concerning any of these facts, as well as death, if the declarant was related to the person by blood, adoption, or marriage or was so intimately associated with the person's family that the declarant's information is likely to be accurate.

(5) [Other Exceptions.] [Transferred to Rule 807.]

(6) Statement Offered Against a Party That Wrongfully Caused the Declarant's Unavailability. A statement offered against a party that wrongfully caused—or acquiesced in wrongfully causing—the declarant's unavailability as a witness, and did so intending that result.

(Pub.L. 93–595, § 1, Jan. 2, 1975, 88 Stat. 1942; Pub.L. 94–149, § 1(12), (13), Dec. 12, 1975, 89 Stat. 806; Mar. 2, 1987, eff. Oct. 1, 1987; Pub.L. 100–690, Title VII, § 7075(b), Nov. 18, 1988, 102 Stat. 4405; Apr. 11, 1997, eff. Dec. 1, 1997; Apr. 28, 2010, eff. Dec. 1, 2010; Apr. 26, 2011, eff. Dec. 1, 2011.)

RULE 805.　HEARSAY WITHIN HEARSAY

Hearsay within hearsay is not excluded by the rule against hearsay if each part of the combined statements conforms with an exception to the rule.

(Pub.L. 93–595, § 1, Jan. 2, 1975, 88 Stat. 1943; Apr. 26, 2011, eff. Dec. 1, 2011.)

RULE 806.　ATTACKING AND SUPPORTING THE DECLARANT'S CREDIBILITY

When a hearsay statement—or a statement described in Rule 801(d)(2)(C), (D), or (E)—has been admitted in evidence, the declarant's credibility may be attacked, and then supported, by any evidence that would be admissible for those purposes if the declarant had testified as a witness. The court may admit evidence of the declarant's inconsistent statement or conduct, regardless of when it occurred or whether the declarant had an opportunity to explain or deny it. If the party against whom the statement was admitted calls the declarant as a witness, the party may examine the declarant on the statement as if on cross-examination.

(Pub.L. 93–595, § 1, Jan. 2, 1975, 88 Stat. 1943; Mar. 2, 1987, eff. Oct. 1, 1987; Apr. 11, 1997, eff. Dec. 1, 1997; Apr. 26, 2011, eff. Dec. 1, 2011.)

RULE 807.　RESIDUAL EXCEPTION

(a) In General. Under the following circumstances, a hearsay statement is not excluded by the rule against hearsay even if the statement is not specifically covered by a hearsay exception in Rule 803 or 804:

(1) the statement has equivalent circumstantial guarantees of trustworthiness;

(2) it is offered as evidence of a material fact;

(3) it is more probative on the point for which it is offered than any other evidence that the proponent can obtain through reasonable efforts; and

(4) admitting it will best serve the purposes of these rules and the interests of justice.

(b) Notice. The statement is admissible only if, before the trial or hearing, the proponent gives an adverse party reasonable notice of the intent to offer the statement and its particulars, including the declarant's name and address, so that the party has a fair opportunity to meet it.

(Added Apr. 11, 1997, eff. Dec. 1, 1997; Apr. 26, 2011, eff. Dec. 1, 2011.)

ARTICLE IX.　AUTHENTICATION AND IDENTIFICATION

RULE 901.　AUTHENTICATING OR IDENTIFYING EVIDENCE

(a) In General. To satisfy the requirement of authenticating or identifying an item of evidence, the proponent must produce evidence sufficient to support a finding that the item is what the proponent claims it is.

(b) Examples. The following are examples only—not a complete list—of evidence that satisfies the requirement:

(1) Testimony of a Witness with Knowledge. Testimony that an item is what it is claimed to be.

(2) Nonexpert Opinion About Handwriting. A nonexpert's opinion that handwriting is genuine, based on a familiarity with it that was not acquired for the current litigation.

(3) Comparison by an Expert Witness or the Trier of Fact. A comparison with an authenticated specimen by an expert witness or the trier of fact.

(4) Distinctive Characteristics and the Like. The appearance, contents, substance, internal patterns, or other distinctive characteristics of the item, taken together with all the circumstances.

(5) Opinion About a Voice. An opinion identifying a person's voice—whether heard firsthand or through mechanical or electronic transmission or recording—based on hearing the voice at any time under circumstances that connect it with the alleged speaker.

(6) Evidence About a Telephone Conversation. For a telephone conversation, evidence that a call was made to the number assigned at the time to:

(A) a particular person, if circumstances, including self-identification, show that the person answering was the one called; or

(B) a particular business, if the call was made to a business and the call related to business reasonably transacted over the telephone.

(7) Evidence About Public Records. Evidence that:

(A) a document was recorded or filed in a public office as authorized by law; or

(B) a purported public record or statement is from the office where items of this kind are kept.

(8) Evidence About Ancient Documents or Data Compilations. For a document or data compilation, evidence that it:

(A) is in a condition that creates no suspicion about its authenticity;

(B) was in a place where, if authentic, it would likely be; and

(C) is at least 20 years old when offered.

(9) Evidence About a Process or System. Evidence describing a process or system and showing that it produces an accurate result.

(10) Methods Provided by a Statute or Rule. Any method of authentication or identification allowed by a federal statute or a rule prescribed by the Supreme Court.

(Pub.L. 93–595, § 1, Jan. 2, 1975, 88 Stat.1943; Apr. 26, 2011, eff. Dec. 1, 2011.)

RULE 902. EVIDENCE THAT IS SELF–AUTHENTICATING

The following items of evidence are self-authenticating; they require no extrinsic evidence of authenticity in order to be admitted:

(1) Domestic Public Documents That Are Sealed and Signed. A document that bears:

(A) a seal purporting to be that of the United States; any state, district, commonwealth, territory, or insular possession of the United States; the former Panama Canal Zone; the Trust Territory of the Pacific Islands; a political subdivision of any of these entities; or a department, agency, or officer of any entity named above; and

(B) a signature purporting to be an execution or attestation.

(2) Domestic Public Documents That Are Not Sealed but Are Signed and Certified. A document that bears no seal if:

(A) it bears the signature of an officer or employee of an entity named in Rule 902(1)(A); and

(B) another public officer who has a seal and official duties within that same entity certifies under seal—or its equivalent—that the signer has the official capacity and that the signature is genuine.

(3) Foreign Public Documents. A document that purports to be signed or attested by a person who is authorized by a foreign country's law to do so. The document must be accompanied by a final certification that certifies the genuineness of the signature and official position of the signer or attester—or of any foreign official whose certificate of genuineness relates to the signature or attestation or is in a chain of certificates of genuineness relating to the signature or attestation. The certification may be made by a secretary of a United States embassy or legation; by a consul general, vice consul, or consular agent of the United States; or by a diplomatic or consular official of the foreign country assigned or accredited to the United States. If all parties have been given a reasonable opportunity to investigate the document's authenticity and accuracy, the court may, for good cause, either:

(A) order that it be treated as presumptively authentic without final certification; or

(B) allow it to be evidenced by an attested summary with or without final certification.

(4) Certified Copies of Public Records. A copy of an official record—or a copy of a document that was recorded or filed in a public office as authorized by law—if the copy is certified as correct by:

(A) the custodian or another person authorized to make the certification; or

(B) a certificate that complies with Rule 902(1), (2), or (3), a federal statute, or a rule prescribed by the Supreme Court.

(5) Official Publications. A book, pamphlet, or other publication purporting to be issued by a public authority.

(6) Newspapers and Periodicals. Printed material purporting to be a newspaper or periodical.

(7) Trade Inscriptions and the Like. An inscription, sign, tag, or label purporting to have been affixed in the course of business and indicating origin, ownership, or control.

(8) Acknowledged Documents. A document accompanied by a certificate of acknowledgment that is lawfully executed by a notary public or another officer who is authorized to take acknowledgments.

(9) Commercial Paper and Related Documents. Commercial paper, a signature on it, and related documents, to the extent allowed by general commercial law.

(10) Presumptions Under a Federal Statute. A signature, document, or anything else that a federal statute declares to be presumptively or prima facie genuine or authentic.

(11) Certified Domestic Records of a Regularly Conducted Activity. The original or a copy of a domestic record that meets the requirements of Rule 803(6)(A)–(C), as shown by a certification of the custodian or another qualified person that complies with a federal statute or a rule prescribed by the Supreme Court. Before the trial or hearing, the proponent must give an adverse party reasonable written notice of the intent to offer the record—and must make the record and certification available for inspection—so that the party has a fair opportunity to challenge them.

(12) Certified Foreign Records of a Regularly Conducted Activity. In a civil case, the original or a copy of a foreign record that meets the requirements of Rule 902(11), modified as follows: the certification, rather than complying with a federal statute or Supreme Court rule, must be signed in a manner that, if falsely made, would subject the maker to a criminal penalty in the country where the certification is signed. The proponent must also meet the notice requirements of Rule 902(11).

(Pub.L. 93–595, § 1, Jan. 2, 1975, 88 Stat. 1944; Mar. 2, 1987, eff. Oct. 1, 1987; Apr. 25, 1988, eff. Nov. 1, 1988; Apr. 17, 2000, eff. Dec. 1, 2000; Apr. 26, 2011, eff. Dec. 1, 2011.)

RULE 903.　SUBSCRIBING WITNESS'S TESTIMONY

A subscribing witness's testimony is necessary to authenticate a writing only if required by the law of the jurisdiction that governs its validity.

(Pub.L. 93–595, § 1, Jan. 2, 1975, 88 Stat.1945; Apr. 26, 2011, eff. Dec. 1, 2011.)

ARTICLE X.　CONTENTS OF WRITINGS, RECORDINGS, AND PHOTOGRAPHS

RULE 1001.　DEFINITIONS THAT APPLY TO THIS ARTICLE

In this article:

(a) A "writing" consists of letters, words, numbers, or their equivalent set down in any form.

(b) A "recording" consists of letters, words, numbers, or their equivalent recorded in any manner.

(c) A "photograph" means a photographic image or its equivalent stored in any form.

(d) An "original" of a writing or recording means the writing or recording itself or any counterpart intended to have the same effect by the person who executed or issued it. For electronically stored information, "original" means any printout—or other output readable by sight—if it accurately reflects the information. An "original" of a photograph includes the negative or a print from it.

(e) A "duplicate" means a counterpart produced by a mechanical, photographic, chemical, electronic, or other equivalent process or technique that accurately reproduces the original.

(Pub.L. 93–595, § 1, Jan. 2, 1975, 88 Stat. 1945; Apr. 26, 2011, eff. Dec. 1, 2011.)

RULE 1002.　REQUIREMENT OF THE ORIGINAL

An original writing, recording, or photograph is required in order to prove its content unless these rules or a federal statute provides otherwise.

(Pub.L. 93–595, § 1, Jan. 2, 1975, 88 Stat. 1946; Apr. 26, 2011, eff. Dec. 1, 2011.)

RULE 1003.　ADMISSIBILITY OF DUPLICATES

A duplicate is admissible to the same extent as the original unless a genuine question is raised about the original's authenticity or the circumstances make it unfair to admit the duplicate.

(Pub.L. 93–595, § 1, Jan. 2, 1975, 88 Stat. 1946; Apr. 26, 2011, eff. Dec. 1, 2011.)

RULE 1004.　ADMISSIBILITY OF OTHER EVIDENCE OF CONTENT

An original is not required and other evidence of the content of a writing, recording, or photograph is admissible if:

(a) all the originals are lost or destroyed, and not by the proponent acting in bad faith;

(b) an original cannot be obtained by any available judicial process;

(c) the party against whom the original would be offered had control of the original; was at that time put on notice, by pleadings or otherwise, that the original would be a subject of proof at the trial or hearing; and fails to produce it at the trial or hearing; or

(d) the writing, recording, or photograph is not closely related to a controlling issue.

(Pub.L. 93–595, § 1, Jan. 2, 1975, 88 Stat. 1946; Mar. 2, 1987, eff. Oct. 1, 1987; Apr. 26, 2011, eff. Dec. 1, 2011.)

RULE 1005. COPIES OF PUBLIC RECORDS TO PROVE CONTENT

The proponent may use a copy to prove the content of an official record—or of a document that was recorded or filed in a public office as authorized by law—if these conditions are met: the record or document is otherwise admissible; and the copy is certified as correct in accordance with Rule 902(4) or is testified to be correct by a witness who has compared it with the original. If no such copy can be obtained by reasonable diligence, then the proponent may use other evidence to prove the content.

(Pub.L. 93–595, § 1, Jan. 2, 1975, 88 Stat. 1946; Apr. 26, 2011, eff. Dec. 1, 2011.)

RULE 1006. SUMMARIES TO PROVE CONTENT

The proponent may use a summary, chart, or calculation to prove the content of voluminous writings, recordings, or photographs that cannot be conveniently examined in court. The proponent must make the originals or duplicates available for examination or copying, or both, by other parties at a reasonable time and place. And the court may order the proponent to produce them in court.

(Pub.L. 93–595, § 1, Jan. 2, 1975, 88 Stat. 1946; Apr. 26, 2011, eff. Dec. 1, 2011.)

RULE 1007. TESTIMONY OR STATEMENT OF A PARTY TO PROVE CONTENT

The proponent may prove the content of a writing, recording, or photograph by the testimony, deposition, or written statement of the party against whom the evidence is offered. The proponent need not account for the original.

(Pub.L. 93–595, § 1, Jan. 2, 1975, 88 Stat. 1947; Mar. 2, 1987, eff. Oct. 1, 1987; Apr. 26, 2011, eff. Dec. 1, 2011.)

RULE 1008. FUNCTIONS OF THE COURT AND JURY

Ordinarily, the court determines whether the proponent has fulfilled the factual conditions for admitting other evidence of the content of a writing, recording, or photograph under Rule 1004 or 1005. But in a jury trial, the jury determines—in accordance with Rule 104(b)—any issue about whether:

(a) an asserted writing, recording, or photograph ever existed;

(b) another one produced at the trial or hearing is the original; or

(c) other evidence of content accurately reflects the content.

(Pub.L. 93–595, § 1, Jan. 2, 1975, 88 Stat. 1947; Apr. 26, 2011, eff. Dec. 1, 2011.)

ARTICLE XI. MISCELLANEOUS RULES

RULE 1101. APPLICABILITY OF THE RULES

(a) To Courts and Judges. These rules apply to proceedings before:

- United States district courts;
- United States bankruptcy and magistrate judges;
- United States courts of appeals;
- the United States Court of Federal Claims; and
- the district courts of Guam, the Virgin Islands, and the Northern Mariana Islands.

(b) To Cases and Proceedings. These rules apply in:

- civil cases and proceedings, including bankruptcy, admiralty, and maritime cases;
- criminal cases and proceedings; and
- contempt proceedings, except those in which the court may act summarily.

(c) Rules on Privilege. The rules on privilege apply to all stages of a case or proceeding.

(d) Exceptions. These rules—except for those on privilege—do not apply to the following:

(1) the court's determination, under Rule 104(a), on a preliminary question of fact governing admissibility;

(2) grand-jury proceedings; and

(3) miscellaneous proceedings such as:

- extradition or rendition;
- issuing an arrest warrant, criminal summons, or search warrant;
- a preliminary examination in a criminal case;
- sentencing;
- granting or revoking probation or supervised release; and
- considering whether to release on bail or otherwise.

(e) Other Statutes and Rules. A federal statute or a rule prescribed by the Supreme Court may provide for admitting or excluding evidence independently from these rules.

(Pub.L. 93–595, § 1, Jan. 2, 1975, 88 Stat. 1947; Pub.L. 94–149, § 1(14), Dec. 12, 1975, 89 Stat. 806; Pub.L. 95–598,

Title II, § 251, Nov. 6, 1978, 92 Stat. 2673; Pub.L. 97–164, Title I, § 142, Apr. 2, 1982, 96 Stat. 45; Mar. 2, 1987, eff. Oct. 1, 1987; Apr. 25, 1988, eff. Nov. 1, 1988; Pub.L. 100–690, Title VII, § 7075(c), Nov. 18, 1988, 102 Stat. 4405; Apr. 22, 1993, eff. Dec. 1, 1993; Apr. 26, 2011, eff. Dec. 1, 2011.)

RULE 1102. AMENDMENTS

These rules may be amended as provided in 28 U.S.C. § 2072.

(Pub.L. 93–595, § 1, Jan. 2, 1975, 88 Stat.1948; Apr. 30, 1991, eff. Dec. 1, 1991; Apr. 26, 2011, eff. Dec. 1, 2011.)

RULE 1103. TITLE

These rules may be cited as the Federal Rules of Evidence.

(Pub.L. 93–595, § 1, Jan. 2, 1975, 88 Stat.1948; Apr. 26, 2011, eff. Dec. 1, 2011.)

INDEX TO FEDERAL RULES OF EVIDENCE

*

FEDERAL RULES OF APPELLATE PROCEDURE

Effective July 1, 1968

Including Amendments Effective December 1, 2011

Research Note

These rules may be searched electronically on Westlaw in the US-RULES database; updates to these rules may be found on Westlaw in US-RULESPDATES. For search tips, and a detailed summary of database content, consult the Westlaw Scope Screen of each database.

TITLE I. APPLICABILITY OF RULES

RULE 1. SCOPE OF RULES; DEFINITION; TITLE

(a) Scope of Rules.

(1) These rules govern procedure in the United States courts of appeals.

(2) When these rules provide for filing a motion or other document in the district court, the procedure must comply with the practice of the district court.

(b) Definition. In these rules, "state" includes the District of Columbia and any United States commonwealth or territory.

(c) Title. These rules are to be known as the Federal Rules of Appellate Procedure.

(As amended Apr. 30, 1979, eff. Aug. 1, 1979; Apr. 25, 1989, eff. Dec. 1, 1989; Apr. 29, 1994, eff. Dec. 1, 1994; Apr. 24, 1998, eff. Dec. 1, 1998; Apr. 29, 2002, eff. Dec. 1, 2002; Apr. 28, 2010, eff. Dec. 1, 2010.)

RULE 2. SUSPENSION OF RULES

On its own or a party's motion, a court of appeals may—to expedite its decision or for other good cause—suspend any provision of these rules in a particular case and order proceedings as it directs, except as otherwise provided in Rule 26(b).

(As amended Apr. 24, 1998, eff. Dec. 1, 1998.)

TITLE II. APPEAL FROM A JUDGMENT OR ORDER OF A DISTRICT COURT

RULE 3. APPEAL AS OF RIGHT— HOW TAKEN

(a) Filing the Notice of Appeal.

(1) An appeal permitted by law as of right from a district court to a court of appeals may be taken only by filing a notice of appeal with the district clerk within the time allowed by Rule 4. At the time of filing, the appellant must furnish the clerk with enough copies of the notice to enable the clerk to comply with Rule 3(d).

(2) An appellant's failure to take any step other than the timely filing of a notice of appeal does not affect the validity of the appeal, but is ground only for the court of appeals to act as it considers appropriate, including dismissing the appeal.

(3) An appeal from a judgment by a magistrate judge in a civil case is taken in the same way as an appeal from any other district court judgment.

(4) An appeal by permission under 28 U.S.C. § 1292(b) or an appeal in a bankruptcy case may be taken only in the manner prescribed by Rules 5 and 6, respectively.

(b) Joint or Consolidated Appeals.

(1) When two or more parties are entitled to appeal from a district-court judgment or order, and their interests make joinder practicable, they may file a joint notice of appeal. They may then proceed on appeal as a single appellant.

(2) When the parties have filed separate timely notices of appeal, the appeals may be joined or consolidated by the court of appeals.

(c) Contents of the Notice of Appeal.

(1) The notice of appeal must:

(A) specify the party or parties taking the appeal by naming each one in the caption or body of the notice, but an attorney representing more than one party may describe those parties with such terms as "all plaintiffs," "the defendants," "the plaintiffs A, B, et al.," or "all defendants except X";

(B) designate the judgment, order, or part thereof being appealed; and

(C) name the court to which the appeal is taken.

(2) A pro se notice of appeal is considered filed on behalf of the signer and the signer's spouse and minor children (if they are parties), unless the notice clearly indicates otherwise.

(3) In a class action, whether or not the class has been certified, the notice of appeal is sufficient if it names one person qualified to bring the appeal as representative of the class.

(4) An appeal must not be dismissed for informality of form or title of the notice of appeal, or for failure to name a party whose intent to appeal is otherwise clear from the notice.

(5) Form 1 in the Appendix of Forms is a suggested form of a notice of appeal.

(d) Serving the Notice of Appeal.

(1) The district clerk must serve notice of the filing of a notice of appeal by mailing a copy to each party's counsel of record—excluding the appellant's—or, if a party is proceeding pro se, to the party's last known address. When a defendant in a criminal case appeals, the clerk must also serve a copy of the notice of appeal on the defendant, either by personal service or by mail addressed to the defendant. The clerk must promptly send a copy of the notice of appeal and of the docket entries—and any later docket entries—to the clerk of the court of appeals named in the notice. The district clerk must note, on each copy, the date when the notice of appeal was filed.

(2) If an inmate confined in an institution files a notice of appeal in the manner provided by Rule 4(c), the district clerk must also note the date when the clerk docketed the notice.

(3) The district clerk's failure to serve notice does not affect the validity of the appeal. The clerk must note on the docket the names of the parties to whom the clerk mails copies, with the date of mailing. Service is sufficient despite the death of a party or the party's counsel.

(e) Payment of Fees. Upon filing a notice of appeal, the appellant must pay the district clerk all required fees. The district clerk receives the appellate docket fee on behalf of the court of appeals.

(As amended Apr. 30, 1979, eff. Aug. 1, 1979; Mar. 10, 1986, eff. July 1, 1986; Apr. 25, 1989, eff. Dec. 1, 1989; Apr. 22, 1993, eff. Dec. 1, 1993; Apr. 29, 1994, eff. Dec. 1, 1994; Apr. 24, 1998, eff. Dec. 1, 1998.)

[RULE 3.1. APPEAL FROM A JUDGMENT OF A MAGISTRATE JUDGE IN A CIVIL CASE (Abrogated Apr. 24, 1998, eff. Dec. 1, 1998)]

RULE 4. APPEAL AS OF RIGHT— WHEN TAKEN

(a) Appeal in a Civil Case.

(1) **Time for Filing a Notice of Appeal.**

(A) In a civil case, except as provided in Rules 4(a)(1)(B), 4(a)(4), and 4(c), the notice of appeal required by Rule 3 must be filed with the district clerk within 30 days after entry of the judgment or order appealed from.

(B) The notice of appeal may be filed by any party within 60 days after entry of the judgment or order appealed from if one of the parties is:

(i) the United States;

(ii) a United States agency;

(iii) a United States officer or employee sued in an official capacity; or

(iv) a current or former United States officer or employee sued in an individual capacity for an act or omission occurring in connection with duties performed on the United States' behalf—including all instances in which the United States represents that person when the judgment or order is entered or files the appeal for that person.

(C) An appeal from an order granting or denying an application for a writ of error coram nobis is an appeal in a civil case for purposes of Rule 4(a).

(2) **Filing Before Entry of Judgment.** A notice of appeal filed after the court announces a decision or order—but before the entry of the judgment or order—is treated as filed on the date of and after the entry.

(3) **Multiple Appeals.** If one party timely files a notice of appeal, any other party may file a notice of appeal within 14 days after the date when the first notice was filed, or within the time otherwise prescribed by this Rule 4(a), whichever period ends later.

(4) **Effect of a Motion on a Notice of Appeal.**

(A) If a party timely files in the district court any of the following motions under the Federal Rules of Civil Procedure, the time to file an appeal runs for all parties from the entry of the order disposing of the last such remaining motion:

(i) for judgment under Rule 50(b);

(ii) to amend or make additional factual findings under Rule 52(b), whether or not granting the motion would alter the judgment;

(iii) for attorney's fees under Rule 54 if the district court extends the time to appeal under Rule 58;

(iv) to alter or amend the judgment under Rule 59;

(v) for a new trial under Rule 59; or

(vi) for relief under Rule 60 if the motion is filed no later than 28 days after the judgment is entered.

(B)(i) If a party files a notice of appeal after the court announces or enters a judgment—but before it disposes of any motion listed in Rule 4(a)(4)(A)—the notice becomes effective to appeal a judgment or order, in whole or in part, when the order disposing of the last such remaining motion is entered.

(ii) A party intending to challenge an order disposing of any motion listed in Rule 4(a)(4)(A), or a judgment's alteration or amendment upon such a motion, must file a notice of appeal, or an amended notice of appeal—in compliance with Rule 3(c)—within the time prescribed by this Rule measured from the entry of the order disposing of the last such remaining motion.

(iii) No additional fee is required to file an amended notice.

(5) Motion for Extension of Time.

(A) The district court may extend the time to file a notice of appeal if:

(i) a party so moves no later than 30 days after the time prescribed by this Rule 4(a) expires; and

(ii) regardless of whether its motion is filed before or during the 30 days after the time prescribed by this Rule 4(a) expires, that party shows excusable neglect or good cause.

(B) A motion filed before the expiration of the time prescribed in Rule 4(a)(1) or (3) may be ex parte unless the court requires otherwise. If the motion is filed after the expiration of the prescribed time, notice must be given to the other parties in accordance with local rules.

(C) No extension under this Rule 4(a)(5) may exceed 30 days after the prescribed time or 14 days after the date when the order granting the motion is entered, whichever is later.

(6) Reopening the Time to File an Appeal. The district court may reopen the time to file an appeal for a period of 14 days after the date when its order to reopen is entered, but only if all the following conditions are satisfied:

(A) the court finds that the moving party did not receive notice under Federal Rule of Civil Procedure 77(d) of the entry of the judgment or order sought to be appealed within 21 days after entry;

(B) the motion is filed within 180 days after the judgment or order is entered or within 14 days after the moving party receives notice under Federal Rule of Civil Procedure 77(d) of the entry, whichever is earlier; and

(C) the court finds that no party would be prejudiced.

(7) Entry Defined.

(A) A judgment or order is entered for purposes of this Rule 4(a):

(i) if Federal Rule of Civil Procedure 58(a) does not require a separate document, when the judgment or order is entered in the civil docket under Federal Rule of Civil Procedure 79(a); or

(ii) if Federal Rule of Civil Procedure 58(a) requires a separate document, when the judgment or order is entered in the civil docket under Federal Rule of Civil Procedure 79(a) and when the earlier of these events occurs:

• the judgment or order is set forth on a separate document, or

• 150 days have run from entry of the judgment or order in the civil docket under Federal Rule of Civil Procedure 79(a).

(B) A failure to set forth a judgment or order on a separate document when required by Federal Rule of Civil Procedure 58(a) does not affect the validity of an appeal from that judgment or order.

(b) Appeal in a Criminal Case.

(1) Time for Filing a Notice of Appeal.

(A) In a criminal case, a defendant's notice of appeal must be filed in the district court within 14 days after the later of:

(i) the entry of either the judgment or the order being appealed; or

(ii) the filing of the government's notice of appeal.

(B) When the government is entitled to appeal, its notice of appeal must be filed in the district court within 30 days after the later of:

(i) the entry of the judgment or order being appealed; or

(ii) the filing of a notice of appeal by any defendant.

(2) Filing Before Entry of Judgment. A notice of appeal filed after the court announces a decision, sentence, or order—but before the entry of the judgment or order—is treated as filed on the date of and after the entry.

(3) Effect of a Motion on a Notice of Appeal.

(A) If a defendant timely makes any of the following motions under the Federal Rules of Criminal Procedure, the notice of appeal from a judgment of conviction must be filed within 14 days after the entry of the order disposing of the last such remaining motion, or within 14 days after the entry of the judgment of conviction, whichever period ends later. This provision applies to a timely motion:

(i) for judgment of acquittal under Rule 29;

(ii) for a new trial under Rule 33, but if based on newly discovered evidence, only if the motion is made no later than 14 days after the entry of the judgment; or

(iii) for arrest of judgment under Rule 34.

(B) A notice of appeal filed after the court announces a decision, sentence, or order—but before it disposes of any of the motions referred to in Rule 4(b)(3)(A)—becomes effective upon the later of the following:

(i) the entry of the order disposing of the last such remaining motion; or

(ii) the entry of the judgment of conviction.

(C) A valid notice of appeal is effective—without amendment—to appeal from an order disposing of any of the motions referred to in Rule 4(b)(3)(A).

(4) **Motion for Extension of Time.** Upon a finding of excusable neglect or good cause, the district court may—before or after the time has expired, with or without motion and notice—extend the time to file a notice of appeal for a period not to exceed 30 days from the expiration of the time otherwise prescribed by this Rule 4(b).

(5) **Jurisdiction.** The filing of a notice of appeal under this Rule 4(b) does not divest a district court of jurisdiction to correct a sentence under Federal Rule of Criminal Procedure 35(a), nor does the filing of a motion under 35(a) affect the validity of a notice of appeal filed before entry of the order disposing of the motion. The filing of a motion under Federal Rule of Criminal Procedure 35(a) does not suspend the time for filing a notice of appeal from a judgment of conviction.

(6) **Entry Defined.** A judgment or order is entered for purposes of this Rule 4(b) when it is entered on the criminal docket.

(c) **Appeal by an Inmate Confined in an Institution.**

(1) If an inmate confined in an institution files a notice of appeal in either a civil or a criminal case, the notice is timely if it is deposited in the institution's internal mail system on or before the last day for filing. If an institution has a system designed for legal mail, the inmate must use that system to receive the benefit of this rule. Timely filing may be shown by a declaration in compliance with 28 U.S.C. § 1746 or by a notarized statement, either of which must set forth the date of deposit and state that first-class postage has been prepaid.

(2) If an inmate files the first notice of appeal in a civil case under this Rule 4(c), the 14–day period provided in Rule 4(a)(3) for another party to file a notice of appeal runs from the date when the district court dockets the first notice.

(3) When a defendant in a criminal case files a notice of appeal under this Rule 4(c), the 30–day period for the government to file its notice of appeal runs from the entry of the judgment or order appealed from or from the district court's docketing of the defendant's notice of appeal, whichever is later.

(d) **Mistaken Filing in the Court of Appeals.** If a notice of appeal in either a civil or a criminal case is mistakenly filed in the court of appeals, the clerk of that court must note on the notice the date when it was received and send it to the district clerk. The notice is then considered filed in the district court on the date so noted.

(As amended Apr. 30, 1979, eff. Aug. 1, 1979; Nov. 18, 1988, Pub.L. 100–690, Title VII, § 7111, 102 Stat. 4419; Apr. 30, 1991, eff. Dec. 1, 1991; Apr. 22, 1993, eff. Dec. 1, 1993; Apr. 27, 1995, eff. Dec. 1, 1995; Apr. 24, 1998, eff. Dec. 1, 1998; Apr. 29, 2002, eff. Dec. 1, 2002; Apr. 25, 2005, eff. Dec. 1, 2005; Mar. 26, 2009, eff. Dec. 1, 2009; Apr. 28, 2010, eff. Dec. 1, 2010; Apr. 26, 2011, eff. Dec. 1, 2011.)

RULE 5. APPEAL BY PERMISSION

(a) Petition for Permission to Appeal.

(1) To request permission to appeal when an appeal is within the court of appeals' discretion, a party must file a petition for permission to appeal. The petition must be filed with the circuit clerk with proof of service on all other parties to the district-court action.

(2) The petition must be filed within the time specified by the statute or rule authorizing the appeal or, if no such time is specified, within the time provided by Rule 4(a) for filing a notice of appeal.

(3) If a party cannot petition for appeal unless the district court first enters an order granting permission to do so or stating that the necessary conditions are met, the district court may amend its order, either on its own or in response to a party's motion, to include the required permission or statement. In that event, the time to petition runs from entry of the amended order.

(b) Contents of the Petition; Answer or Cross–Petition; Oral Argument.

(1) The petition must include the following:

(A) the facts necessary to understand the question presented;

(B) the question itself;

(C) the relief sought;

(D) the reasons why the appeal should be allowed and is authorized by a statute or rule; and

(E) an attached copy of:

(i) the order, decree, or judgment complained of and any related opinion or memorandum, and

(ii) any order stating the district court's permission to appeal or finding that the necessary conditions are met.

(2) A party may file an answer in opposition or a cross-petition within 10 days after the petition is served.

(3) The petition and answer will be submitted without oral argument unless the court of appeals orders otherwise.

(c) Form of Papers; Number of Copies. All papers must conform to Rule 32(c)(2). Except by the court's permission, a paper must not exceed 20 pages, exclusive of the disclosure statement, the proof of service, and the accompanying documents required by Rule 5(b)(1)(E). An original and 3 copies must be filed unless the court requires a different number by local rule or by order in a particular case.

(d) Grant of Permission; Fees; Cost Bond; Filing the Record.

(1) Within 14 days after the entry of the order granting permission to appeal, the appellant must:

(A) pay the district clerk all required fees; and

(B) file a cost bond if required under Rule 7.

(2) A notice of appeal need not be filed. The date when the order granting permission to appeal is entered serves as the date of the notice of appeal for calculating time under these rules.

(3) The district clerk must notify the circuit clerk once the petitioner has paid the fees. Upon receiving this notice, the circuit clerk must enter the appeal on the docket. The record must be forwarded and filed in accordance with Rules 11 and 12(c).

(As amended Apr. 30, 1979, eff. Aug. 1, 1979; Apr. 29, 1994, eff. Dec. 1, 1994; Apr. 24, 1998, eff. Dec. 1, 1998; Apr. 29, 2002, eff. Dec. 1, 2002; Mar. 26, 2009, eff. Dec. 1, 2009.)

[RULE 5.1. APPEAL BY LEAVE UNDER 28 U.S.C. § 636(c)(5) (Abrogated Apr. 24, 1998, eff. Dec. 1, 1998)]

RULE 6. APPEAL IN A BANKRUPTCY CASE FROM A FINAL JUDGMENT, ORDER, OR DECREE OF A DISTRICT COURT OR BANKRUPTCY APPELLATE PANEL

(a) Appeal From a Judgment, Order, or Decree of a District Court Exercising Original Jurisdiction in a Bankruptcy Case. An appeal to a court of appeals from a final judgment, order, or decree of a district court exercising jurisdiction under 28 U.S.C. § 1334 is taken as any other civil appeal under these rules.

(b) Appeal From a Judgment, Order, or Decree of a District Court or Bankruptcy Appellate Panel Exercising Appellate Jurisdiction in a Bankruptcy Case.

(1) Applicability of Other Rules. These rules apply to an appeal to a court of appeals under 28 U.S.C. § 158(d) from a final judgment, order, or decree of a district court or bankruptcy appellate panel exercising appellate jurisdiction under 28 U.S.C. § 158(a) or (b). But there are 3 exceptions:

(A) Rules 4(a)(4), 4(b), 9, 10, 11, 12(b), 13–20, 22–23, and 24(b) do not apply;

(B) the reference in Rule 3(c) to "Form 1 in the Appendix of Forms" must be read as a reference to Form 5; and

(C) when the appeal is from a bankruptcy appellate panel, the term "district court," as used in any applicable rule, means "appellate panel."

(2) Additional Rules. In addition to the rules made applicable by Rule 6(b)(1), the following rules apply:

(A) Motion for rehearing.

(i) If a timely motion for rehearing under Bankruptcy Rule 8015 is filed, the time to appeal for all parties runs from the entry of the order disposing of the motion. A notice of appeal filed after the district court or bankruptcy appellate panel announces or enters a judgment, order, or decree—but before disposition of the motion for rehearing—becomes effective when the order disposing of the motion for rehearing is entered.

(ii) Appellate review of the order disposing of the motion requires the party, in compliance with Rules 3(c) and 6(b)(1)(B), to amend a previously filed notice of appeal. A party intending to challenge an altered or amended judgment, order, or decree must file a notice of appeal or amended notice of appeal within the time prescribed by Rule 4—excluding Rules 4(a)(4) and 4(b)—measured from the entry of the order disposing of the motion.

(iii) No additional fee is required to file an amended notice.

(B) The record on appeal.

(i) Within 14 days after filing the notice of appeal, the appellant must file with the clerk possessing the record assembled in accordance with Bankruptcy Rule 8006—and serve on the appellee—a statement of the issues to be presented on appeal and a designation of the record to be certified and sent to the circuit clerk.

(ii) An appellee who believes that other parts of the record are necessary must, within 14 days after being served with the appellant's designation, file with the clerk and serve on the appellant a designation of additional parts to be included.

(iii) The record on appeal consists of:

• the redesignated record as provided above;

• the proceedings in the district court or bankruptcy appellate panel; and

• a certified copy of the docket entries prepared by the clerk under Rule 3(d).

(C) Forwarding the record.

(i) When the record is complete, the district clerk or bankruptcy appellate panel clerk must number the documents constituting the record and send them promptly to the circuit clerk together with a list of the documents correspondingly numbered and reasonably identified. Unless directed to do so by a party or the circuit clerk, the clerk will not send to the court of appeals documents of unusual bulk or weight, physical exhibits other than documents, or other parts of the record designated for omission by local rule of the court of appeals. If the exhibits are unusually bulky or heavy, a party must arrange with the clerks in advance for their transportation and receipt.

(ii) All parties must do whatever else is necessary to enable the clerk to assemble and forward the record. The court of appeals may provide by rule or order that a certified copy of the docket entries be sent in place of the redesignated record, but any party may request at any time during the pendency of the appeal that the redesignated record be sent.

(D) Filing the record. Upon receiving the record—or a certified copy of the docket entries sent in place of the redesignated record—the circuit clerk must file it and immediately notify all parties of the filing date.

(Added Apr. 25, 1989, eff. Dec. 1, 1989, and amended Apr. 30, 1991, eff. Dec. 1, 1991; Apr. 22, 1993, eff. Dec. 1, 1993; Apr. 24, 1998, eff. Dec. 1, 1998; Mar. 26, 2009, eff. Dec. 1, 2009.)

RULE 7. BOND FOR COSTS ON APPEAL IN A CIVIL CASE

In a civil case, the district court may require an appellant to file a bond or provide other security in any form and amount necessary to ensure payment of costs on appeal. Rule 8(b) applies to a surety on a bond given under this rule.

(As amended Apr. 30, 1979, eff. Aug. 1, 1979; Apr. 24, 1998, eff. Dec. 1, 1998.)

RULE 8. STAY OR INJUNCTION PENDING APPEAL

(a) Motion for Stay.

(1) Initial Motion in the District Court. A party must ordinarily move first in the district court for the following relief:

(A) a stay of the judgment or order of a district court pending appeal;

(B) approval of a supersedeas bond; or

(C) an order suspending, modifying, restoring, or granting an injunction while an appeal is pending.

(2) Motion in the Court of Appeals; Conditions on Relief. A motion for the relief mentioned in Rule 8(a)(1) may be made to the court of appeals or to one of its judges.

(A) The motion must:

(i) show that moving first in the district court would be impracticable; or

(ii) state that, a motion having been made, the district court denied the motion or failed to afford the relief requested and state any reasons given by the district court for its action.

(B) The motion must also include:

(i) the reasons for granting the relief requested and the facts relied on;

(ii) originals or copies of affidavits or other sworn statements supporting facts subject to dispute; and

(iii) relevant parts of the record.

(C) The moving party must give reasonable notice of the motion to all parties.

(D) A motion under this Rule 8(a)(2) must be filed with the circuit clerk and normally will be considered by a panel of the court. But in an exceptional case in which time requirements make that procedure impracticable, the motion may be made to and considered by a single judge.

(E) The court may condition relief on a party's filing a bond or other appropriate security in the district court.

(b) Proceeding Against a Surety. If a party gives security in the form of a bond or stipulation or other undertaking with one or more sureties, each surety submits to the jurisdiction of the district court and irrevocably appoints the district clerk as the surety's agent on whom any papers affecting the surety's liability on the bond or undertaking may be served. On motion, a surety's liability may be enforced in the district court without the necessity of an independent action. The motion and any notice that the district court prescribes may be served on the district clerk, who must promptly mail a copy to each surety whose address is known.

(c) Stay in a Criminal Case. Rule 38 of the Federal Rules of Criminal Procedure governs a stay in a criminal case.

(As amended Mar. 10, 1986, eff. July 1, 1986; Apr. 27, 1995, eff. Dec. 1, 1995; Apr. 24, 1998, eff. Dec. 1, 1998.)

RULE 9. RELEASE IN A CRIMINAL CASE

(a) Release Before Judgment of Conviction.

(1) The district court must state in writing, or orally on the record, the reasons for an order regarding the release or detention of a defendant in a criminal case. A party appealing from the order must file with the court of appeals a copy of the district court's order and the court's statement of reasons as soon as practicable after filing the notice of appeal. An appellant who questions the factual basis for the district court's order must file a transcript of the release proceedings or an explanation of why a transcript was not obtained.

(2) After reasonable notice to the appellee, the court of appeals must promptly determine the appeal on the basis of the papers, affidavits, and parts of the record that the parties present or the court requires. Unless the court so orders, briefs need not be filed.

(3) The court of appeals or one of its judges may order the defendant's release pending the disposition of the appeal.

(b) Release After Judgment of Conviction. A party entitled to do so may obtain review of a district-court order regarding release after a judgment of conviction by filing a notice of appeal from that order in the district court, or by filing a motion in the court of appeals if the party has already filed a notice of appeal from the judgment of conviction. Both the order and the review are subject to Rule 9(a). The papers filed by the party seeking review must include a copy of the judgment of conviction.

(c) Criteria for Release. The court must make its decision regarding release in accordance with the applicable provisions of 18 U.S.C. §§ 3142, 3143, and 3145(c).

(As amended Apr. 24, 1972, eff. Oct. 1, 1972; Oct. 12, 1984, Pub.L. 98–473, Title II, § 210, 98 Stat. 1987; Apr. 29, 1994, eff. Dec. 1, 1994; Apr. 24, 1998, eff. Dec. 1, 1998.)

RULE 10. THE RECORD ON APPEAL

(a) Composition of the Record on Appeal. The following items constitute the record on appeal:

(1) the original papers and exhibits filed in the district court;

(2) the transcript of proceedings, if any; and

(3) a certified copy of the docket entries prepared by the district clerk.

(b) The Transcript of Proceedings.

(1) **Appellant's Duty to Order.** Within 14 days after filing the notice of appeal or entry of an order disposing of the last timely remaining motion of a type specified in Rule 4(a)(4)(A), whichever is later, the appellant must do either of the following:

(A) order from the reporter a transcript of such parts of the proceedings not already on file as the appellant considers necessary, subject to a local rule of the court of appeals and with the following qualifications:

(i) the order must be in writing;

(ii) if the cost of the transcript is to be paid by the United States under the Criminal Justice Act, the order must so state; and

(iii) the appellant must, within the same period, file a copy of the order with the district clerk; or

(B) file a certificate stating that no transcript will be ordered.

(2) **Unsupported Finding or Conclusion.** If the appellant intends to urge on appeal that a finding or conclusion is unsupported by the evidence or is contrary to the evidence, the appellant must include in the record a transcript of all evidence relevant to that finding or conclusion.

(3) **Partial Transcript.** Unless the entire transcript is ordered:

(A) the appellant must—within the 14 days provided in Rule 10(b)(1)—file a statement of the issues that the appellant intends to present on the appeal and must serve on the appellee a copy of both the order or certificate and the statement;

(B) if the appellee considers it necessary to have a transcript of other parts of the proceedings, the appellee must, within 14 days after the service of the order or certificate and the statement of the issues, file and serve on the appellant a designation of additional parts to be ordered; and

(C) unless within 14 days after service of that designation the appellant has ordered all such parts, and has so notified the appellee, the appellee may within the following 14 days either order the parts or move in the district court for an order requiring the appellant to do so.

(4) Payment. At the time of ordering, a party must make satisfactory arrangements with the reporter for paying the cost of the transcript.

(c) Statement of the Evidence When the Proceedings Were Not Recorded or When a Transcript Is Unavailable. If the transcript of a hearing or trial is unavailable, the appellant may prepare a statement of the evidence or proceedings from the best available means, including the appellant's recollection. The statement must be served on the appellee, who may serve objections or proposed amendments within 14 days after being served. The statement and any objections or proposed amendments must then be submitted to the district court for settlement and approval. As settled and approved, the statement must be included by the district clerk in the record on appeal.

(d) Agreed Statement as the Record on Appeal. In place of the record on appeal as defined in Rule 10(a), the parties may prepare, sign, and submit to the district court a statement of the case showing how the issues presented by the appeal arose and were decided in the district court. The statement must set forth only those facts averred and proved or sought to be proved that are essential to the court's resolution of the issues. If the statement is truthful, it—together with any additions that the district court may consider necessary to a full presentation of the issues on appeal—must be approved by the district court and must then be certified to the court of appeals as the record on appeal. The district clerk must then send it to the circuit clerk within the time provided by Rule 11. A copy of the agreed statement may be filed in place of the appendix required by Rule 30.

(e) Correction or Modification of the Record.

(1) If any difference arises about whether the record truly discloses what occurred in the district court, the difference must be submitted to and settled by that court and the record conformed accordingly.

(2) If anything material to either party is omitted from or misstated in the record by error or accident, the omission or misstatement may be corrected and a supplemental record may be certified and forwarded:

(A) on stipulation of the parties;

(B) by the district court before or after the record has been forwarded; or

(C) by the court of appeals.

(3) All other questions as to the form and content of the record must be presented to the court of appeals.

(As amended Apr. 30, 1979, eff. Aug. 1, 1979; Mar. 10, 1986, eff. July 1, 1986; Apr. 30, 1991, eff. Dec. 1, 1991; Apr. 22, 1993, eff. Dec. 1, 1993; Apr. 27, 1995, eff. Dec. 1, 1995; Apr. 24, 1998, eff. Dec. 1, 1998; Mar. 26, 2009, eff. Dec. 1, 2009.)

RULE 11. FORWARDING THE RECORD

(a) Appellant's Duty. An appellant filing a notice of appeal must comply with Rule 10(b) and must do whatever else is necessary to enable the clerk to assemble and forward the record. If there are multiple appeals from a judgment or order, the clerk must forward a single record.

(b) Duties of Reporter and District Clerk.

(1) Reporter's Duty to Prepare and File a Transcript. The reporter must prepare and file a transcript as follows:

(A) Upon receiving an order for a transcript, the reporter must enter at the foot of the order the date of its receipt and the expected completion date and send a copy, so endorsed, to the circuit clerk.

(B) If the transcript cannot be completed within 30 days of the reporter's receipt of the order, the reporter may request the circuit clerk to grant additional time to complete it. The clerk must note on the docket the action taken and notify the parties.

(C) When a transcript is complete, the reporter must file it with the district clerk and notify the circuit clerk of the filing.

(D) If the reporter fails to file the transcript on time, the circuit clerk must notify the district judge and do whatever else the court of appeals directs.

(2) District Clerk's Duty to Forward. When the record is complete, the district clerk must number the documents constituting the record and send them promptly to the circuit clerk together with a list of the documents correspondingly numbered and reasonably identified. Unless directed to do so by a party or the circuit clerk, the district clerk will not send to the court of appeals documents of unusual bulk or weight, physical exhibits other than documents, or other parts of the record designated for omission by local rule of the court of appeals. If the exhibits are unusually bulky or heavy, a party must arrange with the clerks in advance for their transportation and receipt.

(c) Retaining the Record Temporarily in the District Court for Use in Preparing the Appeal. The parties may stipulate, or the district court on motion may order, that the district clerk retain the record temporarily for the parties to use in preparing the papers on appeal. In that event the district clerk must certify to the circuit clerk that the record on appeal is complete. Upon receipt of the appellee's brief, or earlier if the court orders or the parties agree, the appellant must request the district clerk to forward the record.

(d) [Abrogated.]

(e) Retaining the Record by Court Order.

(1) The court of appeals may, by order or local rule, provide that a certified copy of the docket entries be forwarded instead of the entire record. But a party may at any time during the appeal request that designated parts of the record be forwarded.

(2) The district court may order the record or some part of it retained if the court needs it while the appeal is pending, subject, however, to call by the court of appeals.

(3) If part or all of the record is ordered retained, the district clerk must send to the court of appeals a copy of the order and the docket entries together with the parts of the original record allowed by the district court and copies of any parts of the record designated by the parties.

(f) Retaining Parts of the Record in the District Court by Stipulation of the Parties. The parties may agree by written stipulation filed in the district court that designated parts of the record be retained in the district court subject to call by the court of appeals or request by a party. The parts of the record so designated remain a part of the record on appeal.

(g) Record for a Preliminary Motion in the Court of Appeals. If, before the record is forwarded, a party makes any of the following motions in the court of appeals:

- for dismissal;
- for release;
- for a stay pending appeal;
- for additional security on the bond on appeal or on a supersedeas bond; or
- for any other intermediate order—

the district clerk must send the court of appeals any parts of the record designated by any party.

(As amended Apr. 30, 1979, eff. Aug. 1, 1979; Mar. 10, 1986, eff. July 1, 1986; Apr. 24, 1998, eff. Dec. 1, 1998.)

RULE 12. DOCKETING THE APPEAL; FILING A REPRESENTATION STATEMENT; FILING THE RECORD

(a) Docketing the Appeal. Upon receiving the copy of the notice of appeal and the docket entries from the district clerk under Rule 3(d), the circuit clerk must docket the appeal under the title of the district-court action and must identify the appellant, adding the appellant's name if necessary.

(b) Filing a Representation Statement. Unless the court of appeals designates another time, the attorney who filed the notice of appeal must, within 14 days after filing the notice, file a statement with the circuit clerk naming the parties that the attorney represents on appeal.

(c) Filing the Record, Partial Record, or Certificate. Upon receiving the record, partial record, or district clerk's certificate as provided in Rule 11, the circuit clerk must file it and immediately notify all parties of the filing date.

(As amended Apr. 30, 1979, eff. Aug. 1, 1979; Mar. 10, 1986, eff. July 1, 1986; Apr. 22, 1993, eff. Dec. 1, 1993; Apr. 24, 1998, eff. Dec. 1, 1998; Mar. 26, 2009, eff. Dec. 1, 2009.)

RULE 12.1. REMAND AFTER AN INDICATIVE RULING BY THE DISTRICT COURT ON A MOTION FOR RELIEF THAT IS BARRED BY A PENDING APPEAL

(a) Notice to the Court of Appeals. If a timely motion is made in the district court for relief that it lacks authority to grant because of an appeal that has been docketed and is pending, the movant must promptly notify the circuit clerk if the district court states either that it would grant the motion or that the motion raises a substantial issue.

(b) Remand After an Indicative Ruling. If the district court states that it would grant the motion or that the motion raises a substantial issue, the court of appeals may remand for further proceedings but retains jurisdiction unless it expressly dismisses the appeal. If the court of appeals remands but retains jurisdiction, the parties must promptly notify the circuit clerk when the district court has decided the motion on remand.

(Added Mar. 26, 2009, eff. Dec. 1, 2009.)

TITLE III. REVIEW OF A DECISION OF THE UNITED STATES TAX COURT

RULE 13. REVIEW OF A DECISION OF THE TAX COURT

(a) How Obtained; Time for Filing Notice of Appeal.

(1) Review of a decision of the United States Tax Court is commenced by filing a notice of appeal with the Tax Court clerk within 90 days after the entry of the Tax Court's decision. At the time of filing, the appellant must furnish the clerk with enough copies of the notice to enable the clerk to comply with Rule 3(d). If one party files a timely notice of appeal, any other party may file a notice of appeal within 120 days after the Tax Court's decision is entered.

(2) If, under Tax Court rules, a party makes a timely motion to vacate or revise the Tax Court's decision, the time to file a notice of appeal runs from the entry of the order disposing of the motion or from the entry of a new decision, whichever is later.

(b) Notice of Appeal; How Filed. The notice of appeal may be filed either at the Tax Court clerk's office in the District of Columbia or by mail addressed to the clerk. If sent by mail the notice is considered filed on the postmark date, subject to § 7502 of the Internal Revenue Code, as amended, and the applicable regulations.

(c) Contents of the Notice of Appeal; Service; Effect of Filing and Service. Rule 3 prescribes the contents of a notice of appeal, the manner of service, and the effect of its filing and service. Form 2 in the Appendix of Forms is a suggested form of a notice of appeal.

(d) The Record on Appeal; Forwarding; Filing.

(1) An appeal from the Tax Court is governed by the parts of Rules 10, 11, and 12 regarding the record on appeal from a district court, the time and manner of forwarding and filing, and the docketing in the court of appeals. References in those rules and in Rule 3 to the district court and district clerk are to be read as referring to the Tax Court and its clerk.

(2) If an appeal from a Tax Court decision is taken to more than one court of appeals, the original record must be sent to the court named in the first notice of appeal filed. In an appeal to any other court of appeals, the appellant must apply to that other court to make provision for the record.

(As amended Apr. 30, 1979, eff. Aug. 1, 1979; Apr. 29, 1994, eff. Dec. 1, 1994; Apr. 24, 1998, eff. Dec. 1, 1998.)

RULE 14. APPLICABILITY OF OTHER RULES TO THE REVIEW OF A TAX COURT DECISION

All provisions of these rules, except Rules 4–9, 15–20, and 22–23, apply to the review of a Tax Court decision.

(As amended Apr. 24, 1998, eff. Dec. 1, 1998.)

TITLE IV. REVIEW OR ENFORCEMENT OF AN ORDER OF AN ADMINISTRATIVE AGENCY, BOARD, COMMISSION, OR OFFICER

RULE 15. REVIEW OR ENFORCEMENT OF AN AGENCY ORDER—HOW OBTAINED; INTERVENTION

(a) Petition for Review; Joint Petition.

(1) Review of an agency order is commenced by filing, within the time prescribed by law, a petition for review with the clerk of a court of appeals authorized to review the agency order. If their interests make joinder practicable, two or more persons may join in a petition to the same court to review the same order.

(2) The petition must:

   (A) name each party seeking review either in the caption or the body of the petition—using such terms as "et al.," "petitioners," or "respondents" does not effectively name the parties;

   (B) name the agency as a respondent (even though not named in the petition, the United States is a respondent if required by statute); and

   (C) specify the order or part thereof to be reviewed.

(3) Form 3 in the Appendix of Forms is a suggested form of a petition for review.

(4) In this rule "agency" includes an agency, board, commission, or officer; "petition for review" includes a petition to enjoin, suspend, modify, or otherwise review, or a notice of appeal, whichever form is indicated by the applicable statute.

(b) Application or Cross–Application to Enforce an Order; Answer; Default.

(1) An application to enforce an agency order must be filed with the clerk of a court of appeals authorized to enforce the order. If a petition is filed to review an agency order that the court may enforce, a party opposing the petition may file a cross-application for enforcement.

(2) Within 21 days after the application for enforcement is filed, the respondent must serve on the applicant an answer to the application and file it with the clerk. If the respondent fails to answer in time, the court will enter judgment for the relief requested.

(3) The application must contain a concise statement of the proceedings in which the order was entered, the facts upon which venue is based, and the relief requested.

(c) Service of the Petition or Application. The circuit clerk must serve a copy of the petition for review, or an application or cross-application to enforce an agency order, on each respondent as prescribed by Rule 3(d), unless a different manner of service is prescribed by statute. At the time of filing, the petitioner must:

(1) serve, or have served, a copy on each party admitted to participate in the agency proceedings, except for the respondents;

(2) file with the clerk a list of those so served; and

(3) give the clerk enough copies of the petition or application to serve each respondent.

(d) Intervention. Unless a statute provides another method, a person who wants to intervene in a proceeding under this rule must file a motion for leave to intervene with the circuit clerk and serve a copy on all parties. The motion—or other notice of intervention authorized by statute—must be filed within 30 days after the petition for review is filed and must contain a concise statement of the interest of the moving party and the grounds for intervention.

(e) Payment of Fees. When filing any separate or joint petition for review in a court of appeals, the petitioner must pay the circuit clerk all required fees.

(As amended Apr. 22, 1993, eff. Dec. 1, 1993; Apr. 24, 1998, eff. Dec. 1, 1998; Mar. 26, 2009, eff. Dec. 1, 2009.)

RULE 15.1. BRIEFS AND ORAL ARGUMENT IN A NATIONAL LABOR RELATIONS BOARD PROCEEDING

In either an enforcement or a review proceeding, a party adverse to the National Labor Relations Board proceeds first on briefing and at oral argument, unless the court orders otherwise.

(Added Mar. 10, 1986, eff. July 1, 1986, and amended Apr. 24, 1998, eff. Dec. 1, 1998.)

RULE 16. THE RECORD ON REVIEW OR ENFORCEMENT

(a) Composition of the Record. The record on review or enforcement of an agency order consists of:

(1) the order involved;

(2) any findings or report on which it is based; and

(3) the pleadings, evidence, and other parts of the proceedings before the agency.

(b) Omissions From or Misstatements in the Record. The parties may at any time, by stipulation, supply any omission from the record or correct a misstatement, or the court may so direct. If necessary, the court may direct that a supplemental record be prepared and filed.

(As amended Apr. 24, 1998, eff. Dec. 1, 1998.)

RULE 17. FILING THE RECORD

(a) Agency to File; Time for Filing; Notice of Filing. The agency must file the record with the circuit clerk within 40 days after being served with a petition for review, unless the statute authorizing review provides otherwise, or within 40 days after it files an application for enforcement unless the respondent fails to answer or the court orders otherwise. The court may shorten or extend the time to file the record. The clerk must notify all parties of the date when the record is filed.

(b) Filing—What Constitutes.

(1) The agency must file:

(A) the original or a certified copy of the entire record or parts designated by the parties; or

(B) a certified list adequately describing all documents, transcripts of testimony, exhibits, and other material constituting the record, or describing those parts designated by the parties.

(2) The parties may stipulate in writing that no record or certified list be filed. The date when the stipulation is filed with the circuit clerk is treated as the date when the record is filed.

(3) The agency must retain any portion of the record not filed with the clerk. All parts of the record retained by the agency are a part of the record on review for all purposes and, if the court or a party so requests, must be sent to the court regardless of any prior stipulation.

(As amended Apr. 24, 1998, eff. Dec. 1, 1998.)

RULE 18. STAY PENDING REVIEW

(a) Motion for a Stay.

(1) Initial Motion Before the Agency. A petitioner must ordinarily move first before the agency for a stay pending review of its decision or order.

(2) Motion in the Court of Appeals. A motion for a stay may be made to the court of appeals or one of its judges.

(A) The motion must:

(i) show that moving first before the agency would be impracticable; or

(ii) state that, a motion having been made, the agency denied the motion or failed to afford the relief requested and state any reasons given by the agency for its action.

(B) The motion must also include:

(i) the reasons for granting the relief requested and the facts relied on;

(ii) originals or copies of affidavits or other sworn statements supporting facts subject to dispute; and

(iii) relevant parts of the record.

(C) The moving party must give reasonable notice of the motion to all parties.

(D) The motion must be filed with the circuit clerk and normally will be considered by a panel of the court. But in an exceptional case in which time requirements make that procedure impracticable, the motion may be made to and considered by a single judge.

(b) Bond. The court may condition relief on the filing of a bond or other appropriate security.

(As amended Apr. 24, 1998, eff. Dec. 1, 1998.)

RULE 19. SETTLEMENT OF A JUDGMENT ENFORCING AN AGENCY ORDER IN PART

When the court files an opinion directing entry of judgment enforcing the agency's order in part, the agency must within 14 days file with the clerk and serve on each other party a proposed judgment conforming to the opinion. A party who disagrees with the agency's proposed judgment must within 10 days file with the clerk and serve the agency with a proposed judgment that the party believes conforms to the opinion. The court will settle the judgment and direct entry without further hearing or argument.

(As amended Mar. 10, 1986, eff. July 1, 1986; Apr. 24, 1998, eff. Dec. 1, 1998; Mar. 26, 2009, eff. Dec. 1, 2009.)

RULE 20. APPLICABILITY OF RULES TO THE REVIEW OR ENFORCEMENT OF AN AGENCY ORDER

All provisions of these rules, except Rules 3–14 and 22–23, apply to the review or enforcement of an agency order. In these rules, "appellant" includes a petitioner or applicant, and "appellee" includes a respondent.

(As amended Apr. 24, 1998, eff. Dec. 1, 1998.)

TITLE V. EXTRAORDINARY WRITS

RULE 21. WRITS OF MANDAMUS AND PROHIBITION, AND OTHER EXTRAORDINARY WRITS

(a) Mandamus or Prohibition to a Court: Petition, Filing, Service, and Docketing.

(1) A party petitioning for a writ of mandamus or prohibition directed to a court must file a petition with the circuit clerk with proof of service on all parties to the proceeding in the trial court. The party must also provide a copy to the trial-court judge. All parties to the proceeding in the trial court other than the petitioner are respondents for all purposes.

(2)(A) The petition must be titled "In re [name of petitioner]."

(B) The petition must state:

(i) the relief sought;

(ii) the issues presented;

(iii) the facts necessary to understand the issue presented by the petition; and

(iv) the reasons why the writ should issue.

(C) The petition must include a copy of any order or opinion or parts of the record that may be essential to understand the matters set forth in the petition.

(3) Upon receiving the prescribed docket fee, the clerk must docket the petition and submit it to the court.

(b) Denial; Order Directing Answer; Briefs; Precedence.

(1) The court may deny the petition without an answer. Otherwise, it must order the respondent, if any, to answer within a fixed time.

(2) The clerk must serve the order to respond on all persons directed to respond.

(3) Two or more respondents may answer jointly.

(4) The court of appeals may invite or order the trial-court judge to address the petition or may invite an amicus curiae to do so. The trial-court judge may request permission to address the petition but may not do so unless invited or ordered to do so by the court of appeals.

(5) If briefing or oral argument is required, the clerk must advise the parties, and when appropriate, the trial-court judge or amicus curiae.

(6) The proceeding must be given preference over ordinary civil cases.

(7) The circuit clerk must send a copy of the final disposition to the trial-court judge.

(c) Other Extraordinary Writs. An application for an extraordinary writ other than one provided for in Rule 21(a) must be made by filing a petition with the circuit clerk with proof of service on the respondents. Proceedings on the application must conform, so far as is practicable, to the procedures prescribed in Rule 21(a) and (b).

(d) Form of Papers; Number of Copies. All papers must conform to Rule 32(c)(2). Except by the court's permission, a paper must not exceed 30 pages, exclusive of the disclosure statement, the proof of service, and the accompanying documents required by Rule 21(a)(2)(C). An original and 3 copies must be filed unless the court requires the filing of a different number by local rule or by order in a particular case.

(As amended Apr. 29, 1994, eff. Dec. 1, 1994; Apr. 23, 1996, eff. Dec. 1, 1996; Apr. 24, 1998, eff. Dec. 1, 1998; Apr. 29, 2002, eff. Dec. 1, 2002.)

TITLE VI. HABEAS CORPUS; PROCEEDINGS IN FORMA PAUPERIS

RULE 22. HABEAS CORPUS AND SECTION 2255 PROCEEDINGS

(a) Application for the Original Writ. An application for a writ of habeas corpus must be made to the appropriate district court. If made to a circuit judge, the application must be transferred to the appropriate district court. If a district court denies an application made or transferred to it, renewal of the application before a circuit judge is not permitted. The applicant may, under 28 U.S.C. § 2253, appeal to the court of appeals from the district court's order denying the application.

(b) Certificate of Appealability.

(1) In a habeas corpus proceeding in which the detention complained of arises from process issued by a state court, or in a 28 U.S.C. § 2255 proceeding, the applicant cannot take an appeal unless a circuit justice or a circuit or district judge issues a certificate of appealability under 28 U.S.C. § 2253(c). If an applicant files a notice of appeal, the district clerk must send to the court of appeals the certificate (if any) and the statement described in Rule 11(a) of the Rules Governing Proceedings Under 28 U.S.C. § 2254 or § 2255 (if any), along with the notice of appeal and the file of the district-court proceedings. If the district judge has denied the certificate, the applicant may request a circuit judge to issue it.

(2) A request addressed to the court of appeals may be considered by a circuit judge or judges, as the court prescribes. If no express request for a certificate is filed, the notice of appeal constitutes a request addressed to the judges of the court of appeals.

(3) A certificate of appealability is not required when a state or its representative or the United States or its representative appeals.

(As amended Pub.L. 104–132, Title I, § 103, Apr. 24, 1996, 110 Stat. 1218; Apr. 24, 1998, eff. Dec. 1, 1998; Mar. 26, 2009, eff. Dec. 1, 2009.)

RULE 23. CUSTODY OR RELEASE OF A PRISONER IN A HABEAS CORPUS PROCEEDING

(a) Transfer of Custody Pending Review. Pending review of a decision in a habeas corpus proceeding commenced before a court, justice, or judge of the United States for the release of a prisoner, the person having custody of the prisoner must not transfer custody to another unless a transfer is directed in accordance with this rule. When, upon application, a custodian shows the need for a transfer, the court, justice, or judge rendering the decision under review may authorize the transfer and substitute the successor custodian as a party.

(b) Detention or Release Pending Review of Decision Not to Release. While a decision not to release a prisoner is under review, the court or judge rendering the decision, or the court of appeals, or the Supreme Court, or a judge or justice of either court, may order that the prisoner be:

(1) detained in the custody from which release is sought;

(2) detained in other appropriate custody; or

(3) released on personal recognizance, with or without surety.

(c) Release Pending Review of Decision Ordering Release. While a decision ordering the release of a prisoner is under review, the prisoner must—unless the court or judge rendering the decision, or the court of appeals, or the Supreme Court, or a judge or justice of either court orders otherwise—be released on personal recognizance, with or without surety.

(d) Modification of the Initial Order on Custody. An initial order governing the prisoner's custody or release, including any recognizance or surety, continues in effect pending review unless for special reasons shown to the court of appeals or the Supreme Court, or to a judge or justice of either court, the order is modified or an independent order regarding custody, release, or surety is issued.

(As amended Mar. 10, 1986, eff. July 1, 1986; Apr. 24, 1998, eff. Dec. 1, 1998.)

RULE 24. PROCEEDING IN FORMA PAUPERIS

(a) Leave to Proceed In Forma Pauperis.

(1) Motion in the District Court. Except as stated in Rule 24(a)(3), a party to a district-court action who desires to appeal in forma pauperis must file a motion in the district court. The party must attach an affidavit that:

    (A) shows in the detail prescribed by Form 4 of the Appendix of Forms the party's inability to pay or to give security for fees and costs;

    (B) claims an entitlement to redress; and

    (C) states the issues that the party intends to present on appeal.

(2) Action on the Motion. If the district court grants the motion, the party may proceed on appeal without prepaying or giving security for fees and costs, unless a statute provides otherwise. If the district court denies the motion, it must state its reasons in writing.

(3) Prior Approval. A party who was permitted to proceed in forma pauperis in the district-court action, or who was determined to be financially unable to obtain an adequate defense in a criminal case, may proceed on appeal in forma pauperis without further authorization, unless:

    (A) the district court—before or after the notice of appeal is filed—certifies that the appeal is not taken in good faith or finds that the party is not otherwise entitled to proceed in forma pauperis and states in writing its reasons for the certification or finding; or

    (B) a statute provides otherwise.

(4) Notice of District Court's Denial. The district clerk must immediately notify the parties and the court of appeals when the district court does any of the following:

    (A) denies a motion to proceed on appeal in forma pauperis;

    (B) certifies that the appeal is not taken in good faith; or

    (C) finds that the party is not otherwise entitled to proceed in forma pauperis.

(5) Motion in the Court of Appeals. A party may file a motion to proceed on appeal in forma pauperis in the court of appeals within 30 days after service of the notice prescribed in Rule 24(a)(4). The motion must include a copy of the affidavit filed in the district court and the district court's statement of reasons for its action. If no affidavit was filed in the district court, the party must include the affidavit prescribed by Rule 24(a)(1).

(b) Leave to Proceed In Forma Pauperis on Appeal or Review of an Administrative–Agency Proceeding. When an appeal or review of a proceeding before an administrative agency, board, commission, or officer (including for the purpose of this rule the United States Tax Court) proceeds directly in a court of appeals, a party may file in the court of appeals a motion for leave to proceed on appeal in forma pauperis with an affidavit prescribed by Rule 24(a)(1).

(c) Leave to Use Original Record. A party allowed to proceed on appeal in forma pauperis may request that the appeal be heard on the original record without reproducing any part.

(As amended Apr. 30, 1979, eff. Aug. 1, 1979; Mar. 10, 1986, eff. July 1, 1986; Apr. 24, 1998, eff. Dec. 1, 1998; Apr. 29, 2002, eff. Dec. 1, 2002.)

TITLE VII. GENERAL PROVISIONS

RULE 25. FILING AND SERVICE

(a) Filing.

(1) Filing with the Clerk. A paper required or permitted to be filed in a court of appeals must be filed with the clerk.

(2) Filing: Method and Timeliness.

    (A) In general. Filing may be accomplished by mail addressed to the clerk, but filing is not timely unless the clerk receives the papers within the time fixed for filing.

    (B) A brief or appendix. A brief or appendix is timely filed, however, if on or before the last day for filing, it is:

        (i) mailed to the clerk by First-Class Mail, or other class of mail that is at least as expeditious, postage prepaid; or

(ii) dispatched to a third-party commercial carrier for delivery to the clerk within 3 days.

(C) Inmate filing. A paper filed by an inmate confined in an institution is timely if deposited in the institution's internal mailing system on or before the last day for filing. If an institution has a system designed for legal mail, the inmate must use that system to receive the benefit of this rule. Timely filing may be shown by a declaration in compliance with 28 U.S.C. § 1746 or by a notarized statement, either of which must set forth the date of deposit and state that first-class postage has been prepaid.

(D) Electronic filing. A court of appeals may by local rule permit or require papers to be filed, signed, or verified by electronic means that are consistent with technical standards, if any, that the Judicial Conference of the United States establishes. A local rule may require filing by electronic means only if reasonable exceptions are allowed. A paper filed by electronic means in compliance with a local rule constitutes a written paper for the purpose of applying these rules.

(3) Filing a Motion with a Judge. If a motion requests relief that may be granted by a single judge, the judge may permit the motion to be filed with the judge; the judge must note the filing date on the motion and give it to the clerk.

(4) Clerk's Refusal of Documents. The clerk must not refuse to accept for filing any paper presented for that purpose solely because it is not presented in proper form as required by these rules or by any local rule or practice.

(5) Privacy Protection. An appeal in a case whose privacy protection was governed by Federal Rule of Bankruptcy Procedure 9037, Federal Rule of Civil Procedure 5.2, or Federal Rule of Criminal Procedure 49.1 is governed by the same rule on appeal. In all other proceedings, privacy protection is governed by Federal Rule of Civil Procedure 5.2, except that Federal Rule of Criminal Procedure 49.1 governs when an extraordinary writ is sought in a criminal case.

(b) Service of All Papers Required. Unless a rule requires service by the clerk, a party must, at or before the time of filing a paper, serve a copy on the other parties to the appeal or review. Service on a party represented by counsel must be made on the party's counsel.

(c) Manner of Service.

(1) Service may be any of the following:

(A) personal, including delivery to a responsible person at the office of counsel;

(B) by mail;

(C) by third-party commercial carrier for delivery within 3 days; or

(D) by electronic means, if the party being served consents in writing.

(2) If authorized by local rule, a party may use the court's transmission equipment to make electronic service under Rule 25(c)(1)(D).

(3) When reasonable considering such factors as the immediacy of the relief sought, distance, and cost, service on a party must be by a manner at least as expeditious as the manner used to file the paper with the court.

(4) Service by mail or by commercial carrier is complete on mailing or delivery to the carrier. Service by electronic means is complete on transmission, unless the party making service is notified that the paper was not received by the party served.

(d) Proof of Service.

(1) A paper presented for filing must contain either of the following:

(A) an acknowledgment of service by the person served; or

(B) proof of service consisting of a statement by the person who made service certifying:

(i) the date and manner of service;

(ii) the names of the persons served; and

(iii) their mail or electronic addresses, facsimile numbers, or the addresses of the places of delivery, as appropriate for the manner of service.

(2) When a brief or appendix is filed by mailing or dispatch in accordance with Rule 25(a)(2)(B), the proof of service must also state the date and manner by which the document was mailed or dispatched to the clerk.

(3) Proof of service may appear on or be affixed to the papers filed.

(e) Number of Copies. When these rules require the filing or furnishing of a number of copies, a court may require a different number by local rule or by order in a particular case.

(As amended Mar. 10, 1986, eff. July 1, 1986; Apr. 30, 1991, eff. Dec. 1, 1991; Apr. 22, 1993, eff. Dec. 1, 1993; Apr. 29, 1994, eff. Dec. 1, 1994; Apr. 23, 1996, eff. Dec. 1, 1996; Apr. 24, 1998, eff. Dec. 1, 1998; Apr. 29, 2002, eff. Dec. 1, 2002; Apr. 12, 2006, eff. Dec. 1, 2006; Apr. 30, 2007, eff. Dec. 1, 2007; Mar. 26, 2009, eff. Dec. 1, 2009.)

RULE 26. COMPUTING AND EXTENDING TIME

(a) Computing Time. The following rules apply in computing any time period specified in these rules, in any local rule or court order, or in any statute that does not specify a method of computing time.

(1) Period Stated in Days or a Longer Unit. When the period is stated in days or a longer unit of time:

   (A) exclude the day of the event that triggers the period;

   (B) count every day, including intermediate Saturdays, Sundays, and legal holidays; and

   (C) include the last day of the period, but if the last day is a Saturday, Sunday, or legal holiday, the period continues to run until the end of the next day that is not a Saturday, Sunday, or legal holiday.

(2) Period Stated in Hours. When the period is stated in hours:

   (A) begin counting immediately on the occurrence of the event that triggers the period;

   (B) count every hour, including hours during intermediate Saturdays, Sundays, and legal holidays; and

   (C) if the period would end on a Saturday, Sunday, or legal holiday, the period continues to run until the same time on the next day that is not a Saturday, Sunday, or legal holiday.

(3) Inaccessibility of the Clerk's Office. Unless the court orders otherwise, if the clerk's office is inaccessible:

   (A) on the last day for filing under Rule 26(a)(1), then the time for filing is extended to the first accessible day that is not a Saturday, Sunday, or legal holiday; or

   (B) during the last hour for filing under Rule 26(a)(2), then the time for filing is extended to the same time on the first accessible day that is not a Saturday, Sunday, or legal holiday.

(4) "Last Day" Defined. Unless a different time is set by a statute, local rule, or court order, the last day ends:

   (A) for electronic filing in the district court, at midnight in the court's time zone;

   (B) for electronic filing in the court of appeals, at midnight in the time zone of the circuit clerk's principal office;

   (C) for filing under Rules 4(c)(1), 25(a)(2)(B), and 25(a)(2)(C)—and filing by mail under Rule 13(b)—at the latest time for the method chosen for delivery to the post office, third-party commercial carrier, or prison mailing system; and

   (D) for filing by other means, when the clerk's office is scheduled to close.

(5) "Next Day" Defined. The "next day" is determined by continuing to count forward when the period is measured after an event and backward when measured before an event.

(6) "Legal Holiday" Defined. "Legal holiday" means:

   (A) the day set aside by statute for observing New Year's Day, Martin Luther King Jr.'s Birthday, Washington's Birthday, Memorial Day, Independence Day, Labor Day, Columbus Day, Veterans' Day, Thanksgiving Day, or Christmas Day;

   (B) any day declared a holiday by the President or Congress; and

   (C) for periods that are measured after an event, any other day declared a holiday by the state where either of the following is located: the district court that rendered the challenged judgment or order, or the circuit clerk's principal office.

(b) Extending Time. For good cause, the court may extend the time prescribed by these rules or by its order to perform any act, or may permit an act to be done after that time expires. But the court may not extend the time to file:

   (1) a notice of appeal (except as authorized in Rule 4) or a petition for permission to appeal; or

   (2) a notice of appeal from or a petition to enjoin, set aside, suspend, modify, enforce, or otherwise review an order of an administrative agency, board, commission, or officer of the United States, unless specifically authorized by law.

(c) Additional Time after Service. When a party may or must act within a specified time after service, 3 days are added after the period would otherwise expire under Rule 26(a), unless the paper is delivered on the date of service stated in the proof of service. For purposes of this Rule 26(c), a paper that is served electronically is not treated as delivered on the date of service stated in the proof of service.

(As amended Mar. 1, 1971, eff. July 1, 1971; Mar. 10, 1986, eff. July 1, 1986; Apr. 25, 1989, eff. Dec. 1, 1989; Apr. 30, 1991, eff. Dec. 1, 1991; Apr. 23, 1996, eff. Dec. 1, 1996; Apr. 24, 1998, eff. Dec. 1, 1998; Apr. 29, 2002, eff. Dec. 1, 2002; Apr. 25, 2005, eff. Dec. 1, 2005; Mar. 26, 2009, eff. Dec. 1, 2009.)

RULE 26.1. CORPORATE DISCLOSURE STATEMENT

(a) Who Must File. Any nongovernmental corporate party to a proceeding in a court of appeals must file a statement that identifies any parent corporation and any publicly held corporation that owns 10% or more of its stock or states that there is no such corporation.

(b) Time for Filing; Supplemental Filing. A party must file the Rule 26.1(a) statement with the principal brief or upon filing a motion, response, petition, or answer in the court of appeals, whichever occurs first, unless a local rule requires earlier filing. Even if the statement has already been filed, the party's principal brief must include the statement before the table of contents. A party must supplement its statement whenever the information that must be disclosed under Rule 26.1(a) changes.

(c) Number of Copies. If the Rule 26.1(a) statement is filed before the principal brief, or if a supplemental statement is filed, the party must file an original and 3 copies unless the court requires a different number by local rule or by order in a particular case.

(Added Apr. 25, 1989, eff. Dec. 1, 1989, and amended Apr. 30, 1991, eff. Dec. 1, 1991; Apr. 29, 1994, eff. Dec. 1, 1994; Apr. 24, 1998, eff. Dec. 1, 1998; Apr. 29, 2002, eff. Dec. 1, 2002.)

RULE 27. MOTIONS

(a) In General.

(1) Application for Relief. An application for an order or other relief is made by motion unless these rules prescribe another form. A motion must be in writing unless the court permits otherwise.

(2) Contents of a Motion.

(A) Grounds and relief sought. A motion must state with particularity the grounds for the motion, the relief sought, and the legal argument necessary to support it.

(B) Accompanying documents.

(i) Any affidavit or other paper necessary to support a motion must be served and filed with the motion.

(ii) An affidavit must contain only factual information, not legal argument.

(iii) A motion seeking substantive relief must include a copy of the trial court's opinion or agency's decision as a separate exhibit.

(C) Documents barred or not required.

(i) A separate brief supporting or responding to a motion must not be filed.

(ii) A notice of motion is not required.

(iii) A proposed order is not required.

(3) Response.

(A) Time to file. Any party may file a response to a motion; Rule 27(a)(2) governs its contents. The response must be filed within 10 days after service of the motion unless the court shortens or extends the time. A motion authorized by Rules 8, 9, 18, or 41 may be granted before the 10–day period runs only if the court gives reasonable notice to the parties that it intends to act sooner.

(B) Request for affirmative relief. A response may include a motion for affirmative re-lief. The time to respond to the new motion, and to reply to that response, are governed by Rule 27(a)(3)(A) and (a)(4). The title of the response must alert the court to the request for relief.

(4) Reply to Response. Any reply to a response must be filed within 7 days after service of the response. A reply must not present matters that do not relate to the response.

(b) Disposition of a Motion for a Procedural Order. The court may act on a motion for a procedural order—including a motion under Rule 26(b)—at any time without awaiting a response, and may, by rule or by order in a particular case, authorize its clerk to act on specified types of procedural motions. A party adversely affected by the court's, or the clerk's, action may file a motion to reconsider, vacate, or modify that action. Timely opposition filed after the motion is granted in whole or in part does not constitute a request to reconsider, vacate, or modify the disposition; a motion requesting that relief must be filed.

(c) Power of a Single Judge to Entertain a Motion. A circuit judge may act alone on any motion, but may not dismiss or otherwise determine an appeal or other proceeding. A court of appeals may provide by rule or by order in a particular case that only the court may act on any motion or class of motions. The court may review the action of a single judge.

(d) Form of Papers; Page Limits; and Number of Copies.

(1) Format.

(A) Reproduction. A motion, response, or reply may be reproduced by any process that yields a clear black image on light paper. The paper must be opaque and unglazed. Only one side of the paper may be used.

(B) Cover. A cover is not required, but there must be a caption that includes the case number, the name of the court, the title of the case, and a brief descriptive title indicating the purpose of the motion and identifying the party or parties for whom it is filed. If a cover is used, it must be white.

(C) Binding. The document must be bound in any manner that is secure, does not obscure the text, and permits the document to lie reasonably flat when open.

(D) Paper size, line spacing, and margins. The document must be on 8½ by 11 inch paper. The text must be double-spaced, but quotations more than two lines long may be indented and single-spaced. Headings and footnotes may be single-spaced. Margins must be at least one inch on all four sides. Page numbers may be placed in the margins, but no text may appear there.

(E) Typeface and type styles. The document must comply with the typeface requirements of Rule 32(a)(5) and the type-style requirements of Rule 32(a)(6).

(2) Page Limits. A motion or a response to a motion must not exceed 20 pages, exclusive of the corporate disclosure statement and accompanying documents authorized by Rule 27(a)(2)(B), unless the court permits or directs otherwise. A reply to a response must not exceed 10 pages.

(3) Number of Copies. An original and 3 copies must be filed unless the court requires a different number by local rule or by order in a particular case.

(e) Oral Argument. A motion will be decided without oral argument unless the court orders otherwise.

(As amended Apr. 30, 1979, eff. Aug. 1, 1979; Apr. 25, 1989, eff. Dec. 1, 1989; Apr. 29, 1994, eff. Dec. 1, 1994; Apr. 24, 1998, eff. Dec. 1, 1998; Apr. 29, 2002, eff. Dec. 1, 2002; Apr. 25, 2005, eff. Dec. 1, 2005; Mar. 26, 2009, eff. Dec. 1, 2009.)

RULE 28. BRIEFS

(a) Appellant's Brief. The appellant's brief must contain, under appropriate headings and in the order indicated:

(1) a corporate disclosure statement if required by Rule 26.1;

(2) a table of contents, with page references;

(3) a table of authorities—cases (alphabetically arranged), statutes, and other authorities—with references to the pages of the brief where they are cited;

(4) a jurisdictional statement, including:

   (A) the basis for the district court's or agency's subject-matter jurisdiction, with citations to applicable statutory provisions and stating relevant facts establishing jurisdiction;

   (B) the basis for the court of appeals' jurisdiction, with citations to applicable statutory provisions and stating relevant facts establishing jurisdiction;

   (C) the filing dates establishing the timeliness of the appeal or petition for review; and

   (D) an assertion that the appeal is from a final order or judgment that disposes of all parties' claims, or information establishing the court of appeals' jurisdiction on some other basis;

(5) a statement of the issues presented for review;

(6) a statement of the case briefly indicating the nature of the case, the course of proceedings, and the disposition below;

(7) a statement of facts relevant to the issues submitted for review with appropriate references to the record (see Rule 28(e));

(8) a summary of the argument, which must contain a succinct, clear, and accurate statement of the arguments made in the body of the brief, and which must not merely repeat the argument headings;

(9) the argument, which must contain:

   (A) appellant's contentions and the reasons for them, with citations to the authorities and parts of the record on which the appellant relies; and

   (B) for each issue, a concise statement of the applicable standard of review (which may appear in the discussion of the issue or under a separate heading placed before the discussion of the issues);

(10) a short conclusion stating the precise relief sought; and

(11) the certificate of compliance, if required by Rule 32(a)(7).

(b) Appellee's Brief. The appellee's brief must conform to the requirements of Rule 28(a)(1)–(9) and (11), except that none of the following need appear unless the appellee is dissatisfied with the appellant's statement:

(1) the jurisdictional statement;

(2) the statement of the issues;

(3) the statement of the case;

(4) the statement of the facts; and

(5) the statement of the standard of review.

(c) Reply Brief. The appellant may file a brief in reply to the appellee's brief. Unless the court permits, no further briefs may be filed. A reply brief must contain a table of contents, with page references, and a table of authorities—cases (alphabetically arranged), statutes, and other authorities—with references to the pages of the reply brief where they are cited.

(d) References to Parties. In briefs and at oral argument, counsel should minimize use of the terms "appellant" and "appellee." To make briefs clear, counsel should use the parties' actual names or the designations used in the lower court or agency proceeding, or such descriptive terms as "the employee," "the injured person," "the taxpayer," "the ship," "the stevedore."

(e) References to the Record. References to the parts of the record contained in the appendix filed with the appellant's brief must be to the pages of the appendix. If the appendix is prepared after the briefs are filed, a party referring to the record must follow one of the methods detailed in Rule 30(c). If the original record is used under Rule 30(f) and is not consecutively paginated, or if the brief refers to an unreproduced part of the record, any reference must be to the page of the original document. For example:

- Answer p. 7;
- Motion for Judgment p. 2;
- Transcript p. 231.

Only clear abbreviations may be used. A party referring to evidence whose admissibility is in controversy must cite the pages of the appendix or of the transcript at which the evidence was identified, offered, and received or rejected.

(f) Reproduction of Statutes, Rules, Regulations, etc. If the court's determination of the issues presented requires the study of statutes, rules, regulations, etc., the relevant parts must be set out in the brief or in an addendum at the end, or may be supplied to the court in pamphlet form.

(g) [Reserved]

(h) [Deleted]

(i) Briefs in a Case Involving Multiple Appellants or Appellees. In a case involving more than one appellant or appellee, including consolidated cases, any number of appellants or appellees may join in a brief, and any party may adopt by reference a part of another's brief. Parties may also join in reply briefs.

(j) Citation of Supplemental Authorities. If pertinent and significant authorities come to a party's attention after the party's brief has been filed—or after oral argument but before decision—a party may promptly advise the circuit clerk by letter, with a copy to all other parties, setting forth the citations. The letter must state the reasons for the supplemental citations, referring either to the page of the brief or to a point argued orally. The body of the letter must not exceed 350 words. Any response must be made promptly and must be similarly limited.

(As amended Apr. 30, 1979, eff. Aug. 1, 1979; Mar. 10, 1986, eff. July 1, 1986; Apr. 25, 1989, eff. Dec. 1, 1989; Apr. 30, 1991, eff. Dec. 1, 1991; Apr. 22, 1993, eff. Dec. 1, 1993; Apr. 29, 1994, eff. Dec. 1, 1994; Apr. 24, 1998, eff. Dec. 1, 1998; Apr. 29, 2002, eff. Dec. 1, 2002; Apr. 25, 2005, eff. Dec. 1, 2005.)

RULE 28.1. CROSS–APPEALS

(a) Applicability. This rule applies to a case in which a cross-appeal is filed. Rules 28(a)-(c), 31(a)(1), 32(a)(2), and 32(a)(7)(A)-(B) do not apply to such a case, except as otherwise provided in this rule.

(b) Designation of Appellant. The party who files a notice of appeal first is the appellant for the purposes of this rule and Rules 30 and 34. If notices are filed on the same day, the plaintiff in the proceeding below is the appellant. These designations may be modified by the parties' agreement or by court order.

(c) Briefs. In a case involving a cross-appeal:

(1) Appellant's Principal Brief. The appellant must file a principal brief in the appeal. That brief must comply with Rule 28(a).

(2) Appellee's Principal and Response Brief. The appellee must file a principal brief in the cross-appeal and must, in the same brief, respond to the principal brief in the appeal. That appellee's brief must comply with Rule 28(a), except that the brief need not include a statement of the case or a statement of the facts unless the appellee is dissatisfied with the appellant's statement.

(3) Appellant's Response and Reply Brief. The appellant must file a brief that responds to the principal brief in the cross-appeal and may, in the same brief, reply to the response in the appeal. That brief must comply with Rule 28(a)(2)–(9) and (11), except that none of the following need appear unless the appellant is dissatisfied with the appellee's statement in the cross-appeal:

(A) the jurisdictional statement;

(B) the statement of the issues;

(C) the statement of the case;

(D) the statement of the facts; and

(E) the statement of the standard of review.

(4) Appellee's Reply Brief. The appellee may file a brief in reply to the response in the cross-appeal. That brief must comply with Rule 28(a)(2)–(3) and (11) and must be limited to the issues presented by the cross-appeal.

(5) No Further Briefs. Unless the court permits, no further briefs may be filed in a case involving a cross-appeal.

(d) Cover. Except for filings by unrepresented parties, the cover of the appellant's principal brief must be blue; the appellee's principal and response brief, red; the appellant's response and reply brief, yellow; the appellee's reply brief, gray; an intervenor's or amicus curiae's brief, green; and any supplemental brief, tan. The front cover of a brief must contain the information required by Rule 32(a)(2).

(e) Length.

(1) Page Limitation. Unless it complies with Rule 28.1(e)(2) and (3), the appellant's principal brief must not exceed 30 pages; the appellee's principal and response brief, 35 pages; the appellant's response and reply brief, 30 pages; and the appellee's reply brief, 15 pages.

(2) Type-Volume Limitation.

(A) The appellant's principal brief or the appellant's response and reply brief is acceptable if:

(i) it contains no more than 14,000 words; or

(ii) it uses a monospaced face and contains no more than 1,300 lines of text.

(B) The appellee's principal and response brief is acceptable if:

(i) it contains no more than 16,500 words; or

(ii) it uses a monospaced face and contains no more than 1,500 lines of text.

(C) The appellee's reply brief is acceptable if it contains no more than half of the type volume specified in Rule 28.1(e)(2)(A).

(3) Certificate of Compliance. A brief submitted under Rule 28.1(e)(2) must comply with Rule 32(a)(7)(C).

(f) Time to Serve and File a Brief. Briefs must be served and filed as follows:

(1) the appellant's principal brief, within 40 days after the record is filed;

(2) the appellee's principal and response brief, within 30 days after the appellant's principal brief is served;

(3) the appellant's response and reply brief, within 30 days after the appellee's principal and response brief is served; and

(4) the appellee's reply brief, within 14 days after the appellant's response and reply brief is served, but at least 7 days before argument unless the court, for good cause, allows a later filing.

(As added April 25, 2005, eff. Dec. 1, 2005, and amended Mar. 26, 2009, eff. Dec. 1, 2009.)

RULE 29. BRIEF OF AN AMICUS CURIAE

(a) When Permitted. The United States or its officer or agency or a state may file an amicus-curiae brief without the consent of the parties or leave of court. Any other amicus curiae may file a brief only by leave of court or if the brief states that all parties have consented to its filing.

(b) Motion for Leave to File. The motion must be accompanied by the proposed brief and state:

(1) the movant's interest; and

(2) the reason why an amicus brief is desirable and why the matters asserted are relevant to the disposition of the case.

(c) Contents and Form. An amicus brief must comply with Rule 32. In addition to the requirements of Rule 32, the cover must identify the party or parties supported and indicate whether the brief supports affirmance or reversal. An amicus brief need not comply with Rule 28, but must include the following:

(1) if the amicus curiae is a corporation, a disclosure statement like that required of parties by Rule 26.1;

(2) a table of contents, with page references;

(3) a table of authorities—cases (alphabetically arranged), statutes, and other authorities—with references to the pages of the brief where they are cited;

(4) a concise statement of the identity of the amicus curiae, its interest in the case, and the source of its authority to file;

(5) unless the amicus curiae is one listed in the first sentence of Rule 29(a), a statement that indicates whether:

(A) a party's counsel authored the brief in whole or in part;

(B) a party or a party's counsel contributed money that was intended to fund preparing or submitting the brief; and

(C) a person—other than the amicus curiae, its members, or its counsel—contributed money that was intended to fund preparing or submitting the brief and, if so, identifies each such person;

(6) an argument, which may be preceded by a summary and which need not include a statement of the applicable standard of review; and

(7) a certificate of compliance, if required by Rule 32(a)(7).

(d) Length. Except by the court's permission, an amicus brief may be no more than one-half the maximum length authorized by these rules for a party's principal brief. If the court grants a party permission to file a longer brief, that extension does not affect the length of an amicus brief.

(e) Time for Filing. An amicus curiae must file its brief, accompanied by a motion for filing when necessary, no later than 7 days after the principal brief of the party being supported is filed. An amicus curiae that does not support either party must file its brief no later than 7 days after the appellant's or petitioner's principal brief is filed. A court may grant leave for later filing, specifying the time within which an opposing party may answer.

(f) Reply Brief. Except by the court's permission, an amicus curiae may not file a reply brief.

(g) Oral Argument. An amicus curiae may participate in oral argument only with the court's permission.

(As amended Apr. 24, 1998, eff. Dec. 1, 1998; Apr. 28, 2010, eff. Dec. 1, 2010.)

RULE 30. APPENDIX TO THE BRIEFS

(a) Appellant's Responsibility.

(1) Contents of the Appendix. The appellant must prepare and file an appendix to the briefs containing:

(A) the relevant docket entries in the proceeding below;

(B) the relevant portions of the pleadings, charge, findings, or opinion;

(C) the judgment, order, or decision in question; and

(D) other parts of the record to which the parties wish to direct the court's attention.

(2) Excluded Material. Memoranda of law in the district court should not be included in the appendix unless they have independent relevance. Parts of the record may be relied on by the court or the parties even though not included in the appendix.

(3) Time to File; Number of Copies. Unless filing is deferred under Rule 30(c), the appellant must file 10 copies of the appendix with the brief and must serve one copy on counsel for each party separately represented. An unrepresented party proceeding in forma pauperis must file 4 legible copies with the clerk, and one copy must be served on counsel for each separately represented party. The court may by local rule or by order in a particular case require the filing or service of a different number.

(b) All Parties' Responsibilities.

(1) Determining the Contents of the Appendix. The parties are encouraged to agree on the contents of the appendix. In the absence of an agreement, the appellant must, within 14 days after the record is filed, serve on the appellee a designation of the parts of the record the appellant intends to include in the appendix and a statement of the issues the appellant intends to present for review. The appellee may, within 14 days after receiving the designation, serve on the appellant a designation of additional parts to which it wishes to direct the court's attention. The appellant must include the designated parts in the appendix. The parties must not engage in unnecessary designation of parts of the record, because the entire record is available to the court. This paragraph applies also to a cross-appellant and a cross-appellee.

(2) Costs of Appendix. Unless the parties agree otherwise, the appellant must pay the cost of the appendix. If the appellant considers parts of the record designated by the appellee to be unnecessary, the appellant may advise the appellee, who must then advance the cost of including those parts. The cost of the appendix is a taxable cost. But if any party causes unnecessary parts of the record to be included in the appendix, the court may impose the cost of those parts on that party. Each circuit

must, by local rule, provide for sanctions against attorneys who unreasonably and vexatiously increase litigation costs by including unnecessary material in the appendix.

(c) Deferred Appendix.

(1) Deferral Until After Briefs Are Filed. The court may provide by rule for classes of cases or by order in a particular case that preparation of the appendix may be deferred until after the briefs have been filed and that the appendix may be filed 21 days after the appellee's brief is served. Even though the filing of the appendix may be deferred, Rule 30(b) applies; except that a party must designate the parts of the record it wants included in the appendix when it serves its brief, and need not include a statement of the issues presented.

(2) References to the Record.

(A) If the deferred appendix is used, the parties may cite in their briefs the pertinent pages of the record. When the appendix is prepared, the record pages cited in the briefs must be indicated by inserting record page numbers, in brackets, at places in the appendix where those pages of the record appear.

(B) A party who wants to refer directly to pages of the appendix may serve and file copies of the brief within the time required by Rule 31(a), containing appropriate references to pertinent pages of the record. In that event, within 14 days after the appendix is filed, the party must serve and file copies of the brief, containing references to the pages of the appendix in place of or in addition to the references to the pertinent pages of the record. Except for the correction of typographical errors, no other changes may be made to the brief.

(d) Format of the Appendix. The appendix must begin with a table of contents identifying the page at which each part begins. The relevant docket entries must follow the table of contents. Other parts of the record must follow chronologically. When pages from the transcript of proceedings are placed in the appendix, the transcript page numbers must be shown in brackets immediately before the included pages. Omissions in the text of papers or of the transcript must be indicated by asterisks. Immaterial formal matters (captions, subscriptions, acknowledgments, etc.) should be omitted.

(e) Reproduction of Exhibits. Exhibits designated for inclusion in the appendix may be reproduced in a separate volume, or volumes, suitably indexed. Four copies must be filed with the appendix, and one copy must be served on counsel for each separately represented party. If a transcript of a proceeding before an administrative agency, board, commission, or officer was used in a district-court action and has been designated for inclusion in the appendix, the transcript must be placed in the appendix as an exhibit.

(f) Appeal on the Original Record Without an Appendix. The court may, either by rule for all cases or classes of cases or by order in a particular case, dispense with the appendix and permit an appeal to proceed on the original record with any copies of the record, or relevant parts, that the court may order the parties to file.

(As amended Mar. 30, 1970, eff. July 1, 1970; Mar. 10, 1986, eff. July 1, 1986; Apr. 30, 1991, eff. Dec. 1, 1991; Apr. 29, 1994, eff. Dec. 1, 1994; Apr. 24, 1998, eff. Dec. 1, 1998; Mar. 26, 2009, eff. Dec. 1, 2009.)

RULE 31. SERVING AND FILING BRIEFS

(a) Time to Serve and File a Brief.

(1) The appellant must serve and file a brief within 40 days after the record is filed. The appellee must serve and file a brief within 30 days after the appellant's brief is served. The appellant may serve and file a reply brief within 14 days after service of the appellee's brief but a reply brief must be filed at least 7 days before argument, unless the court, for good cause, allows a later filing.

(2) A court of appeals that routinely considers cases on the merits promptly after the briefs are filed may shorten the time to serve and file briefs, either by local rule or by order in a particular case.

(b) Number of Copies. Twenty-five copies of each brief must be filed with the clerk and 2 copies must be served on each unrepresented party and on counsel for each separately represented party. An unrepresented party proceeding in forma pauperis must file 4 legible copies with the clerk, and one copy must be served on each unrepresented party and on counsel for each separately represented party. The court may by local rule or by order in a particular case require the filing or service of a different number.

(c) Consequence of Failure to File. If an appellant fails to file a brief within the time provided by this rule, or within an extended time, an appellee may move to dismiss the appeal. An appellee who fails to file a brief will not be heard at oral argument unless the court grants permission.

(As amended Mar. 30, 1970, eff. July 1, 1970; Mar. 10, 1986, eff. July 1, 1986; Apr. 29, 1994, eff. Dec. 1, 1994; Apr. 24, 1998, eff. Dec. 1, 1998; Apr. 29, 2002, eff. Dec. 1, 2002; Mar. 26, 2009, eff. Dec. 1, 2009.)

RULE 32. FORM OF BRIEFS, APPENDICES, AND OTHER PAPERS

(a) Form of a Brief.

(1) Reproduction.

(A) A brief may be reproduced by any process that yields a clear black image on light paper.

The paper must be opaque and unglazed. Only one side of the paper may be used.

(B) Text must be reproduced with a clarity that equals or exceeds the output of a laser printer.

(C) Photographs, illustrations, and tables may be reproduced by any method that results in a good copy of the original; a glossy finish is acceptable if the original is glossy.

(2) Cover. Except for filings by unrepresented parties, the cover of the appellant's brief must be blue; the appellee's, red; an intervenor's or amicus curiae's, green; any reply brief, gray; and any supplemental brief, tan. The front cover of a brief must contain:

(A) the number of the case centered at the top;

(B) the name of the court;

(C) the title of the case (see Rule 12(a));

(D) the nature of the proceeding (e.g., Appeal, Petition for Review) and the name of the court, agency, or board below;

(E) the title of the brief, identifying the party or parties for whom the brief is filed; and

(F) the name, office address, and telephone number of counsel representing the party for whom the brief is filed.

(3) Binding. The brief must be bound in any manner that is secure, does not obscure the text, and permits the brief to lie reasonably flat when open.

(4) Paper Size, Line Spacing, and Margins. The brief must be on 8½ by 11 inch paper. The text must be double-spaced, but quotations more than two lines long may be indented and single-spaced. Headings and footnotes may be single-spaced. Margins must be at least one inch on all four sides. Page numbers may be placed in the margins, but no text may appear there.

(5) Typeface. Either a proportionally spaced or a monospaced face may be used.

(A) A proportionally spaced face must include serifs, but sans-serif type may be used in headings and captions. A proportionally spaced face must be 14–point or larger.

(B) A monospaced face may not contain more than 10½ characters per inch.

(6) Type Styles. A brief must be set in a plain, roman style, although italics or boldface may be used for emphasis. Case names must be italicized or underlined.

(7) Length.

(A) Page limitation. A principal brief may not exceed 30 pages, or a reply brief 15 pages, unless it complies with Rule 32(a)(7)(B) and (C).

(B) Type-volume limitation.

(i) A principal brief is acceptable if:

● it contains no more than 14,000 words; or

● it uses a monospaced face and contains no more than 1,300 lines of text.

(ii) A reply brief is acceptable if it contains no more than half of the type volume specified in Rule 32(a)(7)(B)(i).

(iii) Headings, footnotes, and quotations count toward the word and line limitations. The corporate disclosure statement, table of contents, table of citations, statement with respect to oral argument, any addendum containing statutes, rules or regulations, and any certificates of counsel do not count toward the limitation.

(C) Certificate of compliance.

(i) A brief submitted under Rules 28.1(e)(2) or 32(a)(7)(B) must include a certificate by the attorney, or an unrepresented party, that the brief complies with the type-volume limitation. The person preparing the certificate may rely on the word or line count of the word-processing system used to prepare the brief. The certificate must state either:

● the number of words in the brief; or

● the number of lines of monospaced type in the brief.

(ii) Form 6 in the Appendix of Forms is a suggested form of a certificate of compliance. Use of Form 6 must be regarded as sufficient to meet the requirements of Rules 28.1(e)(3) and 32(a)(7)(C)(i).

(b) Form of an Appendix. An appendix must comply with Rule 32(a)(1), (2), (3), and (4), with the following exceptions:

(1) The cover of a separately bound appendix must be white.

(2) An appendix may include a legible photocopy of any document found in the record or of a printed judicial or agency decision.

(3) When necessary to facilitate inclusion of odd-sized documents such as technical drawings, an appendix may be a size other than 8½ by 11 inches, and need not lie reasonably flat when opened.

(c) Form of Other Papers.

(1) Motion. The form of a motion is governed by Rule 27(d).

(2) Other Papers. Any other paper, including a petition for panel rehearing and a petition for hearing or rehearing en banc, and any response to such a petition, must be reproduced in the manner prescribed by Rule 32(a), with the following exceptions:

(A) A cover is not necessary if the caption and signature page of the paper together contain the information required by Rule 32(a)(2). If a cover is used, it must be white.

(B) Rule 32(a)(7) does not apply.

(d) Signature. Every brief, motion, or other paper filed with the court must be signed by the party filing the paper or, if the party is represented, by one of the party's attorneys.

(e) Local Variation. Every court of appeals must accept documents that comply with the form requirements of this rule. By local rule or order in a particular case a court of appeals may accept documents that do not meet all of the form requirements of this rule.

(As amended Apr. 24, 1998, eff. Dec. 1, 1998; Apr. 29, 2002, eff. Dec. 1, 2002; Apr. 25, 2005, eff. Dec. 1, 2005.)

RULE 32.1. CITING JUDICIAL DISPOSITIONS

(a) Citation Permitted. A court may not prohibit or restrict the citation of federal judicial opinions, orders, judgments, or other written dispositions that have been:

(i) designated as "unpublished," "not for publication," "non-precedential," "not precedent," or the like; and

(ii) issued on or after January 1, 2007.

(b) Copies Required. If a party cites a federal judicial opinion, order, judgment, or other written disposition that is not available in a publicly accessible electronic database, the party must file and serve a copy of that opinion, order, judgment, or disposition with the brief or other paper in which it is cited.

(Added Apr. 12, 2006, eff. Dec. 1, 2006.)

RULE 33. APPEAL CONFERENCES

The court may direct the attorneys—and, when appropriate, the parties—to participate in one or more conferences to address any matter that may aid in disposing of the proceedings, including simplifying the issues and discussing settlement. A judge or other person designated by the court may preside over the conference, which may be conducted in person or by telephone. Before a settlement conference, the attorneys must consult with their clients and obtain as much authority as feasible to settle the case. The court may, as a result of the conference, enter an order controlling the course of the proceedings or implementing any settlement agreement.

(As amended Apr. 29, 1994, eff. Dec. 1, 1994; Apr. 24, 1998, eff. Dec. 1, 1998.)

RULE 34. ORAL ARGUMENT

(a) In General.

(1) Party's Statement. Any party may file, or a court may require by local rule, a statement explaining why oral argument should, or need not, be permitted.

(2) Standards. Oral argument must be allowed in every case unless a panel of three judges who have examined the briefs and record unanimously agrees that oral argument is unnecessary for any of the following reasons:

(A) the appeal is frivolous;

(B) the dispositive issue or issues have been authoritatively decided; or

(C) the facts and legal arguments are adequately presented in the briefs and record, and the decisional process would not be significantly aided by oral argument.

(b) Notice of Argument; Postponement. The clerk must advise all parties whether oral argument will be scheduled, and, if so, the date, time, and place for it, and the time allowed for each side. A motion to postpone the argument or to allow longer argument must be filed reasonably in advance of the hearing date.

(c) Order and Contents of Argument. The appellant opens and concludes the argument. Counsel must not read at length from briefs, records, or authorities.

(d) Cross-Appeals and Separate Appeals. If there is a cross-appeal, Rule 28.1(b) determines which party is the appellant and which is the appellee for purposes of oral argument. Unless the court directs otherwise, a cross-appeal or separate appeal must be argued when the initial appeal is argued. Separate parties should avoid duplicative argument.

(e) Nonappearance of a Party. If the appellee fails to appear for argument, the court must hear appellant's argument. If the appellant fails to appear for argument, the court may hear the appellee's argument. If neither party appears, the case will be decided on the briefs, unless the court orders otherwise.

(f) Submission on Briefs. The parties may agree to submit a case for decision on the briefs, but the court may direct that the case be argued.

(g) Use of Physical Exhibits at Argument; Removal. Counsel intending to use physical exhibits other than documents at the argument must arrange to place them in the courtroom on the day of the argument before the court convenes. After the argument, counsel must remove the exhibits from the courtroom, unless the court directs otherwise. The clerk may destroy or dispose of the exhibits if counsel does not reclaim them within a reasonable time after the clerk gives notice to remove them.

(As amended Apr. 30, 1979, eff. Aug. 1, 1979; Mar. 10, 1986, eff. July 1, 1986; Apr. 30, 1991, eff. Dec. 1, 1991; Apr. 22, 1993, eff. Dec. 1, 1993; Apr. 24, 1998, eff. Dec. 1, 1998; Apr. 25, 2005, eff. Dec. 1, 2005.)

RULE 35. EN BANC DETERMINATION

(a) When Hearing or Rehearing En Banc May Be Ordered. A majority of the circuit judges who are in regular active service and who are not disqualified may order that an appeal or other proceeding be heard or reheard by the court of appeals en banc. An en banc hearing or rehearing is not favored and ordinarily will not be ordered unless:

(1) en banc consideration is necessary to secure or maintain uniformity of the court's decisions; or

(2) the proceeding involves a question of exceptional importance.

(b) Petition for Hearing or Rehearing En Banc. A party may petition for a hearing or rehearing en banc.

(1) The petition must begin with a statement that either:

(A) the panel decision conflicts with a decision of the United States Supreme Court or of the court to which the petition is addressed (with citation to the conflicting case or cases) and consideration by the full court is therefore necessary to secure and maintain uniformity of the court's decisions; or

(B) the proceeding involves one or more questions of exceptional importance, each of which must be concisely stated; for example, a petition may assert that a proceeding presents a question of exceptional importance if it involves an issue on which the panel decision conflicts with the authoritative decisions of other United States Courts of Appeals that have addressed the issue.

(2) Except by the court's permission, a petition for an en banc hearing or rehearing must not exceed 15 pages, excluding material not counted under Rule 32.

(3) For purposes of the page limit in Rule 35(b)(2), if a party files both a petition for panel rehearing and a petition for rehearing en banc, they are considered a single document even if they are filed separately, unless separate filing is required by local rule.

(c) Time for Petition for Hearing or Rehearing En Banc. A petition that an appeal be heard initially en banc must be filed by the date when the appellee's brief is due. A petition for a rehearing en banc must be filed within the time prescribed by Rule 40 for filing a petition for rehearing.

(d) Number of Copies. The number of copies to be filed must be prescribed by local rule and may be altered by order in a particular case.

(e) Response. No response may be filed to a petition for an en banc consideration unless the court orders a response.

(f) Call for a Vote. A vote need not be taken to determine whether the case will be heard or reheard en banc unless a judge calls for a vote.

(As amended Apr. 30, 1979, eff. Aug. 1, 1979; Apr. 29, 1994, eff. Dec. 1, 1994; Apr. 24, 1998, eff. Dec. 1, 1998; Apr. 25, 2005, eff. Dec. 1, 2005.)

RULE 36. ENTRY OF JUDGMENT; NOTICE

(a) Entry. A judgment is entered when it is noted on the docket. The clerk must prepare, sign, and enter the judgment:

(1) after receiving the court's opinion—but if settlement of the judgment's form is required, after final settlement; or

(2) if a judgment is rendered without an opinion, as the court instructs.

(b) Notice. On the date when judgment is entered, the clerk must serve on all parties a copy of the opinion—or the judgment, if no opinion was written—and a notice of the date when the judgment was entered.

(As amended Apr. 24, 1998, eff. Dec. 1, 1998; Apr. 29, 2002, eff. Dec. 1, 2002.)

RULE 37. INTEREST ON JUDGMENT

(a) When the Court Affirms. Unless the law provides otherwise, if a money judgment in a civil case is affirmed, whatever interest is allowed by law is payable from the date when the district court's judgment was entered.

(b) When the Court Reverses. If the court modifies or reverses a judgment with a direction that a money judgment be entered in the district court, the mandate must contain instructions about the allowance of interest.

(As amended Apr. 24, 1998, eff. Dec. 1, 1998.)

RULE 38. FRIVOLOUS APPEAL— DAMAGES AND COSTS

If a court of appeals determines that an appeal is frivolous, it may, after a separately filed motion or notice from the court and reasonable opportunity to respond, award just damages and single or double costs to the appellee.

(As amended Apr. 29, 1994, eff. Dec. 1, 1994; Apr. 24, 1998, eff. Dec. 1, 1998.)

RULE 39. COSTS

(a) Against Whom Assessed. The following rules apply unless the law provides or the court orders otherwise:

(1) if an appeal is dismissed, costs are taxed against the appellant, unless the parties agree otherwise;

(2) if a judgment is affirmed, costs are taxed against the appellant;

(3) if a judgment is reversed, costs are taxed against the appellee;

(4) if a judgment is affirmed in part, reversed in part, modified, or vacated, costs are taxed only as the court orders.

(b) Costs For and Against the United States. Costs for or against the United States, its agency, or officer will be assessed under Rule 39(a) only if authorized by law.

(c) Costs of Copies. Each court of appeals must, by local rule, fix the maximum rate for taxing the cost of producing necessary copies of a brief or appendix, or copies of records authorized by Rule 30(f). The rate must not exceed that generally charged for such work in the area where the clerk's office is located and should encourage economical methods of copying.

(d) Bill of Costs: Objections; Insertion in Mandate.

(1) A party who wants costs taxed must—within 14 days after entry of judgment—file with the circuit clerk, with proof of service, an itemized and verified bill of costs.

(2) Objections must be filed within 14 days after service of the bill of costs, unless the court extends the time.

(3) The clerk must prepare and certify an itemized statement of costs for insertion in the mandate, but issuance of the mandate must not be delayed for taxing costs. If the mandate issues before costs are finally determined, the district clerk must—upon the circuit clerk's request—add the statement of costs, or any amendment of it, to the mandate.

(e) Costs on Appeal Taxable in the District Court. The following costs on appeal are taxable in the district court for the benefit of the party entitled to costs under this rule:

(1) the preparation and transmission of the record;

(2) the reporter's transcript, if needed to determine the appeal;

(3) premiums paid for a supersedeas bond or other bond to preserve rights pending appeal; and

(4) the fee for filing the notice of appeal.

(As amended Apr. 30, 1979, eff. Aug. 1, 1979; Mar. 10, 1986, eff. July 1, 1986; Apr. 24, 1998, eff. Dec. 1, 1998; Mar. 26, 2009, eff. Dec. 1, 2009.)

RULE 40. PETITION FOR PANEL REHEARING

(a) Time to File; Contents; Answer; Action by the Court if Granted.

(1) **Time.** Unless the time is shortened or extended by order or local rule, a petition for panel rehearing may be filed within 14 days after entry of judgment. But in a civil case, unless an order shortens or extends the time, the petition may be filed by any party within 45 days after entry of judgment if one of the parties is:

(A) the United States;

(B) a United States agency;

(C) a United States officer or employee sued in an official capacity; or

(D) a current or former United States officer or employee sued in an individual capacity for an act or omission occurring in connection with duties performed on the United States' behalf— including all instances in which the United States represents that person when the court of appeals' judgment is entered or files the petition for that person.

(2) **Contents.** The petition must state with particularity each point of law or fact that the petitioner believes the court has overlooked or misapprehended and must argue in support of the petition. Oral argument is not permitted.

(3) **Answer.** Unless the court requests, no answer to a petition for panel rehearing is permitted. But ordinarily rehearing will not be granted in the absence of such a request.

(4) **Action by the Court.** If a petition for panel rehearing is granted, the court may do any of the following:

(A) make a final disposition of the case without reargument;

(B) restore the case to the calendar for reargument or resubmission; or

(C) issue any other appropriate order.

(b) Form of Petition; Length. The petition must comply in form with Rule 32. Copies must be served and filed as Rule 31 prescribes. Unless the court permits or a local rule provides otherwise, a petition for panel rehearing must not exceed 15 pages.

(As amended Apr. 30, 1979, eff. Aug. 1, 1979; Apr. 29, 1994, eff. Dec. 1, 1994; Apr. 24, 1998, eff. Dec. 1, 1998; Apr. 26, 2011, eff. Dec. 1, 2011.)

RULE 41. MANDATE: CONTENTS; ISSUANCE AND EFFECTIVE DATE; STAY

(a) Contents. Unless the court directs that a formal mandate issue, the mandate consists of a certified copy of the judgment, a copy of the court's opinion, if any, and any direction about costs.

(b) When Issued. The court's mandate must issue 7 days after the time to file a petition for rehearing expires, or 7 days after entry of an order denying a timely petition for panel rehearing, petition for rehearing en banc, or motion for stay of mandate, whichever is later. The court may shorten or extend the time.

(c) Effective Date. The mandate is effective when issued.

(d) Staying the Mandate.

(1) **On Petition for Rehearing or Motion.** The timely filing of a petition for panel rehearing, petition for rehearing en banc, or motion for stay of mandate, stays the mandate until disposition of the petition or motion, unless the court orders otherwise.

(2) **Pending Petition for Certiorari.**

(A) A party may move to stay the mandate pending the filing of a petition for a writ of certiorari in the Supreme Court. The motion must be served on all parties and must show that the certiorari petition would present a substantial question and that there is good cause for a stay.

(B) The stay must not exceed 90 days, unless the period is extended for good cause or unless the party who obtained the stay files a petition for the writ and so notifies the circuit clerk in writing within the period of the stay. In that case, the stay continues until the Supreme Court's final disposition.

(C) The court may require a bond or other security as a condition to granting or continuing a stay of the mandate.

(D) The court of appeals must issue the mandate immediately when a copy of a Supreme

Court order denying the petition for writ of certiorari is filed.

(As amended Apr. 29, 1994, eff. Dec. 1, 1994; Apr. 24, 1998, eff. Dec. 1, 1998; Apr. 29, 2002, eff. Dec. 1, 2002; Mar. 26, 2009, eff. Dec. 1, 2009.)

RULE 42.   VOLUNTARY DISMISSAL

(a) Dismissal in the District Court. Before an appeal has been docketed by the circuit clerk, the district court may dismiss the appeal on the filing of a stipulation signed by all parties or on the appellant's motion with notice to all parties.

(b) Dismissal in the Court of Appeals. The circuit clerk may dismiss a docketed appeal if the parties file a signed dismissal agreement specifying how costs are to be paid and pay any fees that are due. But no mandate or other process may issue without a court order. An appeal may be dismissed on the appellant's motion on terms agreed to by the parties or fixed by the court.

(As amended Apr. 24, 1998, eff. Dec. 1, 1998.)

RULE 43.   SUBSTITUTION OF PARTIES

(a) Death of a Party.

(1) After Notice of Appeal Is Filed. If a party dies after a notice of appeal has been filed or while a proceeding is pending in the court of appeals, the decedent's personal representative may be substituted as a party on motion filed with the circuit clerk by the representative or by any party. A party's motion must be served on the representative in accordance with Rule 25. If the decedent has no representative, any party may suggest the death on the record, and the court of appeals may then direct appropriate proceedings.

(2) Before Notice of Appeal Is Filed—Potential Appellant. If a party entitled to appeal dies before filing a notice of appeal, the decedent's personal representative—or, if there is no personal representative, the decedent's attorney of record—may file a notice of appeal within the time prescribed by these rules. After the notice of appeal is filed, substitution must be in accordance with Rule 43(a)(1).

(3) Before Notice of Appeal Is Filed—Potential Appellee. If a party against whom an appeal may be taken dies after entry of a judgment or order in the district court, but before a notice of appeal is filed, an appellant may proceed as if the death had not occurred. After the notice of appeal is filed, substitution must be in accordance with Rule 43(a)(1).

(b) Substitution for a Reason Other Than Death. If a party needs to be substituted for any reason other

than death, the procedure prescribed in Rule 43(a) applies.

(c) Public Officer: Identification; Substitution.

(1) Identification of Party. A public officer who is a party to an appeal or other proceeding in an official capacity may be described as a party by the public officer's official title rather than by name. But the court may require the public officer's name to be added.

(2) Automatic Substitution of Officeholder. When a public officer who is a party to an appeal or other proceeding in an official capacity dies, resigns, or otherwise ceases to hold office, the action does not abate. The public officer's successor is automatically substituted as a party. Proceedings following the substitution are to be in the name of the substituted party, but any misnomer that does not affect the substantial rights of the parties may be disregarded. An order of substitution may be entered at any time, but failure to enter an order does not affect the substitution.

(As amended Mar. 10, 1986, eff. July 1, 1986; Apr. 24, 1998, eff. Dec. 1, 1998.)

RULE 44.   CASE INVOLVING A CONSTITUTIONAL QUESTION WHEN THE UNITED STATES OR THE RELEVANT STATE IS NOT A PARTY

(a) Constitutional Challenge to Federal Statute. If a party questions the constitutionality of an Act of Congress in a proceeding in which the United States or its agency, officer, or employee is not a party in an official capacity, the questioning party must give written notice to the circuit clerk immediately upon the filing of the record or as soon as the question is raised in the court of appeals. The clerk must then certify that fact to the Attorney General.

(b) Constitutional Challenge to State Statute. If a party questions the constitutionality of a statute of a State in a proceeding in which that State or its agency, officer, or employee is not a party in an official capacity, the questioning party must give written notice to the circuit clerk immediately upon the filing of the record or as soon as the question is raised in the court of appeals. The clerk must then certify that fact to the attorney general of the State.

(As amended Apr. 24, 1998, eff. Dec. 1, 1998; Apr. 29, 2002, eff. Dec. 1, 2002.)

RULE 45.   CLERK'S DUTIES

(a) General Provisions.

(1) Qualifications. The circuit clerk must take the oath and post any bond required by law. Nei-

FEDERAL RULES OF APPELLATE PROCEDURE — Rule 46

ther the clerk nor any deputy clerk may practice as an attorney or counselor in any court while in office.

(2) When Court Is Open. The court of appeals is always open for filing any paper, issuing and returning process, making a motion, and entering an order. The clerk's office with the clerk or a deputy in attendance must be open during business hours on all days except Saturdays, Sundays, and legal holidays. A court may provide by local rule or by order that the clerk's office be open for specified hours on Saturdays or on legal holidays other than New Year's Day, Martin Luther King, Jr.'s Birthday, Washington's Birthday, Memorial Day, Independence Day, Labor Day, Columbus Day, Veterans' Day, Thanksgiving Day, and Christmas Day.

(b) Records.

(1) The Docket. The circuit clerk must maintain a docket and an index of all docketed cases in the manner prescribed by the Director of the Administrative Office of the United States Courts. The clerk must record all papers filed with the clerk and all process, orders, and judgments.

(2) Calendar. Under the court's direction, the clerk must prepare a calendar of cases awaiting argument. In placing cases on the calendar for argument, the clerk must give preference to appeals in criminal cases and to other proceedings and appeals entitled to preference by law.

(3) Other Records. The clerk must keep other books and records required by the Director of the Administrative Office of the United States Courts, with the approval of the Judicial Conference of the United States, or by the court.

(c) Notice of an Order or Judgment. Upon the entry of an order or judgment, the circuit clerk must immediately serve a notice of entry on each party, with a copy of any opinion, and must note the date of service on the docket. Service on a party represented by counsel must be made on counsel.

(d) Custody of Records and Papers. The circuit clerk has custody of the court's records and papers. Unless the court orders or instructs otherwise, the clerk must not permit an original record or paper to be taken from the clerk's office. Upon disposition of the case, original papers constituting the record on appeal or review must be returned to the court or agency from which they were received. The clerk must preserve a copy of any brief, appendix, or other paper that has been filed.

(As amended Mar. 1, 1971, eff. July 1, 1971; Mar. 10, 1986, eff. July 1, 1986; Apr. 24, 1998, eff. Dec. 1, 1998; Apr. 29, 2002, eff. Dec. 1, 2002; Apr. 25, 2005, eff. Dec. 1, 2005.)

RULE 46. ATTORNEYS

(a) Admission to the Bar.

(1) Eligibility. An attorney is eligible for admission to the bar of a court of appeals if that attorney is of good moral and professional character and is admitted to practice before the Supreme Court of the United States, the highest court of a state, another United States court of appeals, or a United States district court (including the district courts for Guam, the Northern Mariana Islands, and the Virgin Islands).

(2) Application. An applicant must file an application for admission, on a form approved by the court that contains the applicant's personal statement showing eligibility for membership. The applicant must subscribe to the following oath or affirmation:

"I, _____, do solemnly swear [or affirm] that I will conduct myself as an attorney and counselor of this court, uprightly and according to law; and that I will support the Constitution of the United States."

(3) Admission Procedures. On written or oral motion of a member of the court's bar, the court will act on the application. An applicant may be admitted by oral motion in open court. But, unless the court orders otherwise, an applicant need not appear before the court to be admitted. Upon admission, an applicant must pay the clerk the fee prescribed by local rule or court order.

(b) Suspension or Disbarment.

(1) Standard. A member of the court's bar is subject to suspension or disbarment by the court if the member:

(A) has been suspended or disbarred from practice in any other court; or

(B) is guilty of conduct unbecoming a member of the court's bar.

(2) Procedure. The member must be given an opportunity to show good cause, within the time prescribed by the court, why the member should not be suspended or disbarred.

(3) Order. The court must enter an appropriate order after the member responds and a hearing is held, if requested, or after the time prescribed for a response expires, if no response is made.

(c) Discipline. A court of appeals may discipline an attorney who practices before it for conduct unbecoming a member of the bar or for failure to comply with any court rule. First, however, the court must afford the attorney reasonable notice, an opportunity to show cause to the contrary, and, if requested, a hearing.

(As amended Mar. 10, 1986, eff. July 1, 1986; Apr. 24, 1998, eff. Dec. 1, 1998.)

RULE 47. LOCAL RULES BY COURTS OF APPEALS

(a) Local Rules.

(1) Each court of appeals acting by a majority of its judges in regular active service may, after giving appropriate public notice and opportunity for comment, make and amend rules governing its practice. A generally applicable direction to parties or lawyers regarding practice before a court must be in a local rule rather than an internal operating procedure or standing order. A local rule must be consistent with—but not duplicative of—Acts of Congress and rules adopted under 28 U.S.C. § 2072 and must conform to any uniform numbering system prescribed by the Judicial Conference of the United States. Each circuit clerk must send the Administrative Office of the United States Courts a copy of each local rule and internal operating procedure when it is promulgated or amended.

(2) A local rule imposing a requirement of form must not be enforced in a manner that causes a party to lose rights because of a nonwillful failure to comply with the requirement.

(b) Procedure When There Is No Controlling Law. A court of appeals may regulate practice in a particular case in any manner consistent with federal law, these rules, and local rules of the circuit. No sanction or other disadvantage may be imposed for noncompliance with any requirement not in federal law, federal rules, or the local circuit rules unless the alleged violator has been furnished in the particular case with actual notice of the requirement.

(As amended Apr. 27, 1995, eff. Dec. 1, 1995; Apr. 24, 1998, eff. Dec. 1, 1998.)

RULE 48. MASTERS

(a) Appointment; Powers. A court of appeals may appoint a special master to hold hearings, if necessary, and to recommend factual findings and disposition in matters ancillary to proceedings in the court. Unless the order referring a matter to a master specifies or limits the master's powers, those powers include, but are not limited to, the following:

(1) regulating all aspects of a hearing;

(2) taking all appropriate action for the efficient performance of the master's duties under the order;

(3) requiring the production of evidence on all matters embraced in the reference; and

(4) administering oaths and examining witnesses and parties.

(b) Compensation. If the master is not a judge or court employee, the court must determine the master's compensation and whether the cost is to be charged to any party.

(As amended Apr. 29, 1994, eff. Dec. 1, 1994; Apr. 24, 1998, eff. Dec. 1, 1998.)

APPENDIX OF FORMS

FORM 1. NOTICE OF APPEAL TO A COURT OF APPEALS FROM A JUDGMENT OR ORDER OF A DISTRICT COURT

United States District Court for the _____
District of _____
File Number _____

A.B., Plaintiff	)
	)
v.	) *Notice of Appeal*
	)
C.D., Defendant	)

Notice is hereby given that [___ (here name all parties taking the appeal)___, (plaintiffs) (defendants) in the above named case,[1]] hereby appeal to the United States Court of Appeals for the _____ Circuit (from the final judgment) (from an order (describing it)) entered in this action on the _____ day of _____, 20___.

       (s) _____
               Attorney for [_____]
               [Address:_____]

(As amended Apr. 22, 1993, eff. Dec. 1, 1993; Mar. 27, 2003, eff. Dec. 1, 2003.)

[1] See Rule 3(c) for permissible ways of identifying appellants.

FORM 2. NOTICE OF APPEAL TO A COURT OF APPEALS FROM A DECISION OF THE UNITED STATES TAX COURT

UNITED STATES TAX COURT

Washington, D.C.

A.B., *Petitioner*	)
	)
v.	) Docket No. _____
	)
Commissioner of Internal	)
Revenue, Respondent	)

Notice of Appeal

Notice is hereby given that [____ here name all parties taking the appeal [1] ____], hereby appeals to the United States Court of Appeals for the _____ Circuit from (that part of) the decision of this court entered in the above captioned proceeding on the _____ day of _____, 20___ (relating to _____).

(s)   _____

Counsel for [_____]

[Address:_____]

(As amended Apr. 22, 1993, eff. Dec. 1, 1993; Mar. 27, 2003, eff. Dec. 1, 2003.)

[1] See Rule 3(c) for permissible ways of identifying appellants.

FORM 3. PETITION FOR REVIEW OF ORDER OF AN AGENCY, BOARD, COMMISSION OR OFFICER

United States Court of Appeals for the _____ Circuit

A.B., Petitioner   )
)
               v.   )   Petition for Review
XYZ Commission, Respondent   )

[____(here name all parties bringing the petition[1])____] hereby petitions the court for review of the Order of the XYZ Commission (describe the order) entered on _____, 20___.

[(s)] _____

Attorney for Petitioners
Address:_____

(As amended Apr. 22, 1993, eff. Dec. 1, 1993; Mar. 27, 2003, eff. Dec. 1, 2003.)

[1] See Rule 15.

FORM 4.   AFFIDAVIT ACCOMPANYING MOTION FOR PERMISSION TO APPEAL IN FORMA PAUPERIS

United States District Court
for the
_____ District of _____

A.B., Plaintiff
v.   Case No. _____
C.D., Defendant

Affidavit in Support of Motion

I swear or affirm under penalty of perjury that, because of my poverty, I cannot prepay the docket fees of my appeal or post a bond for them. I believe I am entitled to redress. I swear or affirm under penalty of perjury under United States laws that my answers on this form are true and correct. (28 U.S.C. § 1746; 18 U.S.C. § 1621.)

Signed: _____

Instructions

Complete all questions in this application and then sign it. Do not leave any blanks: if the answer to a question is "0," "none," or "not applicable (N/A)," write in that response. If you need more space to answer a question or to explain your answer, attach a separate sheet of paper identified with your name, your case's docket number, and the question number.

Date: _____

My issues on appeal are:

1.   For both you and your spouse estimate the average amount of money received from each of the following sources during the past 12 months. Adjust any amount that was received weekly, biweekly, quarterly, semiannually, or annually to show the monthly rate. Use gross amounts, that is, amounts before any deductions for taxes or otherwise.

Income source	Average monthly amount during the past 12 months		Amount expected next month	
	You	Spouse	You	Spouse
Employment	$_____	$_____	$_____	$_____
Self-employment	$_____	$_____	$_____	$_____
Income from real property (such as rental income)	$_____	$_____	$_____	$_____
Interest and dividends	$_____	$_____	$_____	$_____
Gifts	$_____	$_____	$_____	$_____
Alimony	$_____	$_____	$_____	$_____
Child support	$_____	$_____	$_____	$_____
Retirement (such as social security, pensions, annuities, insurance)	$_____	$_____	$_____	$_____
Disability (such as social security, insurance payments)	$_____	$_____	$_____	$_____
Unemployment payments	$_____	$_____	$_____	$_____
Public-assistance (such as welfare)	$_____	$_____	$_____	$_____
Other (specify): _____	$_____	$_____	$_____	$_____
Total monthly income:	$_____	$_____	$_____	$_____

2. List your employment history, most recent employer first. (Gross monthly pay is before taxes or other deductions.)

Employer	Address	Dates of employment	Gross monthly pay
_____	_____	_____	_____
_____	_____	_____	_____

3. List your spouse's employment history, most recent employer first. (Gross monthly pay is before taxes or other deductions.)

Employer	Address	Dates of employment	Gross monthly pay
_____	_____	_____	_____
_____	_____	_____	_____
_____	_____	_____	_____

4. How much cash do you and your spouse have? $_____
Below, state any money you or your spouse have in bank accounts or in any other financial institution.

Financial institution	Type of account	Amount you have	Amount your spouse has
_____	_____	$_____	$_____
_____	_____	$_____	$_____
_____	_____	$_____	$_____

If you are a prisoner, you must attach a statement certified by the appropriate institutional officer showing all receipts, expenditures, and balances during the last six months in your institutional accounts. If you have multiple accounts, perhaps because you have been in multiple institutions, attach one certified statement of each account.

5. List the assets, and their values, which you own or your spouse owns. Do not list clothing and ordinary household furnishings.

Home	(Value)	**Other real estate**	(Value)	**Motor vehicle #1**	(Value)
_____		_____			
_____		_____		Make & year: _____	
_____		_____		Model: _____	
				Registration #: _____	

Motor vehicle #2	(Value)	**Other assets**	(Value)	**Other assets**	(Value)
Make & year: _____		_____		_____	
Model: _____		_____		_____	
Registration #: _____		_____		_____	

6. State every person, business, or organization owing you or your spouse money, and the amount owed.

Person owing you or your spouse money	**Amount owed to you**	**Amount owed to your spouse**
_____	_____	_____
_____	_____	_____
_____	_____	_____

7. State the persons who rely on you or your spouse for support.

Name [or, if under 18, initials only]	**Relationship**	**Age**
_____	_____	_____
_____	_____	_____
_____	_____	_____

8. Estimate the average monthly expenses of you and your family. Show separately the amounts paid by your spouse. Adjust any payments that are made weekly, biweekly, quarterly, semiannually, or annually to show the monthly rate.

	You	**Your Spouse**
Rent or home-mortgage payment (include lot rented for mobile home)	$_____	$_____
Are real-estate taxes included? ☐ Yes ☐ No		
Is property insurance included? ☐ Yes ☐ No		
Utilities (electricity, heating fuel, water, sewer, and Telephone)	$_____	$_____
Home maintenance (repairs and upkeep)	$_____	$_____
Food	$_____	$_____
Clothing	$_____	$_____
Laundry and dry-cleaning	$_____	$_____
Medical and dental expenses	$_____	$_____
Transportation (not including motor vehicle payments)	$_____	$_____
Recreation, entertainment, newspapers, magazines, etc.	$_____	$_____
Insurance (not deducted from wages or included in Mortgage payments)		
Homeowner's or renter's	$_____	$_____
Life	$_____	$_____
Health	$_____	$_____
Motor Vehicle	$_____	$_____
Other: _____	$_____	$_____
Taxes (not deducted from wages or included in Mortgage payments) (specify): __	$_____	$_____
Installment payments		
Motor Vehicle	$_____	$_____
Credit card (name): _____	$_____	$_____
Department store (name): _____	$_____	$_____
Other: _____	$_____	$_____
Alimony, maintenance, and support paid to others	$_____	$_____
Regular expenses for operation of business, profession, or farm (attach detailed statement)	$_____	$_____
Other (specify): _____	$_____	$_____
Total monthly expenses:	$_____	$_____

9. Do you expect any major changes to your monthly income or expenses or in your assets or liabilities during the next 12 months?

☐ Yes ☐ No   If yes, describe on an attached sheet.

10. Have you paid—or will you be paying—an attorney any money for services in connection with this case, including the completion of this form? Yes No

If yes, how much? $_____

If yes, state the attorney's name, address, and telephone number:

_____

_____

_____

11. Have you paid—or will you be paying—anyone other than an attorney (such as a paralegal or a typist) any money for services in connection with this case, including the completion of this form?

☐ Yes ☐ No

If yes, how much? $_____

If yes, state the person's name, address, and telephone number:

_____

_____

12. Provide any other information that will help explain why you cannot pay the docket fees for your appeal.

13. State the city and state of your legal residence.

_____
_____

Your daytime phone number: (___) _____
Your age: _____ Your years of schooling: _____
Last four digits of your social-security number: _____

(As amended Apr. 24, 1998, eff. Dec. 1, 1998; Apr. 28, 2010, eff. Dec. 1, 2010.)

FORM 5. NOTICE OF APPEAL TO A COURT OF APPEALS FROM A JUDGMENT OR ORDER OF A DISTRICT COURT OR A BANKRUPTCY APPELLATE PANEL

United States District Court for the ....
District of ....

<pre>
In re   )
)
.... ,)
            Debtor   )
) File No...........
.... ,)
           Plaintiff   )
)
          v.   )
)
.... ,)
          Defendant   )
</pre>

Notice of Appeal to
United States Court of Appeals
for the .... Circuit
........................., the plaintiff [or defendant or other party] appeals to
the United States Court of Appeals for the .... Circuit from
the final judgment [or order or decree] of the district court for the district of ...
[or bankruptcy appellate panel of the .... circuit], entered in this case
on ...., 20.... [here describe the judgment, order, or decree] ....
    The parties to the judgment [or order or decree] appealed from and the names
and addresses of their respective attorneys are as follows:

Dated ....
Signed ....
Attorney for Appellant

Address: ....
....

(Added Apr. 25, 1989, eff. Dec. 1, 1989; Mar. 27, 2003, eff. Dec. 1, 2003.)

FORM 6.   CERTIFICATE OF COMPLIANCE WITH RULE 32(a)

Certificate of Compliance With Type-Volume Limitation, Typeface Requirements, and Type Style Requirements

1. This brief complies with the type-volume limitation of Fed. R. App. P. 32(a)(7)(B) because:

☐ this brief contains [*state the number of*] words, excluding the parts of the brief exempted by Fed. R. App. P. 32(a)(7)(B)(iii), *or*

☐ this brief uses a monospaced typeface and contains [*state the number of*] lines of text, excluding the parts of the brief exempted by Fed. R. App. P. 32(a)(7)(B)(iii).

2. This brief complies with the typeface requirements of Fed. R. App. P. 32(a)(5) and the type style requirements of Fed. R. App. P. 32(a)(6) because:

☐ this brief has been prepared in a proportionally spaced typeface using [*state name and version of word processing program*] in [*state font size and name of type style*], *or*

☐ this brief has been prepared in a monospaced typeface using [*state name and version of word processing program*] with [*state number of characters per inch and name of type style*].

(s)_____

Attorney for _____

Dated: _____

(Added Apr. 29, 2002, eff. Dec. 1, 2002.)

*

INDEX TO
FEDERAL RULES OF APPELLATE PROCEDURE

*

UNITED STATES COURT OF APPEALS FOR THE FIRST CIRCUIT

Including Amendments Received Through
January 1, 2012

Research Note

These rules may be searched electronically on Westlaw in the US–RULES database; updates to these rules may be found on Westlaw in US–RULESUPDATES. For search tips, and a detailed summary of database content, consult the Westlaw Scope Screen of each database.

APPENDIX OF FORMS

RULES OF ATTORNEY DISCIPLINARY ENFORCEMENT FOR THE COURT OF APPEALS FOR THE FIRST CIRCUIT

FIRST CIRCUIT LOCAL RULES FOR JUDICIAL–CONDUCT AND JUDICIAL–DISABILITY PROCEEDINGS

INTERNAL OPERATING PROCEDURES

ELECTRONIC CASE FILING

TITLE I.   APPLICABILITY OF RULES

FRAP 1.   SCOPE OF RULES; DEFINITION; TITLE

[For text of rule, see Federal Rules of Appellate Procedure]

FRAP 2.   SUSPENSION OF RULES

[For text of rule, see Federal Rules of Appellate Procedure]

TITLE II. APPEAL FROM A JUDGMENT OR ORDER OF A DISTRICT COURT

FRAP 3. APPEAL AS OF RIGHT—HOW TAKEN

[For text of rule, see Federal Rules of Appellate Procedure]

RULE 3.0. DOCKETING STATEMENT REQUIRED; DISMISSALS FOR WANT OF DILIGENT PROSECUTION

(a) Docketing Statement Required. To provide the clerk of the Court of Appeals at the commencement of an appeal with the information needed for effective case management, within 14 days after the case is docketed in the court of appeals, the person or persons taking the appeal must submit a separate statement listing all parties to the appeal, the last known counsel, and last known addresses and email addresses for counsel and unrepresented parties. Errors or omissions in this separate statement alone shall not otherwise affect the appeal if the notice of appeal itself complies with this rule.

(1) Form. Counsel filing an appeal must complete and file a docketing statement, using the form provided by the clerk of the appeals court.

(2) Service. A copy of the docketing statement and any attachments must be served on the opposing party or parties at the time the docketing statement is filed.

(3) Duty of Opposing Party. If an opposing party concludes that the docketing statement is in any way inaccurate, incomplete, or misleading, the clerk's office must be informed in writing of any errors and any proposed additions or corrections within fourteen days of service of the docketing statement, with copies to all other parties.

(b) If appellant does not pay the docket fee within 14 days of the filing of the notice of appeal, or does not file the docketing statement or any other document within the time set by the court, the appeal may be dismissed for want of diligent prosecution.

[Adopted effective September. 1, 1986. Amended effective September, 1999; October 13, 2009; December 1, 2009.]

FRAP 3.1 APPEAL FROM A JUDGMENT OF A MAGISTRATE JUDGE IN A CIVIL CASE [ABROGATED]

[For text of rule, see Federal Rules of Appellate Procedure]

FRAP 4. APPEAL AS OF RIGHT—WHEN TAKEN

[For text of rule, see Federal Rules of Appellate Procedure]

FRAP 5. APPEAL BY PERMISSION

[For text of rule, see Federal Rules of Appellate Procedure]

FRAP 5.1. APPEAL BY LEAVE UNDER 28 U.S.C. § 636(C)(5) [ABROGATED]

[For text of rule, see Federal Rules of Appellate Procedure]

FRAP 6. APPEAL IN A BANKRUPTCY CASE FROM A FINAL JUDGMENT, ORDER, OR DECREE OF A DISTRICT COURT OR BANKRUPTCY APPELLATE PANEL

[For text of rule, see Federal Rules of Appellate Procedure]

FRAP 7. BOND FOR COSTS ON APPEAL IN A CIVIL CASE

[For text of rule, see Federal Rules of Appellate Procedure]

FRAP 8. STAY OR INJUNCTION PENDING APPEAL

[For text of rule, see Federal Rules of Appellate Procedure]

FRAP 9. RELEASE IN A CRIMINAL CASE

[For text of rule, see Federal Rules of Appellate Procedure]

RULE 9.0. RECALCITRANT WITNESSES

(a) A recalcitrant witness who is held in contempt for refusal to testify is entitled to disposition of the recalcitrant witness's appeal within thirty days if the recalcitrant witness is denied bail, and the government is entitled to equal promptness if bail is granted. The unsuccessful party on the bail issue may waive the thirty day statutory requirement by filing a written waiver with the clerk of this court.

(b) The district court shall allow bail, with or without surety, unless the appeal appears frivolous, but a condition shall be the filing of a notice of appeal forthwith, and obedience to all subsequent orders with respect to briefing and argument. Except for cause shown the district court shall not, in any case, order a witness committed for the first forty-eight hours after the date of the order.

(c) The appeal shall be docketed immediately, and the district court's order on bail may be reviewed by the court of appeals or a judge thereof.

[Adopted effective September 1, 1986.]

FRAP 10. THE RECORD ON APPEAL

*[For text of rule, see Federal Rules
of Appellate Procedure]*

RULE 10.0. ORDERING TRANSCRIPTS

(a) Timely Filing. Fed. R. App. P. 10(b) requires that the transcript be ordered within 14 days of the filing of the notice of appeal. Parties are nevertheless urged to order any necessary transcript immediately after the filing of the notice. If the appellant fails to timely order a transcript in writing from the court reporter, the appeal may be dismissed for want of diligent prosecution.

(b) Transcript Order/Report. A Transcript Order/Report, in the form prescribed by this court, shall be used to satisfy the requirements of Fed. R. App. P. 10(b).

(c) Transcripts under the Criminal Justice Act. If the cost of the transcript is to be paid by the United States under the Criminal Justice Act, counsel must complete and attach CJA form 24 to the Transcript Order/Report so as to satisfy the requirement of Fed. R. App. P. 10(b) (4).

(d) Caveat. The court is of the opinion that in many cases a transcript is not really needed, and makes for delay and expense, as well as unnecessarily large records. The court urges counsel to endeavor, in appropriate cases, to enter into stipulations that will avoid or reduce transcripts. *See* Fed. R. App. P. 30(b). However, if an agreed statement of the evidence is contemplated, counsel are reminded of Fed. R. App. P. 10(c) requiring submission to the district court for approval. The fourteen-day ordering rule will not be suspended because of such activity, however, except by order of the court for good cause shown.

[Adopted effective September 1, 1986. Amended effective October 29, 1990; September, 1999; December 1, 2009.]

FRAP 11. FORWARDING THE RECORD

*[For text of rule, see Federal Rules
of Appellate Procedure]*

RULE 11.0. TRANSMISSION OF THE RECORD, SEALED DOCUMENTS

(a) Duty of Appellant. In addition to an appellant's duties under Fed. R. App. P. 11(a), it is an appellant's responsibility to see that the record, as certified, is complete.

(b) Transmission of the Record. In counseled appeals, the district court will transmit to the circuit clerk electronically a copy of the notice of appeal, the order(s) being appealed, and a certified copy of the district court docket report in lieu of transmitting the entire record. Papers and exhibits which are not electronically available will also be transmitted to the circuit clerk. In pro se cases, the entire record will be transmitted to the circuit clerk.

(c) Sealed Materials.

(1) Materials Sealed by District Court or Agency Order. The court of appeals expects that ordinarily motions to seal all or part of a district court or agency record will be presented to, and resolved by, the lower court or agency. Motions, briefs, transcripts, and other materials which were filed with the district court or agency under seal and which constitute part of the record transmitted to the court of appeals shall be clearly labeled as sealed when transmitted to the court of appeals and will remain under seal until further order of court.

(2) Motions to Seal in the Court of Appeals. In order to seal in the court of appeals materials not already sealed in the district court or agency (e.g., a brief or unsealed portion of the record), a motion to seal must be filed in paper form in the court of appeals; parties cannot seal otherwise public documents merely by agreement or by labeling them "sealed." A motion to seal, which should not itself be filed under seal, must explain the basis for sealing and specify the desired duration of the sealing order. If discussion of confidential material is necessary to support the motion to seal, that discussion shall be confined to an affidavit or declaration, which may be filed provisionally under seal. A motion to seal may be filed before the sealed material is submitted or, alternatively the item to be sealed (e.g., the brief) may be tendered with the motion and, upon request, will be accepted provisionally under seal, subject to the court's subsequent ruling on the motion. Material submitted by a party under seal, provisionally or otherwise must be stamped or labeled by the party on the cover "FILED UNDER SEAL." If the court of appeals denies the movant's motion to seal, any materials tendered under provisional seal will be returned to the movant. Motions to seal or sealed documents should never be filed electronically. See Administrative Order Regarding Case Management/Electronic Case Files System.

(3) Limiting Sealed Filings. Rather than automatically requesting the sealing of an entire brief, motion, or other filing, litigants should consider whether argument relating to sealed materials may be contained in separate supplemental brief, motion, or filing, which may then be sealed in accordance with the procedures in subsection (2).

(d) References to Sealed Materials.

(1) Records or materials sealed by district court, court of appeals, or agency order shall not be included in the regular appendix, but may be submitted in a separate, sealed supplemental volume of appendix. The sealed supplemental volume must be clearly and prominently labeled by the party on the cover "FILED UNDER SEAL."

(2) In addressing material under seal in an unsealed brief or motion or oral argument counsel are expected not to disclose the substance of the sealed material and to apprise the court that the material in question is sealed. If the record contains sealed materials of a sensitive character, counsel would be well advised to alert the court to the existence of such materials and their location by a footnote appended to the "Statement of Facts" caption in the opening or answering brief.

[Adopted effective September 1, 1986. Amended effective September, 1999; October 13, 2009.]

FRAP 12. DOCKETING THE APPEAL; FILING A REPRESENTATION STATEMENT; FILING THE RECORD

[For text of rule, see Federal Rules of Appellate Procedure]

RULE 12.0. APPEARANCE, WITHDRAWAL OF APPEARANCE

(a) Representation Statement, Appearance. A representation statement must take the form of an appearance, in a form prescribed by this court. Attorneys for both appellant and appellee must file appearance forms within 14 days after the case is docketed in the court of appeals. *See also* Local Rule 46.0(a). Additional or new attorneys for the parties may enter an appearance outside the 14 day period. However, in no event may any attorney file a notice of appearance without leave of court after the appellee brief has been filed.

(b) Withdrawal of Appearance. No attorney who has entered an appearance in this court may withdraw without the consent of the court. An attorney who has represented a defendant in a criminal case in the district court will be responsible for representing the defendant on appeal, whether or not the attorney has entered an appearance in the Court of Appeals, until the attorney is relieved of such duty by the court. Procedures for withdrawal in criminal cases are found in Local Rule 46.6. For requirements applying to court-appointed counsel, reference is made to Loc. R. 46.5, para. (c), the Criminal Justice Plan of this Circuit.

[Adopted effective September 1, 1986. Amended effective September, 1999; January 1, 2005.]

FRAP 12.1. REMAND AFTER AN INDICATIVE RULING BY THE DISTRICT COURT ON A MOTION FOR RELIEF THAT IS BARRED BY A PENDING APPEAL

[For text of rule, see Federal Rules of Appellate Procedure]

TITLE III. REVIEW OF A DECISION OF THE UNITED STATES TAX COURT

FRAP 13. REVIEW OF A DECISION OF THE TAX COURT

[For text of rule, see Federal Rules of Appellate Procedure]

FRAP 14. APPLICABILITY OF OTHER RULES TO THE REVIEW OF A TAX COURT DECISION

[For text of rule, see Federal Rules of Appellate Procedure]

TITLE IV. REVIEW OR ENFORCEMENT OF AN ORDER OF AN ADMINISTRATIVE AGENCY, BOARD, COMMISSION, OR OFFICER

FRAP 15. REVIEW OR ENFORCEMENT OF AN AGENCY ORDER—HOW OBTAINED; INTERVENTION

[For text of rule, see Federal Rules of Appellate Procedure]

FRAP 15.1. BRIEFS AND ORAL ARGUMENT IN A NATIONAL LABOR RELATIONS BOARD PROCEEDING

[For text of rule, see Federal Rules of Appellate Procedure]

FRAP 16. THE RECORD ON REVIEW OR ENFORCEMENT

[For text of rule, see Federal Rules of Appellate Procedure]

FRAP 17. FILING THE RECORD

[For text of rule, see Federal Rules of Appellate Procedure]

FRAP 18. STAY PENDING REVIEW

[For text of rule, see Federal Rules of Appellate Procedure]

FRAP 19. SETTLEMENT OF A JUDGMENT ENFORCING AN AGENCY ORDER IN PART

[For text of rule, see Federal Rules of Appellate Procedure]

FRAP 20. APPLICABILITY OF RULES TO THE REVIEW OR ENFORCEMENT OF AN AGENCY ORDER

[For text of rule, see Federal Rules of Appellate Procedure]

TITLE V. EXTRAORDINARY WRITS

FRAP 21. WRITS OF MANDAMUS AND PROHIBITION, AND OTHER EXTRAORDINARY WRITS

[For text of rule, see Federal Rules of Appellate Procedure]

RULE 21.0. PETITIONS FOR SPECIAL WRITS

A petition for a writ of mandamus or writ of prohibition shall be entitled simply "In re _____, Petitioner." To the extent that relief is requested of a particular judge, unless otherwise ordered, the judge shall be represented pro forma by counsel for the party opposing the relief, who shall appear in the name of the party and not that of the judge.

[Adopted effective September 1, 1986. Amended effective January 1, 1992; September, 1999.]

TITLE VI. HABEAS CORPUS; PROCEEDINGS IN FORMA PAUPERIS

FRAP 22. HABEAS CORPUS AND SECTION 2255 PROCEEDINGS

[For text of rule, see Federal Rules of Appellate Procedure]

RULE 22.0. HABEAS CORPUS; CERTIFICATE OF APPEALABILITY

(a) General Procedures. In this circuit, ordinarily neither the court nor a judge thereof will act on a request for a certificate of appealability if the district judge who refused the writ is available and has not ruled first. The general procedures regarding certificates of appealability are set forth in Fed. R. App. P.

22 and Rule 11 of the Rules Governing Proceedings Under 28 U.S.C. § 2254 or § 2255. These latter rules require the district judge to rule on the issuance of a certificate of appealability when a final order issues. If the district court denies a certificate, the petitioner may not appeal the denial but may file a motion for a certificate of appealability before this court. A petitioner wishing to challenge the denial of a § 2254 or § 2255 petition must file a timely notice of appeal whether or not the district court issues a certificate of appealability.

(b) Denial in Full by District Court. If the district court denies a certificate of appealability, the petitioner should promptly apply within the time set by the clerk to the court of appeals for issuance of a certificate of appealability. The motion should be accompanied by a copy of the district court's order and a memorandum giving specific and substantial reasons, and not mere generalizations, why a certificate should be granted. If no sufficient memorandum has been filed by the time set by the clerk, the certificate may be denied without further consideration. The effect of a denial is to terminate the appeal.

(c) Partial Denial by District Court.

(1) If the district court grants a certificate of appealability as to one or more issues, the petitioner's appeal shall go forward only as to the issue or issues for which the district court granted the certificate. *See Grant–Chase v. Commissioner*, 145 F.3d 431 (1st Cir. 1998).

(2) If the petitioner wants appellate review of an issue or issues as to which the district court has denied a certificate of appealability, petitioner must apply promptly, within the time set by the clerk of the court of appeals, to the court of appeals for an expanded certificate of appealability. The request for an expanded certificate of appealability:

(A) must be explicit as to the additional issues the petitioner wishes the court to consider and

(B) should be accompanied by a copy of the district court order and a memorandum giving specific and substantial reasons, and not mere generalizations, why an expanded certificate of appealability should be granted.

If the petitioner fails to apply for an expanded certificate of appealability within the time designated by the clerk, the appeal will proceed only with respect to the issues on which the district court has granted a certificate; this court will not treat an inexplicit notice of appeal, without more, as a request for a certificate of appealability with respect to issues on which the district court has denied a certificate.

(d) Grant in Full by District Court. If the district court grants a certificate of appealability on all issues,

the petitioner's appeal shall go forward. *See Grant–Chase v. Commissioner*, 145 F.3d 431 (1st Cir. 1998).
[Adopted effective September 10, 1996; July 22, 1997. Amended effective September, 1999; September 26, 2000; renumbered and amended effective December 1, 2009.]

RULE 22.1. HABEAS CORPUS; SUCCESSIVE PETITIONS

(a) Motion for Authorization. Any petitioner seeking to file a second or successive petition for relief pursuant to 28 U.S.C. §§ 2254 or 2255 must first file a motion with this court for authorization. A motion for authorization to file a second or successive § 2254 or § 2255 petition must be sufficiently complete on filing to allow the court to assess whether the standard set forth in 28 U.S.C. §§ 2244(b) or 2255, as applicable, has been satisfied. The motion must be accompanied by both:

(1) a completed application form, available from this court, stating the new claims(s) presented and addressing how Section 2244(b) or Section 2255's standard is satisfied; and

(2) copies of all relevant portions of earlier court proceedings, which must ordinarily include:

(A) copies of all § 2254 or § 2255 petitions earlier filed;

(B) the respondent's answer to the earlier petitions (including any portion of the state record the respondent submitted to the district court);

(C) any magistrate-judge's report and recommendation in the earlier § 2254 or § 2255 proceedings;

(D) the district court's decision in the earlier proceedings; and

(E) the portions of the state court record needed to evaluate the claims presented and to show that movant has exhausted state court remedies.

(b) Incomplete Motion. Failure to provide the requisite application and attachments may result in the denial of the motion for authorization with or without prejudice to refiling. At its discretion, the court may instead treat the motion as lodged, the filing being deemed complete when the deficiency is remedied.

(c) Service. The movant shall serve a copy of the motion to file a second or successive petition and all accompanying attachments on the state attorney general (§ 2254 cases) or United States Attorney for the federal judicial district in which movant was convicted (§ 2255 cases) and shall comply with Fed. R. App. P. 25.

(d) Response. The state attorney general (§ 2254 cases) or United States Attorney (§ 2255 cases) is requested to file a response within 14 days of the filing of the motion.

(e) Transfer. If a second or successive § 2254 or § 2255 petition is filed in a district court without the requisite authorization by the court of appeals pursuant to 28 U.S.C. § 2244(b)(3), the district court will transfer the petition to the court of appeals pursuant to 28 U.S.C. § 1631 or dismiss the petition. If the petition is transferred, the petitioner must file a motion meeting the substantive requirements of Loc. R. 22.2(a) within 45 days of the date of notice from the clerk of the court of appeals that said motion is required. If the motion is not timely filed, the court will enter an order denying authorization for the § 2254 or § 2255 petition.

[Adopted effective September 10, 1996; July 22, 1997. Amended effective September, 1999; renumbered effective December 1, 2009.]

TITLE VII. GENERAL PROVISIONS

FRAP 25. FILING AND SERVICE

[For text of rule, see Federal Rules of Appellate Procedure]

RULE 25.0. ELECTRONIC CASE FILING SYSTEM AND FACSIMILE

(a) Electronic Case Filing. Pursuant to Fed. R. App. P. 25(a)(2)(D) and (c)(2), the court has established procedures for electronic filing of documents, with certain exceptions, and authorized electronic service of documents using the court's transmission equipment, as set forth in the Administrative Order Regarding Case Management/Electronic Case Files System and any amendments to that order.

(b) Facsimile. The Clerk of Court is authorized to accept for filing papers transmitted by facsimile equipment in situations determined by the Clerk to be of an emergency nature or other compelling circumstances, subject to such procedures for follow-up filing of electronic or hard copies, as the Clerk may from time to time specify.

[Adopted effective March 18, 1992. Amended effective September, 1999; December 1, 2000; December 16, 2003; October 13, 2009.]

FRAP 26. COMPUTING AND EXTENDING TIME

[For text of rule, see Federal Rules of Appellate Procedure]

FRAP 26.1. CORPORATE DISCLOSURE STATEMENT

[For text of rule, see Federal Rules of Appellate Procedure]

FRAP 27. MOTIONS

FRAP 23. CUSTODY OR RELEASE OF A PRISONER IN A HABEAS CORPUS PROCEEDING

[For text of rule, see Federal Rules of Appellate Procedure]

FRAP 24. PROCEEDING IN FORMA PAUPERIS

[For text of rule, see Federal Rules of Appellate Procedure]

[For text of rule, see Federal Rules of Appellate Procedure]

RULE 27.0. MOTIONS

(a) Assent. Motions will not necessarily be allowed even though assented to.

(b) Emergency Relief. Motions for stay, or other emergency relief, may be denied for failure to present promptly. Counsel who envisages a possible need for an emergency filing, or emergency action by the court, or both, during a period when the Clerk's Office is ordinarily closed should consult with the Clerk's Office at the earliest opportunity. Failure to consult with the Clerk's Office well in advance of the occasion may preclude such special arrangements. Although documents may be filed electronically at any time through CM/ECF, the filer should not expect that the filing will be addressed outside regular business hours unless the filer contacts the clerk's office in advance to make special arrangements. The business hours for the clerk's office are Mondays through Fridays from 8:30 a.m. to 5:00 p.m.

(c) Summary Disposition. At any time, on such notice as the court may order, on motion of appellee or sua sponte, the court may dismiss the appeal or other request for relief or affirm and enforce the judgment or order below if the court lacks jurisdiction, or if it shall clearly appear that no substantial question is presented. In case of obvious error the court may, similarly, reverse. Motions for such relief should be promptly filed when the occasion appears, and must be accompanied by four copies of a memorandum or brief.

(d) Motions Decided by the Clerk. The clerk is authorized to dispose of certain routine, procedural motions in accordance with the Court's standing instructions. Any party adversely affected by the action of the clerk on a motion may promptly move for reconsideration. Unless the clerk grants reconsideration, the motion for reconsideration will be submitted to a single judge or panel. *See* Internal Operating Procedure V(C).

[Adopted effective September 1, 1986. Amended effective September, 1999; January 2, 2001; March 16, 2006; October 13, 2009.]

FRAP 28. BRIEFS

*[For text of rule, see Federal Rules
of Appellate Procedure]*

RULE 28.0. ADDENDUM TO BRIEFS REQUIRED

(a) Contents. In addition to the requirements of Fed. R. App. P. 28, for the court's convenience, the brief of the appellant must include an addendum containing the following items:

(1) Required. The judgments, decisions, rulings, or orders appealed from, including any supporting explanation (e.g., a written or transcript opinion), and in addition, where the district court or agency whose decision is under review was itself reviewing or acting upon the decision of a lower-level decision-maker, that lower-level decision as well (e.g., a recommended decision by a magistrate judge or an initial decision by an administrative law judge).

Note: If the decision appealed from is a text-only entry upon a docket report, a copy of the relevant entry or page of the docket report should be provided.

(2) Optional, but encouraged. The addendum may also include other items or short excerpts from the record that are either the subject of an issue on appeal (e.g., disputed jury instructions or disputed contractual provisions) or necessary for understanding the specific issues on appeal, up to 25 pages in total. Statutes, rules, regulations, etc. included as part of the addendum pursuant to Fed. R. App. P. 28(f) do not count towards this page limit.

(b) Form. The addendum shall be bound at the rear of the appellant's brief. The addendum must begin with a table of contents identifying the page at which each part begins.

(1) The appellee's brief may include such an addendum to incorporate materials omitted from the appellant's addendum, subject to the same limitations on length and content.

(2) Material included in the addendum need not be reproduced in the appendix also.

(c) Sealed Items. Notwithstanding the above, sealed or non-public items—including a presentence investigation report or statement of reasons in a judgment of criminal conviction—should not be included in a public addendum. Rather, where sealed items are to be included, they should be filed in a separate, sealed addendum.

[Renumbered and amended effective October, 1999. Amended effective April 10, 2006; February 16, 2007.]

[Formerly Local Rule 28.2.]

RULE 28.1. REFERENCES IN BRIEFS TO SEALED MATERIAL

Briefs filed with the court of appeals are a matter of public record. In order to have a brief sealed, counsel must file a specific and timely motion in compliance with Local Rule 11.0(c)(2) and (3) asking the court to seal a brief or supplemental brief. Counsel must also comply with Local Rule 11.0(d), when applicable.

Former Local Rule 28.1 is renumbered 32.2.

[Adopted 1999.]

FRAP 28.1. CROSS–APPEALS

*[For text of rule, see Federal Rules
of Appellate Procedure]*

FRAP 29. BRIEF OF AN AMICUS CURIAE

*[For text of rule, see Federal Rules
of Appellate Procedure]*

FRAP 30. APPENDIX TO THE BRIEFS

*[For text of rule, see Federal Rules
of Appellate Procedure]*

RULE 30.0. APPENDIX TO THE BRIEFS

(a) Number of Copies. Pursuant to Fed. R. App. P. 30(a)(3), only five (5) copies of the appendix need be filed with the clerk and on motion, for cause shown, parties may be allowed to file even fewer copies.

(b) Reproduction. The appendix should be printed on both sides of each page.

(c) Contents. The appendix must include any relevant portions of the pleadings, transcripts, exhibits, or other parts of the record referred to in the briefs as may be necessary to understand the issues on appeal and to preserve context. Material included in the addendum bound with appellant's brief need not be reproduced in the appendix. Guidance to counsel as to the contents of the appendix is set forth in a Notice to Counsel Regarding Contents of the Appendix, which accompanies the briefing schedule and is available on the court's website at www.ca1.uscourts.gov. The required and optional contents of the addendum are set forth in Local Rule 28.0(a).

(d) In Forma Pauperis. All pro se appeals proceeding in forma pauperis shall be considered on the record on appeal as certified by the clerk of the district court without the necessity of filing an appendix unless otherwise ordered by this court in a specific case. An appendix is required in all other appeals unless the court rules otherwise pursuant to Fed. R. App. P. 30(f). Although an appellant may be reimbursed for the cost of preparing an appendix where appellant's counsel is appointed under the Criminal Justice Act, counsel in consolidated multi-defendant appeals should coordinate, to the extent possible, to file a consolidated appendix.

(e) Translations. The court will not receive documents or cited opinions not in the English language unless translations are furnished. Whenever an opinion of the Supreme Court of Puerto Rico (or other Commonwealth of Puerto Rico court) is cited in a brief or oral argument which does not appear in the bound volumes in English, an official, certified or stipulated translation thereof shall be filed. Unless the translation is filed electronically in compliance with the court's electronic filing system, three conformed copies should also be filed. Partial translations will be accepted if stipulated by the parties or if submitted by one party not less than 30 days before the oral argument. Where partial translations are submitted by one party, opposing parties may, prior to oral argument, submit translations of such additional parts as they may deem necessary for a proper understanding of the holding.

(f) Sanctions. This court may impose sanctions against attorneys who unreasonably and vexatiously increase litigation costs by including unnecessary material in the appendix as provided for in Local Rule 38.0.

(g) Inclusion of Sealed Material in Appendices. Appendices filed with the court of appeals are a matter of public record. If counsel conclude that it is necessary to include sealed material in appendix form, then, in order to maintain the confidentiality of materials filed in the district court or agency under seal, counsel must designate the sealed material for inclusion in a supplemental appendix to be filed separately from the regular appendix and must file a specific and timely motion in compliance with Local Rules 11.0(c)(2), 11.0(c)(3), and 11.0(d) asking the court to seal the supplemental appendix.

[Amended effective January 1, 2005; May 14, 2009; October 13, 2009.]

NOTICE TO COUNSEL

The United States Court of Appeals for the First Circuit, in its Notice of Adoption of Amendment to Local Rule 30.0, dated April 14, 2009, eff. May 14, 2009, included the following:

"Notice to Counsel Regarding Contents of the Appendix

"In cases where appellant is represented by counsel, the district courts will no longer transmit the full record except upon the rare request of the circuit clerk. Accordingly, counsel should ensure that the addendum and appendix, combined, include those parts of the record necessary to understand the issues on appeal. At the same time, the appendix should not be unduly large. Pursuant to Fed. R. App. P. 30(a)(2), counsel may cite to parts of the record not included in the appendix.

"The appendix should be printed on two sides of each page. Transcript portions and other portions of the record are not considered relevant merely because they are referred to in the Statement of the Case or Statement of Facts, if not otherwise necessary for an understanding of the issues on appeal. The following is a list of items that typically should be included in the appendix if not already in the addendum:

"● The district court docket report;

"● The notice of appeal;

"● The complaint or indictment, as finally amended;

"● Where the appeal is from the grant or denial of a motion, those portions of any affidavits or exhibits submitted in the district court essential to resolution of an issue on appeal;

"● Where an appeal challenges sufficiency of the evidence to support a verdict or other determination (including an argument that a finding is clearly erroneous), the evidence of record that is relevant to the challenged determination;

"● Where an issue on appeal is based upon a jury instruction given or refused, the instruction or proposed instruction, any other relevant portion of the jury charge, and the specific portions of the transcript recording any discussion by the court or counsel involving the instruction, including the ruling or order, and objections;

"● Where an issue of appeal is based on written exhibits (including affidavits), the exhibit or portion thereof necessary to resolve the issue;

"● Where an issue on appeal concerns matters raised at a suppression hearing or is otherwise based upon a challenge to the admission or exclusion of evidence, relevant portions of the transcript, including any discussion by court or counsel involving the evidence, offer of proof, ruling or order, and objections at issue;

"● If the appeal is a collateral attack on a criminal conviction, copies of all relevant opinions by any federal court or state appellate court previously rendered in the criminal prosecution, any appeal, and any earlier collateral attack;

"● Where an issue on appeal concerns matters raised at a change of plea hearing, a transcript of the proceeding and any plea agreement;

"● If the appeal is a sentencing appeal, the sentencing hearing transcript and pre-sentence report, the latter of which should be filed in a separate sealed volume; and

"● In a proceeding on a petition for review of an administrative agency decision, the relevant portions of the administrative record.

"Pro se appeals proceeding in forma pauperis will be considered on the record without need to file an appendix unless otherwise ordered by the Court. Appendices are required in all other appeals. Although the cost of the appendix is reimbursable where appellant's counsel is appointed under the Criminal Justice Act, counsel in consolidated multi-defendant appeals should coordinate, to the extent possible, to file a joint appendix.

"Other federal and local rules should be carefully consulted and read in conjunction with Loc. R. 30.0. Fed. R. App. P. 30 and 32 provide additional guidance as to the form and content of the appendix. Local Rule 28.0 provides detailed guidance as to the form, content, and size limit of the addendum. Items which are required to be in the addendum include the judgments, decisions, rulings, or orders appealed from, including any supporting explanation (e.g., a written or transcript opinion), and in addition, where the district court or agency whose decision is under review was itself reviewing or acting upon the decision of a lower-level decision-maker; that lower-level decision as well (e.g., a recommended decision by a magistrate judge or an initial decision by an administrative law judge). Local Rule 28.0(b) lists optional, but encouraged items. Material included in the addendum need not be reproduced in the appendix.

"Sealed or otherwise non-public items should not be included in a public appendix or addendum, but rather should be filed in a separate sealed volume. See Local Rules 11.0(d)(1), 28.0(c), 30(g). For example, a pre-sentence report in a criminal case should not be included in a public appendix or addendum. Where a judgment of criminal conviction is required to be included in the addendum, the statement of reasons should be filed in a separate, sealed volume. See Local Rule 28.0(c). Finally, counsel should comply with the privacy protection requirements of Fed. R. App. P. 25(a)(5) and should make appropriate redactions. For more information on redaction requirements see the Notice of Electronic Availability of Case Information on the First Circuit's website at www.ca1.uscourts.gov."

FRAP 31. SERVING AND FILING BRIEFS

[For text of rule, see Federal Rules of Appellate Procedure]

RULE 31.0. FILING BRIEFS

(a) Time to File a Brief.

(1) Briefing schedules will be set in accordance with Fed. R. App. P.31(a) once the record is complete, including any necessary transcripts. When a brief (and addendum required by Local Rule 28.0) is filed electronically in compliance with the court's electronic filing system, the court will review the electronic filing and notify the filer of the due date for the paper copies of the brief. A reply brief may be rejected by the court if it contains matter repetitive of the main brief, or which, in the opinion of the court, should have been in the main brief.

(2) Unavailability of the transcript shall constitute cause for granting extensions, subject, however, to the provisions of Local Rule 10.0, ante.

(b) Number of copies. Only 10 copies of briefs need be filed with the clerk and on motion for cause shown, parties may be allowed to file even fewer copies. The disk required by Local Rule 32.0 for

briefs filed in paper form constitutes one copy for purposes of this rule. If a brief is filed electronically in compliance with the court's electronic filing system, the electronically filed brief counts as one copy and nine paper copies must be filed.

[Adopted effective September 1, 1986. Amended effective September, 1999; October 13, 2009.]

FRAP 32. FORM OF BRIEFS, APPENDICES, AND OTHER PAPERS

[For text of rule, see Federal Rules of Appellate Procedure]

RULE 32.0. COMPUTER GENERATED DISK REQUIREMENT FOR DOCUMENTS FILED IN PAPER FORM

(a) When a party who is represented by counsel files a brief, petition for rehearing or other paper exceeding 10 pages in length in paper form and not electronically, one copy must be submitted on a computer readable disk. The disk shall be filed at the time the party's paper filing is made. The brief on disk must be accompanied by nine paper copies of the brief. The disk shall contain the entire brief in a single electronic file. The label of the disk shall include the case name and docket number and identify the brief being filed (i.e. appellant's brief, appellee's brief, appellant's reply brief, etc.) and the file format utilized.

(b) The brief, petition for rehearing, and, in addition, all other papers exceeding 10 pages in length must be in Portable Document Format (PDF). The electronic version must contain any supplemental material that is bound with the paper version, such as an addendum. Although the main document must be generated by saving in PDF from the original word processing file, supplemental material may be scanned if an original word processing file of that material is unavailable.

(c) One copy of the disk may be served on each party separately represented by counsel. If a party chooses to serve a copy of the disk, the certificate of service must indicate service of the brief, petition for rehearing, and, in addition, all other papers exceeding 10 pages in length in both paper and electronic format.

(d) A party may be relieved from filing and service under this rule by submitting a motion, within fourteen days after the date of the notice establishing the party's initial briefing schedule, certifying that undue hardship or other unusual circumstances preclude compliance. The requirements of this rule shall not apply to parties appearing pro se.

(e) The disk requirement does not apply to electronically filed documents.

[Renumbered and amended effective October, 1999. Amended effective January 2, 2000; January 2, 2001; December 16, 2003; December 27, 2005; April 17, 2008; October 13, 2009.]

RULE 32.2   CITATION OF STATE DECISIONS AND LAW REVIEW ARTICLES

All citations to State or Commonwealth Courts must include both the official state court citation and the National Reporter System citation when such decisions have been published in both reports; *e.g., Coney v. Commonwealth*, 364 Mass. 137, 301 N.E.2d 450 (1973). Law review or other articles unpublished at the time a brief or memorandum is filed may not be cited therein, except with permission of the court.

[Renumbered and amended effective October, 1999.]

[Formerly Local Rule 28.1.]

RULE 32.4.   MOTIONS FOR LEAVE TO FILE OVERSIZED BRIEFS

The First Circuit encourages short, concise briefs. A motion for leave to file an oversized opening brief must be filed at least ten days in advance of the brief's due date, must specify the additional length sought, and must be supported by a detailed statement of grounds. A motion for leave to file an oversized reply brief must be filed at least seven days in advance. Such motions will be granted only for compelling reasons.

[Adopted effective January 1, 2005. Amended effective December 1, 2009.]

FRAP 32.1.   CITING JUDICIAL DISPOSITIONS

[For text of rule, see Federal Rules of Appellate Procedure]

RULE 32.1.0.   CITATION OF UNPUBLISHED DISPOSITIONS

(a) Disposition of this court. An unpublished judicial opinion, order, judgment or other written disposition of this court may be cited regardless of the date of issuance. The court will consider such dispositions for their persuasive value but not as binding precedent. A party must note in its brief or other filing that the disposition is unpublished. The term "unpublished" as used in this subsection and Local Rule 36.0(c) refers to a disposition that has not been selected for publication in the West Federal Reporter series, e.g., F., F.2d, and F.3d.

(b) Dispositions of other courts. The citation of dispositions of other courts is governed by Fed. R. App. P. 32.1 and the local rules of the issuing court. Notwithstanding the above, unpublished or non-precedential dispositions of other courts may always be cited to establish a fact about the case before the court (for example, its procedural history) or when the binding or preclusive effect of the opinion, rather than its quality as precedent, is relevant to support a claim of res judicata, collateral estoppel, law of the case, double jeopardy, abuse of the writ, or other similar doctrine.

[Adopted effective December 16, 2003; Renumbered and amended effective December 1, 2006.]

FRAP 33.   APPEAL CONFERENCES

[For text of rule, see Federal Rules of Appellate Procedure]

RULE 33.0.   CIVIL APPEALS MANAGEMENT PLAN

Pursuant to Rule 47 of the Federal Rules of Appellate Procedure, the United States Court of Appeals for the First Circuit adopts the following plan to establish a Civil Appeals Management Program, said Program to have the force and effect of a local rule.

(a) Pre–Argument Filing; Ordering Transcript.

(1) Upon receipt of the Notice of Appeal in the Court of Appeals, the Clerk of the Court of Appeals shall send notice of the Civil Appeals Management Plan to the appellant. Upon receipt of further notice from the Clerk of the Court of Appeals, appellant shall, within fourteen days:

(A) file with the Clerk of the Court of Appeals, and serve on all other parties a statement, in the form of the Docketing Statement required by Local Rule 3.0(a), detailing information needed for the prompt disposition of an appeal;

(B) certify and file with the Clerk of the Court of Appeals a statement, in the form required by Local Rule 10.0(b), that satisfactory arrangements have been made with the court reporter for payment of the cost of the transcript.

The Parties shall thereafter provide Settlement Counsel with such information about the appeals as Settlement Counsel may reasonably request.

(2) Nothing herein shall alter the duty to order from the court reporter, promptly upon filing of the Notice of Appeal in the District Court, a transcript of the proceedings pursuant to Fed. R. App. P. Rule 10(b).

(b) Pre–Argument Conference; Pre–Argument Conference Order.

(1) In cases where he may deem this desirable, the Settlement Counsel, who shall be appointed by the Court of Appeals, may direct the attorneys, and in certain cases the clients, to attend a pre-argument conference to be held as soon as practicable before him or a judge designated by the Chief Judge to consider the possibility of settlement, the simplification of the issues, and any other matters which the Settlement Counsel determines may aid in the handling or the disposition of the proceeding.

(2) At the conclusion of the conference, the Settlement Counsel shall consult with the Clerk concerning the Clerk's entry of a Conference Order which shall control the subsequent course of the proceeding.

(c) Confidentiality. The Settlement Counsel shall not disclose the substance of the Pre-argument Conference, nor report on the same, to any person or persons whomsoever (including, but not limited to, any judge). The attorneys are likewise prohibited from disclosing any substantive information emanating from the conference to anyone other than their clients or co-counsel; and then only upon receiving due assurance that the recipients will honor the confidentiality of the information. *See In re Lake Utopia Paper Ltd.*, 608 F.2d 928 (2nd Cir. 1979). The fact of the conference having taken place, and the bare result thereof (*e.g.*, "settled," "not settled," "continued"), including any resulting Conference Order, shall not be considered to be confidential.

(d) Non–Compliance Sanctions.

(1) If the appellant has not taken each of the actions set forth in section (a) of this Program, or in the Conference Order, within the time therein specified, the appeal may be dismissed by the Clerk without further notice.

(2) Upon the failure of a party or attorney to comply with the provisions of this rule or the provisions of the court's notice of settlement conference, the court may assess reasonable expenses caused by the failure, including attorney's fees; assess all or a portion of the appellate costs; dismiss the appeal; or take such other appropriate action as the circumstances may warrant.

(e) Grievances. Any grievances as to the handling of any case under the Program will be addressed by the Court of Appeals, and should be sent to the Circuit Executive, One Courthouse Way, Suite 3700, Boston, MA 02210, who will hold them confidential on behalf of the Court of Appeals unless release is authorized by the complainant.

(f) Scope of Program. The Program will include all civil appeals and review of administrative orders, except the following: It will not include original proceedings (such as petitions for mandamus), prisoner petitions, habeas corpus petitions, summary enforcement actions of the National Labor Relations Board or any pro se cases. Nothing herein shall prevent any judge or panel, upon motion or sua sponte, from referring any matter to the Settlement Counsel at any time.

The foregoing Civil Appeals Management Program shall be applicable to all such cases as set forth above, arising from the District Courts in the Districts of Maine, New Hampshire, Massachusetts, and Rhode Island, in which the Notice of Appeal is received in the Court of Appeals on or after January 1, 1992; and all such cases arising from the District Court in the District of Puerto Rico, in which the Notice of Appeal is received in the Court of Appeals on or after January 1, 1993.

[Adopted effective October 15, 1999. Amended effective October 15, 2007; October 13, 2009; December 1, 2009.]

FRAP 34.   ORAL ARGUMENT

*[For text of rule, see Federal Rules
of Appellate Procedure]*

RULE 34.0.   ORAL ARGUMENT

(a) Party's Statement. Any party who desires to do so may include, either in the opening or answering brief as the case may be, a statement limited to one-half page setting forth the reasons why oral argument should, or need not, be heard. If such a statement is included, it must be inserted in the brief immediately after the Table of Contents and Table of Authorities and immediately before the first page of the brief and must be captioned "REASONS WHY ORAL ARGUMENT SHOULD [NEED NOT] BE HEARD" as appropriate. The inclusion of this statement will not be counted in computing the maximum permitted length of the brief.

(b) Notice of Argument. If the court concludes that oral argument is unnecessary based on the standards set forth in Fed. R. App. P. 34(a)(2), counsel shall be so advised. The court's decision to dispense with oral argument may be announced at the time that a decision on the merits is rendered.

(c) Argument.

(1) Presentation. Parties may expect the court to have some familiarity with the briefs. Normally the court will permit no more than 15 minutes per side for oral argument. It is counsel's responsibility to keep track of time. Where more than one counsel argues on one side of a case, it is counsel's further responsibility to assure a fair division of the total time allotted. One or more cases posing the same issues, arising from the same factual context, will be treated as a single case for the purposes of this rule.

(2) Rebuttal. Allowance of time for rebuttal is within the discretion of the presiding judge, but often appellant will be allowed to reserve a few minutes on request made at the outset of opening argument. However, counsel is expected to cover all anticipated issues in opening argument. Reserved rebuttal time is for the purpose of answering contentions made in the other side's oral argument. Any time allowed to be reserved by the presiding judge will be deducted from that party's allotted time for opening argument.

[Adopted effective September 1, 1986; renumbered and amended effective October, 1999. Amended effective January 22, 2010.]

[Formerly Local Rule 34.1.]

RULE 34.1.　TERMS AND SITTINGS

(a) **Terms.** The court shall not hold formal terms but shall be deemed always open for the purpose of docketing appeals and petitions, making motions, filing records, briefs and appendices, filing opinions and entering orders and judgments. Where a federal holiday falls on a Monday, the general order is that the court shall commence its sitting on Tuesday.

(b) **Sittings.**

(1) **Locations.** Sittings will be in Boston except that there will also be sittings in Puerto Rico in November and March and at such other times and places as the court orders. Cases arising in Puerto Rico which are assigned to other sessions may be reassigned to sessions scheduled to be conducted in Puerto Rico. All other cases will be assigned for hearing or submission to the next available session after the briefs have been filed or the time therefor has run.

(2) **Request for Assignment.** Requests for assignment to a specific session, including the March and November sessions, must state reasons justifying special treatment. Assignment to the November and March Puerto Rico session list, so long as space permits, will be made on the basis of statutory priority requirements, hardship that would result from travel to Boston, or other good cause shown.

(c) **Calendaring.** Approximately six weeks prior to hearing, the clerk will contact counsel concerning assignment of the case to a specific day, and request the name of the person who will present the oral argument. Two weeks before the monthly sitting commences the clerk will prepare and distribute an order assigning the cases for that session for hearing. The court reserves the privilege of reducing the allotted time for argument when the case is presented.

(d) **Continuances.** Once a case is scheduled for argument, continuances may be allowed only for grave cause.

[Adopted effective September 1, 1986. Amended effective April 1, 1988; renumbered and amended effective October, 1999. Amended effective December 16, 2003.]

[Formerly Local Rule 34.2.]

FRAP 35.　EN BANC DETERMINATION

[For text of rule, see Federal Rules of Appellate Procedure]

RULE 35.0.　EN BANC DETERMINATION

(a) **Who May Vote; Composition of En Banc Court.** The decision whether a case should be heard or reheard en banc is made solely by the circuit judges of this circuit who are in regular active service. Rehearing en banc shall be ordered only upon the affirmative votes of a majority of the judges of this court in regular active service who are not disqualified, provided that the judges who are not disqualified constitute a majority of the judges who are in regular active service. A court en banc consists solely of the circuit judges of this circuit in regular active service except that any senior circuit judge of this circuit shall be eligible to participate, at that judge's election, in the circumstances specified in 28 U.S.C. § 46(c).

(b) **Petitions for Panel Hearing or Rehearing En Banc.** If a petitioner files a petition for panel rehearing and a petition for rehearing en banc addressed to the same decision or order of the court, the two petitions must be combined into a single document and the document is subject to the 15–page limitation contained in Fed. R. App. P. 35 (b)(2), (3).

(c) **Number of Copies.** When a petition for hearing or rehearing en banc or combined Fed. R. App. P. 35(b)(3) document is filed electronically in compliance with the court's electronic filing system, paper copies are not required and a disk copy is not required. When a petition for hearing or rehearing en banc or combined Fed. R. App. P. 35(b)(3) document is filed in paper form, ten copies must be filed with the clerk, including one copy on a computer generated disk. The disk must be filed regardless of page length but otherwise in accordance with Local Rule 32.0.

(d) **Motions for Leave to File Oversized Petitions.** A motion for leave to file a petition in excess of the page length limitations of Fed. R. App. P. 35(b)(2) and Local Rule 35.0(b) must be filed at least five days in advance of the petition's due date, must specify the additional length sought, and must contain a detailed statement of grounds. Such motions will be granted only for compelling reasons.

[Local Rule 35 adopted effective September 1, 1986; renumbered as Local Rule 35.1 effective April 1, 1988. Renumbered and amended effective October 1999. Amended effective January 2, 2001; December 16, 2003; January 1, 2005; December 1, 2009.]

[Formerly Local Rules 35.1, 35.2, and 35.3. Amended effective October 13, 2009.]

FRAP 36. ENTRY OF JUDGMENT; NOTICE

[For text of rule, see Federal Rules of Appellate Procedure]

RULE 36.0. OPINIONS

(a) Opinions Generally. The volume of filings is such that the court cannot dispose of each case by opinion. Rather it makes a choice, reasonably accommodated to the particular case, whether to use an order, memorandum and order, or opinion. An opinion is used when the decision calls for more than summary explanation. However, in the interests both of expedition in the particular case, and of saving time and effort in research on the part of future litigants, some opinions are rendered in unpublished form; that is, the opinions are directed to the parties but are not published in West's Federal Reporter. As indicated in Local Rule 36.0(b), the court's policy, when opinions are used, is to prefer that they be published; but in limited situations, described in Local Rule 36.0(b), where opinions are likely not to break new legal ground or contribute otherwise to legal development, they are issued in unpublished form.

(b) Publication of Opinions. The United States Court of Appeals for the First Circuit has adopted the following plan for the publication of its opinions.

(1) Statement of Policy. In general, the court thinks it desirable that opinions be published and thus be available for citation. The policy may be overcome in some situations where an opinion does not articulate a new rule of law, modify an established rule, apply an established rule to novel facts or serve otherwise as a significant guide to future litigants. (Most opinions dealing with claims for benefits under the Social Security Act, 42 U.S.C. § 205(g), will clearly fall within the exception.)

(2) Manner of Implementation.

(A) As members of a panel prepare for argument, they shall give thought to the appropriate mode of disposition (order, memorandum and order, unpublished opinion, published opinion). At conference the mode of disposition shall be discussed and, if feasible, agreed upon. Any agreement reached may be altered in the light of further research and reflection.

(B) With respect to cases decided by a unanimous panel with a single opinion, if the writer recommends that the opinion not be published, the writer shall so state in the cover letter or memorandum accompanying the draft. After an exchange of views, should any judge remain of the view that the opinion should be published, it must be.

(C) When a panel decides a case with a dissent, or with more than one opinion, the opinion or opinions shall be published unless all the participating judges decide against publication. In any case decided by the court en banc the opinion or opinions shall be published.

(D) Any party or other interested person may apply for good cause shown to the court for publication of an unpublished opinion.

(E) Periodically the court shall conduct a review in an effort to improve its publication policy and implementation.

(c) Precedential Value of Unpublished Opinions. While an unpublished opinion of this court may be cited to this court in accordance with Fed. R. App. P. 32.1 and Local Rule 32.1.0, a panel's decision to issue an unpublished opinion means that the panel sees no precedential value in that opinion.

(d) Copies of Opinions. Unless subject to a standing order which might apply to classes of subscribers, such as law schools, the charge for a copy of each opinion, after one free copy to counsel for each party, is $5.00. Free copies of opinions are available on the court's website at www.ca1.uscourts.gov.

[Renumbered and amended effective October, 1999. Par. (b)(2)(F) amended on an interim basis, effective September 24, 2001. Amended effective December 16, 2003; December 1, 2006; October 13, 2009.]

[Formerly Local Rules 36.1 and 36.2.]

RULE 36.1 OPINIONS

[Renumbered Local Rule 36(a).]

[Adopted effective September 1, 1986; renumbered October, 1999.]

RULE 36.2 PUBLICATION OF OPINIONS

[Renumbered Local Rule 36(b).]

[Adopted effective September 1, 1986; renumbered effective October, 1999.]

FRAP 37. INTEREST ON JUDGMENT

[For text of rule, see Federal Rules of Appellate Procedure]

FRAP 38. FRIVOLOUS APPEAL— DAMAGES AND COSTS

[For text of rule, see Federal Rules of Appellate Procedure]

RULE 38.0. SANCTIONS FOR VEXATIOUS LITIGATION

When any party to a proceeding before this court or any attorney practicing before the court files a motion, brief, or other document that is frivolous or interposed for an improper purpose, such as to harass or to cause unnecessary delay, or unreasonably or vexatiously increases litigation costs, the court may, on its own motion, or on motion of a party, impose appropriate sanctions on the offending party, the attorney, or both. Any party or attorney on whom sanctions may be imposed under this rule shall be afforded an opportunity to respond within fourteen days of service of a motion or an order to show cause before sanctions are imposed by the court.

[Adopted effective January 1, 2005.]

FRAP 39. COSTS

[For text of rule, see Federal Rules of Appellate Procedure]

RULE 39.0. TAXATION OF REPRODUCTION COSTS

(a) The maximum rate at which costs may be taxed shall be fixed from time to time by the clerk of the court of appeals. See Fed. R. App. P. 39(c). A schedule of Maximum Rates for Taxation of Costs is posted on the court's website at www.ca1.uscourts.gov and is available by request to the clerk's office. Costs are taxed at the maximum rates set by the clerk or at the actual cost, whichever is lower.

(b) Costs may be recovered for reproducing the following number of copies, unless the court directs filing of a different number:

(1) **Briefs.** Nine copies of each brief plus two for the filer and two for each party required to be served with paper copies of the brief. See Local Rule 31.0(b).

(2) **Appendices.** Five copies of each appendix plus one for the filer and one for each unrepresented party and each separately represented party. See Local Rule 30.0(a).

(c) Requests for taxation of costs must be made on the Bill of Costs form available on the court's website at www.ca1.uscourts.gov and by request to the clerk's office, and must be accompanied by a vendor's itemized statement of charges, if applicable, or a statement by counsel if reproduction was performed in-house. Bills of costs must be filed in the clerk's office within fourteen days after entry of judgment, even if a petition for rehearing or other post-judgment motion is filed. See Fed. R. App. P. 39(d)(1). Payment of costs should be made directly to the prevailing party or counsel, not to the clerk's office.

[Adopted effective April 20, 2007. Amended effective October 13, 2009.]

RULE 39.1. FEE APPLICATIONS

(a) Fee Applications under the Equal Access to Justice Act.

(1) **Time for Filing.** An application to a court of appeals for an award of fees and other expenses pursuant to 28 U.S.C. § 2412, in connection with an appeal, must be filed with the clerk of the court of appeals, with proof of service on the United States, within 30 days of final judgment in the action. For purposes of the 30–day limit, a judgment must not be considered final until the time for filing an appeal or a petition for a writ of certiorari has expired, or the government has given written notice to the parties and to the court of appeals that it will not seek further review, or judgment is entered by the court of last resort.

(2) **Content.** The application shall:

(A) identify the applicant and the proceeding for which the award is sought;

(B) show that the party seeking the award is a prevailing party and is eligible to receive an award;

(C) show the nature and extent of services rendered and the amount sought, including an itemized statement from an attorney representing the party or any agent or expert witness appearing on behalf of the party, stating the actual time expended and the rate at which fees are computed, together with a statement of expenses for which reimbursement is sought; and

(D) identify the specific position of the United States that the party alleges was not substantially justified. The court of appeals may, in its discretion, remit any such application to the district court for a determination.

(3) **Objection.** If the United States has any objection to the application for fees and other expenses, such objection must be filed within 30 days of service of the application.

(b) Fee Applications other than under 28 U.S.C. § 2412. An application, under any statute, rule or custom other than 28 U.S.C. § 2412, for an award of fees and other expenses, in connection with an appeal, must be filed with the clerk of the court of appeals within 30 days of the date of entry of the final circuit judgment, whether or not attorney fees had been requested in the trial court, except in those circumstances where the court of appeals has ordered that the award of fees and other expenses be remanded to the district court for a determination. For purposes of the 30–day limit, a judgment must not be considered final until the time for filing an appeal or a petition for a writ of certiorari has expired, or judgment is entered by the court of last resort. If any party against whom an award of fees and other expenses is sought has any objection to the application, such objection must be filed within 30 days of service of the application. The court of appeals may, in its discretion, remit any such application to the district court for a determination.

[Renumbered and amended effective October, 1999; Former Rule 39.0 redesignated Rule 39.1 effective April 20, 2007.]

FRAP 40. PETITION FOR PANEL REHEARING

[For text of rule, see Federal Rules of Appellate Procedure]

RULE 40.0. PETITION FOR PANEL REHEARING

(a) Number of Copies. When a petition for panel rehearing is filed electronically in compliance with the court's electronic filing system, paper copies are not required and a disk copy is not required. When a petition for panel rehearing is filed in paper form, ten copies must be filed with the clerk, including one copy on computer generated disk. The disk must be filed regardless of page length but otherwise in accordance with Local Rule 32.0.

(b) Motions for Leave to File Oversized Petitions. A motion for leave to file a petition for panel rehearing in excess of the page length limitations of Fed. R. App. P. 40(b) must be filed at least five days in advance of the petition's due date, must specify the additional length sought, and must contain a detailed statement of grounds. Such motions will be granted only for compelling reasons.

[Amended effective January 1, 2005; October 13, 2009; December 1, 2009.]

FRAP 41. MANDATE: CONTENTS; ISSUANCE AND EFFECTIVE DATE; STAY

[For text of rule, see Federal Rules of Appellate Procedure]

RULE 41.0. STAY OF MANDATE

Whereas an increasingly large percentage of unsuccessful petitions for certiorari have been filed in this circuit in criminal cases in recent years, in the interests of minimizing unnecessary delay in the administration of justice mandate will not be stayed hereafter in criminal cases following the affirmance of a conviction simply upon request. On the contrary, mandate

will issue and bail will be revoked at such time as the court shall order except upon a showing, or an independent finding by the court, of probable cause to believe that a petition would not be frivolous, or filed merely for delay. *See* 18 U.S.C. § 3148. The court will revoke bail even before mandate is due. A comparable principle will be applied in connection with affirmed orders of the NLRB, *see NLRB v. Athbro Precision Engineering*, 423 F.2d 573 (1st Cir. 1970), and in other cases where the court believes that the only effect of a petition for certiorari would be pointless delay.

[Adopted effective September 1, 1986.]

FRAP 42. VOLUNTARY DISMISSAL

[For text of rule, see Federal Rules of Appellate Procedure]

FRAP 43. SUBSTITUTION OF PARTIES

[For text of rule, see Federal Rules of Appellate Procedure]

FRAP 44. CASE INVOLVING A CONSTITUTIONAL QUESTION WHEN THE UNITED STATES OR THE RELEVANT STATE IS NOT A PARTY

[For text of rule, see Federal Rules of Appellate Procedure]

FRAP 45. CLERK'S DUTIES

[For text of rule, see Federal Rules of Appellate Procedure]

RULE 45.0. DEFAULTS

(a) Appellant. When a cause is in default as to the filing of the brief for appellant or petitioner, and the appendix, if one is required, the clerk must enter an order dismissing the appeal for want of diligent prosecution. The party in default may have the appeal reinstated upon showing special circumstances justifying the failure to comply with the time limit. The motion to set aside the dismissal must be filed within fourteen days.

(b) Appellee. When a cause is in default as to the filing of the brief for appellee or respondent, the cause must be assigned to the next list and the appellee will not be heard at oral argument except by leave of the Court.

(c) Local Rule 3.0. Counsel are reminded of Local Rule 3.0 providing for the dismissal of the appeal for want of diligent prosecution if the docket fee is not paid within 14 days of the filing of the notice of appeal.

[Adopted effective September 1, 1986. Amended effective January 1, 1992; October 15, 1999; December 1, 2009.]

RULE 45.1. THE CLERK

(a) **Business Hours.** The office of the clerk shall be open for business from 8:30 a.m. to 5:00 p.m. except Saturdays, Sundays, and legal holidays.

(b) **Fees and Costs.** The clerk must charge the fees and costs which are fixed from time to time by the Judicial Conference of the United States, pursuant to 28 U.S.C. § 1913.

(c) **Copies of Opinions.** Unless subject to a standing order which might apply to classes of subscribers, such as law schools, the charge for a copy of each opinion, after one free copy to counsel for each party, is $5.00. Free copies of opinions are available on the court's website at www.ca1.uscourts.gov.

[Adopted effective September 1, 1986. Amended effective October 15, 1999; October 13, 2009.]

FRAP 46. ATTORNEYS

[For text of rule, see Federal Rules of Appellate Procedure]

RULE 46.0. ATTORNEYS

(a) **Admission.**

(1) **Admission Fee.** Upon being admitted to practice, an attorney other than government counsel, and court-appointed counsel, must pay a local admission fee of $50.00 to the clerk. The clerk must maintain the proceeds as a court's discretionary fund for the reimbursement of expenses of non-compensable court-appointed counsel and such other purposes as the court may order. This fee is in addition to the $176.00 national admission fee imposed by the Court of Appeals Miscellaneous Fee Schedule, promulgated under 28 U.S.C. § 1913. Attorneys may be admitted in open court on motion or otherwise as the court shall determine.

(2) **Admission as a Prerequisite to Practice.** In order to file motions, pleadings or briefs on behalf of a party or participate in oral argument, attorneys must be admitted to the bar of this court and file an appearance form. The appearance of a member of the bar of any court designated in Fed. R. App. P. 46(a) will be entered subject to filing an application and subsequent admission to practice in this court. Forms for admission and entry of appearance will be provided by the clerk.

(3) **Parties.** A party desiring to appear without counsel shall notify the clerk in writing by completing and filing an entry of appearance on a form approved by the court.

(b) **Temporary Suspension of Attorneys.** When it is shown to the Court of Appeals that any member of its bar has been suspended or disbarred from practice by a final decision issued by any other court of record, or has been found guilty of conduct unbecoming of a member of the bar of this court, the member may be temporarily suspended from representing parties before this court pending the completion of proceedings initiated under Fed. R. App. P. 46 and the Rules of Attorney Disciplinary Enforcement for the Court of Appeals for the First Circuit.

(c) **Disciplinary Rules.** The Rules of Attorney Disciplinary Enforcement for the Court of Appeals for the First Circuit are on file in the clerks's office. A copy may be obtained upon request addressed to the clerk of this court.

(d) **Library Access.** The law library of this court shall be open to members of the Bar, to the United States Attorney of the Circuit and their assistants, to other law officers of the government, and persons having a case in this court, but books may be removed only by government employees, who shall sign therefor.

(e) **Staff Attorneys and Law Clerks.** No one serving as a staff attorney to the court or as a law clerk to a member of this court or employed in any such capacity by this court shall engage in the practice of law while continuing in such position. Nor shall a staff attorney or law clerk after separating from that position practice as an attorney in connection with any case pending in this court during the term of service, or appear at the counsel table or on brief in connection with any case heard during a period of one year following separation from service with the court.

(f) **Standing Rule Governing Appearance and Argument by Eligible Law Students.**

(1) **Scope of Legal Assistance.**

(A) An eligible law student with the written consent of an indigent and the indigent's attorney of record may appear in this court on behalf of that indigent in any case. The attorney of record, for purposes of this paragraph, must be a member of the bar of this court and either appointed as counsel on appeal for the indigent or represent the indigent on a pro bono basis. The written consent must be filed with the clerk.

An eligible law student may also appear in this court on behalf of the United States or a State, or agency thereof, provided that the governmental entity on whose behalf the student appears has consented thereto in writing, and that the attorney of record has also indicated in writing approval of that appearance. The attorney of record must be a member of the bar of this court, and the written consent must be filed with the clerk.

(B) An eligible law student may assist in the preparation of briefs and other documents to be filed in this court, but such briefs or documents must be signed by the attorney of record. Names of students participating in the preparation of briefs may, however, be added to the briefs. The law student may also participate in oral argument with leave of the court, but only in the presence of the attorney of record. The attorney of record must assume personal professional responsibility for the law student's work and for supervising the quality of the law student's work. The attorney of record should be familiar with the case and prepared to supplement or correct any written or oral statements made by the student.

(2) **Student Eligibility Requirements.** In order to appear, the student must:

(A) Be enrolled in a law school approved by the American Bar Association, or be a recent graduate of such a school, awaiting the first bar examination after the student's graduation or the result of that examination;

(B) Have completed legal studies amounting to at least four (4) semesters, or the equivalent if the school is on some basis other than a semester basis;

(C) Be taking, or have taken, a course in appellate advocacy or a course in a supervised clinical program for academic credit;

(D) Be certified by the dean of the student's law school as qualified to provide the legal representation permitted by this rule. This certification, which shall be filed with the clerk, may be withdrawn by the dean at any time by mailing a notice to the clerk or by termination by this court without notice or hearing and without any showing of cause;

(E) Neither ask for nor receive any compensation or remuneration of any kind for the student's services from the person on whose behalf the student renders services, but this shall not prevent an attorney, legal aid bureau, law school, public defender agency, a State, or the United States from paying compensation to the eligible law student;

(F) Certify in writing that the student has read and is familiar with the Code of Professional Responsibility of the American Bar Association, the Federal Rules of Appellate Procedure, and the rules of this court.

(3) **Standards of Supervision.** The supervising attorney of record must:

(A) File with this court the attorney's written consent to supervise the student;

(B) Assume personal professional responsibility for the student's work;

(C) Assist the student to the extent necessary;

(D) Appear with the student in all proceedings before this court and be prepared to supplement any written or oral statement made by the student to this court or opposing counsel.

(4) **Forms Required by Rule.**

(A) **Form to be completed by the party for whom the law student is rendering services:**

I authorize _____, a [law student] or [recent law school graduate awaiting the first bar examination after the student's graduation or the results of that examination], to appear in court or at other proceedings on my behalf, and to prepare documents on my behalf.

| _____ | _____ |
| (Date) | (Signature of Client) |

(If more than one client is involved, approvals from each shall be attached. If services are rendered for the United States or agency thereof, the form should be completed by the United States Attorney or authorized representative. If services are rendered for a State or agency thereof, the form should be completed by the State Attorney General or authorized representative.)

(B) **Form to be completed by the law student's supervising attorney:**

I certify that this student [has completed at least 4 semesters of law school work] or [is a recent law school graduate awaiting the first bar examination or the results of that examination], and is, to the best of my knowledge, of good character and competent legal ability. I will carefully supervise all of this student's work. I authorize this student to appear in court or at other proceedings, and to prepare documents. I will accompany the student at such appearances, sign all documents prepared by the student, assume personal responsibility for the student's work, and be prepared to supplement, if necessary, any statements made by the student to the court or to opposing counsel.

_____	_____
(Name of Student)	(Signature of Supervising Attorney)
_____	_____
(Address & Phone of Above)	(Address & Phone of Above)

Name of Law School Attending _____

(C) Form to be completed by law student:

I certify that I [have completed at least 4 semesters of law school work] or [am a recent law school graduate awaiting the first bar examination or the results of that examination]; that I am taking, or have taken, a course in appellate advocacy or a course in a supervised clinical program for academic credit; that I am familiar and will comply with the Code of Professional Responsibility of the American Bar Association, the Federal Rules of Appellate Procedure, and the Rules of this Court; and that I am receiving no compensation from the party on whose behalf I am rendering services (not including any compensation from an attorney, legal aid bureau, law school, public defender agency, a State, or the United States).

_____   _____
(Date)   (Signature of Student)

(D) Form to be completed by Dean:

I certify that this student [has completed at least 4 semesters of law school work] or [is a recent law school graduate awaiting the first bar examination or the results of that examination]; is taking, or has taken, a course in appellate advocacy or a course in a supervised clinical program for academic credit; and is qualified to fulfill the responsibilities required by First Circuit Rule 46.0(f).

_____   _____
(Name of Student)   (Signature of Dean)

                                   _____

                                   _____
                                   (Address & Phone of Above)

Name of Law School Attending _____

(5) **Exceptions.** The court retains authority to establish exceptions to these requirements in any individual case.

[Renumbered and amended effective October 15, 1999. Amended effective December 16, 2003; January 11, 2005; September 14, 2009; April 13, 2011; November 1, 2011; December 1, 2011.]

RULE 46.5. APPOINTMENT OF COUNSEL IN CRIMINAL CASES

The United States Court of Appeals for the First Circuit adopts the following Plan to implement the Criminal Justice Act of 1964, 18 U.S.C. § 3006A, P.L. 88–455, as amended October 12, 1984, P.L. 98–473, and November 14, 1986, P.L. 99–651 to which references must be made. The purpose of this Plan is to provide adequate representation and defense of all persons to the extent provided therein including cases where a person faces loss of liberty or is in custody as a material witness. The court notes at the outset that the Act does not diminish the traditional responsibility of members of the Bar to accept appointments. It recognizes that compensation will, in most instances, be something less than full, and appreciates that service by counsel will represent a substantial measure of public dedication.

(a) **Request for Counsel.** Every person or eligible witness desiring counsel and that the government pay for the expense of appeal, whether or not the person had court-appointed counsel in the district court, shall address to this court a request in writing and a statement of the person's inability to pay. The court may make such further inquiry of the person's need as it may see fit. This inquiry may also be addressed to previously retained counsel, with the objective of ascertaining that present inability to pay is not a result of past excessive compensation. Such inquiry is not aimed at depriving an indigent of counsel but at the relatively few counsel who might reasonably be considered to have used up all of the available funds for doing only part of the work.

(b) **Appointment of Counsel.** The court may appoint counsel who represented the person in the district court, or counsel from a panel maintained by the court, or otherwise. The addition or deletion of names from the panel and the selection of counsel shall be the sole and exclusive responsibility of the court but the actual administration thereof may be conducted by the clerk of this court. The person may ask for appointment of counsel who represented the defendant in the district court or for the non-appointment of such counsel, but shall not otherwise request any specific individual. The court shall give consideration to such request, but shall not be bound by it. A request for relief by trial counsel, upon a showing of cause, shall be given due consideration. It is recognized that counsel on appeal may require different qualifications than for trial. The substitution of counsel on appeal shall not in any way reflect upon the ability or upon the conduct of prior counsel. The Administration Office shall be notified promptly of each appointment, and of each order releasing counsel.

(c) **Duration and Substitution of Counsel.** The court notes, and incorporates herein, the provisions of section (c) of the Act, except the references therein to magistrates. Except when relieved by the court, counsel's appointment shall not terminate until, if the person loses the appeal, counsel informs the person of that fact and of the person's right to petition for certiorari and the time period, and has prepared and filed the petition if the person requests it and there are reasonable grounds for counsel properly to do so (see Rule 10 of the Rules of the Supreme Court of the United States). If counsel determines that there are no reasonable grounds and declines to file a petition for certiorari requested by the person, counsel shall so inform the Court and request leave to withdraw from the representation by written motion stating that counsel has reviewed the matter and determined that the petition would be frivolous, accompanied by counsel's certification of the date when a copy of the motion was furnished to the person. If the person does not wish to apply for certiorari or does not respond to the notification, counsel shall so inform the court by letter, which action shall terminate the representation. The clerk will inform the person in writing of the fact and effective date of the termination of counsel's appointment.

(d) Payment for Representation and Services other than Counsel. The court notes sections (d) and (e) of the Act and incorporates the pertinent portions herein. Expenses described in the Act do not include overhead and such matters as secretarial expenses not ordinarily billed to clients, but a reasonable charge for copying briefs may be allowed. For additional guidance, see the *Guidelines for the Administration of the Criminal Justice Act and Related Statutes*, Volume VII, *Guide to Judiciary Policies and Procedures.*

All claims, whether for compensation, or for expenditures, shall be submitted promptly after the completion of all duties, at the risk of disallowance. If counsel files a petition for a writ of certiorari, counsel's time and expenses involved in the preparation of the petition should be included on the voucher for services performed in this court. After court approval all orders for payment shall be processed through the Administrative Office.

(e) Receipt of Other Payments. The provisions of section (f) of the Act are incorporated herein. Appointed counsel shall be under a continuing duty to report to the court any circumstances indicating financial ability on behalf of the person to pay part or all of the person's counsel fees or expenses. The court shall in no instance permit counsel who receives payments under the Act to frustrate the intent of the limitations contained in sections (d) and (e) by the receipt of other payment, either during, before, or after such representation.

(f) Forms. For the appointment of counsel, the making of claims, and all other matters for which forms shall have been approved by the Administrative Office, such forms shall be used as a matter of course.

(g) Effective Date and Amendments. This amended Plan shall take effect on November 14, 1986. It may be amended at any time with the approval of the Judicial Council. [The present plan incorporates an amendment made on December 16, 2002.]

[Adopted effective September 1, 1986. Amended effective November 14, 1986; October, 1999; December 16, 2002.]

RULE 46.6. PROCEDURE FOR WITHDRAWAL IN CRIMINAL CASES

(a) Trial Counsel's Duty to Continue to Represent Defendant on Appeal until Relieved by the Court of Appeals. An attorney who has represented a defendant in a criminal case in the district court will be responsible for representing the defendant on appeal, whether or not the attorney has entered an appearance in the court of appeals, until the attorney is relieved of such duty by the court of appeals. *See* Local Rule 12.0(b).

(b) Withdrawal by Counsel Appointed in the District Court. When a defendant has been represented in the district court by counsel appointed under the Criminal Justice Act, the clerk will usually send a "Form for Selection of Counsel on Appeal" to defendant, which asks defendant to select among the following:

(1) representing him or herself on appeal and proceeding pro se;

(2) requesting trial counsel to be appointed on appeal to represent defendant on appeal;

(3) requesting the appointment of new counsel on appeal; and

(4) retaining private counsel for appeal.

If the defendant returns the form and elects to proceed with new counsel to be appointed on appeal, then the court will ordinarily appoint new counsel and allow trial counsel to withdraw.

If counsel wishes to withdraw and either the defendant fails to complete the form or counsel wishes to terminate representation even though the defendant has selected (2) above, counsel may file an affidavit explaining the difficulty and move to withdraw.

An unsworn declaration under the penalty of perjury in the format set forth in 28 U.S.C. § 1746 will suffice in place of an affidavit.

(c) Procedure for Withdrawal in Situations not Governed by Local Rule 46.6(b). Motions to withdraw as counsel on appeal in criminal cases must be accompanied by a notice of appearance of replacement counsel or, in the absence of replacement counsel, such motions must state the reasons for withdrawal and must be accompanied by one of the following:

(1) The defendant's completed application for appointment of replacement counsel under the Criminal Justice Act or a showing that such application has already been filed with the court and, if defendant has not already been determined to be financially eligible, certification of compliance with Fed. R. App. P. 24; or

(2) An affidavit from the defendant showing that the defendant has been advised that the defendant

may retain replacement counsel or apply for appointment of replacement counsel and expressly stating that the defendant does not wish to be represented by counsel but elects to appear pro se; or

(3) An affidavit from the defendant showing that the defendant has been advised of the defendant's rights with regard to the appeal and expressly stating that the defendant elects to withdraw the appeal; or

(4) If the reason for the motion is the frivolousness of the appeal, a brief following the procedure described in *Anders v. California*, 386 U.S. 738 (1967), must be filed with the court. [Counsel's attention is also directed to *McCoy v. Court of Appeals*, 486 U.S. 429 (1988); *Penson v. Ohio*, 488 U.S. 75 (1988)]. Any such brief shall be filed only after counsel has ordered and read all relevant transcripts, including trial, change of plea, and sentencing transcripts, as well as the presentence investigation report. Counsel shall serve a copy of the brief and motion on the defendant and advise the defendant that the defendant has thirty (30) days from the date of service in which to file a brief in support of reversal or modification of the judgment. The motion must be accompanied by proof of service on the defendant and certification that counsel has advised the defendant of the defendant's right to file a separate brief.

If counsel is unable to comply with (1), (2), or (3) and does not think it appropriate to proceed in accordance with (4), counsel may file an affidavit explaining the difficulty and move to withdraw.

An unsworn declaration under the penalty of perjury in the format set forth in 28 U.S.C. § 1746 will suffice in place of an affidavit.

(d) Service. All motions must be accompanied by proof of service on the defendant and the Government and will be determined, without oral argument, by one or more judges.

[Renumbered and amended October, 1999. Amended effective December 16, 2002.]

[Formerly Local Rule 46.4(a). Former Local Rule 46.6 renumbered Local Rule 46(b).]

FRAP 47. LOCAL RULES BY COURTS OF APPEALS

[For text of rule, see Federal Rules of Appellate Procedure]

RULE 47.0. LOCAL RULES OF THE FIRST CIRCUIT

(a) Advisory Committee

(1) Membership. In accordance with 28 U.S.C. § 2077(b) an advisory committee on the rules of practice and internal operating procedures is hereby created for the court. This committee shall consist of members of the Bar of the court as follows: Three members from the District of Massachusetts, two members from the District of Puerto Rico and one each from the Districts of Maine, New Hampshire and Rhode Island. In addition, a ninth member shall be appointed, which position shall rotate among the five districts.

(2) Duties. The advisory committee shall have an advisory role concerning the rules of practice and internal operating procedures of the court. The advisory committee shall, among other things,

(A) provide a forum for continuous study of the rules of practice and internal operating procedures of the court;

(B) serve as a conduit between the bar and the public and the court regarding procedural matters and suggestions for changes;

(C) consider and recommend rules and amendments for adoption; and

(D) render reports from time to time, on its own initiative and on request, to the court.

(3) Terms of Members. The members of the advisory committee shall serve three-year terms, which will be staggered, so that three new members will be appointed every year in such order as the court decides. The court shall appoint one of the members of the committee to serve as chairman.

(b) Comments from Members of the Bar. Prior to the adoption of a proposed amendment to these Rules, if time permits, the court will seek the comments and recommendations of interested members of the bar through the office of the clerk and with the aid of the advisory committee created pursuant to 28 U.S.C. § 2077.

[Renumbered and amended effective October 15, 1999. Amended effective December 16, 2003; May 18, 2009.]

[Formerly Local Rules 47.2, 47.3 and 47.4.]

RULE 47.1. JUDICIAL CONFERENCE OF THE FIRST CIRCUIT

(a) A Judicial Conference of the First Circuit will be held periodically in accordance with 28 U.S.C. § 333. The chief judge shall preside at the Conference.

(b) The chief judge of the circuit shall appoint a Planning Committee consisting of a circuit judge and/or district judge and such members of the Bar as they may designate to plan and conduct the Conference.

(c) Members of the Conference shall include the following:

(1) Presidents of the state bar associations of states and commonwealths within the circuit;

(2) The dean or member of the faculty designated by the dean of each accredited law school within the circuit;

(3) All United States Attorneys of the circuit;

(4) Lawyers to be appointed from each state in numbers to be determined by the Planning Committee, such appointment to be made by the district committee of each district; if such a committee does not exist, such appointments to be made by the district judges as determined by each district court. Such additional members of the Bar may also be invited as the chief circuit judge, in consultation with the other circuit judges, and the Planning Committee shall decide; and

(5) All federal defenders designated by the chief judge of the circuit.

(d) The Circuit Executive of this court shall be the Secretary of the Conference.

[Adopted effective September 1, 1986. Amended effective October, 1999; December 27, 2005.]

FRAP 48. MASTERS

[For text of rule, see Federal Rules of Appellate Procedure]

RULE 48.0. CAPITAL CASES

(a) Applicability of Rule. This rule shall govern all matters in which this Court is requested to rule in any case where the death penalty has been imposed, including, but not limited to, the following:

(1) direct criminal appeals;

(2) appeals from District Court rulings, such as on motions to vacate a sentence, petitions for a writ of habeas corpus, and requests for a stay or other injunction;

(3) original petitions for a writ of habeas corpus;

(4) motions for second or successive habeas corpus applications;

(5) any related civil proceedings challenging the conviction or sentence of death, or the time, place or manner of execution, as being in violation of federal law, whether filed by the prisoner or by someone else on his or her behalf.

Such cases shall be referred to herein as "capital cases" and shall be governed by this rule, except where otherwise specified in a written order by the Court. To the extent that any local rule of this Court is inconsistent with this rule, this rule shall govern. All local rules of this Court, including interim local rules, are otherwise as applicable to capital cases as they would have been absent this rule.

(b) Certificate of Death Penalty Case. A special docket shall be maintained by the Clerk of this Court for all cases filed pursuant to this rule.

(1) Filing. Upon the filing of any proceeding in any District Court in this Circuit challenging a sentence of death imposed pursuant to a federal or a state court judgment, each party to such proceeding shall file a Certificate of Death Penalty Case with the Clerk of this Court. The U.S. Attorney shall file a Certificate of Death Penalty Case with the Clerk of this Court immediately upon notifying the District Court of intent to seek the death penalty in a federal criminal case. The U.S. Attorney shall also update the Certificate immediately upon return of a verdict imposing a sentence of death.

(2) Content of the Certificate. The Certificate shall set forth the names, telephone numbers and addresses of the parties and counsel, the proposed date and place of implementation of the sentence of death, if set, and the emergency nature of the proceedings, if appropriate. It shall be the responsibility of counsel for all parties to apprise the Clerk of this Court of any changes in the information provided on the Certificate as expeditiously as possible.

(c) Certificates of Appealability and Stays.

(1) Certificates of Appealability and Motions for Stays. Certificates of appealability for all habeas matters are addressed in Fed. R. App. P. 22 and Rule 11 of the Rules Governing Proceedings Under 28 U.S.C. § 2254 or § 2255.

(2) Stays of Execution.

(A) Except where otherwise prohibited by 28 U.S.C. § 2262, a sentence of death shall automatically be stayed upon the filing of a notice of appeal. In cases where the petitioner is seeking leave to file a second or successive application under 28 U.S.C. § 2254 or § 2255, a stay of execution shall automatically be issued upon approval by the Court of Appeals of the filing of a second or successive application under 28 U.S.C. § 2244(b). The Clerk shall immediately notify all parties and the state or federal authorities responsible for implementing the defendant's sentence of death of the stay of execution. If notification is oral, it shall be followed as expeditiously as possible by written notice.

(B) Except where otherwise required by law or specified in a written order by the Court, an automatic stay of execution shall remain in effect until the Court issues its mandate, at which time the automatic stay shall expire. In the event that a motion requesting a stay of mandate is filed, the motion should also be accompanied by a motion requesting a case-specific stay of execution.

(C) The assigned panel may grant or modify or vacate any stay of execution at any time and will consider upon request motions for a case-specific stay of execution. All motions for a case-specific stay of execution must be accompanied by a memorandum of law, which must include at a minimum the prevailing standards of review and any relevant facts to advise the Court's decision.

(D) Upon making the necessary findings, the Court may enter a case-specific stay of execution which shall clearly specify the duration of the stay.

(E) The Clerk shall send notice to all the parties and state or federal authorities responsible for implementing the defendant's sentence of death when a stay imposed by this provision, be it automatic or case-specific, is no longer in effect.

[Adopted effective October, 1999. Amended effective December 16, 2003. Amended effective October 6, 2004; December 1, 2009.]

APPENDIX OF FORMS

FORM 1. NOTICE OF APPEAL TO A COURT OF APPEALS FROM A JUDGMENT OR ORDER OF A DISTRICT COURT

[For text of form, see Federal Rules of Appellate Procedure]

FORM 2. NOTICE OF APPEAL TO A COURT OF APPEALS FROM A DECISION OF THE UNITED STATES TAX COURT

[For text of form, see Federal Rules of Appellate Procedure]

FORM 3. PETITION FOR REVIEW OF ORDER OF AN AGENCY, BOARD, COMMISSION OR OFFICER

[For text of form, see Federal Rules of Appellate Procedure]

FORM 4. AFFIDAVIT TO ACCOMPANY MOTION FOR LEAVE TO APPEAL IN FORMA PAUPERIS

[For text of form, see Federal Rules of Appellate Procedure]

FORM 5. NOTICE OF APPEAL TO A COURT OF APPEALS FROM A JUDGMENT OR ORDER OF A DISTRICT COURT OR A BANKRUPTCY APPELLATE PANEL

[For text of form, see Federal Rules of Appellate Procedure]

FORM 6. CERTIFICATE OF COMPLIANCE WITH RULE 32(A)

[For text of form, see Federal Rules of Appellate Procedure]

RULES OF ATTORNEY DISCIPLINARY ENFORCEMENT FOR THE COURT OF APPEALS FOR THE FIRST CIRCUIT

PREFACE

The Court of Appeals for the First Circuit, in furtherance of its inherent power and responsibility to supervise the conduct of attorneys who are admitted to practice before it, or admitted for the purpose of a particular proceeding (pro hac vice), promulgates the following Rules of Attorney Disciplinary Enforcement superseding all of its other Rules pertaining to disciplinary enforcement heretofore promulgated.

RULE 1. ATTORNEYS CONVICTED OF CRIMES

A. Upon filing with this Court of a certified copy of a judgment of conviction demonstrating that any attorney admitted to practice before the Court has been convicted in any Court of the United States, or the District of Columbia, or of any state, territory, commonwealth or possession of the United States of a serious crime as hereinafter defined, the Chief Judge shall refer the matter to a disciplinary panel. The disciplinary panel shall enter an order immediately suspending that attorney, whether the conviction resulted from a plea of guilty or nolo contendere or from a verdict after trial or otherwise, and regardless of the pendency of any appeal, until final disposition of a disciplinary proceeding to be commenced upon such conviction. A copy of such order shall immediately be served by the Clerk of this Court upon the attorney personally or by certified or registered mail. Upon motion and good cause shown, the disciplinary panel may set aside such order when it appears in the interest of justice to do so.

B. The term "serious crime" shall include any felony and any lesser crime, a necessary element of which, as determined by the statutory or common law definition of such crime in the jurisdiction where the judgment was entered, involves false swearing, misrepresentation, fraud, willful failure to file income tax returns, deceit, bribery, extortion, misappropriation, theft, or an attempt or a conspiracy or solicitation of another to commit a "serious crime."

C. Upon the filing of a certified copy of a judgment of conviction of an attorney for a serious crime, the disciplinary panel shall, in addition to suspending that attorney in accordance with the provisions of this Rule, also initiate disciplinary proceedings in which the sole issue to be determined shall be the extent of

the final discipline to be imposed as a result of the conduct resulting in the conviction, provided that no final disposition will be rendered until all direct appeals from the conviction are concluded. The certified copy of the judgment of conviction shall be conclusive evidence of the commission of that crime by the attorney in question.

D. Upon the filing of a certified copy of a judgment of conviction of an attorney for any crime not constituting a "serious crime," the Chief Judge may refer the matter to a disciplinary panel for disciplinary proceedings or may exercise discretion to make no reference with respect to convictions for minor offenses for which discipline would not be appropriate.

E. Any attorney suspended under the first paragraph of this Rule will be reinstated immediately upon the filing of a certificate demonstrating that the underlying conviction has been vacated or reversed on direct appeal, but the reinstatement shall not terminate any disciplinary proceeding then pending against the attorney, the disposition of which shall be determined by the disciplinary panel on the basis of all available evidence pertaining to both guilt and the extent of discipline to be imposed.

[Amended July 17, 2002, effective August 1, 2002.]

RULE 2. DISCIPLINE IMPOSED BY OTHER COURTS

A. Any attorney admitted to practice before this Court shall, upon being subject to public discipline by any other Court of the United States, or the District of Columbia, or of any state, territory, commonwealth or possession of the United States, promptly inform the Clerk of this Court of such action.

B. Upon filing of a certified copy of a judgment, order, or other official document demonstrating that an attorney admitted to practice before this Court has been publicly disciplined by another court, the Chief Judge shall refer the matter to a disciplinary panel and the Clerk of this Court shall serve on the attorney, personally or by certified or registered mail, a notice containing:

  1. a copy of the judgment or order from the other court; and

  2. an order to show cause directing that the attorney inform this Court within 30 days after service of the order of any claim predicated upon the grounds set forth in paragraph (C) of this Rule that the imposition of substantially similar discipline on the attorney would be unwarranted and the reasons therefor. The order shall also state that a hearing on such a claim must be requested within 30 days after service of the order.

C. Upon the expiration of the time to show cause, if no response has been filed, then the disciplinary panel shall enter an order imposing substantially similar discipline. If a timely response is filed, the disciplinary panel shall, after any applicable hearing or other proceedings, impose substantially the same discipline imposed by the other court unless the attorney demonstrates, and the disciplinary panel is persuaded:

1. that the procedure used by the other court was so lacking in notice or opportunity to be heard as to constitute a deprivation of due process; or

2. that there was such an infirmity of proof establishing the misconduct as to give rise to the clear conviction that this Court could not, consistent with its duty, accept as final the conclusion on that subject; or

3. that the imposition of substantially similar discipline by this Court would result in grave injustice; or

4. that the misconduct established is deemed by this Court to warrant different discipline.

Where the disciplinary panel determines that any of these elements exist, it shall enter such other order as it deems appropriate.

D. In all other respects, a final adjudication in another court that an attorney has been guilty of misconduct shall establish conclusively the misconduct for purposes of any disciplinary proceeding in this Court.

[Amended July 17, 2002, effective August 1, 2002.]

RULE 3. DISBARMENT ON CONSENT OR RESIGNATION IN OTHER COURTS

A. Any attorney admitted to practice before this Court who shall be disbarred on consent or resign from the bar of any other court of the United States or the District of Columbia, or from the Bar of any state, territory, commonwealth or possession of the United States while an investigation into allegations of misconduct is pending, shall, upon the filing with this Court of a certified or exemplified copy of the judgment or order accepting such disbarment on consent or resignation, cease to be permitted to practice before this Court and be stricken from the roll of attorneys admitted to practice before this Court.

B. Any attorney admitted to practice before this Court shall, upon being disbarred on consent or resigning from the bar of any other court of the United States or the District of Columbia, or from the Bar of any state, territory, commonwealth or possession of the United States while an investigation into allega-

tions of misconduct is pending, promptly inform the Clerk of this Court of such disbarment on consent or resignation.

[Amended July 17, 2002, effective August 1, 2002.]

RULE 4. STANDARDS FOR PROFESSIONAL CONDUCT

A. For misconduct defined in these Rules, and for good cause shown, and after notice and opportunity to be heard, any attorney admitted to practice before this Court may be disbarred, suspended from practice before this Court, reprimanded or subjected to such other disciplinary action as the circumstances may warrant.

B. Acts or omissions by an attorney admitted to practice before this Court, individually or in concert with any other person or persons, which violate the Code of Professional Responsibility, either of the state, territory, commonwealth or possession of the United States in which the attorney maintains his principal office; or of the state, territory, commonwealth or possession of the United States in which the attorney is acting at the time of the misconduct; or of the state in which the circuit maintains its Clerk's Office, shall constitute misconduct and shall be grounds for discipline, whether or not the act or omission occurred in the course of the attorney-client relationship. The Code of Professional Responsibility means that code adopted by the highest court of the state, territory, commonwealth or possession of the United States, as amended from time to time by that court, except as otherwise provided by specific Rule of this Court after consideration of comments by representatives of bar associations within the state, territory, commonwealth or possession of the United States. Failure to comply with the Federal Rules of Appellate Procedure, the Local Rules of this Court, or the orders of this Court may also constitute misconduct and be grounds for discipline.

[Amended July 17, 2002, effective August 1, 2002.]

RULE 5. DISCIPLINARY PROCEEDINGS

A. When misconduct or allegations of misconduct on the part of an attorney admitted to practice before this Court shall come to the attention of a Judge or officer of this Court, whether by complaint or otherwise, and the applicable procedure is not otherwise mandated by these rules, the Judge or officer shall refer the matter to the Chief Judge for initial review. If the Chief Judge determines that misconduct is alleged which, if substantiated, would warrant discipline by this Court, the Chief Judge shall refer the matter to a disciplinary panel; if not, the Chief Judge may dismiss the matter. A disciplinary panel shall consist of three judges of this Court, whether active or senior, appointed by the Chief Judge. The Chief Judge may serve as a member of the disciplinary panel. In the absence of the Chief Judge, the active judge most senior in service on the Court serves as chair. If no active judge is on the disciplinary panel, the Chief Judge shall appoint the chair. The disciplinary panel may at any time appoint counsel to investigate or to prosecute any disciplinary matter. In a matter in which the Chief Judge is recused, references to "Chief Judge" shall mean the senior active judge who is not recused.

B. If the disciplinary panel determines that cause may exist for disciplinary action, the disciplinary panel will direct the Clerk of the Court to issue an order to the attorney in question to show cause why (1) specified discipline should not be imposed or (2) discipline to be determined later should not be imposed. The order shall be served on the attorney personally or by certified or registered mail, shall notify the attorney of the alleged conduct and the reason the conduct may justify disciplinary action, and shall direct that 5 copies of a response, including any supporting evidence or request for a hearing, be filed within 30 days of service of the order or such other time as the order may specify. The Clerk shall also append a copy of these rules to the order. In any response to the order, the attorney must also (a) include an affidavit listing the other bars to which the attorney is admitted, (b) note which if any of the facts alleged are controverted, and (c) specify the basis on which any controverted facts are disputed. If the disciplinary panel determines on initial investigation and review that cause does not exist for disciplinary action, the disciplinary panel may dismiss the matter.

C. If the attorney fails to timely respond to an order to show cause, or if the attorney's timely response to the order to show cause does not specifically request to be heard in person, the disciplinary panel may direct entry of an order imposing discipline or take any other appropriate action. If the attorney specifically requests to be heard in person, either in defense or in mitigation, the disciplinary panel shall set the matter for such hearing as is appropriate under the circumstances. The disciplinary panel may itself order a hearing whether or not one is requested. Following such a hearing and the receipt of any findings or recommendation that may be required and any further submissions that the disciplinary panel may invite, the disciplinary panel may direct entry of an order imposing discipline or take any other appropriate action.

D. If a hearing is ordered, the disciplinary panel may conduct the hearing itself or designate a special master (including but not limited to a district judge or magistrate judge serving within the circuit) for purposes of conducting any hearing. The disciplinary panel (or the special master, subject to the instruction of the disciplinary panel) may in its discretion adopt appropriate procedural and evidentiary rules for any such hearing. At the conclusion of a hearing held before a special master, the special master shall promptly make a report of findings and—if directed by the disciplinary panel—recommendations to the disciplinary panel. A copy of the report and any recommendations shall be made available to the attorney under investigation. The disciplinary panel may reject or adopt the findings and/or recommendations of the special master in whole or part.

E. Any attorney may file a petition for rehearing by the disciplinary panel or a combined petition for rehearing by the disciplinary panel and suggestion for rehearing en banc by the active judges of the Court. Similarly, the attorney may seek a stay of any disciplinary order entered by the disciplinary panel, the stay to be sought from the disciplinary panel in the first instance and thereafter if desired by the attorney from the Court en banc. The procedures for any such petition will be in accordance with the Federal Rules of Appellate Procedure and the Local Rules of this Court. If en banc review is granted, any senior judge shall be eligible to be a member of the en banc Court, at that judge's election, in the circumstances specified in 28 U.S.C. § 46(c).

F. At any time, the disciplinary panel may in its discretion refer a disciplinary matter pending before it to an appropriate state bar association or state disciplinary board. In such a case, the disciplinary panel is free to dismiss the matter or hold its own proceedings in abeyance pending the completion of the state disciplinary proceedings. Nothing in these rules prevents any disciplinary panel, Judge, or officer of this Court from bringing disciplinary matters to the attention of the appropriate state disciplinary authorities.

G. The provisions of this Rule shall govern disciplinary proceedings addressed to misconduct as defined in Rule IV, and shall also apply to any proceedings under Rule I (Attorneys Convicted of Crimes), Rule II (Discipline Imposed by Other Courts), and Rule VII (Reinstatement) to the extent not inconsistent with the express provisions of those rules.

[Amended July 17, 2002, effective August 1, 2002.]

RULE 6. DISBARMENT ON CONSENT WHILE UNDER DISCIPLINARY INVESTIGATION OR PROSECUTION

A. Any attorney admitted to practice before this Court who is the subject of an investigation into, or a pending proceeding involving, allegations or misconduct may consent to disbarment, but only by delivering to this Court an affidavit stating that the attorney desires to consent to disbarment and that:

1. the attorney's consent is freely and voluntarily rendered; the attorney is not being subjected to coercion or duress; the attorney is fully aware of the implications of so consenting;

2. the attorney is aware that there is a presently pending investigation or proceeding involving allegation that there exist grounds for the attorney's discipline the nature of which the attorney shall specifically set forth;

3. the attorney acknowledges that the material facts so alleged are true; and

4. the attorney so consents because the attorney knows that if charges were predicted upon the matters under investigation, or if the proceeding were prosecuted, the attorney could not successfully defend himself.

B. Upon receipt of the required affidavit, this Court shall enter an order disbarring the attorney.

C. The order disbarring the attorney on consent shall be a matter of public record. However, the affidavit required under the provisions of this Rule shall not be publicly disclosed or made available for use in any other proceeding except upon order of this Court.

[Amended July 17, 2002, effective August 1, 2002.]

RULE 7. REINSTATEMENT

A. Unless this court's suspension order provides otherwise, an attorney who seeks to resume practice before this Court after being disbarred or suspended under these rules must petition for reinstatement. Petitions for reinstatement shall be filed with the Clerk of this Court and contain a concise statement of the circumstances of the disciplinary proceeding, the discipline imposed by this Court, and the grounds that justify reinstatement of the attorney in question. In accordance with Rule V, the Chief Judge shall conduct an initial review, and, as warranted, dismiss the petition or refer it to a disciplinary panel. After whatever investigation it sees fit, the disciplinary panel may set the matter for whatever hearing it deems appropriate under the circumstances.

B. The petitioner shall have the burden of demonstrating by clear and convincing evidence that he or she has the moral qualifications, competency, and learning in the law required for admission to practice law before this Court and that the resumption of the practice of law will not be detrimental to the integrity and standing of the bar or to the administration of justice, or subversive to the public interest.

C. If the disciplinary panel finds that the petitioner is unfit to resume the practice of law, the petition shall be dismissed. If the petitioner is found fit to resume the practice of law, the disciplinary panel shall enter an order of reinstatement, provided that the disciplinary panel may make reinstatement conditional upon the payment of all or part of the costs of the

proceedings, and upon the making of partial or complete restitution to parties harmed by the petitioner whose conduct led to the suspension or disbarment, and the disciplinary panel may impose such other reasonable conditions as it deems meet. Further, if the petitioner has been suspended or disbarred for five or more years, the disciplinary panel may in its discretion condition reinstatement upon the furnishing of proof of competency and learning in the law, which proof may include successful completion of an examination for admission to practice subsequent to the date of suspension or disbarment.

D. No petition for reinstatement under this Rule shall be filed within one year following an adverse final judgment upon a petition for reinstatement filed by or on behalf of the same attorney.

[Amended July 17, 2002, effective August 1, 2002. Amended effective April 13, 2011.]

RULE 8. ATTORNEYS SPECIALLY ADMITTED

Whenever an attorney applies to be admitted or is admitted to this Court for purposes of a particular proceeding (pro hac vice), the attorney shall be deemed thereby to have conferred disciplinary jurisdiction upon this Court for any alleged misconduct of that attorney arising in the course of or in the preparation for such proceeding.

[Amended July 17, 2002, effective August 1, 2002.]

RULE 9. APPOINTMENT OF COUNSEL

Whenever counsel is appointed pursuant to these rules to investigate allegations of misconduct or prosecute disciplinary proceedings or in conjunction with a reinstatement petition filed by a disciplined attorney, a member of the Bar of this Court shall be appointed. Counsel, once appointed, shall not resign without the consent of the disciplinary panel.

[Amended July 17, 2002, effective August 1, 2002.]

RULE 10. DUTIES AND POWERS OF THE CLERK

A. The Clerk of this Court shall promptly notify the National Discipline Data Bank operated by the American Bar Association of any order imposing public discipline upon any attorney admitted to practice before this Court.

B. The Clerk of this Court is empowered, upon being informed that any attorney admitted to practice before this Court has been convicted of any crime or has been subjected to discipline by another court, to obtain and file with this Court a certified or exemplified copy of such conviction or disciplinary judgment or order.

C. Whenever it appears that any person who is disbarred or suspended or censured or disbarred on consent by this Court is admitted to practice law in any other jurisdiction or before any other court, the Clerk of this Court is empowered, to the extent he deems it desirable and necessary to supplement the action taken under clause A, above, to so advise the disciplinary authority in such other jurisdiction or such other court.

[Amended July 17, 2002, effective August 1, 2002.]

RULE 11.   JURISDICTION

Nothing contained in these Rules shall be construed to deny to this Court such powers as are necessary for the Court to maintain control over proceedings conducted before it, such as proceedings for contempt under Title 18 of the United States Code or under Rule 42 of the Federal Rules of Criminal Procedure.

[Amended July 17, 2002, effective August 1, 2002.]

RULE 12.   EFFECTIVE DATE

These Rules shall become effective on August 1, 2002, provided that any formal disciplinary proceedings then pending before the Court shall (unless the Court otherwise directs) be concluded under the Rules existing prior to that date.

[Amended July 17, 2002, effective August 1, 2002.]

FIRST CIRCUIT LOCAL RULES FOR JUDICIAL–CONDUCT AND JUDICIAL–DISABILITY PROCEEDINGS

PREFACE

These Rules were promulgated by the Judicial Conference of the United States, after public comment, pursuant to 28 U.S.C. §§ 331 and 358, to establish standards and procedures for addressing complaints filed by complainants or identified by chief judges, under the Judicial Conduct and Disability Act, 28 U.S.C. §§ 351-364.

ARTICLE I. GENERAL PROVISIONS

RULE 1. SCOPE

These Rules govern proceedings under the Judicial Conduct and Disability Act, 28 U.S.C. §§ 351–364 (the Act), to determine whether a covered judge has engaged in conduct prejudicial to the effective and expeditious administration of the business of the courts or is unable to discharge the duties of office because of mental or physical disability.

[Adopted March 11, 2008, effective April 10, 2008.]

Commentary on Rule 1

In September 2006, the Judicial Conduct and Disability Act Study Committee, appointed in 2004 by Chief Justice Rehnquist and known as the "Breyer Committee," presented a report, known as the "Breyer Committee Report," 239 F.R.D. 116 (Sept. 2006), to Chief Justice Roberts that evaluated implementation of the Judicial Conduct and Disability Act of 1980, 28 U.S.C. §§ 351–364. The Breyer Committee had been formed in response to criticism from the public and the Congress regarding the effectiveness of the Act's implementation. The Executive Committee of the Judicial Conference directed the Judicial Conference Committee on Judicial

Conduct and Disability to consider the recommendations made by the Breyer Committee and to report on their implementation to the Conference.

The Breyer Committee found that it could not evaluate implementation of the Act without establishing interpretive standards, Breyer Committee Report, 239 F.R.D. at 132, and that a major problem faced by chief judges in implementing the Act was the lack of authoritative interpretive standards. Id. at 212–15. The Breyer Committee then established standards to guide its evaluation, some of which were new formulations and some of which were taken from the "Illustrative Rules Governing Complaints of Judicial Misconduct and Disability," discussed below. The principal standards used by the Breyer Committee are in Appendix E of its Report. Id. at 238.

Based on the findings of the Breyer Committee, the Judicial Conference Committee on Judicial Conduct and Disability concluded that there was a need for the Judicial Conference to exercise its power under Section 358 of the Act to fashion standards guiding the various officers and bodies who must exercise responsibility under the Act. To that end, the Judicial Conference Committee proposed rules that were based largely on Appendix E of the Breyer Committee Report and the Illustrative Rules.

The Illustrative Rules were originally prepared in 1986 by the Special Committee of the Conference of Chief Judges of the United States Courts of Appeals, and were subsequently revised and amended, most recently in 2000, by the predecessor to the Committee on Judicial Conduct and Disability. The Illustrative Rules were adopted, with minor variations, by circuit judicial councils, to govern complaints under the Judicial Conduct and Disability Act.

After being submitted for public comment pursuant to 28 U.S.C. § 358(c), the present Rules were promulgated by the Judicial Conference on March 11, 2008.

RULE 2. EFFECT AND CONSTRUCTION

(a) Generally. These Rules are mandatory; they supersede any conflicting judicial-council rules. Judicial councils may promulgate additional rules to implement the Act as long as those rules do not conflict with these Rules.

(b) Exception. A Rule will not apply if, when performing duties authorized by the Act, a chief judge, a special committee, a judicial council, the Judicial Conference Committee on Judicial Conduct and Disability, or the Judicial Conference of the United States expressly finds that exceptional circumstances render application of that Rule in a particular proceeding manifestly unjust or contrary to the purposes of the Act or these Rules.

[Adopted March 11, 2008, effective April 10, 2008.]

Commentary on Rule 2

Unlike the Illustrative Rules, these Rules provide mandatory and nationally uniform provisions governing the substantive and procedural aspects of misconduct and disability proceedings under the Act. The mandatory nature of these Rules is authorized by 28 U.S.C. § 358(a) and (c). Judicial councils retain the power to promulgate rules consistent with

these Rules. For example, a local rule may authorize the electronic distribution of materials pursuant to Rule 8(b).

Rule 2(b) recognizes that unforeseen and exceptional circumstances may call for a different approach in particular cases.

RULE 3. DEFINITIONS

(a) **Chief Judge.** "Chief judge" means the chief judge of a United States Court of Appeals, of the United States Court of International Trade, or of the United States Court of Federal Claims.

(b) **Circuit Clerk.** "Circuit clerk" means a clerk of a United States court of appeals, the clerk of the United States Court of International Trade, the clerk of the United States Court of Federal Claims, or the circuit executive of the United States Court of Appeals for the Federal Circuit.

(c) **Complaint.** A complaint is:

(1) a document that, in accordance with Rule 6, is filed by any person in his or her individual capacity or on behalf of a professional organization; or

(2) information from any source, other than a document described in (c)(1), that gives a chief judge probable cause to believe that a covered judge, as defined in Rule 4, has engaged in misconduct or may have a disability, whether or not the information is framed as or is intended to be an allegation of misconduct or disability.

(d) **Court of Appeals, District Court, and District Judge.** "Courts of appeals," "district court," and "district judge," where appropriate, include the United States Court of Federal Claims, the United States Court of International Trade, and the judges thereof.

(e) **Disability.** "Disability" is a temporary or permanent condition rendering a judge unable to discharge the duties of the particular judicial office. Examples of disability include substance abuse, the inability to stay awake during court proceedings, or a severe impairment of cognitive abilities.

(f) **Judicial Council and Circuit.** "Judicial council" and "circuit,' ' where appropriate, include any courts designated in 28 U.S.C. § 363.

(g) **Magistrate Judge.** "Magistrate judge," where appropriate, includes a special master appointed by the Court of Federal Claims under 42 U.S.C. § 300aa–12(c).

(h) **Misconduct.** Cognizable misconduct:

(1) is conduct prejudicial to the effective and expeditious administration of the business of the courts. Misconduct includes, but is not limited to:

(A) using the judge's office to obtain special treatment for friends or relatives;

(B) accepting bribes, gifts, or other personal favors related to the judicial office;

(C) having improper discussions with parties or counsel for one side in a case;

(D) treating litigants or attorneys in a demonstrably egregious and hostile manner;

(E) engaging in partisan political activity or making inappropriately partisan statements;

(F) soliciting funds for organizations; or

(G) violating other specific, mandatory standards of judicial conduct, such as those pertaining to restrictions on outside income and requirements for financial disclosure.

(2) is conduct occurring outside the performance of official duties if the conduct might have a prejudicial effect on the administration of the business of the courts, including a substantial and widespread lowering of public confidence in the courts among reasonable people.

(3) does not include:

(A) an allegation that is directly related to the merits of a decision or procedural ruling. An allegation that calls into question the correctness of a judge's ruling, including a failure to recuse, without more, is merits-related. If the decision or ruling is alleged to be the result of an improper motive, e.g., a bribe, ex parte contact, racial or ethnic bias, or improper conduct in rendering a decision or ruling, such as personally derogatory remarks irrelevant to the issues, the complaint is not cognizable to the extent that it attacks the merits.

(B) an allegation about delay in rendering a decision or ruling, unless the allegation concerns an improper motive in delaying a particular decision or habitual delay in a significant number of unrelated cases.

(i) Subject Judge. "Subject judge" means any judge described in Rule 4 who is the subject of a complaint.

[Adopted March 11, 2008, effective April 10, 2008.]

Commentary on Rule 3

Rule 3 is derived and adapted from the Breyer Committee Report and the Illustrative Rules.

Unless otherwise specified or the context otherwise indicates, the term "complaint" is used in these Rules to refer both to complaints identified by a chief judge under Rule 5 and to complaints filed by complainants under Rule 6.

Under the Act, a "complaint" may be filed by "any person" or "identified" by a chief judge. See 28 U.S.C. § 351(a) and (b). Under Rule 3(c)(1), complaints may be submitted by a person, in his or her individual capacity, or by a professional organization. Generally, the word "complaint" brings to mind the commencement of an adversary proceeding in which the contending parties are left to present the evidence and legal arguments, and judges play the role of an essentially passive arbiter. The Act, however, establishes an administrative, inquisitorial process. For example, even absent a complaint under Rule 6, chief judges are expected in some

circumstances to trigger the process—"identify a complaint," see 28 U.S.C. § 351(b) and Rule 5—and conduct an investigation without becoming a party. See 28 U.S.C. § 352(a); Breyer Committee Report, 239 F.R.D. at 214; Illustrative Rule 2(j). Even when a complaint is filed by someone other than the chief judge, the complainant lacks many rights that a litigant would have, and the chief judge, instead of being limited to the "four corners of the complaint," must, under Rule 11, proceed as though misconduct or disability has been alleged where the complainant reveals information of misconduct or disability but does not claim it as such. See Breyer Committee Report, 239 F.R.D. at 183–84.

An allegation of misconduct or disability filed under Rule 6 is a "complaint," and the Rule so provides in subsection (c)(1). However, both the nature of the process and the use of the term "identify" suggest that the word "complaint" covers more than a document formally triggering the process. The process relies on chief judges considering known information and triggering the process when appropriate. "Identifying" a "complaint," therefore, is best understood as the chief judge's concluding that information known to the judge constitutes probable cause to believe that misconduct occurred or a disability exists, whether or not the information is framed as, or intended to be an accusation. This definition is codified in (c)(2).

Rule 3(e) relates to disability and provides only the most general definition, recognizing that a fact-specific approach is the only one available.

The phrase "prejudicial to the effective and expeditious administration of the business of the courts" is not subject to precise definition, and subsection (h)(1) therefore provides some specific examples. Although the Code of Conduct for United States Judges may be informative, its main precepts are highly general; the Code is in many potential applications aspirational rather than a set of disciplinary rules. Ultimately, the responsibility for determining what constitutes misconduct under the statute is the province of the judicial council of the circuit subject to such review and limitations as are ordained by the statute and by these Rules.

Even where specific, mandatory rules exist—for example, governing the receipt of gifts by judges, outside earned income, and financial disclosure obligations—the distinction between the misconduct statute and the specific, mandatory rules must be borne in mind. For example, an inadvertent, minor violation of any one of these Rules, promptly remedied when called to the attention of the judge, might still be a violation but might not rise to the level of misconduct under the statute. By contrast, a pattern of such violations of the Code might well rise to the level of misconduct.

An allegation can meet the statutory standard even though the judge's alleged conduct did not occur in the course of the performance of official duties. The Code of Conduct for United States Judges expressly covers a wide range of extra-official activities, and some of these activities may constitute misconduct. For example, allegations that a judge solicited funds for a charity or participated in a partisan political event are cognizable under the Act.

On the other hand, judges are entitled to some leeway in extra-official activities. For example, misconduct may not include a judge being repeatedly and publicly discourteous to a spouse (not including physical abuse) even though this might cause some reasonable people to have diminished confidence in the courts. Rule 3(h)(2) states that conduct of this sort is covered, for example, when it might lead to a "substantial and widespread" lowering of such confidence.

Rule 3(h)(3)(A) tracks the Act, 28 U.S.C. § 352(b)(1)(A)(ii), in excluding from the definition of misconduct allegations "[d]irectly related to the merits of a decision or procedural ruling." This exclusion preserves the independence of judges in the exercise of judicial power by ensuring that the complaint procedure is not used to collaterally attack the substance of a judge's ruling. Any allegation that calls into question the correctness of an official action of a judge—without more—is merits-related. The phrase "decision or procedural ruling" is not limited to rulings issued in deciding Article III cases or controversies. Thus, a complaint challenging the correctness of a chief judge's determination to dismiss a prior misconduct complaint would be properly dismissed as merits-related—in other words, as challenging the substance of the judge's administrative determination to dismiss the complaint—even though it does not concern the judge's rulings in Article III litigation. Similarly, an allegation that a judge had incorrectly declined to approve a Criminal Justice Act voucher is merits-related under this standard.

Conversely, an allegation—however unsupported—that a judge conspired with a prosecutor to make a particular ruling is not merits-related, even though it "relates" to a ruling in a colloquial sense. Such an allegation attacks the propriety of conspiring with the prosecutor and goes beyond a challenge to the correctness—"the merits"—of the ruling itself. An allegation that a judge ruled against the complainant because the complainant is a member of a particular racial or ethnic group, or because the judge dislikes the complainant personally, is also not merits-related. Such an allegation attacks the propriety of arriving at rulings with an illicit or improper motive. Similarly, an allegation that a judge used an inappropriate term to refer to a class of people is not merits-related even if the judge used it on the bench or in an opinion; the correctness of the judge's rulings is not at stake. An allegation that a judge treated litigants or attorneys in a demonstrably egregious and hostile manner while on the bench is also not merits-related.

The existence of an appellate remedy is usually irrelevant to whether an allegation is merits-related. The merits-related ground for dismissal exists to protect judges' independence in making rulings, not to protect or promote the appellate process. A complaint alleging an incorrect ruling is merits-related even though the complainant has no recourse from that ruling. By the same token, an allegation that is otherwise cognizable under the Act should not be dismissed merely because an appellate remedy appears to exist (for example, vacating a ruling that resulted from an improper ex parte communication). However, there may be occasions when appellate and misconduct proceedings overlap, and consideration and disposition of a complaint under these Rules may be properly deferred by a chief judge until the appellate proceedings are concluded in order to avoid, inter alia, inconsistent decisions.

Because of the special need to protect judges' independence in deciding what to say in an opinion or ruling, a somewhat different standard applies to determine the merits-relatedness of a non-frivolous allegation that a judge's language in a ruling reflected an improper motive. If the judge's language was relevant to the case at hand—for example a statement that a claim is legally or factually "frivolous"—then the judge's choice of language is presumptively merits-related and excluded, absent evidence apart from the ruling itself suggesting an improper motive. If, on the other hand, the challenged language does not seem relevant on its face, then an additional inquiry under Rule 11 is necessary.

With regard to Rule 3(h)(3)(B), a complaint of delay in a single case is excluded as merits-related. Such an allegation may be said to challenge the correctness of an official action of the judge—in other words, assigning a low priority to deciding the particular case. But, by the same token, an allegation of a habitual pattern of delay in a significant number of unrelated cases, or an allegation of deliberate delay in a single case arising out of an illicit motive, is not merits-related.

The remaining subsections of Rule 3 provide technical definitions clarifying the application of the Rules to the various kinds of courts covered.

RULE 4.   COVERED JUDGES

A complaint under these Rules may concern the actions or capacity only of judges of United States courts of appeals, judges of United States district courts, judges of United States bankruptcy courts, United States magistrate judges, and judges of the courts specified in 28 U.S.C. § 363.

[Adopted March 11, 2008, effective April 10, 2008.]

Commentary on Rule 4

This Rule tracks the Act. Rule 8(c) and (d) contain provisions as to the handling of complaints against persons not covered by the Act, such as other court personnel, or against both covered judges and noncovered persons.

ARTICLE II.   INITIATION OF A COMPLAINT

RULE 5.   IDENTIFICATION
OF A COMPLAINT

(a) Identification. When a chief judge has information constituting reasonable grounds for inquiry into whether a covered judge has engaged in misconduct or has a disability, the chief judge may conduct an inquiry, as he or she deems appropriate, into the accuracy of the information even if no related complaint has been filed. A chief judge who finds probable cause to believe that misconduct has occurred or that a disability exists may seek an informal resolution that he or she finds satisfactory. If no informal resolution is achieved or is feasible, the chief judge may identify a complaint and, by written order stating the reasons, begin the review provided in Rule 11. If the evidence of misconduct is clear and convincing and no informal resolution is achieved or is feasible, the chief judge must identify a complaint. A chief judge must not decline to identify a complaint merely because the person making the allegation has not filed a complaint under Rule 6. This Rule is subject to Rule 7.

(b) Noncompliance with Rule 6(d). Rule 6 complaints that do not comply with the requirements of Rule 6(d) must be considered under this Rule.

[Adopted March 11, 2008, effective April 10, 2008.]

Commentary on Rule 5

This Rule is adapted from the Breyer Committee Report, 239 F.R.D. at 245–46.

The Act authorizes the chief judge, by written order stating reasons, to identify a complaint and thereby dispense with the filing of a written complaint. See 28 U.S.C. § 351(b). Under Rule 5, when a chief judge becomes aware of information constituting reasonable grounds to inquire into possible misconduct or disability on the part of a covered judge, and no formal complaint has been filed, the chief judge has the power in his or her discretion to begin an appropriate inquiry. A chief judge's decision whether to informally seek a resolution and/or to identify a complaint is guided by the results of that inquiry. If the chief judge concludes that there is probable cause to believe that misconduct has occurred or a disability exists, the chief judge may seek an informal resolution, if feasible, and if failing in that, may identify a complaint. Discretion is accorded largely for the reasons police officers and prosecutors have discretion in making arrests or bringing charges. The matter may be trivial and isolated, based on marginal evidence, or otherwise highly unlikely to lead to a misconduct or disability finding. On the other hand, if the inquiry leads the chief judge to conclude that there is clear and convincing evidence of misconduct or a disability, and no satisfactory informal resolution has been achieved or is feasible, the chief judge is required to identify a complaint.

An informal resolution is one agreed to by the subject judge and found satisfactory by the chief judge. Because an informal resolution under Rule 5 reached before a complaint is filed under Rule 6 will generally cause a subsequent Rule 6 complaint alleging the identical matter to be concluded, see Rule 11(d), the chief judge must be sure that the resolution is fully appropriate before endorsing it. In doing so, the chief judge must balance the seriousness of the matter against the particular judge's alacrity in addressing the issue. The availability of this procedure should encourage attempts at swift remedial action before a formal complaint is filed.

When a complaint is identified, a written order stating the reasons for the identification must be provided; this begins the process articulated in Rule 11. Rule 11 provides that once the chief judge has identified a complaint, the chief judge, subject to the disqualification provisions of Rule 25, will perform, with respect to that complaint, all functions assigned to the chief judge for the determination of complaints filed by a complainant.

In high-visibility situations, it may be desirable for the chief judge to identify a complaint without first seeking an informal resolution (and then, if the circumstances warrant, dismiss or conclude the identified complaint without appointment of a special committee) in order to assure the public that the allegations have not been ignored.

A chief judge's decision not to identify a complaint under Rule 5 is not appealable and is subject to Rule 3(h)(3)(A), which excludes merits-related complaints from the definition of misconduct.

A chief judge may not decline to identify a complaint solely on the basis that the unfiled allegations could be raised by one or more persons in a filed complaint, but none of these persons has opted to do so.

Subsection (a) concludes by stating that this Rule is "subject to Rule 7." This is intended to establish that only: (i) the chief judge of the home circuit of a potential subject judge, or (ii) the chief judge of a circuit in which misconduct is alleged to have occurred in the course of official business while the potential subject judge was sitting by designation, shall have the power or a duty under this Rule to identify a complaint.

Subsection (b) provides that complaints filed under Rule 6 that do not comply with the requirements of Rule 6(d), must be considered under this Rule. For instance, if a complaint has been filed but the form submitted is unsigned, or the truth of the statements therein are not verified in writing under penalty of perjury, then a chief judge must nevertheless consider the allegations as known information, and proceed to follow the process described in Rule 5(a).

RULE 6. FILING A COMPLAINT

(a) Form. A complainant may use the form reproduced in the appendix to these Rules or a form designated by the rules of the judicial council in the circuit in which the complaint is filed. A complaint form is also available on each court of appeals' website or may be obtained from the circuit clerk or any district court or bankruptcy court within the circuit. A form is not necessary to file a complaint, but the complaint must be written and must include the information described in (b).

(b) Brief Statement of Facts. A complaint must contain a concise statement that details the specific facts on which the claim of misconduct or disability is based. The statement of facts should include a description of:

(1) what happened;

(2) when and where the relevant events happened;

(3) any information that would help an investigator check the facts; and

(4) for an allegation of disability, any additional facts that form the basis of that allegation.

(c) Legibility. A complaint should be typewritten if possible. If not typewritten, it must be legible. An illegible complaint will be returned to the complainant with a request to resubmit it in legible form. If a resubmitted complaint is still illegible, it will not be accepted for filing.

(d) Complainant's Address and Signature; Verification. The complainant must provide a contact address and sign the complaint. The truth of the statements made in the complaint must be verified in writing under penalty of perjury. If any of these requirements are not met, the complaint will be accepted for filing, but it will be reviewed under only Rule 5(b).

(e) Number of Copies; Envelope Marking. The complainant shall provide the number of copies of the complaint required by local rule. Each copy should be in an envelope marked "Complaint of Misconduct" or "Complaint of Disability." The envelope must not show the name of any subject judge.

[Adopted March 11, 2008, effective April 10, 2008.]

Commentary on Rule 6

The Rule is adapted from the Illustrative Rules and is self-explanatory.

RULE 7.   WHERE TO INITIATE COMPLAINTS

(a) Where to File. Except as provided in (b),

(1) a complaint against a judge of a United States court of appeals, a United States district court, a United States bankruptcy court, or a United States magistrate judge must be filed with the circuit clerk in the jurisdiction in which the subject judge holds office.

(2) a complaint against a judge of the United States Court of International Trade or the United States Court of Federal Claims must be filed with the respective clerk of that court.

(3) a complaint against a judge of the United States Court of Appeals for the Federal Circuit must be filed with the circuit executive of that court.

(b) Misconduct in Another Circuit; Transfer. If a complaint alleges misconduct in the course of official business while the subject judge was sitting on a court by designation under 28 U.S.C. §§ 291–293 and 294(d), the complaint may be filed or identified with the circuit clerk of that circuit or of the subject judge's home circuit. The proceeding will continue in the circuit of the first-filed or first-identified complaint. The judicial council of the circuit where the complaint was first filed or first identified may transfer the complaint to the subject judge's home circuit or to the circuit where the alleged misconduct occurred, as the case may be.

[Adopted March 11, 2008, effective April 10, 2008.]

Commentary on Rule 7

Title 28 U.S.C. § 351 states that complaints are to be filed with "the clerk of the court of appeals for the circuit." However, in many circuits, this role is filled by circuit executives. Accordingly, the term "circuit clerk," as defined in Rule 3(b) and used throughout these Rules, applies to circuit executives.

Section 351 uses the term "the circuit" in a way that suggests that either the home circuit of the subject judge or the circuit in which misconduct is alleged to have occurred is the proper venue for complaints. With an exception for judges sitting by designation, the Rule requires the identifying or filing of a misconduct or disability complaint in the circuit in which the judge holds office, largely based on the administrative perspective of the Act. Given the Act's emphasis on the future conduct of the business of the courts, the circuit in which the judge holds office is the appropriate forum because that circuit is likely best able to influence a judge's future behavior in constructive ways.

However, when judges sit by designation, the non-home circuit has a strong interest in redressing misconduct in the course of official business, and where allegations also involve a member of the bar—ex parte contact between an attorney and a judge, for example—it may often be desirable to have the judicial and bar misconduct proceedings take place in the same venue. Rule 7(b), therefore, allows transfer to, or filing or identification of a complaint in, the non-home circuit. The proceeding may be transferred by the judicial council of the filing or identified circuit to the other circuit.

RULE 8.   ACTION BY CLERK

(a) Receipt of Complaint. Upon receiving a complaint against a judge filed under Rule 5 or 6, the circuit clerk must open a file, assign a docket number according to a uniform numbering scheme promulgated by the Judicial Conference Committee on Judicial Conduct and Disability, and acknowledge the complaint's receipt.

(b) Distribution of Copies. The clerk must promptly send copies of a complaint filed under Rule 6 to the chief judge or the judge authorized to act as chief judge under Rule 25(f), and copies of complaints filed under Rule 5 or 6 to each subject judge. The clerk must retain the original complaint. Any further distribution should be as provided by local rule.

(c) Complaints Against Noncovered Persons. If the clerk receives a complaint about a person not holding an office described in Rule 4, the clerk must not accept the complaint for filing under these Rules.

(d) Receipt of Complaint about a Judge and Another Noncovered Person. If a complaint is received about a judge described in Rule 4 and a person not holding an office described in Rule 4, the clerk must accept the complaint for filing under these Rules only with regard to the judge and must inform the complainant of the limitation.

[Adopted March 11, 2008, effective April 10, 2008.]

Commentary on Rule 8

This Rule is adapted from the Illustrative Rules and is largely self- explanatory.

The uniform docketing scheme described in subsection (a) should take into account potential problems associated with a complaint that names multiple judges. One solution may be to provide separate docket numbers for each subject judge. Separate docket numbers would help avoid difficulties in tracking cases, particularly if a complaint is dismissed with respect to some, but not all of the named judges.

Complaints against noncovered persons are not to be accepted for processing under these Rules but may, of course, be accepted under other circuit rules or procedures for grievances.

LOCAL RULE 8. ACTION BY CIRCUIT EXECUTIVE UPON RECEIPT OF A COMPLAINT

(a) Receipt of Complaint in Proper Form. Upon receipt of a complaint against a judge filed in proper form under these rules, the clerk of court of appeals will promptly transmit it to the circuit executive. The circuit executive will have custody of the complaint and all related papers and see that the complaint is expeditiously processed. The circuit executive will docket the complaint according to a uniform numbering scheme promulgated by the Judicial Conference Committee on Judicial Conduct and Disability, and acknowledge the complaint's receipt. The circuit executive will promptly distribute copies of the complaint in accordance with Rule 8(b). When the chief judge issues an order identifying a complaint under rule 5(a), the circuit executive will process such complaint as otherwise provided by these rules.

(b) Distribution of Copies. If a district judge or magistrate judge is complained about, the circuit executive will also send a copy of the complaint to the chief judge of the district court in which the judge or magistrate judge holds his or her appointment. If a bankruptcy judge is complained about, the circuit executive will send copies to the chief judges of the district court and the bankruptcy court. However, if the chief judge of the district court or bankruptcy court is a subject of a complaint, the chief judge's copy will be sent to the judge of such court in regular active service who is most senior in date of commission among those who are not subjects of the complaint.

(c) Complaints Against Noncovered Persons. If the circuit executive receives a complaint about a person not holding an office described in Rule 4, the circuit executive will not accept the complaint for filing and will advise the complainant in writing of the procedure for processing such complaints.

(d) Receipt of Complaint About a Judge and Another Noncovered Person. If a complaint is received about a judge described in Rule 4 and a person not holding an office described in Rule 4, the circuit executive will accept the complaint for filing only with regard to the judge, and will advise the complainant accordingly.

(e) Receipt of a Complaint Not in Proper Form. If the circuit executive receives a complaint against a judge described in Rule 4 that does not comply with the requirements of Rule 6, the circuit executive will ensure that the complaint is reviewed under Rule 5(b), will advise the complainant of the appropriate

procedures for refiling the complaint under Rule 6, and will enclose a copy of these rules and the accompanying forms.

[Effective June 1, 2009.]

RULE 9. TIME FOR FILING OR IDENTIFYING A COMPLAINT

A complaint may be filed or identified at any time. If the passage of time has made an accurate and fair investigation of a complaint impractical, the complaint must be dismissed under Rule 11(c)(1)(E).

[Adopted March 11, 2008, effective April 10, 2008.]

Commentary on Rule 9

This Rule is adapted from the Act, 28 U.S.C. §§ 351, 352(b)(1)(A)(iii), and the Illustrative Rules.

RULE 10. ABUSE OF THE COMPLAINT PROCEDURE

(a) Abusive Complaints. A complainant who has filed repetitive, harassing, or frivolous complaints, or has otherwise abused the complaint procedure, may be restricted from filing further complaints. After giving the complainant an opportunity to show cause in writing why his or her right to file further complaints should not be limited, a judicial council may prohibit, restrict, or impose conditions on the complainant's use of the complaint procedure. Upon written request of the complainant, the judicial council may revise or withdraw any prohibition, restriction, or condition previously imposed.

(b) Orchestrated Complaints. When many essentially identical complaints from different complainants are received and appear to be part of an orchestrated campaign, the chief judge may recommend that the judicial council issue a written order instructing the circuit clerk to accept only a certain number of such complaints for filing and to refuse to accept further ones. The clerk must send a copy of any such order to anyone whose complaint was not accepted.

[Adopted March 11, 2008, effective April 10, 2008.]

Commentary on Rule 10

This Rule is adapted from the Illustrative Rules.

Rule 10(a) provides a mechanism for a judicial council to restrict the filing of further complaints by a single complainant who has abused the complaint procedure. In some instances, however, the complaint procedure may be abused in a manner for which the remedy provided in Rule 10(a) may not be appropriate. For example, some circuits have been inundated with submissions of dozens or hundreds of essentially identical complaints against the same judge or judges, all submitted by different complainants. In many of these instances, persons with grievances against a particular judge or judges used the Internet or other technology to orchestrate mass complaint-filing campaigns against them. If each complaint submitted as part of such a campaign were accepted for filing and processed according to these Rules, there would be a serious drain on court resources without any benefit to the adjudication of the underlying merits.

A judicial council may, therefore, respond to such mass filings under Rule 10(b) by declining to accept repetitive complaints for filing, regardless of the fact that the complaints are nominally submitted by different complainants.

When the first complaint or complaints have been dismissed on the merits, and when further, essentially identical submissions follow, the judicial council may issue a second order noting that these are identical or repetitive complaints, directing the circuit clerk not to accept these complaints or any further such complaints for filing, and directing the clerk to send each putative complainant copies of both orders.

ARTICLE III.   REVIEW OF A COMPLAINT BY THE CHIEF JUDGE

RULE 11.   REVIEW BY THE CHIEF JUDGE

(a) Purpose of Chief Judge's Review.   When a complaint is identified by the chief judge or is filed, the chief judge must review it unless the chief judge is disqualified under Rule 25.   If the complaint contains information constituting evidence of misconduct or disability, but the complainant does not claim it as such, the chief judge must treat the complaint as if it did allege misconduct or disability and give notice to the subject judge.   After reviewing the complaint, the chief judge must determine whether it should be:

(1) dismissed;

(2) concluded on the ground that voluntary corrective action has been taken;

(3) concluded because intervening events have made action on the complaint no longer necessary; or

(4) referred to a special committee.

(b) Inquiry by Chief Judge.   In determining what action to take under Rule 11(a), the chief judge may conduct a limited inquiry.   The chief judge, or a designee, may communicate orally or in writing with the complainant, the subject judge, and any others who may have knowledge of the matter, and may review transcripts or other relevant documents.   In conducting the inquiry, the chief judge must not determine any reasonably disputed issue.

(c) Dismissal.

(1) Allowable grounds.   A complaint must be dismissed in whole or in part to the extent that the chief judge concludes that the complaint:

(A) alleges conduct that, even if true, is not prejudicial to the effective and expeditious administration of the business of the courts and does not indicate a mental or physical disability resulting in inability to discharge the duties of judicial office;

(B) is directly related to the merits of a decision or procedural ruling;

(C) is frivolous;

(D) is based on allegations lacking sufficient evidence to raise an inference that misconduct has occurred or that a disability exists;

(E) is based on allegations which are incapable of being established through investigation;

(F) has been filed in the wrong circuit under Rule 7; or

(G) is otherwise not appropriate for consideration under the Act.

(2) Disallowed grounds.   A complaint must not be dismissed solely because it repeats allegations of a previously dismissed complaint if it also contains material information not previously considered and does not constitute harassment of the subject judge.

(d) Corrective Action.   The chief judge may conclude the complaint proceeding in whole or in part if:

(1) an informal resolution under Rule 5 satisfactory to the chief judge was reached before the complaint was filed under Rule 6, or

(2) the chief judge determines that the subject judge has taken appropriate voluntary corrective action that acknowledges and remedies the problems raised by the complaint.

(e) Intervening Events.   The chief judge may conclude the complaint proceeding in whole or in part upon determining that intervening events render some or all of the allegations moot or make remedial action impossible.

(f) Appointment of Special Committee.   If some or all of the complaint is not dismissed or concluded, the chief judge must promptly appoint a special committee to investigate the complaint or any relevant portion of it and to make recommendations to the judicial council.   Before appointing a special committee, the chief judge must invite the subject judge to respond to the complaint either orally or in writing if the judge was not given an opportunity during the limited inquiry.   In the chief judge's discretion, separate complaints may be joined and assigned to a single special committee.   Similarly, a single complaint about more than one judge may be severed and more than one special committee appointed.

(g) Notice of Chief Judge's Action; Petitions for Review.

(1) When special committee is appointed.   If a special committee is appointed, the chief judge must

notify the complainant and the subject judge that the matter has been referred to a special committee and identify the members of the committee. A copy of the order appointing the special committee must be sent to the Judicial Conference Committee on Judicial Conduct and Disability.

(2) When chief judge disposes of complaint without appointing special committee. If the chief judge disposes of the complaint under Rule 11(c), (d), or (e), the chief judge must prepare a supporting memorandum that sets forth the reasons for the disposition. Except as authorized by 28 U.S.C. § 360, the memorandum must not include the name of the complainant or of the subject judge. The order and the supporting memorandum, which may be one document, must be provided to the complainant, the subject judge, and the Judicial Conference Committee on Judicial Conduct and Disability.

(3) Right of petition for review. If the chief judge disposes of a complaint under Rule 11(c), (d), or (e), the complainant and subject judge must be notified of the right to petition the judicial council for review of the disposition, as provided in Rule 18. If a petition for review is filed, the chief judge must promptly transmit all materials obtained in connection with the inquiry under Rule 11(b) to the circuit clerk for transmittal to the judicial council.

(h) Public Availability of Chief Judge's Decision. The chief judge's decision must be made public to the extent, at the time, and in the manner provided in Rule 24.

[Adopted March 11, 2008, effective April 10, 2008.]

Commentary on Rule 11

Subsection (a) lists the actions available to a chief judge in reviewing a complaint. This subsection provides that where a complaint has been filed under Rule 6, the ordinary doctrines of waiver do not apply. A chief judge must identify as a complaint any misconduct or disability issues raised by the factual allegations of the complaint even if the complainant makes no such claim with regard to those issues. For example, an allegation limited to misconduct in fact-finding that mentions periods during a trial when the judge was asleep must be treated as a complaint regarding disability. Some formal order giving notice of the expanded scope of the proceeding must be given to the subject judge.

Subsection (b) describes the nature of the chief judge's inquiry. It is based largely on the Breyer Committee Report, 239 F.R.D. at 243–45. The Act states that dismissal is appropriate "when a limited inquiry ... demonstrates that the allegations in the complaint lack any factual foundation or are conclusively refuted by objective evidence." 28 U.S.C. § 352(b)(1)(B). At the same time, however, Section 352(a) states that "[t]he chief judge shall not undertake to make findings of fact about any matter that is reasonably in dispute." These two statutory standards should be read together, so that a matter is not "reasonably" in dispute if a limited inquiry shows that the allegations do not constitute misconduct or disability, that they lack any reliable factual foundation, or that they are conclusively refuted by objective evidence.

In conducting a limited inquiry under subsection (b), the chief judge must avoid determinations of reasonably disputed issues, including reasonably disputed issues as to whether the facts alleged constitute misconduct or disability, which are ordinarily left to a special committee and the judicial council. An allegation of fact is ordinarily not "refuted" simply because the subject judge denies it. The limited inquiry must reveal something more in the way of refutation before it is appropriate to dismiss a complaint that is otherwise cognizable. If it is the complainant's word against the subject judge's—in other words, there is simply no other significant evidence of what happened or of the complainant's unreliability—then there must be a special-committee investigation. Such a credibility issue is a matter "reasonably in dispute" within the meaning of the Act.

However, dismissal following a limited inquiry may occur when the complaint refers to transcripts or to witnesses and the chief judge determines that the transcripts and witnesses all support the subject judge. Breyer Committee Report, 239 F.R.D. at 243. For example, consider a complaint alleging that the subject judge said X, and the complaint mentions, or it is independently clear, that five people may have heard what the judge said. Id. The chief judge is told by the subject judge and one witness that the judge did not say X, and the chief judge dismisses the complaint without questioning the other four possible witnesses. Id. In this example, the matter remains reasonably in dispute. If all five witnesses say the judge did not say X, dismissal is appropriate, but if potential witnesses who are reasonably accessible have not been questioned, then the matter remains reasonably in dispute. Id.

Similarly, under (c)(1)(A), if it is clear that the conduct or disability alleged, even if true, is not cognizable under these Rules, the complaint should be dismissed. If that issue is reasonably in dispute, however, dismissal under (c)(1)(A) is inappropriate.

Essentially, the standard articulated in subsection (b) is that used to decide motions for summary judgment pursuant to Fed. R. Civ. P. 56. Genuine issues of material fact are not resolved at the summary judgment stage. A material fact is one that "might affect the outcome of the suit under the governing law," and a dispute is "genuine" if "the evidence is such that a reasonable jury could return a verdict for the nonmoving party." *Anderson v. Liberty Lobby*, 477 U.S. 242, 248 (1986). Similarly, the chief judge may not resolve a genuine issue concerning a material fact or the existence of misconduct or a disability when conducting a limited inquiry pursuant to subsection (b).

Subsection (c) describes the grounds on which a complaint may be dismissed. These are adapted from the Act, 28 U.S.C. § 352(b), and the Breyer Committee Report, 239 F.R.D. at 239–45. Subsection (c)(1)(A) permits dismissal of an allegation that, even if true, does not constitute misconduct or disability under the statutory standard. The proper standards are set out in Rule 3 and discussed in the Commentary on that Rule. Subsection (c)(1)(B) permits dismissal of complaints related to the merits of a decision by a subject judge; this standard is also governed by Rule 3 and its accompanying Commentary.

Subsections (c)(1)(C)–(E) implement the statute by allowing dismissal of complaints that are "frivolous, lacking sufficient evidence to raise an inference that misconduct has occurred, or containing allegations which are incapable of being established through investigation." 28 U.S.C. § 352(b)(1)(A)(iii).

Dismissal of a complaint as "frivolous," under Rule 11(c)(1)(C), will generally occur without any inquiry beyond the face of the complaint. For instance, when the allegations are facially incredible or so lacking in indicia of reliability that no further inquiry is warranted, dismissal under this subsection is appropriate.

A complaint warranting dismissal under Rule 11(c)(1)(D) is illustrated by the following example. Consider a complainant who alleges an impropriety and asserts that he knows of it because it was observed and reported to him by a person who is identified. The judge denies that the event occurred. When contacted, the source also denies it. In such a case, the chief judge's proper course of action may turn on whether the source had any role in the allegedly improper conduct. If the complaint was based on a lawyer's statement that he or she had an improper ex parte contact with a judge, the lawyer's denial of the impropriety might not be taken as wholly persuasive, and it would be appropriate to conclude that a real factual issue is raised. On the other hand, if the complaint quoted a disinterested third party and that disinterested party denied that the statement had been made, there would be no value in opening a formal investigation. In such a case, it would be appropriate to dismiss the complaint under Rule 11(c)(1)(D).

Rule 11(c)(1)(E) is intended, among other things, to cover situations when no evidence is offered or identified, or when the only identified source is unavailable. Breyer Committee Report, 239 F.R.D. at 243. For example, a complaint alleges that an unnamed attorney told the complainant that the judge did X. Id. The subject judge denies it. The chief judge requests that the complainant (who does not purport to have observed the judge do X) identify the unnamed witness, or that the unnamed witness come forward so that the chief judge can learn the unnamed witness's account. Id. The complainant responds that he has spoken with the unnamed witness, that the unnamed witness is an attorney who practices in federal court, and that the unnamed witness is unwilling to be identified or to come forward. Id. at 243–44. The allegation is then properly dismissed as containing allegations that are incapable of being established through investigation. Id.

If, however, the situation involves a reasonable dispute over credibility, the matter should proceed. For example, the complainant alleges an impropriety and alleges that he or she observed it and that there were no other witnesses; the subject judge denies that the event occurred. Unless the complainant's allegations are facially incredible or so lacking indicia of reliability warranting dismissal under Rule 11(c)(1)(C), a special committee must be appointed because there is a material factual question that is reasonably in dispute.

Dismissal is also appropriate when a complaint is filed so long after an alleged event that memory loss, death, or changes to unknown residences prevent a proper investigation.

Subsection (c)(2) indicates that the investigative nature of the process prevents the application of claim preclusion principles where new and material evidence becomes available. However, it also recognizes that at some point a renewed investigation may constitute harassment of the subject judge and should be foregone, depending of course on the seriousness of the issues and the weight of the new evidence.

Rule 11(d) implements the Act's provision for dismissal if voluntary appropriate corrective action has been taken. It is largely adapted from the Breyer Committee Report, 239 F.R.D. 244–45. The Act authorizes the chief judge to conclude the proceedings if "appropriate corrective action has been taken." 28 U.S.C. § 352(b)(2). Under the Rule, action taken after the complaint is filed is "appropriate" when it acknowledges and remedies the problem raised by the complaint. Breyer Committee Report, 239 F.R.D. at 244. Because the Act deals with the conduct of judges, the emphasis is on correction of the judicial conduct that was the subject of the complaint. Id. Terminating a complaint based on corrective action is premised on the implicit understanding that voluntary self-correction or redress of misconduct or a disability is preferable to sanctions. Id. The chief judge may facilitate this process by giving the subject judge an objective view of the appearance of the judicial conduct in question and by suggesting appropriate corrective measures. Id. Moreover, when corrective action is taken under Rule 5 satisfactory to the chief judge before a complaint is filed, that informal resolution will be sufficient to conclude a subsequent complaint based on the identical conduct.

"Corrective action" must be voluntary action taken by the subject judge. Breyer Committee Report, 239 F.R.D. at 244. A remedial action directed by the chief judge or by an appellate court without the participation of the subject judge in formulating the directive or without the subject judge's subsequent agreement to such action does not constitute the requisite voluntary corrective action. Id. Neither the chief judge nor an appellate court has authority under the Act to impose a formal remedy or sanction; only the judicial council can impose a formal remedy or sanction under 28 U.S.C. § 354(a)(2). Id. Compliance with a previous council order may serve as corrective action allowing conclusion of a later complaint about the same behavior. Id.

Where a judge's conduct has resulted in identifiable, particularized harm to the complainant or another individual, appropriate corrective action should include steps taken by that judge to acknowledge and redress the harm, if possible, such as by an apology, recusal from a case, or a pledge to refrain from similar conduct in the future. Id. While the Act is generally forward-looking, any corrective action should, to the extent possible, serve to correct a specific harm to an individual, if such harm can reasonably be remedied. Id. In some cases, corrective action may not be "appropriate" to justify conclusion of a complaint unless the complainant or other individual harmed is meaningfully apprised of the nature of the corrective action in the chief judge's order, in a direct communication from the subject judge, or otherwise. Id.

Voluntary corrective action should be proportionate to any plausible allegations of misconduct in the complaint. The form of corrective action should also be proportionate to any sanctions that a judicial council might impose under Rule 20(b), such as a private or public reprimand or a change in case assignments. Breyer Committee Report, 239 F.R.D at 244–45. In other words, minor corrective action will not suffice to dispose of a serious matter. Id.

Rule 11(e) implements Section 352(b)(2) of the Act, which permits the chief judge to "conclude the proceeding," if "action on the complaint is no longer necessary because of intervening events," such as a resignation from judicial office. Ordinarily, however, stepping down from an administrative post such as chief judge, judicial-council member, or court-committee chair does not constitute an event rendering unnecessary any further action on a complaint alleging judicial misconduct. Breyer Committee Report, 239 F.R.D. at 245. As long as the subject of the complaint performs judicial duties, a complaint alleging judicial misconduct must be addressed. Id.

If a complaint is not disposed of pursuant to Rule 11(c), (d), or (e), a special committee must be appointed. Rule 11(f) states that a subject judge must be invited to respond to the complaint before a special committee is appointed, if no earlier response was invited.

Subject judges, of course, receive copies of complaints at the same time that they are referred to the chief judge, and they are free to volunteer responses to them. Under Rule 11(b), the chief judge may request a response if it is thought necessary. However, many complaints are clear candidates for dismissal even if their allegations are accepted as true, and there is no need for the subject judge to devote time to a defense.

The Act requires that the order dismissing a complaint or concluding the proceeding contain a statement of reasons and that a copy of the order be sent to the complainant. 28 U.S.C. § 352(b). Rule 24, dealing with availability of information to the public, contemplates that the order will be made public, usually without disclosing the names of the complainant or the subject judge. If desired for administrative purposes, more identifying information can be included in a non-public version of the order.

When complaints are disposed of by chief judges, the statutory purposes are best served by providing the complainant with a full, particularized, but concise explanation, giving reasons for the conclusions reached. See also Commentary on Rule 24, dealing with public availability.

Rule 11(g) provides that the complainant and subject judge must be notified, in the case of a disposition by the chief judge, of the right to petition the judicial council for review. A copy of a chief judge's order and memorandum, which may be one document, disposing of a complaint must be sent by the circuit clerk to the Judicial Conference Committee on Judicial Conduct and Disability.

ARTICLE IV. INVESTIGATION AND REPORT BY SPECIAL COMMITTEE

RULE 12. COMPOSITION OF SPECIAL COMMITTEE

(a) Membership. Except as provided in (e), a special committee appointed under Rule 11(f) must consist of the chief judge and equal numbers of circuit and district judges. If the complaint is about a district judge, bankruptcy judge, or magistrate judge, then, when possible, the district-judge members of the committee must be from districts other than the district of the subject judge. For the courts named in 28 U.S.C. § 363, the committee must be selected from the judges serving on the subject judge's court.

(b) Presiding Officer. When appointing the committee, the chief judge may serve as the presiding officer or else must designate a committee member as the presiding officer.

(c) Bankruptcy Judge or Magistrate Judge as Adviser. If the subject judge is a bankruptcy judge or magistrate judge, he or she may, within 14 days after being notified of the committee's appointment, ask the chief judge to designate as a committee adviser another bankruptcy judge or magistrate judge, as the case may be. The chief judge must grant such a request but may otherwise use discretion in naming the adviser. Unless the adviser is a Court of Federal Claims special master appointed under 42 U.S.C. § 300aa–12(c), the adviser must be from a district other than the district of the subject bankruptcy judge or subject magistrate judge. The adviser cannot vote but has the other privileges of a committee member.

(d) Provision of Documents. The chief judge must certify to each other member of the committee and to any adviser copies of the complaint and statement of facts in whole or relevant part, and any other relevant documents on file.

(e) Continuing Qualification of Committee Members. A member of a special committee who was qualified to serve when appointed may continue to serve on the committee even though the member relinquishes the position of chief judge, active circuit judge, or active district judge, as the case may be, but only if the member continues to hold office under Article III, Section 1, of the Constitution of the United States, or under 28 U.S.C. § 171.

(f) Inability of Committee Member to Complete Service. If a member of a special committee can no longer serve because of death, disability, disqualification, resignation, retirement from office, or other reason, the chief judge must decide whether to appoint a replacement member, either a circuit or district judge as needed under (a). No special committee appointed under these Rules may function with only a single member, and the votes of a two-member committee must be unanimous.

(g) Voting. All actions by a committee must be by vote of a majority of all members of the committee.

[Adopted March 11, 2008, effective April 10, 2008.]

Commentary on Rule 12

This Rule is adapted from the Act and the Illustrative Rules.

Rule 12 leaves the size of a special committee flexible, to be determined on a case-by-case basis. The question of committee size is one that should be weighed with care in view of the potential for consuming the members' time; a large committee should be appointed only if there is a special reason to do so.

Although the Act requires that the chief judge be a member of each special committee, 28 U.S.C. § 353(a)(1), it does not require that the chief judge preside. Accordingly, Rule 12(b) provides that if the chief judge does not preside, he or she must designate another committee member as the presiding officer.

Rule 12(c) provides that the chief judge must appoint a bankruptcy judge or magistrate judge as an adviser to a special committee at the request of a bankruptcy or magistrate subject judge.

Subsection (c) also provides that the adviser will have all the privileges of a committee member except a vote. The adviser, therefore, may participate in all deliberations of the committee, question witnesses at hearings, and write a separate statement to accompany the special committee's report to the judicial council.

Rule 12(e) provides that a member of a special committee who remains an Article III judge may continue to serve on the committee even though the member's status otherwise changes. Thus, a committee that originally consisted of the chief judge and an equal number of circuit and district judges, as required by the law, may continue to function even though changes of status alter that composition. This provision reflects the belief that stability of membership will contribute to the quality of the work of such committees.

Stability of membership is also the principal concern animating Rule 12(f), which deals with the case in which a special committee loses a member before its work is complete. The Rule permits the chief judge to determine whether a replacement member should be appointed. Generally, appointment of a replacement member is desirable in these situations unless the committee has conducted evidentiary hearings before the vacancy occurs. However, cases may arise in which a committee is in the late stages of its work, and in which it would be difficult for a new member to play a meaningful role. The Rule also preserves the collegial character of the committee process by prohibiting a single surviving member from serving as a committee and by providing that a committee of two surviving members will, in essence, operate under a unanimity rule.

Rule 12(g) provides that actions of a special committee must be by vote of a majority of all the members. All the members of a committee should participate in committee decisions. In that circumstance, it seems reasonable to require that committee decisions be made by a majority of the membership, rather than a majority of some smaller quorum.

RULE 13. CONDUCT OF AN INVESTIGATION

(a) Extent and Methods of Special–Committee Investigation. Each special committee must determine the appropriate extent and methods of the investigation in light of the allegations of the complaint. If, in the course of the investigation, the committee has cause to believe that the subject judge may have engaged in misconduct or has a disability that is beyond the scope of the complaint, the committee must refer the new matter to the chief judge for action under Rule 5 or Rule 11.

(b) Criminal Conduct. If the committee's investigation concerns conduct that may be a crime, the committee must consult with the appropriate prosecutorial authorities to the extent permitted by the Act to avoid compromising any criminal investigation. The committee has final authority over the timing and extent of its investigation and the formulation of its recommendations.

(c) Staff. The committee may arrange for staff assistance to conduct the investigation. It may use existing staff of the judicial branch or may hire special staff through the Director of the Administrative Office of the United States Courts.

(d) Delegation of Subpoena Power; Contempt. The chief judge may delegate the authority to exercise the committee's subpoena powers. The judicial council or special committee may institute a contempt proceeding under 28 U.S.C. § 332(d) against anyone who fails to comply with a subpoena.

[Adopted March 11, 2008, effective April 10, 2008.]

Commentary on Rule 13

This Rule is adapted from the Illustrative Rules.

Rule 13, as well as Rules 14, 15, and 16, are concerned with the way in which a special committee carries out its mission. They reflect the view that a special committee has two roles that are separated in ordinary litigation. First, the committee has an investigative role of the kind that is characteristically left to executive branch agencies or discovery by civil litigants. 28 U.S.C. § 353(c). Second, it has a formalized fact-finding and recommendation-of-disposition role that is characteristically left to juries, judges, or arbitrators. Id. Rule 13 generally governs the investigative stage. Even though the same body has responsibility for both roles under the Act, it is important to distinguish between them in order to ensure that appropriate rights are afforded at appropriate times to the subject judge.

One of the difficult questions that can arise is the relationship between proceedings under the Act and criminal investigations. Rule 13(b) assigns responsibility for coordination to the special committee in cases in which criminal conduct is suspected, but gives the committee the authority to determine the appropriate pace of its activity in light of any criminal investigation.

Title 28 U.S.C. § 356(a) provides that a special committee will have full subpoena powers as provided in 28 U.S.C. § 332(d). Section 332(d)(1) provides that subpoenas will be issued on behalf of judicial councils by the circuit clerk "at the direction of the chief judge of the circuit or his designee." Rule 13(d) contemplates that, where the chief judge designates someone else as presiding officer of a special committee, the presiding officer also be delegated the authority to direct the circuit clerk to issue subpoenas related to committee proceedings. That is not intended to imply, however, that the decision to use the subpoena power is exercisable by the presiding officer alone. See Rule 12(g).

RULE 14. CONDUCT OF HEARINGS BY SPECIAL COMMITTEE

(a) Purpose of Hearings. The committee may hold hearings to take testimony and receive other evidence, to hear argument, or both. If the committee is investigating allegations against more than one judge, it may hold joint or separate hearings.

(b) Committee Evidence. Subject to Rule 15, the committee must obtain material, nonredundant evidence in the form it considers appropriate. In the committee's discretion, evidence may be obtained by committee members, staff, or both. Witnesses offering testimonial evidence may include the complainant and the subject judge.

(c) Counsel for Witnesses. The subject judge has the right to counsel. The special committee has discretion to decide whether other witnesses may have counsel present when they testify.

(d) Witness Fees. Witness fees must be paid as provided in 28 U.S.C. § 1821.

(e) Oath. All testimony taken at a hearing must be given under oath or affirmation.

(f) Rules of Evidence. The Federal Rules of Evidence do not apply to special-committee hearings.

(g) Record and Transcript. A record and transcript must be made of all hearings.

[Adopted March 11, 2008, effective April 10, 2008.]

Commentary on Rule 14

This Rule is adapted from Section 353 of the Act and the Illustrative Rules.

Rule 14 is concerned with the conduct of fact-finding hearings. Special-committee hearings will normally be held only after the investigative work has been completed and the committee has concluded that there is sufficient evidence to warrant a formal fact-finding proceeding. Special-committee proceedings are primarily inquisitorial rather than adversarial. Accordingly, the Federal Rules of Evidence do not apply to such hearings. Inevitably, a hearing will have something of an adversary character. Nevertheless, that tendency should be moderated to the extent possible. Even though a proceeding will commonly have investigative and hearing stages, committee members should not regard themselves as prosecutors one day and judges the next. Their duty—and that of their staff—is at all times to be impartial seekers of the truth.

Rule 14(b) contemplates that material evidence will be obtained by the committee and presented in the form of affidavits, live testimony, etc. Staff or others who are organizing the hearings should regard it as their role to present evidence representing the entire picture. With respect to testimonial evidence, the subject judge should normally be called as a committee witness. Cases may arise in which the judge will not testify voluntarily. In such cases, subpoena

powers are available, subject to the normal testimonial privileges. Although Rule 15(c) recognizes the subject judge's statutory right to call witnesses on his or her own behalf, exercise of this right should not usually be necessary.

RULE 15. RIGHTS OF SUBJECT JUDGE

(a) Notice.

(1) Generally. The subject judge must receive written notice of:

(A) the appointment of a special committee under Rule 11(f);

(B) the expansion of the scope of an investigation under Rule 13(a);

(C) any hearing under Rule 14, including its purposes, the names of any witnesses the committee intends to call, and the text of any statements that have been taken from those witnesses.

(2) Suggestion of additional witnesses. The subject judge may suggest additional witnesses to the committee.

(b) Report of the Special Committee. The subject judge must be sent a copy of the special committee's report when it is filed with the judicial council.

(c) Presentation of Evidence. At any hearing held under Rule 14, the subject judge has the right to present evidence, to compel the attendance of witnesses, and to compel the production of documents. At the request of the subject judge, the chief judge or the judge's designee must direct the circuit clerk to issue a subpoena to a witness under 28 U.S.C. § 332(d)(1). The subject judge must be given the opportunity to cross-examine committee witnesses, in person or by counsel.

(d) Presentation of Argument. The subject judge may submit written argument to the special committee and must be given a reasonable opportunity to present oral argument at an appropriate stage of the investigation.

(e) Attendance at Hearings. The subject judge has the right to attend any hearing held under Rule 14 and to receive copies of the transcript, of any documents introduced, and of any written arguments submitted by the complainant to the committee.

(f) Representation by Counsel. The subject judge may choose to be represented by counsel in the exercise of any right enumerated in this Rule. As provided in Rule 20(e), the United States may bear the costs of the representation.

[Adopted March 11, 2008, effective April 10, 2008.]

Commentary on Rule 15

This Rule is adapted from the Act and the Illustrative Rules.

The Act states that these Rules must contain provisions requiring that "the judge whose conduct is the subject of a complaint ... be afforded an opportunity to appear (in person or by counsel) at proceedings conducted by the investigating panel, to present oral and documentary evidence, to compel the attendance of witnesses or the production of documents, to cross-examine witnesses, and to present argument orally or in writing." 28 U.S.C. § 358(b)(2). To implement this provision, Rule 15(e) gives the judge the right to attend any hearing held for the purpose of receiving evidence of record or hearing argument under Rule 14.

The Act does not require that the subject judge be permitted to attend all proceedings of the special committee. Accordingly, the Rules do not give a right to attend other proceedings—for example, meetings at which the committee is engaged in investigative activity, such as interviewing persons to learn whether they ought to be called as witnesses or examining for relevance purposes documents delivered pursuant to a subpoena duces tecum, or meetings in which the committee is deliberating on the evidence or its recommendations.

RULE 16. RIGHTS OF COMPLAINANT IN INVESTIGATION

(a) **Notice.** The complainant must receive written notice of the investigation as provided in Rule 11(g)(1). When the special committee's report to the judicial council is filed, the complainant must be notified of the filing. The judicial council may, in its discretion, provide a copy of the report of a special committee to the complainant.

(b) **Opportunity to Provide Evidence.** If the committee determines that the complainant may have evidence that does not already exist in writing, a representative of the committee must interview the complainant.

(c) **Presentation of Argument.** The complainant may submit written argument to the special committee. In its discretion, the special committee may permit the complainant to offer oral argument.

(d) **Representation by Counsel.** A complainant may submit written argument through counsel and, if permitted to offer oral argument, may do so through counsel.

(e) **Cooperation.** In exercising its discretion under this Rule, a special committee may take into account the degree of the complainant's cooperation in preserving the confidentiality of the proceedings, including the identity of the subject judge.

[Adopted March 11, 2008, effective April 10, 2008.]

Commentary on Rule 16

This Rule is adapted from the Act and the Illustrative Rules.

In accordance with the view of the process as fundamentally administrative and inquisitorial, these Rules do not give the complainant the rights of a party to litigation, and leave the complainant's role largely to the discretion of the special committee. However, Rule 16(b) provides that, where a special committee has been appointed and it determines that the complainant may have additional evidence, the complainant must be interviewed by a representative of the committee. Such an interview may be in person or by telephone, and the representative of the committee may be either a member or staff.

Rule 16 does not contemplate that the complainant will ordinarily be permitted to attend proceedings of the special committee except when testifying or presenting oral argument. A special committee may exercise its discretion to permit the complainant to be present at its proceedings, or to permit the complainant, individually or through counsel, to participate in the examination or cross-examination of witnesses.

The Act authorizes an exception to the normal confidentiality provisions where the judicial council in its discretion provides a copy of the report of the special committee to the complainant and to the subject judge. 28 U.S.C. § 360(a)(1). However, the Rules do not entitle the complainant to a copy of the special committee's report.

In exercising their discretion regarding the role of the complainant, the special committee and the judicial council should protect the confidentiality of the complaint process. As a consequence, subsection (e) provides that a special committee may consider the degree to which a complainant has cooperated in preserving the confidentiality of the proceedings in determining what role beyond the minimum required by these Rules should be given to that complainant.

RULE 17. SPECIAL–COMMITTEE REPORT

The committee must file with the judicial council a comprehensive report of its investigation, including findings and recommendations for council action. The report must be accompanied by a statement of the vote by which it was adopted, any separate or dissenting statements of committee members, and the record of any hearings held under Rule 14. A copy of the report and accompanying statement must be sent to the Judicial Conference Committee on Judicial Conduct and Disability.

[Adopted March 11, 2008, effective April 10, 2008.]

Commentary on Rule 17

This Rule is adapted from the Illustrative Rules and is self-explanatory. The provision for sending a copy of the special-committee report and accompanying statement to the Judicial Conference Committee is new.

ARTICLE V. JUDICIAL–COUNCIL REVIEW

RULE 18. PETITIONS FOR REVIEW OF CHIEF JUDGE DISPOSITIONS UNDER RULE 11(c), (d), or (e)

(a) Petitions for Review. After the chief judge issues an order under Rule 11(c), (d), or (e), a complainant or subject judge may petition the judicial council of the circuit to review the order. By rules promulgated under 28 U.S.C. § 358, the judicial council may refer a petition for review filed under this Rule to a panel of no fewer than five members of the council, at least two of whom must be district judges.

(b) When to File; Form; Where to File. A petition for review must be filed in the office of the circuit clerk within 35 days of the date on the clerk's letter informing the parties of the chief judge's order. The petition should be in letter form, addressed to the circuit clerk, and in an envelope marked "Misconduct Petition" or "Disability Petition." The name of the subject judge must not be shown on the envelope. The letter should be typewritten or otherwise legible. It should begin with "I hereby petition the judicial council for review of . . ." and state the reasons why the petition should be granted. It must be signed.

(c) Receipt and Distribution of Petition. A circuit clerk who receives a petition for review filed within the time allowed and in proper form must:

(1) acknowledge its receipt and send a copy to the complainant or subject judge, as the case may be;

(2) promptly distribute to each member of the judicial council, or its relevant panel, except for any member disqualified under Rule 25, or make available in the manner provided by local rule, the following materials:

(A) copies of the complaint;

(B) all materials obtained by the chief judge in connection with the inquiry;

(C) the chief judge's order disposing of the complaint;

(D) any memorandum in support of the chief judge's order;

(E) the petition for review; and

(F) an appropriate ballot;

(3) send the petition for review to the Judicial Conference Committee on Judicial Conduct and Disability. Unless the Judicial Conference Committee requests them, the clerk will not send copies of the materials obtained by the chief judge.

(d) Untimely Petition. The clerk must refuse to accept a petition that is received after the deadline in (b).

(e) Timely Petition Not in Proper Form. When the clerk receives a petition filed within the time allowed but in a form that is improper to a degree that would substantially impair its consideration by the judicial council—such as a document that is ambiguous about whether it is intended to be a petition for review—the clerk must acknowledge its receipt, call the filer's attention to the deficiencies, and give the filer the opportunity to correct the deficiencies within 21 days of the date of the clerk's letter about the deficiencies or within the original deadline for filing the petition, whichever is later. If the deficiencies are corrected within the time allowed, the clerk will proceed according to paragraphs (a) and (c) of this Rule. If the deficiencies are not corrected, the clerk must reject the petition.

[Adopted March 11, 2008, effective April 10, 2008.]

Commentary on Rule 18

Rule 18 is adapted largely from the Illustrative Rules.

Subsection (a) permits a subject judge, as well as the complainant, to petition for review of a chief judge's order dismissing a complaint under Rule 11(c), or concluding that appropriate corrective action or intervening events have remedied or mooted the problems raised by the complaint pursuant to Rule 11(d) or (e). Although the subject judge may ostensibly be vindicated by the dismissal or conclusion of a complaint, a chief judge's order may include language disagreeable to the subject judge. For example, an order may dismiss a complaint, but state that the subject judge did in fact engage in misconduct. Accordingly, a subject judge may wish to object to the content of the order and is given the opportunity to petition the judicial council of the circuit for review.

Subsection (b) contains a time limit of thirty-five days to file a petition for review. It is important to establish a time limit on petitions for review of chief judges' dispositions in order to provide finality to the process. If the complaint requires an investigation, the investigation should proceed; if it does not, the subject judge should know that the matter is closed.

The standards for timely filing under the Federal Rules of Appellate Procedure should be applied to petitions for review. See Fed. R. App. P. 25(a)(2)(A) and (C).

Rule 18(e) provides for an automatic extension of the time limit imposed under subsection (b) if a person files a petition that is rejected for failure to comply with formal requirements.

LOCAL RULE 18. PETITIONS FOR REVIEW OF CHIEF JUDGE DISPOSITIONS UNDER RULE 11(c), (d), OR (e)

(a) Receipt and Distribution of Petitions for Review. Upon receipt of a petition for review filed within the time allowed and in proper form under these rules, the clerk of the court of appeals will promptly transmit such petition to the circuit execu-

tive, who will acknowledge receipt of the petition. The circuit executive will promptly make available to each member of the Judicial Council review panel, as set forth in Local Rule 19(a), except for any member disqualified under Rule 25, copies of the materials identified in Rule 18(c)(2). The circuit executive will also send the same materials, except for the ballot, to the chief judge of the circuit and each judge whose conduct is at issue, except the materials previously sent to a person may be omitted.

(b) Receipt of Untimely Petition. *The circuit executive will not accept a petition that is received after the deadline set forth in Rule 18(b).*

(c) Receipt of Timely Petition Not in Proper Form. *Upon receipt of a petition filed within the time allowed but not in proper form under these rules (including a document that is ambiguous about whether a petition for review is intended), the circuit executive will acknowledge receipt of the petition, call the petitioner's attention to the deficiencies, and give the petitioner the opportunity to correct the deficiencies within 21 days of the date of the circuit executive's letter or within the original deadline for filing the petition, whichever is later. If the deficiencies are corrected within the time allowed, the circuit executive will proceed in accordance with paragraph (a) of this rule. If the deficiencies are not corrected, the circuit executive will reject the petition.*

[Effective June 1, 2009.]

RULE 19. JUDICIAL–COUNCIL DISPOSITION OF PETITIONS FOR REVIEW

(a) Rights of Subject Judge. At any time after a complainant files a petition for review, the subject judge may file a written response with the circuit clerk. The clerk must promptly distribute copies of the response to each member of the judicial council or of the relevant panel, unless that member is disqualified under Rule 25. Copies must also be distributed to the chief judge, to the complainant, and to the Judicial Conference Committee on Judicial Conduct and Disability. The subject judge must not otherwise communicate with individual council members about the matter. The subject judge must be given copies of any communications to the judicial council from the complainant.

(b) Judicial–Council Action. After considering a petition for review and the materials before it, a judicial council may:

(1) affirm the chief judge's disposition by denying the petition;

(2) return the matter to the chief judge with directions to conduct a further inquiry under Rule 11(b) or to identify a complaint under Rule 5;

(3) return the matter to the chief judge with directions to appoint a special committee under Rule 11(f); or

(4) in exceptional circumstances, take other appropriate action.

(c) Notice of Council Decision. Copies of the judicial council's order, together with any accompanying memorandum in support of the order or separate concurring or dissenting statements, must be given to the complainant, the subject judge, and the Judicial Conference Committee on Judicial Conduct and Disability.

(d) Memorandum of Council Decision. If the council's order affirms the chief judge's disposition, a supporting memorandum must be prepared only if the judicial council concludes that there is a need to supplement the chief judge's explanation. A memorandum supporting a council order must not include the name of the complainant or the subject judge.

(e) Review of Judicial–Council Decision. If the judicial council's decision is adverse to the petitioner, and if no member of the council dissented on the ground that a special committee should be appointed under Rule 11(f), the complainant must be notified that he or she has no right to seek review of the decision. If there was a dissent, the petitioner must be informed that he or she can file a petition for review under Rule 21(b) solely on the issue of whether a special committee should be appointed.

(f) Public Availability of Judicial–Council Decision. Materials related to the council's decision must be made public to the extent, at the time, and in the manner set forth in Rule 24.

[Adopted March 11, 2008, effective April 10, 2008.]

Commentary on Rule 19

This Rule is largely adapted from the Act and is self-explanatory.

The council should ordinarily review the decision of the chief judge on the merits, treating the petition for review for all practical purposes as an appeal. The judicial council may respond to a petition by affirming the chief judge's order, remanding the matter, or, in exceptional cases, taking other appropriate action.

LOCAL RULE 19. JUDICIAL-COUNCIL DISPOSITION OF PETITIONS FOR REVIEW

(a) Review Panel. *Pursuant to Rule 18(a), the chief judge shall annually designate two review panels to act for the Judicial Council on all petitions for review of the chief judge's dismissal order, except for those petitions referred to the full membership of the Judicial Council pursuant to Local Rule 19(b). Each review panel will serve alternating six-month terms and shall be comprised of five members of the Judi-*

cial Council, excluding the chief judge. In order of seniority, each circuit judge council member shall be alternately assigned to each of the two review panels. The district judge council members shall also be alternately assigned in order of seniority to each of the two panels so as to ensure that at least two of the members of each review panel shall be district judges.

In the event of the absence of a panel member, or the recusal or disqualification of a panel member under Rule 25 from ruling on a particular petition for review, the circuit executive will select a judge in order of seniority from the other review panel to replace the unavailable panel member. An unavailable circuit judge will be replaced by the next available circuit judge in rotation. An unavailable district judge will be replaced by the next available district judge in rotation. If necessary, an unavailable circuit judge may be replaced by a district judge and an unavailable district judge may be replaced by a circuit judge but in no event will the panel be composed of fewer than two district judges.

In the event of a change in Judicial Council membership, the new council member shall take the place of his or her predecessor pending the review panels' annual reorganization.

(b) Mail Ballot. *Each member of the review panel to whom a ballot was sent will return a signed ballot, or otherwise communicate the member's vote, to the circuit executive. The ballot form will provide opportunities to vote to: (1) affirm the chief judge's disposition, or (2) refer the petition to the full membership of the Judicial Council for disposition in accordance with Rule 19(b). The form will also provide an opportunity for members to indicate that they have disqualified themselves from participating in consideration of the petition.*

Upon the vote of any member of the review panel, the petition for review shall be referred to the full membership of the Judicial Council. Any member of the review panel who votes to refer the petition to the full council shall include a brief statement of the reasons for the referral with the ballot. The review panel may act only by vote of all five members. If, because of absence, recusal or disqualification, all five members of the panel cannot participate, the petition shall be referred to the full membership of the Judicial Council for disposition in accordance with Rule 19(b).

Upon referral of a petition to the full membership of the Judicial Council, the circuit executive shall send the referring judge's ballot and brief statement to each member of the Judicial Council. The circuit executive will also make available the documents specified in Rule 18(c) to council members not then serving on the reviewing panel, unless disqualified under Rule 25. Every voting member of the Judicial Council will return a signed ballot, or otherwise

communicate the member's vote, to the circuit executive.

[Effective June 1, 2009.]

RULE 20. JUDICIAL–COUNCIL CONSIDERATION OF REPORTS AND RECOMMENDATIONS OF SPECIAL COMMITTEES

(a) Rights of Subject Judge. Within 21 days after the filing of the report of a special committee, the subject judge may send a written response to the members of the judicial council. The judge must also be given an opportunity to present argument through counsel, written or oral, as determined by the council. The judge must not otherwise communicate with council members about the matter.

(b) Judicial–Council Action.

(1) *Discretionary Actions.* Subject to the judge's rights set forth in subsection (a), the judicial council may:

(A) dismiss the complaint because:

(i) even if the claim is true, the claimed conduct is not conduct prejudicial to the effective and expeditious administration of the business of the courts and does not indicate a mental or physical disability resulting in inability to discharge the duties of office;

(ii) the complaint is directly related to the merits of a decision or procedural ruling;

(iii) the facts on which the complaint is based have not been established; or

(iv) the complaint is otherwise not appropriate for consideration under 28 U.S.C. §§ 351–364.

(B) conclude the proceeding because appropriate corrective action has been taken or intervening events have made the proceeding unnecessary.

(C) refer the complaint to the Judicial Conference of the United States with the council's recommendations for action.

(D) take remedial action to ensure the effective and expeditious administration of the business of the courts, including:

(i) censuring or reprimanding the subject judge, either by private communication or by public announcement;

(ii) ordering that no new cases be assigned to the subject judge for a limited, fixed period;

(iii) in the case of a magistrate judge, ordering the chief judge of the district court to take action specified by the council, including the initiation of removal proceedings under 28 U.S.C. § 631(i) or 42 U.S.C. § 300aa–12(c)(2);

(iv) in the case of a bankruptcy judge, removing the judge from office under 28 U.S.C. § 152(e);

(v) in the case of a circuit or district judge, requesting the judge to retire voluntarily with the provision (if necessary) that ordinary length-of-service requirements will be waived; and

(vi) in the case of a circuit or district judge who is eligible to retire but does not do so, certifying the disability of the judge under 28 U. S.C. § 372(b) so that an additional judge may be appointed.

(E) take any combination of actions described in (b)(1)(A)–(D) of this Rule that is within its power.

(2) *Mandatory Actions.* A judicial council must refer a complaint to the Judicial Conference if the council determines that a circuit judge or district judge may have engaged in conduct that:

(A) might constitute ground for impeachment; or

(B) in the interest of justice, is not amenable to resolution by the judicial council.

(c) **Inadequate Basis for Decision.** If the judicial council finds that a special committee's report, recommendations, and record provide an inadequate basis for decision, it may return the matter to the committee for further investigation and a new report, or it may conduct further investigation. If the judicial council decides to conduct further investigation, the subject judge must be given adequate prior notice in writing of that decision and of the general scope and purpose of the additional investigation. The judicial council's conduct of the additional investigation must generally accord with the procedures and powers set forth in Rules 13 through 16 for the conduct of an investigation by a special committee.

(d) **Council Vote.** Council action must be taken by a majority of those members of the council who are not disqualified. A decision to remove a bankruptcy judge from office requires a majority vote of all the members of the council.

(e) **Recommendation for Fee Reimbursement.** If the complaint has been finally dismissed or concluded under (b)(1)(A) or (B) of this Rule, and if the subject judge so requests, the judicial council may recommend that the Director of the Administrative Office of the United States Courts use funds appropriated to the Judiciary to reimburse the judge for reasonable expenses incurred during the investigation, when those expenses would not have been incurred but for the requirements of the Act and these Rules. Reasonable expenses include attorneys' fees and expenses related to a successful defense or prosecution of a proceeding under Rule 21(a) or (b).

(f) **Council Action.** Council action must be by written order. Unless the council finds that extraor-

dinary reasons would make it contrary to the interests of justice, the order must be accompanied by a memorandum setting forth the factual determinations on which it is based and the reasons for the council action. The order and the supporting memorandum must be provided to the complainant, the subject judge, and the Judicial Conference Committee on Judicial Conduct and Disability. The complainant and the subject judge must be notified of any right to review of the judicial council's decision as provided in Rule 21(b).

[Adopted March 11, 2008, effective April 10, 2008.]

Commentary on Rule 20

This Rule is largely adapted from the Illustrative Rules.

Rule 20(a) provides that within twenty-one days after the filing of the report of a special committee, the subject judge may address a written response to all of the members of the judicial council. The subject judge must also be given an opportunity to present oral argument to the council, personally or through counsel. The subject judge may not otherwise communicate with council members about the matter.

Rule 20(c) provides that if the judicial council decides to conduct an additional investigation, the subject judge must be given adequate prior notice in writing of that decision and of the general scope and purpose of the additional investigation. The conduct of the investigation will be generally in accordance with the procedures set forth in Rules 13 through 16 for the conduct of an investigation by a special committee. However, if hearings are held, the council may limit testimony or the presentation of evidence to avoid unnecessary repetition of testimony and evidence before the special committee.

Rule 20(d) provides that council action must be taken by a majority of those members of the council who are not disqualified, except that a decision to remove a bankruptcy judge from office requires a majority of all the members of the council as required by 28 U.S.C. § 152(e). However, it is inappropriate to apply a similar rule to the less severe actions that a judicial council may take under the Act. If some members of the council are disqualified in the matter, their disqualification should not be given the effect of a vote against council action.

With regard to Rule 20(e), the judicial council, on the request of the subject judge, may recommend to the Director of the Administrative Office of the United States Courts that the subject judge be reimbursed for reasonable expenses, including attorneys' fees, incurred. The judicial council has the authority to recommend such reimbursement where, after investigation by a special committee, the complaint has been finally dismissed or concluded under subsection (b)(1)(A) or (B) of this Rule. It is contemplated that such reimbursement may be provided for the successful prosecution or defense of a proceeding under Rule 21(a) or (b), in other words, one that results in a Rule 20(b)(1)(A) or (B) dismissal or conclusion.

Rule 20(f) requires that council action normally be supported with a memorandum of factual determinations and reasons and that notice of the action be given to the complainant and the subject judge. Rule 20(f) also requires that the notification to the complainant and the subject judge include notice of any right to petition for review of the council's decision under Rule 21(b).

ARTICLE VI. REVIEW BY JUDICIAL CONFERENCE COMMITTEE ON CONDUCT AND DISABILITY

RULE 21. COMMITTEE ON JUDICIAL CONDUCT AND DISABILITY

(a) Review by Committee. The Committee on Judicial Conduct and Disability, consisting of seven members, considers and disposes of all petitions for review under (b) of this Rule, in conformity with the Committee's jurisdictional statement. Its disposition of petitions for review is ordinarily final. The Judicial Conference of the United States may, in its sole discretion, review any such Committee decision, but a complainant or subject judge does not have a right to this review.

(b) Reviewable Matters.

(1) Upon Petition. A complainant or subject judge may petition the Committee for review of a judicial-council order entered in accordance with:

(A) Rule 20(b)(1)(A), (B), (D), or (E); or

(B) Rule 19(b)(1) or (4) if one or more members of the judicial council dissented from the order on the ground that a special committee should be appointed under Rule 11(f); in that event, the Committee's review will be limited to the issue of whether a special committee should be appointed.

(2) Upon Committee's Initiative. At its initiative and in its sole discretion, the Committee may review any judicial-council order entered under Rule 19(b)(1) or (4), but only to determine whether a special committee should be appointed. Before undertaking the review, the Committee must invite that judicial council to explain why it believes the appointment of a special committee is unnecessary, unless the reasons are clearly stated in the judicial council's order denying the petition for review. If the Committee believes that it would benefit from a submission by the subject judge, it may issue an appropriate request. If the Committee determines that a special committee should be appointed, the Committee must issue a written decision giving its reasons.

(c) Committee Vote. Any member of the Committee from the same circuit as the subject judge is disqualified from considering or voting on a petition for review. Committee decisions under (b) of this Rule must be by majority vote of the qualified Committee members. If only six members are qualified to vote on a petition for review, the decision must be made by a majority of a panel of five members drawn from a randomly selected list that rotates after each decision by a panel drawn from the list. The members who will determine the petition must be selected based on committee membership as of the date on which the petition is received. Those members selected to hear the petition should serve in that capacity until final disposition of the petition, whether or not their term of committee membership has ended. If only four members are qualified to vote, the Chief Justice must appoint, if available, an ex-member of the Committee or, if not, another United States judge to consider the petition.

(d) Additional Investigation. Except in extraordinary circumstances, the Committee will not conduct an additional investigation. The Committee may return the matter to the judicial council with directions to undertake an additional investigation. If the Committee conducts an additional investigation, it will exercise the powers of the Judicial Conference under 28 U.S.C. § 331.

(e) Oral Argument; Personal Appearance. There is ordinarily no oral argument or personal appearance before the Committee. In its discretion, the Committee may permit written submissions from the complainant or subject judge.

(f) Committee Decisions. Committee decisions under this Rule must be transmitted promptly to the Judicial Conference of the United States. Other distribution will be by the Administrative Office at the direction of the Committee chair.

(g) Finality. All orders of the Judicial Conference or of the Committee (when the Conference does not exercise its power of review) are final.

[Adopted March 11, 2008, effective April 10, 2008.]

Commentary on Rule 21

This Rule is largely self-explanatory.

Rule 21(a) is intended to clarify that the delegation of power to the Judicial Conference Committee on Judicial Conduct and Disability to dispose of petitions does not preclude review of such dispositions by the Conference. However, there is no right to such review in any party.

Rules 21(b)(1)(B) and (b)(2) are intended to fill a jurisdictional gap as to review of dismissals or conclusions of complaints under Rule 19(b)(1) or (4). Where one or more members of a judicial council reviewing a petition have dissented on the ground that a special committee should have been appointed, the complainant or subject judge has the right to petition for review by the Committee but only as to that issue. Under Rule 21(b)(2), the Judicial Conference Committee on Judicial Conduct and Disability may review such a dismissal or conclusion in its sole discretion, whether or not such a dissent occurred, and only as to the appointment of a special committee. No party has a right to such review, and such review will be rare.

Rule 21(c) provides for review only by Committee members from circuits other than that of the subject judge. To avoid tie votes, the Committee will decide petitions for review by rotating panels of five when only six members are qualified. If only four members are qualified, the Chief Justice must appoint an additional judge to consider that petition for review.

Under this Rule, all Committee decisions are final in that they are unreviewable unless the Judicial Conference, in its discretion, decides to review a decision. Committee decisions, however, do not necessarily constitute final action on a complaint for purposes of Rule 24.

RULE 22. PROCEDURES FOR REVIEW

(a) Filing a Petition for Review. A petition for review of a judicial-council decision may be filed by sending a brief written statement to the Judicial Conference Committee on Judicial Conduct and Disability, addressed to:

> Judicial Conference Committee on Judicial Conduct and Disability
> Attn: Office of General Counsel
> Administrative Office of the United States Courts
> One Columbus Circle, NE
> Washington, D.C. 20544

The Administrative Office will send a copy of the petition to the complainant or subject judge, as the case may be.

(b) Form and Contents of Petition for Review. No particular form is required. The petition must contain a short statement of the basic facts underlying the complaint, the history of its consideration before the appropriate judicial council, a copy of the judicial council's decision, and the grounds on which the petitioner seeks review. The petition for review must specify the date and docket number of the judicial-council order for which review is sought. The petitioner may attach any documents or correspondence arising in the course of the proceeding before the judicial council or its special committee. A petition should not normally exceed 20 pages plus necessary attachments.

(c) Time. A petition must be submitted within 63 days of the date of the order for which review is sought.

(d) Copies. Seven copies of the petition for review must be submitted, at least one of which must be signed by the petitioner or his or her attorney. If the petitioner submits a signed declaration of inability to pay the expense of duplicating the petition, the Administrative Office must accept the original petition and must reproduce copies at its expense.

(e) Action on Receipt of Petition for Review. The Administrative Office must acknowledge receipt of a petition for review submitted under this Rule, notify the chair of the Judicial Conference Committee on Judicial Conduct and Disability, and distribute the petition to the members of the Committee for their deliberation.

[Adopted March 11, 2008, effective April 10, 2008.]

Commentary on Rule 22

Rule 22 is self-explanatory.

ARTICLE VII. MISCELLANEOUS RULES

RULE 23. CONFIDENTIALITY

(a) General Rule. The consideration of a complaint by the chief judge, a special committee, the judicial council, or the Judicial Conference Committee on Judicial Conduct and Disability is confidential. Information about this consideration must not be disclosed by any judge or employee of the judicial branch or by any person who records or transcribes testimony except as allowed by these Rules. In extraordinary circumstances, a chief judge may disclose the existence of a proceeding under these Rules when necessary to maintain public confidence in the federal judiciary's ability to redress misconduct or disability.

(b) Files. All files related to complaints must be separately maintained with appropriate security precautions to ensure confidentiality.

(c) Disclosure in Decisions. Except as otherwise provided in Rule 24, written decisions of the chief judge, the judicial council, or the Judicial Conference Committee on Judicial Conduct and Disability, and dissenting opinions or separate statements of members of the council or Committee may contain information and exhibits that the authors consider appropriate for inclusion, and the information and exhibits may be made public.

(d) Availability to Judicial Conference. On request of the Judicial Conference or its Committee on Judicial Conduct and Disability, the circuit clerk must furnish any requested records related to a complaint. For auditing purposes, the circuit clerk must provide access to the Committee to records of proceedings under the Act at the site where the records are kept.

(e) Availability to District Court. If the judicial council directs the initiation of proceedings for removal of a magistrate judge under Rule 20(b)(1)(D)(iii), the circuit clerk must provide to the chief judge of the district court copies of the report of the special committee and any other documents and records that were before the judicial council at the time of its decision. On request of the chief judge of the district court, the judicial council may authorize release to that chief judge of any other records relating to the investigation.

(f) Impeachment Proceedings. If the Judicial Conference determines that consideration of impeachment may be warranted, it must transmit the record of all relevant proceedings to the Speaker of the House of Representatives.

(g) Subject Judge's Consent. If both the subject judge and the chief judge consent in writing, any materials from the files may be disclosed to any person. In any such disclosure, the chief judge may require that the identity of the complainant, or of witnesses in an investigation conducted by a chief judge, a special committee, or the judicial council, not be revealed.

(h) Disclosure in Special Circumstances. The Judicial Conference, its Committee on Judicial Conduct and Disability, or a judicial council may authorize disclosure of information about the consideration of a complaint, including the papers, documents, and transcripts relating to the investigation, to the extent that disclosure is justified by special circumstances and is not prohibited by the Act. Disclosure may be made to judicial researchers engaged in the study or evaluation of experience under the Act and related modes of judicial discipline, but only where the study or evaluation has been specifically approved by the Judicial Conference or by the Judicial Conference Committee on Judicial Conduct and Disability. Appropriate steps must be taken to protect the identities of the subject judge, the complainant, and witnesses from public disclosure. Other appropriate safeguards to protect against the dissemination of confidential information may be imposed.

(i) Disclosure of Identity by Subject Judge. Nothing in this Rule precludes the subject judge from acknowledging that he or she is the judge referred to in documents made public under Rule 24.

(j) Assistance and Consultation. Nothing in this Rule precludes the chief judge or judicial council acting on a complaint filed under the Act from seeking the help of qualified staff or from consulting other judges who may be helpful in the disposition of the complaint.

[Adopted March 11, 2008, effective April 10, 2008.]

Commentary on Rule 23

Rule 23 was adapted from the Illustrative Rules.

The Act applies a rule of confidentiality to "papers, documents, and records of proceedings related to investigations conducted under this chapter" and states that they may not be disclosed "by any person in any proceeding," with enumerated exceptions. 28 U.S.C. § 360(a). Three questions arise: Who is bound by the confidentiality rule, what proceedings are subject to the rule, and who is within the circle of people who may have access to information without breaching the rule?

With regard to the first question, Rule 23(a) provides that judges, employees of the judicial branch, and those persons involved in recording proceedings and preparing transcripts are obliged to respect the confidentiality requirement. This of course includes subject judges who do not consent to identification under Rule 23(i).

With regard to the second question, Rule 23(a) applies the rule of confidentiality broadly to consideration of a complaint at any stage.

With regard to the third question, there is no barrier of confidentiality among a chief judge, judicial council, the Judicial Conference, and the Judicial Conference Committee on Judicial Conduct and Disability. Each may have access to any of the confidential records for use in their consideration of a referred matter, a petition for review, or monitoring the administration of the Act. A district court may have similar access if the judicial council orders the district court to initiate proceedings to remove a magistrate judge from office, and Rule 23(e) so provides.

In extraordinary circumstances, a chief judge may disclose the existence of a proceeding under these Rules. The disclosure of such information in high-visibility or controversial cases is to reassure the public that the federal judiciary is capable of redressing judicial misconduct or disability. Moreover, the confidentiality requirement does not prevent the chief judge from "communicat[ing] orally or in writing with . . . [persons] who may have knowledge of the matter," as part of a limited inquiry conducted by the chief judge under Rule 11(b).

Rule 23 recognizes that there must be some exceptions to the Act's confidentiality requirement. For example, the Act requires that certain orders and the reasons for them must be made public. 28 U.S.C. § 360(b). Rule 23(c) makes it explicit that memoranda supporting chief judge and council orders, as well as dissenting opinions and separate statements, may contain references to information that would otherwise be confidential and that such information may be made public. However, subsection (c) is subject to Rule 24(a) which provides the general rule regarding the public availability of decisions. For example, the name of a subject judge cannot be made public in a decision if disclosure of the name is prohibited by that Rule.

The Act makes clear that there is a barrier of confidentiality between the judicial branch and the legislative. It provides that material may be disclosed to Congress only if it is believed necessary to an impeachment investigation or trial of a judge. 28 U.S.C. § 360(a)(2). Accordingly, Section 355(b) of the Act requires the Judicial Conference to transmit the record of the proceeding to the House of Representatives if the Conference believes that impeachment of a subject judge may be appropriate. Rule 23(f) implements this requirement.

The Act provides that confidential materials may be disclosed if authorized in writing by the subject judge and by the chief judge. 28 U.S.C. § 360(a)(3). Rule 23(g) implements this requirement. Once the subject judge has consented to the disclosure of confidential materials related to a complaint, the chief judge ordinarily will refuse consent only to the extent necessary to protect the confidentiality interests of the complainant or of witnesses who have testified in investigatory proceedings or who have provided information in response to a limited inquiry undertaken pursuant to Rule 11. It will generally be necessary, therefore, for the chief judge to require that the identities of the complainant or of such witnesses, as well as any identifying information, be shielded in any materials disclosed, except insofar as the chief judge has secured the consent of the complainant or of a particular witness to disclosure, or there is a demonstrated need for disclosure of the information that, in the judgment of the chief judge, outweighs the confidentiality interest of the complainant or of a particular witness (as may be the case where the complainant is delusional or where the complainant or a particular witness has already demonstrated a lack of concern about maintaining the confidentiality of the proceedings).

Rule 23(h) permits disclosure of additional information in circumstances not enumerated. For example, disclosure may be appropriate to permit a prosecution for perjury based on testimony given before a special committee. Another example might involve evidence of criminal conduct by a judge discovered by a special committee.

Subsection (h) also permits the authorization of disclosure of information about the consideration of a complaint, including the papers, documents, and transcripts relating to the investigation, to judicial researchers engaged in the study or evaluation of experience under the Act and related modes of judicial discipline. The Rule envisions disclosure of information from the official record of complaint proceedings to a limited category of persons for appropriately authorized research purposes only, and with appropriate safeguards to protect individual identities in any published research results that ensue. In authorizing disclosure, the judicial council may refuse to release particular materials when such release would be contrary to the interests of justice, or that constitute purely internal communications. The Rule does not envision disclosure of purely internal communications between judges and their colleagues and staff.

Under Rule 23(j), chief judges and judicial councils may seek staff assistance or consult with other judges who may be helpful in the process of complaint disposition; the confidentiality requirement does not preclude this. The chief judge, for example, may properly seek the advice and assistance of another judge who the chief judge deems to be in the best position to communicate with the subject judge in an attempt to bring about corrective action. As another example, a new chief judge may wish to confer with a predecessor to learn how similar complaints have been handled. In consulting with other judges, of course, the chief judge should disclose information regarding the complaint only to the extent the chief judge deems necessary under the circumstances.

RULE 24. PUBLIC AVAILABILITY OF DECISIONS

(a) General Rule; Specific Cases. When final action has been taken on a complaint and it is no longer subject to review, all orders entered by the chief judge and judicial council, including any supporting memoranda and any dissenting opinions or separate statements by members of the judicial council, must be made public, with the following exceptions:

(1) if the complaint is finally dismissed under Rule 11(c) without the appointment of a special committee, or if it is concluded under Rule 11(d) because of voluntary corrective action, the publicly available materials must not disclose the name of the subject judge without his or her consent.

(2) if the complaint is concluded because of intervening events, or dismissed at any time after a special committee is appointed, the judicial council must determine whether the name of the subject judge should be disclosed.

(3) if the complaint is finally disposed of by a privately communicated censure or reprimand, the publicly available materials must not disclose either the name of the subject judge or the text of the reprimand.

(4) if the complaint is finally disposed of under Rule 20(b)(1)(D) by any action other than private censure or reprimand, the text of the dispositive order must be included in the materials made public, and the name of the subject judge must be disclosed.

(5) the name of the complainant must not be disclosed in materials made public under this Rule unless the chief judge orders disclosure.

(b) Manner of Making Public. The orders described in (a) must be made public by placing them in a publicly accessible file in the office of the circuit clerk or by placing the orders on the court's public website. If the orders appear to have precedential value, the chief judge may cause them to be published. In addition, the Judicial Conference Committee on Judicial Conduct and Disability will make available on the Federal Judiciary's website, www.uscourts.gov, selected illustrative orders described in paragraph (a), appropriately redacted, to provide additional information to the public on how complaints are addressed under the Act.

(c) Orders of Judicial Conference Committee. Orders of this Committee constituting final action in a complaint proceeding arising from a particular circuit will be made available to the public in the office of the clerk of the relevant court of appeals. The Committee will also make such orders available on the Federal Judiciary's website, www.uscourts.gov. When authorized by the Committee, other orders related to complaint proceedings will similarly be made available.

(d) Complaints Referred to the Judicial Conference of the United States. If a complaint is referred to the Judicial Conference under Rule 20(b)(1)(C) or 20(b)(2), materials relating to the complaint will be made public only if ordered by the Judicial Conference.

[Adopted March 11, 2008, effective April 10, 2008.]

Commentary on Rule 24

Rule 24 is adapted from the Illustrative Rules and the recommendations of the Breyer Committee.

The Act requires the circuits to make available only written orders of a judicial council or the Judicial Conference imposing some form of sanction. 28 U.S.C. § 360(b). The Judicial Conference, however, has long recognized the desirability of public availability of a broader range of orders and other materials. In 1994, the Judicial Conference "urge[d] all circuits and courts covered by the Act to submit to the West Publishing Company, for publication in Federal Reporter 3d, and to Lexis all orders issued pursuant to [the Act] that are deemed by the issuing circuit or court to have significant precedential value to other circuits and courts covered by the Act." Report of the Proceedings of the Judicial Conference of the United States, Mar. 1994, at 28. Following this recommendation, the 2000 revision of the Illustrative Rules contained a public availability provision very similar to Rule 24. In 2002, the Judicial Conference again voted to encourage the circuits "to submit non-routine public orders disposing of complaints of judicial misconduct or disability for publication by on-line and print services." Report of the Proceedings of the Judicial Conference of the United States, Sept. 2002, at 58. The Breyer Committee Report further emphasized that "[p]osting such orders on the judicial branch's public website would not only benefit judges directly, it would also encourage scholarly commentary and analysis of the orders." Breyer Committee Report, 239 F.R.D. at 216. With these considerations in mind, Rule 24 provides for public availability of a wide range of materials.

Rule 24 provides for public availability of orders of the chief judge, the judicial council, and the Judicial Conference Committee on Judicial Conduct and Disability and the texts of any memoranda supporting their orders, together with any dissenting opinions or separate statements by members of the judicial council. However, these orders and memoranda are to be made public only after final action on the complaint has been taken and any right of review has been exhausted. The provision that decisions will be made public only after final action has been taken is designed in part to avoid public disclosure of the existence of pending proceedings. Whether the name of the subject judge is disclosed will then depend on the nature of the final action. If the final action is an order predicated on a finding of misconduct or disability (other than a privately communicated censure or reprimand) the name of the judge must be made public. If the final action is dismissal of the complaint, the name of the subject judge must not be disclosed. Rule 24(a)(1) provides that where a proceeding is concluded under Rule 11(d) by the chief judge on the basis of voluntary corrective action, the name of the subject judge must not be disclosed. Shielding the name of the subject judge in this circumstance should encourage informal disposition.

If a complaint is dismissed as moot, or because intervening events have made action on the complaint unnecessary, after appointment of a special committee, Rule 24(a)(2) allows the judicial council to determine whether the subject judge will be identified. In such a case, no final decision has been rendered on the merits, but it may be in the public interest—particularly if a judicial officer resigns in the course of an investigation—to make the identity of the judge known.

Once a special committee has been appointed, and a proceeding is concluded by the full council on the basis of a remedial order of the council, Rule 24(a)(4) provides for disclosure of the name of the subject judge.

Finally, Rule 24(a)(5) provides that the identity of the complainant will be disclosed only if the chief judge so

orders. Identifying the complainant when the subject judge is not identified would increase the likelihood that the identity of the subject judge would become publicly known, thus circumventing the policy of nondisclosure. It may not always be practicable to shield the complainant's identity while making public disclosure of the judicial council's order and supporting memoranda; in some circumstances, moreover, the complainant may consent to public identification.

RULE 25.   DISQUALIFICATION

(a) General Rule. Any judge is disqualified from participating in any proceeding under these Rules if the judge, in his or her discretion, concludes that circumstances warrant disqualification. If the complaint is filed by a judge, that judge is disqualified from participating in any consideration of the complaint except to the extent that these Rules provide for a complainant's participation. A chief judge who has identified a complaint under Rule 5 is not automatically disqualified from considering the complaint.

(b) Subject Judge. A subject judge is disqualified from considering the complaint except to the extent that these Rules provide for participation by a subject judge.

(c) Chief Judge Not Disqualified from Considering a Petition for Review of a Chief Judge's Order. If a petition for review of a chief judge's order entered under Rule 11(c), (d), or (e) is filed with the judicial council in accordance with Rule 18, the chief judge is not disqualified from participating in the council's consideration of the petition.

(d) Member of Special Committee Not Disqualified. A member of the judicial council who serves on a special committee, including the chief judge, is not disqualified from participating in council consideration of the committee's report.

(e) Subject Judge's Disqualification After Appointment of a Special Committee. Upon appointment of a special committee, the subject judge is automatically disqualified from participating in any proceeding arising under the Act or these Rules as a member of any special committee, the judicial council of the circuit, the Judicial Conference of the United States, and the Judicial Conference Committee on Judicial Conduct and Disability. The disqualification continues until all proceedings on the complaint against the subject judge are finally terminated with no further right of review.

(f) Substitute for Disqualified Chief Judge. If the chief judge is disqualified from participating in consideration of the complaint, the duties and responsibilities of the chief judge under these Rules must be assigned to the most-senior active circuit judge not disqualified. If all circuit judges in regular active service are disqualified, the judicial council may determine whether to request a transfer under Rule 26, or, in the interest of sound judicial administration, to permit the chief judge to dispose of the complaint on the merits. Members of the judicial council who are named in the complaint may participate in this determination if necessary to obtain a quorum of the judicial council.

(g) Judicial–Council Action When Multiple Judges Are Disqualified. Notwithstanding any other provision in these Rules to the contrary,

(1) a member of the judicial council who is a subject judge may participate in its disposition if:

(A) participation by one or more subject judges is necessary to obtain a quorum of the judicial council;

(B) the judicial council finds that the lack of a quorum is due to the naming of one or more judges in the complaint for the purpose of disqualifying that judge or judges, or to the naming of one or more judges based on their participation in a decision excluded from the definition of misconduct under Rule 3(h)(3); and

(C) the judicial council votes that it is necessary, appropriate, and in the interest of sound judicial administration that one or more subject judges be eligible to act.

(2) otherwise disqualified members may participate in votes taken under (g)(1)(B) and (g)(1)(C).

(h) Disqualification of Members of the Judicial Conference Committee. No member of the Judicial Conference Committee on Judicial Conduct and Disability is disqualified from participating in any proceeding under the Act or these Rules because of consultations with a chief judge, a member of a special committee, or a member of a judicial council about the interpretation or application of the Act or these Rules, unless the member believes that the consultation would prevent fair-minded participation.

[Adopted March 11, 2008, effective April 10, 2008.]

Commentary on Rule 25

Rule 25 is adapted from the Illustrative Rules.

Subsection (a) provides the general rule for disqualification. Of course, a judge is not disqualified simply because the subject judge is on the same court. However, this subsection recognizes that there may be cases in which an appearance of bias or prejudice is created by circumstances other than an association with the subject judge as a colleague. For example, a judge may have a familial relationship with a complainant or subject judge. When such circumstances exist, a judge may, in his or her discretion, conclude that disqualification is warranted.

Subsection (e) makes it clear that the disqualification of the subject judge relates only to the subject judge's participation in any proceeding arising under the Act or these Rules as a member of a special committee, judicial council, Judicial Conference, or the Judicial Conference Committee. The Illustrative Rule, based on Section 359(a) of the Act, is ambiguous and could be read to disqualify a subject judge from service of any kind on each of the bodies mentioned.

This is undoubtedly not the intent of the Act; such a disqualification would be anomalous in light of the Act's allowing a subject judge to continue to decide cases and to continue to exercise the powers of chief circuit or district judge. It would also create a substantial deterrence to the appointment of special committees, particularly where a special committee is needed solely because the chief judge may not decide matters of credibility in his or her review under Rule 11.

While a subject judge is barred by Rule 25(b) from participating in the disposition of the complaint in which he or she is named, Rule 25(e) recognizes that participation in proceedings arising under the Act or these Rules by a judge who is the subject of a special committee investigation may lead to an appearance of self-interest in creating substantive and procedural precedents governing such proceedings; Rule 25(e) bars such participation.

Under the Act, a complaint against the chief judge is to be handled by "that circuit judge in regular active service next senior in date of commission." 28 U.S.C. § 351(c). Rule 25(f) provides that seniority among judges other than the chief judge is to be determined by date of commission, with the result that complaints against the chief judge may be routed to a former chief judge or other judge who was appointed earlier than the chief judge. The Rules do not purport to prescribe who is to preside over meetings of the judicial council. Consequently, where the presiding member of the judicial council is disqualified from participating under these Rules, the order of precedence prescribed by Rule 25(f) for performing "the duties and responsibilities of the chief circuit judge under these Rules" does not apply to determine the acting presiding member of the judicial council. That is a matter left to the internal rules or operating practices of each judicial council. In most cases the most senior active circuit judge who is a member of the judicial council and who is not disqualified will preside.

Sometimes a single complaint is filed against a large group of judges. If the normal disqualification rules are observed in such a case, no court of appeals judge can serve as acting chief judge of the circuit, and the judicial council will be without appellate members. Where the complaint is against all circuit and district judges, under normal rules no member of the judicial council can perform the duties assigned to the council under the statute.

A similar problem is created by successive complaints arising out of the same underlying grievance. For example, a complainant files a complaint against a district judge based on alleged misconduct, and the complaint is dismissed by the chief judge under the statute. The complainant may then file a complaint against the chief judge for dismissing the first complaint, and when that complaint is dismissed by the next senior judge, still a third complaint may be filed. The threat is that the complainant will bump down the seniority ladder until, once again, there is no member of the court of appeals who can serve as acting chief judge for the purpose of the next complaint. Similarly, complaints involving the merits of litigation may involve a series of decisions in which many judges participated or in which a rehearing en banc was denied by the court of appeals, and the complaint may name a majority of the judicial council as subject judges.

In recognition that these multiple-judge complaints are virtually always meritless, the judicial council is given discretion to determine: (1) whether it is necessary, appropriate, and in the interest of sound judicial administration to permit the chief judge to dispose of a complaint where it would otherwise be impossible for any active circuit judge in the circuit to act, and (2) whether it is necessary, appropriate, and in the interest of sound judicial administration, after appropriate findings as to need and justification are made, to permit subject judges of the judicial council to participate in the disposition of a petition for review where it would otherwise be impossible to obtain a quorum.

Applying a rule of necessity in these situations is consistent with the appearance of justice. See, e.g., In re Complaint of Doe, 2 F.3d 308 (8th Cir. Jud. Council 1993) (invoking the rule of necessity); In re Complaint of Judicial Misconduct, No. 91–80464 (9th Cir. Jud. Council 1992) (same). There is no unfairness in permitting the chief judge to dispose of a patently insubstantial complaint that names all active circuit judges in the circuit.

Similarly, there is no unfairness in permitting subject judges, in these circumstances, to participate in the review of a chief judge's dismissal of an insubstantial complaint. The remaining option is to assign the matter to another body. Among other alternatives, the council may request a transfer of the petition under Rule 26. Given the administrative inconvenience and delay involved in these alternatives, it is desirable to request a transfer only if the judicial council determines that the petition is substantial enough to warrant such action.

In the unlikely event that a quorum of the judicial council cannot be obtained to consider the report of a special committee, it would normally be necessary to request a transfer under Rule 26.

Rule 25(h) recognizes that the jurisdictional statement of the Judicial Conference Committee contemplates consultation between members of the Committee and judicial participants in proceedings under the Act and these Rules. Such consultation should not automatically preclude participation by a member in that proceeding.

RULE 26. TRANSFER TO ANOTHER JUDICIAL COUNCIL

In exceptional circumstances, a chief judge or a judicial council may ask the Chief Justice to transfer a proceeding based on a complaint identified under Rule 5 or filed under Rule 6 to the judicial council of another circuit. The request for a transfer may be made at any stage of the proceeding before a reference to the Judicial Conference under Rule 20(b)(1)(C) or 20(b)(2) or a petition for review is filed under Rule 22. Upon receiving such a request, the Chief Justice may refuse the request or select the transferee judicial council, which may then exercise the powers of a judicial council under these Rules.

[Adopted March 11, 2008, effective April 10, 2008.]

Commentary on Rule 26

Rule 26 is new; it implements the Breyer Committee's recommended use of transfers. Breyer Committee Report, 239 F.R.D. at 214–15.

Rule 26 authorizes the transfer of a complaint proceeding to another judicial council selected by the Chief Justice. Such transfers may be appropriate, for example, in the case of a serious complaint where there are multiple disqualifications among the original council, where the issues are highly visible and a local disposition may weaken public confidence in the process, where internal tensions arising in the council as a result of the complaint render disposition by a less involved council appropriate, or where a complaint calls into question policies or governance of the home court of appeals. The power to effect a transfer is lodged in the Chief Justice to avoid disputes in a council over where to transfer a sensitive matter and to ensure that the transferee council accepts the matter.

Upon receipt of a transferred proceeding, the transferee council shall determine the proper stage at which to begin consideration of the complaint—for example, reference to the transferee chief judge, appointment of a special committee, etc.

RULE 27. WITHDRAWAL OF COMPLAINTS AND PETITIONS FOR REVIEW

(a) Complaint Pending Before Chief Judge. With the chief judge's consent, a complainant may withdraw a complaint that is before the chief judge for a decision under Rule 11. The withdrawal of a complaint will not prevent a chief judge from identifying or having to identify a complaint under Rule 5 based on the withdrawn complaint.

(b) Complaint Pending before Special Committee or Judicial Council. After a complaint has been referred to a special committee for investigation and before the committee files its report, the complainant may withdraw the complaint only with the consent of both the subject judge and either the special committee or the judicial council.

(c) Petition for Review. A petition for review addressed to a judicial council under Rule 18, or the Judicial Conference Committee on Judicial Conduct and Disability under Rule 22 may be withdrawn if no action on the petition has been taken.

[Adopted March 11, 2008, effective April 10, 2008.]

Commentary on Rule 27

Rule 27 is adapted from the Illustrative Rules and treats the complaint proceeding, once begun, as a matter of public business rather than as the property of the complainant. Accordingly, the chief judge or the judicial council remains responsible for addressing any complaint under the Act, even a complaint that has been formally withdrawn by the complainant.

Under subsection 27(a), a complaint pending before the chief judge may be withdrawn if the chief judge consents. Where the complaint clearly lacked merit, the chief judge may accordingly be saved the burden of preparing a formal order and supporting memorandum. However, the chief judge may, or be obligated under Rule 5, to identify a complaint based on allegations in a withdrawn complaint.

If the chief judge appoints a special committee, Rule 27(b) provides that the complaint may be withdrawn only with the consent of both the body before which it is pending (the special committee or the judicial council) and the subject judge. Once a complaint has reached the stage of appointment of a special committee, a resolution of the issues may be necessary to preserve public confidence. Moreover, the subject judge is given the right to insist that the matter be resolved on the merits, thereby eliminating any ambiguity that might remain if the proceeding were terminated by withdrawal of the complaint.

With regard to all petitions for review, Rule 27(c) grants the petitioner unrestricted authority to withdraw the petition. It is thought that the public's interest in the proceeding is adequately protected, because there will necessarily have been a decision by the chief judge and often by the judicial council as well in such a case.

RULE 28. AVAILABILITY OF RULES AND FORMS

These Rules and copies of the complaint form as provided in Rule 6(a) must be available without charge in the office of the clerk of each court of appeals, district court, bankruptcy court, or other federal court whose judges are subject to the Act. Each court must also make these Rules and the complaint form available on the court's website, or provide an Internet link to the Rules and complaint form that are available on the appropriate court of appeals' website.

[Adopted March 11, 2008, effective April 10, 2008.]

RULE 29. EFFECTIVE DATE

These Rules will become effective 30 days after promulgation by the Judicial Conference of the United States.

[Adopted March 11, 2008, effective April 10, 2008.]

APPENDIX A. 28 U.S.C §§ 351–364

[*Publisher's Note: For text of Appendix A, see 28 U.S.C. §§ 351–364.*]

APPENDIX B. COMPLAINT FORM

Judicial Council of the _____ Circuit

COMPLAINT OF JUDICIAL MISCONDUCT OR DISABILITY

To begin the complaint process, complete this form and prepare the brief statement of facts described in item 5 (below). The RULES FOR JUDICIAL-CONDUCT AND JUDICIAL-DISABILITY PROCEEDINGS, adopted by the Judicial Conference of the United States, contain information on what to include in a complaint (Rule 6), where to file a complaint (Rule 7), and other important matters. The rules are available in federal court clerks' offices, on individual federal courts' Web sites, and on www.uscourts.gov.

Your complaint (this form and the statement of facts) should be typewritten and must be legible. For the number of copies to file, consult the local rules or clerk's office of the court in which your complaint is required to be filed. Enclose each copy of the complaint in an envelope marked "COMPLAINT OF MISCONDUCT" or "COMPLAINT OF DISABILITY" and submit it to the appropriate clerk of court. **Do not put the name of any judge on the envelope.**

1. Name of Complainant: _____
    Contact Address: _____
    _____
    Daytime telephone: (__) _____

2. Name(s) of Judge(s): _____
    Court: _____

3. Does this complaint concern the behavior of the judge(s) in a particular lawsuit or lawsuits?
    [ ] Yes   [ ] No
    If "yes," give the following information about each lawsuit:
    Court: _____
    Case Number: _____
    Docket number of any appeal to the _____ Circuit: _____
    Are (were) you a party or lawyer in the lawsuit?
    [ ] Party   [ ] Lawyer   [ ] Neither

If you are (were) a party and have (had) a lawyer, give the lawyer's name, address, and telephone number:

_____

_____

_____

4. Have you filed any lawsuits against the judge?
       [ ] Yes   [ ] No
    If "yes," give the following information about each lawsuit:
    Court: _____
    Case Number: _____
    Present status of lawsuit: _____
    Name, address, and telephone number of your lawyer for the lawsuit against the judge:

_____

_____

_____

Court to which any appeal has been taken in the lawsuit against the judge:

_____

Docket number of the appeal: _____
Present status of the appeal: _____

5. **Brief Statement of Facts.** Attach a brief statement of the specific facts on which the claim of judicial misconduct or disability is based. Include what happened, when and where it happened, and any information that would help an investigator check the facts. If the complaint alleges judicial disability, also include any additional facts that form the basis of that allegation.

6. **Declaration and signature:**

  I declare under penalty of perjury that the statements made in this complaint are true and correct to the best of my knowledge.

    (Signature)_____ (Date)_____

[Adopted March 11, 2008, effective April 10, 2008.]

INTERNAL OPERATING PROCEDURES
OF THE
FIRST CIRCUIT

INTRODUCTION

This publication outlines the procedures followed in this Court, and its Clerk's Office, for the processing of appeals, petitions for review and other appellate matters in this Circuit. New techniques and procedures are continually tried and, when improvements are found, such procedures are adopted so that at any given time the procedures set forth herein may be in a state of change.

IOP I. COURT ORGANIZATION

A. Facilities. The Clerk's Office and the appellate courtrooms are located in the John Joseph Moakley United States Courthouse at 1 Courthouse Way in Boston. The staff attorneys, the Court of Appeals library, the Circuit Executive and some of the appellate judges are located in the courthouse.

B. Clerk's Office. The office hours for the Clerk's Office are from 8:30 a.m. to 5:00 p.m., Monday through Friday. In case of an emergency, the Clerk or the Chief Deputy Clerk may be contacted after hours; however, appropriate arrangements should be made with the Clerk's Office in advance. Although documents may be filed electronically at any time through the court's Case Management/Electronic Case Files ("CM/ECF") system, the filer should not expect that the filing will be addressed outside regular business hours unless the filer contacts the Clerk's Office in advance to make special arrangements.

C. Library. The Court of Appeals library is open from 8:30 a.m. to 5:00 p.m. and attorneys practicing in the federal courts may use the library, but books and materials may not be removed.

D. Staff Attorneys. The office of the staff attorneys assists the Court in many ways including research, drafting memoranda and other forms of legal assistance to the Court.

[Amended September 14, 2009, effective October 13, 2009.]

IOP II. ATTORNEYS

A. Admission. Attorneys seeking admission to the bar of the First Circuit Court of Appeals should obtain an application from the court's website at www. ca1.uscourts.gov or write to the Clerk's Office. The admission fee imposed by Local Rule 46.0(a)(1) is $50.00. There is an additional $176.00 admission fee prescribed by the Court of Appeals Miscellaneous Fee Schedule, promulgated under 28 U.S.C. § 1913. The combined fee of $226.00 should be paid in a single check or money order, made payable to: "Clerk, United States Court." Qualified attorneys should mail the completed application, along with the admission fee to the Clerk's Office. Once verification of the application is complete, which may take up to 14 days, a Certificate of Admission will be returned by mail. Incomplete applications will not be considered. Requests to be admitted in person must be made on the application form and will be allowed at the Court's discretion. Successful applicants to be admitted in court will be electronically notified of the time and place of admission. Such applicants will receive their Certificate of Admission by mail at a later date. Where an application raises questions about the applicant's qualification for admission, the Clerk will refer the matter to the Chief Judge. If the Chief Judge concludes that denial may be warranted, the matter will be referred to a panel for determination.

B. Discipline. Procedures to be followed in this Court are covered by Fed. R. App. P. 46(b) and the Rules of Attorney Disciplinary Enforcement for the Court of Appeals for the First Circuit. Copies of the latter rules may be obtained at the Clerk's Office.

[Amended effective June 19, 2009; November 1, 2011; December 1, 2011.]

IOP III. INITIAL PROCEDURES

A. Appeals, Petitions for Review and Fees. In cases appealed from the district court, the notice of appeal is filed in the district court in accordance with the Fed. R. App. P. and the combined docketing and filing fees are paid to the district court clerk. In administrative agency cases and petitions for mandamus, the docketing fee is paid to the Clerk of the Court of Appeals at the time the petition is filed in the Court of Appeals. The relevant fees can be found in the Schedule of Fees posted on this court's website at www.ca1.uscourts.gov.

B. Ordering Transcripts. The transcripts must be ordered from the court reporter(s) on Transcript Order/Report Form which is available from the district court clerks and from the Clerk of the Court of Appeals. The order for the transcript must be given within 14 days after the filing of the notice of appeal and satisfactory financial arrangements must be made with the court reporter. *See* Fed. R. App. P. 10, 11; Local Rule 10.0. Counsel are required to complete these arrangements *before* the copy of the Transcript Order/Report is filed with the Court of Appeals. If counsel are being paid under the Criminal Justice Act ("CJA"), the CJA form must first be approved and then attached to the Transcript Order/Report Form.

C. Reporter's Duties. If the reporter cannot complete the transcript by the date set by the court, then pursuant to Fed. R. App. P. 11(b) the reporter must file a motion in the Court of Appeals for an enlargement of time for filing the transcript. Counsel for appellants, however, would be well advised to check with the court reporter to see that the transcript will be timely filed and that the reporter is making such a request, if it will not be so completed.

[Amended June 23, 2004, effective June 23, 2004; April 10, 2006; September 14, 2009, effective October 13, 2009. Amended effective December 1, 2009.]

IOP IV. DOCKETING PROCEDURES

A. Docketing. Pursuant to Fed. R. App. P. 12, appeals are docketed in the Court of Appeals upon receipt from the Clerk of the district court of copies of the notice of appeal and the district court docket report. If the docketing fee has not been paid in the district court, the failure to pay is grounds for dismissal of the appeal pursuant to Local Rule 3.0. Local Rule 3.0 also requires the filing of a Docketing Statement within 14 days after the case is docketed in the court of appeals.

B. Screening. In the First Circuit a preliminary screening takes place upon the docketing of the appeal and procedural defects are often called to the Court's attention for sua sponte action by the Court including dismissal of the appeal.

C. Briefing. Once the record on appeal is complete, including the filing of all necessary transcripts, the Clerk's Office sends to counsel a notice advising appellant of the filing dates for the brief and the appendix. After the brief for appellant is filed, the Clerk's Office likewise gives notice to the appellee.

[Amended June 23, 2004, effective June 23, 2004; September 14, 2009, effective October 13, 2009.]

IOP V. MOTION PROCEDURES

A. General. In accordance with Fed. R. App. P. 27(d) (3), all motions must be accompanied by 3 copies unless the motion is filed electronically in compliance with the court's electronic filing system, and a proof of service showing the type of service that was made, i.e., by mail or by hand delivery or electronically. The date of service establishes the due date for filing the response per Fed. R. App. P. 27(a)(3).

B. Processing. All motions must be filed with the clerk. The single judge matters are transmitted to a single judge and the matters calling for three judge action are transmitted to a three judge panel. The motion judge and the motion panel duties are rotated among the judges of this Court. All motions are decided without oral argument, unless the Court orders otherwise. The motions are submitted to the Court after the response time provided in Fed. R. App. P. 27(a)(3)(A) has run except for (1) routine procedural motions which are usually processed forthwith, and (2) emergency motions which may be handled on an expedited basis. The court will not ordinarily await the filing of a reply to a response before acting on a motion and response. If a movant intends to file a reply to a response, the movant shall promptly notify the clerk of the intended filing.

C. Disposition By the Clerk. Pursuant to Fed. R. App. P. 27(b) and 1st Cir. R. 27.0(d), the clerk is authorized to dispose of certain routine, procedural motions in accordance with the Court's standing instructions. Typical examples include motions for an enlargement of time, to consolidate, to correct filings, to correct captions, and to withdraw as counsel. Effective March 16, 2006, clerk's orders are identifiable by their form: a clerk's order states on its face that it is entered pursuant to 1st Cir. R. 27.0(d).

D. Emergencies. If counsel anticipates that a matter may arise requiring emergency action by the court outside of ordinary business hours, the court's local rules advise counsel to contact the Clerk's Office at the earliest opportunity to discuss the matter. Depending on the circumstances, the Clerk's Office, in consultation with the duty judge and the Staff Attorney's Office, may make special arrangements for after hours filings and responses, issuance of orders after hours, and similar matters. Counsel are further advised that in all emergency matters, whether or not action outside of ordinary business hours is required, the process is facilitated if counsel contacts the Clerk's Office in advance and the motion seeking expedited relief clearly indicates the date by which a ruling is requested and the reasons supporting expedition. Although documents may be filed electronically at any time through CM/ECF, the filer should not expect that the filing will be addressed outside regular business hours unless the filer contacts the Clerk's Office in advance to make special arrangements. The business hours for the Clerk's Office are Mondays through Fridays from 8:30 a.m. to 5:00 p.m.

[Amended June 23, 2004, effective June 23, 2004; September 14, 2009, effective October 13, 2009.]

IOP VI. BRIEFS AND APPENDICES

A. General. The court's website, www.ca1.uscourts.gov, contains guidelines and a checklist to assist counsel in preparing briefs. Counsel are advised that any brief that does not conform to the requirements of the rules may be rejected. For information regarding electronic document filing pursuant to the court's electronic filing system, see Administrative Order Regarding Case Management/Electronic

Case Files System ("CM/ECF"), a copy of which is available on the court's website. Electronic filing is permitted after October 13, 2009 and is required for all attorney filings after January 1, 2010.

B. Modifications. The following modifications of the Fed. R. App. P. apply in the First Circuit:

1. One copy of the brief or petition must be filed electronically or on a computer generated disk. See Local Rule 32.0.

2. Only 10 copies, including the disk or electronic filing, need be filed.

C. Deferred Appendix. Note the Local Rules of this Court do not provide for the proceeding on a deferred appendix pursuant to Fed. R. App. P. 30(c). If special leave to proceed under this method is sought, and the Court grants such leave, the leave will be conditioned upon a shorter time schedule than the Fed. R. App. P. generally allow so that the processing of the appeal will not take any longer time than it would under the regular procedure.

D. Defaults. If the appellant fails to file the brief and appendix on time, the Clerk is authorized to enter an order dismissing the appeal, and when an appellee is in default as to filing a brief, the appellee will not be heard at oral argument. The party in default may remove the default by showing special circumstance justifying the failure to comply. Any motion to set aside a dismissal should be filed within fourteen days. See Local Rule 45.0.

[Amended June 23, 2004, effective June 23, 2004; September 14, 2009, effective October 13, 2009. Amended effective December 1, 2009.]

IOP VII. SCREENING AND CALENDARING

A. General. Initially, the staff attorney reviews the briefs in the cases the Clerk has assigned for a particular session. If a panel of 3 judges, in accordance with Fed. R. App. P. 34 and after consultation with the staff attorney, is of the opinion that a case does not warrant oral argument, the Clerk so advises counsel. Shortly after the decision as to hearing is made, the amount of time to be allotted for oral argument is also set by the Court. Before the hearing list is finally established, the Clerk notifies the parties by letter of the proposed date for hearing the case so that counsel may contact the Clerk if it appears that a scheduling conflict exists.

B. Expedited Schedule. Expedited scheduling is provided automatically in those cases where it is required by statute, such as recalcitrant witness cases. In other cases a request for expedited processing may be filed, but the motion should be made shortly after the case is docketed in the Court of Appeals.

C. Dates of Sessions. In January through June, and October through December, the Court usually sits for one week starting on the first Monday of the month. In either July or August, the Court sits for one week. In September the Court starts on the Wednesday after Labor Day and sits for the 3 days in that week and the 5 days in the following week. In November and March the Court sits two weeks, with one week in Boston and one week in Puerto Rico.

D. Judges and Case Assignment. In accordance with long-standing practice, cases are assigned to panels on a random basis provided, however, that a case may be assigned to a particular panel or to a panel including a particular judge in the following circumstances:

(1) where the case is a sequel to, or offshoot of, a case previously decided by the court (e.g., following a remand);

(2) where the case was presented to the duty panel in the regular course of duties, see, e.g., *Bui v. DiPaolo*, 170 F.3d 232, 238 (1st Cir. 1999) ("[a]s an administrative measure, we advise litigants that, to the extent practicable, the panel that determines whether to issue a complementary COA also will be the panel that adjudicates the appeal on the merits"), cert. denied, 529 U.S. 1086 (2000);

(3) where a case has been assigned to a panel, but scheduling changes (e.g., postponement of oral argument) or changes in the procedural handling of the case (e.g., a case intended for summary disposition is thereafter set for oral argument) require rescheduling;

(4) where a case has been assigned to a panel, but the subsequent recusal of a judge (or other unavailability of a judge, e.g., due to illness) makes it appropriate to transfer the case to a different panel or to find a replacement judge.

No other non-random assignments of cases shall be made except for special cause and with the concurrence of the duty judge.

E. Judges and Case Assignment in Capital Cases.

(1) **Capital Case Panel.** Capital cases, as defined in Local Rule 48.0, shall be randomly assigned to a panel of three judges, of whom at least one is an active judge of this Court, from the capital case pool. The capital case pool of judges shall consist of all active judges of this Court and those senior judges who have filed with the Clerk a statement of willingness to serve on capital case panels.

(2) **Duties of Capital Case Panel.** Notwithstanding the practices identified in Internal Operating Procedure V, the assigned capital case panel handles all matters relating to the case, including but not limited to, the merits of a direct appeal, all case management, all petitions for collateral review,

motions for stay of execution, motions to vacate a stay of execution, applications for a certificate of appealability, motions for an order authorizing the district court to consider a second or successive application for habeas corpus, appeals from subsequent petitions, and remands from the United States Supreme Court.

F. Timing. The Court will hear up to six cases per day. Generally, it is the practice of this Court to schedule cases in which the brief for appellee is filed by the fifteenth day of one month, so as to have the case screened and assigned to the list for hearing or submission on the second month thereafter.

IOP VIII. ORAL ARGUMENT

A. General. The Court establishes the times allotted for oral argument and the Clerk so notifies the parties at least one week before argument starts. Though the calendar is not called at the beginning of the court day, counsel should be present at the opening or make arrangements to ascertain whether there is any change in the order of the cases at the opening of Court. It is counsel's responsibility to be present and be prepared should earlier cases take less time for oral argument than was anticipated. *See* Local Rule 34.1.

B. Disclosure of Panel in Advance of Oral Argument. The names of the judges on each panel may be disclosed for a particular session seven (7) days in advance of the session. Once the panel is made public, the Court will not normally grant motions for continuances or for a change in argument date during the same session.

C. Lights. The signal lights are located on the Clerk's desk and they are set so that an amber light turns on when there are five minutes left and it remains on until the red light turns on indicating that the time for oral argument has ended.

D. Recording. Oral arguments in all cases are digitally recorded for the use of the Court and are not part of the permanent record of the case. A disk copy of the recording of an oral argument may be obtained by submitting a request in writing to the Clerk with a check in the amount prescribed by the Judicial Conference of the United States. The Schedule of Fees is posted on this court's website at www.ca1.uscourts.gov. Audio recordings of the court's oral arguments are also available on the court's website.

[Amended June 23, 2004, effective June 23, 2004; September 16, 2005, effective September 16, 2005; September 14, 2009, effective October 13, 2009. Amended effective January 22, 2010.]

IOP IX. OPINIONS & JUDGMENTS

A. Processing. When the opinion of the Court (and concurring and dissenting opinions, if any) are completed, they are turned over to the Clerk for reproducing and release. Copies of the opinion and copies of the judgment are sent to one counsel for each side. They are also released in electronic format on the same day.

B. Publication. The manner of deciding whether an opinion is to be published and the Court's policy with respect to publication are set forth in Local Rule 36.0.

C. Electronic Access. The Court's dockets and opinions are available electronically through the PACER network supported by the Administrative Office for the United States Courts. Details are available in the Clerk's Office. Opinions are also available on the court's website at www.ca1.uscourts.gov.

[Amended September 14, 2009, effective October 13, 2009.]

IOP X. PETITIONS FOR PANEL REHEARING AND PETITIONS FOR HEARING OR REHEARING EN BANC

A. General. Fed. R. App. P. 40 and 35 should be consulted with respect to the procedures. Petitions for rehearing are intended to bring to the attention of the panel claimed errors in the opinion and they are not to be used for reargument of an issue previously presented.

B. No Response. Unless the court requests, no response to a petition is permitted.

C. En Banc Processing. A petition for a hearing or rehearing en banc is submitted by the Clerk to the panel that heard the case and to the other active First Circuit judges. A petition for rehearing en banc will also be treated as a petition for rehearing before the original panel.

D. Vacation of Previous Opinion and Judgment. Usually when an en banc rehearing is granted, the previous opinion and judgment will be vacated.

IOP XI. COMPLAINTS AGAINST JUDGES

The procedure for filing complaints against judges is set forth in the Rules for Judicial–Conduct and Judicial–Disability Proceedings. A copy of these Rules may be obtained from the Clerk of this Court and are also on the Court's website.

Office of the Clerk

U.S. Court of Appeals for the First Circuit

John Joseph Moakley Courthouse

1 Courthouse Way, Suite 2500

Boston, Massachusetts 02210

[Amended June 23, 2004, effective June 23, 2004; September 14, 2009, effective October 13, 2009.]

IOP XII. NOTIFICATION OF CHANGES OR NOTIFICATIONS OF THE COURT'S LOCAL RULES AND INTERNAL OPERATING PROCEDURES

Changes in the Local Rules of this Court or its Internal Operating Procedures will be publicized by circulating for comment the entire text of the proposed change to the following state legal publishers:

a. Massachusetts Lawyers Weekly, 10 Milk Street, Suite 1000, Boston, Massachusetts 02108.

b. Rhode Island Lawyers Weekly, c/o Massachusetts Lawyers Weekly, 10 Milk Street, Suite 1000, Boston, MA 02108.

c. New Hampshire Bar News, 112 Pleasant Street, Concord, New Hampshire 03301.

d. Maine Bar Journal, P.O. Box 788, Augusta, Maine 04332.

e. Puerto Rico Bar Association, P.O. Box 1900, San Juan, PR 00903.

Notice of the changes will also be placed in all federal court bulletin boards and to all state bar associations within the Circuit. Comments should be forwarded to the Clerk's Office within thirty days from the date of the notice.

ELECTRONIC CASE FILING

ADMINISTRATIVE ORDER REGARDING CASE MANAGEMENT/ELECTRONIC CASE FILES SYSTEM ("CM/ECF")— RULES GOVERNING ELECTRONIC FILING

Entered September 14, 2009

The United States Court of Appeals for the First Circuit adopts the following provisions to govern the electronic filing of documents in cases before the court. Effective October 13, 2009, the court will permit filings to be made by means of the court's electronic filing system. Effective January 1, 2010, use of the electronic filing system is mandatory for all attorneys filing in this court, unless they are granted an exemption, and is voluntary for all non-incarcerated pro se litigants proceeding without counsel. These provisions may be amended from time to time, with or without prior notice, by further order of the court. The clerk may make changes to the procedures for electronic filing to adapt to changes in technology or to facilitate electronic filing. Any changes to procedures will be posted on the court's website. The court may deviate from these procedures in specific cases if deemed appropriate in the exercise of its discretion.

Rule 1—Scope of Electronic Filing

Except as otherwise prescribed by local rule or order, all cases will be assigned to the court's electronic filing system. Upon motion and a showing of good cause, the court may exempt an attorney from the provisions of this Rule and authorize filing by means other than use of the electronic filing system. After January 1, 2010, all documents filed by counsel must be filed electronically using the electronic filing system unless counsel obtains an exemption, except for the following types of documents, which must be filed only in paper form:

a. documents filed in the court of appeals which initiate cases, including for example, petitions for review, petitions for permission to appeal, applications to enforce an agency order, petitions for a writ of mandamus or prohibition, and applications for leave to file a second or successive petition for relief pursuant to 28 U.S.C. § 2254 or § 2255;

b. any document filed before a case is docketed by the court;

c. motions to seal;

d. sealed, ex parte, or otherwise non-public documents, including for example, pre-sentence reports and statements of reasons in a judgment of criminal conviction;

e. appendices to briefs; and

f. vouchers filed in accordance with the Criminal Justice Act, 18 U.S.C. § 3006A, and other documents relating to compensation and reimbursement for representation and for ancillary services and expenses.

Notices of appeal, although they initiate appeals, are filed in the district court and, thus, are subject to the relevant district court's procedures governing electronic filing.

Although a brief (including the addendum, required by 1st Cir. R. 28.0) must be filed electronically after January 1, 2010, paper copies of briefs are still required to be filed. The clerk's office will review the electronically filed brief and, if the brief is compliant with federal and local rules, will send a notification requiring the attorney or party filing electronically ("ECF Filer") to file nine identical paper copies so that they are received by the court within seven days of the notification. The court may shorten the period for filing paper copies of a brief if it becomes necessary in a particular case. At the time a brief is filed electronically, it must be served on all other parties, as required by Federal Rules of Appellate Procedure 25(b) and 31(b). See Rule 4 of this Order. Parties do not need to serve the brief again when identical paper copies are filed with the court. Appendices must be filed and served in paper form at the time the electronic version of the brief is filed.

Paper copies of other electronically filed documents (including petitions for rehearing or rehearing en banc) are not required and should not be filed unless specifically requested by the clerk. The clerk may direct the ECF Filer to provide the court with paper copies of electronically filed documents, or with an identical electronic version of any paper document previously filed in the same case by that filer, in a format designated by the court.

Documents must be formatted for electronic filing by converting the original word processing document into Portable Document Format ("PDF") (resulting in what is referred to as a "native PDF" or "text PDF"). PDF images created by scanning paper documents do not comply with this order. However, exhibits which are submitted as attachments to an electronically filed pleading may be scanned and attached if the filer does not possess a word-processing file version of the document.

Rule 2—Eligibility, Registration, Passwords

Attorneys who practice in this court must register as ECF Filers. Registration is required to obtain a login and password for use of the electronic case filing system. Attorneys and non-incarcerated pro se litigants may register at www.ca1.uscourts.gov. Before filing an electronic document using the court's electronic filing system, ECF Filers must complete the computer-based training modules listed as mandatory on the court's website. ECF Filers should also familiarize themselves with the CM/ECF User's Guide. The computer-based training modules and the CM/ECF User's Guide, together with other training materials concerning electronic filing in the First Circuit, including Frequently Asked Questions, are available on the court's website at www.ca1.uscourts.gov.

A non-incarcerated party to a pending case who is not represented by an attorney may, but is not required to, register as an ECF Filer for purposes of that case. If a pro se party retains an attorney, the attorney must advise the clerk by filing an appearance form and, after January 1, 2010, must also register as an ECF Filer if he or she has not already done so.

Registration as an ECF Filer constitutes consent to electronic service of all documents as provided in these rules and in the Federal Rules of Appellate Procedure. All ECF Filers have an affirmative duty to inform the clerk immediately of any change in their e-mail address. Any changes to an ECF Filer's contact information, including physical address, telephone, fax number or e-mail address, should be made through the PACER system, which can be accessed at http://pacer.psc.uscourts.gov.

ECF Filers agree to protect the security of their logins and passwords and immediately notify the PACER Service Center and the clerk if they learn, or have reason to suspect, that their login or password has been compromised. ECF Filers may be sanctioned for failure to comply with this provision. In addition to other sanctions imposed by the court, the clerk may terminate without notice the electronic filing privileges of any ECF Filer who uses the electronic filing system inappropriately.

Rule 3—Consequences of Electronic Filing

Electronic transmission of a document to the electronic filing system in compliance with these rules, together with the transmission of a Notice of Docket Activity from the court, constitutes filing of the document under the Federal Rules of Appellate Procedure and the local rules of this court, and constitutes entry of the document on the docket kept by the clerk under Fed. R. App. P. 36 and 45(b). If leave of court is required to file a document and the document may be filed electronically under Rule 1 of this Order, both the motion and document at issue should be submitted electronically. If leave is granted, the docket will so reflect.

Before filing a document with the court, an ECF Filer must verify its legibility and completeness. When a document has been filed electronically, the official record is the electronic document stored by the court. Except in the case of documents first filed in paper form and subsequently submitted electronically, an electronically filed document is deemed filed at the date and time stated on the Notice of Docket Activity

from the court. Unless otherwise required by statute, rule, or court order, filing must be completed by midnight in the time zone of the circuit clerk's office in Boston to be considered timely filed that day.

ECF Filers are advised that they should contact the clerk's office if they transmit a document to the electronic filing system but do not receive a Notice of Docket Activity. If a Notice of Docket Activity was not transmitted by the court, the ECF Filer's filing attempt failed and the document was not filed.

Rule 4—Service of Documents by Electronic Means

The Notice of Docket Activity that is generated by the court's electronic filing system constitutes service of the filed document on all ECF Filers. The system identifies which parties in a particular case are ECF filers. Parties who are not registered as ECF Filers must be served with a copy of any electronically filed document in some other way authorized by Fed. R. App. P. 25(c)(1). Similarly, a document filed in paper form pursuant to Rule 1 of this Order must be served using an alternate method of service prescribed by Fed. R. App. P. 25(c)(1). However, paper copies of briefs filed electronically and already served on all parties do not need to be served.

The Notice of Docket Activity does not replace the certificate of service required by Fed. R. App. P. 25(d). ECF Filers must include certificates of service with any electronically filed document which state whether the parties being served are ECF Filers being served electronically by the Notice of Docket Activity or whether they are being served using an alternate method of service permitted by Fed. R. App. P. 25(c)(1), and, if so, which method. The certificate must also provide the other information required by Fed. R. App. P. 25(d)(1).

Rule 5—Entry of Court–Issued Documents

Except as otherwise provided by local rule or court order, all public orders, opinions, judgments, and proceedings of the court in cases assigned to the electronic filing system will be filed in accordance with these rules, which will constitute entry on the docket kept by the clerk under Fed. R. App. P. 36 and 45(b). Any order or document electronically issued by the court without the original signature of a judge or authorized court personnel has the same force and effect as if the judge or clerk had signed a paper copy of the order.

Orders also may be issued as "text-only" entries on the docket, without an attached document. Such orders are official and binding.

Rule 6—Attachments and Exhibits to Electronically Filed Documents

All documents referenced as exhibits or attachments to an electronically filed document must also be filed electronically, unless the court permits or requires traditional paper filing. An ECF Filer must submit as exhibits or attachments only those excerpts of the referenced documents that are directly germane to the matter under consideration by the court. Excerpted material must be clearly and prominently identified as such. The court may require parties to file additional excerpts or the complete document. This Rule does not apply to appendices to briefs. See Rule 1.e of this Order.

Rule 7—Sealed Documents

As required by Rule 1 of this Order, sealed documents and motions for permission to file a document under seal should be filed only in paper form. Sealed documents must be filed in compliance with 1st Cir. R. 11.0(c) and 1st Cir. R. 30.0(f). If an entire case is sealed, all documents in the case are considered sealed unless the court orders otherwise or, in the case of a court order, opinion, or judgment, the court releases the order, opinion or judgment for public dissemination.

Rule 8—Retention Requirements

Electronically filed documents which require original signatures other than that of the ECF Filer must be maintained in paper form by the ECF Filer until final disposition of the case. For purposes of this rule, a disposition is not final until the time for filing a petition for a writ of certiorari has expired, or, if a petition for a writ of certiorari is filed, until the Supreme Court disposes of the matter, and, if a remand is ordered, the case is finally resolved. Upon request by the court, ECF Filers must provide original documents for review.

Rule 9—Signatures

The user login and password required to submit documents to the electronic filing system serve as the ECF Filer's signature on all electronic documents filed with the court. They also serve as a signature for purposes of the Federal Rules of Appellate Procedure, the local rules of court, and any other purpose for which a signature is required in connection with proceedings before the court. The name of the ECF Filer under whose login and password the document is submitted must be preceded by an "s/" and typed in the space where the signature would otherwise appear. No ECF Filer or other person may knowingly permit or cause to permit an ECF Filer's login and password to be used by anyone other than an authorized agent of the ECF Filer. ECF Filers are reminded that pursuant to Rule 2 of this Order they must immediately notify the PACER Service Center and the clerk if they learn, or have reason to know, that their login or password has been compromised.

The filer of any electronically filed document requiring multiple signatures (for example, stipulations) must list thereon all the names of other signatories by means of an "s/ [name]" block for each. By submitting such a document, the ECF Filer certifies that each of the other signatories has expressly agreed to the form and substance of the document, and that the ECF Filer has their authority to submit the document electronically. In the alternative, the ECF Filer may submit a scanned document containing all necessary signatures. If any person objects to the representation of his or her signature on an electronic document as described above, he or she must, within 14 days of the electronic filing, file a notice setting forth the basis of the objection.

Rule 10—Notice of Court Orders and Judgments

Immediately upon the entry of a public order, opinion or judgment in a case assigned to the electronic filing system, the clerk will electronically transmit a Notice of Docket Activity to ECF Filers in the case. Electronic transmission of the Notice of Docket Activity constitutes the notice and service of the order, opinion, or judgment required by Fed. R. App. P. 36(b) and 45(c). The clerk must give notice in paper form to a person who has not consented to electronic service in accordance with the Federal Rules of Appellate Procedure.

Rule 11—Technical Failures

An ECF Filer whose filing is made untimely as the result of a technical failure may seek appropriate relief from the court.

Rule 12—Privacy Protections and Public Access

Filers, whether filing electronically or in paper form, must refrain from including or must redact certain personal data identifiers from all documents filed with the court whenever such redaction is required by Fed. R. App. P. 25(a)(5). The responsibility for redacting these personal identifiers rests solely with counsel and the parties. The clerk will not review any document for compliance with this rule. Filers are advised that it is the experience of this court that failure to comply with redaction requirements is most apt to occur in attachments, addenda, or appendices, and, thus, special attention should be given to them.

Rule 13—Hyperlinks

Electronically filed documents may contain hyperlinks except as stated herein. Hyperlinks may not be used to link to sealed or restricted documents. Hyperlinks to cited authority may not replace standard citation format. Complete citations must be included in the text of the document. A hyperlink, or any site to which it refers, will not be considered part of the record. Hyperlinks are simply convenient mechanisms for accessing material in a document. The court accepts no responsibility for the availability or functionality of any hyperlink, and does not endorse any product, organization, or content at any hyperlinked site, or at any site to which that site might be linked.

[Adopted September 14, 2009, effective October 13, 2009.]

INDEX TO
THE FIRST CIRCUIT RULES

251

*

UNITED STATES BANKRUPTCY APPELLATE PANEL FOR THE FIRST CIRCUIT

Effective May 13, 2010

Including Amendments Received Through January 1, 2012

Research Note

These rules may be searched electronically on Westlaw in the US-RULES database; updates to these rules may be found on Westlaw in US-RULESUPDATES. For search tips, and a detailed summary of database content, consult the Westlaw Scope Screen of each database.

RULE 8001–1. TITLE AND EFFECTIVE DATE

(a) **Title.** These local rules, promulgated under Fed. R. Bankr. P. 8018, shall govern practice before the United States Bankruptcy Appellate Panel for the First Circuit (the "BAP" or the "Panel") and shall be known as the First Circuit BAP Local Rules. They shall be cited as "1st Cir. BAP L.R. ___."

(b) **Effective Date.** These rules shall take effect on May 13, 2010, with respect to pending cases and those filed thereafter insofar as is just and practicable. [Effective May 13, 2010.]

RULE 8001–2. NOTICE OF APPEAL

(a) **Filing Requirements.** A notice of appeal, substantially in conformance with Official Bankruptcy Form 17, shall be filed with the appropriate bankruptcy court with the filing fee in the total amount provided in 28 U.S.C. § 1930(c) and the Bankruptcy Court

Miscellaneous Fee Schedule promulgated pursuant to 28 U.S.C. § 1930(b). The appellant shall attach to the notice of appeal a copy of the bankruptcy court judgment, order, or decree from which the appeal is taken.

(b) Separate Notices. A separate notice of appeal and filing fee shall be filed for each bankruptcy court judgment, order, or decree being appealed.

(c) Consequence of Noncompliance. The BAP may dismiss an appeal for failure to cure any defect in the notice of appeal within the time period prescribed by the BAP.

[Effective May 13, 2010.]

RULE 8001–3. VOLUNTARY DISMISSAL OF APPEAL

If an appeal has been docketed with the BAP, it may be dismissed by the parties in the manner set forth in Fed. R. Bankr. P. 8001(c)(2). An appeal may also be dismissed on motion of the appellant(s), if no response or opposition is filed within fourteen (14) days after service of the motion, on terms and conditions determined by the BAP.

[Effective May 13, 2010.]

RULE 8001–4. FORUM FOR APPEAL

(a) Appeals to the BAP. Pursuant to 28 U.S.C. § 158(c)(1), all appeals from bankruptcy courts are to the BAP, unless one of the parties to the appeal files an election to have the district court hear the appeal as set forth in subsection (b) of this Rule.

(b) Election to Have District Court Hear Appeal.

(1) *Appellant Election.* An appellant electing to have the district court hear the appeal shall file with the bankruptcy court, concurrently with the notice of appeal, a separate written statement of election to have the district court hear the appeal. Failure to elect at the time of filing the notice of appeal will result in a waiver of the right of election under 28 U.S.C. § 158(c)(1) and Fed. R. Bankr. P. 8001(e). The statement of election shall substantially conform with 1st Cir. BAP L.R. Official Form 1.

(2) *Appellee Election.* An appellee electing to have the district court hear the appeal shall file with the BAP, within thirty (30) days from service of the notice of appeal, a separate written statement of election to have the district court hear the appeal. Failure to elect within the time provided will result in a waiver of the right of election under 28 U.S.C. § 158(c)(1) and Fed. R. Bankr. P. 8001(e). The statement of election shall substantially conform with 1st Cir. BAP L.R. Official Form 2.

(A) Waiver. Unless the Panel orders otherwise, the filing of any document(s) (other than a notice of appearance) by an appellee with the BAP or with the bankruptcy court in connection with an appeal prior to filing a statement of election will result in a waiver of any time remaining in the thirty (30) day election period.

(c) Procedure Upon Election. Upon an effective election by an appellant, the bankruptcy court clerk shall direct the appeal to the district court in accordance with any established rules in the district. Upon an effective election by an appellee, the BAP Clerk shall transfer to the bankruptcy court all pleadings filed with the BAP and a certified copy of the BAP docket.

(d) Challenge(s) to Election. Any challenge to an election shall be brought by motion within fourteen (14) days after an election is filed. The motion shall be filed with the BAP unless the bankruptcy court clerk or the BAP Clerk has transmitted the appeal to the district court in which case the motion shall be filed with the district court.

(e) Transfer. The BAP may transfer an appeal to the district court to further the interests of justice or for any other reason the BAP deems appropriate including circumstances where a timely statement of election has been filed in a related appeal.

(f) Election and Motion for Leave to Appeal. If an appellant moves for leave to appeal pursuant to Fed. R. Bankr. P. 8003, and fails to file a separate notice of appeal concurrently with filing the motion for leave, the motion for leave shall be treated as if it were a notice of appeal for purposes of calculating the time period for filing an election.

[Effective May 13, 2010.]

RULE 8003–1. MOTION FOR LEAVE TO FILE INTERLOCUTORY APPEAL

(a) Motion Required. Parties seeking leave to appeal an interlocutory judgment, order, or decree shall file in the bankruptcy court a motion, containing the matters set forth in Fed. R. Bankr. P. 8003(a), together with the notice of appeal.

(b) Response. Unless the BAP orders otherwise, any party opposing a motion for leave to appeal an interlocutory judgment, order, or decree shall file its response with the bankruptcy court within fourteen (14) days of service of the motion. Unless the BAP orders otherwise, the filing of any document(s) prior to making the election, including a response to the motion for leave to appeal, will result in a waiver of any time remaining in the thirty (30) day election period. See 1st Cir. BAP L.R. 8001—4(b)(2)(A).

(c) Clerk to Transmit. Unless there is an election to have the district court hear the appeal, the bankruptcy court clerk shall forward the motion and any responses to the BAP for decision.

(d) Decision on Motion. The BAP may render its decision on the motion with or without a hearing. Upon the entry of the BAP decision or order, the BAP Clerk shall serve the same on the parties and the bankruptcy court clerk.

[Effective May 13, 2010.]

RULE 8005–1. STAY PENDING APPEAL

(a) Appendix. In addition to the requirements set forth in Fed. R. Bankr. P. 8005, a motion for stay pending appeal shall be accompanied by an appendix containing the following:

(1) a copy of the bankruptcy court's order denying a motion for stay or a copy of the transcript of the bankruptcy court's hearing on the motion, unless the motion was not first presented to the bankruptcy court; and

(2) a copy of any document(s) filed in the bankruptcy court that is relevant to the motion for stay.

[Effective May 13, 2010.]

RULE 8006–1. RECORD ON APPEAL

(a) Consequence of Noncompliance. Failure to include in the record on appeal all of the items listed in Fed. R. Bankr. P. 8006 may result in dismissal of the appeal.

(b) Copy of Record on Appeal. Upon request of the BAP, a party shall provide four (4) copies of its designation and each item designated to the BAP.

(c) Challenge(s) to Designation. A party challenging a designation shall file a motion with the BAP within fourteen (14) days of the filing of the designation.

[Effective May 13, 2010.]

RULE 8007–1. DOCKETING OF APPEAL; COMPLETION OF THE RECORD

(a) Preliminary Transmission. Promptly after a notice of appeal is filed, the bankruptcy court clerk shall transmit to the BAP Clerk a copy of the following:

(1) a certified copy of the dockets in the main case and adversary proceeding, if applicable;

(2) the notice of appeal with the attached bankruptcy court judgment, order, or decree being appealed;

(3) any motion to extend time to file the notice of appeal and the order disposing of the motion;

(4) any written findings and conclusions or opinion of the bankruptcy court; and

(5) any post-judgment motion regarding the appealed judgment, order, or decree and any order disposing of the motion.

(b) Supplemental Transmission. If after the bankruptcy court clerk has transmitted the preliminary transmission, a motion regarding the appealed judgment, order, or decree is filed, the bankruptcy court clerk promptly shall transmit to the BAP Clerk a copy of the motion, any order disposing of the motion, and the related docket entries. The bankruptcy court clerk shall transmit to the BAP Clerk a copy of the transcript immediately after it is filed.

(c) Completion of the Record. After the parties have completed the record pursuant to the deadlines and requirements set forth in Fed. R. Bankr. P. 8006, the bankruptcy court clerk shall promptly transmit the completed record to the BAP.

(d) Docketing of Appeal. An appeal is deemed to be docketed at the BAP, for purposes of Fed. R. Bankr. P. 8007(b), upon the docketing of the completed record received from the bankruptcy court clerk. The BAP Clerk shall give notice promptly to all parties of the date of the docketing of the appeal.

[Effective May 13, 2010.]

RULE 8008–1. FILING AND SERVICE

(a) Filing. Unless the BAP orders otherwise, any document(s), other than briefs and appendices, which are not filed electronically are timely filed if received in the office of the BAP Clerk by 5:00 p.m. All documents filed shall be received and docketed by the BAP Clerk, whether or not timely filed. The BAP has established procedures for electronic filing of documents, with certain exceptions, as set forth in General Order No. 2 and any amendments to that order. General Order No. 2 is posted on the website at http://www.bap1.uscourts.gov. Upon request, the BAP Clerk will provide a hard copy of General Order No. 2.

(b) Translation(s) Required. The BAP will disregard any document(s) not in the English language unless a translation(s) is furnished. Whenever a party cites to a statute, rule, or regulation of the Commonwealth of Puerto Rico ("Puerto Rico"), an opinion of the Supreme Court of Puerto Rico, or other court of Puerto Rico in an appendix, brief, or at oral argument and the cited authority is not available in the bound English language volumes, an official, certified, or stipulated translation thereof shall be filed. Translations of pertinent and relevant excerpts of the foregoing may be accepted if stipulated to by the parties or submitted by a party not less than thirty (30) days before oral argument. Where translations of excerpts are submitted by one party, opposing parties may submit, prior to oral argument, translations of such additional parts as they deem necessary for a proper understanding of the substance of any such statute, rule, regulation, or holding.

(c) Service. A party shall serve all other parties to the appeal with an exact copy of any document(s) the party files with the BAP, with the exception of the designated record, and shall attach to the document(s) a signed certificate of service. Although the BAP Clerk shall accept for filing any document(s) lacking a certificate of service, failure to effect service properly or to file such certificate shall be grounds for such sanctions as the BAP may deem appropriate.

(d) Facsimile Filing. The BAP Clerk is authorized to accept any document(s) via facsimile if the BAP Clerk determines that the situation presents an emergency or is otherwise compelling. Any document(s) filed by facsimile must be served on all other parties by facsimile or hand delivery within 24 hours after the facsimile filing and may be subject to such procedures for follow-up filing of electronic or hard copies as the BAP Clerk may from time to time specify. Under no circumstances will the BAP Clerk accept for filing by facsimile briefs and appendices. The facsimile number for the BAP is posted on the website at http://www.bap1.uscourts.gov.

[Effective May 13, 2010.]

RULE 8009–1. TIME FOR FILING BRIEFS AND RELATED DOCUMENTS

(a) Filing of Briefs. After the BAP dockets the appeal pursuant to 1st Cir. BAP L.R. 8007–1(d), it shall issue a briefing order setting forth the deadlines for the filing of all briefs. The briefs shall be filed in the form set forth in 1st Cir. BAP L.R. 8010–1. Briefs filed electronically must be filed on or before the date provided in the briefing order. Briefs not filed electronically may be filed by mail, but the filing is not timely unless the briefs are received by the BAP Clerk within the time fixed for filing, except that briefs are deemed filed on the day of mailing.

(b) Motion for Extension of Time for Filing a Brief.

(1) *Requirements.* A motion for extension of time for filing a brief shall:

(A) be made within the time limit established by the briefing order for the filing of such brief;

(B) be supported by a declaration setting forth any previous briefing deadlines; how many extensions of time, if any, have been granted; and whether any previous requests for extensions of time have been denied or denied in part; and

(C) briefly recite the reasons why such an extension is necessary and the amount of time requested. Any motion for an extension of time to file a brief on the ground that the transcript is unavailable shall affirmatively show that the transcript was timely ordered and paid for or shall state why the transcript was not ordered.

(c) Consequence of Failure to File Brief Timely. An appellant's failure to file a brief timely may result in dismissal of the appeal. An appellee's failure to file a brief timely may result in loss of the right to be heard at oral argument. Briefs filed late shall be accompanied by a motion in accordance with subsection (b) of this Rule. The Panel has no obligation to grant an untimely motion for an extension of time to file a brief or consider a late brief.

[Effective May 13, 2010.]

RULE 8009–2. APPENDICES

(a) Filing of Appendix. Appendices are due pursuant to the deadlines set forth in the briefing order issued by the BAP. Appellant briefs shall be accompanied by relevant appendices containing the documents set forth in Fed. R. Bankr. P. 8009(b). An appellee may serve and file a supplemental appendix as provided in Fed. R. Bankr. P. 8009(b). In addition to the other items required by Fed. R. Bankr. P. 8009(b), an appellant shall include in its appendix a copy of the judgment, order, or decree from which the appeal is taken, and, where applicable, a copy of the transcript containing the findings of fact and the conclusions of law orally delivered by the bankruptcy court. The parties shall include in their respective appendices all portions of the transcript required for adequate review of the issues before the BAP. Appendices filed electronically must be filed on or before the date provided in the briefing order. Appendices not filed electronically may be filed by mail, but the filing is not timely unless the appendices are received by the BAP Clerk within the time fixed for filing, except that appendices are deemed filed on the day of mailing.

(b) Format of Appendix.

(1) *Paper and Margin Standards.* The appendix must be separate from the brief and must be printed on 8 ½″ × 11″ white paper with a one-inch margin on all four sides of text.

(2) *Table of Contents and Page Numbering.* Any appendix shall be sequentially paginated and shall contain a table of contents with reference to the numbered pages.

(3) *Covers.* Unless filed electronically, appendix covers shall be white. They shall contain the case caption, substantially in the format set forth in 1st Cir. BAP L.R. Official Forms 1-4, identify the party submitting the appendix with the name, address, telephone number, fax number, and bar number of any counsel filing the appendix.

(4) *Binding.* Unless filed electronically, any appendix shall be firmly bound along the left margin.

(5) *Relevant Statutes, Rules, and Regulations.* A party may include copies of relevant statutes, rules,

and regulations either in the appendix or in pamphlet form.

(c) Consequence of Noncompliance. The Panel may reject or disregard any appendices that fail to comply with any of the requirements set forth in this Rule or in Fed. R. Bankr. P. 8009(b).

[Effective May 13, 2010.]

RULE 8010–1. FORM OF BRIEFS

(a) Length. Unless the BAP orders otherwise, opening briefs may not exceed 30 pages and reply briefs may not exceed 20 pages. Copies may be double sided.

(b) Content.

(1) *Briefs.* All briefs shall contain the matter set forth in Fed. R. Bankr. P. 8010(a).

(2) *References to Appendix.* Statements in briefs regarding background facts shall be supported by citation to the appendix. Citations to documents in the appendix shall be to pages of the appendix (e.g., App. at 27, or Appellee App. at 14) rather than to page numbering that appear on original papers.

(3) *Statement of Related Cases.* Any party filing a brief shall file a statement, attached to the last page of its brief and substantially in the form of 1st Cir. BAP L.R. Official Form 3, indicating whether the party knows of a related case pending before the Supreme Court of the United States or any United States Court of Appeals, United States District Court, or BAP.

(A) Related Case. A related case is one that involves substantially the same litigants and substantially the same fact pattern or legal issues as the pending appeal.

(4) *Statement of Interested Parties.* Any party filing a brief, other than governmental parties, shall file a statement, attached to the last page of its brief and substantially in the form of 1st Cir. BAP L.R. Official Form 4, indicating whether the party knows of any interested party who is not listed in the notice of appeal.

(A) Interested Party. An "interested party" includes all persons, associations, firms, partnerships, corporations, guarantors, insurers, affiliates, or other legal entities that are financially interested in the outcome of the appeal. When a corporation is a party to an appeal, the Statement of Interested Parties shall identify any parent corporation and any publicly held corporation that owns 10 per cent or more of its stock or state that there is no such corporation. An individual listing is not necessary if a large group of persons or firms can be specified by a generic description. The Statement of Interested Parties shall include the names of attorneys who have previously appeared for a party in the

case or proceeding below but who have not entered an appearance with the BAP.

(c) Format.

(1) *Paper and Margins Standard.* Briefs shall be printed on 8½″ by 11″ paper with a one-inch margin on all four sides of text, including pagination and footnotes.

(2) *Line Spacing and Type.* Briefs shall use the following line format: single spacing for the caption and footnotes, and double-spacing for the main text. All printed matter shall appear in at least 12 point type.

(3) *Page Numbering.* All pages of briefs shall be sequentially numbered.

(4) *Table of Contents.* Briefs shall contain a table of contents.

(5) *Covers.*

(A) Form. The covers of all briefs shall provide the following information, substantially in the format set forth in 1st Cir. BAP L.R. Official Forms 1–4:

(i) Name of court;

(ii) Case numbers (BAP and bankruptcy court);

(iii) Name of debtor(s);

(iv) Names of appellant(s) and appellee(s);

(v) Title of document;

(vi) Name, address, telephone number, facsimile number, and bar number of counsel filing document, or of pro se party.

(B) Color. Unless filed electronically, all briefs shall have a color cover depending on the respective party. The covers of briefs shall be as follows:

(i) appellant's brief shall have a blue cover;

(ii) appellee's brief shall have a red cover; and

(iii) appellant's reply brief shall have a gray cover.

(6) *Binding.* Unless filed electronically, briefs shall be firmly bound along the left margin.

(d) Consequence of Noncompliance. The Panel may reject or disregard any briefs that fail to comply with any of the requirements set forth in this Rule.

[Effective May 13, 2010.]

RULE 8011–1. MOTION PRACTICE

(a) Written Motion Required. All motions to the BAP shall be in writing and filed with the BAP Clerk and served in accordance with 1st Cir. BAP L.R. 8008–1(c). Any brief, affidavit, or other document(s) necessary to support the motion shall be filed with the motion.

(1) *Statement Regarding Opposition.* A motion shall state whether any party to the appeal opposes the relief sought, if known.

(b) Responses. Unless the BAP orders otherwise, responses or oppositions to a motion shall be filed within fourteen (14) days after service of the motion.

(c) Telephone Number and Facsimile Number. A motion or response shall include the telephone and, if applicable, the facsimile number of the person signing the motion.

(d) Procedural Motions.

(1) *Clerk Authorized.* The BAP Clerk may act on the following motions without submission to the Panel:

(A) Motions relating to the production or filing of the record, transcripts, appendices, or briefs on appeal;

(B) Motions for voluntary dismissal of appeals;

(C) Motions to dismiss for want of prosecution;

(D) Motions for extension of time;

(E) Motions for leave to consolidate appeals; and

(F) Such other motions as the BAP may designate and that are subject to disposition by a single judge under Fed. R. Bankr. P. 8011(e).

(2) *Reconsideration.* A BAP Clerk order shall be subject to reconsideration by a single judge or a three-judge Panel if, within fourteen (14) days of service of notice of the entry of the order, a party adversely affected moves for reconsideration.

(e) Substantive Motions. The BAP Clerk shall forward substantive motions (e.g., motions for leave to appeal, to dismiss an appeal, or to reduce bond) to the appropriate judge(s) for determination. Unless the BAP otherwise directs, oral argument will not be held on motions.

(f) Summary Disposition. At any time, on such notice as the Panel may direct, on motion of any appellant, any appellee, or sua sponte, the Panel may:

(1) dismiss the appeal if the BAP lacks jurisdiction;

(2) dismiss the appeal, grant any other request for relief, or affirm and enforce the judgment, order, or decree below if it appears that no substantial question is presented; or

(3) reverse in the case of obvious error.

[Effective May 13, 2010.]

RULE 8011–2. EMERGENCY MOTIONS

(a) Notice. Emergency motions and responses shall be filed and served by the quickest method available. Although documents may be filed any time through CM/ECF, the filer should not expect that the filing will be addressed outside regular business hours.

(b) Form and Content. A party requesting emergency determination shall plainly title its motion as one for emergency relief. The motion shall set forth a date or period within which it seeks such determination and request that the period for response be reduced to a specified date or period. The circumstances warranting emergency determination shall be fully disclosed and explained by a verified statement of counsel accompanying the motion, or by the party if not represented by counsel.

[Effective May 13, 2010.]

RULE 8012–1. ORAL ARGUMENT

(a) Statement Regarding Oral Argument. Any party may include, either in the opening or answering brief, a statement limited to one-half page setting forth the reasons oral argument should, or need not, be heard (the "Statement"). The Statement shall be inserted immediately after the Table of Contents and Table of Authorities, and before the first page of the brief, and shall bear the caption "Statement Regarding Oral Argument." The Statement shall not be considered in determining the maximum number of pages in the brief.

(b) Waiver of Oral Argument. Oral argument may be waived upon written stipulation of the parties, unless the Panel orders otherwise.

(c) Telephonic Appearance. A party may request in the Statement, or the Panel may determine, that oral argument be conducted telephonically.

(d) Notice of Argument. If the Panel concludes that oral argument is unnecessary, based on the standards set forth in Fed. R. Bankr. P. 8012, the parties shall be so advised. The Panel's decision to dispense with oral argument may be announced by the Panel at the time the decision on the merits is rendered.

(e) Presentation of Oral Argument. At oral argument the parties may expect the Panel to be familiar with the briefs and the record on appeal. The Panel will permit no more than 15 minutes per side for oral argument unless the Panel announces a different time at the commencement of argument. Counsel shall adhere to the prescribed time limit by their own devices. Where more than one counsel argues on one side of a case, it is their responsibility to assure a fair division of the total time allotted. One or more cases posing the same issues arising from the same factual context may be treated as a single case for the purposes of this Rule.

(f) Location of Oral Argument. The BAP generally conducts oral argument monthly in Boston. For cases originating in Puerto Rico, Maine, New Hampshire, and Rhode Island, the BAP may conduct oral argument in those districts. The parties may set forth their preference for the timing or location of oral argument in the Statement. The BAP may accommodate those preferences depending on considerations of scheduling and caseload.

[Effective May 13, 2010.]

RULE 8016–1. CLERK OF THE BANKRUPTCY APPELLATE PANEL

(a) Communication with the BAP. All communication with the BAP shall be addressed to the BAP Clerk at the following address:

U.S. Bankruptcy Appellate Panel
for the First Circuit
John W. McCormack
Post Office and Court House
5 Post Office Square, Suite 910
Boston, MA 02109
(617) 748-9650

(b) Hours of the BAP. The office of the BAP Clerk shall be open for business during the hours posted at the website located at http://www.bap1.uscourts.gov except for legal holidays as that term is defined in Fed. R. Bankr. P. 9006(a). For information regarding emergency closings, parties may telephone the Office of the Clerk of the United States Court for Appeals for the First Circuit at (617) 748-9057.

[Effective May 13, 2010. Amended effective October 12, 2010.]

RULE 8018–1. SILENCE OF LOCAL RULES

To the extent the Federal Rules of Bankruptcy Procedure and these rules are silent as to a particular matter of practice, the BAP may apply the First Circuit Local Rules and the Federal Rules of Appellate Procedure.

[Effective May 13, 2010.]

RULE 8070–1. DILIGENT PROSECUTION OF APPEALS

(a) Reporting Changes. Attorneys who are not filing electronically and pro se parties shall immediately file with the BAP a statement of any address, telephone number, or facsimile number changes.

(b) Dismissal for Failure to Prosecute. If no party has elected to proceed before the district court and no appellant prosecutes the appeal in accordance with the requirements of the Federal Rules of Bankruptcy Procedure and these rules, the BAP Clerk may enter an order dismissing the appeal for failure to prosecute.

(1) *Discretion to Reinstate.* The BAP may reinstate the appeal upon a motion by a defaulting party, within fourteen (14) days of service of the order.

Such a motion shall not be allowed absent a verified statement by counsel for the defaulting party or by the defaulting party, if pro se, showing special circumstances justifying the failure to comply with the requirements of the Federal Rules of Bankruptcy Procedure or these rules.

[Effective May 13, 2010.]

RULE 9009–1. OFFICIAL FORMS

The BAP adopts the 1st Cir. BAP L.R. Official Forms appended hereto and such forms shall be utilized in cases and proceedings filed with the BAP under Title 11 of the United States Code. The 1st Cir. BAP L.R. Official Forms may be amended and supplemented from time to time.

[Effective May 13, 2010.]

RULE 9010–1. ENTRY OF APPEARANCE AND ADMISSION TO PRACTICE

(a) Notice of Appearance. An attorney who represents a party in an appeal, and who is not identified in the notice of appeal or a notice of substitution of attorney, shall immediately file and serve a notice of appearance containing the attorney's name, address, telephone number, bar number, and facsimile number.

(b) Appearance. Notwithstanding the previous subsection, an attorney who authorizes his or her name to appear on any pleading filed with the BAP has entered an appearance.

(c) Withdrawal and Substitution. An attorney who has entered an appearance may not withdraw without either:

(1) filing and serving a Notice of Substitution of Attorney. The notice shall contain substitute counsel's name, bar number, address, telephone number, facsimile number, and signature; or

(2) obtaining an order of the Panel allowing the attorney to withdraw. The Panel may grant such an order if an attorney files and serves on opposing counsel and the attorney's client a motion to withdraw as counsel. Any motion to withdraw shall include the client's current address and telephone number. Where an attorney appeared on behalf of a corporation, the motion to withdraw will be considered in conjunction with 1st Cir. BAP L.R. 9010-2.

(d) Admission. An attorney is admitted to practice before the BAP if the attorney is:

(1) admitted to practice by and a member in good standing of the United States Court of Appeals for the First Circuit;

(2) admitted to practice by and a member in good standing of a United States District Court within the First Circuit; or

(3) admitted to practice by a United States Bankruptcy Court in the case or proceeding on appeal.

(e) Pro Hac Vice. Any attorney not admitted to practice by the United States Court of Appeals for the First Circuit, a United States District Court within the First Circuit, or a United States Bankruptcy Court in the case or proceeding on appeal may, upon a motion, appear and practice before the BAP in a particular action at the BAP's discretion. All such motions shall have attached a supporting affidavit containing the following:

(1) the attorney's address, telephone number, and facsimile number;

(2) a listing of the court(s) to which the attorney has been admitted to practice and the date(s) of admission;

(3) a statement that the attorney is in good standing and eligible to practice in the court(s);

(4) a statement that the attorney is not currently suspended or disbarred in any jurisdiction;

(5) a statement describing the nature and status of any pending disciplinary matters involving the attorney; and

(6) a statement that the attorney is familiar with the requirements of Rule VIII of the Rules of Attorney Disciplinary Enforcement for the Court of Appeals for the First Circuit, made applicable through 1st Cir. BAP L.R. 8018–1.

[Effective May 13, 2010.]

RULE 9010–2. PRO SE PARTIES

The signature of an individual not represented by counsel on a pleading shall constitute a pro se appearance. All other parties shall appear only through counsel. Pro se parties shall ensure their appeal is perfected in a manner and within the time limits prescribed in these rules and shall prosecute the appeal with diligence.

[Effective May 13, 2010.]

FORM 1.   APPELLANT'S STATEMENT OF ELECTION TO HAVE THE UNITED STATES DISTRICT COURT HEAR APPEAL

UNITED STATES BANKRUPTCY APPELLATE PANEL
FOR THE FIRST CIRCUIT

BAP No. 00–000

Bankruptcy Case No. 00–00000

,

Debtor(s).

,

Appellant(s),

v.

,

Appellee(s).

APPELLANT'S STATEMENT OF ELECTION TO HAVE THE UNITED STATES DISTRICT COURT HEAR APPEAL

Appellant, _____, hereby elects, pursuant to 28 U.S.C. § 158(c)(1)(a), Fed. R. Bankr. P. 8001(e), and 1st Cir. BAP L.R. 8001–4(b)(1), to have the United States District Court for the District of _____ hear this appeal.

> _____
> Attorney for the Appellant or Pro Se
> Appellant
> Address
> Telephone Number
> Facsimile Number

[Effective May 13, 2010.]

FORM 2. APPELLEE'S STATEMENT OF ELECTION TO HAVE THE UNITED STATES DISTRICT COURT HEAR APPEAL

UNITED STATES BANKRUPTCY APPELLATE PANEL FOR THE FIRST CIRCUIT

_____

BAP No. 00–000

_____

Bankruptcy Case No. 00–00000

_____

,

Debtor(s).

_____

,

Appellant(s),

v.

,

Appellee(s).

_____

APPELLEE'S STATEMENT OF ELECTION TO HAVE THE UNITED STATES DISTRICT COURT HEAR APPEAL

Appellee, _____, hereby elects, pursuant to 28 U.S.C. § 158(c)(1)(B), Fed. R. Bankr. 8001(e), and 1st Cir. BAP L.R. 8001–4(b)(1), to have the United States District Court for the District of _____ hear this appeal.

_____
Attorney for the Appellee or Pro Se
Appellee
Address
Telephone Number
Facsimile Number

[Effective May 13, 2010.]

FORM 3.   STATEMENT REGARDING RELATED CASES—1ST CIR. BAP L.R.8010–1(b)(3)

UNITED STATES BANKRUPTCY APPELLATE PANEL
FOR THE FIRST CIRCUIT

BAP No. 00–000

Bankruptcy Case No. 00–00000

,

Debtor(s).

,

Appellant(s),

v.

,

Appellee(s).

STATEMENT REGARDING RELATED CASES
1st Cir. BAP L.R. 8010–1(b)(3)

☐ The undersigned certifies that the following are known related cases and appeals:

Case Name	Court	Status of Case

☐ The undersigned certifies that the undersigned knows of no related cases or appeals as that term is defined in 1st Cir. BAP L.R. 8010–1(b)(3)(A).

Attorney or Pro Se Party
Address
Telephone Number
Facsimile Number

[Effective May 13, 2010.]

FORM 4.   STATEMENT REGARDING INTERESTED PARTIES—1ST CIR. BAP L.R.8010–1(b)(4)

UNITED STATES BANKRUPTCY APPELLATE PANEL
FOR THE FIRST CIRCUIT

_____

BAP No. 00–000

_____

Bankruptcy Case No. 00–00000

_____

,

Debtor(s).

_____

,

Appellant(s),

v.

,

Appellee(s).

_____

STATEMENT REGARDING INTERESTED PARTIES
1st Cir. BAP L.R. 8010–1(b)(4)

☐ The undersigned certifies that the following parties have an interest in the outcome of this appeal. These representations are made to enable the judges of the Panel to evaluate possible disqualification or recusal.

☐ The undersigned certifies that the undersigned knows of no interested party as that term is defined in 1st Cir. BAP L.R. 8010–1(b)(4)(A).

_____

Attorney or Pro Se Party
Address
Telephone Number
Facsimile Number

[Effective May 13, 2010.]

ELECTRONIC CASE FILING

GENERAL ORDER NO. 2 REGARDING CASE MANAGEMENT/ELECTRONIC CASE FILES SYSTEM ("CM/ECF")

Before HAINES, Chief Judge, VOTOLATO, LAMOUTTE, DE JESÚS, HILLMAN, FEENEY, VAUGHN, BOROFF, DEASY, ROSENTHAL, KORNREICH, AND TESTER

The United States Bankruptcy Appellate Panel for the First Circuit ("BAP") adopts the following provisions to govern the electronic filing of documents in cases before the BAP. Effective **May 13, 2010,** the BAP will permit filings to be made by means of the BAP's electronic filing system. Effective **July 13, 2010,** use of the electronic filing system is *mandatory* for all attorneys unless they are granted an exemption. These provisions may be amended from time to time, with or without prior notice, by further order of the BAP. The BAP Clerk may make changes to the procedures for electronic filing to adapt to changes in technology or to facilitate electronic filing. Any changes to procedures will be posted on the BAP's website. The BAP may deviate from these procedures in specific cases if deemed appropriate in the exercise of its discretion.

RULE 1.   SCOPE OF ELECTRONIC FILING

(a) **Scope.** Except as otherwise prescribed by local rule or order, all cases will be part of the BAP's CM/ECF System. All motions, briefs, appendices, or other pleadings and documents must be filed electronically except for:

(1) documents filed by parties in interest who are pro se;

(2) motions to seal and the document(s) subject to the motion;

(3) any document exceeding 6.5 megabytes; and

(4) documents filed by an attorney who has sought and received an exemption from the BAP via a motion demonstrating good cause. A previously received exemption from a bankruptcy court will constitute good cause.

(b) **Format of Document.** Documents must be formatted for electronic filing by converting the original word-processing document into Portable Document Format ("PDF"). PDF images created by scanning paper documents do not comply with this order. Exhibits which are submitted as attachments to an electronically filed pleading, however, may be scanned and attached if the ECF Filer does not possess a word-processing file version of the document.

(c) **Briefs and Appendices.** ECF Filers must file briefs and appendices electronically and it is not necessary to supply the BAP with additional paper copies. An electronically filed appendix may contain multiple attachments. The description of each attachment as entered by the ECF Filer should identify the page numbers within the appendix, for example "Appendix, pages 51–100." 1st Cir. BAP L.R. 8009–2 and 8010–1 apply to electronically filed briefs and appendices with the exception of the cover colors and binding.

RULE 2.   REGISTRATION AND TRAINING

(a) **Generally.** Attorneys who practice before the BAP must register with the BAP's electronic case filing system. Registration is required to obtain a login and password for use of the BAP's electronic case filing system. Attorneys may register at http://www.bap1.uscourts.gov. An ECF Filer is an attorney who has obtained a login and password to file documents electronically. Before filing an electronic document using the BAP's electronic filing system, ECF Filers must have previously completed an electronic case filing training in any federal court. The BAP recommends that ECF Filers also complete the computer-based training modules listed on the BAP's website. ECF Filers should also familiarize themselves with the CM/ECF User's Guide, together with other training materials concerning electronic filing at the BAP, including Frequently Asked Questions, all of which are available on the BAP's website at http://www.bap1.uscourts.gov.

(b) **Effect of Registration.** Registration as an ECF Filer constitutes consent to electronic service of all documents as provided in these rules and in the Federal Rules of Bankruptcy Procedure. All ECF Filers have an affirmative duty to inform the BAP Clerk immediately of any change in their e-mail address. Any changes to an ECF Filer's contact information, including physical address, telephone, facsimile number, or e-mail address, should be made through the PACER system.

(c) **Protecting the Password.** ECF Filers agree to protect the security of their logins and passwords and immediately notify the PACER Service Center and the BAP Clerk if they learn, or have reason to suspect, that their login or password has been compromised. ECF Filers may be sanctioned for failure to comply with this provision. In addition to other sanctions imposed by the BAP, the BAP may terminate with notice the electronic filing privileges of any ECF Filer who uses the electronic filing system inappropriately.

(d) **Revocation.** The BAP may revoke an ECF Filer's authority to file documents electronically for violating subsection (c) above, this general order, or otherwise misusing the BAP's electronic case filing system.

RULE 3. CONSEQUENCES OF ELECTRONIC FILING

(a) Generally. Electronic transmission of a document to the electronic filing system in compliance with these rules, together with the transmission of a Notice of Docket Activity from the BAP, constitutes filing of the document under the Federal Rules of Bankruptcy Procedure and the First Circuit BAP Local Rules, and constitutes entry of the document on the docket kept by the BAP Clerk.

(b) Timing of Filing. Electronic filing is permitted at all times, except when the system is temporarily unavailable due to routine or emergency maintenance. When a document has been filed electronically, the official record is the electronic document stored by the BAP. An electronically filed document is deemed filed at the date and time stated on the Notice of Docket Activity from the BAP. Unless otherwise required by statute, rule, or order of the BAP, electronic filing must be completed by midnight in the time zone of the BAP Clerk's office in Boston to be considered timely filed that day. The ECF Filer, however, should not expect that the filing will be addressed outside of regular business hours.

(c) Failure to Receive Notice of Docketing Activity. ECF Filers are advised that they should contact the BAP Clerk's office if they transmit a document to the electronic filing system but do not receive a Notice of Docket Activity. If the BAP does not transmit a Notice of Docket Activity, the ECF Filer's filing attempt failed and the document was not filed. If a technical failure prevents timely electronic filing of any document, the filing party should promptly seek relief from the BAP.

RULE 4. SIGNATURE

(a) Generally. The user login and password required to submit documents to the electronic filing system serve as the ECF Filer's signature on all electronic documents filed with the Panel. They also serve as a signature for purposes of the Federal Rules of Bankruptcy Procedure, the First Circuit BAP Local Rules, and any other purpose for which a signature is required. No ECF Filer or other person may knowingly permit or cause to permit an ECF Filer's login and password to be used by anyone other than an authorized agent of the ECF Filer.

(b) Multiple Signatures. The filer of any electronically filed document requiring multiple signatures (for example, stipulations) must list thereon all the names of other signatories by means of an "/s/ [name]" block for each. By submitting such a document, the ECF Filer certifies that each of the other signatories has expressly agreed to the form and substance of the document, and that the ECF Filer has their authority to submit the document electronically. In the alternative, the ECF Filer may submit a scanned document containing all necessary signatures.

RULE 5. SERVICE

(a) Generally. The CM/ECF system will generate a Notice of Docket Activity when any document is filed electronically. This notice constitutes service of the document on all parties who have registered as BAP electronic filers pursuant to Rule 2. Such registration constitutes consent to service via Notice of Docket Activity.

(b) Non–Registrants. Parties who are not registered as ECF Filers must be served with a copy of any electronically filed document in some other way authorized by Fed. R. Bankr. P. 8008 and 1st Cir. BAP L.R. 8008–1. Similarly, a document filed in paper form pursuant to Rule 1 of this Order must be served using an alternate method of service prescribed by Fed. R. Bankr. P. 8008 and 1st Cir. BAP L.R. 8008–1.

(c) Certificate of Service. The Notice of Docket Activity does not replace the certificate of service required by Fed. R. Bankr. P. 8008(d) and 1st Cir. BAP L.R. 8008–1. ECF Filers must include certificates of service with any electronically filed document which state whether the parties being served are ECF Filers being served electronically by the Notice of Docket Activity or whether they are being served using an alternate method of service and, if so, which method. The certificate must also provide the other information required by Fed. R. Bankr. P. 8008(d) and 1st Cir. BAP L.R. 8008–1.

RULE 6. TECHNICAL REQUIREMENTS

(a) Searchable Text. Except as otherwise specified in this Rule, or as otherwise ordered, the text of all electronic filings must be searchable using Adobe Acrobat's text search function.

(b) Non–Searchable Text. For some documents, primarily exhibits, a text searchable version might not be available. If so, the electronic filer may upload a version that is not text searchable.

(c) Technical Failures. An ECF Filer whose filing is made untimely as the result of a technical failure may seek appropriate relief from the BAP.

RULE 7. PRIVACY

(a) Personal Data Identifiers. In compliance with Fed. R. App. P. 25(a)(5) and Fed. R. Bankr. P. 9037, parties must refrain from including, or must partially redact where inclusion is necessary, the following personal data identifiers from all documents filed with the BAP:

(1) Minors' names (use initials only);

(2) Social Security numbers (use last four digits only);

(3) Dates of birth (use year of birth only);

(4) Financial account numbers (identify the type of account and institution and provide the last four digits of the account number).

(b) Redaction Responsibility. The ECF Filer bears sole responsibility for redaction.

RULE 8. OTHER LIMITATIONS AND RESTRICTIONS CONCERNING CM/ECF

(a) Counsel of Record. Except as otherwise specified in this Rule, or as otherwise ordered, the ECF Filer duly registered pursuant to Rule 2, above, may only file documents in BAP appeals where he or she is counsel of record.

(b) Additional Copies. Except as otherwise specified in this Rule, or as otherwise ordered, an ECF Filer need not and may not submit (by U.S. Mail, other mail services, facsimile, or by e-mail) additional copies of any documents filed electronically through CM/ECF.

(c) Hyperlinks. Documents filed electronically may contain hyperlinks except as stated herein. Hyperlinks may not be used to link to sealed or restricted documents. Hyperlinks to cited authority may not replace standard citation format. Complete citations must be included in the text of the document. A hyperlink, or any site to which it refers, will not be considered part of the record. Hyperlinks are simply convenient mechanisms for accessing material in a document. The BAP accepts no responsibility for the availability of functionality of any hyperlink, and does not endorse any product, organization, or content at any hyperlinked site, or at any site to which that site might be linked.

RULE 9. PACER

(a) Pacer Docket. Unless otherwise ordered, all documents that are filed electronically will be attached to the PACER docket.

(b) Paper Filing. Unless otherwise ordered, when the BAP receives a document only in paper format, the BAP will scan the document, convert it to a PDF, and attach it to the PACER docket.

[Dated: May 10, 2010.]

UNITED STATES DISTRICT COURT FOR THE DISTRICT OF MASSACHUSETTS

Summary of Contents

Local Rules of the United States District Court for the District of Massachusetts.

Rules for United States Magistrates in the United States District Court for the District of Massachusetts.

Index.

LOCAL RULES OF THE UNITED STATES DISTRICT COURT FOR THE DISTRICT OF MASSACHUSETTS

Effective September 1, 1990

Including Amendments Received Through January 1, 2012

Research Note

These rules may be searched electronically on Westlaw in the MA-RULES database; updates to these rules may be found on Westlaw in MA-RULESUPDATES. For search tips, and a detailed summary of database content, consult the Westlaw Scope Screen of each database.

LOCAL RULES

PREFACE

At the request of the Committee on Rules and Practice of the Judicial Conference of the United States, local rules dealing with civil practice have been renumbered to key them to the Federal Rules of Civil Procedure. Accordingly, the numbering is not sequential. Criminal Rules will be numbered from 100 to 199, and district court rules relating to bankruptcy from 200 to 299.

RULE 1.1 TITLE

These rules shall be known as Local Rules of the United States District Court for the District of Massachusetts and cited as "LR, D.Mass." or "LR."

[Effective September 1, 1990.]

RULE 1.2 APPLICATION

(a) In General. These rules shall apply to all proceedings in the United States District Court for the District of Massachusetts.

(b) Cases Pending When Rules Adopted and Amended. These rules became effective in this form on September 1, 1990, and have been amended from time to time thereafter. They shall, except as applicable time periods may have run, govern all actions and proceedings pending on or commenced after the date of adoption or amendment. Where justice so requires, proceedings in designated cases or other matters before the court on the effective date of the adoption or amendment of these rules shall be governed by the practice of the court before the adoption of these rules.

[Effective September 1, 1990. Amended effective October 1, 1992.]

RULE 1.3 SANCTIONS

Failure to comply with any of the directions or obligations set forth in, or authorized by, these Local Rules may result in dismissal, default, or the imposition of other sanctions as deemed appropriate by the judicial officer.

[Adopted effective October 1, 1992.]

RULE 3.1 CIVIL COVER SHEET

The party filing the initial pleading shall also file a civil cover sheet in the form prescribed by the Judicial Conference of the United States (JS 44) and the local category sheet.

[Effective September 1, 1990.]

RULE 4.1 SERVICE OF PROCESS—DISMISSAL FOR FAILURE TO MAKE SERVICE

(A) Any summons not returned with proof that it was served within one hundred twenty (120) days of the filing of the complaint is deemed to be unserved for the purpose of Fed.R.Civ.P. 4(m).

(B) Counsel and parties appearing pro se who seek to show good cause for the failure to make service within the 120 day period prescribed by Fed.R.Civ.P. 4(m) shall do so by filing a motion for enlargement of time under Fed.R.Civ.P. 6(b), together with a supporting affidavit. If on the 14th day following the expiration of the 120 day period good cause has not been shown as provided herein, the clerk shall forthwith automatically enter an order of dismissal for failure to effect service of process, without awaiting any further order of the court. The clerk shall furnish a copy of this local rule to counsel or pro se plaintiffs, together with the summons, and delivery of this copy by the clerk will constitute the notice required by Rule 4(m) Federal Rules of Civil Procedure. Such notice shall constitute the notice required by Fed.R.Civ.P. 4(m). No further notice need be given by the court.

(C) In those cases where the Federal Rules of Civil Procedure authorize service of process to be made in accordance with state practice, it shall be the duty of counsel for the party seeking such service to furnish to the Clerk of Court forms of all necessary orders and sufficient copies of all papers to comply with the requirements of the state practice, together with specific instructions for the making of such service, if such service is to be made by the United States marshal.

[Effective September 1, 1990. Amended effective January 2, 1995; December 1, 2009.]

RULE 4.5 FEES

(a) Except as otherwise provided by law, the clerk and other officers and employees of the court shall not be required to perform any service for a party other than the United States for which a fee is lawfully prescribed, unless the amount of the fee, if it is known, or an amount sufficient to cover the fee reasonably expected by the officer to come due for performance of the service has been deposited with the court.

(b) This provision shall not apply to the United States or a party who is proceeding in forma pauperis, or in any other situation where, in the judgment of the officer entitled to a fee, it is unnecessary to ensure payment of the fee and would work hardship or an injustice.

(c) The clerk shall receive for filing all complaints accompanied by a request to proceed in forma pauperis, and note the date thereon. If the request is denied, the matter will be noted on the miscellaneous business docket. If the request is allowed, or the denial is reversed, the clerk shall file the complaint on the civil docket. Requests to proceed in forma pauperis shall be accompanied by an affidavit containing details of the individual's financial status. (The recommended form is available without charge from the clerk's office.)

(d) In seamen's cases, or cases in which the plaintiff is granted leave to proceed in forma pauperis, the plaintiff remains liable for filing and other fees in the event he is the prevailing party at settlement or otherwise, and he collects a money judgment or any costs taxed by the court or clerk. These fees are payable forthwith upon collection of any sums from the defendant.

(e) The clerk shall on request file notices of appeal whether or not accompanied by the required filing fee.

[Effective September 1, 1990.]

[**Publisher's Note:** See also, "Appendix A. Local Rule 4.5 Supplement."]

RULE 5.1   FORM AND FILING OF PAPERS

(a) Form and Signing of Papers.

(1) The provisions of the Federal Rules of Civil Procedure pertaining to the form and signing of pleadings, motions, and other papers shall be applicable to all papers filed in any proceeding in this court. The board of bar overseers registration number of each attorney signing such documents, except the United States Attorney and his staff, shall be inscribed below the signature.

(2) All papers filed in the court shall be adapted for flat filing, be filed on 8½″ × 11″ paper without backers and be bound firmly by staple or some such other means (excluding paper or binder clip or rubber band). All papers, except discovery requests and responses, shall be double-spaced except for the identification of counsel, title of the case, footnotes, quotations and exhibits. Discovery requests and responses shall be single-spaced. Except for complaints and notices of appeal, papers that do not conform to the requirements of this subsection shall be returned by the clerk.

(b) Time and Place of Filing. Except as noted in Rule 33–36(f), the original of all papers required to be served under Fed. R. Civ. P. 5(d) shall, unless otherwise submitted to the court, be filed in the office of the clerk within seven (7) days after service has been made.

(c) Requests for Special Action. When any pleading or other paper filed in the court includes a request for special process or relief, or any other request such that, if granted, the court will proceed other than in the ordinary course, the request shall, unless it is noted on the category sheet [see Rule 40.1(a)(1)], be noted on the first page to the right of or immediately beneath the caption.

(d) Additional Copies. Whenever, because of the nature of a proceeding, such as a proceeding before a three-judge district court under 28 U.S.C. § 2284, additional copies of a paper required to be filed are necessary either for the use of the court or to enable the clerk to carry out his duties, it is the responsibility of the party filing or having filed the paper to provide the necessary copies.

(e) Removal of Papers. Except as otherwise provided, papers filed in the office of the clerk shall not be removed from the office except by a judge, official, or employee of the court using the papers in official capacity, or by order of the court. All other persons removing papers from the office of the clerk shall prepare, sign and furnish to the clerk a descriptive receipt therefor in a form satisfactory to the clerk.

[Effective September 1, 1990. Amended effective December 1, 2009.]

RULE 5.2   SERVICE AND FILING OF PLEADINGS AND OTHER PAPERS

(a) Manner of Service. Service of all pleadings subsequent to the original complaint and of all other papers required to be served shall be made in the manner specified by Rule 5, Federal Rules of Civil Procedure.

(b) Proof of Service.

(1) Except as otherwise provided by the Federal Rules of Civil Procedure, proof of service of all pleadings and other papers required to be served (except discovery papers that in accordance with Rule 33–36(f) are not to be filed) shall be filed in the office of the clerk promptly after service has been made. The proof shall show the time and manner of service, and may be made by written acknowledgment of service, a certificate of a member of the bar of this court, or an affidavit of the person who served the paper.

(2) A certificate of service of a member of the bar shall appear at the bottom of or on the margin of the last page of the paper to which it relates. The certificate shall be a brief, single-spaced statement and may be in the following form:

I hereby certify that a true copy of the above document was served upon (each party appearing pro se and) the attorney of record for each other party by mail (by hand) on (date). (Signature)

On or after the effective date of these local rules, documents not conforming to the requirements of this rule (except notices of appeal) shall be returned by the clerk.

(3) Failure to make proof of service does not affect the validity of the service.

(c) Service on Nonresident Attorney or Party Acting Pro Se.

(1) *Nonresident Attorney.* On application of a party, the court may order an attorney who represents any other party and who does not maintain an office within this district where service can be made on him by delivery as provided by Rule 5(b), Federal Rules of Civil Procedure, to designate a member of the bar of this court who does maintain such an office to receive service of all pleadings and other papers in his behalf.

(2) *Party Acting Pro Se.* On application of a party, the court may order any other party who is appearing without an attorney and who does not maintain an office or residence within this district where service can be made on him by delivery as provided by Rule 5(b), Federal Rules of Civil Procedure, to designate an address within the district at which service can be made on him by delivery.

[Effective September 1, 1990.]

RULE 5.3   PERSONAL DATA IDENTIFIERS

(A) Restrictions on Personal Identifiers in Filings. In compliance with the policy of the Judicial Conference of the United States, and the E-Government Act of 2002, and in order to promote electronic access to case files while also protecting personal privacy and other legitimate interests, parties shall refrain from including, or shall partially redact where inclusion is necessary, the following personal data identifiers from all filings submitted to the court, including exhibits thereto, whether filed electronically or in paper, unless otherwise ordered by the Court.

(1) *Social Security Numbers.* If an individual's social security number must be included in a filing, only the last four digits of that number should be used.

(2) *Names of Minor Children.* If the involvement of a minor child must be mentioned, only the initials of that child should be used.

(3) *Dates of Birth.* If an individual's date of birth must be included in a pleading, only the year should be used.

(4) *Financial Account Numbers.* If financial account numbers are relevant, only the last four digits of these numbers should be used.

(B) Non-Redacted Filings Under Seal. In compliance with the E-Government Act of 2002, a party wishing to file a document containing the personal data identifiers listed above may file an unredacted document under seal, pursuant to Local Rule 7.2. This document shall be retained by the court as part of the record. The court may, however, still require the party to file a redacted copy for the public file.

(C) Responsibility for Redaction. The responsibility for redacting these personal identifiers rests solely with counsel and the parties. The Clerk will not review each pleading for compliance with this rule.

[Effective May 6, 2003.]

RULE 5.4   FILING AND SERVICE BY ELECTRONIC MEANS

(A) Electronic Filing Generally. Unless exempt or otherwise ordered by the court, all pleadings and other papers submitted to the court must be filed, signed, and verified by electronic means as provided herein.

(B) ECF Administrative Procedures. Subject to the supervision of the court, the clerk will maintain Electronic Case Filing (ECF) Administrative Procedures, including procedures for the registration of attorneys and other authorized users and for distribution of passwords to permit electronic filing. All electronic filings must be made in accordance with the ECF Administrative Procedures. The ECF Administrative Procedures will be generally available to the public and shall be posted on the court's web site.

(C) Service of Pleadings. Unless exempt or otherwise ordered by the court, all pleadings and other papers must be served on other parties by electronic means. Transmission of the Notice of Electronic Filing (NEF) through the court's transmission facilities will constitute service of the filed document upon a registered ECF user. Any pleading or other paper served by electronic means must bear a certificate of service in accordance with Local Rule 5.2(b).

(D) Deadlines. Although the ECF system is generally available 24 hours a day for electronic filing, that availability will not alter filing deadlines, whether set by rule, court order, or stipulation. All electronic transmissions of documents must be completed prior to 6:00 p.m. to be considered timely filed that day.

(E) Civil Case Opening Documents. All ECF filers registered in the District of Massachusetts must file civil case opening documents, such as a complaint (or petition or notice of removal), civil action cover sheet, or category sheet, electronically. Cases which include sealed or ex parte documents and supporting materials presented contemporaneously with civil case opening documents may be filed and served initially in paper format and not electronically. Pro se filers, others exempt from electronic filing, or otherwise ordered by the court, may file case opening documents in paper format and not electronically. Whenever possible, at the time a civil case is submitted in paper format, the filing party may also file a disk with the clerk's office containing in PDF format the opening documents and any emergency motions and supporting papers not filed electronically.

(F) State Court Record in Removal Proceedings. Within twenty-eight days after filing a notice of removal in a civil action, a party removing an action under 28 U.S.C. §§ 1441–52 must file certified or attested copies of all docket entries, records, and proceedings in the state court in paper format. Unless exempt or otherwise ordered by the court, the removing party must also file a disk with the clerk's office containing the state court record in PDF format.

(G) Exemptions.

(1) *Documents That Should Not Be Filed Electronically.* The following types of documents must not be filed electronically, and will not be scanned into the ECF system by the clerk's office:

(a) sealed documents;

(b) ex parte motions;

(c) documents generated as part of an alternative dispute resolution (ADR) process;

(d) the administrative record in social security and other administrative proceedings;

(e) the state court record in proceedings under 28 U.S.C. § 2254; and

(f) such other types of documents as the clerk may direct in the ECF Administrative Procedures.

(2) *Documents That Need Not Be Filed Electronically.* The following types of documents need not be filed electronically, but may be scanned into the ECF system by a filing party or the clerk's office:

(a) handwritten pleadings;

(b) documents filed by pro se litigants who are incarcerated or who are not registered ECF users;

(c) indictments, informations, criminal complaints, and the criminal JS45 form;

(d) affidavits for search or arrest warrants and related documents;

(e) documents received from another court under Fed. R. Crim. P. 20 or 40;

(f) appearance bonds;

(g) any document in a criminal case containing the original signature of a defendant, such as a waiver of indictment or a plea agreement;

(h) petitions for violations of supervised release;

(i) executed service of process documents under Rule 4; and

(j) such other types of documents as the clerk may direct in the ECF Administrative Procedures.

[Adopted effective January 1, 2006. Amended effective January 1, 2009; December 1, 2009; September 7, 2011.]

RULE 7.1 MOTION PRACTICE

(A) Control of Motion Practice.

(1) *Plan for the Disposition of Motions.* At the earliest practicable time, the judicial officer shall establish a framework for the disposition of motions, which, at the discretion of the judicial officer, may include specific deadlines or general time guidelines for filing motions. This framework may be amended from time to time by the judicial officer as required by the progress of the case.

(2) *Motion Practice.* No motion shall be filed unless counsel certify that they have conferred and have attempted in good faith to resolve or narrow the issue.

(3) *Unresolved Motions.* The court shall rule on motions as soon as practicable, having in mind the reporting requirements set forth in the Civil Justice Reform Act.

(B) Submission of Motion and Opposition to Motion.

(1) *Submission of Motion.* A party filing a motion shall at the same time file a memorandum of reasons, including citation of supporting authorities, why the motion should be granted. Affidavits and other documents setting forth or evidencing facts on which the motion is based shall be filed with the motion.

(2) *Submission of Opposition to a Motion.* A party opposing a motion, shall file an opposition within 14 days after the motion is served, unless (1) the motion is for summary judgment, in which case the opposition shall be filed within 21 days after the motion is served, or (2) another period is fixed by rule or statute, or by order of the court. A party opposing a motion shall file, in the same (rather than a separate), document a memorandum of reasons, including citation of supporting authorities, why the motion should not be granted. Affidavits and other documents setting forth or evidencing facts on which the opposition is based shall be filed with the opposition. The fourteen day period is intended to include the period specified by the civil rules for mailing time and provide for a uniform period regardless of the use of the mails.

(3) *Additional Papers.* All other papers not filed as indicated in subsections (B)(1) and (2), whether in the form of a reply brief or otherwise, may be submitted only with leave of court.

(4) *Length of Memoranda.* Memoranda supporting or opposing allowance of motions shall not, without leave of court, exceed twenty (20) pages, double-spaced.

(C) Service. All papers filed pursuant to section (B) shall be served unless the moving party indicates in writing on the face of the motion that ex parte consideration is requested. Motions filed "ex parte" and related papers need not be served until the motion has been ruled upon or the court orders that service be made.

(D) Request for Hearing. Any party making or opposing a motion who believes that oral argument may assist the court and wishes to be heard shall include a request for oral argument in a separate paragraph of the motion or opposition. The request should be set off with a centered caption, "REQUEST FOR ORAL ARGUMENT."

(E) Hearing. If the court concludes that there should be a hearing on a motion, the motion will be set down for hearing at such time as the court determines.

(F) Decision of Motion Without Hearing. Motions that are not set down for hearing as provided in subsection (E) will be decided on the papers submitted after an opposition to the motion has been filed, or, if no opposition is filed, after the time for filing an opposition has elapsed.

[Effective September 1, 1990. Amended effective October 1, 1992; December 1, 2009.]

RULE 7.2 IMPOUNDED AND CONFIDENTIAL MATERIALS

(a) Whenever a party files a motion to impound, the motion shall contain a statement of the earliest date on which the impounding order may be lifted, or a statement, supported by good cause, that the material should be impounded until further order of the court. The motion shall contain suggested custody arrangements for the post-impoundment period.

(b) The clerk shall attach a copy of the order to the envelope or other container holding the impounded material.

(c) If the impound order provides a cut-off date but no arrangements for custody, the clerk (without further notice to the court or the parties) shall place the material in the public information file upon expiration of the impoundment period. If the order provides for post-impoundment custody by counsel or the parties, the materials must be retrieved immediately upon expiration of the order, or the clerk (without further notice to the court or the parties) shall place the material in the public file.

(d) Motions for impoundment must be filed and ruled upon prior to submission of the actual material sought to be impounded, unless the court orders otherwise.

(e) The court will not enter blanket orders that counsel for a party may at any time file material with the clerk, marked confidential, with instructions that the clerk withhold the material from public inspection. A motion for impoundment must be presented each time a document or group of documents is to be filed.

[Effective September 1, 1990.]

RULE 7.3 CORPORATE DISCLOSURE STATEMENT

(A) A nongovernmental corporate party to a civil action or proceeding in this court must file a statement identifying any parent corporation and any publicly held company that owns 10% or more of the party's stock.

(B) A party must file the Local Rule 7.3(A) statement upon its first appearance, pleading, petition, motion, response, or other request addressed to the court and must promptly supplement the statement upon any change in the information that the statement requires.

[Adopted effective January 1, 2001.]

RULE 10.1 SOCIAL SECURITY APPEALS [DELETED]

[Effective September 1, 1990. Deleted effective May 6, 2003.]

RULE 15.1 ADDITION OF NEW PARTIES

(A) Amendments Adding Parties. Amendments adding parties shall be sought as soon as an attorney reasonably can be expected to have become aware of the identity of the proposed new party.

(B) Service on New Party. A party moving to amend a pleading to add a new party shall serve, in the manner contemplated by Fed.R.Civ.P. 5(b), the motion to amend upon the proposed new party at least 14 days in advance of filing the motion, together with a separate document stating the date on which the motion will be filed. A motion to amend a pleading to add a new party shall be accompanied by a certificate stating that it has been served in advance on the new party as required by this rule.

[Adopted effective October 1, 1992. Amended effective January 2, 1995; December 1, 2009.]

RULE 16.1 EARLY ASSESSMENT OF CASES

(A) Scheduling Conference in Civil Cases. In every civil action, except in categories of actions exempted by LR 16.2 as inappropriate for scheduling procedures, the judge or, in the interests of the efficient administration of justice, a designated magistrate judge shall convene a scheduling conference as soon as practicable, but in any event within ninety (90) days after the appearance of a defendant and within one hundred twenty (120) days after the complaint has been served on a defendant. In cases removed to this court from a state court or transferred from any other federal court, the judge or designated magistrate judge shall convene a scheduling conference within sixty (60) days after removal or transfer.

(B) Obligation of Counsel to Confer. Unless otherwise ordered by the judge, counsel for the parties must, pursuant to Fed.R.Civ.P. 26(f), confer at least 21 days before the date for the scheduling conference for the purpose of:

(1) preparing an agenda of matters to be discussed at the scheduling conference,

(2) preparing a proposed pretrial schedule for the case that includes a plan for discovery, and

(3) considering whether they will consent to trial by magistrate judge.

(C) Settlement Proposals. Unless otherwise ordered by the judge, the plaintiff shall present written settlement proposals to all defendants no later than 14 days before the date for the scheduling conference. Defense counsel shall have conferred with their clients on the subject of settlement before the scheduling conference and be prepared to respond to the proposals at the scheduling conference.

(D) Joint Statement. Unless otherwise ordered by the judge, the parties are required to file, no later than seven (7) days before the scheduling conference and after consideration of the topics contemplated by Fed.R.Civ.P. 16(b) & (c) and 26(f), a joint statement containing a proposed pretrial schedule, which shall include:

(1) a joint discovery plan scheduling the time and length for all discovery events, that shall

    (a) conform to the obligation to limit discovery set forth in Fed.R.Civ.P. 26(b), and

    (b) take into account the desirability of conducting phased discovery in which the first phase is limited to developing information needed for a realistic assessment of the case and, if the case does not terminate, the second phase is directed at information needed to prepare for trial; and

(2) a proposed schedule for the filing of motions; and

(3) certifications signed by counsel and by an authorized representative of each party affirming that each party and that party's counsel have conferred:

    (a) with a view to establishing a budget for the costs of conducting the full course—and various alternative courses—of the litigation; and

    (b) to consider the resolution of the litigation through the use of alternative dispute resolution programs such as those outlined in LR 16.4.

To the extent that all parties are able to reach agreement on a proposed pretrial schedule, they shall so indicate. To the extent that the parties differ on what the pretrial schedule should be, they shall set forth separately the items on which they differ and indicate the nature of that difference. The purpose of the parties' proposed pretrial schedule or schedules shall be to advise the judge of the parties' best estimates of the amounts of time they will need to accomplish specified pretrial steps. The parties' proposed agenda for the scheduling conference, and their proposed pretrial schedule or schedules, shall be considered by the judge as advisory only.

(E) Conduct of Scheduling Conference. At or following the scheduling conference, the judge shall make an early determination of whether the case is "complex" or otherwise appropriate for careful and deliberate monitoring in an individualized and case-specific manner. The judge shall consider assigning any case so categorized to a case management conference or series of conferences under LR 16.3. The factors to be considered by the judge in making this decision include:

(1) the complexity of the case (the number of parties, claims, and defenses raised, the legal difficulty of the issues presented, and the factual difficulty of the subject matter);

(2) the amount of time reasonably needed by the litigants and their attorneys to prepare the case for trial;

(3) the judicial and other resources required and available for the preparation and disposition of the case;

(4) whether the case belongs to those categories of cases that:

    (a) involve little or no discovery,

    (b) ordinarily require little or no additional judicial intervention, or

    (c) generally fall into identifiable and easily managed patterns;

(5) the extent to which individualized and case-specific treatment will promote the goal of reducing cost and delay in civil litigation; and

(6) whether the public interest requires that the case receive intense judicial attention.

In other respects, the scheduling conference shall be conducted according to the provisions for a pretrial conference under Federal Rule of Civil Procedure 16 and for a case management conference under LR 16.3.

(F) Scheduling Orders. Following the conference, the judge shall enter a scheduling order that will govern the pretrial phase of the case. Unless the judge determines otherwise, the scheduling order shall include specific deadlines or general time frameworks for:

(1) amendments to the pleadings;

(2) service of, and compliance with, written discovery requests;

(3) the completion of depositions, including, if applicable, the terms for taking and using videotape depositions;

(4) the identification of trial experts;

(5) the sequence of disclosure of information regarding experts contemplated by Fed.R.Civ.P. 26(b);

(6) the filing of motions;

(7) a settlement conference, to be attended by trial counsel and, in the discretion of the judge, their clients;

(8) one or more case management conferences and/or the final pretrial conference;

(9) a final pretrial conference, which shall occur within eighteen months after the filing of the complaint;

(10) the joinder of any additional parties;

(11) any other procedural matter that the judge determines is appropriate for the fair and efficient management of the litigation.

(G) Modification of Scheduling Order. The scheduling order shall specify that its provisions, including any deadlines, having been established with the participation of all parties, can be modified only by order of the judge, or the magistrate judge if so authorized by the judge, and only upon a showing of good cause supported by affidavits, other evidentiary materials, or references to pertinent portions of the record.

(H) Definition of Judge. As used in this rule, "judge" refers to the United States District Judge to whom the case is assigned or to the United States Magistrate Judge who has been assigned the case pursuant to 28 U.S.C. § 636(c), if the Magistrate Judge has been assigned the case prior to the convening of the scheduling conference mandated by this rule.

[Adopted effective October 1, 1992. Amended effective January 2, 1995; December 10, 1996; December 4, 2000; January 2, 2001; December 1, 2009.]

Publisher's Note

See "Attachment C," infra, for the form "Notice of Scheduling Conference" which Judges of the District Court utilize in connection with the conference mandated by LR 16.1.

RULE 16.2 EXEMPTIONS FROM Fed. R. Civ. P. 16(b)

Pursuant to Rule 16(b), Federal Rules of Civil Procedure, as amended, the following categories of actions (based upon the numbered "Nature of Suit" list on form JS 44) are exempted in this district from the scheduling and planning provisions of Rule 16(b), Federal Rules of Civil Procedure, as inappropriate actions for such scheduling and planning:

CONTRACT

150 Recovery of Overpayment & Enforcement of Judgment

152 Recovery of Defaulted Student Loans

153 Recovery of Overpayment of Veterans Benefits

REAL PROPERTY

210 Condemnation

220 Foreclosure

230 Rent Lease & Ejectment

245 Tort Product Liability—Asbestos Cases Only

PRISONER PETITIONS

510 Vacate Sentence (2255)

530 Habeas Corpus

535 Death Penalty

540 Mandamus & Other

550 Civil Rights

555 Prison Condition Cases

560 Civil Detainee—Conditions of Confinement

FORFEITURE/PENALTY

625 Drug Related Seizure

BANKRUPTCY

422 Appeal (22 U.S.C. 158)

423 Withdrawal (28 U.S.C. 157)

SOCIAL SECURITY

861 HIA (1395ff)

862 Black Lung (923)

863 DIWC/DIWW (405(g))

864 SSID Title XVI

865 RSI (405(g))

TAX SUITS

871 IRS—Third Party (26 U.S.C. 7609)

OTHER STATUTES

400 State Reapportionment

450 Commerce

[Effective September 1, 1990. Amended effective January 3, 2012.]

RULE 16.3   CASE MANAGEMENT CONFERENCES

(A) Conduct of Case Management Conferences. Case management conferences shall be presided over by a judicial officer who, in furtherance of the scheduling order required by LR 16.1(f) may:

(1) explore the possibility of settlement;

(2) identify or formulate (or order the attorneys to formulate) the principal issues in contention;

(3) prepare (or order the attorneys to prepare) a specific discovery schedule and discovery plan that, if the presiding judicial officer deems appropriate, might:

    (a) identify and limit the volume of discovery available in order to avoid unnecessary or unduly burdensome or expensive discovery;

    (b) sequence discovery into two or more stages; and

    (c) include time limits set for the completion of discovery;

(4) establish deadlines for filing motions and a time framework for their disposition;

(5) provide for the "phased resolution" or "bifurcation of issues for trial" consistent with Federal Rule 42(b); and

(6) explore any other matter that the judicial officer determines is appropriate for the fair and efficient management of the litigation.

(B) Obligation of Counsel to Confer. The judicial officer may require counsel for the parties to confer before the case management conference for the purpose of preparing a joint statement containing:

(1) an agenda of matters that one or more parties believe should be addressed at the conference; and

(2) a report advising the judicial officer whether the case is progressing within the allotted time limits and in accord with the specified pretrial steps.

This statement is to be filed with the court no later than seven (7) days before the case management conference.

(C) Additional Case Management Conferences. Nothing in this rule shall be construed to prevent the convening of additional case management conferences by the judicial officer as may be thought appropriate in the circumstances of the particular case. In any event, a conference should not terminate without the

parties being instructed as to when and for what purpose they are to return to the court.

[Adopted effective October 1, 1992. Amended effective December 1, 2009.]

RULE 16.4   ALTERNATIVE DISPUTE RESOLUTION

(A) The judicial officer shall encourage the resolution of disputes by settlement or other alternative dispute resolution programs.

(B) Settlement. At every conference conducted under these rules, the judicial officer shall inquire as to the utility of the parties conducting settlement negotiations, explore means of facilitating those negotiations, and offer whatever assistance may be appropriate in the circumstances. Assistance may include a reference of the case to another judicial officer for settlement purposes. Whenever a settlement conference is held, a representative of each party who has settlement authority shall attend or be available by telephone.

(C) Other Alternative Dispute Resolution Programs.

(1) *Discretion of Judicial Officer.* The judicial officer, following an exploration of the matter with all counsel, may refer appropriate cases to alternative dispute resolution programs that have been designated for use in the district court or that the judicial officer may make available. The dispute resolution programs described in subdivisions (2) through (4) are illustrative, not exclusive.

(2) *Mini-Trial.*

    (a) The judicial officer may convene a mini-trial upon the agreement of all parties, either by written motion or their oral motion in open court entered upon the record.

    (b) Each party, with or without the assistance of counsel, shall present his or her position before:

        (1) selected representatives for each party, or

        (2) an impartial third party, or

        (3) both selected representatives for each party and an impartial third party.

    (c) An impartial third party may issue an advisory opinion regarding the merits of the case.

    (d) Unless the parties agree otherwise, the advisory opinion of the impartial third party is not binding.

    (e) The impartial third party's advisory opinion is not appealable.

    (f) Neither the advisory opinion of an impartial third party nor the presentations of the parties shall be admissible as evidence in any subsequent proceeding, unless otherwise admissible under the rules of evidence. Also, the occurrence of the mini-trial shall not be admissible.

(3) *Summary Jury Trial.*

(a) The judicial officer may convene a summary jury trial:

(1) with the agreement of all parties, either by written motion or their oral motion in court entered upon the record, or

(2) upon the judicial officer's determination that a summary jury trial would be appropriate, even in the absence of the agreement of all the parties.

(b) There shall be six (6) jurors on the panel, unless the parties agree otherwise.

(c) The panel may issue an advisory opinion regarding:

(1) the respective liability of the parties, or

(2) the damages of the parties, or

(3) both the respective liability and the damages of the parties.

Unless the parties agree otherwise, the advisory opinion is not binding and it shall not be appealable.

(d) Neither the panel's advisory opinion nor its verdict, nor the presentations of the parties shall be admissible as evidence in any subsequent proceeding, unless otherwise admissible under the rules of evidence. Also, the occurrence of the summary jury trial shall not be admissible.

(4) *Mediation.*

(a) The judicial officer may grant mediation upon the agreement of all parties.

(b) The mediator selected may be an individual, group of individuals or institution. The mediator shall be compensated as agreed by the parties.

(c) The mediator shall meet, either jointly or separately, with each party and counsel for each party and shall take any other steps that may appear appropriate in order to assist the parties to resolve the impasse or controversy.

(d) If mediation does not result in a resolution of the dispute, the parties shall promptly report the termination of mediation to the judicial officer.

(e) If an agreement is reached between the parties on any issues, the mediator shall make appropriate note of that agreement and refer the parties to the judicial officer for entry of a court order.

(f) Any communication related to the subject matter of the dispute made during the mediation by any participant, mediator, or any other person present at the mediation shall be a confidential communication to the full extent contemplated by Fed. R.Evid. 408. No admission, representation, state-ment, or other confidential communication made in setting up or conducting the proceedings not otherwise discoverable or obtainable shall be admissible as evidence or subject to discovery.

[Adopted effective October 1, 1992.]

RULE 16.5 FINAL PRETRIAL CONFERENCE

(A) Schedule of Conference. The judicial officer to whom the case is assigned for trial may set a new date for the final pretrial conference if that judicial officer determines that resolution of the case through settlement or some other form of alternative dispute resolution is imminent.

(B) Representation by Counsel; Settlement. Unless excused by the judicial officer to whom the case is assigned for trial, each party shall be represented at the final pretrial conference by counsel who will conduct the trial. Counsel shall have full authority from their clients with respect to settlement and shall be prepared to advise that judicial officer as to the prospects of settlement.

(C) Disclosures Preliminary to the Pretrial Conference. As provided in LR 26.4(A), the disclosure regarding experts required by Fed.R.Civ.P. 26(a)(2) shall be made at least 90 days before the final pretrial conference. No later than 28 days before the date of the pretrial conference the parties shall make the pretrial disclosures required by Fed.R.Civ.P. 26(a)(3). Any objections to the use of the evidence identified in the pretrial disclosure required by Fed.R.Civ.P. 26(a)(3) shall be made before counsel confer regarding the pretrial memorandum, shall be a subject of their conference and shall not be filed with the court unless the objections cannot be resolved. Filing of such objections shall be made pursuant to subsection (D)(12) of this rule.

(D) Obligation of Counsel to Confer and Prepare Pretrial Memorandum. Unless otherwise ordered by the judicial officer to whom the case is assigned for trial, counsel for the parties shall confer no later than 14 days before the date of the final pretrial conference for the purpose of jointly preparing a pretrial memorandum for submission to the judicial officer. Unless otherwise ordered by the judicial officer to whom the case is assigned for trial, the parties are required to file, no later than seven (7) days prior to the pre-trial conference, a joint pretrial memorandum which shall set forth:

(1) a concise summary of the evidence that will be offered by:

(a) plaintiff;

(b) defendant; and

(c) other parties;

with respect to both liability and damages (including special damages, if any);

(2) the facts established by pleadings or by stipulations or admissions of counsel;

(3) contested issues of fact;

(4) any jurisdictional questions;

(5) any questions raised by pending motions;

(6) issues of law, including evidentiary questions, together with supporting authority;

(7) any requested amendments to the pleadings;

(8) any additional matters to aid in the disposition of the action;

(9) the probable length of the trial;

(10) the names, addresses and telephone numbers of witnesses to be called (expert and others) and whether the testimony of any such witness is intended to be presented by deposition;

(11) the proposed exhibits; and

(12) the parties' respective positions on any remaining objections to the evidence identified in the pretrial disclosure required by Fed.R.Civ.P. 26(a)(3).

(E) Conduct of Conference. The agenda of the final pretrial conference, when possible and appropriate, shall include:

(1) a final and binding definition of the issues to be tried;

(2) the disclosure of expected and potential witnesses and the substance of their testimony;

(3) the exchange of all proposed exhibits;

(4) a pretrial ruling on objections to evidence;

(5) the elimination of unnecessary or redundant proof, including the limitation of expert witnesses;

(6) a consideration of the bifurcation of the issues to be tried;

(7) the establishment of time limits and any other restrictions on the trial;

(8) a consideration of methods for expediting jury selection;

(9) a consideration of means for enhancing jury comprehension and simplifying and expediting the trial;

(10) a consideration of the feasibility of presenting direct testimony by written statement;

(11) the exploration of possible agreement among the parties on various issues and encouragement of a stipulation from the parties, when that will serve the ends of justice, including:

(a) that direct testimony of some or all witnesses will be taken in narrative or affidavit form, with right of cross-examination reserved;

(b) that evidence in affidavit form will be read to the jury by the witnesses, or by counsel or another reader with court approval; and (C) that time limits shorter than those set forth in Rule 43.1 be used for trial; and

(12) a consideration of any other means to facilitate and expedite trial.

(F) Trial Brief. A trial brief, including requests for rulings or instructions, shall be filed by each party seven (7) days before the commencement of trial. Each party may supplement these requests at the trial if the evidence develops otherwise than as anticipated.

[Adopted effective October 1, 1992. Amended effective January 2, 1995; December 1, 2009.]

RULE 16.6 SCHEDULING AND PROCEDURES IN PATENT INFRINGEMENT CASES

(A) Additional Items for Consideration by the Court and the Parties. In addition to the parties' obligations under Fed. R. Civ. P. 26 (f) and LR 16.1, the parties in cases raising issues of patent infringement shall consider and address in their joint statement under L.R. 16.1 the following issues:

(1) The timing for disclosing initial infringement and invalidity positions;

(2) The process for identifying disputed claim terms, exchanging proposed claim constructions, and claim construction briefing;

(3) The timing of and procedure for the claim construction hearing, including:

(a) whether the Court will decide claim construction through live testimony at a hearing or based on the papers and attorney argument; and

(b) the timing of claim construction relative to summary judgment, expert discovery, and the close of fact discovery.

(4) The need for tutorials on the relevant technology, including:

(a) the form and scope of any such tutorials; and

(b) the timing for such tutorials.

(5) The identification of dispositive issues that may lead to an early resolution of the litigation.

(6) Whether the court should authorize the filing under seal of any documents that contain confidential information.

(7) Procedures for, and limits (if any) to be placed on, the preservation and discovery of electronically stored information, including:

(a) whether preservation and discovery of electronically stored information should be limited to that located on the parties' active computer systems or extended to backup systems;

(b) the identification of key persons, if any, who should have their electronically stored information produced;

(c) whether production of electronically stored information should be limited to discrete time periods;

(d) whether costs of producing electronically stored information should be shifted, particularly costs of preserving and producing information stored on backup systems.

(B) Scheduling Order. The Scheduling Conference in cases raising issues of patent infringement should result in a special tailored Scheduling Order. A template for such a Scheduling Order is set forth as a default in the Appendix.

Adopted effective November 4, 2008. [See Appendix E. Local Rule 16.6 Supplement].

[Effective November 4, 2008. Amended effective September 7, 2011.]

RULE 26.1 CONTROL OF DISCOVERY

(A) Cooperative Discovery. The judicial officer should encourage cost effective discovery by means of voluntary exchange of information among litigants and their attorneys. This may be accomplished through the use of:

(1) informal, cooperative discovery practices in which counsel provide information to opposing counsel without resort to formal discovery procedures; or

(2) stipulations entered into by the parties with respect to deposition notices, waiver of signing, and other matters, except that the parties may not enter into stipulations extending the time for responding to discovery requests or otherwise modify discovery procedures ordered by the judicial officer.

(B) Disclosure Orders. The judicial officer may order the parties to submit at the scheduling conference, or at any subsequent time the officer deems appropriate, sworn statements disclosing certain information to every other party. At the discretion of the judicial officer, this order may direct the submission of:

(1) a sworn statement from a claimant, whether plaintiff, third-party plaintiff, cross-claimant, or counter-claimant, that:

(a) itemizes all economic loss and provides a computation of damages for which recovery is sought, if any, sustained before the date of service of process;

(b) identifies all persons then known to the claimant or the claimant's attorney who witnessed or participated in the transaction or occurrence giving rise to the claim or otherwise known or believed to have substantial discoverable information about the claim or defenses, together with a statement of the subject and a brief summary of that information;

(c) identifies all opposing parties, and all officers, directors, and employees of opposing parties, from whom statements have been obtained by or on behalf of the claimant regarding the subject matter of the claim; and

(d) identifies all governmental agencies or officials then known to the claimant or the claimant's attorney to have investigated the transaction or occurrence giving rise to the claim; and

(2) a sworn statement from a defendant, whether the direct defendant, third-party defendant, cross-claim defendant, or counterclaim defendant, that identifies:

(a) all persons then known to the defendant or the defendant's attorneys who witnessed the transaction or occurrence giving rise to the claim or otherwise is known or believed to have substantial discoverable information about the claims or defenses, together with a statement of the subject and a brief summary of that information;

(b) all opposing parties, and all officers, directors, and employees of opposing parties, from whom statements have been obtained by or on behalf of the defendant regarding the subject matter of the claims or defenses; and

(c) all government agencies or officials then known to the defendant or the defendant's attorneys to have investigated the transaction or occurrence giving rise to the claims or defenses.

Noncompliance may be excused only by order of the judicial officer.

(C) Discovery Event Limitations. Unless the judicial officer orders otherwise, the number of discovery events shall be limited for each side (or group of parties with a common interest) to ten (10) depositions, twenty-five (25) interrogatories, twenty-five (25) requests for admissions, and two (2) separate sets of requests for production. For purposes of determining the number of interrogatories propounded, subparts of a basic interrogatory which are logical extensions of the basic interrogatory and seek only to obtain specified additional particularized information with respect to the basic interrogatory shall not be counted separately from the basic interrogatory.

[Adopted effective October 1, 1992. Amended effective January 2, 1995.]

RULE 26.2 SEQUENCES OF DISCOVERY

(A) Automatic Required Disclosure. Unless otherwise ordered by the judge, or by the United States

Magistrate Judge who has been assigned the case pursuant to 28 U.S.C. § 636(c), disclosure required by Fed.R.Civ.P. 26(a)(1) should be made as soon as practicable and in any event must be made at or within 14 days after the meeting required by Fed.R.Civ.P. 26(f) and LR 16.1(B). Unless otherwise ordered by such a judicial officer, before a party may initiate discovery, that party must provide to other parties disclosure of the information and materials called for by Fed. R.Civ.P. 26(a)(1).

(B) Further Discovery. Should a party exhaust the opportunities for any type of discovery events under LR 26.1(C), any requests that such party may make for additional interrogatories, depositions, admissions or the production of documents beyond that allowed pursuant to LR 26.1(C) shall be by discovery motion. All requests for additional discovery events, extensions of deadlines, for the completion of discovery or for postponement of the trial must be signed by the attorney and the party making the request.

(C) Certification of Discovery Motions. The judicial officer shall not consider any discovery motion that is not accompanied by a certification, as required by LR 7.1(A)(2) and LR 37.1(B), that the moving party has made a reasonable and good faith effort to reach agreement with opposing counsel on the matters set forth in the motion. In evaluating any discovery motion, the judicial officer may consider the desirability of conducting phased discovery, as contemplated by LR 26.3.

(D) Removed and Transferred Actions. In all actions removed to this court or transferred to this court from another federal court, the submission required by subdivision (A) shall be made as prescribed in that subdivision, and if discovery was initiated before the action being removed or transferred to this court, then the submission required by subdivision (A) shall be made within 21 days of the date of removal or transfer.

[Adopted effective October 1, 1992. Amended effective January 2, 1995; December 10, 1996; December 4, 2000; December 1, 2009.]

RULE 26.3   PHASING OF DISCOVERY

In order to facilitate settlement and the efficient completion of discovery, the judicial officer has discretion to structure discovery activities by phasing and sequencing the topics which are the subject of discovery. For example, an order may be framed limiting the first phase to developing information needed for a realistic assessment of the case. If the case does not terminate, the second phase would be directed at information needed to prepare for trial.

[Adopted effective October 1, 1992. Amended effective January 2, 1995.]

RULE 26.4   SPECIAL PROCEDURES FOR HANDLING EXPERTS

(A) Objections to Expert Witnesses. Unless otherwise directed by the judicial officer, the disclosure regarding experts required by Fed.R.Civ.P. 26(a)(2) shall be made at least 90 days before the final pretrial conference. A party who intends to object to the qualifications of an expert witness, or to the introduction of any proposed exhibit related to that expert's testimony, shall give written notice of the grounds of objection, together with supporting authority, to all other parties no later than the time for such objections provided in LR 16.5(c).

(B) Setting Terms and Conditions. At the final pretrial conference, the judge shall consider:

(1) precluding the appearance of expert witnesses not timely identified;

(2) precluding use of any trial testimony by an expert at variance with any written statement or any deposition testimony;

(3) making a ruling concerning the use of expert depositions, including videotaped depositions at trial; and

(4) making any other ruling on the admissibility of expert testimony at the trial.

[Adopted effective October 1, 1992. Amended effective January 2, 1995.]

RULE 26.5   UNIFORM DEFINITIONS IN DISCOVERY REQUESTS

(A) Incorporation by Reference and Limitations. The full text of the definitions set forth in paragraph (C) is deemed incorporated by reference into all discovery requests, but shall not preclude

(1) the definition of other terms specific to the particular litigation;

(2) the use of abbreviations; or

(3) a narrower definition of a term defined in paragraph (C).

(B) Effect on Scope of Discovery. This rule is not intended to broaden or narrow the scope of discovery permitted by the Federal Rules of Civil Procedure.

(C) Definitions. The following definitions apply to all discovery requests:

(1) *Communication.* The term "communication" means the transmittal of information (in the form of facts, ideas, inquiries, or otherwise).

(2) *Document.* The term "document" is defined to be synonymous in meaning and equal in scope to the usage of this term in Fed.R.Civ.P. 34(a). A draft or

non-identical copy is a separate document within the meaning of this term.

(3) *Identify (With Respect to Persons).* When referring to a person, "to identify" means to give, to the extent known, the person's full name, present or last known address, and, when referring to a natural person, the present or last known place of employment. Once a person has been identified in accordance with this subparagraph, only the name of that person need be listed in response to subsequent discovery requesting the identification of that person.

(4) *Identify (With Respect to Documents).* When referring to documents, "to identify" means to give, to the extent known, the

 (a) type of document;

 (b) general subject matter;

 (c) date of the document; and

 (d) author(s), addressee(s), and recipient(s).

(5) *Parties.* The terms "plaintiff" and "defendant" as well as a party's full or abbreviated name or a pronoun referring to a party mean the party and, where applicable, its officers, directors, employees, partners, corporate parent, subsidiaries, or affiliates. This definition is not intended to impose a discovery obligation on any person who is not a party to the litigation.

(6) *Person.* The term "person" is defined as any natural person or any business, legal, or governmental entity or association.

(7) *Concerning.* The term "concerning" means referring to, describing, evidencing, or constituting.

(8) *State the Basis.* When an interrogatory calls upon a party to "state the basis" of or for a particular claim, assertion, allegation, or contention, the party shall

 (a) identify each and every document (and, where pertinent, the section, article, or subparagraph thereof), which forms any part of the source of the party's information regarding the alleged facts or legal conclusions referred to by the interrogatory;

 (b) identify each and every communication which forms any part of the source of the party's information regarding the alleged facts or legal conclusions referred to by the interrogatory;

 (c) state separately the acts or omissions to act on the part of any person (identifying the acts or omissions to act by stating their nature, time, and place and identifying the persons involved) which form any part of the party's information regarding the alleged facts or legal conclusions referred to in the interrogatory; and

 (d) state separately any other fact which forms the basis of the party's information regarding the alleged facts or conclusions referred to in the interrogatory.

[Adopted effective October 1, 1992.]

RULE 26.6 COURT FILINGS AND COSTS

(A) Nonfiling of Discovery Materials. Automatic or voluntary disclosure materials, depositions upon oral examinations and notices thereof, depositions upon written questions, interrogatories, requests for documents, requests for admissions, answers and responses thereto, and any other requests for or products of the discovery process shall not be filed unless so ordered by the court or for use in the proceeding. The party taking a deposition or obtaining any material through discovery is responsible for its preservation and delivery to the court if needed or so ordered. If for any reason a party or concerned citizen believes that any of the named documents should be filed, an ex parte request may be made that such document be filed, stating the reasons therefor. The court may also order filing sua sponte. If relief is sought under Fed.R.Civ.P. 26(c) or 37, copies of the relevant portions of disputed documents shall be filed with the court contemporaneously with any motion. If the moving party under Fed.R.Civ.P. 56 or the opponent relies on discovery documents, copies of the pertinent parts thereof shall be filed with the motion or opposition.

(B) Copying Expense for Discovery Materials.

(1) *Inspection of Documents.* Except as otherwise provided in an order entered pursuant to Fed.R.Civ.P. 26(c), all parties to an action shall be entitled to inspect documents produced by another party pursuant to Fed.R.Civ.P. 33(c) or 34 at the location where they are produced.

(2) *Copies of Documents.* Except as otherwise provided in an order entered pursuant to Fed.R.Civ.P. 26(c), upon request of any party, and upon that party's agreement to pay the copying costs at the time of delivery, a party who produces documents pursuant to Fed.R.Civ.P. 33(c) or 34 shall provide copies of all or any specified part of the documents. No party shall be entitled to obtain copies of documents produced by another party pursuant to Fed.R.Civ.P. 33(c) or 34 without paying the costs thereof.

[Adopted effective October 1, 1992. Amended effective January 2, 1995.]

RULE 30.1 PLACE FOR TAKING DEPOSITIONS

Unless the court orders otherwise,

(a) Boston is deemed a convenient place for taking of a deposition of any person who resides, is employed, or transacts business in person in Suffolk,

Bristol, Essex, Middlesex, Norfolk or Plymouth Counties;

(b) Springfield is deemed a convenient place for taking the deposition of any person who resides, is employed, or transacts business in person in Berkshire, Franklin, Hampden or Hampshire Counties; and

(c) Worcester is deemed a convenient place for taking the deposition of any person who resides, is employed, or transacts business in person in Worcester County.

[Effective September 1, 1990. Amended effective March 6, 2007.]

RULE 30.2 OPENING OF DEPOSITIONS

(a) If filed, unless the court directs otherwise, depositions taken pursuant to Rule 26, Federal Rules of Civil Procedure, in a pending action shall be opened by the clerk and made available for inspection and copying on request of any party or counsel for any party to the proceeding.

(b) Depositions before action or pending appeal taken pursuant to Rule 27, Federal Rules of Civil Procedure, shall be opened by the clerk and made available for inspection and copying on request of any person served with notice pursuant to subsection (a)(2) of that rule, or by counsel for such person.

[Effective September 1, 1990.]

RULE 33.1 INTERROGATORIES

(A) Form of Response.

(1) Answers and objections in response to interrogatories, served pursuant to Fed.R.Civ.P. 33 shall be made in the order of the interrogatories propounded.

(2) Each answer, statement, or objection shall be preceded by the interrogatory to which it responds.

(3) Each objection and the grounds therefor shall be stated separately.

(B) Reference to Records. Whenever a party answers any interrogatory by reference to records from which the answer may be derived or ascertained, as permitted in Federal Rule of Civil Procedure 33(c):

(1) the specification of documents to be produced shall be in sufficient detail to permit the interrogating party to locate and identify the records and to ascertain the answer as readily as could the party from whom discovery is sought;

(2) the producing party shall make available any computerized information or summaries thereof that it either has, or can adduce by a relatively simple procedure, unless these materials are privileged or otherwise immune from discovery;

(3) the producing party shall provide any relevant compilations, abstracts, or summaries in its custody or readily obtainable by it, unless these materials are privileged or otherwise immune from discovery; and

(4) the documents shall be made available for inspection and copying within fourteen (14) days after service of the answers to interrogatories or at a date agreed upon by the parties.

(C) Objections to Interrogatories.

(1) When an objection is made to any interrogatory, or subpart thereof, it shall state with specificity all grounds upon which the objecting party relies. Any ground not stated in an objection within the time provided by the Federal Rules of Civil Procedure, or any extensions thereof, shall be deemed waived.

(2) No part of an interrogatory shall be left unanswered merely because an objection is interposed to another part of the interrogatory.

(D) Answers to Interrogatories Following Objections. Answers to interrogatories with respect to which objections were served and which are subsequently required to be answered shall be served within fourteen (14) days after it is determined that they should be answered, unless the court directs otherwise.

(E) Claims of Privilege. When a claim of privilege is asserted in objection to any interrogatory, or any sub-part thereof, and an answer is not provided on the basis of that assertion, the attorney asserting the privilege shall identify in the objection the nature of the privilege that is being claimed. If the privilege is being asserted in connection with a claim or defense governed by state law, the attorney asserting the privilege shall indicate the particular privilege rule that is being invoked.

[Adopted effective October 1, 1992. Amended effective January 2, 1995.]

RULE 34.1 DOCUMENT PRODUCTION

(A) Form of Response.

(1) Answers and objections in response to requests for document production, served pursuant to Fed. R.Civ.P. 34 shall be made in the order of the requests propounded.

(2) Each answer, statement, or objection shall be preceded by the request to which it responds.

(3) Each objection and the grounds therefor shall be stated separately.

(B) [RESERVED].

(C) Objections to Document Request.

(1) When an objection is made to any document request, or sub-part thereof, it shall state with specificity all grounds upon which the objecting party

relies. Any ground not stated in an objection within the time provided by the Federal Rules of Civil Procedure, or any extensions thereof, shall be deemed waived.

(2) No part of a document request shall be left unanswered merely because an objection is interposed to another part of the document request.

(D) Answers to Document Request Following Objections. Answers to a document request with respect to which objections were served and which are subsequently required to be answered shall be served within fourteen (14) days after it is determined that they should be answered, unless the court directs otherwise.

(E) Claims of Privilege. When a claim of privilege is asserted in objection to any document request, or any sub-part thereof, and any document is not provided on the basis of that assertion, the attorney asserting the privilege shall identify in the objection the nature of the privilege that is being claimed with respect to each such document. If the privilege is being asserted in connection with a claim or defense governed by state law, the attorney asserting the privilege shall indicate the particular privilege rule that is being invoked.

[Adopted effective October 1, 1992. Amended effective January 2, 1995.]

RULE 35.1 DISCLOSURE OF MEDICAL INFORMATION IN PERSONAL INJURY CASES

(A) Disclosure by Claimants. Fourteen (14) days after an issue is joined by a responsive pleading, a claimant, whether plaintiff, third-party plaintiff, cross-claimant, or counter-claimant, who asserts a claim for personal injuries shall serve defendant, whether the direct defendant, third-party defendant, cross-claim defendant, or counterclaim defendant with

(1) an itemization of all medical expenses incurred before the date of service of the pleading containing the claim for which recovery is sought. If the claimant anticipates that recovery will be sought for future medical expenses, the itemization shall so state, but need not set forth an amount for the anticipated future medical expenses;

(2) a statement that either:

(a) identifies a reasonably convenient location and date, within no more than fourteen (14) days, at which the defendant may inspect and copy, at the defendant's expense, all non-privileged medical records pertaining to the diagnosis, care, or treatment of injuries for which recovery is sought; or

(b) identifies all health care providers from which the claimant has received diagnosis, care, or treatment of injuries for which recovery is sought to-

gether with executed releases directed at each provider authorizing disclosure to the defendant or its counsel of all non-privileged medical records in the provider's possession.

(B) Assertion of Privilege. Insofar as medical records are not produced in accordance with subdivision (a)(2) on the ground of privilege, the claimant shall identify the privileged documents and state the privilege pursuant to which they are withheld.

(C) Removed and Transferred Actions. In all actions removed to this court from a state court or transferred to this court from another federal court, claimants seeking recovery for personal injuries shall provide the information and materials described in subdivision (A) within 21 days after the date of removal or transfer.

[Adopted effective October 1, 1992. Amended effective December 1, 2009.]

RULE 36.1 ADMISSIONS

(A) Requests for Admission—Form of Response.

(1) Statements and objections in response to requests for admission served pursuant to Fed.R.Civ.P. 36 shall be made in the order of the requests for admission propounded.

(2) Each answer, statement, or objection shall be preceded by the request for admission to which it responds.

(3) Each objection and the grounds therefor shall be stated separately.

(B) Statements in Response to Requests for Admission Following Objections. When there is objection to a request for admission and it is subsequently determined that the request is proper, the matter, the admission of which is requested, shall be deemed admitted unless within 14 days after such determination such party to whom the request was directed serves a statement denying the matter or setting forth the reasons why that party cannot admit or deny the matter, as provided in Fed.R.Civ.P. 36.

[Adopted effective October 1, 1992. Amended effective January 2, 1995; December 1, 2009.]

RULE 37.1 DISCOVERY DISPUTES

(A) Before filing any discovery motion, including any motion for sanctions or for a protective order, counsel for each of the parties shall confer in good faith to narrow the areas of disagreement to the greatest possible extent. It shall be the responsibility of counsel for the moving party to arrange for the conference. Conferences may be conducted over the telephone. Failure of opposing counsel to respond to a request for a discovery conference within seven (7) days of the request shall be grounds for sanctions, which may include automatic allowance of the motion.

(B) If (I) opposing counsel has failed to respond to a request for a discovery conference within the seven day period set forth in subdivision (A), (II) opposing counsel has failed to attend a discovery conference within fourteen (14) calendar days of the request, or (III) if disputed issues are not resolved at the discovery conference, a dissatisfied party may file a motion and supporting memorandum. The motion shall include a certificate in the margin of the last page that the provisions of this rule have been complied with. The memorandum shall state with particularity the following:

(1) If a discovery conference was not held, the reasons why it was not;

(2) If a discovery conference was held, the time, date, location and duration of the conference; who was present for each party; the matters on which the parties reached agreement; and the issues remaining to be decided by the court;

(3) The nature of the case and the facts relevant to the discovery matters to be decided;

(4) Each interrogatory, deposition question, request for production, request for admission or other discovery matter raising an issue to be decided by the court, and the response thereto; and

(5) A statement of the moving party's position as to each contested issue, with supporting legal authority, which statement shall be set forth separately immediately following each contested item.

(C) The opposing party may respond to the memorandum within fourteen (14) calendar days after service thereof. The response, if any, shall conform to the requirements of subdivision (B)(5) of this Rule.

[Adopted effective October 1, 1992.]

RULE 40.1   ASSIGNMENT OF CASES

(A) Civil Cases.

(1) *Categories of Cases.* All civil cases shall be divided into the following three categories for purposes of assignment, based upon the numbered Nature of the Suit listed in the civil cover sheet used by the clerk in initiating the civil docket:

I. 410, 441, 470, 535, 830, 891, 893, 895, R.23, regardless of nature of suit.

II. 110, 130, 140, 160, 190, 196, 230, 240, 290, 320, 362, 370, 371, 380, 430, 440, 442, 443, 445, 446, 448, 710, 720, 740, 790, 820, 840, 850

III. 120, 150, 151, 152, 153, 195, 210, 220, 245, 310, 315, 330, 340, 345, 350, 355, 360, 365, 367, 368, 375, 385, 400, 422, 423, 450, 460, 462, 463, 465, 480, 490, 510, 530, 540, 550, 555, 560, 625, 690, 751, 791, 861–865, 890, 896, 899, 950

A copy of the local civil category sheet form referred to is attached as an appendix to this rule.

(2) *Designation of Nature of Suit.* The party filing the initial pleading shall complete a civil cover sheet, Form JS 44, or any successor forms, and file it with the initial pleading. If the clerk should determine that the designation of Nature of Suit is in error, the clerk shall correctly classify the suit and notify the party filing the initial pleading. A designation shall not thereafter be changed except by order of the Chief Judge or the judge to whom the case is assigned.

(3) *Assignment.* The clerk shall place a case in one of the three categories described in subsection (A)(1) and, unless otherwise ordered by the Court, assign it by lot among the judges of the court in active service at their respective duty stations in accordance with this rule in such manner that each such judge shall be assigned as nearly as possible the same number of cases in each category. A senior judge may limit the category of case and nature of suit assigned to that judge and, within the categories of cases or suits that senior judge will accept, assignment shall be by lot in accordance with this rule.

(B) Criminal Cases.

(1) *Categories of Cases.* All criminal cases shall be divided into the following three categories:

I – Felony cases expected to require a combined total of fifteen (15) days or more for pretrial hearings and trial before a district judge.

II – All other felony cases.

III – All misdemeanor and petty offense cases where a district judge has been requested; all Rule 20 cases; cases involving waivers of indictment; and all matters involving alleged violations of conditions of release by persons transferred to this District for supervision.

(2) *Designation of Category.* The attorney for the United States shall identify the appropriate category on Form JS 45, as modified for the District of Massachusetts, or any successor form, and submit the form contemporaneously with the document that initiates the case. If the clerk should determine that the designation of category is in error, the clerk shall correctly classify the case and notify the attorney for the United States. The designation shall not thereafter be changed except by order of the Chief Judge or the judge to whom the case is assigned.

(3) *Assignment.* The clerk shall place a case in one of the three categories described in subsection (B)(1) and, unless otherwise ordered by the Court, assign it by lot among the judges of the court in active service

at their respective active duty stations within the divisions of the court in accordance with this rule in such manner that each judge shall be assigned as nearly as possible the same number of cases in each category. A senior judge may limit the category of cases or types of alleged criminal offenses assigned to that judge and within the categories of cases or offenses that senior judge will accept, assignment shall be in accordance with this rule.

(C) Designation of Divisions. The District of Massachusetts constitutes one judicial district comprising three divisions.

(1) *Eastern Division*. The Eastern Division of the District of Massachusetts comprises the counties of Barnstable, Bristol, Dukes, Essex, Middlesex, Nantucket, Norfolk, Plymouth, and Suffolk. Cases assigned to the Eastern Division and all pleadings and documents therein shall be filed in the clerk's office in Boston.

(2) *Central Division*. The Central Division of the District of Massachusetts is Worcester County. Cases assigned to the Central Division and all pleadings and documents therein shall be filed in the clerk's office in Worcester.

(3) *Western Division*. The Western Division of the District of Massachusetts comprises the counties of Berkshire, Franklin, Hampden and Hampshire. Cases shall be assigned to the Western Division and all pleadings and documents therein shall be filed at the clerk's office in Springfield.

(D) Assignment of Civil Cases.

(1) Civil cases shall be assigned to the respective divisions if:

(a) All of the parties reside in that division.

(b) All of the parties reside in the District of Massachusetts and the majority of the plaintiff(s) reside(s) in that division.

(c) The only parties residing in the District of Massachusetts reside in that division; or

(d) Any of the parties are the United States, the Commonwealth of Massachusetts, or any governmental agency of either the United States or the Commonwealth of Massachusetts and a majority of all other parties resident in the District of Massachusetts reside in that division.

(2) Except as otherwise ordered by the Court, cases not governed by section (D)(1) may be filed, subject to reassignment and transfer, in the division chosen by the plaintiff.

(E) Assignment of Criminal Cases. Criminal cases shall be assigned to that division in which the most significant criminal conduct related to the alleged violations occurred within the District of Massachusetts. All documents in each criminal case shall be

filed in the clerk's office administering cases for the division to which that case is assigned.

(F) Transfer between Divisions. Any case may be transferred from one division to another division on motion of any party for good cause shown or sua sponte for good cause by the judge to whom the case is assigned.

(G) Related Civil Cases.

(1) For purposes of this rule, a civil case is related to one previously filed in this court if some or all of the parties are the same and if one or more of the following similarities exist also: the cases involve the same or similar claims or defenses; or the cases involve the same property, transaction or event; or the cases involve insurance coverage for the same property, transaction or event; or the cases involve substantially the same questions of fact and law. In addition, two cases, one criminal and one civil, are related if the civil case involves forfeiture of property from a transaction or event which is the subject of a previously filed criminal case, or the civil case seeks enforcement of a restitution order or fine imposed in a previously filed criminal case. This rule shall not apply if more than two (2) years have elapsed since the closing of the previous action.

(2) If the party filing the initial pleading believes that the case is related to a case already assigned, whether or not the case is then pending, that party shall notify the clerk by notation on the local civil category sheet indicating the title and number of each such earlier case.

(3) The clerk shall assign related cases to the same judge without regard to the number of other cases in that category previously assigned to that judge. Related cases shall be counted as cases assigned, except as the Chief Judge may otherwise direct.

(4) The assignment of cases as related by the clerk shall be subject to correction only by the judge to whom they have been assigned, who shall return cases erroneously assigned on that basis to the clerk for reassignment.

(5) The treatment of a case as not related to another case shall be subject to correction only by the joint decision of the judge to whom it has been assigned and the judge to whom it should be assigned, if related to another case. The judges may then transfer the case pursuant to section (I) of this rule, and shall notify the clerk of the reason for the transfer.

(H) Proceedings after Assignment. Unless otherwise ordered by the court, all proceedings in a case after its assignment shall be conducted before the judge to whom it has been assigned, except as otherwise provided in these rules. This section does not preclude reassignment of cases by the court or the clerk, at the direction of the court, without prior notice to the parties.

(I) Reassignment and Transfer of Cases. In the interest of justice or to further the efficient performance of the business of the court, a judge may return a case to the clerk for reassignment, whether or not the case is related to any other case, with the approval of the Chief Judge, or, with respect to civil cases only, may transfer the case to another judge, if the other judge consents to the transfer.

(J) Motion for Consolidation of Cases. A motion for consolidation of two or more cases shall be made in the case first filed in this court.

(K) Proceedings after Appeal.

(1) When an appellate court remands a case to this court for a new trial, the case shall be reassigned to a judge other than the judge before whom the first trial was held.

(2) In all other cases in which the mandate of the appellate court requires further proceedings in this court, such proceedings shall not be conducted before the judge before whom the prior proceedings were conducted unless the terms of the remand require that further proceedings be conducted before the original judge or unless the judge determines that there will result a substantial saving in the time of the whole court and that there is no reason why, in the interest of justice, further proceedings should be conducted before another judge. If the judge before whom the prior proceedings were conducted does not retain the case for further proceedings, that judge shall return it to the clerk for reassignment.

[Effective September 1, 1990. Amended effective January 1, 2001; August 2, 2011; January 3, 2012.]

RULE 40.2   CONFLICT OF COURT APPEARANCES

(A) Order of Preference and Notice to Clerks. In situations where counsel, including Assistant United States Attorneys, have conflicting court appearances among cases pending before different judges or magistrates of this court, the following order of preference shall apply, except as otherwise provided by law:

(1) Trials shall take precedence over all other hearings, and jury trials shall take precedence over nonjury trials.

(2) Criminal cases shall take precedence over civil cases.

(3) Criminal cases involving defendants who are in custody pending trial in the particular case shall take precedence over other criminal cases.

(4) Among civil cases or among criminal cases not involving defendants in custody, the case having the earliest docket number shall take precedence over the others.

When such conflicts appear, the counsel involved shall notify the deputy clerk assigned to each judge concerned, in writing, not later than seven (7) days after the receipt of the notice or calendar giving rise to such conflict. The notice shall contain the names and docket number of each case, the time of the scheduled hearings in each case, the purpose thereof, and advise which case has precedence and the reason therefor. Upon receipt of such notice and a determination that a conflict in fact exists, the case or cases not having precedence shall be rescheduled.

(B) Substitution of Counsel. Counsel, in lieu of giving a notice of conflict, may elect to have a colleague, including another Assistant United States Attorney, handle the matter for the counsel involved. This shall not apply to any appointed defense counsel in the trial of criminal cases, unless the judicial officer orders otherwise.

(C) Primacy of Speedy Trial Plan. In the event of any conflict between the provisions of this rule and the provisions of the Speedy Trial Plan for the District of Massachusetts, the Speedy Trial Plan shall control.

(D) Scheduling Policy Regarding Superior Court Cases. When counsel have engagement conflicts with respect to cases pending in the Massachusetts Superior Court and The United States District Court for the District of Massachusetts, the following scheduling policy shall apply:

(1) Trials shall take precedence over all other hearings.

(2) Jury trials shall take precedence over nonjury trials.

(3) Criminal cases shall take precedence over civil cases.

(4) Criminal cases involving defendants who are in custody pending trial shall take precedence over other criminal cases.

(5) Among civil cases, or among criminal cases not involving defendants in custody, the case having the earliest docket number shall take precedence over the others, except that a trial setting involving numerous parties and counsel will ordinarily take precedence over other trials.

Counsel shall notify the presiding Superior Court Justice and U.S. District Judge of the scheduling conflict, in writing, not later than seven (7) days after the receipt of the scheduling order giving rise to the conflict. Counsel's notification shall include: a) the names and docket numbers of each case, b) the date and time of the scheduled proceedings in each case, and c) a brief statement as to which case has precedence under this policy. The case or cases not having precedence shall be rescheduled, unless the presiding Justice and Judge agree otherwise. In the event of any conflict between the provisions of this policy and the provisions of the Speedy Trial Plan for the District of Massachusetts, the Speedy Trial Plan shall have precedence.

[Effective September 1, 1990. Amended effective January 2, 1995; December 1, 2009.]

RULE 40.3 CONTINUANCES

(A) A motion for the continuance of a trial, evidentiary hearing, or any other proceeding, will be granted only for good cause.

(B) Motions to continue discovery and pretrial conferences will not be entertained unless the date and time of the pretrial conference are set out in the motion as well as a statement of how many other requests, if any, for continuances have been sought and granted.

(C) Illness of parties and material witnesses shall be substantiated by a current medical certificate.

(D) The judicial officer may condition a continuance upon the payment of expenses caused to the other parties and of jury fees incurred by the court.

[Effective September 1, 1990. Amended effective October 1, 1992.]

RULE 40.4 EMERGENCIES AND SPECIAL PROCEEDINGS

(a) Matters and Proceedings Heard by Miscellaneous Business Docket (MBD) Judge. There will be designated an MBD judge to hear and determine:

(1) Emergency matters requiring immediate action in cases already assigned to any judge of the court, if the judge to whom a case had been assigned is unavailable or otherwise unable to hear the matter.

(2) Special proceedings, the nature of which precludes their assignment in the ordinary course, e.g., motions relating to grand jury investigations, discovery in cases pending in other districts, enforcement of administrative subpoenas; and

(3) Any other proceedings, including an admission to the bar and a naturalization, which are not part of or related to a case that should be assigned in the ordinary course.

(b) Disposition of "Emergency" Matters. The MBD judge will dispose of matters pursuant to subsection (a)(1), only to the extent necessary to meet the emergency. So far as practicable, consistent with justice and the efficient performance of the business of the court, the matter will be continued for disposition by the judge to whom the case is assigned.

(c) Subsequent "Emergency" Proceedings. If the MBD judge before whom the proceeding is brought concludes that, for lack of an emergency or otherwise, the proceeding should not be determined under this rule, the party who brought the proceeding shall not thereafter present the same matter to any other judge sitting as MBD judge, unless relevant circumstances change in the interim, in which case he shall bring to the attention of such other judge the prior proceeding and the changed circumstances which warrant resubmission of the matter under this rule.

(d) Special and Other Proceedings. Proceedings pursuant to subsections (a)(2) and (3) shall continue before the judge first handling the matter until conclusion.

[Effective September 1, 1990.]

RULE 41.1 DISMISSAL FOR WANT OF PROSECUTION

(a)(1) Whenever in any civil action the clerk shall ascertain that no proceeding has been docketed therein for a period of one (1) year, he shall then mail notice to all persons who have entered an appearance in such a case that, subject to the provisions of subsection (a)(3), the case will be dismissed without further notice 28 days after the sending of the notice.

(2) After the 28th day following the sending of the notice, without order of the court the clerk shall, subject to the provisions of subsection (a)(3), enter an order of dismissal for all cases on the list. It shall not be necessary for the clerk to send additional notice of the dismissal to any counsel or party.

(3) A case shall not be dismissed for lack of prosecution if within 28 days of the sending of notice an explanation for the lack of proceedings is filed and the judge to whom the case is assigned orders that it not be dismissed.

(b)(1) Additionally, each judge may from time to time give notice of not less than 21 days of hearing on a dismissal calendar for actions or proceedings assigned to that judge that appear not to have been diligently prosecuted. Unless otherwise ordered by the assigned judge, each party shall, not less than 14 days prior to the noticed hearing date, serve and file a certificate describing the status of the action or proceeding and showing that good cause exists for the court to retain the case on the docket. Nothing in this rule precludes the filing of a motion for dismissal under Rule 41(b) of the Federal Rules of Civil Procedure.

(2) Failure on the part of the plaintiff to file the required statement or his failure to appear at the scheduled hearing shall be grounds for the dismissal of the action.

(c) The dismissal of a case pursuant to this rule shall not operate as an adjudication on the merits unless the court on motion of a party directs otherwise.

[Effective September 1, 1990. Amended effective December 1, 2009.]

RULE 43.1 TRIAL

(A) Time Limits for Evidentiary Hearing.

(1) Absent agreement of the parties as to the time limits for the trial acceptable to the judicial officer, the judicial officer may order a presumptive limit of a specified number of hours. This time shall be allocated equally between opposing parties, or groups of aligned parties, unless otherwise ordered for good cause.

(2) A request for added time will be allowed only for good cause. In determining whether to grant a motion for an increased allotment of time, the court will take into account:

(a) whether or not the moving party has

(1) used the time since the commencement of trial in a reasonable and proper way, and

(2) complied with all orders regulating the trial;

(b) the moving party's explanation as to the way in which the requested added time would be used and why it is essential to assure a fair trial; and

(c) any other relevant and material facts the moving party may wish to present in support of the motion.

The court will be receptive to motions for reducing or increasing the allotted time to assure that the distribution is fair among the parties and adequate for developing the evidence.

(B) Evidence at the Evidentiary Hearing.

(1) Each party shall give advance notice to the judicial officer and the other parties, before jury selection, of the identity of all witnesses whose testimony it may offer during trial, whether by affidavit, deposition, or oral testimony.

(2) Not later than seven (7) days before it seeks to use the testimony of any witness, or on shorter notice for good cause shown, a party shall advise the judicial officer and all other parties of its intent to use the testimony of the witness on a specified day.

(3) Except for good cause shown, no party shall be allowed to:

(a) use the testimony of a witness other than the witnesses already listed on the filing with the court before trial commences; or

(b) introduce documentary evidence, during direct examination, other than those exhibits already listed with the judicial officer and furnished to the other parties before trial commences.

[Adopted effective October 1, 1992. Amended effective December 1, 2009.]

RULE 48.1 [DELETED]

[Deleted effective January 2, 1995.]

RULE 54.3 [DELETED]

[Deleted effective January 2, 1995.]

RULE 56.1 MOTIONS FOR SUMMARY JUDGMENT

Motions for summary judgment shall include a concise statement of the material facts of record as to which the moving party contends there is no genuine issue to be tried, with page references to affidavits, depositions and other documentation. Failure to include such a statement constitutes grounds for denial of the motion. Opposition to motions for summary judgment must be filed, unless the court orders otherwise, within 21 days after the motion is served. A party opposing the motion shall include a concise statement of the material facts of record as to which it is contended that there exists a genuine issue to be tried, with page references to affidavits, depositions and other documentation. Copies of all referenced documentation shall be filed as exhibits to the motion or opposition. Material facts of record set forth in the statement required to be served by the moving party will be deemed for purposes of the motion to be admitted by opposing parties unless controverted by the statement required to be served by opposing parties. Unless the court orders otherwise, the moving party may file a reply within 14 days after the response is served.

[Effective September 1, 1990; amended effective December 1, 2009.]

RULE 58.2 SATISFACTION OF JUDGMENTS

(a) Satisfaction of a money judgment shall be entered by the clerk without order of the court:

(1) On payment into court of the amount of the judgment including costs taxed, plus interest, and the amount of any fees due; or

(2) On the filing of a satisfaction of judgment executed by the judgment creditor, or his legal representative or assignees with evidence of their authority, or his attorney in the proceeding in which judgment has been entered; or

(3) On the filing of a satisfaction of judgment executed by the United States Attorney, if the judgment is in favor of the United States; or

(4) On registration of a certified copy of a satisfaction of judgment entered in another district court.

(b) When satisfaction is made by payment of money into court, that fact shall be noted in the entry of satisfaction.

(c) Entry of judgment shall constitute sufficient authorization for the clerk to accept payment into court.

(d) Mandate of an Appellate Court. An order or judgment of an appellate court in a case appealed from this court shall, if further proceedings are not required, become the order or judgment of this court and be entered as such on receipt of the mandate of the appellate court.

[Effective September 1, 1990.]

RULE 62.2 SUPERSEDEAS BOND

A supersedeas bond staying execution of a money judgment shall be in the amount of the judgment plus ten (10%) percent of the amount to cover interest and any award of damages for delay plus Five Hundred and no/100 ($500.00) Dollars to cover costs, unless the court directs otherwise.

[Effective September 1, 1990.]

RULE 67.1 SURETIES

(a) Members of the Bar and Court Officers. No judge, clerk, marshal, member of the bar or other officer or employee of the court may be surety or guarantor of any bond or undertaking in any proceeding in this court.

(b) Form of Bond. Surety bonds shall be signed and acknowledged by the party and his surety or sureties. They shall refer to the statute, rule, or court order under which given, state the conditions of the obligation, and contain a provision expressly subjecting them to all applicable federal statutes and rules.

(c) Security. Except as otherwise provided by law or by order of the court, a bond or similar undertaking must be secured by:

(1) The deposit of cash or obligations of the United States in the amount of the bond (note Rule 67.4 with regard to the court's cash policy); or

(2) The guaranty of a company or corporation holding a certificate of authority from the Secretary of the Treasury pursuant to 6 U.S.C. § 8; or

(3) The guaranty of two (2) individual residents of this district each of whom owns unencumbered real or personal property within the district worth the amount of the bond, in excess of legal obligations and exemptions.

(d) Deposits of cash or obligations of the United States shall be accompanied by a written statement, duly acknowledged, that the signer is owner thereof, that the same is subject to the conditions of the bond, and that the clerk may collect or sell the obligations and apply the proceeds, or the cash deposited, in case of default as provided in the bond. Upon satisfaction of the conditions of the bond, the monies or obligations shall be returned to the owner on the order of a magistrate or district judge.

(e) Individual Sureties. An individual acting as surety, pursuant to subsection (c)(3), shall file an affidavit:

(1) Giving his name, occupation, and residential and business address;

(2) Showing that he is qualified to act as surety; and

(3) [In criminal cases] stating that he will not encumber or dispose of the property on which his qualification as surety depends while the bond remains in effect.

(f) Approval of Bond. Except as otherwise provided by law, the Clerk of Court may approve a bond in the amount fixed by the court or by statute or rule, and secured in the manner provided by subsections (c)(1) or (2). All other bonds must be approved by the court.

(g) Service. The party on whose behalf a bond is given shall promptly, after approval and filing of the bond, serve a copy of it on all other parties to the proceeding, but such service need not be made on the United States in a criminal case.

(h) Modification of Bond. The amount or terms of a bond or similar undertaking may be changed at any time as justice requires, by order of the court on its own motion or on motion of a party.

(i) Further Security. The court may order a party to furnish further or different security, or require personal sureties to furnish further justification.

[Effective September 1, 1990.]

RULE 67.2 DEPOSIT IN COURT

The following procedures apply to deposits into the registry of the Court in civil actions.

(a) Receipt of Funds.

(1) No money may be sent to the Court or its officers for deposit into the Court's registry without a Court order by the presiding judge in the case or proceeding.

(2) All money ordered to be paid to the Court or received by its officers in any case pending or adjudicated shall be deposited with the Treasurer of the United States in the name and to the credit of this

Court pursuant to 28 U.S.C. § 2041 through depositories designated by the Treasury to accept such deposit on its behalf.

(3) The party making the deposit or transferring funds to the Court's registry shall serve the order permitting the deposit or transfer on the Clerk of Court.

(b) Investment of Registry Funds.

(1) Funds on deposit with the Court will be placed in interest-bearing instruments in the Court Registry Investment System (CRIS) administered by the Administrative Office of the United States Courts, which is the only investment mechanism authorized.

(2) Under CRIS, monies deposited in each case under Local Civil Rule 67.2(a) shall be "pooled" together with those on deposit with the Treasury to the credit of other courts in CRIS and used to purchase Government Account Series securities through the Bureau of Public Debt, which will be held at Treasury, in an account in the name and to the credit of the Director of Administrative Office of the United States Courts, hereby designated custodian for the Court Registry Investment System.

(3) An account for each case will be established in CRIS titled in the name of the case giving rise to the investment in the fund. Income generated from fund investments will be distributed to each case based on the ratio each account's principal and earnings has to the aggregate principal and income total in the fund. Reports showing the interest earned and the principal amounts contributed in each case will be prepared and distributed to each court participating in CRIS and made available to litigants and/or their counsel.

(c) Deductions of Fees.

(1) The custodian is authorized and directed by this Local Civil Rule to deduct the registry fee for maintaining accounts in CRIS and the investment service fee for the management of investments. The proper registry fee is to be determined on the basis of the rates published by the Director of the Administrative Office of the United States as approved by the Judicial Conference. The investment service fee is assessed from interest earning according to the Court's Miscellaneous Fee Schedule.

(2) If registry fees were assessed against the case under the old 45–day requirement prior to deposit in CRIS, no additional registry fee will be assessed.

[Effective September 1, 1990. Amended effective October 3, 2005; June 7, 2011.]

RULE 67.3 DISBURSEMENT OF REGISTRY FUNDS

The clerk shall not distribute any registry funds without an order of a district judge of this court. All orders for distribution, unless prepared by a deputy clerk assigned to the financial section of the clerk's office, must be approved by the clerk before presentation to a district judge.

All checks drawn by the Clerk of Court on deposits made in the registry of the court shall be made payable to the order of the payee(s) as the name(s) thereof appear in the orders of this court providing for distribution.

Disbursement from the registry of the court shall be made in accordance with the terms and at the time provided in the order for disbursement, or immediately upon receipt of the order if no time is specified, except in cases where it is necessary to allow time for a check or draft to clear. Prior to distribution, any party claiming an interest in the funds may move the court for a stay of the disbursement order pending appeal.

(a) Payees. If more than one check is to be issued on a single order, the portion due to each payee must be set out separately. In all cases, counsel must furnish the clerk with the address and social security number or taxpayer identification number of each recipient, and this number shall be included in the court order for release of funds.

(b) Disbursement of Monies Other Than Registry Funds. All disbursements to individuals made by the clerk of this court of monies received in his official capacity, other than registry funds, when made by check of the clerk on the Treasury of the United States, shall be made to the payee as the name shall appear in the disbursement voucher certified by the clerk or his designated certifying officer. The name of the payee in the disbursement voucher shall conform to the name appearing in the clerk's records of the case to which the disbursement relates. The clerk shall endeavor to note of record the given name of all individuals making deposits of monies with the clerk, and in those cases where the given name appears of record, disbursement vouchers and checks thereunder shall show the full given name, additional initials, if any, and the surname of the payee.

(c) Escrow Agents. In lieu of these provisions, an interested party may apply to the court for appointment of escrow agents. Such agents may deposit funds in a financial institution in an interest-bearing account and provide for the disposition of interest so earned, as approved by the court.

[Effective September 1, 1990.]

RULE 67.4 PAYMENTS AND DEPOSITS MADE WITH THE CLERK

(a) The clerk will not routinely accept payments or deposits in cash; but the court, on motion of any party, may order that the clerk accept cash in a particular instance.

(b) All checks must be made payable to "Clerk, United States District Court." The clerk is authorized to refuse any check not so made payable.

(c) The clerk may, in his discretion, require any payment to be made by certified check or its equivalent. The clerk shall require payment of bail to be made by certified check or its equivalent, unless otherwise ordered by the court.

(d) When electronically filing any pleading or paper through CM/ECF that requires a fee, all registered ECF users are to pay the fee electronically through the Treasury Department's Internet payment process (pay.gov). Pro se filers and those who have been exempted from electronic filing and/or electronic payment of fees may submit payments by check or money order made payable to "Clerk, U.S. District Court".

[Effective September 1, 1990. Amended effective January 1, 2009.]

RULE 68.2   SETTLEMENT

When a case is settled, the parties shall file in the office of the clerk a signed agreement for judgment or stipulation for dismissal, as appropriate, within 28 days, unless the court otherwise orders.

[Effective September 1, 1990. Amended effective December 1, 2009.]

RULE 77.1   SITTINGS

(a) The court shall be in continuous session for transacting judicial business on all business days throughout the year at Boston, Worcester and Springfield.

(b) Any judge of the court may, in the interest of justice or to further efficient performance of the business of the court, conduct proceedings at a special session at any time, anywhere in the district, on request of a party or otherwise.

[Effective September 1, 1990. Amended effective January 1, 2001.]

RULE 77.2   OFFICE OF THE CLERK

The offices of the Clerk of Court at Boston, Worcester and Springfield shall be open from 8:30 a.m. until 5:00 p.m. on all days except Saturdays, Sundays, legal holidays and other days so ordered by the court and announced in advance, if feasible.

[Effective September 1, 1990.]

RULE 79.1   EXHIBITS

(a) Custody. Unless otherwise ordered by the court, all exhibits marked in evidence or for identification shall remain in the custody of the party that introduced them. Exhibits shall be preserved in the form in which they were offered until the proceeding is finally concluded. The party having custody shall make the exhibits available to all parties.

(b) Any party may move the court for custody arrangements that differ from those in section (a) upon a showing of good cause. The court may, on its own motion, provide for different custody arrangements or modify existing arrangements at any time.

(c) A court order that the clerk take custody of any exhibit shall specify the period during which the clerk shall maintain custody, the party to whom the exhibit shall be returned at the end of the period, and provision for destruction by the clerk without further notice to the parties at a set time after expiration of the custody period, if the party to whom the exhibit is to be returned fails to remove it from the custody of the clerk. Such court order shall constitute the only notice required for the purpose of exhibit disposal.

(d) It shall be sufficient if orders under the above sections are in writing, signed by the court or the clerk at the direction of the court, or are entered orally on the record and the substance of the order is reproduced on the docket sheet.

(e) Photographs of Chalks. In order to make a record of a chalk, the court may permit a party to photograph it or otherwise copy it, on such terms as are just. Unless otherwise ordered by the court, in jury cases chalks may be destroyed by the clerk as soon as the jury verdict has been recorded; in nonjury cases, chalks may be destroyed as soon as the evidence is closed.

[Effective September 1, 1990.]

RULE 81.1   REMOVAL

(a) Within 28 days after filing a notice for removal of an action from a state court to this court pursuant to 28 U.S.C. § 1446, the party filing the notice shall file certified or attested copies of all records and proceedings in the state court and a certified or attested copy of all docket entries in the state court.

(b) If the clerk of this court has not received the papers required to be filed under section (a) within 42 days of the filing of the notice for removal, the case shall be remanded to the state court from which it was removed, unless this court directs otherwise.

(c) When a case is remanded to a state court, the clerk shall mail certified copies of the docket and order of remand, together with the remainder of the original file, to the clerk of the state court.

[Effective September 1, 1990. Amended effective December 1, 2009.]

RULE 81.2   DEFINITION OF JUDICIAL OFFICER

As used in these rules, "judicial officer" refers to either a United States District Court Judge or a

United States Magistrate Judge. For purposes of LR 83.6(5)(A), the term "judicial officer" also refers to a United States Bankruptcy Judge.

[Adopted effective October 1, 1992. Amended effective August 1, 1997.]

RULE 83.1A   PROCEDURE FOR ADOPTING, RESCINDING AND AMENDING RULES [RESCINDED]

[Effective September 1, 1990; rescinded effective March 2, 2010.]

RULE 83.1B   GENERAL ORDER DOCKET

(a) Effective upon the adoption of these local rules, the clerk shall establish and maintain one (1) general order docket for each calendar year.

(b) All rules, administrative orders or directives of the court and amendments thereto shall bear a general order number assigned by the clerk, and be entered on the general order docket.

(c) The clerk shall place all prior administrative orders and directives, if they remain in effect at the time of adoption of these rules, on the general order docket for the year in which these rules are adopted.

(d) Any judge of this court may enter standing orders for his session, and may direct the clerk to maintain a docket therefor in accordance with sections (a) through (c).

[Effective September 1, 1990.]

RULE 83.2A   RELEASE OF INFORMATION BY ATTORNEYS

No lawyer or law firm shall release or authorize the release of information or opinion which a reasonable person would expect to be disseminated by means of public communication, in connection with pending or imminent criminal litigation with which he or the firm is associated, if there is a reasonable likelihood that such dissemination will interfere with a fair trial or otherwise prejudice the due administration of justice.

With respect to a grand jury or other pending investigation of any criminal matter, a lawyer participating in or associated with the investigation shall refrain from making any extrajudicial statement, which a reasonable person would expect to be disseminated by means of public communication, that goes beyond the public record or that is not necessary to inform the public that the investigation is underway, to describe the general scope of the investigation, to obtain assistance in the apprehension of a suspect, to warn the public of any dangers, or otherwise to aid in the investigation.

From the time of arrest, issuance of an arrest warrant, or the filing of a complaint, information, or indictment in any criminal matter until the commencement of trial or disposition without trial, a lawyer or law firm associated with the prosecution or defense shall not release or authorize the release of any extrajudicial statement, which a reasonable person would expect to be disseminated by means of public communication, relating to that matter and concerning:

(1) The prior criminal record (including arrests, indictments, or other charges of crime), or the character or reputation of the accused, except that the lawyer or law firm may make a factual statement of the accused's name, age, residence, occupation, and family status, and if the accused has not been apprehended, a lawyer associated with the prosecution may release any information necessary to aid in his apprehension or to warn the public of any dangers he may present;

(2) The existence or contents of any confession, admission, or statement given by the accused, or the refusal or failure of the accused to make any statement;

(3) The performance of any examinations or tests or the accused's refusal or failure to submit to an examination or test;

(4) The identity, testimony, or credibility of prospective witnesses, except that the lawyer or law firm may announce the identity of the victim if the announcement is not otherwise prohibited by law;

(5) The possibility of a plea of guilty to the offense charged or a lesser offense; and

(6) Any opinion as to the accused's guilt or innocence as to the merits of the case or the evidence in the case.

The foregoing shall not be construed to preclude the lawyer or law firm during this period, in the proper discharge of his or its official or professional obligations, from announcing the facts and circumstances of arrest (including time and place of arrest, resistance, pursuit, and use of weapons), the identity of the investigating and arresting officer or agency, and the length of the investigation; from making an announcement, at the time of seizure of any physical evidence other than a confession, admission or statement, which is limited to a description of the evidence seized; from disclosing the nature, substance, or text of the charge, including a brief description of the offense charged; from quoting or referring without comment to public records of the court in the case; from announcing the scheduling or result of any stage in the judicial process; from requesting assistance in obtaining evidence; or from announcing without further comment that the accused denies the charges made against him.

During the trial of any criminal matter, including the period of selection of the jury, no lawyer or law firm associated with the prosecution or defense shall give or authorize any extrajudicial statement or interview relating to the trial or the parties or issues in the trial which a reasonable person would expect to be disseminated by means of public communication, except that the lawyer or law firm may quote from or refer without comment to public records of the court in the case.

After the completion of a trial or disposition without trial of any criminal matter, and prior to the imposition of sentence, a lawyer or law firm associated with the prosecution or defense shall refrain from making or authorizing any extrajudicial statement which a reasonable person would expect to be disseminated by means of public communication if there is a reasonable likelihood that such dissemination will affect the imposition of sentence.

Nothing in this rule is intended to preclude the formulation or application of more restrictive rules relating to the release of information about juvenile or other offenders, to preclude the holding of hearings or the lawful issuance of reports by legislative, administrative, or investigative bodies, or to preclude any lawyer from replying to charges of misconduct that are publicly made against him.

A lawyer or law firm associated with a civil action shall not during its investigation or litigation make or participate in making an extrajudicial statement, other than a quotation from or reference to public records, which a reasonable person would expect to be disseminated by means of public communication if there is a reasonable likelihood that such dissemination will interfere with a fair trial and which relates to:

(1) Evidence regarding the occurrence or transaction involved

(2) The character, credibility, or criminal record of a party, witness, or prospective witness

(3) The performance or results of any examination or tests or the refusal or failure of a party to submit to such

(4) His opinion as to the merits of the claims or defenses of a party, except as required by law or administrative rule

(5) Any other matter reasonably likely to interfere with a fair trial of the action

[Effective September 1, 1990.]

RULE 83.2B SPECIAL ORDERS FOR THE PROTECTION OF THE ACCUSED OR THE LITIGANTS IN WIDELY PUBLICIZED OR SENSATIONAL CRIMINAL OR CIVIL CASES

In a widely publicized or sensational criminal or civil case, the court, on motion of either party or on its own motion, may issue a special order governing such matters as extrajudicial statements by parties and witnesses likely to interfere with the rights of the accused or the litigants to a fair trial by an impartial jury, the seating and conduct in the courtroom of spectators and news media representatives, the management and sequestration of jurors and witnesses, and any other matters which the court may deem appropriate for inclusion in such an order.

[Effective September 1, 1990.]

RULE 83.3 PHOTOGRAPHING, RECORDING, AND BROADCASTING

(a) **Photographing, Recording, and Broadcasting Generally Prohibited.** Except as specifically provided in these rules or by order of the court, no person shall take any photograph, make any recording, or make any broadcast by any means, in the course of or in connection with any proceedings in this court, on any floor of any building on which proceedings of this court are or, in the regular course of the business of the court, may be held.

(b) **Exceptions.**

(1) *Court Reporters.* Official court reporters are not prohibited from making voice recordings for the sole purpose of discharging their official duties. No recording made for that purpose shall be used for any other purpose by any person.

(2) *Presentation of Evidence.* The court may permit the use of electronic or photographic means for the preservation of evidence or the perpetuation of a record.

(3) *Miscellaneous Proceedings.* The court may permit the broadcasting, televising, recording, or photographing of investitive, ceremonial, or naturalization proceedings.

(4) *File Review.* The use of dictation equipment is permitted in the clerk's office by persons reviewing files in that office.

[Effective September 1, 1990. Amended effective September 6, 2011.]

RULE 83.3.1 RULE GOVERNING THE PILOT PROGRAM ON PHOTOGRAPHING, RECORDING AND BROADCASTING CIVIL PROCEEDINGS IN THE COURTROOM [EXPIRED JUNE 30, 1994]

(A) **General Provisions.**

(1) This rule applies to all civil proceedings in any session of the United States District Court and the Bankruptcy Court of the District of Massachusetts. The term "presiding judicial officer" applies to the judicial officer presiding in any such session.

(2) Reasonable advance notice is required from the media of a request to be present to broadcast, televise, record electronically, or take photographs at a particular session. Where possible, such notice should be given prior to the end of the preceding business day, but in no event later than one hour prior to the commencement of the proceedings. In the absence of such notice, the presiding judicial officer may refuse to permit media coverage. The presiding judicial officer may also waive such notice requirement.

(3) A presiding judicial officer may refuse, limit, or terminate media coverage of an entire case, portions thereof, or testimony of particular witnesses, in the interests of justice to protect the rights of the parties, witnesses, and the dignity of the court; to assure the orderly conduct of the proceedings; or for any other reason considered necessary or appropriate by the presiding judicial officer.

(4) No direct public expense is to be incurred for equipment, wiring, or personnel needed to provide media coverage.

(5) Nothing in this rule shall prevent the court from placing additional restrictions, or prohibiting altogether, photographing, recording, or broadcasting in designated areas of the courthouse. The provisions of this experimental rule pertain only to photographing, recording, and broadcasting in the courtroom. In all other areas of the courthouse, the provisions of Local Rule 83.3 remain in full force and effect.

(6) This rule takes effect July 1, 1991, and expires June 30, 1994.

(B) Limitations.

(1) Coverage of criminal proceedings is prohibited.

(2) There shall be no audio pickup or broadcast of conferences which occur in a court facility between attorneys and their clients, between co-counsel of a client, or between counsel and the presiding judicial officer, at the bench or in chambers.

(3) No coverage of the jury, or of any juror or alternate juror, while in the jury box, in the courtroom, in the jury deliberation room, or during recess, or while going to or from the deliberation room at any time, shall be permitted. Coverage of the prospective jury during voir dire is also prohibited.

(C) Equipment and Personnel.

(1) Not more than one television camera, operated by not more than one camera person and related equipment at any one time, shall be permitted in any court proceeding.

(2) Not more than one still photographer, utilizing not more than one camera and related equipment at any one time, shall be permitted in any court proceeding. More than one camera may be brought into the courtroom, provided that only one camera may be used at any one time.

(3) If two or more media representatives apply to cover a proceeding, no such coverage may begin until all such representatives have agreed upon a pooling arrangement for their respective news media. Such pooling arrangements shall include the designation of pool operators, procedures for cost sharing, access to and dissemination of material and selection of a pool representative if appropriate. The presiding judicial officer may not be called upon to mediate or resolve any dispute as to such arrangements.

(4) Equipment or clothing shall not bear the insignia or marking of a media agency. Camera operators shall wear appropriate business attire.

(D) Sound and Light Criteria.

(1) Equipment shall not produce distracting sound or light. Signal lights or devices to show when equipment is operating shall not be visible. Motorized drives, moving lights, flash attachments, or sudden light changes shall not be used. All equipment shall use existing light only.

(2) Except as otherwise approved by the presiding judicial officer, existing courtroom sound and light systems shall be used without modification. Audio pickup for all media purposes shall be accomplished from existing audio systems present in the court facility, or from a television camera's built-in microphone. If no technically suitable audio system exists in the court facility, microphones and related wiring essential for media purposes shall be unobtrusive and shall be located in places designated in advance of any proceeding by the presiding judicial officer.

(E) Location of Equipment and Personnel.

(1) The presiding judicial officer shall designate the location in the courtroom for the camera equipment and operators. Such location may be designated in advance of any request, and where possible, should be outside of the direct line of sight between the jury box and the witness stand.

(2) During the proceedings, operating personnel shall not move about nor shall there be placement, movement, or removal of equipment. All such activities shall take place each day before the proceeding begins, after it ends, or during a recess.

(F) Compliance. Any media representative who fails to comply with the rule shall be subject to appropriate sanction, as determined by the presiding judicial officer.

(G) Review. This rule shall not be construed to create any litigable rights or right to appellate review.

Accordingly, a grant or denial of media coverage shall not be litigable or appealable, except as otherwise provided by law.

(H) Compliance With Rule 83.3. Except as specifically provided in this rule, the prohibitions contained in LR 83.3 shall remain in full force and effect.

[Adopted September 1, 1990; expired June 30, 1994.]

RULE 83.3.2 PARTICIPATION IN PILOT PROGRAM

Notwithstanding the general prohibition on photographing, recording, and broadcasting of district court proceedings set forth in Local Rule 83.3, the District Court may participate in the three year pilot program established by the Judicial Conference of the United States in September 2010 (JCUS–SEP 10, pp. 3–4) to study the use of cameras in district courtrooms for civil case proceedings.

Any recording and broadcasting conducted pursuant to the pilot program must comply with the program guidelines issued by the Judicial Conference Committee on Court Administration and Case Management, pursuant to the pilot program (available at www. uscourts.gov).

[Effective September 6, 2011.]

RULE 83.4 COURTROOM SEARCHES; COURTROOM SEATING

(a) All persons entering a courtroom are subject to search by the United States Marshal, a Deputy United States Marshal, or any other officer authorized by the court, as are all briefcases, parcels or other containers carried by persons entering a courtroom.

(b) Except by leave of the judge or magistrate presiding at a particular session of this court, only members of the bar of this court may be seated within the bar enclosure.

(c) With the exception of weapons carried by the United States Marshal, Deputy United States Marshals, or Federal Protective Officers, no weapons, other than exhibits, are permitted in any courtroom. No other person, including any federal law enforcement agent, shall bring a weapon other than an exhibit into any courtroom, except as specifically set forth below with respect to the courtrooms of the United States District Judges or United States Magistrates. No firearms intended for introduction as an exhibit may be brought into any courtroom unless it is first presented to the marshal for a safety check and the marshal reports to the clerk that the check has been completed.

Nothing in this rule shall be construed as precluding a federal law enforcement officer having custody or being in charge of the transportation of a federal prisoner from carrying a firearm in a courtroom assigned to a United States District Judge or United States Magistrate on the occasion of proceedings under Rule 5, Federal Rules of Criminal Procedure, or as precluding a duly authorized Correctional Officer of the Commonwealth of Massachusetts, entrusted with responsibility of transporting a state prisoner to proceedings before a United States Magistrate for civil or criminal proceedings where a Deputy United States Marshal is unavailable for such purpose, provided that the judge or magistrate is first advised of that fact.

[Effective September 1, 1990.]

RULE 83.5.1 BAR OF THE DISTRICT COURT

(a) Admission to the District Bar.

(1) An attorney is qualified for admission to the district bar of this district if the attorney (i) is currently in good standing as an attorney admitted to practice before the Supreme Judicial Court of Massachusetts; (ii) has satisfied the examination requirements as defined by the District Committee on Admissions relating to familiarity with the Federal Rules of Civil Procedure, the Federal Rules of Evidence, principles of federal jurisdiction and venue, and rules relating to professional responsibility; and (iii) has filed a certificate in a form approved by the District Committee on Admissions attesting to familiarity with the local rules of this district. For so long as the Rules of the Board of Bar Examiners of the Commonwealth of Massachusetts include for examination the subjects named in this rule, proof of good standing as an attorney admitted to practice before the Supreme Judicial Court of Massachusetts satisfies the examination requirement set out in this rule. An attorney admitted to practice in this court before the effective date of this rule and in good standing upon that date is a member of this district bar as of that date without further action on the attorney's part.

(2) All applicants for admission to practice before this court shall complete, verify, and file an application on an official form provided by the clerk.

(3) The clerk shall examine the application and if it is in order transmit it to the United States Attorney.

(4) Within 21 days after the application is transmitted to the United States Attorney, if concluding on the basis of the information contained in the application that the application should be granted, the United States Attorney shall return the application to the clerk with written approval. The clerk shall place the name of the applicant on the list for the first available admissions ceremony.

(5) The United States Attorney, if concluding on the basis of the information contained in the application or otherwise that the application should not be granted, shall return the application to the clerk with written objection. The clerk shall deny the application without prejudice and send notice of the denial together with a copy of the United States Attorney's objection to the applicant.

(6) Any applicant denied admission may ask the court by motion to approve the application. The motion shall be presented to the Miscellaneous Business Docket (MBD) judge, who may rule on the motion ex parte, invite a response from the United States Attorney and the clerk, or schedule the matter for hearing. If the court approves the application, the clerk shall proceed as under subsection (a)(4).

(7) Approved applicants must appear at an admissions ceremony and make the following oath or affirmation before the judge presiding over the admissions ceremony:

I solemnly swear (affirm) that I shall conduct myself as a member of the bar of the United States District Court for the District of Massachusetts uprightly and according to the law.

Approved applicants shall be admitted to the district bar of this district upon signing the register of attorneys and paying to the "Clerk, United States District Court" the approved attorney admission fee.

(b) Student Practice Rule.

(1) A senior law student in a law school who has successfully completed a course for credit or who is enrolled in a course for credit in evidence or trial practice, with the written recommendation of the dean of such school of the law student's character, legal ability, and training, may appear without compensation (i) on behalf of the government or any governmental agency, if the conduct of the case is under the supervision of a member of the district bar; (ii) on behalf of indigent defendants in criminal proceedings, if the defendant consents (as provided in subsection (b)(6)) and if the conduct of the case is under the supervision of a member of the district bar assigned by the court or employed by a nonprofit program of legal aid, legal assistance or defense, or a law school clinical instruction program; and (iii) on behalf of indigent parties in civil proceedings, if the party consents (as provided in subsection (b)(6)), and if the conduct of the case is under the supervision of a member of the district bar assigned by the court or employed by a nonprofit program of legal aid, legal assistance or defense, or a law school clinical instruction program.

(2) A student may not appear in a criminal proceeding, either for the defense or for the prosecution, unless the dean's recommendation indicates that the student, in addition to satisfying all other requisites of this rule, has also successfully completed for credit a course in criminal procedure.

(3) The expression "supervision" shall be construed to require the attendance in court of the supervising member of the district bar. The term "senior law student" shall mean a student who has completed successfully the next-to-the-last year of law school study.

(4) The written recommendation described in subsection (b)(1) shall be filed with the Clerk of Court and shall be in effect, unless withdrawn earlier, until the date of the student's graduation from law school.

(5) A student who has begun the next-to-the-last year of law study in a law school, qualified and supervised as provided in subsections (b)(1), (3) and (4), may appear in civil proceedings under the same conditions as a senior law student, if the written approval referred to in subsections (b)(1) and (4) states that the law student is currently participating in a law school clinical instruction program.

(6) Before acting or appearing for any client, the student shall: (i) file with the clerk a certificate stating that the student has read and will abide by the standards of professional conduct set out in Rules 3:07 and 3:08 of the Rules of the Supreme Judicial Court of Massachusetts and is familiar with the local rules of this district; (ii) disclose to the client the student's status as a law student; (iii) obtain from the client a signed document in which the client acknowledges having been informed of the student's status and authorizes the named student to appear for and represent the client in the litigation or proceedings identified in the document; (iv) have the document approved by the supervising attorney; and (v) file the document and the written appearance of the supervising attorney with the Clerk of Court.

(7) The rules of law and of evidence relating to communications between attorney and client shall govern communications made or received by any student acting under the provisions of this rule.

(8) A student acting under this rule shall comply with the standards of professional conduct set out in Rules 3:07 and 3:08 of the Rules of the Supreme Judicial Court of Massachusetts. Failure of an attorney supervising students to provide proper training or supervision may be grounds for disciplinary action or revocation or restriction of the attorney's authority to supervise students.

(9) The expression "without compensation" used in this rule shall not be construed to prohibit the receipt of a fixed compensation paid regularly by a governmental agency or legal assistance program or law school clinical instruction program acting as the employer of a law student. It shall, however, be construed to prohibit the receipt of a fee by a law student from a client for work on a particular case.

[Effective September 1, 1990. Amended effective December 1, 2009.]

RULE 83.5.2 APPEARANCES

(a) Generally. The filing of the complaint shall constitute an appearance by the attorney who signs it. All other appearances in a case shall be made by filing a notice of appearance containing the docket number of the case, name, address and telephone number of the person entering an appearance, in compliance with Rule 5.1(a)(1).

(b) Appearance Pro Se. A party who appears pro se shall so state in the initial pleading or other paper filed by him or in his notice of appearance. The words "pro se" shall follow his signature on all papers subsequently filed by him in the same case.

(c) Withdrawal of Appearance. An attorney may withdraw from a case by serving notice of his withdrawal on his client and all other parties and filing the notice, provided that (1) such notice is preceded or accompanied by notice of the appearance of other counsel; (2) there are no motions pending before the court; (3) no trial date has been set; and (4) no hearings or conferences are scheduled, and no reports, oral or written, are due. Unless these conditions are met, an attorney (including one whose services have been terminated by his client) may withdraw from a case only by leave of court.

(d) Firms and Corporations. The court will not recognize the appearance of a firm or professional corporation unless it is accompanied by the appearance of at least one (1) attorney. In the event that a party is represented by more than one (1) attorney, whether or not from the same firm, the clerk shall not be required to send notice of orders, judgments, trial settings, etc., to more than one (1) attorney for any party, unless the attorneys represent different interests and this fact is noted on the record.

(e) Change of Address. Each attorney appearing and each party appearing pro se is under a continuing duty to notify the clerk of any change of address and telephone number. Notice under this rule shall be filed in every case. Any attorney or party appearing pro se who has not filed an appearance or provided the clerk with his current address in accordance with this rule shall not be entitled to notice. Notice mailed to an attorney's or party's last address of record shall constitute due notice contestable only upon proof of a failure to mail delivery.

[Effective September 1, 1990.]

RULE 83.5.3. PRACTICE BY PERSONS NOT MEMBERS OF THE BAR

(a) Attorneys for the United States and the Federal Defender's Office. An attorney in good standing as a member of the bar in every jurisdiction where he or she has been admitted to practice and not subject to pending disciplinary proceedings as a member of the bar of any United States District Court may appear and practice in this court as the attorney for the United States or any agency of the United States or an officer of the United States in his official capacity, or as an attorney employed in the Federal Defender's Office for this District.

(b) Other Attorneys. An attorney who is a member of the bar of any United States District Court or the bar of the highest court of any state may appear and practice in this court in a particular case by leave granted in the discretion of the court, provided he files a certificate that (1) he is a member of the bar in good standing in every jurisdiction where he has been admitted to practice; (2) there are no disciplinary proceedings pending against him as a member of the bar in any jurisdiction; and (3) he is familiar with the Local Rules of the United States District Court for the District of Massachusetts; and provided, further, his application for leave to practice in this court is on motion of a member of the bar of this court, who shall also file an appearance. An attorney seeking admission under this subsection may not enter an appearance or sign any papers until his application has been granted, except that the attorney may sign a complaint or any paper necessary to prevent entry of default for failure to answer or otherwise plead, provided such complaint or other paper is accompanied by his application for admission in proper form.

(c) Other Persons. A person who is not a member of the bar of this court, and to whom sections (a) and (b) are not applicable, will be allowed to appear and practice before the court only in his own behalf.

[Effective September 1, 1990. Amended effective February 1, 2012.]

RULE 83.6 RULES OF DISCIPLINARY ENFORCEMENT

(1) Attorneys Convicted of Crimes.

(A) Upon the filing with this court of a certified copy of a judgment of conviction demonstrating that any attorney admitted to practice before the court has been convicted in any court of the United States, or of any state, the District of Columbia, territory, commonwealth, or possession of the United States of a serious crime as hereinafter defined, the court shall enter an order immediately suspending that attorney, whether the conviction resulted from a plea of guilty, or nolo contendere, or from a verdict after trial or otherwise, and regardless of the pendency of any appeal, until final disposition of a disciplinary proceeding to be commenced upon such conviction. A copy of such order shall immediately be served upon the attorney. Upon good cause shown, the court may set aside such order when it appears in the interest of justice to do so.

(B) The term "serious crime" shall include any felony and any lesser crime, a necessary element of which, as determined by the statutory or common law definition of such crime in the jurisdiction where the judgment was entered, involves false swearing, misrepresentation, fraud, willful failure to file income tax returns, deceit, bribery, extortion, misappropriation, theft, or an attempt of a conspiracy or solicitation of another to commit a "serious crime."

(C) A certified copy of a judgment of conviction of an attorney for any crime shall be conclusive evidence of the commission of that crime in any disciplinary proceeding instituted against that attorney based upon the conviction.

(D) Upon the filing of a certified copy of a judgment of conviction of an attorney for a serious crime, the court shall, in addition to suspending that attorney in accordance with the provisions of this rule, also refer the matter to counsel for the institution of a disciplinary proceeding before the court in which the sole issue to be determined shall be the extent of the final discipline to be imposed as a result of the conduct resulting in the conviction, provided that a disciplinary proceeding so instituted will not be brought to final hearing until all appeals from the conviction are concluded.

(E) Upon the filing of a certified copy of a judgment of conviction of an attorney for a crime not constituting a "serious crime," the court may refer the matter to counsel for whatever action counsel may deem warranted, including the institution of a disciplinary proceeding before the court; provided, however, that the court may in its discretion make no reference with respect to convictions for minor offenses.

(F) An attorney suspended under the provisions of this rule will be reinstated immediately upon the filing of a certificate demonstrating that the underlying conviction of a serious crime has been reversed but the reinstatement will not terminate any disciplinary proceeding then pending against the attorney, the disposition of which shall be determined by the court on the basis of all available evidence pertaining to both guilt and the extent of discipline to be imposed.

(2) Discipline Imposed by Other Courts.

(A) Any attorney admitted to practice before this court shall, upon being subject to public discipline by any other court of the United States, or by a court of any state, the District of Columbia, territory, commonwealth, or possession of the United States, promptly inform the clerk of this court of such action.

(B) Upon the filing of a certified or exemplified copy of a judgment or order demonstrating that an attorney admitted to practice before this court has been disciplined by another court, this court shall forthwith issue a notice directed to the attorney containing:

    (i) a copy of the judgment or order from the other court; and

    (ii) an order to show cause directing that the attorney inform this court within 28 days after service of that order upon the attorney, personally or by mail, of any claim by the attorney predicated upon the grounds set forth in subsection (2)(D) hereof that the imposition of the identical discipline by this court would be unwarranted and the reasons therefor. The order shall state that a hearing on such a claim may be had if requested within 14 days after service of the order; otherwise the matter will be determined on the papers without hearing.

(C) In the event the discipline imposed in the other jurisdiction has been stayed there, any reciprocal discipline imposed in this court shall be deferred until such stay expires.

(D) Upon the expiration of 28 days from service of the notice issued pursuant to the provisions of subsection (2)(B), or any longer period needed for a hearing and consideration by the court, this court shall impose the identical discipline unless the respondent-attorney demonstrates, or this court finds, that upon the face of the record upon which the discipline in another jurisdiction is predicated it clearly appears:

    (i) that the procedure was so lacking in notice or opportunity to be heard as to constitute a deprivation of due process; or

    (ii) that there was such an infirmity of proof establishing the misconduct as to give rise to the clear conviction that this court could not, consistent with its duty, accept as final the conclusion on that subject; or

    (iii) that the imposition of the same discipline by this court would result in grave injustice; or

    (iv) that the misconduct established is deemed by this court to warrant substantially different discipline. Where this court determines that any of said elements exist, it shall enter such other order as it deems appropriate.

(E) In all other respects, a final adjudication in another court that an attorney has been guilty of misconduct shall establish conclusively the misconduct for purposes of a disciplinary proceeding in this court.

(F) This court may at any stage appoint counsel to prosecute the disciplinary proceedings.

(3) Disbarment on Consent or Resignation in Other Courts.

(A) Any attorney admitted to practice before this court who shall be disbarred on consent or resign from the bar of any other court of the United States, or from the bar of any state, the District of Columbia, territory, commonwealth, or possession of the United

States while an investigation into allegations of misconduct is pending, shall, upon the filing with this court of a certified or exemplified copy of the judgment or order accepting such disbarment on consent or resignation, cease to be permitted to practice before this court and be stricken from the roll of attorneys admitted to practice before this court.

(B) Any attorney admitted to practice before this court shall, upon being disbarred on consent or resigning from the bar of any other court of the United States, or from the bar of any state, the District of Columbia, territory, commonwealth, or possession of the United States while an investigation into allegations of misconduct is pending, promptly inform the clerk of this court of such disbarment on consent or resignation.

(4) Standards for Professional Conduct.

(A) For misconduct defined in these rules, and for good cause shown, and after notice and opportunity to be heard, any attorney admitted to practice before this court may be disbarred, suspended from practice before this court, reprimanded or subjected to such other disciplinary action as the circumstances may warrant.

(B) Acts or omissions by an attorney admitted to practice before this court pursuant to this Rule 83.6, or appearing and practicing before this court pursuant to Rule 83.7, individually or in concert with any other person or persons, that violate the ethical requirements and rules concerning the practice of law of the Commonwealth of Massachusetts, shall constitute misconduct and shall be grounds for discipline, whether or not the act or omission occurred in the course of an attorney-client relationship. The ethical requirements and rules concerning the practice of law mean those canons and rules adopted by the Supreme Judicial Court of Massachusetts, embodied in Rules 3:05, 3:07 and 3:08 of said court, as they may be amended from time to time by said court, except as otherwise provided by specific rule of this court after consideration of comments by representatives of bar associations within the Commonwealth.

(5) Disciplinary Proceedings.

(A) When misconduct or allegations of misconduct that, if substantiated, would warrant discipline as to an attorney admitted to practice before this court, is brought to the attention of a judicial officer, whether by complaint or otherwise, and the applicable procedure is not otherwise mandated by these rules, the judicial officer may refer the matter to counsel for investigation, the prosecution of a formal disciplinary proceeding or the formulation of such other recommendation as may be appropriate.

(B) Should counsel conclude after investigation and review that a formal disciplinary proceeding should not be initiated against the respondent-attorney because sufficient evidence is not present, or because there is pending another proceeding against the respondent-attorney, the disposition of which in the judgment of counsel should be awaited before further action by this court is considered or for any other valid reason, counsel shall file with the court a recommendation for disposition of the matter, whether by dismissal, admonition, deferral, or otherwise, setting forth the reasons therefor.

(C) To initiate formal disciplinary proceedings, counsel shall obtain an order of this court upon a showing of probable cause, requiring the respondent-attorney to show cause within 28 days after service of that order upon that attorney, personally or by mail, why the attorney should not be disciplined. The order to show cause shall include a certification of all courts before which the respondent-attorney is admitted to practice, as specified in the form appended to these rules.

(D) Upon the respondent-attorney's answer to the order to show cause, if any issue of fact is raised or the respondent-attorney wishes to be heard in mitigation, the Chief Judge of this court or, in his absence, the next senior district judge shall set the matter for prompt hearing before three (3) judges of this court, provided however that if the disciplinary proceeding is predicated upon the complaint of a judge of this court the complaining judge shall not sit, and if the Chief Judge is the complainant, the member of the court who is next senior shall assume his responsibilities in the matter. An en banc hearing may be granted on the affirmative vote of five (5) judges. Nothing herein shall prevent the court from using a master for purposes of fact finding and to make recommendations in a suitable case. The respondent-attorney shall execute the certification of all courts before which that respondent-attorney is admitted to practice, and file the certification with the answer.

(6) Disbarment on Consent While Under Disciplinary Investigation or Prosecution.

(A) Any attorney admitted to practice before this court who is the subject of an investigation into, or a pending proceeding involving, allegations of misconduct may consent to disbarment, but only by delivering to this court an affidavit stating that the attorney desires to consent to disbarment and that:

(i) the attorney's consent is freely and voluntarily rendered; the attorney is not being subjected to coercion or duress; the attorney is fully aware of the implications of so consenting;

(ii) the attorney is aware that there is a presently pending investigation or proceeding involving allegation that there exist grounds for the attorney's discipline, the nature of which the attorney shall specifically set forth;

(iii) the attorney acknowledges that the material facts so alleged are true; and

(iv) the attorney so consents because the attorney knows that if charges were predicated upon the matters under investigation, or if the proceedings were prosecuted, the attorney could not successfully defend himself.

(B) Upon receipt of the required affidavit, this court shall enter an order disbarring the attorney.

(C) The order disbarring the attorney on consent shall be a matter of public record. However, the affidavit required under the provisions of this rule shall not be publicly disclosed or made available for use in any other proceeding except upon order of this court.

(7) Reinstatement.

(A) *After Disbarment or Suspension.* An attorney who is suspended shall be automatically reinstated at the end of the period of suspension upon the filing with the court of an affidavit of compliance with the provisions of the order. An attorney who is suspended indefinitely or disbarred may not resume practice until reinstated by order of this court. Suspensions may be directed to run concurrently with a suspension mandated by other state or federal courts, in which event the attorney shall be eligible for reinstatement in this court when said suspension expires, and will be automatically reinstated upon filing with this court an affidavit indicating that the period of suspension has run.

(B) *Hearing on Application.* Petitions for reinstatement by a disbarred or indefinitely suspended attorney under this rule shall be filed with the Chief Judge of this court. Upon receipt of the petition, the Chief Judge shall promptly refer the petition to counsel and shall assign the matter for prompt hearing before one or more judges of this court provided, however, that if the disciplinary proceeding was predicated upon the complaint of a judge of this court, the complaining judge shall not sit, and if the Chief Judge is the complainant, the judge next senior shall assume his responsibilities in the matter. The judge or judges assigned to the matter shall within 28 days after referral schedule a hearing at which the petitioner shall have the burden of demonstrating by clear and convincing evidence that he has the moral qualifications, competency and learning in the law required for admission to practice law before this court and that his resumption of the practice of law will not be detrimental to the integrity and standing of the bar or to the administration of justice, or subversive of the public interest.

(C) *Duty of Counsel.* In all proceedings upon a petition for reinstatement, cross-examination of the witnesses of the respondent-attorney and the submission of evidence, if any, in opposition to the petition shall be conducted by counsel.

(D) *Conditions of Reinstatement.* If the petitioner is found unfit to resume the practice of law, the petition shall be dismissed. If the petitioner is found fit to resume the practice of law, the judgment shall reinstate him, provided that the judgment may make reinstatement conditional upon the payment of all or part of the costs of the proceedings, and upon the making of partial or complete restitution to parties harmed by the disbarment. Provided further, that if the petitioner has been suspended or disbarred for five (5) years or more, reinstatement may be conditioned, in the discretion of the judge or judges before whom the matter is heard, upon furnishing proof of competency and learning in the law, which proof may include certification by the bar examiners of a state or other jurisdiction of the attorney's successful completion of an examination for admission to practice subsequent to the date of suspension or disbarment.

(E) *Successive Petitions.* No petition for reinstatement under this rule shall be filed within one (1) year following an adverse judgment upon a petition for reinstatement filed by or on behalf of the same person.

(8) Attorneys Specially Admitted.

(A) Whenever an attorney applies to be admitted or is admitted to this court for purposes of a particular proceeding (pro hac vice), the attorney shall be deemed thereby to have conferred disciplinary jurisdiction upon this court for any alleged misconduct of that attorney arising in the course of or in preparation for such proceeding.

(9) Appointment of Counsel.

(A) Whenever counsel is to be appointed pursuant to these rules to investigate allegations of misconduct or prosecute disciplinary proceedings or in conjunction with a reinstatement petition filed by a disciplined attorney, this court shall appoint as counsel the disciplinary agency of the highest court of the state or commonwealth in which the attorney is maintaining his principal office, or other disciplinary agency which the court deems suitable, including the United States Attorney for this district. If no such disciplinary agency exists or such disciplinary agency declines appointment, or such appointment is clearly inappropriate, this court shall appoint as counsel one or more members of the bar of this court to investigate allegations of misconduct or to prosecute disciplinary proceedings under these rules, provided, however, that the respondent-attorney may move to disqualify an attorney so appointed who is or has been engaged as an adversary of the respondent-attorney in any matter. Counsel, once appointed, may not resign without permission of this court.

(10) Duties and Powers of the Clerk.

(A) The clerk of this court shall promptly notify the National Discipline Data Bank operated by the American Bar Association of any order imposing public discipline upon any attorney admitted to practice before this court.

(B) The clerk of this court shall, upon being informed that any attorney admitted to practice before this court has been convicted of any crime or has been subjected to discipline by another court, obtain and file with this court a certified or exemplified copy of such conviction or disciplinary judgment or order.

(C) Whenever it appears that any person who is disbarred or suspended or censured or disbarred on consent by this court is admitted to practice law in any other jurisdiction or before any other court, the clerk of this court may, if necessary to supplement the action taken under subsection (10)(A), so advise the disciplinary authority in such other jurisdiction or such other court.

(11) Jurisdiction.

(A) Nothing contained in these rules shall be construed to deny to the court such powers as are necessary for the court to maintain control over proceedings conducted before it, such as proceedings for contempt under Title 18 of the United States Code or under Rule 42 of the Federal Rules of Criminal Procedure.

[Effective September 1, 1990. Amended effective August 1, 1997; December 1, 2009.]

RULE 106.1   GRAND JURIES

(a) The names of any jurors drawn from the qualified jury wheel and selected to sit on a grand jury shall be kept confidential and not made public or disclosed to any person not employed by the district court, except as otherwise authorized by a court order in an individual case pursuant to 28 U.S.C. § 1867(f).

(b) All subpoenas, motions, pleadings, and other documents filed with the clerk concerning or contesting grand jury proceedings shall be sealed and impounded unless otherwise ordered by the court based upon a showing of particularized need. Impoundment under this rule shall not preclude necessary service of papers on opposing parties or their counsel nor prohibit the clerk from providing copies of papers to the party or counsel filing same.

[Effective September 1, 1990.]

RULE 106.2   RELEASE OF INFORMATION BY COURTHOUSE PERSONNEL IN CRIMINAL CASES

All court supporting personnel, including the United States Marshal, Deputy United States Marshals, the Clerk of Court, deputy clerks, probation officers, assistant probation officers, bailiffs, court reporters, and employees or subcontractors retained by the court-appointed official reporters, judges' secretaries and law clerks and student assistants, and other employees are prohibited from disclosing without authorization by the court, information relating to a pending grand jury proceeding or criminal case that is not part of the public records of the court. Divulging information concerning in camera hearings is also prohibited.

[Effective September 1, 1990.]

RULE 112.1   MOTION PRACTICE

Unless otherwise specified in these Local Rules or by order of the court, motion practice in criminal cases shall be subject to Local Rule 7.1.

[Adopted September 8, 1998, effective December 1, 1998. Amended effective February 1, 2012.]

RULE 112.2   EXCLUDABLE DELAY PURSUANT TO THE SPEEDY TRIAL ACT

(a) Excludable Delay Generally. The Court, having found that a fair and prompt resolution of criminal cases is best served by minimizing formal motion practices and establishing the system of discovery set forth in these Local Rules, has determined that the following periods of time may be excluded, under 18 U.S.C. §§ 3161(h)(1)(D) & (H) and (h)(7)(A), to serve the ends of justice in order to accomplish such purposes:

(1) the period from arraignment to the Initial Status Conference conducted under Local Rule 116.5(a), during which period the parties shall produce the automatic discovery required under Local Rule 116.1(b) and (c) and develop their discovery plans, and defendants shall consider the need for pretrial motions under Fed. R. Crim. P. 12;

(2) no more than 14 days from the filing of a copy of a letter requesting discovery under Local Rule 116.3(a);

(3) no more than 14 days from the date on which a written response to a letter requesting discovery under Local Rule 116.3(a) is due to the filing of a motion seeking the discovery, provided that the party receiving the discovery request either refuses to furnish the requested discovery or fails to respond to the request, and the party requesting the discovery actually files a motion seeking discovery.

(b) Requirement of Order of Excludable Delay. The time periods indicated above will not be automatically excluded. All such periods of excludable delay must be included in an order issued by the District Judge or Magistrate Judge.

(c) Exclusion of Additional Periods. Nothing in this rule shall preclude the Court from excluding additional periods of time as appropriate under 18 U.S.C. § 3161(h).

(d) Procedure Under Waiver of Automatic Discovery. If a defendant files the Waiver provided under Local Rule 116.1(b), all periods of excludable delay shall be calculated pursuant to the Speedy Trial Act without regard to the provisions of this Local Rule.

[Adopted September 8, 1998, effective December 1, 1998. Amended effective February 1, 2012.]

RULE 112.4   CORPORATE DISCLOSURE STATEMENT

(a) A nongovernmental corporate party to a criminal proceeding in this court must file a statement that identifies any parent corporation and any publicly held corporation that owns 10% or more of its stock or states there is no such corporation.

(b) If an organization is a victim of the alleged criminal activity, the government must file a statement identifying the victim. If the organizational victim is a corporation, the statement must also disclose the information required by Local Rule 112.4 (a) charged in any indictment or information.

(c) A party must file the Local Rule 112.4 (a) statement upon its first appearance, pleading, petition, motion, response or other request addressed to the court and must promptly supplement the statement upon any change in the identification that the statement requires.

[Adopted effective January 1, 2001. Amended effective February 1, 2012.]

RULE 116.1   DISCOVERY IN CRIMINAL CASES

(a) Discovery Alternatives.

(1) *Automatic Discovery.* In all felony cases and Class A misdemeanor cases (except those within the Central Violations Bureau), unless a defendant waives automatic discovery in accordance with paragraph (b) below, all discoverable material and information in the possession, custody, or control of the government and the defendant, the existence of which is known, or by the exercise of due diligence may become known, to the attorneys for those parties, must be disclosed to the opposing party without formal motion practice at the times and under the automatic procedures specified in these Local Rules.

(2) *Non–Automatic Discovery.* In petty offense cases and Class A misdemeanor cases within the Central Violations Bureau, and in cases where the defendant waives automatic discovery in accordance with paragraph (b) below, the defendant must obtain

discovery directly through the provisions of the Federal Rules of Criminal Procedure in the manner provided under Local Rule 116.3.

(b) Waiver. A defendant shall be deemed to have requested all the discovery authorized by Fed. R. Crim. P. 16(a)(1)(A)–(F) unless that defendant files a Waiver of Request for Disclosure (the "Waiver") at arraignment or within such additional time as the Court may allow upon motion made by the defendant at arraignment. If the Waiver is not timely filed, the defendant shall be subject to the correlative reciprocal discovery obligations of Fed. R. Crim. P. 16(b) and this rule and shall be deemed to have consented to the exclusion of time for Speedy Trial Act purposes as provided in Local Rule 112.2(a). If the Court allows the defendant additional time in which to file the Waiver, and no Waiver is timely filed, the 28–day period for providing automatic discovery established in Subdivision (c) of this rule shall begin to run on the last date allowed for filing the Waiver, and all dates for filing discovery letters and motions established in Local Rule 116.3 shall be adjusted accordingly.

(c) Automatic Discovery Provided by the Government.

(1) *Following Arraignment.* Unless a defendant has filed the Waiver in accordance with paragraph (b) above, within 28 days of arraignment(except a Rule 11 arraignment on an information), absent a contrary schedule established by the Court pursuant to paragraphs (e) and (f) below, the government must produce to the defendant:

(A) Fed. R. Crim. P. 16 Materials. All of the information to which the defendant is entitled under Fed. R. Crim. P. 16(a)(1)(A)–(F).

(B) Search Materials. A copy of any search warrant (with supporting application, affidavit, and return) and a written description of any consent search or warrantless search (including an inventory of items seized):

(i) that resulted in the seizure of evidence or led to the discovery of evidence that the government intends to use in its case-in-chief; or

(ii) that was obtained for or conducted of the defendant's property, residence, place of business, or person, in connection with investigation of the charges contained in the indictment.

(C) Electronic Surveillance.

(i) a written description of any interception of wire, oral, or electronic communications as defined in 18 U.S.C. § 2510, relating to the charges in the indictment in which the defendant was intercepted and a statement whether the government intends to use any such communications as evidence in its case-in-chief; and

(ii) a copy of any application for authorization to intercept such communications relating to the charges contained in the indictment in which the defendant was named as an interceptee or pursuant to which the defendant was intercepted, together with all supporting affidavits, the Court orders authorizing such interceptions, and the Court orders directing the sealing of intercepted communications under 18 U.S.C. § 2518(a).

(D) Consensual Interceptions.

(i) a written description of any interception of wire, oral, or electronic communications, relating to the charges contained in the indictment, made with the consent of one of the parties to the communication ("consensual interceptions"), in which the defendant was intercepted or which the government intends to use in its case-in-chief.

(ii) nothing in this subsection is intended to determine the circumstances, if any, under which, or the time at which, the attorney for the government must review and produce communications of a defendant in custody consensually recorded by the institution in which that defendant is held.

(E) Unindicted Coconspirators. As to each conspiracy charged in the indictment, the name of any person asserted to be a known unindicted coconspirator. If subsequent litigation requires that the name of any such unindicted coconspirator be referenced in any filing directly with the Court, that information must be redacted from any public filing and be filed under Local Rule 7.2 pending further order of the Court.

(F) Identifications.

(i) A written statement whether the defendant was a subject of an investigative identification procedure used with a witness the government anticipates calling in its case-in-chief involving a line-up, show-up, photospread or other display of an image of the defendant.

(ii) If the defendant was a subject of such a procedure, a copy of any, recording, photospread, image or other tangible evidence reflecting, used in or memorializing the identification procedure.

(2) *Exculpatory Information.* The timing and substance of the disclosure of exculpatory evidence is governed by Local Rule 116.2.

(d) **Automatic Discovery Provided by the Defendant.** Unless a defendant has filed the Waiver in accordance with paragraph (b) above, within 28 days after arraignment (except a Rule 11 arraignment on an information), absent a contrary schedule established by the Court pursuant to paragraphs (e) and (f) below, the defendant must produce to the government all material described in Fed. R. Crim. P. 16(b)(1)(A) and (B).

(e) **Deadline for Automatic Discovery.** At arraignment, the Magistrate Judge shall set a date for completion of automatic discovery in accordance with this rule. The date may be extended on motion or request of any party.

(f) **Alternative Discovery Schedule.** The parties shall inform the court at arraignment, or as soon as practicable thereafter, of any issues that might require an alternative discovery schedule. Requests for an alternative discovery schedule in complex cases shall be liberally granted. The Court shall not allow an alternative discovery schedule without providing a date for the completion of automatic discovery.

(g) **Non–Automatic Discovery Provided by the Parties.** If the defendant files the Waiver, all requests for discovery and reciprocal discovery, and all responses to such requests, shall be made in writing and filed with the court. Unless a greater or lesser amount of time is established by the court upon motion and for good cause shown, within 28 days of receiving a letter or motion requesting discovery, a party shall produce all discovery responsive to those requests to which it does not object and shall file a written response to those requests (if any) to which it does object, explaining the basis for its objections.

[Effective September 1, 1990. Amended September 8, 1998, effective December 1, 1998. Amended effective February 1, 2012.]

RULE 116.2   DISCLOSURE OF EXCULPATORY EVIDENCE

(a) **Definition.** Exculpatory information is information that is material and favorable to the accused and includes, but is not necessarily limited to, information that tends to:

(1) cast doubt on defendant's guilt as to any essential element in any count in the indictment or information;

(2) cast doubt on the admissibility of evidence that the government anticipates using in its case-in-chief, that might be subject to a motion to suppress or exclude, which would, if allowed, be appealable pursuant to 18 U.S.C. § 3731;

(3) cast doubt on the credibility or accuracy of any evidence that the government anticipates using in its case-in-chief; or

(4) diminish the degree of the defendant's culpability or the defendant's Offense Level under the United States Sentencing Guidelines.

(b) **Timing of Disclosure by the Government.** Unless the government invokes the declination procedure under Local Rule 116.6, the government must produce to the defendant exculpatory information in accordance with the following schedule:

(1) Within the time period designated in Local Rule 116.1(c)(1), or by any alternative date established by the Court:

(A) information that would tend directly to negate the defendant's guilt concerning any count in the indictment or information;

(B) information that would cast doubt on the admissibility of evidence that the government anticipates using in its case-in-chief and that could be subject to a motion to suppress or exclude, which would, if allowed, be appealable pursuant to 18 U.S.C. § 3731; and

(C) a statement whether any promise, reward, or inducement has been given to any witness whom the government anticipates calling in its case-in-chief, identifying by name each such witness and each promise, reward, or inducement, and a copy of any promise, reward, or inducement reduced to writing

(D) a copy of any criminal record of any witness whom the government anticipates calling in its case-in-chief, identifying by name each such witness;

(E) a written description of any criminal cases pending against any witness whom the government anticipates calling in its case-in-chief, identifying by name each such witness.

(F) a written description of the failure of any percipient witness identified by name to make a positive identification of a defendant, if any identification procedure has been held with such a witness with respect to the crime at issue.

(2) Not later than 21 days before the trial date established by the judge who will preside at the trial:

(A) any information that tends to cast doubt on the credibility or accuracy of any witness or evidence that the government anticipates calling or offering in its case-in-chief,

(B) any inconsistent statement, or a description of such a statement, made orally or in writing by any witness whom the government anticipates calling in its case-in-chief, regarding the alleged criminal conduct of the defendant;

(C) any statement or a description of such a statement, made orally or in writing by any person, that is inconsistent with any statement made orally or in writing by any witness the government anticipates calling in its case-in-chief, regarding the alleged criminal conduct of the defendant;

(D) information reflecting bias or prejudice against the defendant by any witness whom the government anticipates calling in its case-in-chief;

(E) a written description of any prosecutable federal offense known by the government to have been committed by any witness whom the government anticipates calling in its case-in-chief;

(F) a written description of any conduct that may be admissible under Fed. R. Evid. 608(b) known by the government to have been committed by a witness whom the government anticipates calling in its case-in-chief; and

(G) information known to the government of any mental or physical impairment of any witness whom the government anticipates calling in its case-in-chief, that may cast doubt on the ability of that witness to testify accurately or truthfully at trial as to any relevant event.

(3) No later than the close of the defendant's case: exculpatory information regarding any witness or evidence that the government intends to use in rebuttal.

(4) Before any plea or to the submission by the defendant of any objections to the Pre–Sentence Report, whichever first occurs: a written summary of any information in the government's possession that tends to diminish the degree of the defendant's culpability or the defendant's Offense Level under the United States Sentencing Guidelines.

(5) If an item of exculpatory information can reasonably be deemed to fall into more than one of the foregoing categories, it shall be deemed for purposes of determining when it must be produced to fall into the category which requires the earliest production.

[Adopted September 8, 1998, effective December 1, 1998. Amended effective February 1, 2012.]

RULE 116.3 DISCOVERY MOTION PRACTICE

(a) **Letter Request for Discovery.** Within 14 days of the completion of automatic discovery, any party by letter to the opposing party may request additional discovery. The opposing party shall reply in writing to the requests contained in such letter, no later than 14 days after its receipt, stating whether that party agrees or does not agree to furnish the requested discovery and, if that party agrees, when the party will furnish the requested discovery. A copy of the discovery request letter and any response must also be filed with the Clerk's Office.

(b) **Agreement to Provide Discovery.** If a party agrees in writing to provide the requested discovery, the agreement shall be enforceable to the same extent as a court order requiring the agreed-upon disclosure.

(c) **Explanation for Lack of Agreement.** If a party does not agree to provide the requested information, that party must provide a written statement of the basis for its position.

(d) **No Need to Request Automatic Discovery.** A defendant participating in automatic discovery should not request information expressly required to be produced under Local Rule 116.1, because all such information is required to be produced automatically in any event.

(e) No Motion Before Response to Request. Except in an emergency, no discovery motion, or request for a bill of particulars, shall be filed until the opposing party has declined in writing to provide the requested discovery or has failed to respond in writing within 14 days of receipt of a written discovery request.

(f) No Motion Before Conference with Opponent. Except in an emergency, no discovery motion, or request for a bill of particulars, shall be filed before, the moving party has conferred, or attempted in good faith to confer, with opposing counsel to attempt to eliminate or narrow the areas of disagreement. In the motion or request, the moving party shall certify that a good faith attempt was made to eliminate or narrow the issues raised in the motion through a conference with opposing counsel or that a good faith attempt to comply with the requirement was precluded by the opposing party's unwillingness or inability to confer.

(g) Timing of Motion. Any discovery motion shall be filed within 14 days of receipt of the opposing party's written reply to the letter requesting discovery described in subdivision (a) of this rule or within 14 days of the passage of the period within which the opposing party has the obligation to reply pursuant to subsection (a). The discovery motion shall state with particularity each request for discovery, followed by a concise statement of the moving party's position with respect to such request, including citations of authority.

(h) Multi–Defendant Cases. In multi-defendant cases, except with leave of court, the defendant parties must confer and, to the maximum extent possible in view of any potentially differing positions of the defendants, consolidate their written requests to the government for any discovery. If a discovery motion is to be filed, the defendant parties must endeavor to the maximum extent possible to file a single consolidated motion. Each defendant need not join in every written request submitted to the government or filed in a consolidated motion, but all defense requests and motions, whether of not joined in by each defendant must to the maximum extent possible be contained within a single document or filing.

(i) Timing of Response to Motions. The opposing party must file its response to all discovery motions within 14 days of receipt. In its response, the opposing party, as to each request, shall make a concise statement of the opposing party's basis for opposing that request, including citations to authority.

(j) Subsequent Requests. The procedure set forth in this rule shall apply to any subsequent requests for discovery. When filing a discovery motion that is based on a subsequent discovery request, the moving party must additionally certify that the discovery request resulting in the motion was prompted by information not known, or issues not reasonably foreseeable, to the moving party before the deadline for discovery motions, or that the delay in making the request was for other good cause, which the moving party must describe with particularity.

[Adopted September 8, 1998, effective December 1, 1998. Amended effective February 1, 2012.]

RULE 116.4 SPECIAL PROCEDURE FOR AUDIO AND VIDEO RECORDINGS

(a) Availability of Audio and Video Recordings.

(1) The government must provide at least one copy of all audio and video recordings in its possession that are discoverable for examination and review by the defendant parties.

(2) If a defendant requests additional copies, the government must make arrangements to provide or to enable that defendant to make such copies at that defendant's expense.

(3) If in a multi-defendant case any defendant is in custody, the government must insure that an extra copy of all audio and video recordings is available for review by the defendant(s) in custody.

(b) Composite Recordings, Preliminary Transcripts and Final Transcripts. The parties must make arrangements promptly to provide or make available for inspection and copying by opposing counsel all:

(1) Composite electronic surveillance or consensual interception recordings to be used in that party's case-in-chief at trial, once prepared.

(2) Preliminary transcripts, once prepared. A preliminary transcript may not be used at trial or in any hearing on a pretrial motion without the prior approval of the Court based on a finding that the preliminary transcript is accurate in material respects and it is in the interests of the administration of justice to use it.

(3) Final transcripts, once prepared.

(4) Nothing in this Local Rule shall be construed to require a party to prepare composite recordings, or preliminary or final transcripts, of any recording.

[Adopted September 8, 1998, effective December 1, 1998. Amended effective February 1, 2012.]

RULE 116.5 STATUS CONFERENCES AND STATUS REPORT PROCEDURE

(a) Initial Status Conference. On or about the 14th day following the date scheduled for the completion of automatic discovery, the Magistrate Judge shall convene an Initial Status Conference with the attorneys for the parties who will conduct the trial. Unless otherwise ordered by the court, counsel shall confer and file a joint memorandum no later than 7 days before the Initial Status Conference. The joint memorandum must include the following issues and any other issues relevant to the progress of the case, which counsel must be prepared to discuss at the conference:

(1) the status of automatic discovery and any pending discovery requests;

(2) the timing of any additional discovery to be produced;

(3) the timing of any additional discovery requests;

(4) whether any protective orders addressing the disclosure or dissemination of sensitive information concerning victims, witnesses, defendants, or law enforcement sources or techniques may be appropriate;

(5) the timing of any pretrial motions under Fed. R. Crim. P. 12(b);

(6) the timing of expert witness disclosures;

(7) periods of excludable delay under the Speedy Trial Act;

(8) the timing of an Interim Status Conference or Final Status Conference, as the case may require.

If the defendant indicates an intention to change his/her plea to guilty, or if discovery is complete and the only issues that remain or are anticipated are ones appropriately resolved by the District Judge, the Magistrate Judge may, at the parties' request, treat the Initial Status Conference as a Final Status Conference under Subsection (c) of this Local Rule and transfer the case to the District Judge along with the Final Status Report required by Subsection (d) of this Local Rule. Otherwise, the Magistrate Judge shall issue a scheduling order and an order of excludable delay that reflect the deadlines and periods of excludable delay established at the Initial Status Conference.

(b) Interim Status Conference. At the Initial Status Conference, unless the Magistrate Judge decides to transfer the case to the District Judge under subsection (a) of this rule, the Magistrate Judge shall schedule an Interim Status Conference or a Final Status Conference, as needed, giving due regard to the complexity of the case and the period of time that the parties expect will be required to complete discovery and pretrial motions.

Unless otherwise ordered by the court, counsel shall confer and file a joint memorandum no later than 7 days before the Interim Status Conference. The joint memorandum must address the following issues, and any other issues relevant to the progress of the case, which counsel must be prepared to discuss at the conference:

(1) the status of automatic discovery and any pending discovery requests;

(2) the timing of any additional discovery to be produced;

(3) the timing of any additional discovery requests;

(4) whether any protective orders addressing the disclosure or dissemination of sensitive information concerning victims, witnesses, defendants, or law enforcement sources or techniques may be appropriate;

(5) the status of any pretrial motions under Fed. R. Crim. P. 12(b);

(6) the timing of expert witness disclosures;

(7) defenses of insanity, public authority, or alibi;

(8) periods of excludable delay under the Speedy Trial Act;

(9) the status of any plea discussions and likelihood and estimated length of trial;

(10) the timing of the Final Status Conference or any further Interim Status Conference.

The Magistrate Judge may waive the Interim Status Conference if the parties request such a waiver and the Magistrate Judge determines that the information in the joint memorandum obviates the need for the conference.

If the defendant indicates an intention to change his/her plea to guilty, or if discovery is complete and the only issues that remain or are anticipated are ones appropriately resolved by the District Judge, the Magistrate Judge may, at the parties' request, treat an Interim Status Conference as a Final Status Conference under Subsection (c) of this Local Rule and transfer the case to the District Judge along with the Final Status Report required by Subsection (d) of this Local Rule. Otherwise, the Magistrate Judge shall issue a scheduling order and an order of excludable delay that reflect the deadlines and periods of excludable delay established at the Interim Status Conference or in the parties' joint memorandum, as the case may be.

(c) Final Status Conference. In all felony cases and Class A misdemeanor cases to be heard by a District Judge, before the Magistrate Judge issues the Final Status Report required by subdivision (d) of this rule, the Magistrate Judge shall, if necessary, convene a Final Status Conference with the attorneys who will conduct the trial. Counsel shall confer and file a joint memorandum no later than 7 days before the Final Status Conference. The joint memorandum must address the following issues, and any other issues relevant to the progress of the case, which counsel must be prepared to discuss at the conference:

(1) whether the defendant requests that the case be transferred to the District Judge for a Rule 11 hearing;

(2) whether, alternatively, the parties move for a pretrial conference before the District Judge in order to resolve pretrial motions (if any) and schedule a trial date and, if so:

(A) whether the parties have produced all discovery they intend to produce and, if not, the identity of any additional discovery and its expected production date;

(B) whether all discovery requests and motions have been made and resolved and, if not, the nature of the outstanding requests or motions and the date they are expected to be resolved;

(C) whether all motions under Fed. R. Crim. P. 12(b) have been filed and responded to and, if not, the motions that are expected to be filed and the date they will ready for resolution;

(D) whether the Court should order any additional periods of excludable delay, the number of nonexcludable days remaining, and whether any matter is currently tolling the running of the time period under the Speedy Trial Act; and

(E) the estimated number of trial days; and

(3) any other matters specific to the particular case that would assist the District Judge upon transfer of the case from the Magistrate Judge.

If the joint memorandum permits the Magistrate Judge to prepare the Final Status Report without the necessity of an additional status conference, the Magistrate Judge may waive the Final Status Conference and issue an order transferring the case to the District Judge.

(d) Final Status Report. After the Final Status Conference, or upon receipt of the Joint Final Status Memorandum if no conference is deemed necessary, the Magistrate Judge shall transfer the case to the District Judge along with a Final Status Report that incorporates the information provided by the parties at the Final Status Conference or in the Joint Final Status Memorandum, as the case may be.

[Adopted September 8, 1998, effective December 1, 1998; December 1, 2009. Amended effective February 1, 2012.]

RULE 116.6 DECLINATION OF DISCLOSURE AND PROTECTIVE ORDERS

(a) Declination. If in the judgment of a party it would be detrimental to the interests of justice to make any of the disclosures required by these Local Rules, such disclosures may be declined, before or at the time that disclosure is due, and the opposing party advised in writing, with a copy filed in the Clerk's Office, of the specific matters on which disclosure is declined and the reasons for declining. If the oppos-

ing party seeks to challenge the declination, that party shall file a motion to compel that states the reasons why disclosure is sought. Upon the filing of such motion, except to the extent otherwise provided by law, the burden shall be on the party declining disclosure to demonstrate, by affidavit and supporting memorandum citing legal authority, why such disclosure should not be made. The declining party may file its submissions in support of declination under seal pursuant to Local Rule 7.2 for the Court's in camera consideration. Unless otherwise ordered by the Court, a redacted version of each such submission shall be served on the moving party, which may reply.

(b) Ex Parte Motions for Protective Orders. This Local Rule does not preclude any party from moving under Local Rule 7.2 and ex parte (i.e. without serving the opposing party) for leave to file an ex parte motion for a protective order with respect to any discovery matter. Nor does this Local Rule limit the Court's power to accept or reject an ex parte motion or to decide such a motion in any manner it deems appropriate.

[Adopted September 8, 1998, effective December 1, 1998. Amended effective February 1, 2012.]

RULE 116.7 DUTY TO SUPPLEMENT

The duties established by these Local Rules are continuing. Each party is under a duty, when it learns that a prior disclosure was in some respect inaccurate or incomplete to supplement promptly any disclosure required by these Local Rules or by the Federal Rules of Criminal Procedure.

[Adopted September 8, 1998, effective December 1, 1998.]

RULE 116.8 NOTIFICATION TO RELEVANT LAW ENFORCEMENT AGENCIES OF DISCOVERY OBLIGATIONS

The attorney for the government shall inform all federal, state, and local law enforcement agencies formally participating in the criminal investigation that resulted in the case of the discovery obligations set forth in these Local Rules and obtain any information subject to disclosure from each such agency.

[Adopted September 8, 1998, effective December 1, 1998.]

RULE 116.9 PRESERVATION OF NOTES

(a) General Rule. All contemporaneous notes, memoranda, statements, reports, surveillance logs, recordings, and other documents (regardless of the medium in which they are stored) memorializing matters relevant to the charges contained in the indictment made by or in the custody of any law enforcement officer whose agency at the time was formally participating in an investigation intended, in whole or in part, to result in a federal indictment shall be preserved until the entry of judgment unless otherwise ordered by the Court.

(b) Rough Drafts. These Local Rules do not require the preservation of rough drafts of reports after a subsequent draft of final report is prepared.

(c) Established Retention Procedures. These Local Rules do not require modification of a government agency's established procedure for the retention and disposal of documents when the agency does not reasonably anticipate a criminal prosecution.

[Adopted September 8, 1998, effective December 1, 1998. Amended effective February 1, 2012.]

RULE 116.10   REQUIREMENTS OF TABLE OF CONTENTS FOR VOLUMINOUS DISCOVERY

Any party producing more than 1,000 pages of discovery in a criminal case shall provide a table of contents that describes, in general terms, the type and origin of the documents (for example, "bank records from Sovereign Bank for John Smith"; "grand jury testimony of Officer Jones") and the location of the documents so described within the larger set (for example, by Bates number).

[Adopted January 3, 2012; effective February 1, 2012.]

RULE 117.1   PRETRIAL CONFERENCES

(a) Initial Pretrial Conference. Within 14 days of receiving the Magistrate Judge's Final Status Report, or at the earliest practicable time before trial consistent with the Speedy Trial Act, the District Judge to whom the case is assigned must conduct a Rule 11 hearing, if the defendant has requested one, or else must convene an Initial Pretrial Conference, which counsel who will conduct the trial must attend. At the Initial Pretrial Conference the District Judge must:

(1) determine the number of days remaining before trial must begin under the Speedy Trial Act;

(2) confirm that all discovery has been produced, all discovery disputes have been resolved, and all pretrial motions under Fed. R. Crim. P. 12(b) have been filed and briefed, and schedule any necessary hearings or additional briefing on any pretrial motions under Fed. R. Crim. P. 12(b);

(3) establish a reliable trial date, which should not, except upon motion of the defendant, be less than 30 days after any evidentiary hearing on a pretrial motion under Fed. R. Crim. P. 12(b);

(4) unless the declination procedure provided by Local Rule 116.6 has previously been invoked, order the government to disclose to the defendant no later than 21 days before the trial date:

(A) the exculpatory information identified in Local Rule 116.2 (b)(2); and

(B) a general description (including the approximate date, time and place) of any crime, wrong, or act the government proposes to use pursuant to Fed. R. Evid. 404(b);

(5) determine whether the parties have furnished statements, as defined by 18 U.S.C. § 3500(e) and Fed. R. Crim. P. 26.2(f), of witnesses they intend to call in their cases-in-chief and, if not, when they propose to do so;

(6) determine whether any party objects to complying with the presumptive timing directives of subsections (a)(8) and (a)(9) for the disclosure of witnesses and identification of exhibits and materials. If any party expresses an objection, the court may decide the issues(s) presented at the Initial Pretrial Conference or may order briefing and/or later argument on such issue(s);

(7) establish a schedule for the filing and briefing of possible motions in limine and for the filing of proposed voir dire questions, proposed jury instructions, and, if appropriate, trial briefs;

(8) unless an objection has been made pursuant to subsection (a)(6), order that at least 7 days before the trial date the government must:

(A) provide the defendant with the names and addresses of witnesses the government intends to call at trial (i) in its case-in-chief, and (ii) in its rebuttal to the defendant's alibi defense (if the defendant serves a Rule 12.1(a)(2) notice). If the government subsequently forms an intent to call any other witness, the government shall promptly notify the defendant of the names and address of that prospective witness. The government shall not, however, provide the defendant the addresses of any victims whom it intends to call in its rebuttal to the defendant's alibi defense (if the defendant serves a Rule 12.1(a)(2) notice) except pursuant to subsection (a)(9).

(B) provide the defendant with copies of the exhibits and a premarked list of the exhibits the government intends to use in its case-in-chief. If the government subsequently decides to offer any additional exhibit in its case-in-chief, the government shall promptly provide the opposing party with a copy of the exhibit and a supplemental exhibit list;

(9) if the defendant establishes a need for the address of a victim the government intends to call as a witness in its rebuttal to the defendant's alibi defense (if the defendant serves a Rule 12.1(a)(2) notice), the court may:

(A) order the government to provide the information in writing to the defendant or the defendant's attorney; or

(B) fashion a reasonable procedure that allows preparation of the defense and also protects the victim's interests.

(10) unless an objection has been made pursuant to subsection (a)(6), order that at least 7 days before the trial the defendant must provide the government with witness and exhibit identification and materials to the same extent the government is obligated to do so under subsection (a)(8);

(11) determine whether the parties will stipulate to any facts that are not in dispute;

(12) establish a date for a Final Pretrial Conference, to be held not more than 7 days before the trial date, to resolve any matters that must be decided before trial, unless all parties advise the Court that such a conference is not necessary and the District Judge concurs.

(b) Special Orders. The District Judge who will preside at trial may, upon motion of a party or on the judge's own initiative, modify any of the requirements of subsection (a) of this rule in the interests of justice

(c) Interim Pretrial Conferences. If, at the conclusion of the Initial Pretrial Conference, a reliable trial date cannot be established, or if a trial date is established but later continued by the Court, the Court shall schedule an Interim Status Conference at which the District Judge, in consultation with the parties, must determine the time remaining under the Speedy Trial Act before which trial must begin and must adjust, as needed, the scheduling dates called for by subsections (a)(4)–(12).

[Adopted September 8, 1998, effective December 1, 1998; December 1, 2009. Amended effective February 1, 2012.]

RULE 117.2 SUBPOENAS IN CRIMINAL CASES INVOLVING COURT-APPOINTED COUNSEL

(a) Issuance of Subpoenas. In any criminal matter in which the defendant is represented by the Federal Public Defender or other court-appointed counsel, upon request of such counsel the Clerk of Court shall issue a subpoena for hearing or trial in blank, signed and sealed, to counsel without the necessity for an individual court order.

(b) Service of Subpoenas. Upon presentation of such a subpoena, the United States Marshal shall serve it in the same manner as in other criminal cases pursuant to Fed. R. Crim. P. 17(b).

(c) Process Costs and Witness Fees. Subpoenas issued under subdivision (a) of this Rule are issued upon approval of the court. The United States Marshal shall pay the process costs and fees of any witness subpoenaed pursuant to this Rule as provided in Fed. R. Crim. P. 17(b) and 28 U.S.C. § 1825.

(d) Subpoenas in Certain Hearings. A subpoena may not be issued under this rule to compel the attendance of a witness in

(1) a preliminary hearing pursuant to Rule 5.1 or Rule 32.1(b)(1), Fed. R. Crim. P.;

(2) a detention hearing held pursuant to 18 U.S.C. § 3142(f); or

(3) or a hearing concerning the revocation of release as provided in 18 U.S.C. § 3148, without first seeking leave from the presiding judicial officer.

[Effective February 1, 2012.]

RULE 118.1 EFFECTIVE DATE

These Local Rules shall become effective on December 1, 1998. They shall, except as applicable time periods may have run, govern all actions pending or commenced after the effective date. Where justice so requires, proceedings in cases on the effective date shall be governed by the practice of the court before the adoption of these Local Rules.

[Adopted September 8, 1998, effective December 1, 1998.]

RULE 200 [RENUMBERED AND AMENDED EFFECTIVE JANUARY 2 1995; SEE RULE 203]

RULE 201 REFERENCE TO BANKRUPTCY COURT

Pursuant to 28 U.S.C. § 157(a), any and all cases arising under Title 11 United States Code and any and all proceedings arising under Title 11 or arising in or related to a case under Title 11 shall be referred to the judges of the bankruptcy court for the District of Massachusetts.

[Adopted effective January 2, 1995.]

RULE 202 BANKRUPTCY COURT JURY TRIALS

Pursuant to 28 U.S.C. § 157(e), the judges of the bankruptcy court for the District of Massachusetts are specially designated to conduct jury trials with the express consent of the parties in any proceeding which may be heard by a bankruptcy judge to which a right to jury trial applies.

[Adopted effective January 2, 1995.]

RULE 203 BANKRUPTCY APPEALS

(A) The bankruptcy court is authorized and directed to dismiss an appeal filed after the time specified in Bankruptcy Rule 8002 or an appeal in which the appellant has failed to file a designation of the items for the record or a statement of the issues as required by Bankruptcy Rule 8006. The bankruptcy court is also authorized and directed to decide motions to extend the foregoing deadlines and to consolidate appeals which present similar issues from a common record. Bankruptcy court orders entered under this subsection may be reviewed by the district court on motion filed within 14 days of the entry of the order.

(B) The briefing schedule specified by Bankruptcy Rule 8009 may be altered only by order of the district court. If the clerk of the district court does not receive appellant's brief within the time specified by said Rule 8009, he shall forthwith provide the district judge to whom the appeal has been assigned with a proposed order for dismissal of the appeal.

(C) Upon receipt of the district court's opinion disposing of the appeal, the district court clerk shall enter judgment in accordance with Bankruptcy Rule 8016(a) and shall immediately transmit to each party and to the clerk of the bankruptcy court a notice of entry together with a copy of the court's opinion.

(D) The bankruptcy court clerk shall enclose a copy of this rule with the notice of appeal given to each party in accordance with Bankruptcy Rule 8004; provided, however, that failure of the clerk to enclose a copy of this rule shall not suspend its operation.

(E) This rule is not intended to restrict the district court's discretion as to any aspect of any appeal.

[Effective September 1, 1990. Amended effective January 2, 1995; December 1, 2009.]

RULE 204 BANKRUPTCY COURT LOCAL RULES

Pursuant to Rule 9029(a) of the Federal Rules of Bankruptcy Procedure, the judges of the bankruptcy court for the District of Massachusetts are authorized to make and amend rules of practice and procedure as they may deem appropriate, subject to the requirements of Fed.R.Civ.P. 83. A certified copy of any rules and/or amendments as adopted by the judges of the bankruptcy court, together with a copy of the notice and all comments received regarding the rule, shall be provided to the Clerk of the District Court within 14 days of the date adopted. Once each year, the judges of the district court will review all changes to the local rules of the bankruptcy court. If, after review, the judges of the district court determine that modifications need to be made to any rule, a report will be provided to the judges of the bankruptcy court by March 31.

[Adopted effective August 1, 1997. Amended effective September 15, 2006.]

RULE 205 DISCIPLINARY REFERRALS BY BANKRUPTCY JUDGES

A judge of the bankruptcy court for the District of Massachusetts is authorized as a judicial officer to make referrals for disciplinary proceedings as provided under LR 83.6(5)(a).

[Adopted effective August 1, 1997.]

APPENDICES
APPENDIX A.   LOCAL RULE 4.5 SUPPLEMENT
FEE SCHEDULE—DISTRICT OF MASSACHUSETTS*

The fees included in the District Court Miscellaneous Fee Schedule are to be charged for services provided by the district courts.

- The United States should not be charged fees under this schedule, with the exception of those specifically prescribed in Items 2, 4 and 5, when the information requested is available through remote electronic access.

- Federal agencies or programs that are funded from judiciary appropriations (agencies, organizations, and individuals providing services authorized by the Criminal Justice Act, 18 U.S.C. § 3006 and bankruptcy administrators) should not be charged any fees under this schedule.

A.   Filing Fees—New Civil Action

1.   The filing fee for a complaint is $350.00.

2.   The filing fee for a notice of removal is $350.00.

3.   The filing fee for an application for writ of habeas corpus is $5.00.

B.   Filing Fee—Appeal

1.   For docketing a case on appeal or review, or docketing any other proceeding, $455.   A separate fee shall be paid by each party filing a notice of appeal in the district court, but parties filing a joint notice of appeal in the district court are required to pay only one fee.   A docketing fee shall not be charged for the docketing of an application for the allowance of an interlocutory appeal under 28 U.S.C. § 1292(b), unless the appeal is allowed.   The costs will be broken down as follows: $450 as specified in the revised Miscellaneous Fee Schedule, and the $5.00 fee required by 28 U.S.C. § 1917.   These fees are payable TO THE DISTRICT COURT CLERK when the notice of appeal is filed.

C.   Filing Fee—Miscellaneous Fees

1.   For filing any document that is not related to a pending case or proceeding, $46.

2.   For conducting a search of the district court records, $30 per name or item searched.   This fee applies to services rendered on behalf of the United States if the information requested is available through electronic access.

3.   For certification of any document, $11.   For exemplification of any document, $18.

4.   For reproducing any record or paper, $.50 per page.   This fee shall apply to paper copies made from either:

(1) original documents; or (2) microfiche or microfilm reproductions of the original records.   This fee shall apply to services rendered on behalf of the United States if the record or paper requested is available through electronic access.

5.   For reproduction of an audio recording of a court proceeding, $30.   This fee applies to services rendered on behalf of the United States, if the recording is available electronically.

6.   For each microfiche sheet of film or microfilm jacket copy of any court record, where available, $6.

7.   For retrieval of a record from a Federal Records Center, National Archives, or other storage location removed from the place of business of the court, $53.

8.   For a check paid into the court which is returned for lack of funds, $53.

9. For an appeal to a district judge from a judgment of conviction by a magistrate judge in a misdemeanor case, **$37**.

10. For original admission of attorneys to practice, **$226** each, including a certificate of admission. For reregistration to continue admission for those attorneys admitted prior to January 1, 2001, $25.00. For a duplicate certificate of admission or certificate of good standing, **$18**. The fee for filing a motion for leave to appear and practice in a particular case in the District of Massachusetts is $50.00.

11. The court may charge and collect fees commensurate with the cost of providing copies of the local rules of court. The court may also distribute copies of the local rules without charge.

12. The clerk shall assess a charge for the handling of registry funds deposited with the court, to be assessed from interest earnings and in accordance with the detailed fee schedule issued by the Director of the Administrative Office of the United States Courts.

    For management of registry funds invested through the Court Registry Investment System (CRIS), a fee at a rate of 2.5 basis points shall be assessed from interest earnings.

13. For filing an action brought under Title III of the Cuban Liberty and Democratic Solidarity (LIBERTAD) Act of 1996, P.L. 104–114, 110 Stat. § 785 (1996), **$6,355**. (This fee is in addition to the filing fee prescribed in 28 U.S.C. 1914(a) for instituting any civil action other than a writ of habeas corpus.)

(Eff. 9/7/2011)

ELECTRONIC PUBLIC ACCESS FEE SCHEDULE

(Issued in accordance with 28 U.S.C. § 1913, 1914, 1926, 1930, 1932)

As directed by Congress, the Judicial Conference has determined that the following fees are necessary to reimburse expenses incurred by the judiciary in providing electronic public access to court records. These fees shall apply to the United States unless otherwise stated. No fees under this schedule shall be charged to federal agencies or programs which are funded from judiciary appropriations, including, but not limited to, agencies, organizations, and individuals providing services authorized by the Criminal Justice Act, 18 U.S.C. § 3006A, and bankruptcy administrator programs.

I. For electronic access to court data via a federal judiciary Internet site: eight cents per page, with the total for any document, docket sheet, or case-specific report not to exceed the fee for thirty pages- provided however that transcripts of federal court proceedings shall not be subject to the thirty-page fee limit. For electronic access to an audio file of a court hearing via a federal judiciary Internet site: $2.40 per audio file. Attorneys of record and parties in a case (including pro se litigants) receive one free electronic copy of all documents filed electronically, if receipt is required by law or directed by the filer. No fee is owed under this provision until an account holder accrues charges of more than $10 in a quarterly billing cycle. Consistent with Judicial Conference policy, courts may, upon a showing of cause, exempt indigents, bankruptcy case trustees, individual researchers associated with educational institutions, courts, section 501(c)(3) not-for-profit organizations, court appointed pro bono attorneys, and pro bono ADR neutrals from payment of these fees. Courts must find that parties from the classes of persons or entities listed above seeking exemption have demonstrated that an exemption is necessary in order to avoid unreasonable burdens and to promote public access to information. For individual researchers, courts must also find that the defined research project is intended for academic research, and not for commercial purposes or internet redistribution. Any user granted an exemption agrees not to sell for profit the data obtained as a result. Any transfer of data obtained as the result of a fee exemption is prohibited unless expressly authorized by the court. Exemptions may be granted for a definite period of time and may be revoked at the discretion of the court granting the exemption.

II.   For printing copies of any record or document accessed electronically at a public terminal in the courthouse: ten cents per page. This fee shall apply to services rendered on behalf of the United States if the record requested is remotely available through electronic access.

III. For every search of court records conducted by the PACER Service Center, $26 per name or item searched.

IV.   For the PACER Service Center to reproduce on paper any record pertaining to a PACER account, if this information is remotely available through electronic access, 50 cents per page.

V.   For a check paid to the PACER Service Center which is returned for lack of funds, $45.

JUDICIAL CONFERENCE POLICY NOTES

Courts should not exempt local, state or federal government agencies, members of the media, attorneys or others not members of one of the groups listed above. Exemptions should be granted as the exception, not the rule. A court may not use this exemption language to exempt all users. An exemption applies only to access related to the case or purpose for which it was given. The prohibition on transfer of information received without fee is not intended to bar a quote or reference to information received as a result of a fee exemption in a scholarly or other similar work.

The electronic public access fee applies to electronic court data viewed remotely from the public records of individual cases in the court, including filed documents and the docket sheet. Audio files of court hearings do not include naturalization ceremonies or appellate oral arguments. Electronic court data may be viewed free at public terminals at the courthouse and courts may provide other local court information at no cost. Examples of information that can be provided at no cost include: local rules, court forms, news items, court calendars, opinions, and other information—such as court hours, court location, telephone listings—determined locally to benefit the public and the court.

Academic Researcher Exemption Request—Sample

APPLICATION FOR EXEMPTION FROM
THE JUDICIAL CONFERENCE'S ELECTRONIC PUBLIC ACCESS FEES
IN THE DISTRICT OF _____

In support of this application, I provide the following:

1) I am an individual researcher associated with _____.

2) The data received will be used in my research project:

_____

_____

_____ (Attach additional sheets as necessary)

3) An exemption from the Judicial Conference's Electronic Public Access Fee is necessary in order to avoid unreasonable burdens and to promote public access to information.

4) I understand that this fee exemption will apply only to me, will be valid only for the purposes stated above, and will apply only to the electronic case files of this court that are available through the PACER service.

5) I agree that any data received through this exemption will not be sold for profit, will not be transferred, will not be used for commercial purposes, and will not be redistributed via the Internet.

Declaration: I declare that the above information is true and understand that a false statement may result in abolishment of my exempt access and an assessment of Electronic Public Access usage fees.

Date: _____

_____
Applicant's signature

_____
Printed name

[Effective September 1, 1990. Amended effective December 18, 1996; January 1, 1998; June 1, 1999; February 1, 2001; February 12, 2008; September 7, 2011; November 1, 2011.]

* Issued in accordance with 28 U.S.C. § 1914(b), last modification November 1, 2011. Fees changed are noted in bold text.

APPENDIX B. CIVIL COVER SHEET

CIVIL COVER SHEET

℘JS 44 (Rev. 12/07)

The JS 44 civil cover sheet and the information contained herein neither replace nor supplement the filing and service of pleadings or other papers as required by law, except as provided by local rules of court. This form, approved by the Judicial Conference of the United States in September 1974, is required for the use of the Clerk of Court for the purpose of initiating the civil docket sheet. (SEE INSTRUCTIONS ON THE REVERSE OF THE FORM.)

I. (a) PLAINTIFFS

DEFENDANTS

(b) County of Residence of First Listed Plaintiff _____
     (EXCEPT IN U.S. PLAINTIFF CASES)

County of Residence of First Listed Defendant _____
     (IN U.S. PLAINTIFF CASES ONLY)

NOTE: IN LAND CONDEMNATION CASES, USE THE LOCATION OF THE LAND INVOLVED.

(c) Attorney's (Firm Name, Address, and Telephone Number)

Attorneys (If Known)

II. BASIS OF JURISDICTION (Place an "X" in One Box Only)

☐ 1 U.S. Government Plaintiff

☐ 2 U.S. Government Defendant

☐ 3 Federal Question (U.S. Government Not a Party)

☐ 4 Diversity (Indicate Citizenship of Parties in Item III)

III. CITIZENSHIP OF PRINCIPAL PARTIES (Place an "X" in One Box for Plaintiff and One Box for Defendant)
(For Diversity Cases Only)

	PTF	DEF		PTF	DEF
Citizen of This State	☐ 1	☐ 1	Incorporated or Principal Place of Business In This State	☐ 4	☐ 4
Citizen of Another State	☐ 2	☐ 2	Incorporated and Principal Place of Business In Another State	☐ 5	☐ 5
Citizen or Subject of a Foreign Country	☐ 3	☐ 3	Foreign Nation	☐ 6	☐ 6

IV. NATURE OF SUIT (Place an "X" in One Box Only)

CONTRACT	TORTS		FORFEITURE/PENALTY	BANKRUPTCY	OTHER STATUTES
☐ 110 Insurance	**PERSONAL INJURY**	**PERSONAL INJURY**	☐ 610 Agriculture	☐ 422 Appeal 28 USC 158	☐ 400 State Reapportionment
☐ 120 Marine	☐ 310 Airplane	☐ 362 Personal Injury - Med. Malpractice	☐ 620 Other Food & Drug	☐ 423 Withdrawal 28 USC 157	☐ 410 Antitrust
☐ 130 Miller Act	☐ 315 Airplane Product Liability		☐ 625 Drug Related Seizure of Property 21 USC 881		☐ 430 Banks and Banking
☐ 140 Negotiable Instrument	☐ 320 Assault, Libel & Slander	☐ 365 Personal Injury - Product Liability	☐ 630 Liquor Laws	**PROPERTY RIGHTS**	☐ 450 Commerce
☐ 150 Recovery of Overpayment & Enforcement of Judgment	☐ 330 Federal Employers' Liability	☐ 368 Asbestos Personal Injury Product Liability	☐ 640 R.R. & Truck	☐ 820 Copyrights	☐ 460 Deportation
☐ 151 Medicare Act	☐ 340 Marine		☐ 650 Airline Regs.	☐ 830 Patent	☐ 470 Racketeer Influenced and Corrupt Organizations
☐ 152 Recovery of Defaulted Student Loans (Excl. Veterans)	☐ 345 Marine Product Liability	**PERSONAL PROPERTY**	☐ 660 Occupational Safety/Health	☐ 840 Trademark	☐ 480 Consumer Credit
☐ 153 Recovery of Overpayment of Veteran's Benefits	☐ 350 Motor Vehicle	☐ 370 Other Fraud	☐ 690 Other		☐ 490 Cable/Sat TV
☐ 160 Stockholders' Suits	☐ 355 Motor Vehicle Product Liability	☐ 371 Truth in Lending	**LABOR**	**SOCIAL SECURITY**	☐ 810 Selective Service
☐ 190 Other Contract	☐ 360 Other Personal Injury	☐ 380 Other Personal Property Damage	☐ 710 Fair Labor Standards Act	☐ 861 HIA (1395ff)	☐ 850 Securities/Commodities/ Exchange
☐ 195 Contract Product Liability		☐ 385 Property Damage Product Liability	☐ 720 Labor/Mgmt. Relations	☐ 862 Black Lung (923)	☐ 875 Customer Challenge 12 USC 3410
☐ 196 Franchise			☐ 730 Labor/Mgmt.Reporting & Disclosure Act	☐ 863 DIWC/DIWW (405(g))	☐ 890 Other Statutory Actions
REAL PROPERTY	**CIVIL RIGHTS**	**PRISONER PETITIONS**	☐ 740 Railway Labor Act	☐ 864 SSID Title XVI	☐ 891 Agricultural Acts
☐ 210 Land Condemnation	☐ 441 Voting	☐ 510 Motions to Vacate Sentence	☐ 790 Other Labor Litigation	☐ 865 RSI (405(g))	☐ 892 Economic Stabilization Act
☐ 220 Foreclosure	☐ 442 Employment	**Habeas Corpus:**	☐ 791 Empl. Ret. Inc. Security Act	**FEDERAL TAX SUITS**	☐ 893 Environmental Matters
☐ 230 Rent Lease & Ejectment	☐ 443 Housing/ Accommodations	☐ 530 General		☐ 870 Taxes (U.S. Plaintiff or Defendant)	☐ 894 Energy Allocation Act
☐ 240 Torts to Land	☐ 444 Welfare	☐ 535 Death Penalty		☐ 871 IRS—Third Party 26 USC 7609	☐ 895 Freedom of Information Act
☐ 245 Tort Product Liability	☐ 445 Amer. w/Disabilities - Employment	☐ 540 Mandamus & Other	**IMMIGRATION**		☐ 900 Appeal of Fee Determination Under Equal Access to Justice
☐ 290 All Other Real Property	☐ 446 Amer. w/Disabilities - Other	☐ 550 Civil Rights	☐ 462 Naturalization Application		
	☐ 440 Other Civil Rights	☐ 555 Prison Condition	☐ 463 Habeas Corpus - Alien Detainee		☐ 950 Constitutionality of State Statutes
			☐ 465 Other Immigration Actions		

V. ORIGIN (Place an "X" in One Box Only)

☐ 1 Original Proceeding
☐ 2 Removed from State Court
☐ 3 Remanded from Appellate Court
☐ 4 Reinstated or Reopened
☐ 5 Transferred from another district (specify)
☐ 6 Multidistrict Litigation
☐ 7 Appeal to District Judge from Magistrate Judgment

VI. CAUSE OF ACTION

Cite the U.S. Civil Statute under which you are filing (Do not cite jurisdictional statutes unless diversity):

Brief description of cause:

VII. REQUESTED IN COMPLAINT:

☐ CHECK IF THIS IS A CLASS ACTION UNDER F.R.C.P. 23

DEMAND $

CHECK YES only if demanded in complaint:
JURY DEMAND: ☐ Yes ☐ No

VIII. RELATED CASE(S) IF ANY

(See instructions):

JUDGE

DOCKET NUMBER

DATE

SIGNATURE OF ATTORNEY OF RECORD

FOR OFFICE USE ONLY

RECEIPT # _____ AMOUNT _____ APPLYING IFP _____ JUDGE _____ MAG. JUDGE _____

[Print]   [Save As...]   [Export as FDF]   [Retrieve FDF File]   [Reset]

Authority For Civil Cover Sheet

The JS 44 civil cover sheet and the information contained herein neither replaces nor supplements the filings and service of pleading or other papers as required by law, except as provided by local rules of court. This form, approved by the Judicial Conference of the United States in September 1974, is required for the use of the Clerk of Court for the purpose of initiating the civil docket sheet. Consequently, a civil cover sheet is submitted to the Clerk of Court for each civil complaint filed. The attorney filing a case should complete the form as follows:

I. **(a) Plaintiffs-Defendants.** Enter names (last, first, middle initial) of plaintiff and defendant. If the plaintiff or defendant is a government agency, use only the full name or standard abbreviations. If the plaintiff or defendant is an official within a government agency, identify first the agency and then the official, giving both name and title.

(b) County of Residence. For each civil case filed, except U.S. plaintiff cases, enter the name of the county where the first listed plaintiff resides at the time of filing. In U.S. plaintiff cases, enter the name of the county in which the first listed defendant resides at the time of filing. (NOTE: In land condemnation cases, the county of residence of the "defendant" is the location of the tract of land involved.)

(c) Attorneys. Enter the firm name, address, telephone number, and attorney of record. If there are several attorneys, list them on an attachment, noting in this section "(see attachment)".

II. **Jurisdiction.** The basis of jurisdiction is set forth under Rule 8(a), F.R.C.P., which requires that jurisdictions be shown in pleadings. Place an "X" in one of the boxes. If there is more than one basis of jurisdiction, precedence is given in the order shown below.

United States plaintiff. (1) Jurisdiction based on 28 U.S.C. 1345 and 1348. Suits by agencies and officers of the United States are included here.

United States defendant. (2) When the plaintiff is suing the United States, its officers or agencies, place an "X" in this box.

Federal question. (3) This refers to suits under 28 U.S.C. 1331, where jurisdiction arises under the Constitution of the United States, an amendment to the Constitution, an act of Congress or a treaty of the United States. In cases where the U.S. is a party, the U.S. plaintiff or defendant code takes precedence, and box 1 or 2 should be marked.

Diversity of citizenship. (4) This refers to suits under 28 U.S.C. 1332, where parties are citizens of different states. When Box 4 is checked, the citizenship of the different parties must be checked. (See Section III below; federal question actions take precedence over diversity cases.)

III. **Residence (citizenship) of Principal Parties.** This section of the JS 44 is to be completed if diversity of citizenship was indicated above. Mark this section for each principal party.

IV. **Nature of Suit.** Place an "X" in the appropriate box. If the nature of suit cannot be determined, be sure the cause of action, in Section VI below, is sufficient to enable the deputy clerk or the statistical clerks in the Administrative Office to determine the nature of suit. If the cause fits more than one nature of suit, select the most definitive.

V. **Origin.** Place an "X" in one of the seven boxes.

Original Proceedings. (1) Cases which originate in the United States district courts.

Removed from State Court. (2) Proceedings initiated in state courts may be removed to the district courts under Title 28 U.S.C., Section 1441. When the petition for removal is granted, check this box.

Remanded from Appellate Court. (3) Check this box for cases remanded to the district court for further action. Use the date of remand as the filing date.

Reinstated or Reopened. (4) Check this box for cases reinstated or reopened in the district court. Use the reopening date as the filing date.

Transferred from Another District. (5) For cases transferred under Title 28 U.S.C. Section 1404(a). Do not use this for within district transfers or multidistrict litigation transfers.

Multidistrict Litigation. (6) Check this box when a multidistrict case is transferred into the district under authority of Title 28 U.S.C. Section 1407. When this box is checked, do not check (5) above.

Appeal to District Judge from Magistrate Judgment. (7) Check this box for an appeal from a magistrate judge's decision.

VI. **Cause of Action.** Report the civil statute directly related to the cause of action and give a brief description of the cause. **Do not cite jurisdictional statutes unless diversity.** Example: U.S. Civil Statute: 47 USC 553
                                              Brief Description: Unauthorized reception of cable service

VII. **Requested in Complaint.** Class Action. Place an "X" in this box if you are filing a class action under Rule 23, F.R.Cv.P.

Demand. In this space enter the dollar amount (in thousands of dollars) being demanded or indicate other demand such as a preliminary injunction.

Jury Demand. Check the appropriate box to indicate whether or not a jury is being demanded.

VIII. **Related Cases.** This section of the JS 44 is used to reference related pending cases if any. If there are related pending cases, insert the docket numbers and the corresponding judge names for such cases.

Date and Attorney Signature. Date and sign the civil cover sheet.

APPENDIX C.   LOCAL CIVIL CATEGORY SHEET
UNITED STATES DISTRICT COURT
DISTRICT OF MASSACHUSETTS*

1.   Title of case (name of first party on each side only) _____
_____

2.   Category in which the case belongs based upon the numbered nature of suit code
     listed on the civil cover sheet. (See local rule 40.1(a) (1)).

     ___   I.   410, 441, 470, 535, 830*, 891, 893, 895, R.23, REGARDLESS OF NATURE
                OF SUIT.

     ___   II. 110, 130, 140, 160, 190, 196, 230, 240, 290,320,362, 370, 371, 380, 430, 440, 442,
                443, 445, 446, 448, 710, 720, 740, 790, 820*, 840*, 850, 870, 871.

     ___   III. 120, 150, 151, 152, 153, 195, 210, 220, 245, 310, 315, 330, 340, 345, 350, 355, 360,
                365, 367, 368, 375, 385, 400, 422, 423, 450, 460, 462, 463, 465, 480, 490, 510, 530,
                540, 550, 555, 625, 690, 751, 791, 861–865, 890, 896, 899, 950.

                *Also complete AO 120 or AO 121. for patent, trademark or copyright
                cases.

3.   Title and number, if any, of related cases. (See local rule 40.1(g)). If more than one
     prior related case has been filed in this district please indicate the title and number
     of the first filed case in this court.

     _____

4.   Has a prior action between the same parties and based on the same claim ever been
     filed in this court?

                                                   YES ☐   NO ☐

5.   Does the complaint in this case question the constitutionality of an act of congress
     affecting the public interest? (See 28 USC § 2403)

                                                   YES ☐   NO ☐

     If so, is the U.S.A. or an officer, agent or employee of the U.S. a party?

                                                   YES ☐   NO ☐

6.   Is this case required to be heard and determined by a district court of three judges
     pursuant to title 28 USC § 2284?

                                                   YES ☐   NO ☐

7.   Do all of the parties in this action, excluding governmental agencies of the united
     states and the Commonwealth of Massachusetts ("governmental agencies"), residing
     in Massachusetts reside in the same division?—(See Local Rule 40.1(d)).   YES ☐
     NO ☐

     (a)   If yes, in which division do all of the non- governmental parties reside?

           Eastern Division   ☐   Central Division   ☐   Western Division   ☐

     (b)   If no, in which division do the majority of the plaintiffs or the only
           parties, excluding governmental agencies, residing in Massachusetts re-
           side?

           Eastern Division   ☐   Central Division   ☐   Western Division   ☐

(8)   If filing a Notice of Removal—are there any motions pending in the state court requiring the attention of this Court? (If yes, submit a separate sheet identifying the motions)

YES ☐   NO ☐

(PLEASE TYPE OR PRINT)
ATTORNEY'S NAME _____
ADDRESS _____
TELEPHONE NO. _____

[Amended effective September 7, 2011; January 3, 2012.]

APPENDIX D. NOTICE OF SCHEDULING CONFERENCE

UNITED STATES DISTRICT COURT
DISTRICT OF MASSACHUSETTS

_____
Plaintiff(s)

vs.   Civil Action No.: _____

_____
Defendant(s)

NOTICE OF SCHEDULING CONFERENCE

An initial scheduling conference will be held in Courtroom No. ___ on the ___ floor at ____.m. on _____, in accordance with Fed.R.Civ.P. 16(b) and Local Rules (LR) 16.1 and 16.6 (for patent cases). The court considers attendance of the senior lawyers ultimately responsible for the case and compliance with sections (B), (C), and (D) of LR 16.1[1] and LR 16.6 for patent cases to be of the utmost importance. Counsel may be given a continuance only if actually engaged on trial. Failure to comply fully with this notice and with sections (B), (C), and (D) of LR 16.1 and section (A) of LR 16.6 for patent cases may result in sanctions under LR 1.3. Counsel for the plaintiff is responsible for ensuring that all parties and/or their attorneys, who have not filed an answer or appearance with the court, are notified of the scheduling conference date.

_____
Date

By: _____
Deputy Clerk

_____

[1] These sections of Local Rule 16.1 (See LR 16.6 for additional provisions for patent cases) provide:

(B) Obligation of Counsel to Confer. Unless otherwise ordered by the judge, counsel for the parties shall, pursuant to Fed.R.Civ.P. 26(f), confer no later than twenty-one (21) days before the date for the scheduling conference for the purpose of:

(1) preparing an agenda of matters to be discussed at the scheduling conference,

(2) preparing a proposed pretrial schedule for the case that includes a plan for discovery, and

(3) considering whether they will consent to trial by magistrate judge.

(C) Settlement Proposals. Unless otherwise ordered by the judge, the plaintiff shall present written settlement proposals to all defendants no later than fourteen (14) days before the date for the scheduling conference. Defense counsel shall have conferred with their clients on the subject of settlement before the scheduling conference and be prepared to respond to the proposals at the scheduling conference.

(D) Joint Statement. Unless otherwise ordered by the judge, the parties are required to file, no later than seven (7) business days before the scheduling conference and after consideration of the topics contemplated by Fed.R.Civ.P. 16(b) and 26(f), a joint statement containing a proposed pretrial schedule, which shall include:

(1) a joint discovery plan scheduling the time and length for all discovery events, that shall

(a) conform to the obligation to limit discovery set forth in Fed.R.Civ.P. 26(b), and

(b) take into account the desirability of conducting phased discovery in which the first phase is limited to developing information needed for a realistic assessment of the case and, if the case does not terminate, the second phase is directed at information needed to prepare for trial; and

(2) a proposed schedule for the filing of motions; and

(3) certifications signed by counsel and by an authorized representative of each party affirming that each party and that party's counsel have conferred:

(a) with a view to establishing a budget for the costs of conducting the full course—and various alternative courses—of the litigation; and

(b) to consider the resolution of the litigation through the use of alternative dispute resolution programs such as those outlined in Local Rule 16.4.

To the extent that all parties are able to reach agreement on a proposed pretrial schedule, they shall so indicate. To the extent that the parties differ on what the pretrial schedule should be, they shall set forth separately the items on which they differ and indicate the nature of that difference. The purpose of the parties' proposed pretrial schedule or schedules shall be to advise the judge of the parties' best estimates of the amounts of time they will need to accomplish specified pretrial steps. The parties' proposed agenda for the scheduling conference, and their proposed pretrial schedule or schedules, shall be considered by the judge as advisory only.

[Revised effective December, 2000; June 14, 2010.]

APPENDIX E.　LOCAL RULE 16.6 SUPPLEMENT SAMPLE SPECIAL SCHEDULING ORDER FOR PATENT INFRINGEMENT CASES

SAMPLE SPECIAL SCHEDULING ORDER FOR PATENT INFRINGEMENT CASES

This appendix sets forth a sample scheduling order for claim construction and related procedures in patent cases *[with suggested timing in brackets]*. These procedures should be viewed as supplementing, not replacing, the LR 16.1 schedule. The Court and parties may incorporate such suggested procedures into the LR 16.1 scheduling order.

(A) Preliminary Disclosures

(1) Preliminary Infringement Disclosure

No later than _____ [30] days after the Rule 16 Case Management Conference, the patentee shall serve and file preliminary disclosure of the claims infringed. The patentee shall specify which claims are allegedly infringed and identify the accused product(s) or method(s) that allegedly infringe those claims. The patentee shall also specify whether the alleged infringement is literal or falls under the doctrine of equivalents. If the patentee has not already done so, the patentee shall produce all documents supporting its contentions and/or identify any such supporting documents produced by the accused infringer. Such disclosures may be amended and supplemented up to _____ [30] days before the date of the Markman Hearing. After that time, such disclosures may be amended or supplemented only pursuant to ¶ D(1) or by leave of court, for good cause shown.

The patentee may use a table such as that represented below.

CLAIM LIMITATION	ACCUSED COMPONENT	BASIS OF INFRINGEMENT CONTENTION

(2) Preliminary Invalidity and Non–Infringement Disclosures No later than _____ [60] days after service of the patentee's preliminary infringement contentions, the accused infringer shall serve and file Preliminary Invalidity and Non-Infringement Contentions. The accused infringer shall identify prior art that anticipates or renders obvious the identified patent claims in question and, for each such prior art reference, shall specify whether it anticipates or is relevant to the obviousness inquiry. If applicable, the accused infringer shall also specify any other grounds for invalidity, such as indefiniteness, best mode, enablement, or written description. If the accused infringer has not already done so, the accused infringer shall produce documents relevant to the invalidity defenses and/or identify any such supporting documents produced by the patentee. Further, if the accused infringer has not already done so, the accused infringer shall produce documents sufficient to show operation of the accused product(s) or method(s) that the patentee identified in its preliminary infringement disclosures. Such disclosures may be amended and supplemented up to _____ [30] days before the date of the Markman Hearing. After that time, such disclosures may be amended or supplemented only pursuant to ¶ D(1) or by leave of court, for good cause shown, except that, if the patentee amends or supplements its preliminary infringement disclosures, the accused infringer may likewise amend or supplement its disclosures within _____ [30] days of service of the amended or supplemented infringement disclosures.

The accused infringer may use the charts shown below.

324

CLAIM LIMITATION	PRIOR ART OR OTHER EVIDENCE	BASIS OF INVALIDITY CONTENTION

CLAIM LIMITATION	ACCUSED COMPONENT	BASIS OF NON–INFRINGEMENT CONTENTION

(2) Disclosures in Declaratory Judgment Actions

In declaratory judgment actions initially filed by potential infringers(*i.e.*, as opposed to being stated by way of answer, counterclaim, or other response to a first-filed complaint for patent infringement), the disclosure requirements of subsections (A)(1) and (2) above apply as if the action had been initiated by the patent holder, except that (a) the preliminary infringement disclosure of the declaratory judgment defendant/patent holder shall be due not less than 90 days after the Rule 16 Case Management Conference and (b), if the declaratory judgment defendant/patent holder does not state a claim for infringement, then only the declaratory judgment plaintiff/potential infringer's disclosure requirements shall apply.

(B) Claim Construction Proceedings

(1) No later than [120] days after completion of the preliminary disclosures, the parties shall simultaneously exchange a list of claim terms to be construed and proposed constructions.

(2) No later than [21] days after exchanging the list of claims, the parties shall simultaneously exchange and file preliminary claim construction briefs. Each brief shall contain a list of terms construed, the party's proposed construction of each term, and evidence and argument supporting each construction. Absent leave of court, preliminary claim construction briefs shall be limited to _____ [25] pages, double spaced, of at least 12–point Times New Roman font or equivalent, including footnotes.

(3) No later than [14] days following exchange and filing of the preliminary claim construction briefs, parties shall simultaneously exchange reply briefs. Absent leave of court, reply briefs shall be limited to [15] pages, double spaced, of at least 12–point Times New Roman font or equivalent, including footnotes.

(4) No later than [14] days following exchange and filing of the reply briefs, the parties shall finalize the list of disputed terms for the court to construe. The parties shall prepare and file a joint claim construction and prehearing statement (hereafter the "joint statement") that identifies both agreed and disputed terms.

(a) The joint statement shall note the anticipated length of time necessary for the claim construction hearing and whether any party proposes to call witnesses, including a statement that such extrinsic evidence does not conflict with intrinsic evidence.

(b) The joint statement shall also indicate whether the parties will present tutorials on the relevant technology, the form of such tutorials, and the timing for such tutorials in relation to the claim construction hearing. If the parties plan to provide tutorials in the form of briefs, declarations, computer animations, slide presentations, or other media, the parties shall exchange such materials _____ [7] days before the claim construction hearing. In the alternative, the parties may present tutorials through presentations by the attorneys or experts at the claim construction hearing.

(c) The joint statement shall include a proposed order in which parties will present their arguments at the claim construction hearing, which may be term-by-term or party-by-party, depending on the issues in the case.

(d) The joint statement shall limit the number of claim terms to be construed and shall prioritize the disputed terms in order of importance. The Court suggests that, ordinarily, no more than ten (10) terms per patent be identified as requiring construction.

(e) The joint statement shall include a joint claim construction chart, noting each party's proposed construction of each term, and supporting evidence. The parties may use the form shown below.

TERM	PATENTEE'S CONSTRUCTION	ACCUSED INFRINGER'S CONSTRUCTION	COURT'S CONSTRUCTION

(C) The Claim Construction Hearing (a.k.a. "*Markman* Hearing")

The Court shall schedule a hearing date promptly after the filing of the joint claim construction statement.

(D) After the Hearing

(1) If necessary, the parties may amend their preliminary infringement/non-infringement and invalidity disclosures, noting whether any infringement or invalidity contentions are withdrawn, within [30] days after the Court's ruling on the claim construction.

(2) If the fact discovery period has expired before a ruling on claim construction, and upon motion or stipulation of the parties, the Court may grant additional time for discovery. Such additional discovery shall be limited to issues of infringement, invalidity, or unenforceability dependent on the claim construction.

(E) Expert Discovery

(1) Ordinarily, expert discovery, including expert reports and depositions, shall be scheduled to occur after the close of fact discovery.

(2) If expert discovery has been substantially conducted before a claim construction ruling, then the Court may grant additional time for supplemental expert discovery. Such additional discovery shall be limited to issues of infringement, invalidity, or unenforceability dependent on the claim construction.

[Effective September 7, 2011.]

ELECTRONIC CASE FILING
GENERAL ORDER RE: ELECTRONIC CASE FILING

Fed. R. Civ. P. 5(e) authorizes this Court to establish practices and procedures for the filing, signing and verification of documents by electronic means.

Accordingly, the United States District Court for the District of Massachusetts hereby orders that all cases filed within this District are eligible for electronic case filing according to the rules and procedures outlined in the following:

A) The Electronic Case Filing Administrative Procedures

B) Electronic Case Filing User's Manual

C) Standing Orders concerning ECF implementation and the provision of courtesy copies.* Unless otherwise specified by the particular court in its session order, each session will adopt a standing order of the form attached.

Please Note: Counsel should pay particular attention to the rules with regard to sealed documents and ex parte submissions. Under ECF, if sealed documents or ex parte submissions are inadvertently filed electronically, they become immediately available to the public.

After September 8, 2003, counsel who have registered for ECF and who have received information concerning login and passwords will receive electronic notice of court orders and decisions. After October 1, 2003, counsel who have registered for ECF and have received login and password information will be eligible to file documents electronically, according to the rules and procedures outlined above.

* [**Publisher's Note:** Counsel should consult specific Sessions of Court for Standing Order requirements on CM/ECF that may apply in practice before a specific judge.]

CM/ECF CASE MANAGEMENT/ELECTRONIC CASE FILES ADMINISTRATIVE PROCEDURES

ELECTRONIC FILING AND PDF

Electronic Filing is the process of uploading a document from the registered user's computer, using the court's Internet-based Case Management/Electronic Case Files (CM/ECF) system, to file the document in the court's official case file. The CM/ECF system only accepts documents in 'portable document format' (PDF). There are two types of PDF documents:

Electronically converted PDF documents are created from word processing documents (MS Word, WordPerfect, etc.) using any appropriate software. These documents are text searchable and the file size is generally smaller than a scanned document. CM/ECF users may use any brand of software to convert documents to PDF.

Scanned PDF documents are created from paper documents run through an optical scanner. Scanned PDF documents are generally not searchable and have a larger file size. Please note that software used to create scanned documents may (and should) be set in such a way that the document is "text-searchable."

Documents converted to PDF, rather than scanned, are preferred for filing in CM/ECF.

NOTE: the court will begin requiring submission of documents in PDF/A format in the foreseeable future. PDF/A is an enhanced version of the traditional PDF format. Newer versions of most PDF software will be able to convert to this format. Additional information on PDF/A documents may be found on the court's website at http ://www.mad.uscourts.gov/training/pdf/pdfa.pdf.

ADMINISTRATIVE PROCEDURES

A. Effective Dates and Other General Information.

1. The court began accepting filings electronically through the CM/ECF system on October 1, 2003. Local Rule 5.4, (LR) as modified on January 1, 2006, mandates that all documents submitted for filing in all civil and criminal cases, except those documents specifically exempted in subsection L of these procedures, must be filed electronically using the ECF system. Any variation of these requirements can be made only by orders issued by individual judges.

2. On January 1, 2006 the court integrated the United States Treasury's "pay.gov" service into CM/ECF to accept case-related fees. LR 67.4, effective January 1, 2009 requires that all CM/ECF users pay case-related fees through CM/ECF and pay.gov.

3. The clerk's office will not maintain a paper document file in any civil or criminal case commenced after October 1, 2003, except as otherwise provided herein or as ordered by the judge in a particular session. (The official case files in actions commenced prior to October 1, 2003 may contain both paper versions of those documents filed prior to October 1, 2003 and electronic files of the documents filed on or after October 1, 2003). The official court record in ECF cases shall be the electronic file maintained on the court's database servers together with any paper documents, attachments and exhibits filed in accordance with these procedures.

Documents delivered to the court as a courtesy copy will not be maintained in the official court record.

4. The clerk's office will maintain a paper case file for cases involving pro se litigants, but may discard any original document after it has been scanned and uploaded to ECF.

5. All documents filed by electronic means must comply with technical standards established by the Judicial Conference of the United States or by this court.

6. The court adopted its Transcript Redaction Policy effective May 5, 2008.

7. The procedures governing electronic case filing shall be known as the "Administrative Procedures for Electronic Case Filing in the United States District Court for the District of Massachusetts." They shall be cited as "APECF."

8. These administrative procedures are intended to supplement the local rules of the United States District Court for the District of Massachusetts to the extent necessary to establish procedures for the signing, filing, service, maintenance and verification of documents by electronic means. Unless modified by an order of the court, all Federal Rules of Civil/Criminal Procedure, local rules, and standing orders of the court shall continue to apply to cases that are subject to electronic case filing.

B. Modifications. The court may modify these administrative procedures without prior notice as justice may require.

C. Relief From Administrative Procedures; Failure to Comply.

1. *Relief From Administrative Procedures.* The court may deviate from these procedures in specific cases, without prior notice, if deemed appropriate in the exercise of discretion, considering the need for the just, speedy, and inexpensive determination of matters pending before the court.

2. *Relief From Failure to Comply.* The court may excuse a failure to comply with any administrative procedure whenever justice so requires.

3. *Sanctions for Failure to Comply.* Except as provided by law, the court may impose sanctions as provided in LR 1.3 for failure to comply with these administrative procedures or with LR 5.4.

D. Definitions. CM/ECF means the court's Case Management/Electronic Case Filing System, which is an automated system that receives and stores documents in electronic form.

Document means any written matter filed by or with the court, whether filed conventionally or electronically, including but not limited to motions, pleadings, applications, petitions, notices, declarations, affidavits, exhibits, briefs, memoranda of law, orders, and deposition transcripts.

Electronic Filing or Electronically Filed means the transmission of a document in a portable document format ("PDF") for filing using the ECF system facilities.

Electronic Order or Electronic Notice means any order (or notice) of the court that is not accompanied by a PDF document.

Event is the term used to describe the menu items that may be selected to file documents in CM/ECF. For example, a memorandum in opposition is an event.

Filer means the attorney (or pro se litigant) with a CM/ECF login and password.

MBD means cases filed on the Miscellaneous Business Docket. (With a docket type of "mc")

Notice of Electronic Filing or NEF means the notice automatically generated by CM/ECF each time a document is electronically filed.

PDF or PDF/A means Portable Document Format. This includes both "Electronically Converted PDF Documents," and "Scanned PDF Documents." Electronically converted PDF documents are created from a word processing system (MS Word, WordPerfect, etc.) using PDF creation software and are text searchable. Scanned PDF documents are created from paper documents run through an optical scanner. Scanned documents may not be text-searchable.

E. Registration.

1. *Attorneys Admitted to the Bar of this Court.* Attorneys admitted to the bar of this court, including attorneys admitted pro hac vice, are required to register as users of the court's CM/ECF system prior to filing any pleadings electronically. Registration can be accomplished by using the on-line CM/ECF registration or by completing a CM/ECF Registration Form, a copy of which is on the court's website (www.mad.uscourts.gov). If not submitted on-line, completed CM/ECF registration forms should be mailed or hand delivered to:

Clerk, United States District Court
Attn: CM/ECF Registration
John Joseph Moakley United States Courthouse
1 Courthouse Way, Suite 2300
Boston, MA 02210

Once an account has been established by the court, the CM/ECF login and password will be sent to the registered user by the clerk's office via email.

Failure to file electronically. The clerk's office shall issue a notice regarding the mandatory use of CM/ECF to any attorney who files a document on paper, except as provided by subsection L. If the attorney continues to file documents on paper, the clerk's office shall prepare an Order to Show Cause for consideration by the judge to whom the case is assigned.

2. *Pro Se Litigants.* Anyone who is a party to a civil action, and not a prisoner, and who is not represented by an attorney may register as a filer in the CM/ECF system. The party must (1) have the approval of the judicial officer assigned to the case; and (2) attend a training session offered by the clerk's office on the ECF system or otherwise prove their proficiency on the use of the CM/ECF system before an ECF login will be issued.

The pro se litigant's filing access will be restricted to just those pending cases in which he/she is appearing pro se. Pro se litigants will be given access to all pending cases he or she has filed once written notice of these additional cases has been made to the clerk's office at the address above. The pro se litigant is obligated to notify the clerk's office should he or she obtain counsel for any case pending in this court.

3. *Use of the Login and Password.* A registered user shall not allow another person to file a document using the user's login and password, except for an

authorized agent of the filing user. Use of a user's login and password by an authorized agent shall be deemed to be the act of the registered user.

4. *Obligation to Update Information.* Each registered user has an obligation to maintain his/her CM/ECF account, following the instructions found in this court's CM/ECF Attorney User Manual. The user must maintain current information for his/her: name; mailing address (street and email); firm name or affiliation; and telephone number. If participating in an active CM/ECF case, the user shall inform the court and parties of such a change through the use of the "Notice of Change of Address" event in CM/ECF in each active case as directed in LR 83.5.2(e).

NOTE: due to system configuration, some attorneys are unable to update law firm affiliation and street address information. Attorneys unable to update account information are asked to contact the contact the Bar Liaison clerk at 617–748–9165 for assistance.

5. *PACER Registration.* All registered CM/ECF users also shall apply for a PACER account, and maintain a current user ID and password.

6. *Service.* Registering to use CM/ECF constitutes consent to service of all documents by electronic means as provided in these procedures and Federal Rule of Civil Procedure (Fed.R.Civ.P.) 5(b) and 77(d), and Federal Rule of Criminal Procedure (Fed.R.Crim.P.) 49(b).

7. *Email.* Every registered user must maintain an electronic mailbox of sufficient capacity, with the appropriate email permissions, to receive electronic notice of case-related transmissions.

F. Filing and Service of Civil and Miscellaneous Case Opening Documents.

1. Registered CM/ECF users shall file electronically any and all civil ("cv" case type) and miscellaneous (sometimes referred to as MBD or "mc" case type) case opening documents, such as a complaint, petition, or notice of removal in accordance with the guidelines and restrictions described in subsection L of this document. For civil cases only, filers shall submit the required civil cover and category sheets, both available on the court's website. Pursuant to LR 67.4, all case-related fees shall be paid by credit card in conjunction with CM/ECF and the United States Treasury's pay.gov service.

2. The clerk's office shall create an electronic summons, when appropriate, and provide it to counsel via CM/ECF. Recipients are directed to download the PDF file from the Notice of Electronic Filing (NEF) and create a summons for each party to be served. A party may not electronically serve a civil complaint but shall affect service in the manner required by Fed.R.Civ.P. 4. The return of service of the summons (or other acknowledgment of service) shall be filed with the court electronically.

3. If the attorney filing the new case is not yet registered to use CM/ECF, the clerk's office will issue the summons on paper, along with a notice regarding LR 5.4 and the mandatory use of CM/ECF.

G. Electronic Filing.

1. Electronic transmission of a document to the CM/ECF system, together with the transmission of a Notice of Electronic Filing (NEF) from the court at the completion of the transaction, constitutes the filing of the document for all purposes of the Federal Rules of Procedure and constitutes entry of the document on the docket maintained by the clerk pursuant to Fed.R.Civ.P. 58 and 79 and Fed.R.Crim.P. 55.

2. A document filed electronically shall be deemed filed as of the time and date stated on the NEF received from the court.

3. All pleadings filed electronically shall be titled in accordance with the approved dictionary of civil or criminal events of the CM/ECF system of this court. A list of events is available on the CM/ECF Training Information page of the court's website. The clerk's office may, when necessary and appropriate, modify the docket

entry description, or delete and re-enter the docket entry in order to comply with the court's quality assurance standards.

4. Any memorandum of law or other attachment filed in support of a main document shall be filed as a separate document, using the proper event.

5. If the filer is contemporaneously filing an objection or opposition with a cross motion, the cross motion must be filed as a separate docket entry.

6. The filer shall verify the accuracy and readability of any PDF file before electronically filing it in CM/ECF.

7. Electronically filed documents may contain the following types of hyperlinks:

(1) Hyperlinks to other portions of the same document;

(2) Hyperlinks to other documents filed within the CM/ECF system; and

(3) Hyperlinks to a location on the Internet that contains a source document for a citation. Hyperlinks to cited authority may not replace standard citation format. Complete citations must be included in the text of the filed document. Neither a hyperlink, nor any site to which it refers, shall be considered part of the record, but are simply convenient mechanisms for accessing material cited in a document filed in CM/ECF. Instructions on creating hyperlinks may be found in the CM/ECF User Manual.

The court accepts no responsibility for, and does not endorse, any product, organization, or content at any hyperlinked site, or at any site to which that site may be linked. The court accepts no responsibility for the availability or functionality of any hyperlink.

NOTE regarding PDF/A: In the near future, the CM/ECF software will be upgraded to require filers to submit documents in PDF/A.

One feature of PDF/A documents is that hyperlinks are commonly "masked," meaning that the full address of the referenced file is not written out; for example, clicking the word brief may open a brief which was previously filed in CM/ECF.

An "unmasked" hyperlink has the full address visible to the user, such as "https://ecf.dcd.uscourts.gov/doc1/4512244142".

Masked hyperlinks may or may not work in a PDF/A document, depending on how it was created. Currently, masked hyperlinks are preserved in PDF/A documents produced by the "Save As" method in Microsoft Word 2007 and 2010; the "PDFMaker" method in Microsoft Word 2007; and OpenOffice 2.4 ("PDF Export"). With other production methods, such as WordPerfect, the PDF/A document includes underlined words that appear to be links, but clicking them has no effect.

8. CM/ECF will not accept PDF documents containing tracking tags, embedded systems commands, password protections, access restrictions or other security features, special tags or dynamic features.

H. Service of Electronically Filed Documents.

1. Whenever a pleading or other document is filed electronically, the CM/ECF system will automatically generate and send an NEF (via email) to the filer and all CM/ECF registered users of record in the case.

2. Unless exempt or otherwise ordered by the court, all pleadings and other papers must be served on other parties by electronic means, through CM/ECF. Any pleading or other document filed with the court must bear a certificate of service in accordance with LR 5.2(b). The certificate of service shall state that the filer: (1) filed the document electronically, (2) that it will be served electronically to registered CM/ECF participants via the NEF and (3) that the filer will send paper copies to non-registered participants as indicated on the NEF.

Example:

Certificate of Service

I hereby certify that this document filed through the CM/ECF system will be sent electronically to the registered participants as identified on the NEF (NEF) and paper copies will be sent to those indicated as non registered participants on (date).

3. Transmission of the NEF through the court's transmission facilities will constitute service of the filed document upon a registered CM/ECF user and shall be deemed to satisfy the requirements of Fed.R.Civ.P. 5(b)(2)(E) and 77(d) and Fed.R.Crim.P. 49(b). The party filing the document electronically is responsible for serving a paper copy of the document by mail in accordance with Rule 5(b) to those case participants who have not been identified on the NEF as electronic recipients.

4. Service by electronic means shall be treated the same as service by mail. In accordance with LR 7.1, a party opposing a motion, shall file an opposition within 14 days after the motion is served, unless (1) the motion is for summary judgment, in which case the opposition shall be filed within 21 days after the motion is served or (2) another period is fixed by rule or statute, or by order of the court.

NOTE regarding NEFs received in error: CM/ECF users are obligated not to disseminate any notices received in error, electronically or on paper. Such notices shall be deleted immediately from the recipient's email. The recipient shall notify the clerk's office immediately.

5. In general, the court does not accept documents by email or by fax. If the court, in special circumstances, does authorize the submission of a document in that manner, the document shall not be considered files until an NEF is generated by CM/ECF at the completion of the transaction.

I. Documents with Fee Requirement. Documents filed in a case that require a fee, such as new civil and miscellaneous cases, notices of appeal and motions for leave to appear pro hac vice shall be electronically filed. The court uses the United States Treasury's pay.gov service to process the payment of case-related fees during the transaction, by credit or debit card. There is no additional registration required to use this service.

Should the filer not pay the fee during the entry of the fee-related document, the filer will be notified by the clerk's office to pay the fee electronically. To do that, the filer must first create a PDF document for filing captioned as "Notice of Attorney Payment of Fees" (see Appendix II) and then file that document on the CM/ECF docket using the docket entry of the same name, found under the Notices menu. That entry will allow the user to identify what fee is being paid, and process the credit card information.

J. Courtesy Copies for Judicial Officers. COURTESY COPIES OF DOCUMENTS FILED ELECTRONICALLY SHALL NOT BE SUBMITTED ROUTINELY.

Judicial officers, on a case-by-case basis, may require courtesy copies for specific cases, or types of motions, etc. A few Judicial Officers have entered Standing Orders, which may be found on their respective pages on the court's website (under Divisions). Any document filed on paper with the court as a courtesy copy must be clearly labeled as such (Example: COURTESY COPY—DO NOT SCAN). Documents delivered to the court as a courtesy copy will not be maintained in the official court record.

K. Deadlines. Filing documents electronically does not alter any filing deadlines.

Although CM/ECF is generally available 24 hours a day for filing, all electronic transmissions of documents must be completed prior to 6:00 PM, Eastern Standard (or Daylight Savings) Time, on the date on which it is due, in order to be considered timely filed that day. When a specific time of day deadline is set by court order or stipulation, the electronic filing must be completed by that time. Documents may be filed at any time of the day on days prior to the date on which it is due.

Documents are not considered filed with the court until the NEF is generated by CM/ECF.

L. Special Filing Requirements and Exceptions.

1. The following documents **shall be filed only on paper**:

a. Sealed documents. These documents shall be conventionally filed, clearly labeled as a "Sealed Document," following the requirements of LR 7.2. The filer shall also contemporaneously provide the court with a compact disk of the main document and any accompanying memorandum of law or exhibits as separate documents in PDF format, which shall be named and organized in a manner that clearly identifies each document.

A party shall electronically file a motion, pursuant to LR 7.2, to file a document under seal (unless the motion to seal itself is to be filed under seal). Motions for impoundment shall be specific about what is to be sealed (the document and/or the related docket entries). The motion for impoundment shall be filed and ruled upon prior to submission of the actual material sought to be impounded, unless the court orders otherwise. If the motion is granted, the assigned judge will electronically file an order authorizing the filing of the document under seal. The filing party shall then deliver the document to the clerk's office for conventional filing under seal. A paper copy of the order shall be attached to the documents filed under seal and delivered to the clerk.

b. Ex parte motions and applications. Ex parte motions and documents shall be filed on paper. These will be handled by CM/ECF in a similar fashion as sealed documents (except for the requirement to file a separate motion to seal for each document).

c. Pretrial hearing and trial exhibits.

d. Voluminous documents.

e. Medical Records.

2. The following documents shall be filed on paper. As a rule, they will be scanned and filed into the CM/ECF system by the clerk's office:

a. The charging document in a criminal case, such as the complaint (and supporting affidavit), indictment, and information, as well as the criminal JS45 form for the District of Massachusetts.

b. Applications and affidavits for search, seizure or arrest warrants and related papers.

3. The following types of documents *may* be filed on paper. However, the documents may be scanned and filed into the CM/ECF system by a filing party or the clerk's office, and will be accessible through PACER, where appropriate.

a. The state court record filed in 28 U.S.C. § 1446 removal proceedings.

b. The state court record filed in habeas corpus (28USC§ 2254) proceedings.

c. All handwritten pleadings.

d. Pleadings and documents filed by pro se litigants.

e. Papers received from another court pursuant to Fed.R.Crim.P. 5, 20 and 21.

f. Appearance bonds.

g. Any pleading or document in a criminal case containing the signature of a defendant, such as a waiver of indictment or plea agreement.

4. The following documents may be received by the clerk's office, but are not filed, electronically or otherwise, unless ordered by the court:

a. Pretrial service reports.

b. Pre-sentencing reports and other papers submitted prior to sentencing.

c. Documents filed in relation to Alternative Dispute Resolution (ADR) proceedings. Other than the Order of Reference to ADR and the subsequent reports from the ADR Provider, all documents generated by the parties in the ADR process should be sent or delivered on paper (or email, if directed to do so) to the

ADR Provider, clearly identified as a document for the ADR Provider. ADR documents are not part of the public case file and are not to be filed electronically.

M. Signature.

1. *Attorneys.* The user login and password required to submit documents to the CM/ECF system shall serve as that user's signature for purposes of Fed.R.Civ.P. 11 and for all other purposes under the Federal Rules of Civil and Criminal Procedure and the local rules of this court. All electronically filed documents must include a signature block and must set forth the attorney's name, bar number, address, telephone number and email address. The name of the CM/ECF user under whose log-in and password the document is submitted must be preceded by a "/s/" and typed in the space where the signature would otherwise appear. For example:

/s/ John A. Smith

John A. Smith BBO#123456

123 Main Street

Boston, MA 02210

617–987–6543

jasmith@internetprovider.com

2. *Multiple Signatures.* The filer of any document requiring more than one signature (e.g, stipulations, joint motions, joint status reports, magistrate judge consent forms, etc.) must list thereon all the names of other signatories by means of a "/s/ name of signatory" block for each. By submitting such a document, the filing attorney certifies that each of the other signatories has expressly agreed to the form and substance of the document and that the filing attorney has their actual authority to submit the document electronically. The filing attorney shall retain any records evidencing this concurrence for future production, if necessary, until two (2) years after the expiration of the time for filing a timely appeal. A non-filing signatory or party who disputes the authenticity of an electronically filed document containing multiple signatures must file an objection to the document within fourteen (14) days of the date on the NEF.

3. *Affidavits.* Except as provided in subsection L, affidavits shall be filed electronically; however, the electronically filed version must contain a "/s/ name of signatory" block indicating that the paper document bears an original signature. The filing attorney shall retain the original for future production, if necessary, for two (2) years after the expiration of the time for filing a timely appeal. The court will also accept a scanned version of the original, signed document.

N. Privacy. Sensitive information including any subsequent amendments, should not be included in any document filed with the court, in compliance with Fed.R.Civ.P. 5.2, Fed.R.Crim.P. 49.1 and the E–Government Act of 2002, unless such inclusion is necessary and relevant to the case. Personal information not otherwise protected will be made available over the Internet via PACER. Personal data identifiers must be partially redacted from the pleading, whether it is filed traditionally or electronically.

The following personal identifiers shall not be included:

1. Minors' names (Use the minors' initials only)

2. Social security numbers (Use the last four numbers only)

3. Dates of birth (Use the year of birth only)

4. Financial account numbers (Identify the type of account and the financial institution, but use only the last four numbers of the account number)

5. Home addresses (Use the city and state only)—in criminal proceedings only.

The clerk's office is not responsible for reviewing documents filed with the court to determine whether pleadings have been redacted and are in the proper form.

CM/ECF now includes a reminder on the login screen to all external filers regarding the requirements of Fed.R.Civ.P. 5.2 and Fed.R.Crim.P. 49:

"**IMPORTANT NOTICE OF REDACTION RESPONSIBILITY:** All filers must redact: Social Security or taxpayer-identification numbers; dates of birth; names of minor children; financial account numbers; and, in criminal cases, home addresses, in compliance with Fed. R. Civ. P. 5.2 or Fed. R. Crim. P. 49.1. This requirement applies to all documents, including attachments.

I understand that, if I file, I must comply with the redaction rules. I have read this notice."

The Judicial Conference adopted Fed.R.Civ.P. 5.2 that specifically changes this access in social security and immigration cases, allowing public Internet access to "an opinion, order, judgment, or other disposition of the court, but not any other part of the case file or administrative record."

Therefore, remote electronic access to documents in certain types of cases (social security and immigration matters) is limited to case participants with CM/ECF logins. However, these cases and documents are available electronically to anyone wishing to view the record at the public terminals found in the clerk's office.

O.   Attachments to Filings and Exhibits.

1.   Attachments to filings and exhibits must be filed in accordance with the court's CM/ECF User Manual, unless otherwise ordered by the court.

2.   Filers must submit as attachments only those excerpts of the referenced documents that are directly germane to the matter under consideration by the court. Excerpted material must be clearly and prominently identified as such. Users who file excerpts of documents do so without prejudice to their right to timely file additional excerpts or the complete document, as may be allowed by the court. Responding parties may timely file additional excerpts or the complete document that they believe are directly germane.

3.   Filers shall not attach as an exhibit any pleading or other paper already on file with the court in that case, but shall merely refer to that document. (See subsection G for information on using hyperlinks in PDF documents filed in CM/ECF.)

P.   File Size Limitations and Conventional Filing of Documents.

1.   Documents submitted electronically or on paper are subject to the page limitations set by LR 7.1(b)(4) or by order of the court.

2.   A filing party shall limit the size of each PDF file to no more than seven (7) megabytes. PDF files larger than seven megabytes will be rejected by the CM/ECF system. The filer will see a message advising of the size limitation.

Larger documents or exhibits may be submitted electronically if split into separate PDF files each less than seven megabytes, attached to the main document and clearly labeled.

3.   The filing party is required to verify the accuracy and readability of scanned documents before filing the documents electronically with the court.

4.   Documents or exhibits submitted conventionally shall be served on other parties by the filer using traditional means.

5.   When documents or exhibits (other than those filed ex parte or under seal) are submitted conventionally, a "Notice of Filing with clerk's office" shall be filed electronically and attached to the main document. A paper copy of the "Notice of Filing with clerk's office" must accompany the documents submitted to the court. The "Notice of Filing with clerk's office" (see Appendix I) shall describe each of the documents that will be filed as paper copies in the clerk's office, or shall include an index of the documents if those documents are voluminous.

6.   If an attachment or exhibit is conventionally filed, it shall be maintained and available for inspection in the clerk's office and will not be scanned and added to the court's electronic docket unless specifically directed to do so by the court. However,

the clerk's office will make an entry on the docket stating that the manual filing has been received.

Q. Orders and Judgments.

1.   The assigned judge, chambers staff or deputy clerk shall file electronically all signed orders. Any order signed electronically has the same force and effect as if the judge had affixed his/her signature to a paper copy of the order and it had been entered on the docket conventionally. An electronically signed order shall include, but is not limited to, the signatory's name preceded by a "/s/" typed in the document. Both judicial officers and deputy clerks may electronically sign orders, as appropriate.

2.   A judge, or deputy clerk, may rule on routine motions and enter other orders by a text-only entry upon the docket entitled "Electronic Order" or "Endorsed Order." In such cases, no PDF document will be created or attached to the docket entry; the text-only entry shall constitute the court's only order on the matter and counsel will receive a system-generated NEF. The clerk's office will send a hard copy of the NEF to any attorney or party listed on the NEF as not receiving email notice. The clerk's office will also send the attorney a reminder of his/her obligation to register for CM/ECF.

R. Motions for Leave to File.
If a party electronically files a motion, pursuant to LR 7.1, for leave to file a document, or amend a previously filed document, the party shall attach a copy of the proposed document to the motion for leave to file or amend. The attachment must be marked "Proposed [document designation]." Once leave to file is granted, the party proposing the document shall electronically file the original document, indicating in the caption when leave was granted. Example:

JOHN DOE	)	
	)	09–12345–MLW
v.	)	Amended Complaint
	)	(Leave to file granted 5/20/11)
ABC CORP.	)	

S. Submitting Redacted Documents.
The parties may request or the court may require the submission of documents that have been redacted/stripped of sensitive or confidential information. The redacted document prepared for electronic filing shall include the original caption of the document, and be clearly labeled as "Redacted Document." A specific event is available for this purpose ("Redacted Document"), found under the Other Filings/Other Documents menu option.

Attorneys and pro se litigants are advised to take extra care when creating PDF documents intended for submission to CM/ECF. Steps shall be taken to ensure the documents are free of any hidden data (metadata) that may contain redacted information, or traces of information edited or deleted are not hidden in the final document. Even PDF content that has been encrypted may be recovered. An advisory document with additional information on this topic may be found on the court's website.

T. Submitting Proposed Order.
Proposed orders usually are not required by this court. However, the court may request the party to submit such a document. In those situations, unless otherwise directed by the clerk's office, electronically file the proposed document/order using the entry for "Proposed Documents submitted to the court," found under the Other Documents menu, or as an attachment to the motion to which it relates.

U. Transcripts.

1.   *Proceedings of this Court.* A transcript of a proceeding of this court shall be prepared in PDF format and submitted to the clerk's office by the court reporter. The transcript will be filed electronically, following the practices established by the court's Transcript Redaction Policy. Within twenty-one (21) days after the date on

the NEF of a Transcript, any party who purchased an original or a copy of the transcript shall:

    a. Review the transcript to determine whether it contains any personal identifiers listed in Fed.R.Civ.P. 5.2 and Fed.R.Crim.P. 49.1, whichever is applicable, and

    b. Electronically file a Transcript Redaction Request if that party concludes the transcript contains personal identifiers that must be redacted.

    2. *Transcripts from Other Courts and Depositions.* A transcript of a proceeding of another court, or a deposition transcript shall be filed electronically, if so available, otherwise on paper.

V. Correcting Docket Entries.

    1. Once a document is submitted and becomes part of the official record, corrections to the docket are made only by the clerk's office. The CM/ECF system will not permit the filing party to make changes to the document(s) or docket entry once the transaction has been accepted.

    2. A document incorrectly filed in a case may be the result of posting an incorrect PDF file to a docket entry, selecting an incorrect document type from the menu, or entering an incorrect case number and not recognizing the error before the transaction is completed. The filing party shall not attempt to refile the document unless specifically instructed to do so by clerk's office staff.

    3. As soon as possible after an error is discovered, the filing party should contact the docket clerk assigned to support the presiding judicial officer, and provide the docket clerk with the case number and document number for which the correction is being requested. If appropriate, the court will make an entry indicating that the document was filed in error. The filing party will be advised whether the document should be refiled.

W. Technical Failures and Planned Unavailability of System.

    1. From time to time, CM/ECF will be taken off line so that upgrades and other maintenance may be performed.

    2. Scheduled systems outages will be posted on the court's website, at http://www.mad.uscourts.gov, whenever possible. A user whose filing is made untimely as the result of a technical failure of the court's CM/ECF system may seek appropriate relief from the court.

    3. Technical difficulties on the filer's end, with telephone, cable lines, the filer's Internet Service Provider (ISP), or hardware or software problems, will not constitute a technical failure under these procedures nor excuse an untimely filing. A filer who cannot file a document electronically because of such technical difficulty on the filer's end shall file the document conventionally along with a copy of the document in PDF format on a compact disk or contact the clerk's office for permission to submit the PDF document via email. As help desk support is available during normal business hours, filers are strongly urged to electronically file any documents during that period.

    The court has made available a public terminal (computers and scanner) in each clerk's office for registered users to scan and electronically file documents. This equipment is available during normal business hours. Users should bring their prepared document and a valid CM/ECF login and password.

X. Access to Electronically Stored Documents.
The public may review at public terminals in the clerk's office all case documents that have not been filed under seal. The public may access case files in CM/ECF through the court's website (www.mad.uscourts.gov) by obtaining a PACER login and password. PACER logins are available through the PACER Service Center, at 800–676–6856 or at http://www.pacer.uscourts.gov.

Y. Retention. Unless otherwise ordered by the court, documents that are filed on paper and subsequently uploaded to the CM/ECF system may be destroyed and need not be maintained in its paper form by the clerk's office. Any document requiring an original signature shall be maintained by the attorney until two (2) years after the expiration of the time for filing a timely appeal. (See subsection M)

APPENDIX I

UNITED STATES DISTRICT COURT
DISTRICT OF MASSACHUSETTS

_____

V.   CASE NO. _____

_____

NOTICE OF FILING WITH CLERK'S OFFICE

Notice is hereby given that the documents, exhibits or attachments listed below have been manually filed with the court and are available in paper form only:

The original documents are maintained in the case file in the clerk's office.

_____   _____

Date   Attorney for

                                         _____

                                         _____

                                         _____

APPENDIX II

UNITED STATES DISTRICT COURT
DISTRICT OF MASSACHUSETTS

_____

V.   CASE NO. _____

_____

NOTICE OF FILING FEE PAYMENT

Notice is hereby given that the required fee for the:

☐ A. Notice of Appeal—$455.00   document # _____

☐ B. Initiating document (civil case)—$350.00   document # _____

☐ C. Petition for Writ of Habeas Corpus/new case—$5.00 document # _____

☐   D.   Initiating document (MBD)—$39.00   document # _____

☐   Motion for leave to appear pro hac vice ($50.00 per attorney)

☐   1   ☐   2   ☐   3   ☐   4   ☐   5   ☐   6

for a total of $ _____   document # _____

in the above entitled case is submitted through CM/ECF and pay.gov

_____   _____
Date   Attorney for

                             _____

                             _____

                             _____

[Effective October 24, 2003. Amended effective January 1, 2006; July 31, 2011.]

GENERAL ORDER 09–1. REGARDING THE E–GOVERNMENT ACT AND PERSONAL IDENTIFIERS

In compliance with the Policy of the Judicial Conference of the United States and the E–Government Act of 2002, in all civil and criminal actions, counsel and pro se litigants shall read and comply with Local Rule 5.3 governing personal data identifiers (that is: social security numbers; dates of birth; names of minor children; and financial account numbers). These personal identifiers shall be redacted before documents, including exhibits, are filed for the public file within the CM/ECF system. Failure to comply with the Local Rule may result in sanctions (such as the striking of a pleading or the imposition of monetary penalties).

[Dated: January 6, 2009.]

NOTICE AND TRANSCRIPT REDACTION POLICY

Effective May 5, 2008, the District of Massachusetts, in accordance with Judicial Conference Policy and the amendments to Rule 5.2 of the FRCvP and Rule 49.1 of the FRCrP, will implement a *Transcript Redaction Policy* regarding official court transcripts.

A copy of the policy is attached to this notice, and may be found on the court's web site at www.mad.uscourts.gov.

Summary of the Policy:

1. Counsel of record are obligated to review the transcript for personal identifying information.

2. Any transcript filed with the clerk of court by a court reporter or transcriber will be available electronically at the office of the clerk of court, for inspection only, for a period of ninety (90) days.

3. During the ninety (90) day period, a copy of the transcript may be obtained from the court reporter or transcriber at the rate established by the Judicial Conference. The transcript will be available electronically at the public terminal at the courthouse and remotely available through PACER to any attorneys of record who have purchased a copy from the court reporter.

4. If personal identifiers are found in the transcript, a "Notice of Intent to Redact" must be filed with the clerk (via CM/ECF) within seven (7) business days of the date the transcript was filed.

5. A "Redaction Request" that includes the specific page and line numbers to be redacted must be filed with the clerk (via CM/ECF) within twenty one (21) calendar days of the date the transcript was filed.

6. The transcript (or redacted transcript) will be made available electronically to the public ninety (90) days after the transcript was filed, without further notice to the parties.

Counsel are urged to share this notice with their clients so that an informed decision about the inclusion of certain materials may be made. Every transcript filed electronically in the Court's CM/ECF database will be accompanied by a notice to counsel regarding their duties under the policy. **The responsibility for redacting personal identifiers rests solely with counsel and the parties.** Neither the clerk nor the court reporter will review transcripts for compliance with this policy.

TRANSCRIPT REDACTION POLICY—AMENDED MAY 5, 2008

INTRODUCTION

The United States District Court for the District of Massachusetts shall make transcripts of court proceedings, filed on and after May 5, 2008, available through its electronic case files (CM/ECF) system.

The primary purpose of the Transcript Redaction Policy is to provide guidance to the Court's Official Court Reporters and the attorneys of this bar when preparing and reviewing transcripts of official court proceedings to be filed with the Court.

AUTHORITY

At its September 2007 session, the Judicial Conference approved a new policy regarding the availability of transcripts of court proceedings.

In addition, amendments to the Federal Civil and Criminal Rules of Procedure implementing requirements of the E–Government Act of 2002 to protect the privacy and security of publicly available electronic filings took effect on December 1, 2007. The amendments to Rule 5.2 of FRCvP and Rule 49.1 of FRCrP require that personal identification information (social security numbers, names of minor children, financial account numbers, dates of birth, and, in criminal cases, home addresses) be redacted from documents filed with the Court.

POLICY DESCRIPTION

The effective date of this Policy is May 5, 2008.

It applies only to transcripts of proceedings held before a Judicial Officer of this Court, not depositions taken outside of court or proceedings of state courts or other jurisdictions.

It establishes a procedure for counsel to request the redaction from the transcript of specific personal data identifiers before the transcript is made electronically available to the general public.

It does not change any rules or policies with respect to sealing or redaction of court records for any other purpose.

It does not affect or limit the right of any party (or any other person or entity) to order production of a transcript on an expedited basis. This policy does not affect any court rules or ruling requiring the sealing of materials or the protection of sealed materials.

There is no obligation on the part of the Office of the Clerk to perform any redaction. It is the responsibility of counsel to advise the court reporter what to redact, and the responsibility of the court reporter to perform the redaction.

Redaction responsibilities apply to counsel, even if the requestor of the transcript is a judge or a member of the public or media.

Unless otherwise ordered by the Court, counsel shall review the following portions of the transcript:

- opening and closing statements made on the party's behalf;
- statements of the party;
- the testimony of any witnesses called by the party; and
- any other portion of the transcript as ordered by the Court.

PROCEDURES

Notice of Intent to Redact

Within seven (7) business days of the filing of an official court transcript, each party wishing to redact a transcript shall inform the Court by filing (via CM/ECF) with the Clerk's Office a "Notice of Intent to Redact." A sample form is available on the Court's website and is attached to this policy.

Redaction Request

If a redaction is requested, unless the Court shall otherwise order, counsel shall file (via CM/ECF) with the Clerk's Office, a "Redaction Request" within twenty one (21) days from the filing of the transcript, indicating where the personal identifiers appear in the transcript by page and line, and how they are to be redacted. A sample form is available on the Court's website and is attached to this policy.

This procedure is limited to the redaction of the specific personal data identifiers listed below:

- Social security numbers to the last four digits;
- Financial account numbers to the last four digits;
- Dates of birth to the year;
- Names of minor children to the initials; and
- Home addresses to the city and state.

If counsel files a "Notice of Intent to Redact," but later determines that no redaction is necessary, counsel shall file a "Withdrawal of Notice of Intent To Redact."

If counsel fails to timely file a Redaction Request or Motion to Extend Time or a Withdrawal of the Intent to Redact, the Office of the Clerk shall issue an Order to Show Cause requiring the attorney to file the redaction request, a notice of withdrawal of the intent to redact, or show cause why the transcript should not be released to the public after ninety (90) calendar days from the date the original transcript was filed.

Additional Copies of Transcript Purchased

The court reporter shall notify the court reporter supervisor if additional copies of the transcript are purchased by other counsel of record. The court reporter supervisor will provide electronic access for those additional attorneys during the ninety (90) day period.

Redacted Transcript

If a redaction is requested, the court reporter shall file the redacted transcript with the Office of the Clerk within thirty one (31) days after the filing of the original transcript. The title page of the redacted transcript shall indicate that it is a redacted transcript by including "REDACTED TRANSCRIPT" immediately below the case caption and before the volume number and the name and title of the Judge.

Sealed and Partially Sealed Transcripts

If a transcript is to be filed under seal, the court reporter shall submit that transcript clearly labeled as "SEALED." The court reporter supervisor shall electronically file the PDF document with the appropriate restrictive setting.

If only a portion of a transcript has been ordered sealed, the court reporter shall extract the sealed portions from the original transcript as a separate PDF document (clearly labeled as "SEALED"). The remaining public portion of the transcript shall be created and both PDF documents, clearly labeled, submitted to the court reporter supervisor for electronic filing.

Counsel shall review the remaining public portion of the transcript for any necessary redactions.

Requests for Additional Redactions

Further redactions require the filing of a "Motion for Redaction of Electronic Transcript." Until the Court has ruled on any such motion, the transcript shall not be electronically available, even though the ninety (90) day restriction period may have expired.

Remote Public Access to Transcripts

If the original transcript is filed without redaction, that original transcript shall be remotely electronically available through PACER after ninety (90) calendar days.

If a redacted transcript is filed with the Court, that redacted transcript shall be remotely electronically available through PACER ninety (90) calendar days from the date of filing of the original transcript. The original transcript shall not be made publicly available.

CJA Panel Attorneys

An attorney who is serving as appointed "standby" counsel for a pro se litigant must review the transcript as if the pro se party were his/her client. If an attorney represents a client pursuant to the Criminal Justice Act (CJA), including serving as standby counsel, the attorney conducting the review of the transcript is entitled to compensation under the CJA for functions reasonably performed to fulfill that obligation, and for reimbursement of reasonable expenses related to the transcript review.

PACER Fees

PACER fees shall be applied both during and after the ninety (90) day restriction period. Charges shall accrue for all pages of the transcript. The user shall incur PACER charges each time the transcript is accessed even though he/she may have purchased it from the court reporter and obtained remote access through CM/ECF. Unlike other documents filed electronically, there is no 'free look' for transcripts.

UNITED STATES DISTRICT COURT
DISTRICT OF MASSACHUSETTS

_____
Plaintiff(s)

vs.   Docket No.: _____

_____
Defendant(s)

NOTICE OF INTENT TO REQUEST REDACTION

Notice is hereby given that a Redaction Request shall be filed electronically with the Court, via CM/ECF, within 21 days from the filing of the transcript. The transcript for proceedings on _____ was transcribed by _____, Official Court Reporter.

Submitted by

_____
(Party name)

Through Counsel:

Date: _____

/s/ _____
BBO: _____
_____
_____
_____

CERTIFICATE OF SERVICE

I hereby certify that this document(s) filed through the ECF system shall be sent electronically to the registered participants as identified on the Notice of Electronic Filing (NEF) and paper copies shall be sent to those indicated as non-registered participants on _____.

/s/ _____

NOTE: *This Notice should be filed electronically using "Notice of Intent to Request Redaction" found under the Other Documents menu in CM/ECF. It will be available only to Court staff and case participants.*

UNITED STATES DISTRICT COURT
DISTRICT OF MASSACHUSETTS

_____
Plaintiff(s)

vs.   Docket No.: _____

_____
Defendant(s)

REDACTION REQUEST

Now comes _____, by counsel and submits this Redaction Request. The transcript for proceedings on _____ was transcribed by _____, Official Court Reporter. The Transcript Redaction Policy requires redaction of the following personal identifiers from the transcripts made electronically available:

- Social security numbers to the last four digits,
- Financial account numbers to the last four digits,
- Dates of birth to the year,
- Names of minor children to the initials, and
- Home addresses to the city and state.

It is requested that consistent with the Court's Transcript Redaction Policy, the following information be redacted prior to the transcript being made remotely electronically available:

Document # of Transcript (from docket)	Page	Line(s)	Identifier (Example: SSN 009–99–9999)	Reaction Requested (Example: SSN XXX–XX–1234)	Court Reporter

(Use additional sheets if necessary)

The undersigned understands that redactions other than the personal identifiers listed in the Transcript Redaction Policy require a separate Motion for Additional Redactions be filed within 21 days of the filing of the transcript and requires court approval.

/s/ _____

Attorney for _____

Date: _____

NOTE: *This Request should be filed electronically using "Redaction Request—Transcript" found under the Other Documents menu in CM/ECF. It will be available only to Court staff and case participants.*

[Effective May 5, 2008.]

NOTICE OF ELECTRONIC AVAILABILITY OF CASE FILE INFORMATION

January 1, 2006

The office of the Clerk is now accepting electronically-filed pleadings and making the content of these pleadings available on the Court's Internet web site via WebPACER. Any subscriber to WebPACER will be able to read, download, store, and print the full content of electronically-filed documents. The Clerk's Office will not make electronically available documents that have been sealed or otherwise restricted by court order.

In compliance with the Policy of the Judicial Conference of the United States and the E-Government Act of 2002, do not include sensitive information in any document filed with the Court unless such inclusion is necessary and relevant to the case. Any personal information not otherwise protected will be made available over the Internet via WebPACER. If sensitive information must be included, the following personal data identifiers must be partially redacted from the pleading, regardless of whether the document is filed traditionally or electronically: social security numbers; financial account numbers; dates of birth; names of minor children; and home addresses.

a. Social Security Numbers. If an individual's social security number must be included in a pleading,

only the last four digits of that number should be identified.

b. Names of Minor Children. If the involvement of a minor child must be mentioned, only the initials of that child should be identified.

c. Dates of Birth. If an individual's date of birth must be included in a pleading, only the year should be identified.

d. Financial Account Numbers. If financial account numbers are relevant, only the last four digits of these numbers should be identified.

e. Home Addresses. If a home address must be included, only the city and state should be identified.

In compliance with the E-Government Act of 2002, and the August 2, 2004 Amendments, a party filing a document that contains the personal data identifiers specified above may:

a. File an unredacted document under seal pursuant to LR 7.2. This document shall be retained by the Court as part of the record; or

b. File a reference list under seal pursuant to LR 7.2. The reference list shall contain the complete personal data identifier(s) used in its place in the filing. All references in the case to the redacted identifiers included in the reference list will be construed to refer to the corresponding complete identifier. The reference list must be filed under seal, and may be amended as of right. It shall be retained by the Court as part of the record.

The Court may, however, still require the party to file a redacted copy for the public file. In addition, exercise caution when filing documents that contain the following:

a. Personal identifying number, such as driver's license number;

b. Medical records, treatment and diagnosis;

c. Employment history;

d. Individual financial information; and

e. Proprietary or trade secret information.

Counsel is requested to share this notice with all clients so that an informed decision about the inclusion of certain materials may be made. **If a redacted document is filed, it is the sole responsibility of counsel and the parties to be sure that all pleadings comply with the rules of this Court requiring redaction of personal data identifiers. The Clerk will not review each pleading for redaction.**

Special Notice to Social Security Attorneys. It is your responsibility to provide the U.S. Attorney's Office with the social security number of the plaintiff upon the filing of a social security action.

[January 2006.]

PLAN FOR RANDOM SELECTION OF JURORS

(Effective March 3, 2009)

Pursuant to the Jury Selection and Service Act of 1968, as amended, 28 U.S.C. § 1863, the Court adopts the following Plan for the Random Selection of Jurors (the "Plan").

This Court utilizes the one-step summoning and qualification procedure, as authorized by 28 U.S.C. § 1878. Accordingly, jurors shall be qualified and summoned in a single procedure.

1. DEFINITIONS. For purposes of the Plan, the Clerk shall mean the Clerk of the Court, any authorized deputy clerks, and any other person authorized by the Court to assist the Clerk in the performance of functions under this Plan. The "Jury Commissioner" shall mean the Jury Commissioner for the Commonwealth of Massachusetts or his designees. The Jury Commissioner is hereby authorized to assist the Clerk in the performance of producing the Master Jury Wheel.

2. APPLICABILITY. Pursuant to 28 U.S.C. § 1869(e), the Master Jury Wheel for the District of Massachusetts is hereby divided into three divisions for petit and grand jury selection, as follows: Eastern Division: The Counties of Essex, Middlesex, Suffolk, Norfolk, Bristol, Plymouth, Barnstable, Dukes, Nantucket. Central Division: The County of Worcester. Western Division: The Counties of Franklin, Hampshire, Hampden, and Berkshire.

3. DISCRIMINATION PROHIBITED. No citizen shall be excluded from service as a grand or petit juror on account of race, color, religion, sex, national origin or economic status.

4. MANAGEMENT AND SUPERVISION OF JURY SELECTION PROCESS. The Clerk shall manage the jury selection process under the general supervision of the Chief Judge or his designee.

5. RANDOM SELECTION FROM CROSS-SECTION OF THE COMMUNITY

a. It is the policy of this Court that all citizens of this district shall have the opportunity to be considered for service on grand and petit juries and to ensure, to the greatest extent possible, that all grand and petit juries in the three divisions of the District of Massachusetts are drawn at random from source lists in the relevant division, that represent a fair cross-section of the community of that division. All citizens shall have an obligation to serve as jurors when summonsed for the purpose of serving on grand and petit juries.

b. In order to implement the Court's policy, the Clerk shall take the following steps, beginning on or after the effective date of this Plan. In the first step, described as the "initial" draw in paragraph 7 of this Plan, the Clerk, or his or her designee, shall select at random, from the Master Jury Wheel, the names of persons to whom summonses will be issued for service as grand or petit jurors. The Master Jury Wheel in use as of the effective date of this Plan, however, may be used until it is emptied according to law. In the second step, described as the "supplemental draw," in paragraph 8 of this Plan, the Clerk shall select the name of a person at random, from the Supplemental Jury Wheel, to whom an additional summons will be issued, according to the procedures described in paragraph 8, for each summons returned to the Court as "undeliverable" by the United States Postal Service. The source and composition of the Master Jury Wheel and the Supplemental Jury Wheel are described in paragraph 6 of this Plan.

6. MASTER JURY WHEEL, SUPPLEMENTAL JURY WHEEL

a. *Master Jury Wheel.*

i. The Clerk shall request that the Massachusetts Jury Commissioner ("MJC") utilize the random selection procedures outlined in the MJC's regulation entitled "Specification of Random Selection Methods and Procedures" (describing the use by the MJC of the Marsaglia Random Number Generator) for the selection of the names to be placed in the Master Jury Wheel for each division, so that each county shall be represented in proportion to the number of names on its resident lists.

ii. The Court finds that electronic data processing methods can be advantageously used for selecting and copying names from the municipal resident lists for inclusion in the Master Jury Wheel. Therefore, the Clerk shall use a purely randomized process, through a properly programmed electronic data processing system, to obtain names from the municipal resident lists for inclusion in the Master Jury Wheel. In selecting names for the Master Jury Wheel, however, the Clerk shall maintain the substantial proportionality of names for each county in accordance with 28 U.S.C. § 1863(b)(3).

iii. The Master Jury Wheel shall consist of the names and addresses of all persons randomly selected from the municipal resident lists as described above. The physical form of record on which names from the Master Jury Wheel are kept may include labels or such electronic devices as magnetic tapes or disc files.

iv. Initially, the Clerk shall place in the Master Jury Wheel the number of names that are perceived to be needed in order to provide qualified jurors for the Court, but this number shall always be at least 35,000 names for the Eastern division, 4,000 names for the Central division and 4,000 names for the Western division. The Clerk shall empty and refill the Master Jury Wheel once every year during the period between January 1st and April 30th in conformance with this Plan or at more frequent intervals as deemed necessary or expedient by the Clerk under the supervision of the Chief Judge. The Chief Judge, or his designee, may order additional names to be placed in the Master Jury Wheel at other times, as needed, in accordance with Paragraph 6(a)(i) of this Plan.

b. *The Supplemental Jury Wheel.* Using the procedures described in paragraph 6(a)(i)-(iv) above, the Clerk shall create a Supplemental Jury Wheel for the purposes described in paragraphs 5(b) and 8 of this Plan.

c. *National Change of Address Database.* The Clerk shall submit the names on the Master Jury Wheel and the Supplemental Jury Wheel twice a year to be updated through the national change-of-address system of the United States Postal Service and corrected as appropriate before issuing summonses.

7. METHOD AND MANNER OF RANDOM SELECTION FOR INITIAL DRAW

a. The Clerk, either at one time or at periodic intervals, shall draw at random from the Master Jury Wheel, the names of as many persons as may be required based upon the anticipated juror demands by the Court. The number of names, plus additional names sufficient to compensate for the estimated number of prospective jurors who will be unavailable or ineligible, shall be determined by the Court.

b. The Jury Administrator shall post the Court's Jury Plan for public review in the Clerk's Office for each division of the Court and on the Court's website, so that the process by which names are periodically and randomly drawn will be public knowledge.

c. The Clerk, by automated or manual means, shall prepare and cause to be mailed to every person whose name is drawn, a one-step juror summons/qualification form, accompanied by instructions to complete and return the form to the Clerk by first class mail, duly signed and sworn, within ten days from the receipt of the form, in accordance with 28 U.S.C. § 1864(a).

d. The Clerk shall issue summonses to the persons so drawn and serve the summonses by registered, certified or first class mail, as the Clerk shall determine with the approval of the Chief Judge, addressed to each such person at his or her usual residence or business address.

8. METHOD AND MANNER OF RANDOM SELECTION FOR SUPPLEMENTAL DRAW FOR "UNDELIVERABLES"

a. For each summons returned by the United States Postal Service to the Court as "undeliverable," the Clerk shall draw at random from the Supplemental Jury Wheel the name of a resident who lives in the same zip code area to which the undeliverable summons had been sent and prepare and cause to be mailed to such resident a new one-step juror summons/qualification form.

b. The Clerk shall submit the names and addresses of the "undeliverables" to the Office of the Jury Commissioner of Massachusetts ("OJC"), so that the OJC may also update its lists.

9. QUALIFICATIONS, EXEMPTIONS, AND EXCUSES FROM JURY SERVICE

a. *Qualifications.* Under the supervision of the Court, the Clerk, shall determine, solely on the basis of information provided on the juror qualification form and other competent evidence, whether a person is unqualified for, or exempt, or to be excused from jury service. The determination shall be noted in the space provided on the juror qualification form or on supporting documentation. Any person shall be deemed qualified for jury service unless he or she:

i. is not a citizen of the United States;

ii. is less than eighteen years of age;

iii. has not resided within the judicial district for a period of one year or more;

iv. is unable to read, write, and understand the English language with a degree of proficiency sufficient to fill out satisfactorily the juror qualification form;

v. is unable to speak the English language;

vi. is unable, by reason of mental or physical infirmity, to render satisfactory jury service; or

vii. has a charge pending against him/her for the commission of, or has been convicted in a State or Federal Court of record of, a crime punishable by imprisonment for more than one year, and his/her civil rights have been lost and have not been restored.

b. *Exemptions.* The following classes of persons are exempt from jury service:

i. members in active service in the armed forces of the United States;

ii. members of the fire or police departments of any state, district, territory, possession or subdivision thereof;

iii. public officers in the executive, legislative, or judicial branches of the government of the United States, or any state, district, territory, or possession or subdivision thereof, who are actively engaged in the performance of official duties. Public officer shall mean a person who is either elected to public office or who is directly appointed by the person elected to public office.

c. *Excuses.* The Clerk, upon individual request, shall excuse the following classes of persons:

i. any person over the age of 70 years old;

ii. any person who has served at least 5 days of state jury service or any federal jury service within the last 3 years;

iii. volunteer safety personnel who serve without compensation as firefighters or members of a rescue squad or ambulance crew for a public agency in accordance with 28 U.S.C. § 1863(b)(5)(B). (Public agency shall mean the United States, the Commonwealth of Massachusetts, or any unit of municipal government, department, or instrumentality of the foregoing.)

Under the supervision of the Court, the Clerk, upon individual request showing undue hardship or extreme inconvenience, may excuse any person from jury service for the period that such extreme hardship or inconvenience exists. "Undue hardship or extreme inconvenience" shall mean illness of the juror or a member of the juror's household; the active care and custody of a child under ten years of age; the active full-time care of an aged or infirm person; or business or recreational travel plans established before the receipt of the summons for jury service.

10. MISCELLANEOUS

a. No person shall make public or disclose to any person not employed by this Court the names drawn from the Master Jury Wheel until the jurors have been summoned and have appeared, or failed to appear, in response to the summons. Any judge of this Court may order that the names of jurors remain confidential thereafter if the interests of justice so require.

b. The names of any jurors drawn from the Master Jury Wheel and selected to sit on a Grand Jury shall be kept confidential and not made public or disclosed to any person not employed by the Court, except as otherwise authorized by a court order in an individual case pursuant to 28 U.S.C. § 1867(f).

c. If a judge of this Court finds that a case requires a large array of jurors but it later appears that the array is larger than necessary, the Clerk shall draw by lots the surplus jurors and assign them as is or appears appropriate. Jurors left over in the array of jurors summoned for grand jury or petit jury service may be called in at the next impaneling of a grand jury or petit jury, together with those jurors who were temporarily excused.

d. From time to time, the Court may direct the Clerk to draw from the Master Jury Wheel, in accordance with Paragraph 7 of this Plan, such number of persons as may be required for additional arrays. An "additional array" shall mean a small list of prospective grand or petit jurors which may be added to a regular array of such jurors as necessary when a regular array requires additional names because of excused or increased jury requirements. When added to the regular array, the additional array shall then become a part of the regular array.

[Effective March 1, 2007. Revised effective March 3, 2009.]

PLAN FOR PROMPT DISPOSITION OF CRIMINAL CASES

(December 2008)

Pursuant to the requirements of the Federal Speedy Trial Act of 1974 (18 U.S.C. §§ 3161–3174), the Speedy Trial Act Amendments Act of 1979 (Pub. L. No. 96–43), the Federal Juvenile Delinquency Act (18 U.S.C. §§ 5036, 5037), and the Local Rules concerning criminal cases (LR 112.1 et seq.) the judges of the United States District Court for the District of Massachusetts have adopted the following time limits and procedures to minimize undue delay and to further the prompt disposition of criminal cases and certain juvenile proceedings.

1. Applicability.

(a) *Offenses.* The time limits set forth herein apply to any criminal offense triable in this court, including any offense triable by a United States magistrate judge, except for petty offenses as defined in 18 U.S.C. § 19. Except as specifically provided herein, the following time limits are not applicable to juvenile delinquency proceedings under 18 U.S.C. § 5031–42.

(b) *Persons.* The time limits set forth herein are applicable to any person accused who has not been indicted or informed against as well as any person who has. The word "person" shall include any natural person, corporation, or unincorporated association; the word "defendant" shall include any person so defined unless a contrary intent clearly appears from the context.

2. Priorities in Scheduling Criminal Cases.
Preference shall be given to criminal proceedings as far as practicable as required by Rule 50 of the Federal Rules of Criminal Procedure. The trial or other disposition of cases in which the defendant is detained solely because the defendant is awaiting trial or a released person awaiting trial who has been designated by the United States Attorney as being of high risk shall be accorded priority. (18 U.S.C. § 3164(a))

The preference to be given criminal cases shall not be unduly prejudicial to civil litigation.

3. Time Within Which an Indictment or Information Must Be Filed.

(a) *Time Limits.* If a person is arrested or served with a summons and the complaint charges an offense to be prosecuted in this district, any indictment or information subsequently filed in connection with such charge shall be filed within thirty days after the arrest or service of summons. (18 U.S.C. § 3161(b))

(b) *Attachment of Time Limits.* If a person has not been arrested or served with a summons on an outstanding federal charge, an arrest shall be deemed to have been made when that person (i) is first held in custody in this district solely for the purpose of responding to that federal charge; (ii) is delivered to the custody of a federal official in this district in connection with that federal charge; or (iii) first appears before a judicial officer of this district in connection with that federal charge.

(c) *Related Procedures.* At the time of the earliest appearance before a judicial officer of a person who has been arrested for or served with a summons in connection with an offense not charged in an indict-

ment or information, that judicial officer shall establish for the record the date on which the arrest took place or on which the summons was served.

4. Time Within Which Trial Must Commence.

(a) *Time Limits.*

(1) Original Trials.

(A) The trial of a defendant who is not in custody solely awaiting trial or who has not been designated as high risk shall, subject to the periods of excludable delay enumerated in subsection 5 (b), commence within seventy days after the date of the last to occur of the following events: (i) the filing of an indictment or information in this district; (ii) the making public of a sealed indictment or information; or (iii) the defendant's first appearance before a judicial officer of this district. (18 U.S.C. § 3161(c)(1))

(B) If a defendant consents in writing to be tried before a magistrate judge on a complaint charging a misdemeanor, the trial shall commence within seventy days after the date of that consent. (18 U.S.C. § 3161(c)(1))

(C) If a defendant is to be tried upon an indictment or information which was reinstated following an appeal after dismissal by the district court, the trial shall commence within seventy days after the date the action occasioning the trial becomes final, subject to the period of excludable delay enumerated in subsection 5(b), except that the court retrying the case may enlarge the period for trial if absence or unavailability of witnesses or other factors resulting from the passage of time shall make trial within seventy days impractical, but such enlargement shall not extend more than one hundred eighty days after the date upon which the action occasioning the trial becomes final. (18 U.S.C. § 3161(d)(2))

(D) Without the written consent of the defendant no trial shall commence less than thirty days after the date on which the defendant first appears through counsel or expressly waives counsel and elects to proceed pro se, or if trial is to be by a magistrate judge, within thirty days after the defendant consents thereto. (18 U.S.C. § 3161(c)(2))

(2) Retrials.

(A) If a defendant is to be tried again following the declaration by a trial judge of a mistrial or following the order of a trial judge for a new trial, the trial shall commence within seventy days after the date the declaration or order becomes final, subject to the periods of excludable delay enumerated in subsection 5(b). (18 U.S.C. § 3161(e))

(B) If a defendant is to be tried again following an appeal or collateral attack, the trial shall commence within seventy days after the date the action occasioning the retrial becomes final, subject to the periods of excludable delay enumerated in subsection 5(b), except that the court retrying the case may enlarge the period for retrial if absence or unavailability of witnesses or other factors resulting from the passage of time shall make retrial within seventy days impractical, but such enlargement shall not extend more than one hundred eighty days after the date upon which the action occasioning the retrial becomes final.

(b) *Defendants in Custody and High–Risk Defendants.*

(1) Definitions. As used in this subsection, the following terms shall have the following meanings:

(A) "Defendant in custody" shall mean a person being held in detention for the sole purpose of awaiting trial on the federal charge contained in the pertinent complaint, information or indictment. (18 U.S.C. § 3161(a)(1))

(B) "High-risk defendant" shall mean a person who is awaiting trial on the federal charge contained in the pertinent complaint, information or indictment, but who is not in custody and has been designated by the United States Attorney as being of high risk. (18 U.S.C. § 3164(a)(2))

(2) Time Limits. The following time limits, as extended by the periods of excludable delay enumerated in subsection 5(b), apply to defendants in custody and defendants designated as high-risk:

(A) The trial of a defendant in custody shall commence within ninety days after the beginning of continuous detention for the sole purpose of awaiting trial. (18 U.S.C. § 3164(b))

(B) The trial of a high-risk defendant shall commence within ninety days after he is designated as high-risk. (18 U.S.C. § 3164(b))

(c) *Superseding Charges.* If after an indictment or information has been filed, a subsequent complaint, indictment or information is filed which charges the defendant with the same offense or an offense required to be joined with that offense, the time limits applicable to the subsequent charge shall be determined as follows:

(1) In the case of a subsequent complaint, the time limit within which an indictment or information shall be obtained upon a subsequent charge shall be computed without regard to the existence of the original indictment or information. (18 U.S.C. § 3161(d)(1))

(2) If the original indictment or information was dismissed on motion of the defendant before the filing of the subsequent charge, the time limit for commencement of trial on subsequent charge shall be computed without regard to the existence of the original charge. (18 U.S.C. § 3161(d)(1))

(3) If the original indictment or information is pending at the time the subsequent charge is filed, the time limit for commencement of trial on the subsequent charge shall be the time limit for commencement of trial on the original indictment or information.

(4) If the original indictment or information was dismissed on motion of the United States Attorney before the filing of the subsequent charge, the time limit for commencement of trial on the subsequent charge shall be the time limit for commencement of trial on the original indictment or information, as extended by a period equal to that during which charges were not outstanding. (18 U.S.C. § 3161(h)(6))

(5) The provisions of this subsection 4(c) shall apply to any criminal case in which the JS 45 Form for the District of Massachusetts (Criminal Case Cover Sheet adapted for use in the District of Massachusetts) indicates that the case is related to a pending indictment or information unless on motion of the United States Attorney the court finds that the subsequent indictment or information is not, by double jeopardy standards, for the same offense or is not, pursuant to the Federal Rules of Criminal Procedure, required to be prosecuted in a single proceeding.

(d) *Related Procedures.*

(1) At the time of a defendant's earliest appearance before a judicial officer of this district, that officer shall take appropriate steps to ascertain whether the defendant is represented by counsel and shall, when appropriate, appoint counsel pursuant to the Criminal Justice Act of 1964 (18 U.S.C. § 3006A), Rule 44 of the Federal Rules of Criminal Procedure and the Local Plan for the Administration of the Criminal Justice Act (CJA Plan). If a defendant appears for arraignment without counsel, his/her arraignment may be continued for not more than one week to permit him to consult with his/her chosen counsel. No additional delay of the arraignment may be permitted on the ground that the defendant's chosen counsel is unavailable. The judicial officer may continue an arraignment to enable a defendant to obtain counsel, and the period of the continuance may be excluded if the judicial officer makes the findings required by 18 U.S.C. § 3161(h)(8). When appropriate a judicial officer may cause a plea of not guilty to be entered on behalf of the defendant.

(2) An arraignment shall be deemed to take place at the time a plea is taken or is entered by a judicial officer on behalf of the defendant.

(3) If a defendant enters a plea of guilty or nolo contendere to any or all charges in an indictment or information and is subsequently permitted to withdraw it, the time limit shall be determined for all counts as if the indictment or information were filed on the day the order permitting withdrawal of the plea becomes final. (18 U.S.C. § 3161(i))

(4) In the event of a transfer to this district under Rule 20 or Rule 21 of the Federal Rules of Criminal Procedure, the indictment or information shall be deemed filed in this district when the papers in the proceeding or certified copies thereof are received by the clerk.

(5) The court shall have sole responsibility for setting cases for trial in the manner provided by Local Rule 117.1. After receiving the Magistrate Judge's Final Status Report, and at least thirty (30) days before trial, or at the earliest practicable shorter time before trial consistent with the Speedy Trial Act, the judge who will preside at trial must conduct an Initial Pretrial Conference, at which a reliable trial date will be established.

(6) Each judge shall schedule criminal trials at such times as are necessary to assure prompt disposition of criminal cases. Individual calendars shall be managed so that it can be reasonably anticipated that every criminal case set for trial will be reached during the week for which it was originally set. A continuance shall be granted only as provided by 18 U.S.C. § 3161(h) and this plan. A conflict in schedules of Assistant United States Attorneys shall not be grounds for a delayed setting or for a continuance of the date set, unless the requirements of Local Rule 40.2 concerning conflicts of court appearances have been met.

(7) All status conferences and pretrial hearings shall be conducted in a timely manner consistent with Local Rule 116.5 and 117.1 and with the priorities of other matters on the criminal docket.

(8) For the purpose of this section: (A) a trial in a jury case shall be deemed to have commenced at the beginning of voir dire; (B) a trial in a non-jury case shall be deemed to have commenced on the day the case is called, provided that some step in the trial procedure immediately followed.

(9) If a defendant is being held in custody for the sole purpose of awaiting trial, the United States Attorney shall advise the court at the earliest practicable time of the date of the beginning of such continuous custody.

(10) If the clerk has been advised that a defendant is in custody for the sole purpose of awaiting trial and that the defendant is thereafter released from custody before the commencement of trial, the United States Attorney shall notify the clerk of the change in status.

(11) If a defendant is determined by the United States Attorney to be a high-risk, the United States Attorney shall advise the court and shall notify the defendant and his/her counsel at the earliest practicable time of that designation. The designation shall be made known to the defendant and his/her counsel, but shall not be made known to other persons without the permission of the court.

5. Exclusions of Time From Computations.

(a) *Applicability.* Excludable periods of delay, as defined in subsection 5(b), shall toll the time limits within which an indictment or information must be filed (Section 3), and within which trial must commence (Section 4). (18 U.S.C. § 3161(h))

No excludable period which is based solely upon the consent of the parties may be allowed.

(b) *Excludable Periods.*

(1) Any period of delay resulting from other proceedings concerning the defendant, including, but not limited to:

(A) Delay resulting from any proceeding to determine the mental competency or physical capacity of the defendant, including any examination or hearing. (18 U.S.C. § 3161(h)(1)(A))

(i) The excludable period shall commence on the date upon which any proceeding in the above paragraph is initiated by written or oral motion and shall conclude on the date the court has received the report of examination, all briefs have been filed and any necessary hearing has been completed. In the case of an examination under Fed.R.Crim.P. 12.2(c), if there is no question before the court for ruling, the excludable period shall conclude on the date on which the report of the examination is received by the attorney for the Government.

(ii) Upon the arrival of the defendant at the place of examination, the examiner shall notify the clerk of this court of the date of that arrival and the date on which the examination is to begin and shall estimate the length of the examination. The examiner shall further notify the clerk of the date on which the examination is concluded and of the date on which the defendant is discharged.

(iii) If a defendant is in federal custody, the U.S. Marshal shall notify the clerk of this court of the transfer of the defendant to the custody of the examiner and of the examiner's return of the defendant to the custody of the U.S. Marshal.

(B) Delay resulting from trial of the defendant on other charges in any state or federal court, including this court. (18 U.S.C. § 3161(h)(1)(D))

(i) The excludable period shall commence on the date that such other trial begins and shall conclude fourteen days after the termination of that trial.

(ii) As used in this subparagraph, "trial" shall be deemed to include the impanelling of the jury, a hearing on any motion which has been deferred for hearing to the trial date and any time during which the trial is suspended.

(C) Delay resulting from an interlocutory appeal in the case.

(i) The excludable period shall commence on the date the notice of appeal if filed. (18 U.S.C. § 3161(h)(1)(E))

(ii) The excludable period shall conclude on the date the mandate of the Court of Appeals is received by the clerk of this court.

(D) Delay resulting from the hearing and disposition of a pretrial motion. (18 U.S.C. § 3161(h)(1)(F))

(i) The excludable period shall commence on the date the court grants a period of time to file a pretrial motion or the date on which a pretrial motion is filed, whichever is earlier.

(ii) The excludable period shall conclude on the date on which the Court has received all forthcoming briefs from the parties and any necessary hearing on the motion has been concluded.

(E) Delay resulting from proceedings relating to transfer of cases among districts pursuant to the Federal Rules of Criminal Procedure. (18 U.S.C. § 3161(h)(1)(G))

(i) If a case is transferred back to this district for trial pursuant to Rule 20(c) of the Federal Rules of Criminal Procedure, the time limits of this plan shall commence to run on the date on which the clerk of this court receives the papers in the proceeding from the clerk of the court to which the case was transferred originally.

(ii) If a defendant moves for transfer of a case from this district to another district for trial pursuant to Rule 21 of the Federal Rules of Criminal Procedure, an excludable period shall commence on the date on which the motion is filed and conclude on the last day of any hearing on the motion or a decision on the motion, whichever is sooner. If the court takes the matter under advisement the excludable period shall be determined pursuant to Section H infra. The excludable period shall conclude on the date of decision of that motion if it is denied or, if the motion is allowed and the case is transferred, the concluding date shall be determined by the district court to which the case is transferred.

(iii) If on motion of a defendant pursuant to Rule 21 of Federal Rules of Criminal Procedure a case is ordered transferred to this district, an excludable period shall commence on the date of the first day of the hearing on that motion in that other district and shall conclude on the date on which the defendant first arrives in this district in custody or the date on which the clerk receives the papers in the case, whichever is later.

(iv) If a defendant is removed to this district pursuant to Rule 5(c) of the Federal Rules of Criminal Procedure, the excluded period shall commence on the date of the arrest in another district on charges pending or for a crime committed in this district and shall conclude on the date of the arrival of the defendant in this district if in custody or the date of the first appearance of the defendant before a judicial officer in this district if not in custody.

(F) A reasonable period of delay resulting from transportation of the defendant from another district or to and from places of examination or hospitalization. (18 U.S.C. § 3161(h)(1)(H))

(i) The excluded period shall commence upon the date the order of removal or order directing transportation of the defendant is entered.

(ii) The excluded period shall conclude on the date of the arrival of the defendant in this district pursuant to an order of removal or at the destination stated in an order directing transportation.

(iii) Any time consumed by the transportation in excess of ten days shall be presumed to be unreasonable.

(G) Delay resulting from consideration by the court of a proposed plea agreement to be entered into by the defendant and the attorney for the government pursuant to Rule 11(e) of the Federal Rules of Criminal Procedure. (18 U.S.C. § 3161(h)(1)(I))

(i) The excluded period shall commence on the date of disclosure of the plea agreement to the appropriate judicial officer.

(ii) The excluded period shall conclude on the date the court's decision on the plea agreement is filed or announced in open court.

(H) Delay resulting from proceedings concerning the defendant being under advisement. (18 U.S.C. § 3161(h)(1)(J))

(i) The excludable period shall commence on the date on which any proceeding concerning the defendant is actually taken under advisement.

(ii) The excludable period shall conclude on the date on which an order or ruling on the matter is entered, but in no event shall the excludable period exceed thirty days.

(2) Any period of delay after the filing of an indictment or information during which prosecution is deferred by the United States Attorney, pursuant to a written agreement with the defendant which is approved by the court, for the purpose of allowing the defendant to demonstrate his/her good conduct. (18 U.S.C. § 3161(h)(2))

(A) The excluded period shall commence on the date on which the court approves the agreement for deferral of prosecution.

(B) The excluded period shall conclude on the date on which the United States Attorney resumes prosecution.

(3) Any period of delay resulting from the absence or unavailability of the defendant or an essential witness. (18 U.S.C. § 3161(h)(3))

(A) The excludable period shall commence on the date on which a motion for a continuance of the proceedings is allowed or on such other date as the court may determine.

(B) The excludable period shall conclude on the date on which the court is notified that the defendant or essential witness is available to appear in the proceedings.

(C) If the court finds that the defendant or essential witness was reasonably available on a date earlier than that of which it was notified, the court may order that the excludable period be deemed to have concluded on that earlier date.

(D) For purposes of this paragraph:

(i) The term "essential witness" means a witness so necessary to the proceeding that continuing without that witness would be impossible or would be likely to result in a miscarriage of justice.

(ii) A defendant or an essential witness shall be considered "absent" when (1) his/her whereabouts are unknown and, in addition, (2) he is attempting to avoid apprehension or prosecution or (b) his/her whereabouts cannot be determined by due diligence. (18 U.S.C. § 3161(h)(3)(B))

(iii) A defendant or an essential witness shall be considered "unavailable" when his/her whereabouts are known, but (1) his/her presence at the proceedings cannot be obtained by due diligence or (2) he resists appearing at or being returned for the proceedings. (18 U.S.C. § 3161(h)(3)(B))

An essential witness shall not be considered "unavailable" when he is present at the proceedings or his/her presence could be obtained by due diligence and he is or would be unable to testify due to temporary incompetence or incapacity, but such a condition may be grounds for a continuance under subparagraph 6(b)(h)(8).

(E) The Government shall have the burden of going forward with the evidence in connection with any exclusion of time under this paragraph.

(4) A period of delay resulting from the fact that the defendant is mentally incompetent or physically unable to stand trial. (18 U.S.C. § 3161(h)(4))

(A) The excludable period shall commence on the date on which the defendant is found mentally incompetent or physically unable to stand trial.

(B) The excludable period shall conclude on the date on which the defendant is found mentally competent or physically able to stand trial and the court allows prosecution to resume.

(5) A period of delay resulting from a dismissal of the charges upon motion of the attorney for the government and the subsequent filing of new charges for the same offense or for an offense required to be joined with that offense. (18 U.S.C. § 3161(h)(6))

(A) The excludable period shall commence on the date on which the court orders dismissal of an indictment or information upon motion of the attorney for the government.

(B) The excludable period shall conclude on the date on which new charges are filed for the offense charged in the original indictment or information or for an offense which is, pursuant to the Federal Rules of Criminal Procedure, required to be joined with that offense.

(C) This paragraph shall be governed by the provisions of subsection 5(c) insofar as applicable.

(6) A period of delay resulting from the fact that the defendant is joined for trial with a co-defendant as to whom the time for trial has not run and as to whom no motion for severance has been granted. (18 U.S.C. § 3161(h)(7))

(A) The excluded period shall commence on the date of the expiration of the time limit for trial as computed pursuant to section 5 and shall conclude on the date on which trial is commenced, or on which the time limits for trial as to all co-defendants have expired, or on which motion for severance is granted.

(B) All defendants who are named in a single indictment or information should be tried at a single trial unless a motion for severance has been granted.

(C) The provisions of this paragraph shall not apply to a defendant who is in custody if a co-defendant as to whom the time limit for trial has not expired is not in custody.

(7)(A) A period of delay authorized by L.R. 112.2(A) which is set forth in an electronic or a separate order issued by a judicial officer. The order must specify the time period to be excluded and the subsection of L.R. 112.2(A) which is applicable.

(B) A period of delay resulting from a continuance, granted by a judge on his/her own motion or on the motion of any party, upon a finding that the ends of justice outweigh the best interests of the public and the defendant in a speedy trial. The excluded period shall commence on the date on which a continuance is granted or on such other date as the Court may determine and shall conclude on the date to which proceedings are continued by the order of the Court or on which the proceedings are resumed, whichever is earlier. (18 U.S.C. § 3161(h)(8)(A))

(C) In ordering a continuance under subparagraph (7)(B), the Court shall set forth on the record its specific reasons for finding that the ends of justice outweigh the best interests of the public and the defendant in a speedy trial. The factors, among others, which the court shall consider are:

(i) Whether a failure to grant a continuance would be likely to make a continuation of the proceeding impossible or result in a miscarriage of justice. (18 U.S.C. § 3161(h)(8)(B)(i))

(ii) Whether the case is so unusual or so complex due to the number of defendants, the nature of the prosecution or the existence of novel questions of fact or law, that it is unreasonable to expect adequate preparation for pretrial proceedings or for the trial itself within the time limits established by this section. (18 U.S.C. § 3161(h)(8)(B)(ii))

(iii) Whether, in a case in which arrest precedes indictment, delay in the filing of the indictment is caused because the facts upon which the grand jury must base its determination are unusual or complex or because of events beyond the control of the court or the government. (18 U.S.C. § 3161(h)(8)(B)(iii))

(iv) Whether the failure to grant such a continuance in a case which, taken as a whole, is not so unusual or so complex as to fall within clause (ii), would deny the defendant reasonable time to obtain counsel, would unreasonably deny the defendant or the Government continuity of counsel, or would deny counsel for the defendant or the attorney for the Government the reasonable time necessary for effective preparation, taking into account the exercise of due diligence. (18 U.S.C. § 3161(h)(8)(B)(iv))

(D) No time may be excluded because of general congestion of the court's calendar or a lack of diligent preparation or a failure to obtain available witnesses to either party. (18 U.S.C. § 3161(h)(8)(C))

(8) A period of delay resulting from a continuance which is ordered by the court to promote the efficient administration of justice because the judge to whom the case is assigned is unavailable to commence trial of the defendant within the time limits of this plan when that unavailability is due to the involvement of the judge in an ongoing trial and neither the transfer of the case to another judge nor the interruption of such other trial would serve the best interests of justice.

(A) The excluded period shall commence on the date on which a continuance is ordered.

(B) The excluded period shall conclude fourteen days after the termination of such other trial or on such earlier date as the court may determine.

(9) A reasonable period of delay resulting from a transfer of the defendant from a state or federal penal institution to this court for trial.

(A) The excludable period shall commence on the date on which the attorney for the government files a petition for a writ of habeas corpus ad prosequendum with the Clerk.

(B) The excludable period shall conclude on the date on which the United States Marshal notifies the attorney for the government and the clerk of the availability of the defendant for trial in this district.

(c) *Continuances.*

(1) Pre–Indictment.

(A) If the United States Attorney anticipates that an indictment or information will not be filed within the time limit set forth in section 3, he may file a written motion for a continuance with the judge assigned to the miscellaneous business docket.

(B) The motion of the United States Attorney shall state (i) the period of time proposed for exclusion, and (ii) the grounds for the proposed exclusion. If the motion is for a continuance under paragraph 5(b)(7), it shall also state whether or not the defendant is being held in custody on the basis of the complaint. In appropriate circumstances, the motion may include a request that some or all of the supporting material be considered ex parte and in camera.

(2) Post–Indictment. If after indictment it is determined that a continuance of an arraignment or trial beyond the time limit set forth in section 4 is justified, the court shall set forth its findings in the record, either orally or in writing.

(3) Conditions on Continuance. The court may grant a continuance under this plan for either a specific period of time or a period to be determined by reference to a future event (such as recovery from illness) not within the control of the government. If any continuance is to a date not certain, the court shall require one or both parties to inform the court promptly when the circumstances that justify the continuance no longer exist. In addition, the court shall require one or both parties to file periodic reports on the continued existence of the circumstances. The court shall determine the frequency of such reports in the light of the facts of the particular case.

(d) *Computation of Time Limits.* In computing any time limit other than an excluded period, the day upon which an act or event occurs which causes a designated period of time to commence to run shall not be included. Computation of an excluded period shall include both the first and the last day of the excludable act or event.

(e) *Record Keeping.* A single automated docket covering both proceedings before magistrate judges and district judges in misdemeanor and felony cases shall be maintained by the clerk of court and shall contain a record of excludable time. A magistrate judge's courtroom deputy clerk shall take minutes of the magistrate's orders and shall record them in the same manner as does a courtroom deputy clerk for a district judge. A record of the proceedings in a Class A misdemeanor case shall be maintained upon a docket by the magistrate judge's courtroom deputy clerk until final disposition, if the parties have waived trial before a district judge and jury. At the conclusion of a Class A misdemeanor offense case or at such time as the defendant refuses to consent to trial before the magistrate judge, the magistrate judge's courtroom deputy clerk shall transmit the case file to the clerk of court for the purpose of redrawing the case to a district judge.

(f) *Establishing Excludable Periods.*

(1) Delay Recorded By Magistrate Judge. At the conclusion of the pretrial phases of a case before a magistrate judge, the magistrate judge shall compute the time remaining for trial and shall record the time limit in the Magistrate Judge's Status Report as required by LR 116.5(A)(5) and 116.5(B)(4) and 116.5(C)(8) and 116.5(D(4). In computing the time limit, the magistrate judge may take into account any periods of excludable delay which have occurred to that date, including periods of delay enumerated in LR 112.2, whether based upon his/her own knowledge of the case or upon motion of the parties, and shall issue an Order On Excludable Delay, specifying the amount of time to be excluded and the reasons for the exclusion. A copy of the order shall accompany the Magistrate Judge's Status Report.

(2) Delay Recorded By Courtroom Deputy. The courtroom deputy or a clerk serving as the courtroom deputy shall calculate the amount of excludable delay, if any, based upon his/her own knowledge of the case, and shall submit a report thereof, to the judge for his/her approval. The clerk shall then make an entry on the case docket of the Excludable Delay by specifying the start and end dates for the time to be excluded and the basis for the exclusion in the CM/ECF docketing system. The statement of the reasons for an exclusion based on 18 U.S.C. § 3161(h)(8)(A) and § 5(h)(7)(B) of this Plan as required by 18 U.S.C. § 3161(h)(8)(A) and § 5(h)(7)(C) of this Plan may be made either in the CM/ECF docketing system, in a separate order or on the record in open Court.

(3) Delay Recorded By Judge Acting Sua Sponte. If a judge acts sua sponte to cause delay which is excludable under this plan, the amount thereof shall be calculated by the judge and the excludable period shall be recorded at his/her direction by the courtroom deputy who shall make an entry on the case docket of the Excludable Delay specifying the start and end dates for the time to be excluded and the basis for the exclusion in the CM/ECF docketing system. The statement of the reasons for an exclusion based on 18 U.S.C. § 3161(h)(8)(A) and § 5(h)(7)(B) of this Plan as required by 18 U.S.C. § 3161(h)(8)(A) and § 5(h)(7)(C) of this Plan may be made either in the CM/ECF docketing system, in a separate order or on the record in open Court.

(4) Delay Recorded Pursuant to Motion of Parties.

(A) Any motion to exclude a period of delay shall be filed forthwith upon the occurrence of the act or event which would result in a period of excludable delay. A motion to exclude a period of delay shall conform to the requirements of LR 7.1 as made applicable to criminal cases by LR 112.1. Notwithstanding the provisions of LR 7.1(b)(2), opposition to a motion to exclude a period of delay shall be filed within five court days after the filing of the motion.

(B) In ruling on a motion to exclude a period of delay, a district judge or magistrate judge may rely on the facts stated in the motion, in any opposition filed thereto, and in the accompanying affidavits, or may order a hearing on the motion.

(C) If a motion to exclude a period of delay is granted, the excludable period shall be deemed to have commenced on the date on which the motion was filed in proper form or on such other date as the district judge or magistrate judge may determine and shall conclude on the date ordered by the district judge or magistrate judge.

(D) Nothing in this paragraph may be deemed to limit the power of a district judge or magistrate judge to determine excludable periods of delay without the requirements of motion or hearing, provided that notice of any such action is given to all parties.

(5) Stipulation by the Parties.

(A) The attorney for the government and the attorney for the defendant may at any time enter into stipulations with respect to the accuracy of the docket entries recording excludable time.

(B) To the extent that the amount of time stipulated does not exceed the amount recorded on the docket for any excluded period of delay, the stipulation shall be conclusive as between the parties unless it has no basis in fact or law. It shall likewise be conclusive as to a co-defendant for the limited purpose of determining, pursuant to paragraph 5(b)(6), whether the time limit for trial has run as to the defendant who is a party to the stipulation.

(C) To the extent that the amount of time stipulated exceeds the amount recorded on the docket, the stipulation shall have no effect unless approved by the court.

(6) Objections: Waiver of Objections.

(A) A party who wishes to object to a computation by a magistrate judge shall file an objection pursuant to Rule 59(a) of the Federal Rules of Criminal Procedure with the magistrate judge within the time period specified in that Rule.

(B) A party who wishes to object to a computation by a district judge shall file an objection with the district judge within seven days after service of notice of the computation on that party.

(C) The disposition of an objection shall be final.

(D) A party who fails to object to a computation within the prescribed period shall be deemed to have waived his/her objection.

(7) Time: Computation. Time shall be computed pursuant to Rule 45 (a) of the Federal Rules of Criminal Procedure.

6. Juvenile Proceedings.

(a) *Time Within Which Trial Must Commence.* The trial of an alleged delinquent who is in detention pending trial shall commence within thirty days after the beginning of such detention as required by 18 U.S.C. § 5036 and subject to the exceptions stated therein.

(b) *Time of Dispositional Hearing.* If a juvenile is adjudicated delinquent, a separate dispositional hearing shall be held no later than twenty court days after

trial, unless the court has ordered further study of the juvenile pursuant to 18 U.S.C. § 5037(e).

(c) *Sanctions.* If the trial of an alleged delinquent who is in detention has not commenced within thirty days he shall, pursuant to 18 U.S.C. § 5036 and subject to the exceptions stated therein, be entitled to dismissal of his/her case.

7. Effect of Noncompliance with Time Limits.

(a) *Dismissal.* The sanction of dismissal for noncompliance with the time limits set forth in the Speedy Trial Act of 1974 may entitle the defendant to dismissal of the charges against him pursuant to 18 U.S.C. § 3162(a). Nothing in this plan may be construed so as to require that a case be dismissed in circumstances in which dismissal would not be required by 18 U.S.C. § 3162. Notwithstanding the foregoing, the court shall retain the power to dismiss a case for unnecessary delay pursuant to Rule 48(b) of the Federal Rules of Criminal Procedure.

(b) *Defendant Responsible for Noncompliance.* If the court finds after hearing that any defendant who is not in custody is responsible for a failure to comply with the time limits of this plan, the court may, unless there is good cause shown for the failure to comply, modify or revoke the conditions of the defendant's release consistently with the provisions of 18 U.S.C. § 3148.

(c) *Attorney Misconduct.* In any case in which counsel for either party knowingly fails to disclose the fact that an essential witness is absent or unavailable, files a meritless motion solely for the purpose of delay, knowingly makes a false statement for the purpose of obtaining a continuance, or otherwise willfully fails to proceed to trial without justification consistent with the provisions of 18 U.S.C. § 3161, the court may, in addition to any other authority or power available to it, punish counsel within the terms of 18 U.S.C. §§ 3162 (b) (A)–(E) according to the court's determination of the degree of culpability of counsel.

8. Persons Serving Terms of Imprisonment.
If the United States Attorney knows that a person charged with a federal criminal offense is serving a term of imprisonment in any penal institution, it shall be his/her duty promptly:

(a) to undertake to obtain the presence of the prisoner for plea and trial (18 U.S.C. § 3161(j)(1)(A); or,

(b) if the United States Attorney is unable to obtain the presence of the defendant, to cause a detainer to be filed with the person having custody of the prisoner and request him to so advise the prisoner of his/her right to demand trial. (18 U.S.C. § 3161(j)(1)(B))

9. Monitoring Compliance with Time Limits.

(a) The office of the clerk is responsible for entering and verifying Speedy Trial Act information in the

Court's automated database. In addition, that office is also responsible for maintaining any statistical data required by the Administrative Office of the United States Courts.

(b) The office of the clerk is also responsible for preparing orders of excludable delay as may be required for the Judicial Officer's signature.

(c) At not more than one-month intervals, the office of the clerk shall review the status of all persons awaiting trial. The clerk shall immediately notify the presiding Judicial Officer of any case in which the maximum time for trial has been exceeded or is within

thirty days of being exceeded. Cases shall be reassigned as appropriate to carry out the purpose of this plan. The United States Attorney shall be advised of any case in which his/her office appears to have been responsible for unnecessary delay.

10. Effective Date. After approval by the Reviewing Panel designated in accordance with 18 U.S.C. § 3165 (c), the time limits and procedures set forth herein shall become effective on December 9, 2008, and shall supersede those previously in effect.

[Effective December 9, 2008.]

CRIMINAL JUSTICE ACT PLAN

PLAN FOR IMPLEMENTING THE CRIMINAL JUSTICE ACT OF 1964, AS AMENDED 18 U.S.C. § 3006A

Pursuant to the Report Of The Committee To Evaluate The Performance Of The Criminal Justice Act Plan For The District of Massachusetts, presented on April 27, 1993, the April 2009 Report of the Criminal Justice Act Board on Revisions to the Criminal Justice Act Plan, and pursuant to the provisions of the Criminal Justice Act of 1964, as amended, 18 U.S.C.§ 3006A ("CJA"), the judges of the United States District Court for the District of Massachusetts (the "District Court") have adopted the following plan (the "Plan") for the adequate representation of any person otherwise financially unable to obtain adequate representation, and:

(1) who is charged with a felony, misdemeanor (other than a Class B or C misdemeanor or infraction, as defined in 18 U.S.C. § 3559(a), unless the defendant faces the likelihood of loss of liberty), juvenile delinquency (see 18 U.S.C. § 5034), a violation of probation or parole; or

(2) who is under arrest, when such representation is required by law; or

(3) who is in custody as a material witness, or seeking collateral relief, as provided in 18 U.S.C § 3006A(a)(1)(G); or

(4) for whom the Sixth Amendment to the Constitution requires the appointment of counsel or for whom, in a case in which defendant faces loss of liberty, any federal law requires the appointment of counsel; or

(5) who is facing a parole termination hearing pursuant to 18 U.S.C. § 4211(c); or

(6) who is charged with a violation of supervised release or faces modification, reduction, or enlargement of a condition, or extension or revocation of a term of supervised release.; or

(7) who is subject to a mental condition hearing or sexually dangerous person hearing under 18 U.S.C. §§ 4241 et seq or 4248; or

(8) who is entitled to the appointment of counsel under 18 U.S.C. § 4109; or

(9) who needs representation in a miscellaneous matter, such as a crack cocaine sentencing reduction motion, a grand jury witness, or a pre-charge target; or

(10) who is otherwise eligible for the appointment of counsel, in the interests of justice.

Representation shall include counsel and investigative, expert and other services necessary for an adequate defense [see 18 U.S.C. § 3006A(e)].

I. PROVISION FOR FURNISHING COUNSEL

A. Federal Public Defender and Private Counsel. This Plan provides for the furnishing of legal services by a Federal Public Defender Organization, supervised by a Federal Public Defender ("FPD"). In addition, this Plan provides for the continued appointment and compensation of private counsel in a substantial proportion of cases.

B. Allocation of Representation. The court in its discretion will determine whether any party eligible for representation will be represented by the Federal Public Defender Organization or by private counsel. Insofar as practicable, private attorney appointments will be made in up to sixty-five (65) percent of the cases. For the sole purpose of allocation of cases as between private attorneys and the Federal Public Defender Organization, a "case" shall be deemed to be each defendant or other individual for whom counsel is appointed under the terms of the Criminal Justice Act, as amended, 18 U.S.C. § 3006A.

II. THE CRIMINAL JUSTICE ACT BOARD

A. The Board. The District Court shall establish a Criminal Justice Act Board ("CJA Board") consisting of ten private attorneys who agree to serve without compensation, and the FPD, who shall serve ex officio. A district judge, a magistrate judge, and the Clerk of the District Court, or the Clerk's designee, shall be appointed as liaisons with the CJA Board. The CJA Board shall be responsible for:

(1) Implementing the Mentoring Program described below;

(2) Annually evaluating applications and recommending to the District Court reappointments and new appointments to the CJA Panel of private attorneys for the Eastern Division of the District of Massachusetts (the "District");

(3) Periodically evaluating applications and recommending to the District Court reappointments and new appointments to the CJA Panels of private attorneys for the Central and Western Divisions of the District;

(4) Periodically evaluating applications and recommending to the District Court reappointments and appointments to the CJA Panel of private attorneys to provide representation in habeas corpus cases;

(5) Providing guidance concerning the FPD's office in response to requests from the FPD and on its own initiative;

(6) Working with the FPD to provide training programs for CJA Panel attorneys and other members of the criminal defense bar;

(7) Generally representing the interests of the CJA program in the District;

(8) Receiving, reviewing and making recommendations to the District Court concerning any comments or concerns regarding: (a) the performance of CJA Panel attorneys, (b) the fairness or functioning of the CJA Panel appointment process, or (c) the processing of CJA Panel payment vouchers; and

(9) Annually reporting to the District Court on the performance of the CJA Plan and, if appropriate, recommending revisions to it.

The ten private attorneys on the CJA Board shall be appointed by the District Court to serve staggered three-year terms. At least four members shall not be on any CJA Panel. Also, at least one member shall be from the Western Division of the District, and at least one member shall be from the Central Division of the District. The District Court shall designate the Chair of the CJA Board from among these ten members, to serve for a two-year term. The Chair may create one or more subcommittees of the CJA Board to handle specific areas of responsibility. The District Court shall also designate the district judge and the magistrate judge to serve as liaisons to the CJA Board. The Clerk of the District Court shall either serve as liaison, or designate a member of the Clerk's staff to serve as liaison to the CJA Board, and shall provide administrative support to the CJA Board.

III. FEDERAL PUBLIC DEFENDER ORGANIZATION

A. Establishment. The District Court has determined that the use of a Federal Public Defender Organization, as defined in 18 U.S.C. § 3006A(g)(2)(A), serving the District of Massachusetts, will facilitate the representation of persons entitled to the appointment of counsel under the Criminal Justice Act of 1964, as amended, and that the District of Massachusetts is a district in which at least two hundred (200) persons annually require the appointment of counsel, pursuant to 18 U.S.C. § 3006A(a) pertaining to the qualifications necessary to establish such an organization. A Federal Public Defender Organization has been established, with headquarters in Boston, Massachusetts, capable of rendering defense services on appointment throughout the District of Massachusetts.

B. New Hampshire and Rhode Island Branch Offices. The FPD is authorized to establish branch offices in Concord, New Hampshire, to provide defense services on appointment throughout the District of New Hampshire, and in Providence, Rhode Island, to provide defense services on appointment throughout the District of Rhode Island. Such branch offices shall be under the supervision of the FPD for the District of Massachusetts, and to the extent the caseload in each district permits, and pursuant to the direction of the FPD, the staff of any office shall be available to assist the staff of the other offices.

C. Governing Provisions. The FPD shall operate pursuant to the provisions of 18 U.S.C. § 3006A(g)(2)(A), as well as the Guidelines for the Administration of the Criminal Justice Act, promulgated by the United States Judicial Conference pursuant to 18 U.S.C. § 3006A(h).

D. Private Practice. Neither the FPD nor any appointed staff attorney may engage in the private practice of law.

E. Reports and Budget. The FPD shall submit to the Director of the Administrative Office of the United States Courts, at the time and in the form prescribed by the Director, reports of the activities and the financial position and proposed budget of the office. Copies of such reports shall be furnished to the District Court and to the Judicial Council of the First Circuit.

F. Roster of Staff. The FPD shall furnish to the District Court the roster of Assistant Federal Defenders in the FPD's office and shall report any changes thereto to the District Court.

G. Staffing and Recruitment. The FPD's Boston office shall be staffed to accept at least thirty-five (35) percent of the appointments in the Eastern and Central Divisions annually. Efforts should be made to assure that the FPD and the staff of the FPD's office are both highly qualified and sensitive to the diverse population they represent. This should include efforts to assure that minorities and women are appropriately represented in these positions.

H. Training and Resources. The FPD's office shall take the lead in providing educational programs for the CJA Panel and other members of the bar. Such training is important to enhancing the quality of representation of indigents and to making the CJA Panel accessible to able attorneys who have limited federal criminal experience. Similarly, the FPD's office shall serve as a central repository for materials which may be valuable to members of the CJA Panel, such as legal memoranda on recurring issues and jury instructions.

IV. PANEL OF PRIVATE ATTORNEYS

A. Panel List—Eastern Division of the District. The District Court shall approve, and regularly review and revise a list of private attorneys to serve as the CJA Panel for the Eastern Division of the District of Massachusetts, based at Boston, and shall annually approve a list of attorneys to fill the vacancies of those CJA Panel members whose terms have expired. The size of the Panel should be such that each panel member will receive at least two appointments each year. CJA Panel members shall serve for staggered, three year terms. The CJA Board shall annually solicit and review new applications for the Panel, as possible replacements for the approximately one third of the panel whose term expires each year, and shall make appropriate recommendations to the District Court. Incumbent panel attorneys may be reappointed to further three-year terms, but must complete a new application, and shall not be assured reappointment.

B. Panel List—Western and Central Divisions of the District. The District Court shall approve, and regularly review and revise a list of private attorneys to serve as the CJA Panels for the Central Division of the District of Massachusetts, based in Worcester, and the Western Division of the District of Massachusetts, based in Springfield. When any judicial officers are sitting in the Eastern Division of the District, they shall utilize the panel and procedures set forth herein for the Eastern Division.

C. Criteria for Panel Membership. The minimum criteria for membership on any CJA Panel are that each attorney:

(1) Be a member in good standing of the bar of the United States District Court for the District of Massachusetts and the bar of the Massachusetts Supreme Judicial Court;

(2) Have at least five years experience as a member of the bar;

(3) Have sufficient experience to furnish high quality representation to criminal defendants in the District Court;

(4) Be familiar with (a) the Federal Rules of Criminal Procedure; (b) the Federal Rules of Evidence; (c) the Bail Reform Act of 1984, (d) the Federal Sentencing Guidelines; and (e) such other statutes and rules as may be enacted from time to time with respect to criminal cases in the District Court (This requirement may be satisfied by attendance at the mandatory introductory training session);

(5) Agree to accept appointments in the full range of CJA cases (other than attorneys who are only members of the habeas or other specialized panel);

(6) For the Boston panel, agree to take part in the duty day system by accepting at least two duty days per year;

(7) Demonstrate an interest and experience in the practice of criminal law, or have other equivalent experience;

(8) Be registered for CM/ECF; and,

(9) Agree to attend continuing legal education programs.

D. Application Process. The application process shall be publicized in the Massachusetts Lawyers Weekly and other relevant publications, and local bar associations shall be enlisted in the effort to solicit applications, with particular emphasis on recruiting members of minority groups and women. Each revision of a list should seek to assure that the CJA Panel is accessible to newcomers and reflects the diversity of the defendant population and of the bar.

E. Mentoring Program. A Mentoring Program, based in Boston, shall be established by the CJA Board to provide an opportunity for attorneys, who at present lack the experience to serve on the CJA Panel, who apply to work without compensation on CJA cases with members of the Panel who agree to serve as mentors, and with the FPD's office. Applicants to the Mentoring Program may be accepted from the Western and Central Divisions of the District, but may be required to travel to Boston to participate in the program. Participation in this program would contribute to the development of the qualifications necessary to serve on the CJA Panel, but should not assure automatic future admission to the CJA Panel. In selecting participants for this program, however, consideration should be given to whether an individual would, if eventually made a member, contribute to the diversity of the CJA Panel.

F. Special Lists of Panel Attorneys. Based on the recommendation of the CJA Board, the District Court has established a panel of attorneys to represent indigent petitioners in habeas corpus cases, brought pursuant to 28 U.S.C. §§ 2254 and 2255, when the judicial officer exercises discretion to appoint counsel.

The CJA Board may, as part of its continuing evaluation of this Plan, consider the possible need for additional lists, based on foreign language fluency, or expertise in specialized areas of the law, such as immigration matters and sexually dangerous person litigation. The CJA Board may then make appropriate recommendations to the District Court, which may adopt such further lists as it deems appropriate.

G. Record Keeping

1. The Clerk of the District Court shall maintain a current computerized roster of all attorneys included on the CJA Panel list for the Eastern Division of the District, as approved by the District Court with current office addresses and telephone numbers. The deputy clerk in charge in the Western Division, and the deputy clerk in charge in the Central Division, shall each also maintain a current roster of all attorneys included on the CJA Panel list for such division. Records shall also be maintained by the Clerk of the District Court and his or her deputies in a manner which will permit judicial officers and the CJA Board to monitor the rate of appointments to the FPD's office and to the CJA Panel, and to monitor the distribution of appointments among members of the CJA Panel.

H. Use of Associates and Others. Counsel appointed from the CJA Panel may use associates, paralegals, legal assistants, and law students in the course of providing representation; however, the CJA Panel member is the lawyer responsible for the client's matter. All court appearances must be attended by the appointed CJA Panel member, unless specifically excused by the judicial officer. Appointed counsel may claim compensation for services furnished by associate counsel, paralegals, legal assistants, and law students in accordance with §§ 2.11 and 3.16 of Chapter VII of the Guide to Judiciary Policy and Procedure: Appointment of Counsel in Criminal Cases.

V. APPOINTMENT OF COUNSEL

A. Selection of Counsel—Eastern Division of the District. The judicial officers sitting in the Eastern Division of the District shall appoint counsel for indigent individuals in criminal matters. In general, appointments will be made using a duty day system. Under the duty day system, a member of the CJA Panel and a lawyer from the FPD will be available to accept appointments on each day that the District Court is open. The Clerk's Office will assign a CJA Panel member to have responsibility to be CJA duty attorney. The Federal Defender will assign a lawyer from that office to be FPD duty attorney. The Clerk's Office shall strive to ensure that duty days are evenly spread among Panel members, to the extent practicable.

The CJA duty attorney shall be expected to accept appointments to at least one case, if one is available for the CJA duty attorney, on the day when the CJA Panel member is serving as duty attorney. If multiple cases require appointment of counsel on a single day, and if the CJA and FPD duty attorneys cannot accept appointment to all of the cases on the particular day, the judicial officer shall appoint counsel for the excess cases from the CJA Panel. Those appointments shall be made to CJA Panel members in accordance with the CJA Assignment Program.

In exceptional circumstances, a judicial officer shall have the discretion to appoint an attorney not on the CJA Panel, or a CJA Panel member other than the duty attorney, in order to serve the interests of justice, judicial economy, continuity in representation, or if there is some other compelling circumstance warranting such appointment. A record concerning any such exceptional appointment shall be prepared by the appointing judicial officer, and the Clerk's office shall maintain such record and other documentation, separate from the case file, concerning each appointment and containing sufficient information to monitor the performance of the appointment process.

B. Selection of Counsel—Western and Central Divisions of the District. The judicial officers sitting in the Western and Central Divisions of the District shall appoint counsel for indigent individuals in criminal matters. Such appointment shall normally be made from the FPD or from the list of CJA Panel attorneys maintained in each division. The appointing judicial officers shall attempt to provide a fair distribution of appointments among the CJA Panel attorneys. In exceptional circumstances, a judicial officer shall have the discretion to appoint an attorney not on the CJA Panel, in order to serve the interests of justice, judicial economy, continuity in representation, or if there is some other compelling circumstance warranting such appointment. A record concerning any such exceptional appointment shall be prepared by the appointing judicial officer, and the deputy clerk in charge in each division shall maintain and regularly forward to the Clerk's office such record and other documentation, separate from the case file, concerning each appointment and containing sufficient information to monitor the performance of the appointment process.

C. Process of Appointment. In every criminal case in which the defendant is charged with a felony or a misdemeanor (other than a petty offense as defined in 18 U.S.C. § 1, unless the defendant faces the likelihood of loss of liberty), or with juvenile delinquency by the commission of an act which, if committed by an adult would be such a felony or misdemeanor, or with a violation of probation, supervised release, or parole, or for whom the Sixth Amendment to the Constitution requires the appointment of counsel or for whom, in a case in which he or she faces loss of liberty, any federal law requires the appointment of counsel, and the defendant appears without counsel, the judicial officer shall advise the defendant that he or she has the right to be represented by counsel and that counsel will be appointed if the defendant is financially unable to afford adequate representation. Unless the defendant waives representation by counsel in writing, the judicial officer, if satisfied after appropriate inquiry and after a financial affidavit has been executed by the defendant, that he or she is financially unable to obtain counsel, shall appoint counsel to represent the defendant. A defendant may not choose the counsel who shall provide representation, but may state any objection to a counsel whose appointment is under consideration. Appointment of counsel may be made retroactive to include representation furnished pursuant to the Plan prior to appointment. The judicial officer shall appoint separate counsel for defendants having interests that cannot be represented by the same counsel or when other good cause is shown. All statements made by a defendant in requesting counsel or during the inquiry into eligibility shall be either (a) by affidavit sworn to before a judicial officer, a court clerk or his or her deputy, or a notary public, or (b) under oath before a judicial officer. A financial affidavit shall not be considered part of the public record, unless so ordered by the judicial officer, after notice and a hearing.

D. Scope of Representation. A person for whom counsel is appointed shall be represented at every stage of the proceedings from the initial appearance before the judicial officer through appeal, including ancillary matters appropriate to the proceedings. If at any time after appointment of counsel the judicial officer finds that the person is financially able to obtain counsel or to make partial payment for the representation, the judicial officer may terminate the appointment of counsel or authorize payment as provided in the Criminal Justice Act of 1964, as amended, 18 U.S.C. § 3006A(f), as the interests of justice may dictate. If at any stage of the proceedings in the district court, the judicial officer finds that a person is financially unable to pay counsel whom he or she retained, the judicial officer may appoint counsel as provided in the Criminal Justice Act of 1964, as amended, and authorize payment as therein provided, as the interests of justice may dictate. The judicial officer in the interests of justice may substitute one appointed counsel for another at any stage of the proceedings.

Counsel who represented a defendant in the district court is obligated to continue the representation through the filing of any post-trial motions and the filing of a notice of appeal. Once a notice of appeal is docketed in the Court of Appeals, the continuing obligations of counsel shall be governed by the Local Rules of the United States Court of Appeals for the First Circuit, including the appointment of counsel and changes in representation. A proceeding under 28 U.S.C. 2255, or other collateral challenge, is not a post-trial motion for these purposes. With leave of court, counsel may also represent a defendant with respect to the placement or a prisoner in the prison system or any related issues. If a former client contacts counsel after representation terminates regarding a matter that may require the assistance of counsel, former counsel is required either to seek leave of court to resume representation, or to advise the client how to request new counsel by contacting the court. Nothing in this provision is intended to create a new right to counsel with respect to post-trial matters where such a right is not otherwise established by law.

E. Discretionary Appointments. Any person seeking relief under §§ 2241, 2254, or 2255 of title 28, or individuals who are subjects, or targets, or who have received a grand jury subpoena may be furnished representation pursuant to this Plan whenever the judicial officer determines that the interests of justice so require and such person is financially unable to afford adequate representation. Such appointments are discretionary and payment for such representation shall be in accordance with the provisions of the Act and this Plan.

VI. PAYMENT FOR REPRESENTATION BY PRIVATE COUNSEL

A. Hourly Rates. Any private attorney appointed under this Plan shall, at the conclusion of the representation or on an interim basis, if authorized by the judicial officer, be compensated at the rate set by the Judicial Conference of the United States for the District, and funded by the Congress of the United States, as provided in 18 U.S.C. § 3006A(d)(1). Such attorney shall be reimbursed for expenses reasonably incurred.

B. Maximum Amounts. The maximum amount of compensation to be paid to a private attorney appointed under this Plan shall not exceed the amounts set forth in 18 U.S.C. § 3006A(d)(2), unless waived by the judicial officer.

C. Waiving Maximum Amounts. Payment in excess of any maximum amount set forth in 18 U.S.C. § 3006A (d)(2) may be made for extended or complex representation whenever the district judge before whom the representation was rendered, or the magistrate judge, if the representation was furnished exclusively before the magistrate judge, certifies that the amount of the excess payment is necessary to provide fair compensation and the payment is approved by the Chief Judge of the Court of Appeals for the First Circuit or the Chief Judge's designee.

E.* Filing Claims. A claim for compensation and reimbursement shall be made to the District Court for representation before the judicial officer. Within forty-five (45) days of final disposition the claimant shall file the claim with the Clerk of the District Court for the District of Massachusetts who is authorized to select a deputy to coordinate duties assigned under this Plan. Each claim shall be supported by a sworn written statement specifying the time expended, services rendered, and expenses incurred while the case was pending before the judicial officer, and the compensation and reimbursement applied for or received in the same case from any other source. The judicial officer shall fix the compensation and reimbursement to be paid to the attorney. In cases where representation is furnished exclusively before a magistrate judge, the claim shall be submitted to the magistrate judge who shall fix the compensation and reimbursement to be paid to the attorney. In cases where representation is furnished other than before the magistrate judge, the district court, or an appellate court, the district court shall fix the compensation and reimbursement to be paid.

Whenever compensation is to be fixed by the court, the judge most familiar with the matter shall have authority to act, or in that judge's absence or in the event of any uncertainty, the chief judge or the Miscellaneous Business Docket (MBD) judge may act for the court.

If the compensation claimed exceeds the maximum amount set forth in § 3006A(d)(2), counsel seeking compensation shall submit a memorandum explaining why the judicial officer should approve a waiver of the maximum amount, as provided in § 3006A(d)(3).

If the judicial officer contemplates reducing the requested compensation, the attorney shall be given an opportunity to justify in writing the amount claimed. This paragraph does not afford any right to a hearing.

F. New Trials. For purposes of compensation and other payments authorized under the Criminal Justice Act of 1964, as amended, and this Plan, an order by a court granting a new trial shall be deemed to initiate a new case.

G. Appeals. If a defendant is convicted following trial or is sentenced following a plea, counsel appointed hereunder shall advise the defendant regarding the right to appeal and of the right to counsel on appeal, including the effect of any appeal waiver, and this obligation shall not be affected or diminished by similar advice given to the defendant by the judicial officer. If a defendant does wish to appeal, counsel shall file a timely notice of appeal and shall continue to represent the defendant unless or until relieved by the court of appeals.

VII. SERVICES OTHER THAN COUNSEL
[18 U.S.C. § 3006A(e)]

A. Upon Request. Counsel for any person who is financially unable to obtain investigative, expert, or other services necessary for an adequate defense may request them in an ex parte application. Upon finding, after appropriate inquiry in an ex parte proceeding, that the services are necessary and that the person is financially unable to obtain them, the district judge, or the magistrate judge if the services are required in connection with a matter over which the magistrate judge has jurisdiction, shall authorize counsel to obtain the services requested. The maximum which may be paid to a person for services so authorized shall not exceed the amount set forth in § 3006A(e)(3), exclusive of reimbursement for expenses reasonably incurred, unless payment in excess of that limit is certified by the district judge, or by the magistrate judge if the services were rendered in connection with a case disposed of entirely before the magistrate judge, as necessary to provide fair compensation for services of an unusual character or duration, and the amount of the excess payment is approved by the Chief Judge of the Court of Appeals for the First Circuit or the Chief Judge's delegate

B. Without Prior Request. Counsel appointed under the Criminal Justice Act, as amended, and this Plan may obtain, subject to later review, investigative, expert, or other services without prior authorization if necessary for an adequate defense. The total cost of services obtained without prior authorization may not exceed the amount set forth in § 3006A(e)(2) and expenses reasonably incurred, and payment in excess of that amount may not be approved.

C. Federal Public Defender Organization. The provisions of this section do not apply to the Federal Public Defender Organization established by and operating under this Plan.

VIII. RECEIPT OF OTHER PAYMENTS

Whenever the judicial officer finds that funds are available for payment from or on behalf of a person furnished representation under the Criminal Justice Act, as amended, and this Plan, the judicial officer may authorize or direct that such funds be paid to the appointed attorney, to any person authorized to render investigative, expert, or other services, or to the District Court for deposit in the Treasury. Except as so authorized or directed, no appointed attorney may request or accept any payment or promise of payment for providing services or representation to a defendant.

IX. MISCELLANEOUS

A. Forms. Where standard forms have been approved by the Judicial Conference of the United States or an appropriate Committee thereof and have been distributed by the Administrative Office of the United States Courts, such forms shall be used by the District Court, the Clerk, the judicial officers, the Federal Public Defender Organization, and private counsel appointed under the Criminal Justice Act, as amended, and this Plan.

B. Guidelines for the Administration of the Criminal Justice Act. The judicial officers, Clerk of the District Court, Federal Public Defender Organization, and private attorneys appointed under the Criminal Justice Act, as amended, and this Plan, shall comply with the provisions of the Judicial Conference's Guidelines for the Administration of the Criminal Justice Act.

X. EFFECTIVE DATE

This plan shall take effect immediately upon its approval by the Judicial Council of the First Circuit, or on September 1, 2009, whichever is later. It shall supersede the Plan for Implementing the Criminal Justice Act of 1964, as amended, adopted by this District Court on June 1, 1993, effective on July 1, 1993, and amended on July 10, 2001, except counsel appointed under the earlier Plan to represent particular defendants shall be authorized to complete the services for which they were appointed and shall be entitled to be paid under the earlier Plan for such services and expenses.

THE FOREGOING PLAN IS APPROVED BY THE JUDICIAL COUNCIL OF THE FIRST CIRCUIT AS OF THE 1st DAY OF September, 2009.

[Effective July 1, 1993. Amended effective September 1, 2009.]

* [Publisher's Note: So in original.]

PUBLIC NOTICE REGARDING AMENDMENTS TO THE CRIMINAL JUSTICE ACT

Subject: AMENDMENTS TO THE CRIMINAL JUSTICE ACT

The "Judicial Administration and Technical Amendments Act of 2008," Pub. L. No. 110–406, was enacted on October 13, 2008, and amends the Criminal Justice Act (CJA), 18 U.S.C. § 3006A, to (1) raise the case compensation maximums applicable to appointed private "panel" attorneys, and (2) expand the authority of the chief judge of the court of appeals to delegate the approval of excess compensation vouchers of attorneys and investigative, expert, and other service providers to include senior circuit judges. The Act amends this same delegation provision in the Antiterrorism and Effective Death Penalty Act of 1996 (AEDPA), recodified in part at 18 U.S.C. § 3599, with respect to investigative, expert, and other service provider excess compensation vouchers. Prior to the amendment, the

CJA and AEDPA delegation was limited to active circuit judges.

The impact of this legislation is to raise the case compensation maximums, which had last been revised in December 2004 to reflect the then-prevailing hourly rate of $90. The new maximums include:

$7,800 for felonies at the trial court level and $5,600 for appeal (previously $7,000/$5,000);

$2,200 for misdemeanors at the trial court level and $5,600 for appeal (previously $2,000/$5,000);

$7,800 for non-capital post-conviction proceedings under 18 U.S.C. §§ 2241, 2254 or 2255 and $5,600 for appeal (previously $7,000/$5,000).

In addition, the amendment to subsection (d)(2) of the CJA provides for the case maximums to increase "simultaneously" with changes in the maximum hourly compensation rate. (This obviates the need to amend the amounts in the statute itself, as had been necessary with previous statutory amendments.)

The text of the amended CJA and AEDPA provisions is appended as Attachment 1. The revised paragraphs of the Guidelines for the Administration of the Criminal Justice Act and Related Statutes (CJA Guidelines), Volume 7, *Guide to Judiciary Policies and Procedures* are included as Attachment 2.

The CJA amendment to the attorney case compensation maximums applies to cases pending on or after the date of enactment, which is the effective date of the legislation. **Specifically, the new case compensation maximums apply to a voucher submitted by appointed counsel if that person furnished any CJA-compensable work on or after October 13, 2008.** The former case compensation maximums apply to a voucher submitted by appointed counsel if that person's CJA-compensable work on the representation was completed **before October 13, 2008.** These same dates govern the expanded delegation authority of the chief judge of the court of appeals.

[Dated November 14, 2008.]

ATTACHMENT 1

Provisions of the Criminal Justice Act and Antiterrorism and Effective Death Penalty Act of 1996, as amended by the Judicial Administration and Technical Amendments Act of 2008

Pub. L. No. 110–406

[New language in **bold italics**]

Criminal Justice Act, 18 U.S.C. § 3006A. Adequate representation of defendants

* * *

(d) Payment for Representation.

* * *

(2) *Maximum Amounts.* For representation of a defendant before the United States magistrate judge or the district court, or both, the compensation to be paid to an attorney or to a bar association or legal aid agency or community defender organization shall not exceed $7,000 for each attorney in a case in which one or more felonies are charged, and $2,000 for each attorney in a case in which only misdemeanors are charged. For representation of a defendant in an appellate court, the compensation to be paid to an attorney or to a bar association or legal aid agency or community defender organization shall not exceed $5,000 for each attorney in each court. For representation of a petitioner in a noncapital habeas corpus proceeding, the compensation for each attorney shall not exceed the amount applicable to a felony in this paragraph for representation of a defendant before a judicial officer of the district court. For representation of such petitioner in an appellate court, the compensation for each attorney shall not exceed the amount applicable for representation of a defendant in an appellate court. For representation of an offender before the United States Parole Commission in a proceeding under section 4106A of this title, the compensation shall not exceed $1,500 for each attorney in each proceeding; for representation of an offender in an appeal from a determination of such Commission under such section the compensation shall not exceed $5,000 for each attorney in each court. For any other representation required or authorized by this section, the compensation shall not exceed $1,500 for each attorney in each proceeding. *The compensation maximum amounts provided in this subsection shall increase simultaneously by the same percentage, rounded to the nearest multiple of $100, as the aggregate percentage increases in the maximum hourly compensation rate paid pursuant to paragraph (1) for time expended since the case maximum amounts were last adjusted.*

(3) *Waiving Maximum Amounts.* Payment in excess of any maximum amount provided in paragraph (2) of this subsection may be made for extended or complex representation whenever the court in which the representation was rendered, or the United States magistrate judge if the representation was furnished exclusively before him, certifies that the amount of the excess payment is necessary to provide fair compensation and the payment is approved by the chief judge of the circuit. The chief judge of the circuit may delegate such approval authority to an active *or senior* circuit judge.

* * *

(e) Services Other Than Counsel.

* * *

(3) *Maximum Amounts.* Compensation to be paid to a person for services rendered by him to a person under this subsection, or to be paid to an organization for services rendered by an employee thereof, shall not exceed $1,600, exclusive of reimbursement for expenses reasonably incurred, unless payment in excess of that limit is certified by the court, or by the United States magistrate judge if the services were rendered in connection with a case disposed of entirely before him, as necessary to provide fair compensation for services of an unusual character or duration, and the amount of the excess payment is approved by the chief judge of the circuit. The chief judge of the circuit may delegate such approval authority to an active *or senior* circuit judge.

* * *

Antiterrorism and Effective Death Penalty Act of 1996, recodified in part in Title 18, United States Code, Section 3599

18 U.S.C. § 3599. Counsel for financially unable defendants.

(g)(2) Fees and expenses paid for investigative, expert, and other reasonably necessary services authorized under subsection (f) shall not exceed $7,500 in any case, unless payment in excess of that limit is certified by the court, or by the United States magistrate judge, if the services were rendered in connection with the case disposed of entirely before such magistrate judge, as necessary to provide fair compensation for services of an unusual character or duration, and the amount of the excess payment is approved by the chief judge of the circuit. The chief judge of the circuit may delegate such approval authority to an active *or senior* circuit judge.

ATTACHMENT 2

Guidelines for the Administration of the Criminal Justice Act and Related Statutes (CJA Guidelines), Volume 7, *Guide to Judiciary Policies and Procedures*

ADJUSTMENT OF THE PANEL ATTORNEY CASE COMPENSATION MAXIMUM AMOUNTS

Chapter II. Appointment and Payment of Counsel

* * *

2.22 Limitations.

* * *

B. *Case Compensation Maximums*

* * *

(2) Specific Proceedings.

(i) Felonies [except federal capital prosecutions].

7,800 for trial court level.

5,600 for appeal.

(ii) Misdemeanors [including petty offenses (class B or C misdemeanors or infractions) as set forth in subsection (a)(2)(A) of the Act].

2,200 for trial court level.

5,600 for appeal.

(iii) Proceedings under section 4106A of title 18, United States Code [in connection with paroled prisoners transferred to the United States].

1,700 for representation before the United States Parole Commission.

5,600 for appeal.

(iv) Proceedings under sections 4107 or 4108 of title 18, United States Code [for counsel and guardians ad litem providing services in connection with prisoner transfer proceedings. See Regulations for the Appointment of Counsel Pursuant to a Prisoner Transfer Treaty, which appears at Section B of this Volume, regarding appointment of counsel or guardians ad litem under 18 U.S.C. § 4109].

2,200 for each verification proceeding.

(v) Pre–Trial Diversion.

7,800 if offense alleged by the U.S. Attorney is a felony.

2,200 if offense alleged by the U.S. Attorney is a misdemeanor.

(vi) Proceedings under section 983 of title 18, United States Code [for services provided by counsel appointed under 18 U.S.C. § 983(b)(1) in connection with certain judicial civil forfeiture proceedings].

7,800 for trial court level.

5,600 for appeal.

(vii) Non-capital Post–Conviction Proceedings under sections 2241, 2254 or 2255 of title 18, United States Code.

7,800 for trial court level.

5,600 for appeal.

(viii) Proceedings to Protect Federal Jurors Employment under section 1875 of title 28, United States Code.

7,800 for trial court level.

5,600 for appeal.

(ix) Other Representations required or authorized by the CJA.

1,700 for trial court level.

1,700 for each level of appeal.

This category includes but is not limited to the following representations:

(a) Probation Violation:

(b) Supervised Release Hearing [for persons charged with a violation of supervised release or facing modification, reduction or enlargement of a condition or extension or revocation of a term of supervised release];

(c) Parole Proceedings under chapter 311 of title 18, U.S.C.;

(d) Material Witness in Custody;

(e) Mental Condition Hearings Pursuant to chapter 313 of title 18, U.S.C. [with the exception of hearings pursuant to sections 4241 and 4244 of title 18, U.S.C., which are considered part of the case in chief with no separate compensation maximums applying. (A chart detailing the treatment for the purpose of compensation of representation at each hearing pursuant to chapter 313 is included as Appendix H.];

(f) Civil or Criminal Contempt [Where the person faces loss of liberty];

(g) Witness [before a grand jury, a court, the Congress, or a federal agency or commission which has the power to compel testimony, where there is a reason to believe either prior to or during testimony, that the witness could be subject to a criminal prosecution, a civil or criminal contempt proceeding, or face loss of liberty];

(h) International Extradition [under chapter 209 of title 8, U.S.C.].

EXPANSION OF THE DELEGATION AUTHORITY OF THE CHIEF JUDGE OF THE COURT OF APPEALS TO APPROVE EXCESS COMPENSATION AMOUNTS

CJA Guidelines 2.22B(1)(i), 2.22B(3), 3.02A, and 6.03B

All references in the above-referenced CJA Guidelines to the chief judge of the court of appeals having authority to delegate to an "active circuit judge" the approval of vouchers in excess of the statutory maximum compensation have been revised to read an "active or senior circuit judge."

[Effective October 13, 2008.]

SELECTED ORDERS AND NOTICES

POLICY REGARDING ELECTRONIC DEVICES

The general public is prohibited from bringing cameras, pagers, cellular telephones, personal data assistants (PDA's), laptop computers, tape recorders, and other electronic devices into any United States Courthouse in the District of Massachusetts. Persons bringing these devices into the courthouse must check them at the security screening station in order to gain access to the building. Attorneys who present a valid bar card from any jurisdiction, together with two valid forms of identification, at least one with a photograph, are permitted to bring PDA's, laptop computers, and cellular telephones into the courthouse for business use. Attorneys carrying these items will be required to submit them for x-ray and such other examination as deemed appropriate by court security personnel. Laptop computers with silent keyboards may be used in the courtroom with the prior permission of the presiding judge. Cellular telephones and PDA's must be turned off or placed in silent mode while in the courtroom. Violation of this provision may result in severe sanctions. Cellular telephones may only be used in public areas of the courthouse no less than twenty feet from the entrance to any courtroom. Attorneys are reminded that the recording of court proceedings by any electronic or photographic means is strictly forbidden.

Members of the public invited to after court-hours public events are permitted to bring cellular telephones into the Boston Moakley Courthouse. Public events are held after 6:00 PM on weekdays, weekends, and federal holidays.

[Dated: June 6, 2008.]

NOTICE RE: IMPLEMENTATION OF HOURLY RATE INCREASE FOR CRIMINAL JUSTICE ACT PANEL ATTORNEYS

Congress recently passed, and the President signed into law on December 26, 2007, the Consolidated Appropriations Act of 2008, the 11-bill omnibus spending measure which includes fiscal year 2008 funding for the Judiciary. Congress authorized and provided funds to raise the non-capital hourly panel attorney compensation rate from $94 to $100, and the maximum hourly capital rate from $166 to $170 (for federal capital prosecutions and capital post-conviction proceedings). These rates apply to attorneys appointed to represent eligible persons under the Criminal Justice Act, 18 U.S.C. § 3006A, and the Antiterrorism and Effective Death Penalty Act of 1996, codified in part in 18 U.S.C. § 3599.

The new hourly compensation rates apply to work performed on or after January 1, 2008. Where the appointment of counsel occurred before this effective date, the new compensation rates apply to that portion of services provided on or after January 1, 2008.

If you have any questions concerning this matter, please contact the Office of Defender Services, Legal and Policy Branch Duty Attorney, on (202) 502-3030.

[Dated: January 11, 2008.]

GENERAL ORDER 09–06. REGARDING JURY FEES

Pursuant to the Jury Selection and Service Act, as amended, 28 U.S.C. §§ 1861, et seq., the court hereby reduces the amount of time from (30) to (10) days after which a petit juror shall begin receiving a supplemental daily fee, presently authorized not-to-exceed $10, in addition to the $40 fee per day.

When a grand juror is required to attend more than (45) days of actual grand jury service (including days of travel), said juror may be paid a supplemental daily fee, presently authorized not-to-exceed $10, in addition to the $40 fee per day, unless the presiding judge determines in his or her discretion that such enhanced fees are not appropriate and directs that they not be paid.

[November 3, 2009, effective October 1, 2009, nunc pro tunc.]

GENERAL ORDER 09–08. EM WARRANTS*

In order to more efficiently process the issuance of warrants in the event a defendant or offender in a criminal case violates the terms of his/her electronic monitoring (EM), the District Judge or Magistrate Judge ordering the initial release will also sign an undated warrant for violation of release conditions that will be held in abeyance by the United States Marshals Service (USMS) until such time as the defendant may abscond. Defendants or offenders not referred to a Magistrate Judge at the time the warrant is requested will be deemed automatically referred to the Magistrate Judge for issuance of the EM warrant and initial appearance upon arrest.

The Clerk's office in consultation with the USMS, Pretrial Services and Probation shall establish a protocol for issuance of the EM warrant.

[Adopted effective November 3, 2009.]

* [**Publisher's Note:** Suggested title supplied by publisher.]

EMERGENCY STANDING ORDER 10–2. LOAN MODIFICATION AND FORBEARANCE AGREEMENTS

Unless conspicuously identified and specifically approved by the court in advance, any provision in a loan modification agreement, forbearance agreement, stipulation relating to a motion for relief from the automatic stay under 11 U.S.C. § 362(a) or similar agreement, which provides that, upon default by he debtor, the benefits of the automatic stay will be waived shall be deemed unenforceable and void.

[Dated: March 2, 2010.]

GENERAL ORDER 11–06. TRANSCRIPT RATES, EFFECTIVE JANUARY 1, 2012 *

(Amends General Order 07–3, Adopted November 9, 2007)

Pursuant to Title 28, United States Code, Section 753, and consistent with the action of the Judicial Conference at its September 2011 session, the following transcript rates per page for civil and criminal cases are prescribed by the Court and are effective January 1, 2012.

Maximum Transcript Fee Rates—All Parties Per Page

	Original	First Copy to Each Party	Each Additional Copy to the Same Party
Ordinary Transcript (30 day) A transcript to be delivered within thirty (30) calendar days after receipt of an order.	$3.65	$.90	$.60
14–Day Transcript A transcript to be delivered within fourteen (14) calendar days after receipt of an order.	$4.25	$.90	$.60
Expedited Transcript (7 day) A transcript to be delivered within seven (7) calendar days after receipt of an order.	$4.85	$.90	$.60
Daily Transcript A transcript to be delivered following adjournment and prior to the normal opening hour of the court on the following morning whether or not it actually is a court day.	$6.05	$1.20	$.90
Daily Transcript (CJA Cases)	$6.05	$1.20	$.90
			(CJA Counsel) $.10
Hourly Transcript A transcript of proceedings ordered under unusual circumstances to be delivered within two (2) hours.	$7.25	$1.20	$.90
Realtime Transcript A draft unedited transcript produced by a certified realtime reporter as a by-product of realtime to be delivered electronically during proceedings or immediately following adjournment.	$3.05		One feed,[1] $3.05/page Two-four feeds, $2.10 / page/feed Five or more feeds, $1.50/page/feed

[1] A realtime "feed" is the electronic data flow from the court reporter to the computer of each person or party ordering and receiving the realtime transcription in the courtroom.

[Effective January 1, 2012.]

    * [**Publisher's Note:** Suggested title supplied by publisher.]

RULES FOR UNITED STATES MAGISTRATE JUDGES IN THE UNITED STATES DISTRICT COURT FOR THE DISTRICT OF MASSACHUSETTS

Adopted January 15, 1981

Including Amendments Received Through
January 1, 2012

Research Note

These rules may be searched electronically on WESTLAW *in the MA–RULES database; updates to these rules may be found on* WESTLAW *in MA–RULESUPDATES. For search tips, and a detailed summary of database content, consult the* WESTLAW *Scope Screen of each database.*

I. TITLE AND EFFECT

These rules shall be known as the Rules for United States Magistrates Judges in the United States District Court for the District of Massachusetts.

Proceedings in cases or other matters before the court on the effective date of these Rules will be governed by these Rules unless, in a particular case, the court determines that application of the Rules in that case would be impracticable or unjust.

[Amended effective January 8, 2002.]

II. AUTHORITY OF UNITED STATES MAGISTRATE JUDGES

RULE 1. DUTIES UNDER 28 U.S.C. SECTION 636(a)

Each United States Magistrate Judge appointed by this court is authorized to perform the duties prescribed by 28 U.S.C. Section 636(a) as hereinafter specified and may—

(a) Exercise all the powers and duties conferred or imposed upon United States Commissioners by law or the Federal Rules of Criminal Procedure;

(b) Administer oaths and affirmations, impose conditions of release or detention under 18 U.S.C. Section 3142 et seq., and take acknowledgments, affidavits, and depositions;

(c) When specially designated to exercise such jurisdiction by the district court, try persons accused of, and sentence persons convicted of, misdemeanors (including petty offenses) committed within this district in accordance with 18 U.S.C. Section 3401, Fed. R. Crim P. 58, and Rules 10 through 12 of these Rules, conduct a jury trial in any misdemeanor case (including petty offenses) where the defendant so requests and is entitled to trial by jury under the Constitution and laws of the United States, order a presentence investigative report on any such person who is convicted or pleads guilty or nolo contendere, and sentence such person;

(d) Conduct removal proceedings and issue warrants of removal in accordance with Fed. R. Crim. P. 40;

(e) Conduct extradition proceedings, in accordance with 18 U.S.C. Section 3184; and

(f) Supervise proceedings conducted pursuant to letters rogatory, in accordance with 28 U.S.C. Section 1782.

[Amended effective January 8, 2002.]

RULE 2. NON–DISPOSITIVE PRE–TRIAL MATTERS

(a) A magistrate judge may hear and determine any pretrial motion or other pretrial matter, in accordance with 28 U.S.C. Section 636(b)(1)(A), other than those motions specified in Rule 3 of these Rules.

(b) A party may not assign as error any aspect of the magistrate judge's order made under subsection (a) hereof, unless a timely objection is made. A party must serve and file any objections to the magistrate judge's order within 14 days of being served with a copy of that order unless a different time is prescribed by the magistrate judge or a district judge. The district judge to whom the case is assigned will consider such objections and will modify or set aside any portion of the magistrate judge's order determined to be clearly erroneous or contrary to law.

(c) The ruling or order of a magistrate judge in a matter that is heard and determined under subsection (a) hereof is the ruling of the Court and is final unless reversed, vacated or modified by a district judge as provided in Fed. R. Civ. P. 72(a) and Fed. R. Crim. P. 59(a). The filing of objections under subsection (b) hereof does not operate as a stay of a magistrate judge's ruling or order unless so ordered by the magistrate judge or a district judge, and then only to the extent specifically ordered by the magistrate judge or district judge. Any party desiring a stay of a magistrate judge's ruling or order, or any part thereof, pending ruling on objections filed under subsection (b) hereof, must first apply therefor to the magistrate judge from whose ruling the objection is taken. If the magistrate judge denies a stay, written application therefor may then be made to the district judge to whom the case is assigned. Any application to the district judge for a stay must have appended to it the certificate of counsel that application for the stay sought has been made to the magistrate judge and denied by the magistrate judge, together with a copy of the magistrate judge's denial.

[Amended effective January 8, 2002. Amended effective December 1, 2009.]

RULE 3. DISPOSITIVE PRE–TRIAL MOTIONS AND PRISONER CASES

(a) In accordance with 28 U.S.C. Section 636(b)(B) and (C), a magistrate judge upon a specific referral by the district judge assigned to the case may conduct such evidentiary hearings as are necessary or appropriate, and submit to a district judge proposed findings of fact and recommendations for the disposition of:

(1) applications for post-trial relief made by individuals convicted of criminal offenses;

(2) prisoner petitions challenging conditions of confinement;

(3) motions for injunctive relief (including preliminary injunctions but excluding motions for temporary restraining orders);

(4) motions for judgment on the pleadings;

(5) motions for summary judgment;

(6) motions to dismiss or quash an indictment or information made by a defendant;

(7) motions to suppress evidence in a criminal case;

(8) motions to dismiss or permit the maintenance of a class action;

(9) motions to dismiss for failure to state a claim upon which relief may be granted;

(10) motions to dismiss an action involuntarily;

(11) motions for judicial review of administrative determinations;

(12) motions for review of default judgments;

(13) motions to dismiss or for judgment by default under Fed. R. Civ. P. 37(b);

(14) motions to revoke or modify probation or supervised release under the provisions of Fed. R. Crim. P. 32.1(b), in cases not within the consent jurisdiction of a magistrate judge; and

(15) Such other pretrial matters as are dispositive of a claim or a defense.

(b) In all reports and recommendations filed under the provisions of subsection (a) hereof, the magistrate judge must incorporate therein clear notice to the parties that failure to file timely and appropriate objections to that report and recommendation under the provisions of this Rule will result in preclusion of the right to appeal the district court's order to the United States Court of Appeals. That notice may consist of the following language—

The parties are hereby advised that under the provisions of Fed. R. Civ. P. 72(b) or Fed. R. Crim. P. 59(b), any party who objects to these proposed findings and recommendations must file specific written objections thereto with the Clerk of this Court within 14 days of the party's receipt of this Report and Recommendation. The written objections must specifically identify the portion of the proposed findings, recommendations, or report to which objection is made and the basis for such objections. The parties are further advised that the United States Court of Appeals for this Circuit has repeatedly indicated that failure to comply with Fed. R. Civ. P. 72(b), will preclude further appellate review of the District Court's order based on this Report and Recommendation. See Keating v. Secretary of Health and Human Services, 848 F.2d 271 (1st Cir. 1988); United States v. Emiliano Valencia–Copete, 792 F.2d 4 (1st Cir. 1986); Park Motor Mart, Inc. v. Ford Motor Co., 616 F.2d 603 (1st Cir. 1980); United States v. Vega, 678 F.2d 376, 378–379 (1st Cir. 1982); Scott v. Schweiker, 702 F.2d 13, 14 (1st Cir. 1983); see also, Thomas v. Arn, 474 U.S. 140, 106 S.Ct. 466 (1985).

The notice will be effective if stated in other language that clearly communicates the effect of failure to comply with the provisions of Fed. R. Civ. P. 72(b), as set forth by the United States Court of Appeals for this Circuit in United States v. Emiliano Valencia–Copete, 792 F.2d 4 (1st Cir. 1986).

(c) Within 14 days of being served with a copy of the recommended disposition, a party may serve and file specific, written objections to the proposed findings and recommendations. The written objections must specifically identify the portions of the proposed findings and recommendations or report to which objection is made and the basis for each objection. A party may respond to another party's objections within 14 days after being served with a copy thereof.

The district judge to whom the case is assigned must make a de novo determination upon the record, or after additional evidence, of any portion of the magistrate judge's recommended disposition to which specific written objection has been made in accordance with this Rule. The district judge, however, need not conduct a new hearing and may consider the record developed before the magistrate judge, making a determination on the basis of that record. The district judge may accept, reject or modify the recommended disposition, receive further evidence or recommit the matter to the magistrate judge with instructions.

(d) A magistrate judge may exercise the powers enumerated in Rules 2, 3, 6 and 7 of the Rules Governing Section 2254 and 2255 Proceedings, in accordance with the standards and criteria established in 28 U.S.C. Section 636(b)(1), and may recommend to the district judge appropriate orders under Rules 4, 5, 8 and 9 of the Rules Governing Section 2254 and 2255 Proceedings.

[Amended effective January 8, 2002. Amended effective December 1, 2009.]

RULE 4. SPECIAL MASTER REFERENCES AND TRIALS BY CONSENT

(a) A magistrate judge may serve as a special master subject to the procedures and limitations of 28 U.S.C. Section 636(b)(2) and Fed. R. Civ. P. 53. Unless the district judge orders that a transcript of the proceedings not be filed, any order of reference under this subsection or under Section 4(b) of these Rules must include a directive that the parties, in such proportionate share as the district judge determines to be appropriate, will bear the expense of preparing the transcript required to be filed under Fed. R. Civ. P. 53(e).

(b) With the consent of the parties and the approval of the district judge to whom the case has been assigned, a magistrate judge may serve as special master in any civil case without regard to the provisions of Fed. R. Civ. P. 53(b). The entry of final judgment under this subsection, however, must be ordered by a district judge of the court, or at the direction of a district judge.

(c) Notwithstanding any provision of law to the contrary—

(1) Upon the consent of the parties (including added parties), a magistrate judge, when specially designated to exercise such jurisdiction by the district court, may conduct any and all proceedings in a jury or non-jury civil case and order judgment in the case. A record of the proceedings must be made in accordance with the requirements of 28 U.S.C. § 636(c)(5).

(2) The Clerk of the Court will notify the parties in all civil cases that they may consent to have a magistrate judge conduct any or all proceedings in the case and order the entry of the final judgment. Such notice will be handed or mailed to the plaintiff or plaintiff's representative at the time an action is filed and to the other parties as attachments to copies of the complaint and summons, when served. Additional notices may be furnished to the parties at later stages of the proceedings, and may be included with pretrial notices. If new parties are added after the initial filing, the plaintiff is responsible for obtaining an executed consent form from the new parties.

(3) The Clerk must not accept a consent form unless it has been signed by all the parties in a case. The plaintiff is responsible for obtaining the executed consent form from the parties and filing the form with the Clerk of the Court within 21 days of the filing of an answer or other responsive pleading by the parties, unless the time is enlarged by order of the court. Thereafter, either a district judge or a magistrate judge may again advise the parties of the availability of trial by consent before a magistrate judge, but in so doing, must also advise the parties that they are free to withhold consent without adverse substantive consequences.

(4) Upon entry of judgment of any case reassigned under paragraph (1) of subsection (c) of this Rule, an aggrieved party may appeal directly to the United States Court of Appeals for the First Circuit from the judgment of the magistrate judge in the same manner as if appealing from any other judgment of a district court. Nothing in this paragraph is to be construed as a limitation of any party's right to seek review by the Supreme Court of the United States.

(5) The district court may, for good cause, on its own initiative or under extraordinary circumstances shown by any party, vacate a referral of a civil matter to a magistrate judge under this subsection.

[Amended effective January 8, 2002. Amended effective December 1, 2009.]

RULE 5. OTHER DUTIES

A magistrate judge is also authorized to–

(a) Conduct pretrial conferences, settlement conferences, alternative dispute resolution procedures, and related pretrial proceedings;

(b) Conduct arraignments in cases not triable by the magistrate judge to the extent of taking a not guilty plea or noting a defendant's intention to plead guilty or nolo contendere; and order the preparation of a presentence report when the defendant has expressed a firm intention of entering a plea of guilty and requests that the report be promptly prepared;

(c) Receive grand jury returns in accordance with Fed. R. Crim. P. 6(f);

(d) Conduct a preliminary hearing, if a hearing is required, before revocation of probation or supervised release by a district judge; and may conduct necessary proceedings leading to potential revocation of probation or supervised release imposed by a magistrate judge;

(e) Issue subpoenas, writs of habeas corpus ad testificandum or habeas corpus ad prosequendum, or other orders necessary to obtain the presence of parties or witnesses or evidence needed for court proceedings;

(f) Order the exoneration or forfeiture of bonds;

(g) Conduct examinations of judgment debtors, in accordance with Fed. R. Civ. P. 69;

(h) Conduct evidentiary hearings and prepare findings in employment discrimination cases as a master under Title VII of the Civil Rights Act of 1964, as amended, whenever a district judge cannot schedule a case for trial within 120 days after issue has been joined (42 U.S.C. Section 2000e–5(f)(5));

(i) Administer oath of allegiance to new citizens at naturalization hearings and administer oath of admission to attorneys at admission ceremony;

(j) Conduct evidentiary hearings and prepare recommended findings in civil rights cases brought by prisoners in penal institutions;

(k) Accept petit jury verdicts in civil cases in the absence of a district judge with the consent of the parties;

(l) Conduct proceedings consistent with the provisions of Fed. R. Civ. P. 16(b);

(m) Accept a waiver of indictment pursuant to Fed. R. Crim. P. 7(b); and

(n) Perform any additional duty not inconsistent with the Constitution and laws of the United States.

The enumeration of specific duties in this section is not to be construed as limiting the referral of any other matter otherwise not inconsistent with the Constitution and laws of the United States.

[Amended effective January 8, 2002.]

III. ASSIGNMENT OF DUTIES TO MAGISTRATE JUDGES

RULE 6. GENERALLY

(a) Assignment By Division.

(1) *Eastern Division.* Except as set forth in Rule 8 of these Rules, the Clerk or deputy clerk must assign cases referred in the Eastern Division to the magistrate judges sitting in Boston by lot in such a manner that each magistrate judge is assigned as nearly as possible the same number of cases, except that when a magistrate judge has already ruled on a matter in a particular case, a subsequent referral in that case must be assigned to the same magistrate judge.

(2) *Central Division.* The Clerk or deputy clerk must assign cases referred in the Central Division to the magistrate judge sitting in Worcester.

(3) *Western Division.* The Clerk or deputy clerk must assign cases referred in the Western Division to the magistrate judge sitting in Springfield.

(b) The Clerk must maintain a list of all cases assigned to the magistrate judges.

(c) Each magistrate judge will place assigned cases on a calendar as required by law and in such manner as is most consistent with the just, efficient performance of the business of the court.

(d) The Clerk must designate each referral to a magistrate judge as falling within one of the following categories:

(1) Civil Rule 16(b)/Pretrial Proceedings

(2) Civil and MBD Discovery

(3) Service as a Special Master

(4) Civil Dispositive Motions

(5) Miscellaneous

(6) Criminal Dispositive Motions

(7) Criminal Pretrial or Discovery

(8) Criminal Ex Parte Motions

(9) Post-conviction proceedings

(e) The Clerk must maintain a daily schedule that shows the regular place of business of a magistrate judge during the hours of each business day, and the place where business may be brought to the attention of a magistrate judge at all other times.

(f) It is the continuing duty of each magistrate judge to give the Clerk the information required to maintain the schedule identified in paragraph (e) above.

(g) Every order and decision of a magistrate judge must be entered on the docket of the case in the same manner as orders and decisions of the district judge.

(h) No ex parte motion or ex parte matter in a criminal or civil case will be assigned to a magistrate judge except upon a separate Order of Reference specifically referring the ex parte motion or ex parte matter to a magistrate judge for disposition.

[Amended effective January 8, 2002.]

RULE 7. CRIMINAL CASES

(a) Method of Assignment.

(1) For purposes of assignment of criminal cases to magistrate judges for proceedings consistent with the provisions of Rule 2 of these Rules, all criminal cases are divided into the following categories based upon the category for assignment of the case to the district judge on the JS–45 form:

Category A—Felony cases in which eight (8) or more defendants are named.

Category B—Felony cases in which seven (7) or fewer defendants are named.

Category C—All misdemeanor and petty offense cases; cases involving waivers of indictment; and all matters involving alleged violations of conditions of release by persons transferred to this District for supervision.

(2) Upon the return of an indictment, all criminal cases charging a felony or felonies are automatically assigned by the clerk of the court to a magistrate judge for the conduct of an arraignment and the appointment of counsel to the extent authorized by law, unless the district judge assigned to the case orders otherwise. Upon such referral, the magistrate judge must also conduct such scheduling and status conferences as are necessary and must hear and determine all pretrial procedural and discovery motions, in accordance with Rule 2. Unless such an assignment is made under the provisions of subsection (a)(3) hereof, the Clerk must place a case in one of the categories described in subsection (a)(1) above, and must assign it by lot among the magistrate judges in such manner that each magistrate judge is assigned as nearly as possible the same number of cases in each category, taking into account assignments made under this subsection as well as subsection (a)(3) hereof.

(3) Upon referral by specific order of the district judge to whom the case has been assigned, the magistrate judge may hear motions to suppress evidence and motions to dismiss or quash an indictment or information made by the defendant and must submit a report and recommended disposition of such a motion to the district judge, in accordance with Rule 3 of these Rules. In conducting such proceedings, the mag-

istrate judge must conform to the general procedural Rules of this court and the instructions of the district judge to whom a case is assigned.

(4) For purposes of referral under paragraphs (a)(1) and (a)(2) of this Rule, if a magistrate judge has conducted previous proceedings in connection with the case, including, but not limited to, the receipt of a complaint under Fed. R. Crim. P. 3, or the issuance of a search warrant pursuant to Fed. R. Crim. P. 41, except in the situation described in the second paragraph of Rule 15(d)(1) of these Rules, the United States Attorney must, in a form accompanying the indictment or information, notify the Clerk as to the identity of the magistrate judge conducting such previous proceedings. The Clerk must thereupon refer the matter to the magistrate judge who conducted the previous proceedings. For purposes of this subsection, previous proceedings do not include the approval of applications for pen registers or traps and traces. In all other cases, the referral must be consistent with the provisions set forth in Rule 6(a) of these Rules.

(b) Misdemeanor Cases.

(1) *Initiating Document.* A misdemeanor (other than a petty offense) may be prosecuted by indictment, information, or complaint. A petty offense may be prosecuted by an indictment, information, complaint, citation or violation notice.

(2) An indictment or information charging a misdemeanor other than a petty offense must be filed with the Clerk of the Court, who shall assign the case a docket number, without assigning the case to a district judge until such time as the defendant elects to be tried before a district judge of the district court pursuant to 18 U.S.C. Section 3401(b), or until such time as the case is ordered retained or transferred to a district judge pursuant to the provisions of Fed. R. Crim. P. 58(b)(3)(B).

(3) Upon assigning the case a docket number, the Clerk must thereupon refer the case to the district judge then assigned to the miscellaneous business docket who must, within 48 hours of the referral, review the case and order that the case be continued before the district court, or referred to a magistrate judge.

(4) If the district judge then assigned to the miscellaneous business docket determines that the case is to be retained by the district court, then the Clerk must assign the case to a district judge in accordance with Rule 40.1(B) of the Local Rules of this court and then may be referred to a magistrate judge under the provisions of subsection (a) hereof concerning method of assignment.

(5) If the district judge then assigned to the miscellaneous business docket determines that the case is to be referred to a magistrate judge, then the Clerk must refer the case to a magistrate judge in the same manner as in felony cases under the provisions of subsection (a) above.

(6) Upon receipt of the case, the magistrate judge must proceed under the provisions of Rules 10 through 12 of these Rules.

(7) In the event that the attorney for the government, because of the novelty, importance, or complexity of the case, or other pertinent factors, seeks an order of the district court prohibiting referral of a misdemeanor case pursuant to the provisions of paragraph (5) of this subsection, a petition for such relief, filed in accordance with regulations promulgated by the Attorney General, must be filed at the same time the initiating document is filed with the Clerk.

[Amended effective January 8, 2002.]

RULE 8. CIVIL CASES

(a) Method of Assignment.

(1) *Eastern Division.*

(A) Cases filed After January 1, 2003. Civil cases filed on or after January 1, 2003 shall be randomly assigned to both a district judge and a magistrate judge. The manner of referral to the magistrate judge of specific matters in a case shall be in accordance with the provisions of Rule 8(b) below.

(B) Cases Filed Before January 1, 2003. Effective January 1, 1993 until December 31, 2002, each Eastern Division magistrate judge was paired with two or more district judges for purposes of referral of matters and proceedings in civil cases, with pairing rotating every two years. The pairings in effect on December 31, 2002 shall continue to apply to cases filed before January 1, 2003 except where there has been a prior ruling by a magistrate judge as described in section 1(C) below.

In the event that one or more district judges were not paired, cases referred by those district judges were and will continue to be randomly drawn.

(C) Effect of Prior ruling. When a magistrate judge has already ruled on a matter in a particular case, a subsequent referral in that case is assigned to the same magistrate judge.

(D) Effect of Recusal. In the event that a magistrate judge is recused on a particular matter referred under the provisions of these Rules, the case must be returned to the Clerk to be redrawn to another magistrate judge on a random basis.

(2) *Central and Western Divisions.* All civil and miscellaneous cases as described above are referred in the Central and Western Division to the magistrate judge sitting respectively in Worcester and Springfield.

(b) Manner of Referral.

(1) The following civil matters may be automatically referred to the magistrate judges by the Clerk, if and when timely opposition is filed or the time for opposition has expired, for hearing and decision by a magistrate judge in accordance with Rule 2, unless the district judge orders otherwise in a particular case:

(A) Motions for enlargement of time to file pleadings or complete discovery, except when the time for the completion of discovery has been established after a pretrial conference by order of the district judge;

(B) Motions for more definite statement;

(C) All motions for discovery and for enforcement of discovery orders under Fed. R. Civ. P. 26 through 37, except motions to dismiss or for a judgment by default under Rule 37, and motions for proceedings under Fed. R. Civ. P. 26(f).

(2) The following civil matters may be referred to the magistrate judges by the Clerk for hearing and determination by a magistrate judge as soon as they are filed and docketed, whether opposed or not, in accordance with Rule 2 of these Rules:

(A) Applications to proceed in forma pauperis filed under the provisions of 28 U.S.C. Section 1915 that are not referred to the Pro Se Staff Attorney;

(B) Motions for appointment of counsel in civil cases that are not referred to the Pro Se Staff Attorney;

(C) Supplementary proceedings to enforce a money judgment under Fed. R. Civ. P. 69.

(3) Unopposed non-dispositive motions as defined in 28 U.S.C. Section 636(b)(1)(A) may be decided on the merits by the magistrate judge if referred to the magistrate judge by the Clerk.

(4) All other civil matters may be referred to the magistrate judges only by order of a district judge. The order must specify the matters to be considered and the action to be taken by the magistrate judge.

[Amended effective January 8, 2002; amended effective July 8, 2003.]

RULE 9.   EMERGENCY REVIEW

The miscellaneous business judge may review matters that arise in the administration of the duties of the magistrate judges under these Rules only to the extent necessary to meet an "emergency" as defined by Rule 40.4 of the Local Rules of this court. Unless manifest prejudice to a party will result, the matter will be continued for disposition by the district judge to whom the case is assigned.

[Amended effective January 8, 2002.]

IV.   TRIAL OF MISDEMEANORS

RULE 10.   SCOPE

Magistrate Judges in the District of Massachusetts shall have all powers granted to magistrate judges by the provisions of 18 U.S.C. Section 3401 and proceedings conducted pursuant to those powers must be exercised in conformity with Fed. R. Crim. P. 58.

[Amended effective January 8, 2002.]

RULE 11.   PRETRIAL PROCEDURES FOR CLASS A MISDEMEANORS

(a) Consent and Arraignment. If the defendant consents, either in writing or orally on the record, to be tried before the magistrate judge and the consent specifically waives trial before a district judge, the magistrate judge will take the defendant's plea to the Class A misdemeanor charge. The defendant may plead not guilty, guilty, or, with the consent of the magistrate judge, nolo contendere. If the defendant pleads not guilty, the magistrate judge must either conduct the trial within 30 days upon written consent of the defendant or fix a time for trial, giving due regard to the needs of the parties to consult with counsel and prepare for trial.

(b) Failure to Consent. If the defendant does not, within fourteen days of arraignment (or other reasonable time set by the magistrate judge), indicate an intention to waive the right to a trial before a district judge, then the case must be tried by a district judge unless the defendant shows good cause why the case should be sent back to the magistrate judge for trial. In the event that the defendant does not, in the form and manner prescribed by the magistrate judge at the time of defendant's initial appearance before the magistrate judge, file an intention to waive the right to a trial before a district judge within fourteen days of the arraignment (or other such reasonable time prescribed by the magistrate judge), the case must be returned immediately to the Clerk to be randomly drawn to a district judge. The magistrate judge must explain the terms of this subsection to the defendant at the time of arraignment.

[Amended effective January 8, 2002. Amended effective December 1, 2009.]

RULE 12.   RECORD OF PROCEEDINGS

Proceedings under Rules 10 through 11 must be taken down by a court reporter or recorded by suitable sound recording equipment. In the discretion of the magistrate judge or, in the case of a misdemeanor other than a petty offense, on timely request of either party made not later than fourteen days before the scheduled trial, the proceedings must be taken down by a court reporter. With the consent of the defendant, the keeping of a verbatim record may be waived in petty offense cases.

[Amended effective January 8, 2002. Amended effective December 1, 2009.]

RULE 13. REVOCATION PROCEEDINGS

In any case in which the government seeks revocation or modification of probation or supervised release, consistent with the provisions of Fed. R. Crim. P. 32.1(b), after a defendant has been sentenced by a magistrate judge consistent with these Rules, that application must be determined by the magistrate judge who imposed the sentence; and, in the case of the unavailability of that magistrate judge, by another magistrate judge designated by the Chief Magistrate Judge.

[Amended effective January 8, 2002.]

RULE 14. FORFEITURE OF COLLATERAL IN LIEU OF APPEARANCE

(a) Forfeiture of Collateral—Generally. A person who is charged with a petty offense may, in lieu of appearance, post collateral in the amount indicated for the offense, waive appearance before a magistrate judge, and consent to forfeiture of collateral, unless either the charging document makes appearance mandatory or the offense charged is not posted on the Forfeiture of Collateral Schedule approved by the Court.

(b) Forfeiture of Collateral Schedule. The offenses for which collateral may be posted and forfeited in lieu of appearance by the person charged, together with the amounts of collateral to be posted, are set forth in APPENDIX A SCHEDULE OF FINES.

(c) Excluded Offenses. Under no circumstances may a person charged with operating a motor vehicle under the influence of alcohol or controlled substances in violation of any federal regulation or Massachusetts General Laws ch. 90, Section 24, or other governing statutes, be permitted to post collateral, waive appearance before a magistrate judge, and consent to forfeiture of collateral.

(d) Maximum Penalties in Lieu of Forfeiture of Collateral. If a person charged with an offense under subsection (a) hereof fails to post and forfeit collateral, a punishment, including fine, imprisonment or probation, may be imposed within the limits established by law upon conviction by plea or after trial.

(e) Failure to Appear. If a person charged with an offense under subsection (a) hereof fails to post and forfeit collateral, and then fails to appear for a duly scheduled hearing on the offense charged, and a showing is made consistent with the provisions of Fed. R. Crim. P. 58(d)(3), then the magistrate judge may issue a warrant of arrest for that person. Upon receipt of the warrant of arrest, the United States Marshal for this District may, in lieu of execution thereof, give written notice to the person that a warrant of arrest has issued for his or her arrest, and must state in the notice that the warrant of arrest will not be executed if, within seven (7) days of the notice, (1) the person voluntarily presents himself or herself before the magistrate judge during usual business hours for the purpose of scheduling a hearing on the petty offense; or (2) the person remits as collateral to be posted and forfeited an amount twice that authorized for the violations as set forth in subsection (b) hereof, or the maximum allowable by the applicable statute, whichever is smaller. In the event that the person properly appears before the magistrate judge, or properly remits and forfeits the collateral, as hereinabove set forth, then the magistrate judge must vacate the warrant of arrest; if the person fails to appear or remit as stated above, the United States Marshal must execute the warrant of arrest consistently with applicable law.

(f) Amendments to Forfeiture of Collateral Schedules. A federal agency authorized to issue violation notices for violations within its jurisdiction may petition the United States District Court for the District of Massachusetts for an order authorizing a schedule for forfeiture of collateral or amendments to such schedules under subsection (a) hereof. Such petitions seeking such schedules or amendments thereto must be initiated in the following manner:

(1) *Submission of Proposed Schedule.* The federal agency must first submit the schedule, or proposed amendments to the schedule, to the United States Attorney for the District of Massachusetts for such consideration as the United States Attorney deems appropriate. Upon approval by the United States Attorney or the authorized designee of the United States Attorney, that schedule, or amendments thereto, must be forwarded to the Chief Magistrate Judge for consideration and approval by the magistrate judges. When and if approved by the magistrate judges, the Chief Magistrate Judge must transmit the schedule, and amendments to it, to the district judges for approval of an order authorizing that schedule or amendments thereto.

(2) *New Federal Agencies.* If a federal agency that is not currently authorized by the orders of this court to participate in the forfeiture of collateral provisions seeks authorization for adoption of a schedule, that federal agency is responsible for initiating contact and making arrangements with the Central Violations Bu-

reau in San Antonio, Texas. That federal agency shall also be responsible for obtaining all necessary authorizations from the United States Attorney for this District designating one or more persons within that agency to prosecute matters before magistrate judges in the District of Massachusetts.

(3) *Authority to Prosecute.* In no event will a federal agency be permitted to prosecute a Central Violations Bureau matter before a magistrate judge unless the prosecution is by a member of that agency specifically authorized to do so by the United States Attorney for the District of Massachusetts.

(4) *Agency Preparation of Forfeiture of Collateral Schedules.* In all instances in which a federal agency seeks authorization of a schedule of forfeiture of collateral, or amendments thereto, that agency is responsible for preparation of that schedule in the format prescribed by the Clerk of this Court. In addition to the submission of a hard copy of that proposed schedule or amendments thereto, the federal agency is responsible for the submission to the Clerk of this Court of that schedule, or amendments to it, on electronic media in the manner prescribed by the Clerk of this Court.

[Amended effective January 8, 2002.]

V. MISCELLANEOUS

RULE 15. EMERGENCY MAGISTRATE JUDGE

(a) Generally. One of the magistrate judges is designated as the emergency magistrate judge at Boston for each month of the calendar year. The magistrate judge designated as emergency magistrate judge at Boston during a particular month is the emergency magistrate judge for all emergency matters arising during that month within the territorial jurisdiction of the Eastern Division. The magistrate judge sitting in Worcester is the emergency magistrate judge for all emergency matters within the territorial jurisdiction of the Central Division. The magistrate judge sitting in Springfield is the emergency magistrate judge for all emergency matters within the territorial jurisdiction of the Western Division.

It is the duty of the Chief Magistrate Judge to advise the Clerk of the Court as to which magistrate judge has been designated as the emergency magistrate judge in Boston for any given month of the calendar year.

(b) Original Proceedings. All new original matters within the territorial jurisdiction of the magistrate judges involving the filing of criminal complaints, issuance of warrants of arrest and search warrants, seizure warrants, warrants to permit inspections of worksites sought by or on behalf of OSHA, warrants to inspect sites under CERCLA, presentations for bail or detention, conduct of preliminary examinations pursuant to Fed. R. Crim. P. 5.1, removal proceedings under Fed. R. Crim. P. 40, grand jury returns under Fed. R. Crim. P. 6(f), appointment of counsel in criminal cases in connection with original matters, applications for pen registers, traps and traces, electronic tracking devices, and other matters within the original jurisdiction of magistrate judges, must be filed with the magistrate judge then designated as the emergency magistrate judge.

(c) Referred Proceedings. The following matters not within the original jurisdiction of magistrate judges, or within the concurrent jurisdiction of district judges and magistrate judges, unless otherwise directed by the district judge, must be automatically referred to the emergency magistrate judge:

(1) Applications to proceed in forma pauperis filed under the provisions of 28 U.S.C. section 1915 not otherwise referred to the Pro Se Staff Attorney;

(2) Applications for writs of entry filed by or on behalf of the Internal Revenue Service (see subsection (d)(2), infra);

(3) Motions for appointment of counsel filed in connection with grand jury proceedings;

(4) Applications for tax returns and tax returns information filed under the provisions of 26 U.S.C. section 6103(i)(1)(B)(see subsection (d)(2), infra);

(5) Any other civil motion that the trial judge (or, in the absence of the trial judge, the district judge assigned to the miscellaneous business docket) determines should be resolved before the time that the magistrate judge previously assigned to the case, or in the absence of such previous assignment, the magistrate judge who would normally be assigned the case, could otherwise hear the motion.

(d) Related Procedures.

(1) *Previous Proceedings.* If, on a previous occasion, an emergency magistrate judge has received a criminal complaint or has issued a search warrant under the provisions of Fed. R. Crim. P. 41, in connection with an ongoing investigation, subsequent applications for warrants or arrest, search warrants, or other matters within the original jurisdiction of a magistrate judge, must be made to the magistrate judge who had conducted previous proceedings in the case, unless the new application or matter is not directly related to the previous investigation. If, as a result of that continuing investigation, an indictment is returned, or an information is filed, the attorney for the government must, before the return of the indictment or the filing of the information, record the docket or case num-

ber(s) of those prior proceedings before the magistrate judge on the required Form JS 45.

If the United States Attorney seeks the issuance of a search warrant on the day an indictment is returned in Boston in a case in which no previous proceedings before a magistrate judge have occurred, the United States Attorney must present the application for a search warrant to the magistrate judge to whom the indictment is drawn after the indictment is returned. If the presentation of the application for the search warrant cannot be delayed until the indictment is returned and the indictment is drawn to a magistrate judge, the United States Attorney may present the application for the search warrant to the emergency magistrate judge for issuance. In that instance, the issuance of the search warrant is not treated as a previous proceeding so as to cause the case to be drawn to that magistrate judge when the indictment is returned.

(2) *Applications for Writs of Entry and Tax Information.* Applications for writs of entry filed by or on behalf of the Internal Revenue Service referred to in subsection (c)(2) hereof, motions for appointment of counsel filed in connection with grand jury proceedings referred to in subsection (c)(3) hereof, and applications for returns and returns information filed under the provisions of 26 U.S.C. Section 6103(i)(1)(B) referred to in subsection (c)(4) hereof, must first be filed with the Clerk of the Court to be docketed on the miscellaneous business docket of the court. All such matters must then be referred, unless otherwise directed by the district judge then serving as the miscellaneous business judge, to the magistrate judge who was designated as the emergency magistrate judge at the time of the filing of the application or motion.

(3) *Pen Registers, Traps and Traces, Orders for Telephone Subscriber Information and Electronic Tracking Devices.* Renewals of applications for pen registers, traps and traces, telephone subscriber information, and electronic tracking devices, must be made to the magistrate judge who issued the original order allowing the requested relief. For the purposes of this Rule, however, a renewal does not include an application made after the expiration or termination of the original order. If an order authorizing a pen register, trap and trace, telephone subscriber information, or electronic tracking device, has expired by its terms, a subsequent application must be made to the current emergency magistrate judge.

(4) *Violations of Conditions.* If a person has been arrested for violation of a condition of release, a violation of a condition of probation, or a violation of a condition of supervised release, that matter must be presented to the magistrate judge who conducted previous proceedings in connection with that case; otherwise, the matter must be presented to the current emergency magistrate judge.

(5) *Unavailability of Emergency Magistrate Judge.* For all matters referred under Rule 15(c) above, if the emergency magistrate judge is not available, and the matter so referred requires appropriate action before the emergency magistrate judge, the matter must be referred to another magistrate judge sitting in Boston by random draw.

(6) *Internal Revenue Service Summons Enforcement.* Applications for Orders to Show Cause in matters related to Internal Revenue Service Summonses are **not** emergency matters within the meaning of these Rules. Those applications must be filed with the Clerk of the Miscellaneous Business Docket and must, if ordered referred to a magistrate judge, be drawn to a magistrate judge on a random basis.

(e) Matters Ancillary to Proceedings in Other Districts. The emergency magistrate judge is responsible for all matters in this district ancillary to proceedings in other districts. Such proceedings include the appearance of a Massachusetts resident before a magistrate judge in this district to co-sign a surety bond or post property for a defendant who is being prosecuted in another district. In all such cases, the emergency magistrate judge must assign a Magistrate Judge Docket number to the ancillary proceeding and open a file; the file must be maintained in the same manner as a file maintained in connection with an application for a search warrant.

[Amended effective January 8, 2002.]

RULE 16.   CONTEMPT OF COURT

Magistrate judges in the District of Massachusetts have all powers granted to magistrate judges by the provisions of 28 U.S.C. Section 636(e) with respect to contempt of court, and all proceedings they conduct pursuant to these powers must be in conformity with these statutory provisions.

[Amended effective January 8, 2002.]

RULE 17.   TIMING OF REFERRAL OF CIVIL MOTION

The rule stated here does not apply to those motions referred to in Rule 8(b) of these Rules. In the absence of any extraordinary circumstances warranting prompt referral, no civil motion can be referred to a magistrate judge until such time as the non-moving parties are required to file an opposition under Rule 7.1(B)(2) of the Local Rules of this Court. The order of reference must state whether or not an opposition to the motion or motions has been filed.

[Amended effective January 8, 2002.]

RULE 18. TRANSMITTAL OF PAPERS TO A MAGISTRATE JUDGE

After referral of a case to a magistrate judge, the docket clerk must promptly docket all subsequently filed papers relating to that case and promptly must transmit the filed papers to the magistrate judge for consideration.

[Amended effective January 8, 2002.]

RULE 19. RECORD OF SUBSEQUENT PROCEEDINGS

In any case in which a party has filed objections to a magistrate judge's determination under Rule 2(b) of these Rules, or to a magistrate judge's proposed findings, recommendations or report under Rule 3(b) of these Rules, or has filed an appeal under Fed. R. Crim. P. 58(g)(2), the docket clerk assigned to the district judge to whom the motion for reconsideration, objections, or appeal, has been assigned must promptly transmit to the magistrate judge who conducted the previous proceedings all records and opinions relating to the subsequent action taken by the district judge.

[Amended effective January 8, 2002.]

RULE 20. FORM OF REFERRAL

All referrals to magistrate judges must be made by uniform orders of reference in civil, criminal, miscellaneous, and post-conviction cases in the form annexed to these Rules. In those civil cases referred to a magistrate judge for proceedings consistent with the provisions of Fed. R. Civ. P. 16, however, and in other pretrial management functions, non-dispositive motions may be referred to a magistrate judge under the provisions of Rule 17 of these Rules without a form of reference.

[Amended effective January 8, 2002.]

ORDER OF REFERENCE

UNITED STATES DISTRICT COURT
DISTRICT OF MASSACHUSETTS
ORDER OF REFERENCE

☐ Check if previously referred

_____

V.   CA/CR No. _____

_____   Criminal Category _____

In accordance with 28 U.S.C. § 636 and the Rules for United States Magistrates in the United States District Court for the District of Massachusetts, the above-entitled case is referred to Magistrate Judge _____ for the following proceedings:

___ Referred for full pretrial case management, including all dispositive motions.

___ Referred for full pretrial case management, not including dispositive motions:

___ Referred for discovery purposes only.

___ Referred for Report and Recommendation on:

    ___   ( ) Motion(s) for injunctive relief
    ___   ( ) Motion(s) for judgment on the pleadings
    ___   ( ) Motion(s) for summary judgment
    ___   ( ) Motion(s) to permit maintenance of a class action
    ___   ( ) Motion(s) to suppress evidence
    ___   ( ) Motion(s) to dismiss
    ___   ( ) Post Conviction Proceedings[1]

___ See Documents Numbered: _____

___ Case referred for events only. See Doc. No(s) _____

___ Case referred for settlement.

[1] See reverse side of order for instructions

___ Service as a special master for hearing, determination and report, subject to the terms of the special order filed herewith:

   ___   ( ) In accordance with Rule 53, F.R.Civ.P.
   ___   ( ) In accordance with 42 U.S.C. 2000e–5(f)(5)

___ Special Instructions _____
_____
_____

_____   By: _____
Date   Deputy Clerk

INSTRUCTIONS FOR POST–CONVICTION PROCEEDINGS

In accordance with all rules governing § 2254 and § 2255 cases the magistrate judge to whom this post-conviction proceeding is referred shall:

___ Make a recommendation as to summary dismissal under Rule 4 of the Rules for § 2254 and § 2255 cases

___ Appoint counsel if the interests of justice so require

___ Order issuance of appropriate process, if necessary

___ Hold a hearing to determine whether or not an evidentiary hearing must be held and make a recommendation to the district judge

___ If the magistrate judge expects to recommend that an evidentiary hearing be held, the magistrate judge shall hold a pretrial conference for the purpose of narrowing the issue to be tried and submit a memo to the district judge setting forth:

(a) a concise summary of the ultimate facts claimed by

      (1) petitioner   (2) respondent   (3) other parties;

(b) the facts established by the pleadings or by stipulations of the parties which may be incorporated by reference;

(c) any jurisdictional questions;

(d) issues of law, including evidentiary questions;

(e) the probable length of the evidentiary hearing.

The magistrate judge may also require the parties to submit the names of witnesses whom they intend to produce, and to exhibit to one another, and submit a schedule of, exhibits which they expect to offer in evidence.

___ As to any issue concerning which the magistrate judge does not intend to recommend an evidentiary hearing, the magistrate judge shall submit a memo which shall:

(a) identify the relevant portions of the record or transcript of prior proceedings;

(b) summarize the relevant facts;

(c) summarize the parties' contentions of law with appropriate citations;

(d) state the recommendations as to the disposition of such contentions of law, and the grounds therefore.

APPENDIX A. SCHEDULE OF FINES

[**Publisher's Note:** For the current Schedule of
Fines, please contact the Clerk of Court.]

INDEX TO LOCAL RULES OF THE UNITED STATES DISTRICT COURT FOR THE DISTRICT OF MASSACHUSETTS

*

LOCAL BANKRUPTCY RULES OF THE UNITED STATES BANKRUPTCY COURT FOR THE DISTRICT OF MASSACHUSETTS

Effective August 1, 1997

Including Amendments Received Through January 1, 2012

Research Note

These rules may be searched electronically on Westlaw in the MA-RULES database; updates to these rules may be found on Westlaw in MA-RULESUPDATES. For search tips, and a detailed summary of database content, consult the Westlaw Scope Screen of each database.

LOCAL RULES AND FORMS

RULE 1001–1. TITLE

These Local Bankruptcy Rules, promulgated under Fed. R. Bankr. P. 9029, shall be known as the Local Bankruptcy Rules of the United States Bankruptcy Court for the District of Massachusetts, a unit of the United States District Court for the District of Massachusetts, and shall be referred to in abbreviation as MLBR. These rules shall take effect on December 1, 2009 with respect to pending cases and those filed thereafter, and shall govern all proceedings in bankruptcy cases insofar as is just and practicable.

[Effective August 1, 1997. Amended effective September 1, 1999; January 1, 2002; March 1, 2003; January 1, 2005; October 1, 2006; December 1, 2009.]

RULE 1002–1. STATUS CONFERENCES

(a) The Court shall conduct status conferences, pursuant to 11 U.S.C. § 105(d), as follows:

(1) in any case under Chapter 9 or 11, an initial status conference shall be held within forty-five (45) days of case commencement or as soon thereafter as may be practicable, except that the conference may be combined with any final hearing on the use of cash collateral; and

(2) in all cases, such other or further status conferences, and continuances thereof shall be held, as the Court may determine in its discretion, sua sponte or on motion of a party in interest or the United States trustee, to further the expeditious and economical administration of the case.

(b) Subject to subparagraph (c) below, the Court or any party which it may designate shall give not less than twenty-one (21) days notice of any status conference to the following parties or their counsel of record: the debtor, any committee of unsecured creditors elected under 11 U.S.C. § 705 or appointed under 11 U.S.C. § 1102 (or if none has been appointed the creditors included on the list of creditors filed under Rule 1007(d)), any equity security holders' committee, any secured creditor, all taxing authorities, the United States trustee, any party who requested the conference, any party who filed an appearance in the case, and such other entities as the Court shall direct.

(c) For cause shown, the Court may schedule a status conference on an expedited or emergency basis.

(d) At any status conference, the Court may consider any argument or report, in writing or otherwise, with respect to the status or administration of the case, but shall not issue any order unless (i) the order is of a type specifically enumerated in 11 U.S.C. § 105(d)(2) or (ii) the Court finds that any delay in issuing the order risks immediate and irreparable harm to the estate or a party in interest.

[Effective October 1, 2006. Amended effective December 1, 2009.]

RULE 1006–1. FILING FEES

Applicable filing fees are set forth in Appendix 3.

[Effective August 1, 1997.]

RULE 1006–2. FEES–INSTALLMENT PAYMENTS; IN FORMA PAUPERIS

(a) The Court, upon motion of an individual debtor or joint debtors, may permit payment of the case filing fee in installments. Such debtor(s) shall pay $40.00 at the time of filing, and, except for cause shown upon motion of the debtor; the balance shall be paid in three (3) equal payments in intervals of not greater than thirty (30) days. Failure to make payments shall result in dismissal of the case. No discharge shall enter until all filing fees are paid in full.

(b) In lieu of paying the filing fee or filing an installment application, an individual chapter 7 debtor or joint debtors may file an application for waiver of the filing fee. The application for waiver of the filing fee or any balance thereof must conform substantially to Official Form 3.

(1) The Court may allow the application without a hearing or, in its discretion, schedule a hearing on the application. If a hearing is scheduled, the Court will notify the debtor(s) by mail or telephone as to the date and time of the hearing on the application for the waiver. The debtor(s) must appear at the hearing.

(2) If, with or without a hearing, the Court denies the application for the waiver of the filing fee, then the debtor(s) shall pay the filing fee in installments as provided above. The first installment is due within seven (7) days of the entry of the Court's order denying the application for the waiver. The debtor(s) may also elect to pay the filing fee in full in which case full payment will be due within seven (7) days of the entry of the Court's order denying the application for the waiver.

[Effective August 1, 1997. Amended effective October 1, 2006; December 1, 2009.]

RULE 1007–1. LISTS, SCHEDULES AND STATEMENTS, AND OTHER DOCUMENTS REQUIRED

(a) List of Creditors. Within three (3) court days after entry of the order for relief, the debtor shall file an original matrix of all creditors and their last known complete addresses, in both .txt and PDF format, failing which the Court may dismiss the case pursuant to 11 U.S.C. § 109(g). The form of the matrix shall conform to the specifications of MLBR Official Local Form 1. Any creditors subsequently added to the matrix shall be included in a separate list of only the added creditors filed in compliance with MLBR 1009–1.

(b) Answer "None" to be Stated. Each item in the schedules and statement of affairs shall be completed. Items for which no other entry can be made shall be completed by the entry "none" or "not applicable," whichever response is appropriate.

(c) Schedules, Statements and other Documents Required. In satisfaction of the requirements of 11 U.S.C. § 521 and Fed. R. Bankr. P. 1007, the debtor shall:

(1) At least seven (7) days before the § 341 meeting, provide to the trustee copies of all payment advices or other evidence of payment from all employers, with all but the last four (4) digits of the debtor's social security number redacted. The payment advices shall not be filed with the Court unless otherwise ordered. Payment advices shall include all evidence of payment of any income from all employers the debtor received during the sixty (60) days prior to the filing of the petition; and

(2) File with the Court the certificate of credit counseling pursuant to 11 U.S.C. § 109(h) or a request for an extension in conformity with MLBR Official Local Form 9.

(3) Disclose in the petition other previous or pending bankruptcy cases and adversary proceedings, whether filed in this or any other district, which are related to the bankruptcy case being filed. Related cases and adversary proceedings include those involving (a) a spouse or ex-spouse of the debtor; (b) an affiliate, as defined in 11 U.S.C. § 101(2); or (c) an insider, as defined in 11 U.S.C. § 101(31); or (d) the same debtor using any aliases or fictitious names.

Failure to comply with these disclosure requirements may result in sanctions, including dismissal of the case pursuant to 11 U.S.C. § 109(g).

(4) Complete each item in the schedules and statement of affairs. Items for which no other entry can be made shall be completed by the entry of "none" or "not applicable," whichever response is appropriate.

(5) Complete and file all other documents required by Fed. R. Bankr. P. 1007(b).

(d) Statement of Social Security Number. A Statement of Debtor's Social Security Number (Form B21) not filed with the original petition shall be filed no later than three (3) days from the date of the filing of the petition. Failure to timely comply with this requirement shall result in dismissal of the case without further notice.

(e) Corporate, Partnership or Trust Petitions.

(1) A petition by a corporation shall be signed or verified by an officer or agent of the corporation and shall be accompanied by a copy of the resolution of the board of directors or other evidence of the officer's or agent's authority to file the petition on behalf of the corporation.

(2) A petition by a partnership or a trust shall be signed or verified by a general partner, trustee or appropriate agent and shall be accompanied by evidence of the signing party's authority to file the petition.

(3) A petition filed on behalf of a corporation, partnership or trust shall indicate that the debtor is represented by counsel and shall state the attorney's name, address and telephone number.

(4) Failure to comply with this rule shall result in dismissal of the case within seven (7) days after the Court issues a notice of defective filing.

(f) Homestead Exemption. Individual debtors who claim a homestead exemption under state law shall provide to the trustee such documentary evidence as is necessary to establish the extent of the homestead declared no later than the date scheduled for the § 341 meeting of creditors.

(g) Time Limits. Upon the filing of a motion prior to the expiration of the filing deadlines, and upon a showing of good cause, the Court may excuse the debtor from filing some or all of the documents required in subsection (c). Upon the filing of a motion prior to the expiration of the filing deadlines, and upon a showing of cause, a debtor may seek one or more extensions of the filing deadlines provided that the debtor state the date the petition was filed and the time requested and provide proof of service on the United States trustee and any appointed trustee, committee elected under § 705 or appointed under § 1102 of the Code, and any other party as the court may direct.

[Effective August 1, 1997. Amended effective January 1, 2005; October 1, 2006; December 1, 2009.]

RULE 1009–1. AMENDMENTS

A party filing a document amending a voluntary petition, list, schedule, statement of financial affairs, or statement of executory contracts shall do so by notice as set forth in Fed.R.Bankr.P. 1009(a), except with respect to the following: 1) amendments to the debtor's schedule of liabilities, adding a creditor after the deadline for filing complaints under 11 U.S.C. §§ 523 or 727; and 2) amendments to the schedule of exemptions after the deadline for objecting to the exemptions. If either of these exceptions apply, the debtor shall file a motion with the Court for approval of the amendment. A copy of the amended document shall be attached to the notice or motion and clearly state in the caption that it is an amendment. An amendment to a matrix which adds creditors shall be a separate list of the names and addresses of only the added creditors in compliance with MLBR Official Local Form 1.

[Effective August 1, 1997. Amended effective September 1, 1999; October 1, 2006.]

RULE 1015–1. JOINT ADMINISTRATION OF CASES PENDING IN THE SAME COURT

(a) **Motion for Joint Administration.** A request for an order allowing joint administration of two or more related cases pursuant to Fed.R.Bankr.P. 1015–b shall be made by motion. In the motion for joint administration, the moving party shall 1) designate the name and number of the lead case for conducting proceedings in the jointly administered cases; 2) state the cause warranting joint administration, including the reasons supporting the proposed lead case designation; and 3) state any known facts which may give rise to actual or potential conflicts of interest warranting protection of the interests of creditors of the various estates. A motion for joint administration shall be filed in each case for which joint administration is proposed. A motion for joint administration shall be served by the moving party on all creditors and equity security holders who have requested notice in accordance with Fed.R.Bankr.P. 2002(i), any committee elected under § 705 or appointed under § 1102 of the Bankruptcy Code, the twenty largest unsecured creditors in each case as listed on Official Form 4, all secured creditors and taxing authorities, all attorneys of record, any appointed trustee, and the United States trustee. The court shall grant the motion for joint administration if it is likely to ease the administrative burden on the parties and the court.

(b) **Notice and Effect of Order.** Upon entry of an order authorizing joint administration of cases, or upon the automatic allowance of a motion for joint administration in accordance with (c) below, the moving party shall serve notice of said order upon all creditors and interested parties of all debtors that are the subject of the motion. The court shall enter the order in each of the other related cases in addition to the designated lead case. An order approving joint administration shall not effect substantive consolidation of the respective debtors' estates.

(c) **Automatic Joint Administration of Chapter 11 Cases.** If a motion for joint administration of debtors, other than individual debtors, is filed at the same time as the filing of the petitions commencing the cases proposed to be jointly administered, the motion for joint administration shall be treated as an emergency motion and shall be allowed effective upon filing, subject to reconsideration as set forth in (d) below.

(d) **Reconsideration.** The Court may reconsider an order allowing joint administration upon motion of any party in interest or sua sponte.

[Adopted effective January 1, 2005.]

RULE 1017–1. MOTIONS FOR CONVERSION OR DISMISSAL IN CHAPTER 11; SUBMISSION OF MOTIONS AND OPPOSITIONS TO MOTIONS; HEARING

(a) Prior to filing any motion to dismiss or convert a Chapter 11 case (other than a motion filed by the United States trustee or the debtor), counsel for the prospective movant (if any) shall have a conference, by telephone or in person, with counsel for the debtor-in-possession or counsel for the Chapter 11 trustee (if one is appointed), in a good faith effort to resolve the movant's asserted grounds for dismissal or conversion, and to eliminate as many areas of dispute as possible without the necessity of filing a motion. Unless relieved by order of the Court, such conference shall take place within fourteen (14) days of the prospective movant's service of a letter requesting the conference. Failure of counsel for the debtor-in-possession or counsel for the Chapter 11 trustee to respond to a request for a conference under this Rule shall be grounds for sanctions, which may include substantive and/or monetary sanctions. Any motion filed under this Rule shall contain, or be accompanied by, a statement signed under the penalty of perjury that the movant has complied with the provisions of this section, specifying the time, date and manner of any conference held prior to filing the motion, and certifying that only the issues left unresolved by such conference are included in the motion.

(b) A party in interest (other than the debtor or the United States trustee) who seeks dismissal or conversion of a case under Chapter 11 pursuant to 11 U.S.C. § 1112(b) shall file, in accordance with Fed. R. Bankr. P. 9014, a motion and a proposed order, which motion shall include a concise statement of material undisputed facts pursuant to subsection (c) below. The motion shall include a statement whether the movant does or does not consent to the appointment of a Chapter 11 trustee or examiner in lieu of the requested relief in the motion.

(c) In the movant's statement of undisputed material facts, the movant shall set forth specific undisputed facts that support the movant's allegations of "cause" for the dismissal or conversion set forth in the motion. Such facts shall be supported by references to documents, deposition transcripts (if available) and affidavits, which documentary support shall be filed as exhibits to the motion.

(d) A party opposing a motion for dismissal or conversion of a case under Chapter 11 must file an opposition to the motion within fourteen (14) days, inclusive of the three (3) day mailing period provided in Fed. R. Bankr. P. 9006(f), after service of the motion. The opponent shall include a concise statement of the material facts as to which it is contended that there exists a genuine issue to be tried, supported by references to documents, deposition transcripts (if available) and affidavits, which documentary support shall be filed as exhibits to the statement of disputed material facts. In the opposition, the opponent shall also: (i) set forth facts, supported by references to documents, deposition transcripts (if available) and affidavits, which documentary support shall be filed as exhibits to the opposition, that support the opponent's contentions required under 11 U.S.C. §§ 1112(b)(2)(A) & (B); (ii) state why the relief requested in the motion is not in the best interests of creditors and the estate; (iii) state the basis of any assertion that there is a reasonable likelihood that a plan will be confirmed within the time frames set forth in 11 U.S.C. §§ 1121(e) and/or 1129(e), or within a reasonable time; (iv) state the justification for the act or omission that constitutes the grounds for the relief requested in the motion, and the proposal to cure any such act or omissions that serve as grounds for the motion; and (v) state whether the opposing party does or does not consent to the appointment of a Chapter 11 trustee or an examiner in lieu of the relief requested in the motion.

(e) Responsive pleadings not filed with the motion or in opposition to the motion, whether in the form of a reply memorandum or otherwise, may be submitted only by leave of the Court.

(f) In the absence of a timely filed opposition that complies with subsection (d) of this Rule, and upon evidence of proper service of the motion, the Court, without a hearing and acting within the time limits proscribed by 11 U.S.C. § 1112(b)(3), may allow or deny the motion after the expiration of the fourteen (14) day opposition period. The Court may deny a motion for dismissal or conversion if the moving party is required to, but fails to comply with subsections (a), (b) or (c) of this Rule, and may grant a motion for dismissal or conversion if the opposing party fails to comply with subsection (d) of this Rule. Material facts of record set forth in the statement of the movant will be deemed, for the purposes of the motion, to be admitted by an opposing party unless controverted by the statement of disputed facts set forth in the opposing party's opposition.

(g) Except for any notice of hearing on a motion to dismiss or convert a Chapter 11 case, all documents filed pursuant to this Rule shall be served, in accordance with Fed. R. Bankr. P. 2002(i), 2002(k), and 9006(d)–(f), and MEFR Rule 9, upon the debtor, any committee appointed pursuant to 11 U.S.C. § 1102 or its authorized agent, the twenty (20) largest unsecured creditors of the debtor included on the list filed pursuant to Fed. R. Bankr. P. 1017(d), the United States trustee, all parties who have filed appearances and requested service of all notices and pleadings, and on any other party that the Court may designate. The movant shall serve any notice of hearing on the motion, in accordance with Fed R. Bankr. P. 2002(a)(4), 2002(i), and 2002(k), and MEFR Rule 9, on all creditors, the debtor, any committee appointed pursuant to 11 U.S.C. § 1102 or its authorized agent, the United States trustee, and all parties who have filed appearances and requested service of all notices and pleadings.

(h) Upon the filing of a motion to dismiss or convert a Chapter 11 case, the Clerk shall assign a hearing date. Such hearing shall be a non-evidentiary, preliminary hearing, at which the Court will consider whether there are disputed facts that require an additional, final evidentiary hearing.

(i) The time periods set forth in this Rule for hearings may be: (A) reduced, for good cause shown, by order of the Court; or (B) enlarged to extend to a specified date, either on consent of the movant and opposing parties, or by order of the Court in accordance with 11 U.S.C. § 1112(b)(3). The Court, for good cause shown, may also enter an order excusing compliance with any or all of the procedures and/or time periods set forth in subsections (a)-(d) of this Rule.

[Effective October 1, 2006. Amended effective December 1, 2009.]

RULE 2002–1. NOTICE TO PARTIES

(a) Unless the Court orders otherwise, the moving party shall give notice to all parties entitled to notice under the Bankruptcy Code, the Federal Rules of

Bankruptcy Procedure, MLBR, or an order of the Court, of the following events:

(1) the proposed use, sale or lease of property of the estate;

(2) a proposed compromise or settlement;

(3) a motion for conversion or dismissal;

(4) objections to and the hearing on the adequacy of a disclosure statement;

(5) the order approving a disclosure statement;

(6) a proposed modification of a plan in a chapter 9, 11, or 12 case;

(7) applications for compensation in a chapter 9, 11, or 12 case or a chapter 13 case, except as provided in the chapter 13 rules at paragraph 13–7(b);

(8) the time for filing claims in a chapter 9 or 11 case;

(9) the time for filing objections to and the hearing on confirmation of a chapter 9, 11 or 12 plan;

(10) the order confirming a plan in a chapter 9, 11, or 12 case; and

(11) all other events set forth in Fed. R. Bankr. P. 2002(f).

(b) Unless the Court orders otherwise, motions to limit notice may be served only upon parties who have filed appearances and requested service of all notices and pleadings, any trustee and trustee's counsel, the debtor and debtor's counsel, the twenty (20) largest creditors, the United States trustee and any creditors' committee and its counsel.

[Effective August 1, 1997. Amended effective December 1, 2009.]

RULE 2002–2. NOTICES TO THE UNITED STATES OF AMERICA AND THE COMMONWEALTH OF MASSACHUSETTS

The addresses for service upon federal, and state governmental agencies are set forth in MLBR Appendix 4.

[Effective August 1, 1997.]

RULE 2002–4. ADDRESSES

(a) The debtor or debtor's counsel must notify the Clerk, all creditors, parties in interest and all attorneys who have filed appearances in the case or any proceeding of a mailing address change for the debtor or debtor's counsel within fourteen (14) days of such change.

(b) The Clerk shall direct all returned notices of a § 341(a) meeting of creditors and discharge orders to the debtor's attorney or the debtor, if pro se, to enable that party to locate the correct address and to forward

the notice or order to that address. The responsible party must file a certificate of service of the new mailing with the Clerk and must request, in writing, that the Clerk change the creditor's address on the matrix.

(c) The debtor or debtor's counsel shall maintain, be responsible for the accuracy of, and remit to any party immediately upon request, the master mailing matrix and any amendments to it. The master mailing matrix shall include parties who have filed appearances and requested service of all notices and pleadings, any trustee and trustee's counsel, the debtor and debtor's counsel, all creditors, the United States trustee and any creditors' committee and its counsel. When serving notices, the Clerk and any party may rely exclusively on the master mailing matrix, or amended master mailing matrix.

[Effective August 1, 1997. Amended effective December 1, 2009.]

RULE 2002–5. CONTENT OF NOTICES OF SALE

A notice of proposed sale of estate property shall be in accordance with MLBR 6004–1.

[Effective August 1, 1997. Revised effective May 1, 2008.]

RULE 2003–1. CREDITORS' COMMITTEE

(a) In satisfaction of the requirements of § 1102(b)(3)(A) of the Bankruptcy Code, and subject to subparagraphs (b) and (c) below, the official committee of general unsecured creditors (hereinafter the "Creditors Committee") shall respond to written, telephonic and/or electronically transmitted inquiries received from any general unsecured creditor and provide to such creditor access to documents, pleadings and other materials by any means that the Creditors Committee believes, in its reasonable business judgment, will provide a relevant, informative and complete response. Subject to such enlargement of time as the Court may order, no later than twenty-one (21) days after appointment of its counsel, the Creditors Committee may advise all general unsecured creditors of the preferred means to make any inquiries (e.g., by letter, by telephone, by email, through any website) to the Committee.

(b) The Creditors Committee is not authorized or required, pursuant to § 1102(b)(3)(A) of the Bankruptcy Code, to provide access to any Confidential Information of the Debtor or the Creditors Committee to any creditor. For the purposes hereof, the term "Confidential Information" shall mean any nonpublic information which is the subject of a written confidentiality agreement between the Creditors Committee and the Debtor or another entity or any other nonpublic information, the confidentiality of which in the reasonable business judgment of the Creditors Committee is necessary in order to successfully perform its duties under § 1103(c) and was: 1) otherwise furnished, disclosed, or made known to the Creditors Committee by the Debtor, whether intentionally, unintentionally and in any manner, including in written form, orally, or through any electronic facsimile or computer-related communication or 2) developed by professionals employed by the Creditors Committee and the disclosure of which the Creditors Committee reasonably believes would impair the performance of its duties. Notwithstanding the foregoing, Confidential Information shall not include any information or portion of information that: (i) is or becomes generally available to the public or is or becomes available to the Creditors Committee on a non-confidential basis, in each case to the extent that such information became so available other than by a violation of a contractual legal or fiduciary obligation to the Debtor; or (ii) was in possession of the Creditors Committee prior to its disclosure by the Debtor or the Creditors Committee's professionals and is not subject to any other duty or obligation to maintain confidentiality.

(c) The Creditors Committee is not authorized or required, pursuant to § 1102(b)(3)(A) of the Bankruptcy Code, to provide access to any Privileged Information of the Creditors Committee to any creditor. For the purposes hereof, the term "Privileged Information" shall mean any information subject to the attorney-client privilege or any other state, federal, or other privilege, whether such privilege is solely controlled by the Creditors Committee or is a joint privilege with the Debtor or some other party. Notwithstanding the foregoing, the Creditors Committee shall be permitted, but not required, to provide access to Privileged Information to any party so long as: (1) such Privileged Information is not Confidential Information, and (2) the relevant privilege is held and controlled solely by the Creditors Committee.

(d) In the event that a creditor is dissatisfied with the failure or refusal of the Creditors Committee to provide requested access or information, the creditor may file a motion seeking to compel the Creditors Committee to produce documents and/or information. The dispute shall be deemed to be a discovery dispute and the parties shall comply with the provisions of MLBR 7037–1, insofar as applicable.

[Effective October 1, 2006. Amended effective December 1, 2009.]

RULE 2007.2–1. APPOINTMENT OF PATIENT CARE OMBUDSMAN IN A HEALTH CARE BUSINESS CASE

(a) If the court has not ordered the appointment of an ombudsman or has ordered the termination of the appointment of an ombudsman, the court may, on its own motion, subsequently order such appointment at any time during the case if the court finds that the

appointment of an ombudsman has become necessary to protect patients.

(b) A verified statement of a patient care ombudsman filed pursuant to Rule 2007.2 shall comply with MLBR 2014–1(b) and shall include the following representation: "I shall amend this statement immediately upon my learning that (A) any of the within representations are incorrect or (B) there is any change of circumstances relating thereto."

(c) The United States trustee shall serve notice of appointment of a patient care ombudsman and the verified statement required by Fed. R. Bankr. P. 2007.2(c) upon the debtor, the trustee, any committee elected under § 705 or appointed under § 1102 of the Code or its authorized agent, or, if the case is a chapter 9 municipality case or a chapter 11 reorganization case and no committee of unsecured creditors has been appointed under § 1102, on the creditors included on the list filed under Rule 1007(d), any party who has filed an appearance, and such other entities as the court may direct.

(d) A party opposing the appointment of a patient care ombudsman on the ground that the proposed patient care ombudsman is not disinterested or on any other ground shall file an opposition to the appointment within seven (7) days after the service of the notice of the appointment of the patient care ombudsmen and shall serve such opposition on the United States trustee, the debtor, the trustee, any committee elected under § 705 or appointed under § 1102 of the Code or its authorized agent, or, if the case is a chapter 9 municipality case or a chapter 11 reorganization case and no committee of unsecured creditors has been appointed under § 1102, on the creditors included on the list filed under Rule 1007(d), any party who has filed an appearance, and such other entities as the court may direct.

[Effective October 1, 2006. Amended effective December 1, 2009.]

RULE 2014–1. APPLICATION TO EMPLOY PROFESSIONAL PERSONS

(a) **Application and Statement.** An application of a debtor (other than a chapter 7 debtor), debtor in possession, estate representative, or committee to employ any professional person, including an attorney, accountant, appraiser, broker, auctioneer, consultant or agent, shall include all of the information required to be provided by Fed.R.Bankr.P. 2014(a). In addition, in the statement accompanying the application, the person to be employed (hereinafter the "professional") shall make the following representations and disclosures under penalty of perjury in accordance with section (c):

(1) Neither I nor any member of my firm holds or represents any interest adverse to the estate of the above-named debtor.

(2) My and my firm's connections with the debtor, any creditor, or other party in interest, their respective attorneys and accountants are as follows:

_____

_____

_____

I am and each member of my firm is a "disinterested person" as that term is defined in 11 U.S.C. § 101(14).

(3) I have not agreed to share with any person (except members of my firm) the compensation to be paid for the services rendered in this case, except as follows:

_____

(4) I have received a retainer in this case in the amount of $_____, which sum, upon information and belief, was generated by the debtor from: _____.

(5) I shall amend this statement immediately upon my learning that (A) any of the within representations are incorrect or (B) there is any change of circumstance relating thereto.

(6) I have reviewed the provisions of MLBR 2016–1.

(b) Clarifying Terms.

(1) *Connections and Relationships.* For the purposes of subsection (a)(2) and 11 U.S.C. § 101(14), "connections" and "relationships" shall include, without limitation:

(A) the professional's representation of the debtor or any affiliate of the debtor as that term is defined in 11 U.S.C. § 101(2), or any insider of the debtor as that term is defined in 11 U.S.C. § 101(31), at any time;

(B) the professional's representation of a creditor against the debtor, or any insider or affiliate of the debtor, at any time;

(C) the professional's representation of a creditor on a regular basis or in connection with a substantial matter;

(D) the professional's representation of or by, or employment of or by, another authorized professional specifically in connection with this case or on a regular basis or in connection with a substantial matter in another case; and

(E) a family affiliation to the third degree of consanguinity or marital relationship between the professional or the member(s) of the professional's firm who will actually render services and any party

in interest (or officer, director, or shareholder of such party) or other professional authorized to be employed in the case.

It shall be the duty of the professional to make a preliminary inquiry as to such connections and relationships among the members and employees of the professional's firm.

(2) *Source of Funds.* For the purposes of subsection (a)(4), the professional should disclose whether the funds were generated by the debtor from operations, salary, wages, other income, a loan or capital contribution. If the source is a loan or capital contribution and such loan (other than an advance on a continuing line of credit) or capital contribution was made to the debtor within ninety (90) days prior to the filing of the petition, the identity of the lender or investor/stockholder and the terms of repayment shall be disclosed, as well as any claims by and between the debtor and the lender or investor/stockholder.

(c) Form of Statement. The statement accompanying the application to employ a professional person shall take the form of an affidavit dated and signed under penalty of perjury by the person to be employed, and above such signature the affiant shall include a sworn declaration as provided in 28 U.S.C. § 1746, which states: "I declare (or certify, or verify, or state) under penalty of perjury that the foregoing is true and correct."

(d) Effective Date. If a court approves an application for the employment of a professional person, such approval shall be deemed effective as of the date of the filing of the application. However, if such application is filed within fourteen (14) days from the later of case commencement or the date the professional commenced rendering services, court approval shall be deemed effective commencing the date that services were first rendered. Approval shall not be otherwise retroactive absent extraordinary circumstances.

[Effective August 1, 1997. Amended effective September 1, 1999.]

RULE 2016–1. APPLICATION FOR COMPENSATION

(a) Any professional seeking interim or final compensation for services and reimbursement of expenses under 11 U.S.C. §§ 330, 331, 503(b)(2), 503(b)(4) or 506(b), excluding any broker (other than an investment banker) whose compensation is determined by a commission on the sale price of an asset, shall file an application for compensation and reimbursement. The application shall conform generally to Fed.R.Bankr.P. 2016.

(1) The application and any attachments shall:

(A) be legible and understandable;

(B) identify the time period or periods during which services were rendered;

(C) describe the specific services performed each day by each person with the time broken down into units of tenths of one hour devoted to such services;

(D) include a copy of any contract or agreement reciting the terms and conditions of employment and compensation;

(E) include a copy of the order authorizing the employment;

(F) include the date and amount of any retainer, partial payment or prior interim allowances;

(G) include a brief narrative description of services performed and a summary of hours by professionals and other personnel;

(H) if the trustee is also serving as his or her own attorney, the trustee's attorney's application must contain:

(i) a certification that no compensation has been or will be sought for services as an attorney which are properly trustee services; and

(ii) include a brief biography of each person included in the fee application, stating his or her background and experience.

(2) All applications by professionals shall include a summary chart, which clearly sets forth in columns:

(A) the full names of the attorneys, paralegals and clerks performing services;

(B) the initials used for each person;

(C) the hourly rate charged by each person and, if there is a change in the hourly rate for any such person during the covered period, then that person's name shall be listed as many times as there are changes in the hourly rate and each entry shall show the number of hours at each rate and the date each change became effective; and

(D) the total amount of fees for each person and a column showing a grand total figure (See MLBR Appendix 6 as an example).

(E) the total amount of each type of out-of-pocket expense for which reimbursement is sought, which amounts, subject to subsection (F), shall not exceed the actual cost to the applicant.

(F) In lieu of calculating the actual cost of the expenses set forth below, the applicant may request the rates of reimbursement set forth in MLBR Appendix 2 for:

(i) copies;

(ii) incoming telecopier transmissions; and

(iii) auto mileage.

(b) Any application for compensation by co-counsel shall specify the separate services rendered by each counsel and contain a certification that no compensation is sought for duplicate services.

(c) If an application for compensation and reimbursement by a chapter 7, 11 or 12 trustee exceeds $5,000.00, the trustee shall state:

(1) the total amount received in the estate;

(2) the amount of money disbursed and to be disbursed by the trustee to parties in interest (excluding the debtor) and a calculation of the maximum fee allowable under 11 U.S.C. § 326;

(3) a brief narrative description of services performed;

(4) if the payment sought is interim compensation, why the payment of interim compensation is reasonable and appropriate;

(5) the dividend, expressed as a percentage of funds to be distributed to creditors, if the requested compensation and other requested administrative expenses are allowed in the amounts requested. If a trustee has served both as a chapter 7 and a chapter 11 trustee, separate itemizations must be provided for each period. The amount of compensation shall be stated as a dollar amount, regardless of the calculation of the maximum compensation allowable under 11 U.S.C. § 326(a).

(d)(1) All applications which seek more than $35,000.00 in compensation, or are otherwise very lengthy, must be divided into narrative sections and must utilize the project categories set forth in subsection (2) below. Each narrative section within each project category must represent a task, must describe the task and the benefit to the estate, and must identify the work done by each professional. There shall be attached to each narrative section a specific description of services performed under such project category each day by each person and the time devoted to such services on that day by each person. The end of each narrative section must include a summary chart that conforms to the requirements of section (a)(2)(A)-(F) of this rule.

(2) The following project categories (as described below) are to be utilized in all applications submitted pursuant to this rule. Applications may contain additional categories as may be required in a particular case:

(A) Asset Analysis and Recovery: identification and review of potential assets including causes of action and non–litigation recoveries and appraisals of assets;

(B) Asset Disposition: sales, leases, matters under 11 U.S.C. § 365, abandonment and related transaction work;

(C) Business Operations: issues related to debtor–in–possession operating in chapter 11 cases, such as employee issues, vendor issues, lease and contract issues, and other similar matters, as well as analysis of tax issues and preparation of tax returns;

(D) Case Administration: coordination and compliance activities (including preparation of statements of financial affairs, schedules, lists of contracts, and United States trustee interim statements and operating reports), contacts with the United States trustee, and general creditor inquiries;

(E) Claims Administration and Objections: specific claim inquiries, bar date motions, analyses, objections and allowance of claims;

(F) Employee Benefits and Pensions: issues such as severance, retention, 401(k) coverage and continuance of pension plans;

(G) Employment Applications and Objections: preparation of employment applications, motions to establish interim compensation procedures, and review of and objections to employment applications of others;

(H) Fee Applications and Objections: preparation of fee applications and review of and objections to fee applications of others;

(I) Financing: matters under 11 U.S.C. §§ 361, 363 and 364, including cash collateral and secured claims, and analysis of loan documents;

(J) Litigation: a separate category should be utilized for each litigation matter;

(K) Meetings of Creditors: preparing for and attending conference of creditors, meetings held pursuant to 11 U.S.C. § 341, and other creditors' committee meetings;

(L) Plan and Disclosure Statement: formulation, presentation and confirmation, compliance with confirmation order, related orders and rules, disbursement and case closing activities (except those relating to allowance of any objections to claims); and

(M) Relief from Stay Proceedings: matters relating to termination or continuation of automatic stay under 11 U.S.C. § 362.

[Effective August 1, 1997; amended effective January 1, 2005; October 1, 2006.]

RULE 2082–1. CONFIRMATION OF CHAPTER 12 PLANS

(a) The Clerk, in conjunction with issuing a notice of the initial meeting of creditors, shall issue a notice of the deadline for the filing of claims as established by Fed. R. Bankr. P. 3002.

(b) The Clerk shall schedule the confirmation hearing and establish a plan objection deadline upon the filing of the debtor's plan and notify the debtor of these dates. The debtor shall give at least fourteen (14) days notice of the hearing and the deadline for

filing objections and shall serve a copy of the plan upon all creditors, equity security holders, the chapter 12 trustee, and the United States trustee. The debtor shall file a certificate of service with the Court indicating that service has been made.

[Effective August 1, 1997. Amended effective December 1, 2009.]

RULE 2090–2. DISCIPLINARY PROCEEDINGS

(a) An attorney who appears for any purpose in any case or proceeding submits himself or herself to the Court's disciplinary jurisdiction and shall be held to the standards of professional conduct set forth in District Court Local Rule 83.6.

(b) In any matter in which a bankruptcy judge has reasonable cause to believe that an attorney has committed a violation of any canon or ethical rule, the bankruptcy judge may refer the attorney for disciplinary proceedings to the District Court pursuant to District Court Local Rule 83.6 and to any state disciplinary authority. In connection with any such referral, the bankruptcy judge may recommend expedited interim action by the District Court and the state disciplinary authority if in the opinion of the bankruptcy judge such action is necessary to avoid an imminent risk of harm to the public.

(c) A bankruptcy judge may impose any other sanction the judge deems necessary under the circumstances in accordance with the relevant statutes, rules of this Court and the District Court, or applicable law.

[Effective August 1, 1997. Amended effective September 1, 1999.]

RULE 2091–1. WITHDRAWAL OF APPEARANCE

(a) An attorney may withdraw from a case or proceeding without leave of the Court by serving a notice of withdrawal on the client and all other parties in interest and filing the notice, provided that:

(1) such notice is accompanied by the filing of a notice of appearance of successor counsel;

(2) there are no motions pending before the Court; and

(3) no trial date has been set.

Unless these conditions are met, an attorney may withdraw from a case or proceeding only with leave of the Court.

(b) An attorney granted leave to withdraw shall immediately serve on the client and all other parties in interest the order permitting withdrawal. If the client is a corporation, the order shall contain a provision directing that new counsel file a notice of appearance within twenty-one (21) days from the date of the order or such shorter period as the Court may direct. If a party who has been served with notice of an attorney's withdrawal fails to appear in the case or proceeding either through a newly appointed attorney or, if such party is an individual, in person, within the period prescribed, such failure shall be grounds for entry of a default judgment, dismissal or other appropriate action by the Court.

[Effective August 1, 1997. Amended effective December 1, 2009.]

RULE 3001–1. PROOFS OF CLAIM IN NO ASSET CASES

In any case in which creditors have been advised that there are insufficient assets to pay a dividend, and the trustee, in accordance with Fed.R.Bankr.P. 3002(a)(5), subsequently notifies the Court that payment of a dividend is anticipated, the Clerk shall issue a bar date for the filing of claims and a notice that creditors who previously filed proofs of claims need not file claims again in order to receive a distribution.

[Effective August 1, 1997.]

RULE 3002–1. DEADLINE FOR ASSERTING ADMINISTRATIVE CLAIMS PURSUANT TO 11 U.S.C. § 503(B)(9); RECLAMATION OF GOODS

Unless the Court orders otherwise, any request for allowance of an administrative expense for the value of goods delivered to a debtor in the ordinary course of the debtor's business within twenty (20) days prior to the commencement of a case pursuant to 11 U.S.C. § 503(b)(9) shall be filed with the Court, in writing, within sixty (60) days after the first date set for the meeting of creditors pursuant to 11 U.S.C. § 341(a). Failure to file such a request for allowance within the time period specified in this Rule will result in denial of administrative expense treatment for such claim.

[Effective October 1, 2006. Amended effective December 1, 2009.]

RULE 3007–1. OBJECTIONS TO CLAIMS

(a) A party who files an objection to the allowance of any proof of claim shall state in the objection, with particularity, the factual and legal grounds for the objection, and shall make a recommendation to the Court as to whether the claim should be disallowed or allowed in an amount or with a priority other than as filed. Subject to the provisions of Fed. R. Bankr. P. 3007, a party may file objections to up to 100 claims in any one pleading. The provisions of this rule shall apply to single as well as multiple objections to claims.

(b) The procedures for motion practice and contested matters set forth in Fed. R. Bankr. P. 9013 and 9014 and MLBR 9013–1 shall govern objections to claims. The proposed notice shall be attached to the objection filed with the Court and shall contain blank spaces for the deadline for filing responses, as well as a blank space for the date, time and place of the hearing on the objection. Upon receipt of the proposed notice, the Clerk shall assign a deadline for filing responses, schedule a hearing date, and transmit such date to the objecting party by telephone or such other means as the Clerk deems appropriate. The objecting party shall then serve upon the claimant at the address noted on the proof of claim or any subsequent address provided to the Court by the claimant and upon any other party entitled to notice a copy of the objection and the notice of response deadline and hearing date at least 30 days prior to the hearing, and shall file a certificate of service with respect to the notice. Unless the objecting party requests advance approval of the form of notice, the proposed notice need not be served on any party.

(c) If a claimant contests an objection to claim, the claimant shall file with the Clerk a written response to the objection, which response shall state with particularity why the objection to the claim should be overruled. The response shall be served on the party objecting to the claim and any other party entitled to notice of the response. In addition, at the time of the service of the response, the claimant should also serve on the party objecting to the claim documentation in support of the allowance of the claim not already appended to the claim. A claimant who does not file a timely response to a properly served objection to claim will be deemed to have agreed that the objection to claim may be sustained. The Court, in its discretion, may cancel the hearing on any properly served objection to claim to which a timely response has not been filed and may sustain the objection to claim without further notice or hearing.

(d) A party in interest shall not include a demand for relief of a kind specified in Fed. R. Bankr. P. 7001 in an objection to the allowance of a claim, but an objection to the allowance of a claim may be included in an adversary proceeding.

(e) In the event of one or more timely responses to objections to claims, within fourteen (14) days after the deadline for responses, and at least two (2) days prior to the hearing on objections to claims, the party filing the objection(s) to claims shall file a "Report and Hearing Agenda", setting forth 1) a list of the objections to claims to which no timely responses were filed and the objecting party's recommendations with respect to those claims; 2) a report on the settlement of any objections to claims; 3) the status of any objection to claim to which a timely response was filed and which remains unresolved; 4) whether the objection is likely to be resolved; and 5) the objecting party's recommendation for further proceedings on the objection to claim. If a creditor timely files a response to an objection to claim, the initial hearing on the objection shall be a preliminary nonevidentiary hearing, at which the parties shall appear and be prepared to discuss the need for an evidentiary hearing, discovery, scheduling and settlement.

(f) Within seven (7) days after the Court's action on any objection to claim, the objecting party shall submit a proposed order on the objections to claims.

[Effective August 1, 1997; amended effective January 1, 2005; May 1, 2008; December 1, 2009.]

RULE 3011–1. PROCEDURE FOLLOWING FINAL DISTRIBUTION

(a) One hundred and fifty (150) days after final distribution in a chapter 7 or chapter 13 case, the trustee shall forward to the Clerk:

(1) a list of names and addresses of persons whose checks were not negotiated and the amounts to which they are entitled; and

(2) a check payable to the Clerk in the full amount of all outstanding unpaid checks.

(b) In chapter 7 cases, the trustee shall close out the estate's bank account(s) relating to the case and file with the Clerk a copy of the final bank statement(s) indicating that the bank account(s) has (have) been closed with a zero (0) balance. In chapter 13 cases, the chapter 13 trustee shall file with the Clerk a statement indicating the amount of monies distributed to creditors, the amount of the trustee's commission, the amount of monies being turned over to the Clerk under section (a), and a representation that there is a zero (0) balance in the debtor(s)' account in the records of the chapter 13 trustee.

(c) The trustee shall retain custody of all of the estate's cancelled checks and bank statements for no less than two (2) years from the date the case is closed.

(d) Any check issued by a trustee shall contain a legend stating that the check will not be paid more than ninety (90) days after it is issued.

(e) Prior to the closing of the case, the trustee shall file with the Clerk the Trustee's Final Distribution Report, in such form as may be approved by the United States trustee.

[Effective August 1, 1997.]

RULE 3015–1. CHAPTER 13 CASES

The chapter 13 rules attached hereto as MLBR Appendix 1 are adopted and incorporated herein by reference.

[Effective August 1, 1997.]

RULE 3017–1. APPROVAL OF DISCLOSURE STATEMENTS IN CHAPTER 11 CASES OTHER THAN SMALL BUSINESS CASES

(a) Objections and Hearing on Approval. Notice of the time fixed for filing objections and of the hearing to consider final approval of the disclosure statement shall be given in accordance with Fed. R. Bankr. P. 2002(b). Upon motion and for cause shown, the Court may issue an order combining the hearing on the approval of the disclosure statement with the notice of the hearing on confirmation of the plan.

(b) Prior to filing an objection to a disclosure statement, counsel to the party who intends to object to the adequacy of the disclosure statement shall contact counsel to the plan proponent and confer by telephone or in person in a good faith effort to narrow areas of disagreement.

(c) An objection to the disclosure statement shall be filed and served on the debtor, the United States trustee, the plan proponent, any chapter 11 trustee, any examiner, all members of any committee appointed under the Bankruptcy Code and its counsel and any other entity that has requested service of pleadings in the case or which has been designated by the Court. Any objection to the adequacy of a disclosure statement shall contain a certificate stating that the conference required by section (b) was held, the date and time of the conference and the names of the participating parties, or a statement detailing the reasons why the conference was not held. The Court may overrule without a hearing objections that are not accompanied by the conference certificate.

[Effective August 1, 1997. Amended effective May 1, 2008.]

RULE 3017–2. FILING OF PLAN AND DISCLOSURE STATEMENT IN SMALL BUSINESS CHAPTER 11 REORGANIZATION CASES

(a) In cases filed prior to October 17, 2005 (the "Effective Date"), Fed.R.Bankr.P. 3017.1 as in effect prior to the Effective Date shall apply.

(b) In cases filed on and after the Effective Date Fed.R.Bankr.P. 3017.1 shall apply. A sample Combined Small Business Plan of Reorganization and Disclosure Statement for Small Business Debtor, set forth as Official Local Form 15, may be used and altered to fit the circumstances of the case.

[Effective August 1, 1997. Amended effective May 1, 2008; December 1, 2009.]

RULE 3022–1. CLOSING CHAPTER 11 CASES

(a) Definitions. For purposes of this rule, 11 U.S.C. § 350 and Fed.R.Bankr.P. 3022, a chapter 11 case is "fully administered" unless a matter is pending sixty (60) days following the entry of a final order confirming a plan of reorganization.

(b) Motion for Final Decree. Counsel for the plan proponent shall prepare and file a motion for final decree closing the chapter 11 case within sixty (60) days of the date on which it is fully administered. Preparation and filing of the motion for final decree shall be a continuing post-confirmation duty of counsel to the plan proponent.

(c) Form of Motion for Final Decree. The motion for final decree shall contain the following statements made under oath by an individual with personal knowledge:

(1) that the plan has been substantially consummated in accordance with 11 U.S.C. § 1101(2) and the provisions of the plan and the confirmation order; that any subsequent orders of the Court have been complied with; and that the case may be closed in accordance with Fed.R.Bankr.P. 3022;

(2) that the debtor, trustee or agent has paid all administrative expenses, including court-authorized professional compensation and costs (unless otherwise agreed in writing by the parties or unless otherwise provided for by the confirmed plan), as evidenced by an attached Exhibit "A" listing the names, addresses and amounts paid to each of the recipients;

(3) that the debtor, trustee or agent has commenced making distributions prescribed by the plan, as evidenced by an attached Exhibit "B" listing the names, addresses and amounts paid to each of the recipients;

(4) that all remaining distributions prescribed by the plan shall be made in accordance with an attached Exhibit "C" listing the names, addresses and amounts to be paid to each of the recipients; and

(5) if applicable, that distributions have not been made to recipients set forth on an attached Exhibit "D" listing the names, addresses and amounts tendered but returned and the reasons why payments have not been made, despite reasonable attempts.

(d) Interim Report on Administration Progress. If counsel for the plan proponent cannot file a motion for final decree on or before sixty (60) days after the entry of an order confirming the plan, counsel shall prepare and file an interim report on administration progress, describing the actions taken to consummate the plan and fully administer and close the case. The report shall contain detailed accounts, under subsections (c) (2), (3), and (4), of all amounts paid under the plan, if any, since the entry of the confirmation order. The Court, in its discretion, may direct the filing of additional reports and/or issue an order setting forth a schedule of future reporting.

(e) Service of Motion for Final Decree and Interim Report on Administration Progress. Counsel for the plan proponent shall serve copies of any motion for a final decree or interim report on administration progress, together with all supporting documentation, on any committee appointed by the United States trustee, counsel to any committee, and any party who filed an appearance in the case and requested service of all notices and pleadings, the United States trustee and any other parties as the Court may direct.

(f) Objections to Motion for Final Decree. Any party in interest, including the United States trustee, may object to any motion for a final decree or interim report on administration progress.

(g) Hearings. The Court, in its discretion, may schedule a hearing on any motion for a final decree or interim report on administration progress or any objection thereto.

(h) Entry of Final Decree. The Court may enter a final decree closing the case with or without a hearing.

(i) Reopening of Case. Nothing in this rule shall be interpreted as limiting the Court's ability to reopen a case pursuant to 11 U.S.C. § 350 and Fed.R.Bankr.P. 5010.

[Effective August 1, 1997.]

RULE 4001–1. MOTIONS FOR RELIEF FROM STAY; SUBMISSION OF MOTIONS AND OPPOSITIONS TO MOTIONS

(a) A party seeking relief from the automatic stay provided by 11 U.S.C. § 362(a) shall file, in accordance with Fed. R. Bankr. P. 9014, a motion and a proposed order.

(b) If the motion contains a request for authority to foreclose pursuant to a mortgage or security interest, the movant shall provide the following information:

(1) If the movant seeks relief for cause pursuant to 11 U.S.C. § 362(d)(1), then the cause shall be specifically stated in the motion.

(2) If the movant seeks relief with respect to a stay of an act against property pursuant to 11 U.S.C. § 362(d)(1) or (d)(2), then the motion shall state:

(A) the amounts and priority of the debt alleged to be owed to the movant;

(B) the identification, amount, and priority of each other encumbrance affecting the property, including real estate taxes and other municipal charges;

(C) the total of the amounts set forth in subsections (a) and (b);

(D) the fair market value and liquidation value of the collateral, with any available appraisal(s) attached;

(E) either that (i) there is no other collateral securing the obligation, or (ii) there is other collateral securing the obligation, indicating the identity, value and valuation method and attaching any available appraisal(s);

(F) the original holder of the obligations secured by the security interest and/or mortgage and every subsequent transferee, if known to the movant, and whether the movant is the holder of that obligation or an agent of the holder; and

(G) if known to the movant, whether and where any declaration of homestead has been recorded against the property;

(3) If the movant seeks relief from stay pursuant to 11 U.S.C. § 362(d)(3), the motion shall state:

(A) whether a plan of reorganization has been filed in the case;

(B) whether the debtor has commenced monthly payments to creditors with interests in the real estate pursuant to 11 U.S.C. § 362(d)(3)(B); and

(C) the original holder of the obligations secured by the security interest and/or mortgage and every subsequent transferee, if known to the movant, and whether the movant is the holder of that obligation or an agent of the holder.

(4) If the movant seeks in rem relief from stay pursuant to 11 U.S.C. § 362(d)(4), the motion shall include:

(A) the information set forth in Local Rule 4001–1(b)(2); and

(B) the circumstances of the alleged scheme to delay, hinder, and defraud creditors with particularity, including:

(i) the history of bankruptcy filings affecting the real property at issue (including the filing date(s), docket number(s) and disposition of the prior bankruptcy filing(s)); and/or

(ii) the details of any transfers of the real property at issue without court approval or the consent of the movant (including the date of the transfer(s), the stated consideration and the actual consideration, the name of the grantee(s) and the recording information for the deed(s) at issue).

(c) A party opposing a motion for relief from the automatic stay must file an opposition to the motion within fourteen (14) days, inclusive of the three (3) day mailing period provided in Fed. R. Bankr. P. 9006(f), after service of the motion. The opponent shall either admit, deny or state that the opponent has insufficient knowledge to admit or deny each and every allegation of the motion, shall state specifically why the motion should not be granted, and shall state the terms of any offer of adequate protection made by the debtor or trustee. If the value alleged by the movant is disputed, any appraisal available to the opponent shall be attached to the opposition. If the motion is scheduled for an expedited hearing before the expiration of the fourteen (14) day period, then the opposition shall be filed before the expedited hearing.

(d) Any party in interest seeking the continuation of the automatic stay pursuant to 11 U.S.C. § 362 (c)(3)(B) or seeking the imposition of the automatic stay pursuant to 11 U.S.C. § 362 (c)(4)(B) shall file a motion and a proposed order.

(1) The motion should:

(A) identify the prior case(s) filed by the debtor, individually or jointly, within the preceding year and its/their disposition;

(B) state whether any motion for relief was pending in the prior case(s) at the time of dismissal;

(C) if any motion for relief had been filed in the prior case(s), state whether such motion(s) was/were resolved by terminating, conditioning, or limiting the stay;

(D) explain the extent to which the party in interest wishes the automatic stay to be continued or imposed, including the length of the proposed continuation or imposition and the parties affected (i.e. all creditors or only particular creditors); and

(E) set forth facts demonstrating that the filing of the later case is in good faith as to the creditors to be stayed.

(2) The motion shall be filed within fourteen (14) days from the filing of the new petition. If the motion is not timely filed, the Court may deny the motion.

(e) With regard to a motion for an order confirming that no stay is in effect pursuant to 11 U.S.C. § 362 (j) or 11 U.S.C. § 362 (c)(4)(A)(ii), the motion shall:

(1) set forth the debtor's history of bankruptcy filing(s) within the preceding year (including the filing date(s), docket number(s) and disposition of the prior bankruptcy filing(s)); and

(2) state whether the motion is filed pursuant to 11 U.S.C. § 362 (j) or 11 U.S.C. § 362 (c)(4)(A)(ii).

(f) All documents filed pursuant to this rule shall be served in accordance with Fed. R. Bankr. P. 4001(a) and 9006(d)–(f) upon all parties who have filed appearances and requested service of all notices and pleadings, and on any other party that the Court may designate. If the motion seeks relief with respect to an act against property, the motion shall also be served on all entities that claim an interest in the property, including all co-owners, lienholders and taxing authorities.

(g) A preliminary hearing on a motion for relief from the automatic stay will be a consolidated preliminary and final nonevidentiary hearing unless at the conclusion of the preliminary hearing the Court schedules a final evidentiary or nonevidentiary hearing.

(h) If the estate representative fails to file a response within the time prescribed in section (c), then the estate representative shall be deemed to have assented to the motion.

[Effective August 1, 1997; amended effective January 1, 2005; October 1, 2006; December 1, 2009.]

RULE 4001–2. USE OF CASH COLLATERAL, OBTAINING CREDIT AND STIPULATIONS RELATING TO SAME

(a) A motion for use of cash collateral, for authority to obtain credit, or a stipulation relating to same shall be in the forms required by Fed. R. Bankr. P. 4001(b), (c) and (d), respectively. In addition, the movant shall set forth the following information in any motion for use of cash collateral, for authority to obtain credit, or a stipulation regarding same: the total dollar amount of the request for use of funds, the specific uses to which the funds will be put, the debtor's proposed budget for the use of the funds, pricing and economic terms including interest rates and fees, maturity, termination and default provisions, disclosure by the debtor as to whether it has reason to believe that the budget will be adequate to pay all administrative expenses due and payable during the period covered by the budget, the amount of debt asserted to be owed to any creditor claiming an interest in the collateral, the value of the collateral which secures the creditor's asserted interest, any proposal for providing adequate protection including any priority or superpriority provisions, including the effect thereof on existing liens and any carve-outs from liens or superpriorities, and any choice of law provision. If the debtor seeks authority to use cash collateral or to obtain credit on an emergency or expedited basis, the debtor shall state the nature of the emergency requiring an emergency or expedited determination.

(b) A motion for use of cash collateral, for authority to obtain credit, or a stipulation relating to same as well as any proposed orders for which entry is sought shall be served on all creditors who assert an interest in the cash collateral and their attorneys, if known, any taxing authority that has a claim against the debtor, the debtor's twenty (20) largest unsecured creditors, the members of any committee appointed in the case and counsel to any committee, any parties who have filed a request for service of all pleadings and notices and the United States trustee.

(c) Subject to section (d), the following provisions contained in an agreement between the debtor and the holder of a secured claim as to use of cash collateral,

obtaining credit, or adequate protection, or any interim or final order approving or authorizing the use of cash collateral, obtaining credit, or adequate protection, shall be unenforceable:

(1) *Cross–Collateralization Clauses.* Provisions that elevate prepetition debt to administrative expense or higher status or secure the repayment of prepetition debt with postpetition assets, other than (i) a claim arising from postpetition advances which constitute an additional non-replacement extension of credit; or (ii) a claim representing the diminution in value of the secured claim after the commencement of the case;

(2) *Concessions as to the Status of Prepetition Lien or Debt.* Provisions or findings of fact that bind the debtor, the estate representative or other parties in interest with respect to the validity, perfection, priority, enforceability or amount of the secured creditor's prepetition lien or debt;

(3) *Provisions Creating Liens on Bankruptcy Causes of Action.* Provisions that grant liens on the estate's claims arising under 11 U.S.C. sections 506(c), 544, 545, 547, 548 or 549;

(4) *Waivers.* Provisions that seek a waiver of or restrict in any way rights that the debtor or estate representative may have under sections 506(c), 544, 545, 547, 548 or 549; or that purport to release, waive or restrict alleged prepetition claims by the debtor or the estate against the secured creditor; or that in any way restrict the ability of the debtor or the estate representative to file a plan or that prohibit or restrict any proposed treatment of a creditor in that plan;

(5) *Right to Relief from Stay.* Provisions that grant automatic relief from stay upon the occurrence of any event; or that purport to bind the court to an expedited or emergency hearing on a request for such relief; or that limit in any way the court's consideration of issues that may arise under section 362(d) or the debtor's or estate representative's rights to bring those issues before the court;

(6) *Rollups.* Provisions that deem prepetition secured debt to be postpetition debt or that use postpetition loans from a prepetition secured creditor to pay part or all of a secured creditor's prepetition debt;

(7) *Non–Consensual Priming.* Provisions that create a lien senior or equal to any existing lien without the consent of that lienholder;

(8) *Disparate Carveouts.* Provisions that provide fee or expense carveouts for any professional disparate from those provided to any and all professionals whose employment is approved by the court;

(9) *Waiver of Right to Seek Use of Cash Collateral.* Provisions that limit the right of the debtor or the estate representative to move for an order authorizing the use of cash collateral or that seek to prime the secured position of any other secured party under Section 364(d) in the absence of the secured creditor's consent;

(10) *Waiver of procedural requirements for foreclosure:* Provisions that waive the procedural requirements for foreclosure required under applicable non-bankruptcy law;

(11) *Venue in Foreign Jurisdiction.* Provisions that place venue in a jurisdiction other than this court in the event of a dispute under any agreement;

(12) *Payment of Secured Creditor's Expenses.* Provisions that require the debtor to pay a secured creditor's expenses and attorney's fees in connection with a proposed financing or use of cash collateral without any notice or review by the Office of the United States Trustee and the court;

(13) *Termination; Default; Remedies.* Provisions that provide that the use of cash collateral will cease or the financing agreement will default, on (i) the filing of a challenge to lender's prepetition lien or lender's prepetition conduct; (ii) entry of an order granting relief from automatic stay (except as to material assets); (iii) grant of a change of venue with respect to the case or any adversary proceeding; (iv) the making of a motion by a party in interest seeking any relief (as distinct from an order granting such relief); (v) management changes or the departure, from the debtor, of any identified employees;

(14) *Release of Liability.* Provisions that purport to release the prepetition lender's liability for alleged pre-petition torts, breaches of contract, or lender liability, releases of pre-petition defenses and/or counterclaims, and provisions that shorten the period of limitations within which any party in interest (including a successor trustee) may bring causes of action against the lender.

(d) Notwithstanding section (c), the Court may order the enforcement of any terms and conditions on the use of cash collateral or obtaining credit, provided that (i) the proposed order or agreement specifically states that the proposed terms and conditions vary from the requirements of section (c), and (ii) any such proposed terms and conditions are conspicuously and specifically set forth in the proposed agreement or order.

(e) Preliminary and Final Orders; Notice.

(1) A single motion may be filed seeking entry of an interim and final order authorizing use of cash collateral or a borrowing or approving a stipulation relating to same. The motion shall be accompanied by any proposed order for which entry is sought. Notice of the motion and any notice of any hearing shall be served on the United States trustee, as well as those parties required by Fed. R. Bankr. P. 4001(b)(1) and (c)(1).

(2) The Court may enter an Interim Preliminary Order authorizing use of cash collateral or borrowing, or a stipulation relating to same only to the extent necessary to avoid immediate and irreparable harm to the estate pending a final hearing. Any provision of an Interim Preliminary Order may be reconsidered at the Final Hearing. Provisions in an Interim Preliminary Order shall not be binding on the Court with respect to the provisions of the Final Order, except that a lender: (a) will be afforded the benefits and protections of the Interim Preliminary Order for funds advanced during the term of the Interim Preliminary Order, and (b) will not be required to advance funds under a Final Order which contains provisions contrary to or inconsistent with the Interim Preliminary Order.

(3) A final hearing on a motion authorizing use of cash collateral or a borrowing, or a stipulation relating to same shall not be held earlier than fourteen (14) days after service of the notice of hearing.

[Effective August 1, 1997. Amended January 1, 2002; January 1, 2005. Amended effective December 1, 2009.]

RULE 4001-3. PERMITTED BILLING AND SETTLEMENT COMMUNICATIONS

To the extent that the automatic stay under 11 U.S.C. § 362(a) may be applicable to a debtor or property of the estate and has not terminated or been lifted, relief from the automatic stay shall be deemed granted, without hearing or further order, in any case under any chapter of Title 11 of the United States Code, in order to enable a secured creditor or its agent, representative or nominee (excluding its attorney) to:

(a) send WRITTEN correspondence to the debtor, with a copy to debtor's counsel, consisting of statements, payment coupons, notices, analyses or accountings of any payment defaults, the status of insurance coverage, tax payments, and/or municipal charges on property used as collateral and other such correspondence that the creditor typically sends to its non-debtor customers; EXCEPT that such correspondence shall not make demand for payment or threaten foreclosure or dismissal of the case; and

(b) discuss and/or negotiate with a debtor a proposed modification of the terms of any secured indebtedness, including, without limitation, a home mortgage; EXCEPT that all such negotiations and/or discussions shall be conducted through counsel for the debtor, if the debtor is represented by counsel and such counsel has not, in writing, granted permission for such direct communication by creditor representatives with the debtor.

The secured creditor shall terminate the foregoing communications immediately upon receipt of written notice from the debtor or debtor's counsel requesting that such contacts cease. Further, nothing herein shall authorize a debtor or creditor to enter into any loan modification without court authority, so long as the property which is collateral for the loan is property of the estate under § 541(a).

[Effective December 1, 2009.]

RULE 4002–1. DUTIES OF DEBTOR

(a) A debtor is required to bring the personal identification and financial information required by Fed. R. Bankr P. 4002(b) to the § 341 meeting of creditors.

(b) If a creditor requests a copy of the debtor's Federal tax return or transcript under § 521(e)(2)(A)(ii), the creditor shall make such request in writing no fewer than fourteen (14) days before the meeting of creditors and serve a copy of the request upon the debtor and the debtor's attorney. If the debtor disputes that the requesting party is a creditor, the debtor shall file an objection with the Court within 7 days prior to the § 341 meeting and the Court will set a hearing on the objection. If the debtor does not file an objection and fails to comply with the request, the creditor shall file a notice of noncompliance with the Court and serve a copy on the Debtor. Any tax returns or transcripts provided under this section are subject to the provisions set forth in subsection (c) below.

(c) If the United States trustee or a party in interest deems it appropriate that an individual Chapter 7, 11 or 13 debtor file with the Court Federal tax returns or transcripts as described in § 521(f), a request shall be made by motion on notice to the debtor, debtor's attorney, the trustee and United States trustee (if not the movant). If the Court is inclined to order such a filing, it shall first issue an order to show cause with notice to the same parties. Any party in interest, trustee or United States trustee then seeking access to the returns filed with the Court or trustee pursuant to § 521(g), shall file a motion with the Court on notice to the debtor, debtor's attorney, the trustee and the United States trustee. Parties seeking review of the returns filed with the court or trustee shall include in their motion a description of the movant's status in the case, a description of the specific tax information sought and to a statement (i) that the information is unavailable from any other source, (ii) explaining the need for the tax information, and (iii) that the parties attempted to, but failed to resolve the dispute over access to the tax information prior to the filing of the motion. Any motions filed pursuant to 11 U.S.C. § 521(f) or § 521(g) shall comply with Official Form 10 or 11 respectively. If a debtor objects to a motion filed under this subsection, the debtor shall file the objection within 7 days after service of the motion.

(d) The debtor shall redact on any state or federal tax return all but the last four digits of all taxpayer identification numbers (including social security numbers), the names of any minor children referred to within the tax return, all but the year of birth in any dates of birth and all but the last four digits of any account numbers. Any non-debtor tax identification numbers may be redacted in their entirety. The responsibility for redaction rests solely with the filer. The Clerk will not review each document for compliance with this rule. Any tax returns filed with the Court will only be available for inspection by parties in interest by motion. No tax information filed with the Court will be available to the public via the Internet, PACER or CM/ECF.

[Effective October 1, 2006. Amended effective December 1, 2009.]

RULE 4003–1. AVOIDANCE OF JUDICIAL LIEN

(a) A motion to avoid a judicial lien pursuant to 11 U.S.C. § 522(f) shall:

(1) identify the holder of the judicial lien sought to be avoided and provide the name and address of the lien holder;

(2) state the date the judicial lien was granted and identify the court that issued the lien;

(3) state the amount of the judicial lien as of the date of the filing of the petition;

(4) identify the holders of all other liens on the property listed in order of their priority;

(5) state the amount of each other lien on the property and provide a total of same;

(6) state the amount of the exemption that is allegedly impaired and provide the applicable statute for the debtor's claim of exemption;

(7) state the value of the debtor's interest in the property and attach any available appraisal report;

(8) apply the formula under 11 U.S.C. § 522(f)(2)(A);

(9) state whether the debtor contends that the entire lien is voidable, or if the lien can only be partially avoided, the amount of the surviving lien; and

(10) provide such documentary evidence as is necessary to establish the extent of the homestead declared.

(b) Any opposition to a motion to avoid a judicial lien shall admit or deny each and every allegation of the motion, specifically state why the motion should not be granted, and apply the formula under 11 U.S.C. § 522(f)(2)(A). If the opposing party intends to rely on an appraisal report, the report shall be attached to the opposition.

[Effective September 1, 1999. Amended effective October 1, 2006; December 1, 2009.]

RULE 4008–1. REAFFIRMATION AGREEMENTS

(a) A reaffirmation agreement that does not comply with 11 U.S.C. § 524(c) or (d) or is not accompanied by the cover sheet prescribed by Official Form 27 (included in Official Local Form 6 below) shall be unenforceable. The Court may also require that any reaffirmation agreement conform to Official Local Form 6. Fed. R. Bankr. P. 9011 shall apply to an attorney's declaration under 11 U.S.C. § 524(c).

(b) If a debtor is unrepresented by counsel during the course of negotiating of a reaffirmation agreement, or if a presumption that a reaffirmation agreement is an undue hardship has arisen under 11 U.S.C. § 524(m), the Court shall hold a hearing on the approval of the reaffirmation agreement pursuant to 11 U.S.C. § 524(d). The Court may also, in its discretion, schedule a hearing sua sponte on the validity or approval of any other reaffirmation agreement.

[Effective August 1, 1997. Amended effective January 1, 2002; October 1, 2006; December 1, 2009.]

RULE 5001–1. DIVISIONS OF COURT, CASE ASSIGNMENTS AND FILING OF PAPERS

(a) The District of Massachusetts shall contain the divisions comprised of the counties, cities and towns set forth in MLBR Appendix 5.

(b) All documents related to cases and proceedings for the Eastern Division shall be filed in the Clerk's Office in Boston. All documents in cases and proceedings for the Central Division shall be filed in the Clerk's Office in Worcester. All documents in cases and proceedings for the Western Division shall be filed in the Clerk's Office in Springfield.

(c) The debtor or petitioning creditor(s) shall file an original petition only in the appropriate division office. Venue for a division shall be determined in the same fashion as venue for a district under 28 U.S.C. § 1408 and applicable case law. In the event of an emergency, any division office may accept for filing on behalf of the other division office an original petition under any chapter of the Bankruptcy Code, if accompanied by a written request for transfer to the appropriate division.

(d) Any bankruptcy judge may, in the interest of justice or to further the efficient performance of the business of the Court, reassign a case or proceeding to any other bankruptcy judge, except that, when reassignment is required by reason of recusal, the Clerk shall reassign the case or proceeding on a random basis to any available judge within the district.

(e) In the absence of a judge before whom a case or proceeding is pending, emergency matters submitted to the Court may be acted upon by any available judge as determined by the Clerk or as provided for by the absent judge.

(f) The Clerk shall transfer any document pertaining to a case or proceeding mistakenly filed in the wrong division office to the proper division office and any such document shall be deemed to have been filed on the date first received in either office of the Clerk.

(g) Any party filing a document in the Clerk's Office which relates to a matter scheduled for hearing within twenty four (24) hours of the filing shall specifically bring to the attention of the Clerk, through an accompanying cover letter, the fact that the matter is scheduled for a hearing within 24 hours of the filing, and request that it be delivered to the judge immediately. Failure to comply with this rule may result in the document being deemed filed late and not being considered by the Court.

(h) Pleadings and other documents filed in a case or adversary proceeding may be removed from the Clerk's Office only if the Court has allowed a motion to remove the documents.

[Effective August 1, 1997. Amended effective January 1, 2002; December 1, 2009.]

RULE 5001–2. OFFICE OF THE CLERK

(a) The offices of the Clerk of the Court at Boston, Worcester and Springfield shall be open Monday through Friday with the Clerk or Deputy Clerk in attendance in accordance with Fed. R. Bankr. P. 5001(c).

(b) Where filing documents, including petitions, motions, and complaints, are permitted to be filed by paper or facsimile (see Appendix 8, Rule 1), such documents shall be received for filing in the office of the Clerk between the hours of 8:30 AM and 4:30 PM. Filings before 8:30 AM or after 4:30 PM on court days or on weekends or holidays can be made, for cause, by prior arrangements or in emergency circumstances, as determined by the Clerk or his or her designee, by contacting the Clerk at the telephone numbers set forth in Appendix 5.

[Effective August 1, 1997. Amended effective December 1, 2009.]

RULE 5003–1. CLERK'S AUTHORITY TO ENTER MINISTERIAL ORDERS

The clerk and his/her deputies are authorized to sign and enter without further direction by the Court the following orders, deemed to be of a ministerial nature:

(a) Orders permitting the payment of the petition filing fee in installments and fixing the number, amounts and dates of payment;

(b) Orders deferring the payment of an adversary proceeding filing fee;

(c) Orders to correct defects in the documents accompanying the original petition or orders to file or update such documents;

(d) Orders discharging a Chapter 7, 11, 12, or 13 trustee and closing a case after the case has been fully administered;

(e) Orders granting a discharge;

(f) Orders reopening a case that has been closed due to administrative error; and

(g) Orders to show cause regarding inactivity in bankruptcy cases and adversary proceedings and orders dismissing cases for failure to comply with or to respond to an order to show cause.

This rule is not intended to limit a bankruptcy judge's discretion regarding the governance of a case in any way whatsoever. The above orders may, in particular cases, be subject to modification by a bankruptcy judge.

[Effective September 1, 1999.]

RULE 5005–4. FACSIMILE FILINGS

(a) The Court will accept for filing documents transmitted by facsimile machine only if the documents are permitted to be filed non–electronically pursuant to Rule 1 of Appendix 8, except that the following documents may be filed by facsimile machine only with the prior permission of the Clerk, the Deputy Clerk or their designee:

(1) documents constituting a pleading for which a filing fee is required; and

(2) documents which exceed 35 pages, exclusive of the certificate of service.

(b) All documents filed in accordance with subsection (a) shall be deemed originally filed within the meaning of Fed.R.Civ.P. 5(e) and 11, as made applicable by Fed.R.Bankr.P. 9014 and within the meaning of Fed.R.Bankr.P. 9011. No subsequent original shall be filed after the document is filed by facsimile.

(c) Documents received by the Clerk by facsimile after 4:30 P.M. on a court day shall be deemed received as of the following court day.

[Effective August 1, 1997. Amended effective September 1, 1999; January 1, 2005.]

RULE 5009–1. CLOSING CHAPTER 7 CASES

No chapter 7 case in which dividends will be paid to creditors will be closed until the trustee has filed with the Court a statement indicating the following:

(a) there are no pending adversary proceedings;

(b) all claims have been examined and any objections to claims have been resolved;

(c) all applications by any professionals for compensation have been filed and acted upon, including an application by debtor's counsel to approve application of a retainer; and

(d) the United States trustee has approved the final account, unless the Court determines that such approval is not necessary.

[Effective August 1, 1997.]

RULE 5011–1. WITHDRAWAL OF THE REFERENCE

A motion for withdrawal of the reference shall be filed with the Clerk of the Bankruptcy Court, accompanied by a properly completed United States District Court cover sheet and the prescribed filing fee. Upon the filing of such a motion, the Clerk shall docket receipt of the motion and promptly transmit the original motion and cover sheet to the Clerk of the United States District Court for disposition.

[Effective August 1, 1997.]

RULE 5071–1. CONTINUANCES

(a) No continuance shall be effective unless the Court approves it in writing or in open court. Counsel shall not be excused from appearing before the Court absent such approval or an unexpected emergency.

(b) If a matter or proceeding is resolved between the parties prior to the day of the hearing, any motion for the continuation of a trial or nonevidentiary hearing or for the approval of a settlement of any contested matter or adversary proceeding, or any withdrawal of a motion or opposition, shall be filed and served at least one (1) business day prior to the hearing date.

(c) A motion to continue a hearing or withdraw a motion or opposition must be filed and served upon all previously served parties in a manner reasonably sufficient to reach said parties prior to their attendance at the subject hearing.

(d) Sections (a) and (b) shall not apply to motions filed by the chapter 13 trustee to dismiss a case.

[Effective August 1, 1997.]

RULE 6004-1. SALE OF ESTATE PROPERTY

(a) Motion Required. Whenever the Bankruptcy Code or the Federal Rules of Bankruptcy Procedure require an estate representative to seek leave of court to sell property of the estate, by private or public sale, the request shall be made by motion.

(b) Service Required. The motion seeking authority to sell shall be served on:

(1) the debtor and debtor's counsel, if any,

(2) the United States trustee,

(3) any known creditor claiming a lien or security interest in said property and any counsel to that creditor,

(4) all attorneys who have filed appearances in the case,

(5) any attorneys for any approved creditors or equity committee, and

(6) if no creditors committee has been appointed, the 20 largest unsecured creditors.

(c) Private Sale Procedure.

(1) The motion for authority to sell by way of private sale must state:

(A) whether the sale is to be free and clear of liens or interests;

(B) the identity of the holder of any lien or interest in the property to be sold;

(C) the efforts made by the estate representative to market the property;

(D) whether approval is sought for any proposed distribution of proceeds;

(E) why a private sale, rather than a public sale, is in the estate's best interest; and

(F) if all or substantially all of a chapter 11 debtor's assets are to be sold, why the sale is proposed under 11 U.S.C. § 363 rather than through a chapter 11 plan and a practical and abbreviated equivalent of the adequate information required in a disclosure statement to a chapter 11 plan.

(2) *Prior Approval.* The movant

(A) may seek prior approval of any term of the proposed sale;

(B) must obtain prior approval from the court of any terms for the proposed sale protecting the initial proposed purchaser, including the amount of a break-up fee or the minimum increase required for a higher offer, unless

(i) the proposed break-up fee does not exceed the lesser of 5% of the proposed original purchase price or $50,000 and is subject to final court approval upon application by the bidder; and

(ii) the minimum increase required for a higher offer does not exceed 5% of the proposed original purchase price;

(3) *Notice of Sale.*

(A) The motion for authority to sell by private sale must include a proposed Notice of Sale.

(B) Subject to the requirements of Fed. R. Bankr. P. 2002, Fed. R. Bankr. P. 6004 and any other applicable Federal Rules of Bankruptcy Procedure, these Local Rules or any Standing Order of this court, a notice of proposed private sale of property shall conform substantially to Official Local Form 2A suited to the particular circumstances of the case.

(C) The proposed Notice of Sale shall contain blank spaces for the deadline for filing objections and higher offers, as well as a blank space for the date and time of the hearing on the sale.

(D) The proposed Notice of Sale must include:

(i) the name and address of the initial offeror;

(ii) the consideration to be paid for the purchase;

(iii) the time and place of the proposed sale;

(iv) the terms and conditions of the proposed sale;

(v) the time fixed for filing higher offers and/or objections to the proposed sale;

(vi) the hearing date fixed by the court;

(vii) a general description of the property to be sold;

(viii) an itemized list of the asset or assets to be sold;

(ix) the relationship, if any, of the initial offeror and the seller;

(x) a statement as to whether the sale shall be free and clear of liens or interests pursuant to 11 U.S.C. § 363(f);

(xi) a statement noting that the court may modify the method of sale set forth in the notice at or prior to the hearing on the proposed sale;

(xii) a statement that any objection, higher offer, or request for hearing must be filed and served within the time established by the court, which time shall be conspicuously stated in the notice;

(xiii) the following language: "The Court may take evidence at any hearing on approval of the sale to resolve issues of fact."

(xiv) if a proposed sale or lease of personally identifiable information under 11 U.S.C. § 363(b)(1)(A) or (B), a statement as to whether the sale is consistent with a policy of the debtor prohibiting the transfer of such information; and

(xv) a statement that a copy of the motion and any sales agreement will be provided to any interested party upon request and at no cost.

(4) *Procedure upon Receipt by the Clerk of the Motion to Sell.* Upon receipt of the motion to sell and the proposed Notice of Sale, the Clerk shall assign a deadline date for filing objections and making higher offers, schedule a hearing date, and transmit such dates to the moving party by telephone or such other means as the Clerk deems appropriate. The estate representative shall then serve the motion to sell and completed notice as required by subsection (a)(5) of this rule.

(5) *Service of the Completed Notice.*

(A) Unless the court orders otherwise, the completed notice of proposed private sale shall be served upon all creditors in accordance with Fed. R. Bankr. P. 2002 and Fed. R. Bankr. P. 6004. A copy of the completed notice should also be served on parties regarded by the estate representative as potential purchasers, including, if appropriate, dealers in property similar to that proposed to be sold and the debtor's competitors. Unless the Court orders otherwise, the completed notice shall be served no less than twenty-one (21) days (plus such additional time as may be provided in Fed. R. Bankr. P. 9006(f)) prior to the deadline for filing objections or higher offers.

(B) The motion to sell need not be served on all parties until the Clerk has provided the information necessary to complete the notice of sale.

(C) The estate representative shall file a certificate of service no later than seven (7) days following service of the completed notice of sale unless a different deadline is set by the court.

(6) *Court Approval of Sale.*

(A) If there are no objections or higher offers timely filed with the Court by the deadline, the Court may approve the sale without holding the scheduled hearing.

(B) Within seven (7) days of receipt of a written request by the debtor, estate representative, or other party in interest, the Clerk shall issue a certificate of no objections concerning the sale of property of the estate.

(C) The moving party must submit a proposed order approving the sale within seven (7) days after the court's approval of the sale unless a different deadline is set by the court.

(d) Public Auction Procedure.

(1) *The Motion.*

(A) shall state why a public, rather than a private, sale is requested.

(B) must include a proposed Notice of Public Sale, which shall:

(i) be substantially similar to MLBR Official Local Form 2B; and

(ii) shall contain blank spaces for the deadline for filing objections and higher offers, as well as a blank space for the date and time of the hearing on the sale.

(2) *Procedure upon Receipt by the Clerk of the Motion to Sell.* Upon receipt of the proposed notice, the Clerk shall assign a deadline for filing objections, fix a hearing date, and transmit such dates to the moving party by telephone or such other means as the Clerk deems appropriate.

(3) *Service of the Completed Notice.* The estate representative shall then serve the motion to sell and the completed notice in the manner provided in subsection (c)(5) of this rule or other order of the court and shall file a certificate of service within seven (7) days of service, unless a different deadline is set by the court.

(4) *Subsequent confirmation.* Confirmation by the court of the auction is not required unless such confirmation is a condition of the court's approval. Within seven (7) days of receipt of a written request by the estate representative, the debtor, or other party in interest, the Clerk shall issue a certificate of no objections concerning the public auction sale of property of the estate.

(5) *Restrictions.*

(A) Any auction advertisement placed by an auctioneer or estate representative shall conspicuously state the bankruptcy case name and number.

(B) An auctioneer shall not introduce non-bankruptcy estate items at an auction without the court's prior approval.

(C) Neither an auctioneer employed by an estate representative nor any agent of the auctioneer shall bid on property of the estate.

(D) No buyer's premium shall be charged in a sale under this rule.

(E) Failure to comply with this subsection may result in denial of all compensation and/or the issuance of sanctions.

(6) *Qualification and Duties of Auctioneer.*

(A) An auctioneer shall not be authorized to conduct a public auction of property of an estate without first obtaining the court's specific prior approval of the auctioneer's employment.

(B) The auctioneer must file with the court a bond in an amount fixed by the United States trustee, and furnish the United States Trustee with a copy of that bond. The bond shall be conditioned on the faithful performance of the auctioneer's duties and the auctioneer's accounting for all money and property of the estate that comes into his or her possession.

(C) To avoid the necessity of filing separate bonds for smaller auction sales, the auctioneer may file with the court a blanket bond similarly conditioned in a base amount fixed from time to time by the United States trustee to cover various cases in which the auctioneer may act. The auctioneer shall also provide the United States trustee with a copy of the blanket bond.

(D) If at any time the value of goods of various estates in the auctioneer's custody exceeds the amount of the blanket bond, the auctioneer shall obtain a separate bond or bonds so that the full amount of all goods of various bankruptcy estates in the auctioneer's custody is covered.

(E) As a condition of the employment of an auctioneer in any bankruptcy estate, the auctioneer shall file an affidavit under the penalty of perjury that states:

(i) all goods of bankruptcy estates in the auctioneer's custody are fully covered at all times by separate bonds or blanket bonds or both,

(ii) his or her qualifications,

(iii) where the auctioneer is licensed,

(iv) whether the auctioneer is in good standing in all jurisdictions in which he or she is licensed, and

(v) whether the auctioneer is subject to any disciplinary proceedings or has been subject to any disciplinary proceedings in the five years preceding the filing of the application.

(7) *Attendance at Auction Sale.* The estate representative or a representative of the estate representative must be present at the auction sale.

(8) *Auctioneer's Compensation and Expenses.*

(A) The auctioneer shall file and serve an application for compensation and reimbursement of expenses setting forth the amount requested, services rendered, time spent, and actual expenses incurred as required by Fed. R. Bankr. P. 2016(a).

(B) Auctions of Personal Property. Unless otherwise ordered by the court, with respect to auctions of personal property, the auctioneer's compensation shall not exceed the following percentages of gross proceeds:

(i) 10% of the first ten thousand dollars ($10,000) or part thereof;

(ii) 7% of the next ten thousand dollars ($10,000) or part thereof;

(iii) 6% of the next thirty-five thousand dollars ($35,000) or part thereof; and

(iv) 5% of the balance.

(C) Real Estate Auctions. Unless otherwise ordered by the court, with respect to sales of real property, the auctioneer's compensation shall not exceed the greater of:

(i) 10% of the first fifty thousand dollars ($50,000) realized in excess of the amount of encumbrances, plus 2 ½ % of the balance of such excess; or

(ii) $500.00.

(D) Preapproval of Auction Expenses. The auctioneer shall be reimbursed for actual and necessary expenses incurred in connection with an auction, including advertising, if the auctioneer has obtained approval by the court in advance of the auction for these expenses. Unless otherwise ordered by the court, the auctioneer shall not be reimbursed for any overhead expense associated with the auction, including labor, cleaning, setting up, lotting, and tagging.

(e) Internet Auction Procedures.

(1) With prior court approval, after appropriate notice as required by Fed. R. Bankr. P. 2002 (a), the estate representative, or an auctioneer or other professional authorized by the Court to sell estate property, may sell any asset or assets of the estate by public auction through the use of an automated Internet auction, listing, or brokerage mechanism ("Internet Auction Mechanism").

(2) *The Motion.*

(A) In any motion requesting approval of a sale by use of an Internet Auction Mechanism, the estate representative must:

(i) identify name and uniform resource locator (URL) of the proposed Internet Auction Mechanism;

(ii) state why the estate representative believes that use of the Internet Auction Mechanism is in the best interests of the estate;

(iii) disclose whether the estate representative has or any party in interest is known to have any connections with the proposed Internet Auction Mechanism or any expected bidder;

(iv) disclose all fees associated with use of the Internet Auction Mechanism;

(v) disclose whether use of the Internet Auction Mechanism is subject to rules, policies, procedures or terms or conditions and, if so:

(1) provide either a copy thereof or the URL at which they can be examined and

(2) summarize any such rules, policies, procedures or terms or conditions that are likely to result in any restrictions on bidding for the asset(s) proposed to be sold or limitations on the estate representative in offering asset(s) for sale with full or partial reserve or otherwise controlling the determination to sell each asset;

(vi) identify the mechanism for payment to the estate;

(vii) represent that, to the best knowledge of the estate representative, the Internet Auction Mechanism will not provide auction services or any other services beyond access to its automated on-line services and related customer support; and

(viii) request authority to

(1) comply with any rules, policies, procedures, or terms or conditions of the Internet Auction Mechanism disclosed in the motion and enter into any required agreements in support thereof;

(2) consummate such sale(s), and

(3) pay any and all fees identified in the motion, without further order of the Court.

(3) Nothing in this rule shall limit applicability of the requirements of Local Rule 6004–1(b) with respect to any auctioneer hired by an estate representative to provide services beyond access to an Internet Auction Mechanism.

(4) Unless the court orders otherwise, a listing placed on an Internet Auction Mechanism shall state the bankruptcy case name and number and that the sale procedure has been approved by the United States Bankruptcy Court for the District of Massachusetts.

(f) Sales of Personally Identifiable Information.

(1) In the event that an estate representative shall move to sell personally identifiable information as defined in 11 U.S.C. § 101(41A), the motion and any notice of sale thereon shall, in addition to those requirements set forth in Paragraphs (a) and (b) of this rule, conspicuously describe the type(s) of personal identifiable information which are proposed to be sold (without disclosing thereby the content of such information), why the sale of such information is advantageous or necessary and what private agreements, federal laws and/or state laws purport to restrict the sale or use of such information.

(2) Upon the filing of a motion under subparagraph (1) above, the movant shall file a separate motion seeking expedited determination and requesting an order directing the United States trustee to appoint a consumer privacy ombudsman under 11 U.S.C. § 332.

(3) Unless otherwise ordered, the United States trustee shall seek approval of the appointment of the ombudsman within seven (7) court days of the entry of any such order.

(4) The ombudsman shall file a report with his or her recommendations and the basis therefore within seven (7) days of his or her appointment, subject to such enlargement of time as the Court may allow on request of the ombudsman made prior to the expiration of the deadline.

(g) For the purposes of this rule, the term estate representative shall include a chapter 7 trustee, chapter 11 trustee, chapter 11 debtor-in-possession, chapter 12 trustee, and chapter 13 debtor.

[Effective August 1, 1997. Amended effective January 1, 2005; October 1, 2006; May 1, 2008; December 1, 2009.]

RULE 6005–1. APPRAISERS, BROKERS AND INVESTMENT BANKERS

(a) An appraiser may be employed after allowance by the Court of a motion to employ and shall be paid at an hourly rate to be set from time to time by the Court or at a flat rate approved by the Court.

(b) A motion to approve a broker or investment banker, pursuant to MLBR 2014–1, shall also include a recitation of all of the terms and conditions of the broker's or investment banker's engagement, including :

(1) the rate of any commission on the sale of estate assets;

(2) any agreement respecting compensation made by the broker or investment banker with any other party or parties;

(3) whether, in the event that the compensation of the broker or investment banker is based on a commission and such broker or investment banker locates a proposed buyer who is the successful bidder after subsequent competitive bidding with another proposed buyer, the broker's or investment banker's commission from the sale proceeds would be based on the original bid or the final bid; and

(4) whether, in the event that the compensation of the broker or investment banker is based on a commission and such broker or investment banker locates a proposed buyer who is not the successful bidder after subsequent competitive bidding with another proposed buyer, the broker or investment banker may receive a commission limited to the amount of the original bid.

(c) No party or firm may act as an appraiser, and as a broker, and as an auctioneer, in any combination, in the same case.

[Effective August 1, 1997; Amended effective October 1, 2006.]

RULE 6006–1. MOTION FOR ASSUMPTION OR REJECTION OF EXECUTORY CONTRACT OR UNEXPIRED LEASE

(a) A motion seeking an extension of the deadline for assumption or rejection of an executory contract or an unexpired lease of residential real property or personal property in a Chapter 7 case shall be filed prior to the expiration of the sixty (60) day period found in 11 U.S.C. § 365(d)(1). In the event that the Court cannot hear or determine the motion prior to the expiration of the deadline, the extension requested in the motion shall be automatically approved on an interim basis, subject to final determination by the Court after notice and a hearing set as soon as the Court's calendar may permit. Nothing in this rule shall be deemed to limit the Court's ability to grant additional extensions for cause shown.

(b) A motion seeking extension of the deadline for assumption or rejection of an unexpired lease of non-residential real property shall be filed prior to the expiration of the one hundred twenty (120) day period found in 11 U.S.C. § 365(d)(4)(A). In the event that the Court cannot hear or determine the motion prior to the expiration of the deadline, the extension requested in the motion shall be automatically approved on an interim basis, subject to final determination by the Court after notice and a hearing set as soon as the Court's calendar may permit.

[Effective August 1, 1997; Amended effective October 1, 2006.]

RULE 6007–1. ABANDONMENT OF ESTATE PROPERTY

(a) **Requesting Notice.** The Clerk shall include in the initial notice of a meeting of creditors pursuant to 11 U.S.C. § 341 the following language:

Notice is hereby given that any creditor or other interested party who wishes to receive notice of the estate representative's intention to abandon property of the estate pursuant to 11 U.S.C. § 554(a) must file with the Court and serve upon the estate representative and the United States trustee a written request for such notice within fourteen (14) days from the date first scheduled for the meeting of creditors.

(b) **Estate Representative's Abandonment of Property.** After the expiration of the fourteen (14) day period referenced in section (a), the estate representative is authorized to limit notice of an abandonment of property to the debtor, debtor's counsel, any creditor claiming an interest in the property concerned, those creditors who have requested notice of such action in accordance with section (a), and those parties who have filed appearances and requested service of all notices and pleadings, provided that the value to the estate of the property concerned is less than $5,000.00. If the value to the estate of the property concerned is greater than $5,000.00, the estate representative shall provide notice of abandonment to all creditors and parties in interest in accordance with Fed. R. Bankr. P. 6007.

This rule is not intended to imply that estate representatives are required to abandon property with a value to the estate of less than $5,000.00, or that estate representatives are in any manner restricted from liquidating or administering such property in any other fashion.

(c) **Estate Representative's Discretion to Utilize Full Notice.** Nothing in this rule shall be deemed to prevent the estate representative from utilizing greater notice than that set forth for property with a value to the estate of less than $5,000.00 if the estate representative, in his or her discretion, determines that notice of a greater magnitude is warranted.

(d) Within five (5) days of receipt of a written request by the debtor, estate representative, or other party in interest, the Clerk shall issue a certificate of no objections concerning the abandonment of property of the estate.

[Effective August 1, 1997. Amended effective December 1, 2009.]

RULE 6012–1. ADEQUATE ASSURANCE OF PAYMENT FOR UTILITY SERVICE

A tender of adequate assurance of payment for utility service shall be deemed to be satisfactory within the meaning of 11 U.S.C. § 366(c)(2) unless a utility provides written notice to the debtor-in-possession or, in a case in which a chapter 11 trustee has been appointed, both the debtor and the chapter 11 trustee, within fourteen (14) days after such utility's receipt of the tender of adequate assurance that such tender is unsatisfactory and that service will be terminated in accordance with § 366. Upon receipt of such notice, the estate representative may seek appropriate relief from the Court to prevent a termination of utility service or to reinstate utility service in accordance with § 366.

[Effective October 1, 2006. Amended effective December 1, 2009.]

RULE 7003–1. INFORMATION TO ACCOMPANY COMPLAINT IN ADVERSARY PROCEEDINGS

The original complaint commencing an adversary proceeding filed with the Clerk shall be accompanied by a completed adversary proceeding cover sheet.

[Effective August 1, 1997.]

RULE 7016–1. PRETRIAL PROCEDURE

(a) Upon consent of all parties, the Court may enter an order referring a proceeding to mediation or arbitration or other procedure for alternative dispute resolution upon such terms and conditions as the parties may agree in writing. Such terms and conditions shall include the procedure for selection and compensation of the mediator or arbitrator, the power and authority of the mediator or arbitrator, the deadline for the mediator or arbitrator's report to the Court on whether the matter has been resolved, and the procedures for protecting the confidentiality of the information disclosed at mediation or arbitration, including the protection of proprietary information and preservation of privileges.

(b) Any request for an extension of any deadline or for modification of a party's obligations under Fed. R.Bankr.P. 7016 shall be made by written motion which shall state the basis for the relief requested. The Court will not consider any such motion unless consented to or accompanied by a certification made with particularity (time, date and circumstances) that the moving party has made a reasonable and good faith effort to reach agreement with the opposing party on the matter that is the subject of the motion.

(c) If relief is sought under Fed.R.Civ.P. 26(c) (as made applicable by Fed.R.Bankr.P. 7026) or Fed. R.Bankr.P. 7037, copies of the relevant portions of disputed documents shall be filed with the Court contemporaneously with any motion for order compelling disclosure or discovery. In addition, the Court will not consider any such motion unless accompanied by a certification made with particularity (time, date and circumstances) that the moving party has made a reasonable and good faith effort to reach agreement with the opposing party on the matter that is the subject of the motion.

[Effective August 1, 1997. Amended effective January 1, 2002.]

RULE 7024–2. NOTIFICATION OF CLAIM OF UNCONSTITUTIONALITY

(a) Whenever in any action, suit, or proceeding to which the United States or any agency, officer or employee thereof is not a party, the constitutionality of any Act of Congress affecting the public interest is drawn into question, the party raising such question shall file a notice to enable the Court to comply with 28 U.S.C. § 2403(a), and shall serve a copy of the notice upon the United States trustee, giving the title of the cause, a reference to the questioned statute sufficient for its identification, and the respects in which it is claimed to be unconstitutional.

(b) Whenever in any action, suit or proceeding to which a State of the Union or any agency, officer or employee thereof is not a party, the constitutionality of any statute of that State is drawn into question, the party raising such question shall file a notice to enable the Court to comply with 28 U.S.C. § 2403(b), and shall serve a copy of the notice upon the United States trustee, giving the title of the cause, a reference to the questioned statute sufficient for its identification, and the respects in which it is claimed to be unconstitutional.

[Effective August 1, 1997.]

RULE 7026–1. GENERAL PROVISIONS GOVERNING DISCOVERY

(a) Depositions upon oral examinations, transcripts, interrogatories, requests for documents, requests for admissions, and answers and responses thereto, shall not be filed unless so ordered by the Court or for use in the proceeding. The party taking a deposition or obtaining any material through discovery is responsible for its preservation and delivery to the Court if needed or so ordered. If, for any reason, any party believes that any of the above-named documents should be filed, a motion for authority to file such documents may be made together with the reasons for the request. If the moving party under Fed. R.Bankr.P. 7056 or the opponent relies on discovery documents, copies of the pertinent parts thereof shall be filed with the motion or opposition. The Court also may order the filing of documents sua sponte and, in addition, may order the parties to disclose any information and documentation that the Court determines are discoverable by the submission of sworn statements of any party.

(b) Any request for an extension of any deadline or for modification of a party's obligations under Fed. R.Bankr.P. 7026 shall be made by written motion which shall state the basis for the relief requested. The Court will not consider any such motion unless consented to or accompanied by a certification made with particularity (time, date and circumstances) that the moving party has made a reasonable and good faith effort to reach agreement with the opposing party on the matter that is the subject of the motion.

(c) If relief is sought under Fed.R.Civ.P. 26(c) (as made applicable by Fed.R.Bankr.P. 7026) or Fed. R.Bankr.P. 7037, copies of the relevant portions of disputed documents shall be filed with the Court contemporaneously with any motion for order compelling disclosure or discovery. In addition, the Court will not consider any such motion unless accompanied by a certification made with particularity (time, date and circumstances) that the moving party has made a reasonable and good faith effort to reach agreement with the opposing party on the matter that is the subject of the motion.

[Effective August 1, 1997. Amended effective January 1, 2002.]

RULE 7027-1. DEPOSITIONS

For purposes of Fed.R.Civ.P. 45(b)(2), made applicable to bankruptcy cases by Fed.R.Bankr.P. 9016, and without order of the Court:

(a) Boston shall be deemed a convenient place for the taking of a deposition of any person who resides, is employed, or transacts his or her business in person in any of the following counties: Suffolk, Bristol, Essex, Middlesex, Norfolk and Plymouth.

(b) Springfield shall be deemed a convenient place for the taking of a deposition of any person who resides, is employed, or transacts his or her business in person in any of the following counties: Berkshire, Franklin, Hampden and Hampshire.

(c) Depositions of parties residing within the counties of Worcester, Barnstable, Dukes or Nantucket shall be held within their respective counties.

[Effective August 1, 1997.]

RULE 7033-1. INTERROGATORIES

(a) Number of Interrogatories. A party may proffer no more than twenty-five (25) interrogatories to another party without leave of Court.

(b) Form of Response.

(1) Answers and objections in response to interrogatories served pursuant to Fed. R. Bankr. P. 7033 shall be made in the order of the interrogatories.

(2) Each answer, statement, or objection shall be preceded by the interrogatory to which it responds.

(3) Each objection and the grounds for the objection shall be stated separately.

(c) Provisions of MLBR 9013-1 Applicable to Objections. The provisions of MLBR 9013-1(e) shall be applicable to any motions relating to objections to interrogatories.

(d) Answers to Interrogatories Accompanying or Following Objection.

(1) When there is an objection to part of an interrogatory which is separable from the remainder, the part to which there is no objection shall be answered.

(2) Answers to interrogatories with respect to which objections were served and which are subsequently required to be answered shall be served within fourteen (14) days after entry of an order determining that they should be answered, unless the Court directs otherwise.

(e) Supplemental Answers to Certain Interrogatories. If a party has served an answer to an interrogatory which directly requests information concerning the identity and location of persons having knowledge of relevant facts, and the party later learns that the answer is substantially incomplete, that party shall file a supplemental answer or objection within seven (7) days after learning that the answer is substantially incomplete.

[Effective August 1, 1997. Amended effective December 1, 2009.]

RULE 7036-1. REQUESTS FOR ADMISSION

(a) Form of Response.

(1) Answers and objections in response to requests for admission served pursuant to Fed. R. Bankr. P. 7036 shall be made in the order of the requests for admission.

(2) Each answer, statement, or objection shall be preceded by the request for admission to which it responds.

(3) Each objection and the grounds for the objection shall be stated separately.

(b) Provisions of MLBR 9013-1 Applicable to Objections. The provisions of MLBR 9013-1(e) shall be applicable to any motions relating to objections to requests for admission.

(c) Statements in Response to Requests for Admission After Objection. When there is an objection to a request for admission and it is subsequently determined that the request is proper, the matter for which admission is requested shall be deemed admitted unless within fourteen (14) days after entry of an order making such determination, or such other period as the Court directs, the party to whom the request was directed serves a statement denying the matter or setting forth the reasons why the matter cannot be admitted or denied, as provided in Fed. R. Bankr. P. 7036.

[Effective August 1, 1997. Amended effective December 1, 2009.]

RULE 7037-1. FAILURE TO MAKE DISCOVERY; SANCTIONS

(a) Fed. R. Civ. P. 37 applies in adversary proceedings and contested matters, except that any reference to Fed. R. Civ. P. 26 (a) shall be deleted and substituted with a reference to MLBR 7026-1(b).

(b) Prior to the filing of any motion relating to a discovery dispute, including a motion to compel discovery, a motion for a protective order, or a motion for sanctions, counsel for the parties or any pro se party shall confer by telephone or in person in a good faith effort to resolve the discovery dispute and to eliminate as many areas of the dispute as possible without the necessity of filing a motion. It shall be the responsibility of the party seeking the discovery order to arrange for the conference. Unless relieved by order of the Court, the conference shall take place within fourteen (14) days of the service of a letter requesting the conference. Failure of any party to respond to a request for a discovery conference within seven (7) days of a request for the conference shall be grounds for sanctions, which may include substantive and/or monetary sanctions. Any motion relating to discovery must be accompanied by a statement signed under the penalty of perjury that the movant has complied with the provisions of this section.

(c) If the parties are unable to resolve a discovery dispute and a discovery motion is filed, the parties shall file a joint stipulation specifying separately and with particularity (1) the date of the discovery conference and, if it was not held, the reason why; (2) the matters on which the parties reached agreement; (3) each contested discovery issue that remains to be determined by the Court; and (4) a statement of each party's position as to each contested issue, with supporting legal authority. The stipulation shall be filed within seven (7) days after the discovery motion. Notwithstanding the foregoing, if the only discovery dispute constitutes a failure of a party to serve any response, the discovery motion shall so state, and the joint stipulation need not be filed. The failure of any party or attorney to cooperate in resolving discovery disputes may result in the imposition of sanctions, including but not limited to, the sanctions provided in Fed. R. Civ. P. 37.

[Effective August 1, 1997; Amended effective January 1, 2005; December 1, 2009.]

RULE 7052–1. JUDGMENTS—PREPARATION AND ENTRY

Subject to the provisions of Fed.R.Bankr.P. 7054, upon a general verdict of a jury or upon a decision by the Court that a party shall recover only money or costs or that all relief shall be denied, the Clerk, unless the Court orders otherwise, shall forthwith prepare, sign and enter the judgment without further order of the Court; provided, however, that upon either a decision by the Court granting other relief or upon a special or general verdict accompanied by answers to interrogatories, the Court shall enter the judgment. The judgment shall be set forth on a separate document, in accordance with Fed.R.Civ.P. 58, and shall be effective only upon its entry on the docket, pursuant to Fed.R.Civ.P. 79(a). Entry of the judgment shall not be delayed for the taxing of costs.

[Effective August 1, 1997.]

RULE 7055–1. JUDGMENT BY DEFAULT

Judgment by default may be signed and entered by the Clerk in such circumstances as are specified in Fed.R.Civ.P. 55(b)(1) when accompanied by an affidavit that the person against whom judgment is sought

is not an infant, an incompetent person, or serving in the armed forces within the meaning of the Servicemembers Civil Relief Act, 50 App. U.S.C.A. § 521. Upon application of any party, the Clerk shall make and file a certificate of default as to any party in default for the convenience of the Court or of the party applying for the default judgment. When application is made to the Court under Fed.R.Civ.P. 55(b)(2), made applicable through Fed.R.Bankr.P. 7055, for a default judgment, unless the Court orders otherwise, the Clerk shall schedule a hearing and notify counsel of the hearing date. If the party against whom judgment by default is sought has appeared in the action or proceeding, the party seeking the default judgment and the Clerk shall give notice of the hearing as required by Fed.R.Civ.P. 55(b)(2). With leave of the Court, proof may be submitted by affidavit, and the Court may order such further hearing as it deems necessary.

[Effective August 1, 1997.]

RULE 7055–2. DISMISSAL FOR WANT OF PROSECUTION

(a) Dismissal of Proceedings Inactive for Six Months.

(1) The Clerk shall mail notice to all persons who have entered an appearance in any adversary proceeding in which no action was taken by any party during the preceding six months that, subject to the provisions of subsection (3) of this section, the adversary proceeding will be dismissed thirty (30) days after the date of the notice.

(2) After the thirtieth day following the sending of the notice, the Clerk shall, subject to the provisions of subsection (3), enter an order of dismissal without prejudice and serve the order upon the parties.

(3) An adversary proceeding shall not be dismissed by the Clerk for want of prosecution if, within thirty (30) days of the sending of notice:

(A) there are further proceedings in the adversary proceeding; or

(B) a response is filed in opposition to the proposed dismissal.

(b) Effect of Dismissal. The dismissal of an adversary proceeding pursuant to this rule shall be without prejudice and without costs unless the Court on motion of a party directs otherwise.

[Effective August 1, 1997.]

RULE 7056–1. SUMMARY JUDGMENT

District Court Local Rule 56.1[1] is adopted and made applicable to proceedings in the Bankruptcy Court.

[Effective August 1, 1997.]

[1] LR. 56.1 MOTIONS FOR SUMMARY JUDGMENT*

Motions for summary judgment shall include a concise statement of the material facts of record as to which the moving party contends there is no genuine issue to be tried, with page references to affidavits, depositions and other documentation. Failure to include such a statement constitutes grounds for denial of the motion. Opposition to motions for summary judgment shall include a concise statement of the material facts of record as to which it is contended that there exists a genuine issue to be tried, with page references to affidavits, depositions and other documentation. Copies of all referenced documentation shall be filed as exhibits to the motion or opposition. Material facts of record set forth in the statement required to be served by the moving party will be deemed for purposes of the motion to be admitted by opposing parties unless controverted by the statement required to be served by opposing parties.

Effective September 1, 1990.

* [**Publisher's Note:** For the most current version of the LR 56.1, *see* the local rules of the U.S. District Court, *ante.*]

RULE 7067–1. REGISTRY FUNDS

The provisions of U.S. District Court Local Rules 67.2, 67.3, and 67.4 shall be applicable to proceedings in the United States Bankruptcy Court for the District of Massachusetts. References in specific United States District Court Local Rules to the "Clerk, United States District Court" or the "United States District Court" shall be replaced with "Clerk, United States Bankruptcy Court" or the "United States Bankruptcy Court," respectively.

[Effective August 1, 1997.]

RULE 9004–1. FONT SIZE

The font size of all original documents, other than the Petition, Schedules and Statement of Affairs, shall be not less than 12 point type. The font size of the Petition, Schedules and Statement of Affairs shall be not less than 10 point type.

[Effective March 1, 2003.]

RULE 9006–1. EXTENSIONS OF TIME FOR DISCHARGE COMPLAINTS AND OBJECTIONS TO EXEMPTIONS

If the Court is unable to act on any motion to extend any deadline for filing complaints relating to the debtor's discharge or for filing objections to the debtor's claim of exemptions, which motion to extend was filed before the expiration of the deadline, the deadline shall be automatically extended to the date that the Court acts on the motion.

[Effective September 1, 1999.]

RULE 9009–1. OFFICIAL LOCAL FORMS

The forms adopted by this Court as MLBR Official Local Forms and the official forms promulgated by the Judicial Conference of the United States shall be utilized in cases and proceedings filed in this Court under Title 11 of the United States Code. The MLBR Official Local Forms may be amended and supplemented from time to time.

[Effective August 1, 1997.]

RULE 9009–2. CASE MANAGEMENT

Upon motion of the estate representative or *sua sponte*, the Court may order that one or more case management procedures be employed in order to ease the administrative burden on the parties or the Court. Such procedures may relate to, *inter alia*, omnibus hearing dates, notices of agenda, and payment of interim compensation and reimbursement of expenses and other matters typical to Chapter 11 cases or cases under other Chapters with sufficient complexity. Sample case management procedures are contained in Appendix 6. A motion requesting case management orders shall highlight, in bold-faced type, those provisions which would vary from those set forth in Appendix 6.

[Effective January 1, 2005.]

RULE 9010–1. REPRESENTATION AND APPEARANCES

(a) A person who is a member in good standing of the bar of United States District Court for the District of Massachusetts may appear and practice before this Court.

(b) Except as provided in subsection (d) of this rule, an attorney who is not a member of the bar of the United States District Court for the District of Massachusetts, but is a member of the bar of any other United States District Court or the bar of the highest court of any state may appear and practice in this Court in a particular case or adversary proceeding only by leave granted in the discretion of the Court, provided such attorney files a certificate attesting that (1) the attorney is a member of the bar in good standing in every jurisdiction where the attorney has been admitted to practice; (2) there are no disciplinary proceedings pending against such attorney as a member of the bar in any jurisdiction; and (3) the attorney is familiar with the Local Rules of this Court. An attorney seeking admission under this subsection may not enter an appearance or sign any pleadings until admission is granted, except that the attorney may sign a complaint or any other pleading necessary to prevent entry of default or the passage of any deadline, provided such complaint or other pleading is accompanied by the attorney's application for admission under this subsection in proper form. An attorney seeking admission under this subsection more frequently than twice in any 12 month period shall additionally certify (1) the attorney's efforts to seek admission to the bar of the United States District Court for the District of Massachusetts; or (2) why such efforts have not been undertaken.

(c) A corporation, partnership or trust, by and through an officer or agent, or a person authorized by a power of attorney, may file a proof of claim or an application for payment of unclaimed monies due such entity, and may be heard on objections to claims or applications for payment. Otherwise, such entities shall appear only through counsel.

(d) An attorney need not obtain leave to appear and practice in a particular case merely to file a request for service or a proof of claim.

(e) An attorney representing, without compensation, an otherwise pro se debtor may file a notice of limited appearance setting forth the specific contested matter or adversary proceeding in which the attorney appears and may decline representation of that debtor in other matters or proceedings, but may not withdraw without leave of court from the matter or proceeding in which the attorney has chosen to appear until the final disposition thereof.

[Effective August 1, 1997. Amended effective September 1, 1999; December 1, 2009.]

[**Publisher's Note:** See Standing Order 09–01, *post.*]

RULE 9010–3. NOTICE OF APPEARANCE

(a) The filing of any pleading or other document by an attorney shall constitute an appearance in the case or proceeding in which the pleading or document is filed by the attorney who signs it, unless the pleading or document states otherwise.

(b) An appearance in a case or proceeding by a member of the bar of the United States District Court for the District of Massachusetts may be made by filing a notice of appearance which shall contain the name, address, telephone number and any registration number assigned by the Board of Bar Overseers of the Commonwealth of Massachusetts (the "BBO number") of the attorney entering the appearance. If the Court has authorized the attorney to appear pro hac vice with respect to a particular matter pursuant to MLBR 9010–1(b), the Clerk shall assign a Bankruptcy Court registration number (the "PHV number") to the attorney which number must be set forth by the attorney in any pleadings filed in this Court in connection with the matter.

(c) If an attorney wishes to receive copies of all notices and pleadings, the attorney must file an appearance with a specific request to be so served and must serve a copy of such request on the trustee and counsel for the trustee or debtor in possession and counsel for the debtor; otherwise, the attorney will receive only those notices, pleadings and orders that affect his or her client as required by the Federal Rules of Bankruptcy Procedure.

(d) An attorney representing a debtor in a bankruptcy case is required to represent the debtor in any adversary proceeding filed within the bankruptcy case in which the debtor is a named defendant unless the debtor expressly agrees otherwise in writing at the commencement of the representation.

(e) The Clerk shall maintain a general appearance list within each case and make it available to any attorney or party upon request. The Clerk shall also maintain a general appearance list on the PACER system.

[Effective August 1, 1997. Amended effective September 1, 1999.]

[**Publisher's Note:** See Standing Order 09–01, *post.*]

RULE 9011–1. SIGNING OF PAPERS

Any pleading filed with the Court shall set forth the name, address, telephone number, and BBO or PHV number, *see* MLBR 9010–3, of the attorney signing the pleading.

[Effective September 1, 1999.]

RULE 9013–1. MOTIONS

(a) A request for an order shall be made by motion. Unless it is made during the course of a hearing or trial, the motion must be in writing, setting forth each allegation in a numbered paragraph, and must be filed with the Clerk. Any request that is made by letter need not be considered by the Court.

(b) Before the filing of any motion, except a motion for an emergency hearing under MLBR 9013–1(h) or a routine motion unlikely to be opposed by any party in interest, the movant shall make a reasonable and good faith effort to determine whether or not the motion is unopposed.

(c) The movant may file together with the motion a separate supporting memorandum, including argument and citations to authorities. If the motion is based upon affidavits and documents evidencing facts on which the motion is based, the affidavits and documents must be filed with the motion, unless they are unavailable at the time that the motion is filed. Letters from counsel or parties will not be accepted as memoranda in support of a motion and may be disregarded by the Court.

(d) The Court, in its discretion, may schedule a motion for hearing or establish a deadline for filing objections or responses to a motion. Any party opposing entry of the order requested by a motion must file a response to the motion no later than the response date set in the hearing notice, or if no response date is set in the hearing notice, within fourteen (14) days of service of the motion, inclusive of the three (3) day mailing period set forth in Fed. R. Bankr. P. 9006(f). The Clerk shall set all hearing dates and response deadlines. The Clerk shall notify the movant of the hearing date and/or response deadline and the manner of service. Unless otherwise specified in the Court's notice of hearing, the initial hearing on any motion shall be a preliminary, non-evidentiary hearing; however, any notice of a hearing on a proposed sale or confirmation of a plan of reorganization shall include the following language: "The Court may take evidence at any sale or plan confirmation hearing to resolve issues of fact."

(e) The Court may act upon a motion without a hearing under appropriate circumstances, including the following:

(1) if no objection is filed to the motion (A) within fourteen (14) days of the date of service of the motion, or (B) after any specific objection deadline established by the Court, whichever is later, or

(2) prior to the expiration of any applicable objection period, if the motion is:

(A) a non-adversarial motion of a routine nature;

(B) a motion to which all affected parties in interest have consented;

(C) a motion that is without merit in light of the law and the established facts of the case; and

(D) a motion that is opposed only by objections which are, given the law and the established facts of the case, without merit.

(f) The Court, in its discretion, may remove from the hearing list any motion that has been scheduled for hearing if no timely written response or objection has been filed. The Court may consider and act upon such matters without a hearing and may enter the proposed order submitted with the motion, request from the movant a modified order indicating the lack of timely opposition and the fact that no hearing was held, or enter an appropriate order of its own.

(g) Emergency or Expedited Determination.

(1) *Single Motion for Both Relief and Determination.*

(A) If a movant seeks to have the Court consider a motion requesting relief earlier than three (3) days after the motion for relief is filed, the title of the motion for relief shall include also the language "Request for Emergency Determination."

(B) If a movant seeks to have the Court consider a motion requesting relief earlier than seven (7) days after the motion for relief is filed, the title of the motion for relief shall include also the language "Request for Expedited Determination."

(C) The motion for emergency or expedited determination shall include separately numbered paragraphs that set forth in detail all facts and circumstances that justify an emergency or expedited determination and may include, or be accompanied by, documents, affidavits or a memorandum that includes citations to pertinent authority. The movant

shall make a reasonable, good faith effort to advise all affected parties of the substance of the motion for relief, and the request for an emergency or expedited determination, prior to filing the motion for emergency or expedited hearing, and, upon filing the motion, movant shall file a certification attesting to the efforts so made, together with a certificate of service of the motion setting forth the manner of service. Promptly after obtaining the date and time of the hearing from the court, movant shall advise all affected parties of the date and time of the hearing and any objection deadline and shall file a certificate of service setting forth the manner of service. Such reasonable, good faith efforts may include providing notice by telephone, facsimile transmission or email in appropriate circumstances. Federal R. Bankr. P. 2002 and MLBR 2002–1 govern who is an "affected party." Notice, at a minimum, shall be provided to the debtor, the debtor's counsel, any trustee, the trustee's counsel, the United States trustee, any directly affected creditor, and any party that has entered an appearance or has requested notices.

(2) *Limitation of Notice.* If the facts and circumstances leading to the request for an emergency or expedited determination or the nature of the relief requested justify limitation of notice, (a) the title of the motion for relief shall include also the language "Request for Limitation of Notice"; and (b) the motion shall include separately numbered paragraphs that set forth in detail all facts and circumstances that justify limitation of notice, that designate the recipients to whom the notice should be limited, and that recommend a practical manner of notice reasonably calculated to inform affected parties of the pending motion. The movant shall make reasonable, good faith efforts to advise all affected parties of the request for limitation of notice. Such reasonable, good faith efforts may include providing notice by telephone or by fax in appropriate circumstances.

(3) *Responses.*

(A) Notwithstanding any other provisions of these rules, written responses to a motion for emergency determination are not required. However, written responses are encouraged and may be filed up to the time that the hearing is convened.

(B) Written responses to a motion for expedited determination shall be filed within the time established by the Court. The content of responses to a motion for expedited determination, to the extent possible under the existing circumstances, shall include the information required for responses to non-expedited motions. If no response time is established by the Court, responses to a motion for expedited determination shall be filed no later than three (3) days preceding the day of the hearing.

(h) Ex Parte Motions. A motion seeking ex parte relief may be filed only in circumstances in which immediate action is required to maintain the status quo until an appropriate hearing on notice can be conducted. A motion for ex parte relief shall be verified or supported by affidavit and shall set forth specific facts and circumstances necessitating ex parte relief. The motion shall include a statement as to why proceeding under this rule's procedures for expedited or emergency hearing is not practical. All orders or proposed orders providing ex parte relief shall include the finding that the relief requested could not be delayed and that affected parties may request a hearing on the subject matter addressed by the ex parte motion by filing a motion for review of the ex parte action within fourteen (14) days of service of the order for ex parte relief. The Court shall schedule a hearing on such a post-order motion, if appropriate, as soon as is practicable.

(i) Oppositions. In any opposition to a motion, the opposing party shall admit or deny each allegation of the motion, state any affirmative defense to the motion, and state specifically why the relief requested in the motion should not be granted.

[Effective August 1, 1997. Amended effective September 1, 1999; May 1, 2008; December 1, 2009.]

RULE 9013-3. SERVICE OF PLEADINGS AND NOTICES

(a) Motions and Other Documents. Upon filing a motion requesting action by the Court, with the exception of an adversary complaint, counsel (or a pro se party) shall immediately serve the motion upon all interested parties and upon all parties who have filed their appearances and requested service of all pleadings filed in the case. A certificate of service shall be filed with the motion and served in the same manner and on the same parties as the motion, unless otherwise directed by the Court.

(b) Notice of Hearing. Upon receipt of a notice of hearing from the Court, counsel (or a pro se party) shall immediately serve the notice upon all interested parties and parties who have filed their appearances and requested service of all notices in the case. A certificate of service shall be filed with the Clerk at the same time as service of the notice of hearing and shall be served in the same manner and on the same parties as the notice of hearing, unless otherwise directed by the Court.

(c) Statement on Scope of Service. A certificate of service shall list the name and address of each person and attorney being served with the pleading and the name of the party or parties that an attorney represents. If service is required to be made upon all creditors pursuant to Fed.R.Bankr.P. 2002, the certificate of service shall specifically state whether all creditors have been served and shall list the names and addresses of the parties served.

(d) Sanctions. Failure to comply with the provisions of this rule may result in the imposition of monetary sanctions, non-monetary sanctions, or denial of the relief sought as the Court, in its discretion, deems proper.

[Effective August 1, 1997. Amended effective September 1, 1999.]

RULE 9015-1. JURY TRIALS

(a) In any bankruptcy case or proceeding, issues triable by jury shall be tried by a jury if a party timely demands a jury trial in accordance with the provisions of this rule. Nothing in this rule shall be deemed to (1) create or imply a right to jury trial where no such right exists under applicable law or (2) violate a party's right of trial by jury as set forth in the Seventh Amendment to the Constitution or in any statute of the United States. On motion or on its own initiative, the Court may determine whether there is a right to trial by jury in any adversary proceeding or contested matter or whether a jury demand should be granted or stricken.

(b) Any party may demand a jury trial of any issue triable by jury by filing with the Court and serving upon the other parties a written demand for jury trial no later than the deadline for filing the answer or the reply to a counterclaim or cross claim in an adversary proceeding, or in a contested matter no later than the deadline for filing the initial responsive pleading or opposition. A jury demand may be made in any pleading and need not be made in a separate pleading. The failure of a party to file and serve a demand constitutes a waiver of the right to trial by jury. A demand for a jury trial may not be withdrawn without the consent of all parties.

(c) The bankruptcy judge may conduct a jury trial pursuant to 28 U.S.C. § 157(e) if the right to a jury trial applies and a timely demand has been made, provided that the parties file a pleading entitled "Joint Statement of Consent to Jury Trial in the Bankruptcy Court" no later than the date established by the Court for the filing of the Joint Pretrial Memorandum pursuant to MLBR 7016-1 or such other time as the Court may fix. If the parties do not file the Joint Statement of Consent to Jury Trial in the Bankruptcy Court, the Bankruptcy Court shall conduct all pretrial proceedings and thereafter transfer the case or proceeding to the appropriate United States District Court for trial.

[Effective August 1, 1997. Amended effective September 1, 1999.]

RULE 9018–1. IMPOUNDMENT OF PAPERS

(a) For good and sufficient cause the court may order that some or all of the papers in the case be impounded by the Clerk. Such impounded papers shall be maintained under Clerk custody separate and apart from files to which the public has access; no computer or other images thereof shall be made for public viewing.

(b) A request for impoundment shall be made by motion. The papers sought to be impounded shall be placed in a sealed envelope or container conspicuously marked "filed subject to pending impoundment motion," and shall be filed simultaneously with the motion. The motion shall contain (i) a statement under oath setting forth the grounds for impoundment, (ii) a statement of the earliest date on which the impounding order may be lifted, or a statement, supported by good cause, that the material should be impounded until further order of the court, and (iii) suggested custody arrangements for the post-impoundment period, if any.

(c) The court shall review the papers sought to be impounded in camera. If the motion for impoundment is denied, the papers shall be returned to the party requesting impoundment and, if refiled, shall be filed with other pleadings in the case to which public access is allowed. If the motion for impoundment is granted, the order of impoundment shall be filed with the pleadings in the case. The impounded papers shall be transferred to the custody of the clerk for special storage. The clerk shall attach a copy of the order of impoundment to the envelope or other container holding the impounded material. Thereafter, access to the impounded papers shall be limited to the court, the clerk, the party for whose benefit the impoundment order was granted, and any party who, upon motion, notice to the party for whose benefit the impoundment order was granted and an opportunity to be heard, receives relief from the impoundment order in whole or in part.

(d) If the impoundment order expires by its terms but provides no arrangements for post-impoundment custody of the impounded papers, or if the impoundment order provides for post-impoundment custody of the impounded papers, but the impounded papers are not timely retrieved, the clerk shall provide notice of no less than forty-five (45) days to the party for whose benefit the impoundment order was granted, or his, her or its attorney, that the said papers shall, in the absence of timely objection made prior to the expiration of the notice period, be destroyed.

(e) For good cause shown by affidavit attesting to a risk of irreparable harm if advance notice is given to any other party, the motion for impoundment may be heard ex-parte.

(f) The Court may, sua sponte, for good and sufficient cause, impound any document pursuant to this Rule or order that the document not be released for on-line viewing.

[Effective January 1, 2002. Amended effective May 1, 2008; December 1, 2009.]

RULE 9019–1. STIPULATIONS; SETTLEMENTS

(a) All stipulations affecting a case or proceeding before the Court, except stipulations which are made in open court, shall be in writing, signed, and filed with the Court. No stipulation shall have the effect of relieving the parties from a prior order of the Court, including a scheduling order, unless such stipulation is approved by the Court in writing.

(b) When a proceeding or matter is settled, the parties shall, within seven (7) days or such other time as the Court may direct, file a signed stipulation or agreement for judgment or such other document as the Court may direct.

(c) A settlement of any controversy that affects the estate, except the settlement of complaints pursuant to 11 U.S.C. § 523, shall be accompanied by a motion to approve the stipulation pursuant to Fed.R.Bankr.P. 9019 and, unless otherwise ordered by the Court, the stipulation and motion to approve the stipulation shall be served on all creditors and interested parties in accordance with Fed.R.Bankr.P. 2002. The settlement of a complaint under 11 U.S.C. § 523 may be documented by the filing of a stipulation of dismissal or an agreement for judgment in the adversary proceeding. A stipulation with respect to a motion for relief from stay shall be accompanied by a motion and shall be served in accordance with Fed.R.Bankr.P. 4001(d).

[Effective August 1, 1997.]

RULE 9022–1. NOTICE OF ENTRY OF ORDERS AND JUDGMENTS

The Clerk's mailing to either attorneys of record or pro se parties of copies of orders or judgments showing the date such orders or judgments were entered shall constitute notice of entry pursuant to the provisions of Fed.R.Civ.P. 77(d). The Clerk shall indicate the date of such mailing on the Court docket.

[Effective August 1, 1997.]

RULE 9027–1. REMOVAL

Upon motion, the Court, in its discretion, may permit the filing of a certified docket and photocopies of all records and proceedings in a state or federal court, upon the representation of counsel for the party removing the action that the pleadings are true and accurate copies of the pleadings on file with the state or federal court.

[Effective August 1, 1997.]

RULE 9029–1. APPLICATION

(a) These rules shall govern all cases and civil proceedings arising under Title 11 or related to cases under Title 11 that are referred to or otherwise being heard by the bankruptcy judges in this district. All prior local rules are hereby repealed.

(b) To the extent that a conflict appears or arises between these rules and the Federal Rules of Bankruptcy Procedure promulgated by the Supreme Court of the United States, the latter shall govern.

(c) The Appendices annexed hereto may be amended, from time to time, by joint order of the bankruptcy judges. Nothing in these rules shall prohibit the issuance by one or more individual bankruptcy judges of standing orders relative to the conduct of cases and proceedings before them. A copy of any standing order shall be annexed to these rules by the Clerk.

[Effective August 1, 1997.]

RULE 9029–3. APPLICABILITY OF U.S. DISTRICT COURT LOCAL RULES

The following U.S. District Court Local Rules shall be applicable in the United States Bankruptcy Court for the District of Massachusetts:

26.5 (Uniform Definitions in Discovery Requests)

56.1 (Motions for Summary Judgment)

67.2 (Registry Funds)

67.3 (Disbursement of Registry Funds)

67.4 (Payments and Deposits Made With the Clerk)

81.2 (Definition of Judicial Officer)

83.5.1(b) (Student Practice Rule) (insofar as applicable to civil proceedings)

83.6 (Rules of Disciplinary Enforcement)

201 (Reference to Bankruptcy Court)

202 (Bankruptcy Court Jury Trials)

203 (Bankruptcy Appeals)

204 (Bankruptcy Court Local Rules)

205 (Disciplinary Referrals by Bankruptcy Judges)

The other Local Rules of the United States District Court shall not govern cases or proceedings before the United States Bankruptcy Court.

[Effective August 1, 1997. Amended effective September 1, 1999; January 1, 2005.]

RULE 9036–1. ELECTRONIC FILING RULES

All cases open as of the effective date of these rules or filed thereafter will be administered through the Electronic Case Filing System (the "ECF System"). The procedures for electronic filing set forth in Appendix 8 hereof, as amended from time to time, shall be known as the Electronic Filing Rules of the United States Bankruptcy Court for the District of Massachusetts, and shall be referred to in abbreviation as "MEFR." Except as expressly provided in MEFR 1, parties in interest shall file all petitions, motions, applications, memoranda of law or other pleadings, proofs of claim or documents only through the ECF System. To the extent that the MEFR conflict with any other provision of the Massachusetts Local Bankruptcy Rules or their appendices, the provisions of the MEFR shall govern.

[Effective March 1, 2003; Amended effective January 1, 2005; May 1, 2008.]

RULE 9070–1. EXHIBITS

After a trial, exhibits shall remain in the custody of the Court. If there is no appeal from the Court's decision after the time for filing a notice of appeal has elapsed, or after any appeal has been finally determined, the Clerk shall notify the parties that the exhibits should be removed from the Court within thirty (30) days and that if they are not removed within that time, the Clerk will dispose of them. If the exhibits are not removed or another arrangement made with the Clerk within thirty (30) days, the Clerk may, without further notice, destroy or otherwise dispose of them. If a notice of appeal is filed, the Clerk shall make the exhibits available to the parties for duplication for the record on appeal. After any appeal has been finally determined, the Clerk shall make any disposition of the exhibits required by the Clerk of the appellate court or as otherwise permitted under this rule.

[Effective August 1, 1997.]

RULE 9074–1. APPEARANCES BY TELEPHONE OR VIDEOCONFERENCE

Request to Appear By Telephone or Videoconference. A person may appear at a pretrial conference or non–evidentiary hearing by telephone or by videoconference, for good cause shown. The request shall be in writing and timely filed with the Clerk and will be allowed only if appropriate under the circumstances, considering, without limitation, the nature of the hearing, proximity of the person requesting such an appearance and the resulting savings in travel time and reduction of expenses of that person and/or the court.

The telephone numbers and facsimile numbers for the   [Effective January 1, 2005.]
courtroom deputies are set forth in Appendix 5.

APPENDICES
APPENDIX 1.   CHAPTER 13 RULES

13–1.   APPLICABILITY

These chapter 13 rules relate to chapter 13 cases filed in all divisions of the Court, and supersede any previous orders in conflict with these provisions. To the extent that these rules conflict with the provisions of the Massachusetts Local Bankruptcy Rules ("MLBR"), the provisions of these rules shall prevail. In all other respects, the MLBR shall apply in all chapter 13 cases.

[Effective August 1, 1997.]

13–2.   COMMENCEMENT OF CASE

(a) In addition to the requirements of MLBR 1007–1, the debtor shall:

(1) file with the Court and submit to the Chapter 13 trustee:

(A) with the petition:

(i) evidence of current and sufficient liability and property insurance (not including insurance obtained by any secured party) with respect to any real property or vehicle in which the debtor has an interest; and

(ii) an executed copy of the engagement agreement by and between the debtor and any attorney retained by the debtor in the form set forth on Official Local Form 8.

EXCEPT that if the debtor shall fail to file such documents with the petition, the Court shall issue an order notifying the debtor and the debtor's attorney that, if the missing documents are not filed within fourteen (14) days from the date of commencement of the case and the Court has not allowed a motion to extend the time for filing the missing documents, filed pursuant to subsection (b) below, the Court may dismiss the case pursuant to 11 U.S.C. §§ 109(g) or 1307 at the expiration of that period without a hearing.

(B) within three (3) days after the commencement of the case, a matrix of creditors, failing which the Court may dismiss the case pursuant to 11 U.S.C. §§ 109(g) or 1307 at the expiration of that period without a hearing.

(2) if the debtor is a debtor engaged in business, submit to the Chapter 13 trustee:

(A) within seven (7) days after the commencement of the case:

(i) evidence of current and sufficient business insurance; and

(ii) evidence that appropriate debtor-in-possession checking accounts were opened at the time of the filing of the petition;

(B) within fourteen (14) days after the commencement of the case, a profit and loss statement for the calendar year or fiscal year, whichever is applicable, preceding the year in which the case is filed, and a profit and loss statement for the period from the end of the calendar or fiscal year to the date of the filing of the petition;

(C) within thirty (30) days of the close of each quarter, a statement of quarterly income and expenses incurred; and

(b) Any motion requesting an extension of time to file documents required under this rule shall be filed before the expiration of the filing deadline, shall set forth the specific cause for the request, the amount of additional time requested and the date the petition was filed, and shall include a certificate of service evidencing that the motion was served on the chapter 13 trustee.

(c) Any motion to amend a voluntary petition or statement shall be served upon all parties affected by the amendment and the chapter 13 trustee. The motion and proposed amendment shall be accompanied by a certificate of service identifying those parties served. A motion to amend to add a creditor to the debtor's schedules shall be served upon the creditor being added and the chapter 13 trustee. An amendment adding a creditor or party in interest shall be accompanied by 1) the fee prescribed by the Administrative Office of the United States Courts, if applicable, and 2) an amended matrix including the names and addresses of the added parties.

[Effective August 1, 1997. Amended effective March 1, 2003; January 1, 2005; October 1, 2006; May 1, 2008; December 1, 2009.]

13–3.   DISCLOSURE OF RELATED CASES [DELETED]

[Deleted effective October 1, 2006. (Included in rule 1007–1, incorporated by reference in Appendix 1, Rule 13-2(a))]

13–4.   CHAPTER 13 PLAN

(a) Form of Plan. A chapter 13 plan shall conform to MLBR Official Local Form 3, with such alterations as may be appropriate to suit the circumstances.

(b) Service of Plan. Concurrently with the filing of the plan, the debtor or the debtor's attorney shall cause a copy of the plan to be served by first class mail upon the chapter 13 trustee, all creditors of the debtor, all attorneys who have filed appearances and requested service of all pleadings, and other parties in interest. The debtor or his attorney shall file with the plan a certificate of service.

(c) If a debtor proposes payments to creditors over a period that exceeds three (3) years, the debtor shall set forth in the plan the reasons for such longer payment period.

[Effective August 1, 1997.]

13–5. SERVICE OF MOTIONS

All motions and requests for orders must be served on the chapter 13 trustee, the debtor, the debtor's attorney, persons who have filed appearances and requested service of all pleadings, and all creditors with the following exceptions:

(a) a motion for relief from the automatic stay shall be served on debtor, debtor's attorney, and all persons with an interest in or lien on the subject collateral;

(b) a chapter 13 trustee's motion to dismiss shall be served on the debtor and the debtor's attorney;

(c) a debtor's motion to dismiss or notice of conversion to chapter 7 or 11 when there have been no prior conversions shall be served on the chapter 13 trustee;

(d) objections to claims shall be served on the chapter 13 trustee, the claimant, and the claimant's attorney;

(e) objections to confirmation shall be served in accordance with paragraph 13–8.

[Effective August 1, 1997.]

13–6. ATTORNEYS

(a) An attorney who represents a debtor at the time a chapter 13 case is commenced or when a case under another chapter of the Bankruptcy Code is converted to chapter 13 has a continuing duty to represent the debtor in all matters, including the section 341 meeting and court hearings, until the occurrence of the earliest of the following:

(1) dismissal of the case;

(2) closing of the case; or

(3) the entry of an order allowing the attorney to withdraw from further representation of the debtor.

(b) If an attorney for a debtor is unable to contact the debtor in connection with any matter, the attorney shall file a statement informing the Court of this fact, which statement shall include the efforts the attorney has made to contact the debtor. The attorney shall serve a copy of the statement on the debtor at his or her last known address.

(c) The chapter 13 trustee or a representative of the chapter 13 trustee shall be present at any hearing held in a chapter 13 case, unless excused for cause prior to the hearing.

[Effective August 1, 1997.]

13–7. PROFESSIONAL FEES; PREPETITION RETAINERS

(a) Prepetition Retainers. The amount of any retainer received by debtor's counsel shall be included in the Statement of Attorney Compensation filed pursuant to Fed. R. Bankr. P. 2016(b).

(b) Unless otherwise ordered by the Court, if debtor's attorney's total compensation prior to confirmation of a plan is $3,500 or less, the disclosure of the compensation in the Rule 2016(b) Statement shall be sufficient notwithstanding compensation for post confirmation services in amount not exceeding $500, and the filing of an itemized application for compensation shall be excused, unless the Court orders otherwise.

(c) Application for Additional Attorney's Fees. An attorney who proposes to charge a debtor more than $3,500 in the aggregate for legal services in a chapter 13 case prior to confirmation, or $500 in the aggregate for such services after confirmation, shall file an application for compensation in accordance with Fed. R. Bankr. P. 2016 and MLBR 2016–1. Unless otherwise ordered by the Court, debtor's attorney shall serve a copy of the application on all creditors, parties requesting service of all pleadings, and the Chapter 13 trustee and shall file a certificate of service to that effect with the application. If no objections are filed within twenty-one (21) days of service, the Court shall award fees in its discretion, with or without a hearing, in accordance with applicable law.

(d) Nothing in this rule shall be construed to limit the Court's discretion to review the amount of fees paid to or agreed to be paid to a debtor's attorney, and to enter appropriate orders allowing, disallowing, or reducing such attorney's fees.

[Effective August 1, 1997. Amended effective May 1, 2008; December 1, 2009.]

13–8. OBJECTIONS TO CONFIRMATION

(a) Deadline for filing. Any objection to confirmation of a chapter 13 plan shall be filed no later than the later of (i) thirty (30) days after the first date set for the section 341 meeting or (ii) thirty (30) days after service of a modified plan, unless otherwise ordered by the Court.

(b) Service of Objection. An objection to confirmation shall be filed with the Court and served on the chapter 13 trustee, the debtor, the debtor's attorney, and any other party or attorney who has filed an appearance and requested service of pleadings. The objection shall be accompanied by a certificate of service evidencing compliance with this requirement.

(c) Within seven (7) days after filing any response to an objection to confirmation, counsel to the debtor or a pro se debtor shall confer with counsel to the objecting party, either in person or by telephone conference, to make a good faith effort to resolve or narrow disputes as to the contents of an objection to confirmation. Counsel to the objecting party shall be responsible for initiating the conference by telephone, facsimile, email, first class mail, or in person. Counsel to an objecting party does not violate the automatic stay by contacting the pro se debtor in complying with the requirements of this rule. Such communication shall be for the purpose of initiating the conference only, and the conference must be held either in person or by telephone. The court will not schedule a hearing on an objection to confirmation until the objecting party files a certificate stating that the conference was held, together with the date and time of the conference, and the names of the participating parties. If the conference is not held despite timely and reasonable efforts made to initiate the conference, the objecting party must file a statement attesting to the efforts made to initiate the conference. In the event the parties do not hold the required conference, the court may order appropriate sanctions, including sustaining or overruling the objection to confirmation or awarding monetary sanctions. The requirement of a conference shall not apply in the event the court determines that expedited or emergency consideration of the objection to confirmation is warranted.

[Effective August 1, 1997. Amended effective May 1, 2008; December 1, 2009.]

13–9. SECTION 341 MEETING OF CREDITORS

(a) The Clerk shall serve on all creditors notice of the section 341(a) meeting of creditors and initial confirmation hearing date along with a proof of claim form in accordance with Fed.R.Bankr.P. 2002(a) and 2003(a).

(b) If the debtor fails to appear at the section 341 meeting, the case may be dismissed upon motion of a party in interest pursuant to 11 U.S.C. § 109(g).

(c) The debtor shall file tax returns in accordance with the provisions of 11 U.S.C. § 1308. When the tax return is filed, the debtor shall file with the Clerk and serve on the chapter 13 trustee a notice of the filing of the return, which shall disclose the amount of the tax liability or the amount of the refund.

[Effective August 1, 1997.]

13–10. AMENDMENTS TO PLAN PRIOR TO CONFIRMATION

(a) Amendments to a plan which do not adversely affect creditors may be made at or prior to the section 341(a) meeting without leave of court by a separate pleading entitled "Modification of Plan," which shall be filed with the Court and served on the chapter 13 trustee and any party or attorney who has filed an appearance and requested service of pleadings in the case. The modification shall be accompanied by a certificate of service. If no objections to the modification are filed within fourteen (14) days after service, the Court shall consider confirmation of the plan as amended.

(b) Where an amendment to a plan adversely affects creditors, the debtor shall file with the Court an amended plan and a motion to approve the amended plan. The debtor shall serve a copy of the amended plan and motion to approve the amended plan on the chapter 13 trustee, all creditors, and all parties and attorneys who filed appearances and request for service of all pleadings in the case. The motion shall be accompanied by a certificate of service. If no objections to the motion to approve the amended plan or the amended plan are filed within thirty (30) days of the filing of the certificate of service, the Court may allow the motion without a hearing.

[Effective August 1, 1997. Amended effective December 1, 2009.]

13–11. CONFIRMATION

(a) Where no objection to confirmation of a chapter 13 plan is filed within the time limits established by paragraph 13–8(a) of this order, the Court may enter an order confirming the plan without a hearing.

(b) Where a timely objection to a chapter 13 plan is filed, the Court shall hold a hearing on the objection. The Clerk shall schedule a confirmation hearing and advise the objecting party and/or its counsel of the hearing date. The objecting party shall provide notice of the confirmation hearing to the debtor, debtor's counsel, all creditors, interested parties, and all parties who filed appearances and requested service of all pleadings, and shall file a certificate of service regarding the notice of the hearing.

(c) The chapter 13 trustee shall submit a proposed order of confirmation to the Court in conformity with MLBR Official Local Form 4 within twenty-one (21) days after the later of 1) the Court's order overruling any objection to confirmation; 2) the withdrawal of an objection to confirmation; or 3) in the event that there are no objections to confirmation, the deadline for filing objections to confirmation. The chapter 13 trustee shall attach a copy of the plan to the proposed order of confirmation. The chapter 13 trustee shall serve a copy of the proposed order of confirmation on the debtor's attorney, the debtor, and all parties and attorneys who have filed appearances and requests for service of pleadings in the case.

[Effective August 1, 1997. Amended effective December 1, 2009.]

13–12. AMENDMENTS TO PLAN AFTER CONFIRMATION

(a) A debtor who seeks to amend a chapter 13 plan after confirmation shall do so by filing a motion to amend the plan with a copy of the proposed amended plan attached. The motion to amend shall include a summary and statement of the reason for the amendment. In conjunction with the motion to amend, the debtor shall file updated schedules I and J if plan payments are changing under the terms of the amended plan. The chapter 13 trustee, in his or her discretion, may schedule a new section 341 meeting with respect to the amended plan.

(b) The debtor shall serve a copy of the motion, amended plan, updated schedules I and J, and the amended statement on the chapter 13 trustee, all creditors, and parties and attorneys who have filed appearances and requests for service of pleadings in the case. In the event that the debtor proposes more than one amended plan, each amended plan shall be titled "First Amended Plan," "Second Amended Plan," and so on as may be appropriate.

(c) The Court shall not consider any amendments to a plan unless they are set forth in an amended plan that conforms to MLBR Official Local Form 3B.

(d) Approval of an amended plan after confirmation of a prior plan may be granted without a hearing if no objections are timely filed. Objections to an Amended Plan shall be filed no later than thirty (30) days from the date of service of the motion to amend. In the event that no objections to the motion are timely filed, the Court may, in its discretion, allow the motion to amend without a hearing. If a party in interest files a timely objection to the motion, the Court shall set the motion and objection for hearing. The objecting party shall serve a notice of hearing on the debtor, debtor's counsel, all creditors, the chapter 13 trustee, and all parties who filed appearances and requested service of pleadings at least seven (7) days before the hearing date, and shall file a certificate of service.

(e) The trustee shall submit a proposed order confirming an amended plan in conformity with MLBR Official Local Form 4 within twenty-one (21) days after the Court allows the motion to amend the plan. The chapter 13 trustee shall attach a copy of the amended plan to the proposed order of confirmation. The chapter 13 trustee shall serve a copy of the proposed order confirming an amended plan on the debtor, debtor's attorney, and all parties and attor-

neys who have filed appearances and requests for service of pleadings in the case.

[Effective August 1, 1997. Amended effective December 1, 2009.]

13–13. PROOFS OF CLAIM AND OBJECTIONS

(a) All creditors must timely file a proof of claim that conforms with Official Form 10 to participate in distributions under the plan. If the claim relates to a mortgage or security agreement, the creditor shall attach a copy of the original note and mortgage or security agreement to the proof of claim. If the claimant is not the original holder of the note and mortgage or security agreement, in addition to attaching copies of the original note, mortgage or security agreement to the proof of claim, the creditor shall attach copies of any and all assignments or other appropriate documentation sufficient to trace the chain of ownership of the mortgage or security agreement and to establish its standing to assert the claim.

(b) A creditor whose proof of claim relates to a mortgage or security agreement shall set forth a detailed itemization of all amounts asserted to be due. The itemization shall set forth the principal, interest, costs, and all expenses charged under the agreement or statute under which the claim arose, including but not limited to expenses of any notices, foreclosure sales, advertisements and/or appraisals. The itemization also shall include a statement of attorneys' fees charged as an accounting of the amount of the prepetition arrearage. The Court, in its discretion, may order a claimant or a claimant's attorney to file an application for compensation and reimbursement of expenses in accordance with MLBR 2016–1 or an accounting of the amount of any prepetition arrearage.

(c) The provisions of MLBR 3007–1 shall apply to chapter 13 cases.

(d) Within seven (7) days after filing a response to an objection to a proof of claim, the objecting party (whether the trustee, counsel to the debtor, or a pro se debtor) shall confer with counsel to the claimant, either in person or by telephone conference to make a good faith effort to resolve or narrow disputes as to the contents of the objection to claim. Counsel to the objecting party, the Chapter 13 trustee or the pro se debtor shall be responsible for initiating the conference by telephone, facsimile, email, first class mail, or in person. Such communications shall be for the purposes of initiating the conference only, and the conference must be held either in person or by telephone. The court shall not schedule a hearing on an objection to claim unless counsel to the objecting party or a pro se debtor files a certificate stating that the conference was held, together with the date and time of the conference, and the names of the participating parties. If the conference is not held despite timely efforts to initiate the conference, the party initiating the conference must file a statement attesting to the efforts made to initiate the conference. In the event the parties do not hold the required conference, the court may order appropriate sanctions, including sustaining or overruling the objection to claim or awarding monetary sanctions. The requirement of a conference shall not apply in the event the court determines that expedited or emergency consideration of the objection to claim is warranted.

(e) Objections to claims shall be served and filed with the Court within thirty (30) days after the deadline for filing proofs of claim or within such additional time as the Court may allow upon the filing of a motion to extend time and for good cause shown. Any claim to which a timely objection is not filed shall be deemed allowed and paid by the chapter 13 trustee in accordance with the provisions of the confirmed plan. The Court, in its discretion, may overrule an untimely objection to a proof of claim.

(f) If the Court has determined the allowed amount of a secured or unsecured claim in the context of a valuation hearing pursuant to 11 U.S.C. § 506, the debtor or trustee need not file an objection to a secured creditor's proof of claim that varies from the Court's determination, and the chapter 13 trustee shall make distribution in accordance with the Court's order.

[Effective August 1, 1997. Amended effective December 1, 2009; February 2, 2010; October 26, 2011.]

13–14. SALE OF ESTATE PROPERTY

(a) Any sale of the property of the estate outside the ordinary course of business, including but not limited to, the debtor's principal residence, real property, or other property must be approved by the Court after notice and a hearing. A motion for such approval shall be made in accordance with 11 U.S.C. § 363, Fed. R. Bankr. P. 4001 or 6004, and MLBR 6004–1, as applicable, and the notice of sale shall conform to MLBR Official Local Form 2A. The motion to sell shall include a proposed distribution of the proceeds of the sale. All motions to sell shall be served on the chapter 13 trustee, all creditors, all parties who have filed appearances and any other entity as the Court may direct.

(b) If an appraiser or real estate broker is involved in the sale, the debtor must obtain Court authority to employ the appraiser or broker by way of motion. The motion must be accompanied by an affidavit of disinterestedness signed by the broker and comply with the requirements of MLBR 2014(a)–1 and 6005–1.

(c) Within forty-five (45) days after the entry of an order approving a private sale of real estate which is property of the estate, the chapter 13 debtor's attorney or the debtor (if the debtor is unrepresented), shall file with the court a "Status Report Regarding Sale of Estate Property" (the "Report"). The Report shall contain the following information: 1) the date of the closing of the sale, or if no closing has been held as of the date of the Report, the reasons for delay in the closing of the sale; 2) a detailed itemization of the disbursements made at the closing, or in the alternative, the Report shall attach as an exhibit a copy of the executed settlement statement for the closing of the sale. The closing attorney and the debtor's attorney (or the debtor, if the debtor is unrepresented) shall ensure compliance with the terms of the order of the Court approving the sale.

[Effective August 1, 1997. Amended effective May 1, 2008.]

13–15. BORROWINGS OR REFINANCING OF ESTATE PROPERTY

The provisions and requirements of MLBR 4001–2 shall apply in chapter 13 cases. Any motion for approval of a borrowing or refinancing shall include all the material terms of the proposed credit arrangement. A copy of any borrowing agreement shall be attached to the motion.

[Effective August 1, 1997.]

13–16–1. MOTIONS FOR RELIEF FROM STAY

(a) Pre-filing Conference.

(1) At least seven (7) days prior to filing a motion for relief from stay, counsel to the movant shall confer with counsel to the debtor or with the pro se debtor, in person or by telephone, to make a good faith effort to resolve or narrow disputes as to the contents of the motion. Movant's counsel shall be responsible for initiating the conference either by telephone, facsimile, e-mail, or first class mail or in person. Such communications shall be for the purposes of initiating the conference only, and the conference must be held either in person or by telephone. A movant does not violate the automatic stay by contacting the pro se debtor(s) in complying with this Rule.

(2) If the conference is not held despite timely and reasonable good faith efforts made by movant to initiate the conference, movant's counsel shall attest to the efforts made to initiate the conference with counsel to the debtor or with the pro se debtor.

(3) All motions for relief from stay shall be accompanied by a certificate stating that

(i) the conference was held, together with the date and time of the conference and the names of the participating parties; or

(ii) the conference was not held despite the reasonable efforts made by the movant's counsel as set forth in counsel's attestation.

(4) Motions unaccompanied by a certificate may be denied without prejudice to their renewal when accompanied by the certificate.

(5) A pre-filing conference is not required if (a) the movant has obtained the debtor's assent to the motion prior to the motion being filed with the Court and the motion so indicates, or (b) the debtor has indicated an intent to surrender the real property that is the subject of the motion in the debtor's chapter 13 plan filed with the Court.

(b) Emergency or Expedited Motions. Subsection (a) shall not apply if the movant seeks determination of a motion for relief on an expedited or emergency basis, provided that the motion shall contain a statement consistent with the provisions of MLBR 9013–1.

(c) Contents of Motion. In addition to the requirements of MLBR 4001–1, and except for motions governed by Rule 13–16(d), a motion for relief from the automatic stay shall provide the following information:

(1) the date of the filing of the chapter 13 petition;

(2) the total amount owed to the moving party;

(3) the date of confirmation of the plan;

(4) the amount of the monthly payment at issue;

(5) the total amount of the post-petition or post-confirmation payments (principal and interest) in default as of the date of the filing of the motion and due as of the anticipated date of hearing, and the total amount of any other post-petition change due or anticipated as of each of these dates;

(6) the total amount of the prepetition arrearage;

(7) the identity and an estimation of the amounts due all lienholders, in order of their priority;

(8) an opinion of the value of the property (by declaration), if such value is an issue to be determined;

(9) if the motion for relief from stay is based on defaults in payments to or through the chapter 13 trustee, the motion must show that the debtor has not made the payments to the chapter 13 trustee.

The Court, in its discretion, may deny a motion for relief from stay in the absence of an objection, if the above information is not set forth in the motion.

(d) Motion for Relief from Stay—Real Estate Worksheet (the "Worksheet"). In addition to the requirements of MLBR 4001–1(a) and (b) and 13–16(a) and (b), a motion for relief from stay with respect to real property shall be accompanied by MLBR Official Form 13, entitled Motion for Relief from Stay—Real

Estate Worksheet (the "Worksheet"). The Court in its discretion may deny a motion for relief from stay pertaining to real estate notwithstanding the absence of an opposition, if the Worksheet and the documents required to be attached to it do not accompany the motion for relief from stay. A motion for relief from the automatic stay need not be accompanied by a Worksheet if (a) the movant has obtained the debtor's assent to the motion prior to the motion being filed with the Court and the motion so indicates, or (b) the debtor has indicated an intent to surrender the real property that is the subject of the motion in the debtor's chapter 13 plan filed with the Court.

(e) Debtor's Schedule of Payments in Dispute. In addition to the requirements of MLBR 4001–1(c), if a debtor opposes a motion for relief from stay in which the movant seeks to foreclose a mortgage for post-petition defaults, the debtor shall file MLBR Official Form 14, entitled Debtor(s)' Schedule of Payments in Dispute (the "Schedule"). The Court in its discretion may overrule an opposition to a motion for relief from stay in the absence of a timely filed Schedule.

(f) Consolidation of Motion for Relief from Stay with Objection to Claim. If the motion for relief from stay and opposition raise issues in addition to, or other than, the debtor's postpetition payment history, the parties may request, or the court may order, at either the preliminary, nonevidentiary hearing or at the final evidentiary hearing, that the motion for relief from stay be consolidated with any objection filed by the debtor or the trustee to the movant's proof of claim.

(g) Request for Final Evidentiary Hearing. If the parties determine that the motion for relief from stay cannot be resolved and an evidentiary hearing is required, the parties may file a joint request for a final evidentiary hearing in lieu of a preliminary nonevidentiary hearing. The court in its discretion may cancel the preliminary nonevidentiary hearing and extend the automatic stay until the final evidentiary hearing. The final evidentiary hearing shall be scheduled no later than sixty (60) days after the filing of the motion, unless the parties in interest consent to an extension of the periods set forth in 11 U.S.C. § 362(e). In the joint request for a final evidentiary hearing, the movant shall indicate whether or not it waives the time periods for determination of the motion for relief from stay pursuant to § 362(e).

[Effective December 1. 2009.]

13–16–2. STIPULATIONS RELATING TO MOTIONS FOR RELIEF FROM STAY

(a) Service of Stipulation. A stipulation resolving a motion for relief from stay shall be served, together with a motion to approve the stipulation, on the chapter 13 trustee, any other entity with an interest in the property, including any lienholder or co-owner, and an attorney who has filed an appearance requesting service in the case. The party filing the motion to approve the stipulation shall file a certificate of service reflecting compliance with this rule.

(b) Objections to Stipulations. Unless otherwise ordered by the Court, an objection to a stipulation resolving a motion for relief from stay shall be filed within fourteen (14) days from the date of service of the stipulation. Notwithstanding this requirement, the Court, in its discretion, may cancel a hearing scheduled on a motion for relief from stay which is the subject of a stipulation and may approve a stipulation resolving a motion for relief from stay without a hearing.

(c) Defaults under Stipulations. Any provision of a stipulation or agreement filed with the Court through which the debtor stipulates or agrees to dismissal of the Chapter 13 case or the entry of an order granting relief from the automatic stay under 11 U.S.C. § 362(a) upon the failure of the debtor to make payments beyond those necessary to cure a prior postpetition default, shall be deemed void and unenforceable, unless such language in the proposed stipulation or agreement is conspicuously set forth in capital letters and bold type.

(d) If after a prefiling conference, the parties enter into a stipulation without the need for the filing of a motion for relief from stay and the debtor subsequently defaults under the terms of the stipulation, the party filing the motion to approve stipulation must file a motion for relief from the stay, together with an affidavit of noncompliance with the stipulation and a certificate of service attesting to service on the parties as set forth in subsection (a) of this rule, to obtain an order from the court granting relief from the automatic stay.

[Effective December 1. 2009.]

13–17. MOTIONS TO DISMISS AND CONVERT

(a) A party who files a motion to dismiss or convert a chapter 13 case shall serve the motion on the debtor, debtor's attorney, all creditors, any applicable child support enforcement agency, any party who filed an appearance in the case, and the chapter 13 trustee, and shall file a certificate of service. The motion shall state with particularity the cause for dismissal. A party who opposes a motion to dismiss shall file a response to the motion to dismiss within twenty-one (21) days of service of the motion. If no response to the motion to dismiss is filed, the Court, in its discretion, may allow the motion without a hearing.

(b) In a case not previously converted under 11 U.S.C. §§ 706, 1208, or 1112, a debtor electing to have the case dismissed may file a motion to voluntarily dismiss the case, pursuant to 11 U.S.C. § 1307, which motion shall be served on the chapter 13 trustee. The debtor's motion to dismiss shall contain a statement as to whether the case has been converted previously. If the Court enters an order dismissing the case, the Clerk shall provide timely notice of the dismissal to all creditors on the matrix and to the chapter 13 trustee.

(c) If the Court denies confirmation of the debtor's plan, the case shall be dismissed by the Court without further notice unless, within fourteen (14) days after denial of confirmation, or a different time fixed by the Court:

(1) the debtor files an amended plan;

(2) the debtor moves to convert the case to one under another chapter of the Bankruptcy Code;

(3) the debtor files a Motion for Reconsideration or appeals the denial of confirmation, and obtains a stay of the dismissal order; or

(4) the Court otherwise orders.

[Effective August 1, 1997. Amended effective December 1, 2009.]

13–18. CONVERSION FROM CHAPTERS 11 OR 7 TO CHAPTER 13

Within fourteen (14) days after conversion of a case from chapter 11 or chapter 7 to chapter 13, the debtor shall file with the Court those documents required by paragraph 13–2 of these Chapter 13 Rules and serve copies on the chapter 13 trustee.

[Effective August 1, 1997. Amended effective December 1, 2009.]

13–19. COMMENCEMENT AND CONTINUATION OF PAYMENTS TO THE CHAPTER 13 TRUSTEE; LESSORS AND SECURED PARTIES; DISMISSAL FOR FAILURE TO MAKE REQUIRED PAYMENTS

(a) Payments to the chapter 13 trustee pursuant to either 11 U.S.C. § 1326(a) or the terms of a confirmed plan shall be made by certified check or money order. Each payment shall be legibly marked with the bankruptcy case number and the name of the debtor as it appears in the caption of the case.

(b) Payments to the chapter 13 trustee pursuant to either 11 U.S.C. § 1326(a) or the terms of a confirmed plan shall continue until the case has been dismissed, the debtor has completed all payments required by the plan, the debtor has moved for either a hardship discharge pursuant to 11 U.S.C. § 1328(b) or voluntary dismissal, or the debtor has requested that the case be converted to a case under another chapter of the Bankruptcy Code.

(c) Payments of personal property leases governed by 11 U.S.C. § 1326(a)(1)(B) shall only be made directly by the debtor to the lessor if the debtor's plan so provides or if no plan provision addresses payment of the debtor's lease obligation. If the plan provides for payment of the lease obligation by the trustee, the debtor shall make the payment as part of the total payment to the trustee, and the trustee shall pay the lessor, both before and after confirmation.

(d) Pre-confirmation adequate protection payments governed by 11 U.S.C. § 1326(a)(1)(C) shall only be made directly by the debtor to the secured creditor if the debtor's plan so provides or if no plan provision addresses payment of the debtor's secured obligation. If the plan provides for payment of the secured claim by the trustee, the debtor shall make the payment as part of the total payment to the trustee, and the trustee shall pay the secured creditor, both before and after confirmation.

(e) The Court will not consider, allow or approve motions or stipulations for direct payment to the chapter 13 trustee from the debtor's employer or any other entity.

(f) In the event that a chapter 13 case is dismissed or converted prior to confirmation of the plan, the chapter 13 trustee shall be entitled to retain from any monies collected from the debtor the amount of $150.00, which shall constitute an administrative expense pursuant to 11 U.S.C. § 503(b).

[Effective August 1, 1997.]

13–20. DISTRIBUTION

Unless otherwise directed by the Court, the distribution of any proceeds pursuant to a confirmed plan shall be mailed to the address of the creditor as designated pursuant to Fed.R.Bankr.P. 2002(g).

[Effective August 1, 1997.]

13–21. CHAPTER 13 TRUSTEE'S FINAL ACCOUNT

When the chapter 13 trustee determines that the plan has been completed or the Court otherwise orders, the trustee shall file and serve a final report and account on all creditors with allowed claims, all attor-

neys who have filed appearances and requested service of pleadings in the case, the debtor, and debtor's attorney. The report shall state the allowed amount of each claim and the amount paid on each claim. The chapter 13 trustee shall file a certificate of service reflecting service of the final report and account and providing an objection deadline. In the absence of a timely filed objection, the Court may approve the final report and account without a hearing.

[Effective August 1, 1997. Amended effective January 1, 2002; October 1, 2006; May 1, 2008.]

13–22. DISCHARGE

(a) Upon completion of a Chapter 13 plan, a debtor shall file a Motion for Entry of Discharge which conforms with MLBR Official Local Form 12.

(b) The debtor shall serve the Motion for Entry of Discharge upon the beneficiary of the debtor's domestic support obligations, if any, the Chapter 13 trustee, the United States trustee, and all of the debtor's creditors. Any objections to the motion must be filed within fourteen (14) days after service. The Court may, in its discretion, schedule a hearing if an objection is filed. If the debtor fails to file the motion within a reasonable time after completion of plan payments due under the confirmed plan, the case may be closed without the entry of a discharge order.

(c) The order of discharge shall include findings that

(1) all allowed claims have been fully paid in accordance with the provisions of the confirmed plan; or

(2) with respect to secured claims which continue beyond the term of the plan, any pre-petition or post-petition defaults have been cured and such claims are in all respects current, with no escrow balance, late charges, costs or attorneys' fees owing.

(d) The order of discharge shall direct that

(1) creditors who held secured claims which were fully paid execute and deliver to the debtor a release or other discharge certificate suitable for recording; and

(2) creditors who hold secured claims which continue beyond the term of the plan take no action inconsistent with the findings provided for in subsection (a).

[Effective August 1, 1997. Amended effective September 1, 1999; October 1, 2006; December 1, 2009.]

APPENDIX 2.   EXPENSES

In lieu of calculating the actual cost of the following expenses, the applicant may request the rates of reimbursement set forth below:

(a) copies $0.15 per page

(b) incoming telecopier

transmissions $0.15 per page

(c) auto mileage   at the rate set forth from time to time pursuant to 41 CFR § 301–4.2

[Effective August 1, 1997.]

APPENDIX 3. FILING FEES

(a) New Case, Ancillary Proceeding and Case Reopening. The following fees apply to the filing or reopening of cases:

(1)	Chapter 7 (Filing)	$299.00
(2)	Chapter 7 (Reopen or Split)	$260.00
(3)	Chapter 9	$1,039.00
(4)	Chapter 11 Non–Railroad	$1,039.00
(5)	Chapter 11 Non–Railroad (Reopen or Split)	$1,000.00
(6)	Chapter 11 Railroad	$1,039.00
(7)	Chapter 11 Railroad (Reopen or Split)	$1,000.00
(8)	Chapter 12	$239.00
(9)	Chapter 12 (Reopen or Split)	$200.00
(10)	Chapter 13	$274.00
(11)	Chapter 13 (Reopen or Split)	$235.00
(12)	Chapter 15 (formerly 11 U.S.C. § 304 Ancillary Proceeding)	$1,039.00
(13)	Miscellaneous Case (Including registration of judgment and out-of-district subpoenas)	$39.00
(14)	Case conversion from chapter 7 to chapter 11	$755.00
(15)	Case conversion from chapter 13 to chapter 11	$765.00
(16)	Case conversion from chapter 11 to chapter 7	$15.00
(17)	Case conversion from chapter 12 to chapter 7	$60.00
(18)	Case conversion from chapter 12 to chapter 11	$800.00
(19)	Case conversion from chapter 13 to chapter 7	$25.00
(20)	Case conversion from chapter 12 to chapter 13	$35.00

(21) No fee is charged for converting a chapter 7 case to a chapter 13 case. No refund is given for the difference between the filing fees for the representative chapters shall be given.

(b) Motions.

(1) The fee for the filing of a motion for relief from the automatic stay under 11 U.S.C. § 362(d) is $150.00.

(2) The fee for the filing of a motion to withdraw the reference is $155.00.

(3) The fee for the filing of a motion to compel abandonment of property of the estate is $150.00.

(4) The fee for the filing of a motion to convert or a notice of conversion from a chapter 11 case to a chapter 7 case is $15.00.

(5) The fee for the filing of a motion to convert or a notice of conversion from a chapter 12 case to a chapter 7 case is $60.00.

(c) Adversary Proceedings. The filing fee for a complaint is $250.00, except that no fee is required if the United States or the debtor in a chapter 7 or chapter 13 case is the plaintiff. The debtor-in-possession in a chapter 11 case must pay the filing fee. If a trustee in a case under Title 11 is the plaintiff, the fee shall be payable only from the estate to the extent of available funds. The Court may, upon motion of a trustee, defer payment of the filing fee.

(d) Miscellaneous Fees.

(1)	Notice of Appeal from Final Order	$255.00
(2)	Cross Appeal	$255.00
(3)	Notice of Appeal from Interlocutory Order (If a motion for leave to appeal is allowed, an additional $250.00 will be due.)	$ 5.00
(4)	Amendment to Schedules D, E and F or List of Creditors	$ 26.00
(5)	Clerk's Certificate	$ 18.00
(6)	Records Search (If copies are requested, a copy charge also will be assessed.)	$ 26.00

(7)	Retrieval of Closed File from Federal Records Center	$ 45.00
(8)	Certification of Document	$ 9.00
(9)	Document Exemplification	$ 18.00
(10)	Copies per page	$ .50

(11)	Registering a Judgment from another District	$ 39.00
(12)	Reproduction of a Tape Recording	$ 26.00
(13)	Check Returned Due to Insufficient Funds	$ 45.00

[Effective August 1, 1997. Amended effective September 1, 1999; December 29, 1999; March 1, 2003; November 1, 2003; January 1, 2005; October 1, 2006; May 1, 2008; December 1, 2009.]

APPENDIX 4. NOTICES TO THE UNITED STATES OF AMERICA AND THE COMMONWEALTH OF MASSACHUSETTS

(a) Whenever notice is required to be given to the Internal Revenue Service, it shall be mailed to:

Internal Revenue Service
P.O. Box 7346
Philadelphia, PA 19101–7346

(b) Whenever notice is required to be given to the Securities and Exchange Commission, it shall be mailed to:

Securities and Exchange Commission
Boston District Office
73 Tremont Street, 6th Floor
Boston, MA 02108

Securities and Exchange Commission
450 Fifth Street, N.W.
Washington, DC 20549

(c) Whenever notice is required to be given to the United States Attorney, it shall be mailed to:

United States Attorney
John Joseph Moakley United States Courthouse
One Courthouse Way, Suite 9200
Boston, MA 02210

(d) Fed.R.Bankr.P. 7004(a)(4) governs service of process upon the United States in adversary proceedings and contested matters.

(e) Whenever notice is required to be given to the Massachusetts Department of Revenue, it shall be mailed to:

Massachusetts Department of Revenue
Bankruptcy Unit
P.O. Box 9564
Boston, MA 02114–9564

(f) Whenever notice is required to be given to the Massachusetts Division of Unemployment Assistance[2], it shall be mailed to:

Commonwealth of Massachusetts
Division of Unemployment Assistance
Bankruptcy Unit, 5th Floor, Attn: Chief Counsel
19 Staniford Street
Boston, MA 02114–2502

(g) Whenever notice is required to be given to the Massachusetts Attorney General, it shall be mailed to:

Office of the Attorney General
Commonwealth of Massachusetts
One Ashburton Place
Boston, MA 02108

[Effective August 1, 1997. Amended effective September 1, 1999; March 1, 2003; October 1, 2006.]

[2] Formerly known as the Division of Employment and Training.

APPENDIX 5. COURT DIVISIONS AND CLERK'S OFFICE

(a) Divisions. The District of Massachusetts shall contain the following three (3) divisions:

(1) *Eastern Division.* The Eastern Division shall consist of:

(A) the counties of Barnstable, Bristol, Dukes, Nantucket, Norfolk, Plymouth, and Suffolk,

(B) the county of Essex, with the exception of the towns specifically assigned to the Central Division in section (2), and (c) the following towns in Middlesex County: Arlington, Ashland, Belmont, Burlington, Cambridge, Everett, Framingham, Holliston, Lexington, Lincoln, Malden, Medford, Melrose, Natick, Newton, North Reading, Reading, Sherborn, Somerville, Stoneham, Wakefield, Waltham, Watertown, Wayland, Weston, Wilmington, Winchester and Woburn.

The address of the Eastern Division is: Clerk, U.S. Bankruptcy Court, John W. McCormack Post Office and Court House, 5 Post Office Square, Boston, MA 02109–3945.

(2) *Central Division.* the counties of Worcester and Middlesex, with the exception of the towns specifically assigned to the Eastern Division in section (1) and the following towns in Essex County: Andover, Boxboro, Bradford, Haverhill, Lawrence, Methuen, and North Andover.

The address of the Central Division is: Clerk, U.S. Bankruptcy Court, Donohue Federal Building, 595 Main Street, Worcester, MA 01608–2076.

(3) *Western Division.* The Western Division shall consist of the counties of Berkshire, Franklin, Hampden, and Hampshire.

The address of the Western Division is: Clerk, U.S. Bankruptcy Court, United States Courthouse, 300 State Street, Springfield, MA 01105–2925.

(b) Emergency Filings. Filings can be made before 8:30 AM or after 4:30 PM on court days or on weekends or holidays for cause and by prior arrangement or in emergency circumstances, as determined by the Clerk or his or her designee. With respect to Eastern Division cases, parties should contact the Clerk's office at (617) 748–5300 and press (0) during business hours. With respect to Central Division cases, parties should contact the Clerk's office in Worcester at (508) 770–8900 during business hours. With respect to Western Division cases, parties should contact the Clerk's office in Springfield at (413) 785–6900 during business hours. At other times, parties should contact the Clerk or his or her designee by calling **beeper no. (800) 759–8888 and enter PIN # 1309280.**

(c) Emergency Closings or Delayed Opening. Information as to an emergency closing or delayed opening of the Court is available by calling 1–866–419–5695 (Toll Free).

(d) Courtroom Deputies. The telephone numbers, fax numbers and email addresses (to be employed for forwarding proposed orders), for each of the courtroom deputies are set forth below:

For Chief Judge Henry J. Boroff's Session

Telephone: (413) 785–6909
Fax: (413) 781–9477
Email: hjb@mab.uscourts.gov

For Judge William C. Hillman's Session

Telephone: (617) 748–5330
Fax: (617) 748–5335
Email: wch@mab.uscourts.gov

For Judge Joan N. Feeney's Session

Telephone: (617) 748–5320
Fax: (617) 748–5325
Email: jnf@mab.uscourts.gov

For Judge Joel B. Rosenthal's Session

Telephone: (508) 770–8927
Fax: (508) 793–0189
Email: jbr@mab.uscourts.gov

For Judge Frank J. Bailey's Session

Telephone: (617) 748–5340
Fax: (617) 748–5345
Email: fjb@mab.uscourts.gov

[Effective August 1, 1997. Amended effective March 1, 1999; September 1, 1999; March 1, 2003; January 1, 2005; October 1, 2006; December 1, 2009.]

APPENDIX 6. SAMPLE CASE MANAGEMENT PROCEDURES

(a) Omnibus Hearing Dates and Notices of Agenda.

(1) Unless the Court otherwise orders, the Court will conduct omnibus hearings in this case on a (weekly) (bimonthly) (monthly) basis ("Omnibus Hearing Dates").

(2) All matters requiring a hearing shall be set for and be heard on one of the Omnibus Hearing Dates unless alternative hearing dates are approved by the Court for good cause shown.

(3) In order for a pleading to be heard on an Omnibus Hearing Date, a party must first contact the Court's courtroom deputy and request the scheduling of the hearing. The courtroom deputy shall set the pleading for the first available Omnibus Hearing date, taking into account the time required for notice to other parties and the remaining time available on the Omnibus Hearing Date; and shall set an objection deadline, if any. No motion or application shall be set for hearing absent compliance with Fed. R. Bankr. P. 2002(a) nor shall the hearing be set for less than 7 days from service of that motion or application, unless the Court has allowed a request for emergency or expedited determination. The requesting party must file and serve the pleading no later than forty-eight (48) hours after the courtroom deputy has set the pleading for an Omnibus Hearing Date and must indicate on the first page of the pleading the time of the hearing and the deadline for objections, if any.

(4) The provisions of MLBR 9013–1 shall continue to govern, except insofar as they may specifically conflict with the procedures set forth above.

(5) Counsel to the estate representative shall maintain, file and serve a Notice of Agenda for each Omnibus Hearing Date as follows:

(A) A proposed Notice of Agenda shall be filed before 12:00 noon on the day that is three (3) days before the Omnibus Hearing Date.

(B) Resolved or continued matters shall be listed ahead of unresolved matters.

(C) The Notice of Agenda shall be promptly amended as necessary and served on all parties in interest. All amended Notices of Agenda shall list matters as listed in the original Notice of Agenda with all edits and additional information being listed in boldface type.

(D) For each motion or application, the Notice of Agenda shall indicate:

(i) the name of the movant or the applicant, the nature of the motion or application, and the docket number (Supporting papers of the movant or applicant shall be similarly denoted);

(ii) the objection deadline, any objection filed and its docket number, if available; and

(iii) whether the matter is going forward, whether a continuance is requested (and any opposition to the continuance, if known), whether any or all of the objections have been resolved, and any other pertinent status information.

(E) When a matter in an adversary proceeding is scheduled to be heard, the Notice of Agenda shall indicate the adversary proceeding number and the corresponding docket number for pleadings filed in the adversary proceeding, together with the information contained in subparagraph (d) above, insofar as applicable.

(b) Procedures Governing Payment of Interim Compensation and Reimbursement of Expenses to Professionals Pursuant to 11 U.S.C. §§ 105(a) and 331.

(1) *Scope of Applicability.* All professionals retained in a Chapter 11 case pursuant to 11 U.S.C. §§ 327 and 1103 (each, a "Professional") may seek post-petition interim compensation pursuant to these procedures (the "Administrative Fee Order").

(2) *Submission and Monthly Statements.* On or before the twenty-fifth (25th) day of each month following the month for which compensation is sought, each Professional seeking compensation pursuant to the Administrative Fee Order shall serve a monthly fee and expense statement (the "Monthly Fee Statement") upon the following persons:

(A) the officer designated by the debtor to be responsible for such matters;

(B) counsel to the debtor;

(C) any Chapter 7 or 11 trustee;

(D) counsel to all official committees;

(E) the Office of the United States Trustee;

(F) counsel to all post-petition lenders or their agents; and

(G) any other party the Court may so designate.

(3) *Content of Monthly Fee Statement.* Each Monthly Fee Statement shall contain an itemization of time spent and the applicable hourly rate. All timekeepers must maintain contemporaneous time entries in increments of one-tenth (1/10th) of an hour.

(4) *Review Period.* Each person receiving a Monthly Fee Statement shall have twenty-one (21) days after service of the Monthly Fee Statement to

review it and serve an objection (the "Objection Period").

(5) *Payment.* In the absence of a timely served objection, the estate representative will promptly pay each Professional an amount (the "Interim Payment") equal to the lesser of (i) ninety percent (90%) of the fees and 100 percent (100%) of the expenses requested in the Monthly Fee Statement, or (ii) ninety percent (90%) of the fees and 100 percent (100%) of the expenses not subject to any partial objection.

(6) *Objections.*

(A) If any party objects to a Monthly Fee Statement, it must serve a written objection (the "Notice of Objection to Monthly Fee Statement") and serve it upon the Professional and each of the parties served with the Monthly Fee Statement as set forth above, so that the Notice of Objection to Monthly Fee Statement is received on or before the last day of the Objection Period.

(B) The Notice of Objection to Monthly Fee Statement must set forth the nature of the objection and the amount of fees and/or expenses at issue.

(C) If an estate representative receives an objection to a particular Monthly Fee Statement, the estate representative shall withhold payment of that portion of the Monthly Fee Statement to which the objection is directed, and shall promptly pay the remainder of the fees and disbursements in the percentages set forth above.

(D) If the parties to an objection are able to resolve their respective dispute(s) following the service of a Notice of Objection to Monthly Fee Statement, and the Professional and the objecting party serve upon each of the parties served with the Monthly Fee Statement as set forth above a statement indicating that the objection is withdrawn, in whole or in part, describing in detail the terms of the resolution, then the estate representative shall promptly pay in accordance with the percentages listed above that portion of the Monthly Fee Statement which is no longer subject to an objection.

(E) If the parties are unable to reach a resolution to the objection within twenty-one (21) days after service of the objection, the affected Professional may either (a) move to compel the payment with the Court, together with a request for payment of the difference, if any, between the total amount of the Interim Payment sought and the portion of the Interim Payment as to which there is an objection (the "Incremental Amount"); or (b) forgo payment of the Incremental Amount until the next interim or final fee application, or any other date and time so directed by the Court, at which time it will consider and dispose of the objection, if so requested.

(F) Neither an objection to a Monthly Fee Statement nor the failure to object thereto shall preju-

dice a party's right to object to any fee application on any ground.

(G) Failure of a professional to timely serve a Monthly Fee Statement shall not prejudice such professional in seeking interim or final allowance of fees or expenses. Further, any Monthly Fee Statement served after the deadline for such Monthly Fee Statement shall be deemed served at the time that such professional serves a Monthly Fee Statement for the next subsequent period and shall be subject to the Objection Deadline for the Monthly Fee Statement for such subsequent period.

(7) *Fee Applications.*

(A) Parties seeking compensation pursuant to an Administrative Fee Order shall file at four (4) month intervals or such other intervals directed by the Court ("Interim Period") an interim fee application. Each Professional seeking approval of its interim fee application shall file with the Court an interim application for allowance of compensation and reimbursement of expenses, pursuant to 11 U.S.C. § 331, of the amounts sought in the Monthly Fee Statements issued during such period (the "Interim Fee Application").

(B) The Interim Fee Application shall comply with the mandates of the Bankruptcy Code, Rules 2014 and 2016 of the Federal Rules of Bankruptcy Procedure and the Local Rules for the United States Bankruptcy Court for the District of Massachusetts.

(C) The Interim Fee Application must be filed within forty-five (45) days after the conclusion of the Interim Period.

(D) In the event any Professional fails to file an Interim Fee Application when due, such Professional will be ineligible to receive further interim payments or fees or expenses under the Administrative Fee Order until such time as the Interim Fee Application is submitted.

(E) The pendency of a fee application, or a Court order that payment of compensation or reimbursement of expenses was improper as to a particular Monthly Fee Statement, shall not disqualify a Professional from the further payment of compensation or reimbursement of expenses as set forth above, unless otherwise ordered by the Court. Additionally, the pendency of an objection to payment of compensation or reimbursement of expenses will not disqualify a Professional from future payment of compensation or reimbursement of expenses, unless the Court orders otherwise.

(F) Neither the payment of, nor the failure to pay, in whole or in part, monthly compensation and reimbursement as provided herein shall have any effect on the Court's interim or final allowance of compensation and reimbursement of expenses of any Professionals. All compensation is subject to final approval by the Court.

(G) Counsel for each official committee may, in accordance with the foregoing procedure for monthly compensation and reimbursement to professionals, collect and submit statements of actual expenses incurred, with supporting vouchers, from members of the committee such counsel represents, provided, however, that such committee counsel ensures that these reimbursement requests comply with the applicable rules and those guidelines.

(8) *Miscellaneous.*

(A) Any party may object to requests for payments made pursuant to the Administrative Fee Order for good cause, including, without limitation, that the estate representative has not timely filed monthly operating reports or remained current with its administrative expenses and 28 U.S.C. § 1930 fees.

(B) The estate representative shall include all payments to Professionals on its monthly operating reports, including details of the amount paid to each Professional.

(C) All fees and expenses paid to Professionals are subject to disgorgement until final allowance by the Court.

[Effective August 1, 1997. Amended effective January 1, 2005; December 1, 2009.]

APPENDIX 7.   STANDING ORDER 09–04

[Publisher's Note: See Selected Orders, post.]

[Effective November 3, 2009.]

APPENDIX 8.   ELECTRONIC FILING RULES

RULE 1.   SCOPE OF ELECTRONIC FILING

Except as provided below, electronic filing of petitions, motions, applications, memoranda of law or other pleadings, proofs of claim or documents (hereafter "documents") shall be mandatory as set forth in MLBR 9036–1.

The following may be filed in paper form at the Clerk's Office:

(a) proofs of claim filed by a party in interest or creditor other than the United States Internal Revenue Service or the Commonwealth of Massachusetts Department of Revenue;

(b) documents filed by parties in interest who are pro se;

(c) requests for ex parte determination or a request for impoundment, pursuant to MLBR 9018–1.

(d) documents filed by attorneys who:

(1) appear in not more than three (3) cases per year and personally, or by an agent, hand deliver the document(s) to the Clerk's Office and scan the document(s) electronically employing equipment supplied and procedures as directed by Clerk's Office personnel; or

(2) are unable to file electronically on account of temporary equipment or system breakdown in the attorney's office or the Clerk's Office; or

(e) documents in paper form with prior permission of the Clerk, the Deputy Clerk or their designee, leave to be given only on a showing of temporary exigent circumstances other than equipment or system breakdown.

[Effective March 1, 2003. Amended effective January 1, 2005; May 1, 2008; December 1, 2009.]

RULE 2.   ELIGIBILITY, REGISTRATION, PASSWORDS

(a) Registered User. The term "Registered User" as employed in these rules shall be deemed to mean an individual who has registered to use this Court's ECF System, with full or limited access, pursuant to subsection (b) hereof. Limited access allows an attorney or non-attorney to become a Registered User for the sole purpose of filing proofs of claim, notice requests, transfers or assignments of claim, and withdrawals of claims.

(b) Eligibility. Attorneys admitted to the bar of the United States District Court for the District of Massachusetts (including those admitted pro hac vice, pursuant to Local Rule 9010–1(b)), attorneys representing the United States of America or any state, the United States trustee and his/her assistants, Chapter 7, 11, 12, or 13 trustees, limited access users, and others as the Court may allow in its discretion on prior motion and order, may register as Registered Users of the ECF System after completion of such electronic filing training as the Clerk of this Court may establish and require from time to time.

(c) Registration. Application for registration as a Registered User shall be made on a form prescribed by the Clerk as amended from time to time and posted on the Court's website, www.mab.uscourts.gov. All registration application forms shall be mailed or delivered to the Office of the Clerk, United States Bankruptcy Court, John W. McCormack Post Office and Court House, 5 Post Office Square, Suite 1150, Boston, MA 02109–3945 ATTN: SYSTEMS, PERSONAL AND CONFIDENTIAL. Each approved registrant will receive a notice from the Clerk to retrieve from the Clerk's Office (in Boston, Worcester or Springfield, as designated by the registrant) a sealed envelope containing a log-in name and assigned password. Only the applicant or an authorized representative may retrieve the envelope; except that, at the written request of an approved registrant, the Clerk may email the log-in name and password to the registrant. The Clerk is authorized to employ such further precautions which in the Clerk's judgment will ensure security in the distribution of passwords. Each Registered User shall be entitled to only one password, except that additional passwords may be issued to a single user for good cause shown and in the discretion of the Clerk.

(d) Withdrawal or Amendment of Registration. A Registered User who wishes to withdraw or amend a registration shall email a request for such change to the Clerk on a form prescribed by the Clerk as amended from time to time and posted on the Court's website, www.mab.uscourts.gov.

(e) Security. Registration constitutes a Registered User's agreement to protect the security of his or her assigned password and immediately notify the Clerk if the Registered User learns that the security of the password has been compromised. No Registered User shall knowingly permit the password to be utilized by anyone other than an authorized agent of the Registered User. Upon notice to the Clerk that a password has been compromised, the Clerk shall promptly provide a substitute password to the Registered User.

(f) Waivers. Registration constitutes the Registered User's: (1) agreement to receive documents electronically and waiver of the right to receive notice by any other means; and (2) consent to service of all documents electronically and waiver of the right to service by any other means, excepting only service of process in an adversary proceeding or with respect to an involuntary petition, or as otherwise ordered by the Court. The aforesaid waiver of service and notice by non-electronic means shall include waiver of notice by first class mail of the entry of an order or judgment under Fed. R. Bank. P. 9022.

(g) Involuntary Termination of Registration; Sanctions. On notice from the Clerk that a Registered User and/or his or her agents has/have repeatedly and/or egregiously failed to comply with the procedures established by the Court for use of the ECF System or failed to comply with reasonable password security precautions, the Court may, after notice and hearing, sanction a Registered User for such failure, including, without limitation, by suspending the Registered User from use of the ECF System.

[Effective March 1, 2003. Amended effective January 1, 2005; December 1, 2009.]

RULE 3. CONSEQUENCES OF ELECTRONIC FILING

(a) Filing and Entry. Transmission of a document to the ECF System consistent with these rules, together with the transmission of a Notice of Electronic Filing from the Court, constitutes the filing of the document for all purposes of the Federal Rules of Bankruptcy Procedure and the local rules of this Court, and constitutes entry of the document on the docket kept by the Clerk pursuant to Fed. R. Bank. P. 5003.

(b) Official Record. When a document has been filed electronically, the official record is the electronic recording of the document as stored by the Court, and the filing party is bound by the document as filed. A document filed electronically is deemed filed on the date and the time stated on the Notice of Electronic Filing from the Court.

(c) Filing Deadline. A document may be filed at any time, except that:

(1) where the Court orders that filing must be completed by a specific date and time, filing a document electronically does not alter the filing deadline for that document; and

(2) where the Court orders that filing must be completed by a specific date but does not specify the time, entry of the document into the ECF System must be completed before 4:30 p.m. Eastern Standard (or Daylight, if applicable) Time in order to be deemed timely filed.

[Effective March 1, 2003.]

RULE 4. ENTRY OF COURT ORDERS

The Clerk shall enter all orders, judgments, and proceeding memos on the docket kept by the clerk under Fed. R. Bankr. P. 5003 and 9021 in electronic format. Any order entered electronically without the original signature of a judge shall have the same force and effect as if the judge had affixed his or her signature to a paper copy of the order.

[Effective March 1, 2003. Amended effective January 1, 2005.]

RULE 5. ATTACHMENTS AND EXHIBITS

(a) If the exhibit(s) to any document constitute(s) more than 50 pages in the aggregate, the exhibit(s) must be filed separately from the underlying document. In such event, the Registered User must file with the underlying document (a) a list of all of the exhibits, identifying clearly the subject matter of each exhibit, and (b) a summary of the content of each exhibit of 50 or more pages in length. If any recipient is unable to open an exhibit for any reason, it is the responsibility of the recipient to notify the transmitting Registered User of the recipient's inability to open the exhibit and to request paper copies. The Registered User shall respond promptly to any such request.

(b) Exhibits may, but need not, be attached to Proofs of Claim when filed electronically. The claimant shall promptly provide any party in interest all exhibits upon request.

[Effective March 1, 2003.]

RULE 6. SEALED OR IMPOUNDED DOCUMENTS

Any motion to seal or impound a document, pursuant to MLBR 9018–1, and the subject document, shall not be filed electronically, unless specifically authorized by the Court. In the event that the motion to seal or impound is granted, the Court shall determine the extent to which the motion and/or the document(s) shall be electronically filed.

[Effective March 1, 2003.]

RULE 7. STATEMENTS UNDER OATH; RETENTION REQUIREMENTS

(a) Unless the Court orders otherwise, all electronically filed documents, (including, without limitation, affidavits or a debtor's petition, schedules, statement of affairs, or amendments thereof) requiring signatures of a non-Registered User under the penalties of perjury shall also be executed in paper form, together with a Declaration Re: Electronic Filing in the form of Official Local Form 7. The Declaration Re: Electronic Filing shall be filed with the Court as an imaged, and not electronically created, document, together with or in addition to the document electronically filed with the Court. Said Declaration shall be valid for the declarant for all subsequently filed documents requiring a signature in the case.

(b) Notwithstanding subsection (a) above, the paper forms of the electronically filed document(s) and the Declaration Re: Electronic Filing shall be retained by the Registered User until five (5) years after the closing of the case. Said paper documents shall be deemed property of the Court and not property of the declarant or the Registered User. The Registered User must produce all such original documents for review or filing at the request of a party in interest or upon order of the Court.

(c) Any document electronically filed which is signed by a non-Registered User shall be filed as an imaged, and not electronically created, document.

(d) No document signed by a non-Registered User may be electronically filed unless (1) it is accompanied by a Declaration Re: Electronic Filing in the form of Official Local Form 7 or (2) a Declaration Re: Electronic Filing of Official Local Form 7 has previously been filed in the case which shall be valid for the declarant for all subsequently filed documents requiring a signature in the case.

(e) A non-Registered User may file a Declaration Re: Electronic Filing in the form of Official Local Form 7 at any time prior to the electronic filing of a document in the case bearing his or her signature which shall be valid for the declarant for all subsequently filed documents requiring a signature in the case.

[Effective March 1, 2003. Amended effective January 1, 2005; May 1, 2008.]

RULE 8.   SIGNATURES

(a) The user log-in and password required to submit documents to the ECF System serve as the Registered User's signature on all electronic documents filed with the Court including those requiring signatures under the penalties of perjury. They also serve as a signature for purposes of Fed. R. Bankr. P. 9011, the Federal Rules of Bankruptcy Procedure, the local rules of this Court, and any other purpose for which a signature is required. Electronically filed documents must set forth the name, address, telephone number, email address of a Registered User and, if an attorney, his or her BBO or PHV number (see MLBR 9010–3(b)). In addition, the document must include a signature block where the name of the Registered User and/or affiant is typed but preceded by an "/s/" or is set forth as an imaged or electronically created signature.

(b) Where an electronically filed document sets forth the consent of more than one party, the additional consents may be supplied by: (1) a scanned document containing all of the necessary signatures; or (2) a representation that the Registered User has authority to consent on behalf of the other parties who are purported signatories to the document; or (3) a notice of endorsement filed by the other signatories no later than three business days after filing of the document; or (4) any other manner approved by the Court.

(c) All electronic documents filed after the commencement of the case must contain the case caption and number.

(d) Notwithstanding Fed. R. Bankr. P. 9011(a), an attorney may electronically file an application for compensation for a professional who is not a registered user but whose employment in that case has been authorized previously by order of the court.

[Effective March 1, 2003. Amended effective January 1, 2005; May 1, 2008.]

RULE 9.   SERVICE OF DOCUMENT BY ELECTRONIC MEANS

(a) Transmission by the Court of the "Notice of Electronic Filing" constitutes service or notice of the filed document, except that persons not deemed to have consented to electronic notice or service are entitled to conventional notice or service of any electronically filed document according to the Federal Rules of Bankruptcy Procedure and the local rules.

(b) Service by electronic transmission shall be deemed equivalent to service by mail for the purposes of Fed. R. Bankr. P. 9006(f).

[Effective March 1, 2003.]

RULE 10.   NOTICE OF COURT ORDERS AND JUDGMENTS

Upon the entry of an order or judgment in a case or an adversary proceeding, the Clerk will transmit notice to Registered Users in the case or adversary proceeding in electronic form. Transmission of a Notice of Electronic Filing constitutes the notice required by Fed.R.Bankr.P. 9022. The Clerk shall give conventional notice to a person who has not consented to electronic service in accordance with the Federal Rules of Bankruptcy Procedure.

[Effective March 1, 2003.]

RULE 11.   TECHNICAL FAILURES

A Registered User whose filing is made untimely as a result of a technical failure may seek appropriate relief from the Court, including, without limitation, leave to file by facsimile and defer payment of any filing fee.

[Effective March 1, 2003. Amended effective January 1, 2005.]

RULE 12. PUBLIC ACCESS

A person may view electronically filed documents that have not been impounded by the Court at the Clerk's Office. A person may also access the ECF System at the Court's Internet site, *www.mab. uscourts.gov* or directly at https://ecf.mab.uscourts. gov, by obtaining a PACER login and password. A person who has PACER access may retrieve dockets and documents. Only a Registered User may file documents electronically.

[Effective March 1, 2003. Amended effective October 1, 2006.]

OFFICIAL LOCAL FORMS

OFFICIAL LOCAL FORM 1. MATRIX LIST OF CREDITORS

It is the debtor's responsibility to file an accurate creditor mailing matrix, (a list of the names and addresses of creditors) with the petition. This list is used to mail notices to creditors, so it is very important to take care in entering creditor names and addresses correctly.

NOTE: Lack of proper notice may result in no discharge as to a creditor not listed correctly or additional costs to the debtor as changes and corrections are requested.

Rules for properly formatting a creditor mailing matrix:

Non-electronic filers may file this form with the Court as a paper document or on a computer disk (CD). Electronic filers must file this form in .pdf format and upload it in .txt format to the Court's ECF database as well. Both Electronic and non-electronic filers must follow the same guidelines listed below.

1. Creditors must be listed in a single column containing as many pages as are required to list all creditors.
2. The margins at the top and bottom of the page must be at least one inch.
3. Page numbers or page headings must not be included in the list.
4. The matrix shall be produced with a quality computer printer or typewriter. Standard type shall be used.
5. If not filed on disk, an original of the matrix or an amended matrix must be filed with the Clerk's Office. A matrix cannot be filed by fax.
6. If submitting on a CD, please save the file as an ASCII text file, and write the debtor's name and town on the disk.
7. The name and address of each creditor must not exceed five (5) lines and each creditor's name and address must be separated by at least one blank line.
8. Names and addresses must be aligned left (flush against the left margin, no leading blank spaces.)
9. Each line may contain no more than 40 characters.

10. The creditor's name must be on the first line. Put the first name first, any middle initial then the last name.
11. Use the second line for c/o (care of) or Attention: information.
12. If you have a physical address and post office box information, list both the P.O. Box information and the physical address.
13. City and state abbreviation and ZIP code must be on the last line. (If the address only needs to use four lines the city and state are on the fourth line.)
14. All states must be the standard two-letter abbreviations.
15. Nine-digit ZIP codes used must contain a hyphen separating the two of digits.
16. **DO NOT USE SPECIAL CHARACTERS** SUCH AS %, ( ), or [ ]. These characters will interfere with software used by the Bankruptcy Noticing Center.
17. **DO NOT, ABSOLUTELY DO NOT, INCLUDE ACCOUNT NUMBERS.**
18. Lists of amended creditors must only contain the added creditors.
19. Since amended creditors are filed with the motion as a PDF document, lists of more than 50 added creditors must be submitted on disk clearly identifying the case name and number for the Clerk's Office.
20. Do not include the names and address(es) of the debtor, debtor's counsel or the U.S. Trustee on the matrix as the ECF program will add them automatically.

Examples are as follows:

ABC Corp.
123 Main Street
Any town, MA. 02003

Dr. O. W. Holmes, Jr.
Medical Affiliates and Diagnostics
321 First Avenue, Suite 50
Nice town, MA 01006

OFFICIAL LOCAL FORM 2A. NOTICE OF INTENDED PRIVATE SALE OF PROPERTY, SOLICITATION OF COUNTEROFFERS, DEADLINE FOR SUBMITTING OBJECTIONS AND HIGHER OFFERS AND HEARING DATE

UNITED STATES BANKRUPTCY COURT
DISTRICT OF MASSACHUSETTS

In re   Chapter

                                                         Case No.

,

Debtor

NOTICE OF INTENDED PRIVATE SALE OF PROPERTY, SOLICITATION OF COUNTEROFFERS, DEADLINE FOR SUBMITTING OBJECTIONS AND HIGHER OFFERS AND HEARING DATE

_____ IS THE DATE OF THE PROPOSED SALE

_____ **IS THE DATE BY WHICH OBJECTIONS OR COUNTEROFFERS MUST BE MADE**

NOTICE is hereby given, pursuant to 11 U.S.C. Section 363, Fed. R. Bankr. P. 2002(a)(2) and 6004, and MLBR 2002–5 and 6004–1, that the Trustee (or, where applicable, the Debtor), intends to sell at private sale the Debtor's right, title and interest in certain property of the estate.

PROPERTY TO BE SOLD:

(General description)

An itemized list of the property to be sold is attached to this Notice.

THE OFFER:

The Trustee (or where applicable, the Debtor) has received an offer to purchase the property for the sum of _____ ($ __) in cash (or state other consideration).

THE PROPOSED BUYER:

The proposed buyer is _____ (Name and address). The relationship of the proposed buyer to the Debtor (or Trustee, if applicable) is:

THE SALE DATE:

The sale shall take place on or before _____. The proposed buyer has paid a deposit in the sum of $ __. The terms of the proposed sale are more particularly described in a Motion for Order Authorizing and Approving Private Sale of Property of the Estate (the "Motion to Approve Sale") filed with the Court on _____ and a written purchase and sale agreement dated _____. The Motion to Approve Sale and the purchase and sale agreement are available at no charge upon request from the undersigned.

SALE FREE AND CLEAR OF LIENS:

The _____ will be sold free and clear of all liens, claims and encumbrances. Any perfected, enforceable valid liens shall attach to the proceeds of the sale according to priorities established under applicable law.

COUNTEROFFERS OR OBJECTIONS:

Any objections to the sale and/or higher offers must be filed in writing with the Clerk, United States Bankruptcy Court at _____ (Boston, Springfield or Worcester address as applicable) on or before _____ at 4:30 PM (the "Objection Deadline"). A copy of any objection or higher offer also shall be served upon the undersigned. Any objection to the sale must state with particularity the grounds for the objection and why the intended sale should not be authorized. Any objection to the sale shall be governed by Fed. R. Bankr. P. 9014.

Through this Notice, higher offers for the Property are hereby solicited. Any higher offer must be accompanied by a cash deposit of $ _____ in the form of a certified or bank check made payable to the undersigned. Higher offers must be on the same terms and conditions provided in the Purchase and Sale Agreement, other than the purchase price.

HEARING:

A hearing on the Motion to Approve Sale, objections or higher offers is scheduled to take place on _____ at ___ AM/PM before the Honorable _____, United States Bankruptcy Judge, Courtroom ___, _____, _____, Massachusetts. Any party who has filed an objection or higher offer is expected to be present at the hearing, failing which the objection may be overruled or the higher offer stricken. The Court may take evidence at any hearing on approval of the sale to resolve issues of fact. If no objection to the Motion to Approve Sale or higher offer is timely filed, the Court, in its discretion, may cancel the scheduled hearing and approve the sale without hearing.

At the hearing on the sale the Court may 1) consider any requests to strike a higher offer, 2) determine further terms and conditions of the sale, 3) determine the requirements for further competitive bidding, and 4) require one or more rounds of sealed or open bids from the original offeror and any other qualifying offeror.

DEPOSIT:

The deposit will be forfeited to the estate if the successful purchaser fails to complete the sale by the date ordered by the Court. If the sale is not completed by the buyer approved by the Court, the Court, without further hearing, may approve the sale of the Property to the next highest bidder.

Any questions concerning the intended sale shall be addressed to the undersigned.

Respectfully Submitted,

TRUSTEE (or Debtor)

By _____

Dated: _____

[Effective August 1, 1997. Amended effective December 1, 2009.]

OFFICIAL LOCAL FORM 2B. NOTICE OF INTENDED PUBLIC SALE OF ESTATE PROPERTY

UNITED STATES BANKRUPTCY COURT
DISTRICT OF MASSACHUSETTS

In re   Case No.

                    ,   Chapter

              Debtor

NOTICE OF INTENDED PUBLIC SALE OF ESTATE PROPERTY

_____ **IS THE DATE OF THE PROPOSED SALE**

_____ **IS THE DATE BY WHICH OBJECTIONS MUST BE MADE**

NOTICE is hereby given, pursuant to 11 U.S.C. § 363, Fed. R. Bankr. P. 2002(a)(2) and 6004, and MLBR Rule 2002–5 and 6004–1, that the Trustee (or, where applicable, the Debtor) intends to sell at public sale the Debtor's right, title and interest in certain property of the estate consisting of:

PROPERTY TO BE SOLD:

(General description)

THE AUCTION:

The sale will be conducted by _____ at _____
                              (Auctioneer)   (Address)

_____ on _____ at _____
                                    (Date)   (Time)

The website address of the Auctioneer is: _____

The proposed sale procedures are more particularly described in the Debtor's Motion for Order Authorizing and Approving Public Sale of Property of the Estate (the "Motion to Approve Sale"), a copy of which is available at no charge upon request from the undersigned or on the website of the court: www.mab.uscourts.gov.

SALE FREE AND CLEAR OF LIENS:

The property will be sold free and clear of all liens, claims and encumbrances. Any perfected, enforceable valid liens shall attach to the proceeds of the sale according to priorities established under applicable law.

OBJECTIONS:

Any objections to the sale must be filed in writing with the Clerk, United States Bankruptcy Court at _____ (Boston, Springfield or Worcester address as applicable) on or before _____ at 4:30 PM (the "Objection Deadline"). A copy of any objection also shall be served upon the undersigned. Any objection to the sale must state with particularity the grounds for the objection and why the intended sale should not be authorized. Any objection to the sale shall be governed by Fed. R. Bankr. P. 9014.

448

HEARING:

A hearing on objections and the Motion to Approve Sale is scheduled to take place on _____ at _____ AM/PM before the Honorable _____, United States Bankruptcy Judge, Courtroom _____, _____, _____, Massachusetts. At the hearing on approval of the sale the Court may determine further terms and conditions of the sale. Any party who has filed an objection is expected to be present at the hearing, failing which the objection may be overruled. The Court may take evidence at the hearing to resolve issues of fact. If no objection to the Motion to Approve Sale is timely filed, the Court, in its discretion, may cancel the scheduled hearing and approve the sale without a hearing.

> Respectfully Submitted,
> TRUSTEE (or Debtor)
> By _____

[Effective August 1, 1997. Amended effective December 1, 2009.]

OFFICIAL LOCAL FORM 3.   CHAPTER 13 PLAN AND COVER SHEET

UNITED STATES BANKRUPTCY COURT
DISTRICT OF MASSACHUSETTS

CHAPTER 13 PLAN COVER SHEET

Filing Date: _____   Docket #: _____

Debtor(s): _____   Co–Debtor: _____

SS#: _____   SS#: _____

Address: _____   Address: _____

_____   _____

_____   _____

Debtor's Counsel: _____

Address: _____

_____

_____

Telephone #: _____

Facsimile #: _____

ATTACHED TO THIS COVER SHEET IS THE CHAPTER 13 PLAN FILED BY THE DEBTOR(S) IN THIS CASE. THIS PLAN SETS OUT THE PROPOSED TREATMENT OF THE CLAIMS OF CREDITORS. THE CLAIMS ARE SET FORTH IN THE BANKRUPTCY SCHEDULES FILED BY DEBTOR(S) WITH THE BANKRUPTCY COURT.

YOU WILL RECEIVE A SEPARATE NOTICE FROM THE BANKRUPTCY COURT OF THE SCHEDULED CREDITORS' MEETING PURSUANT TO 11 U.S.C. § 341. THAT NOTICE WILL ALSO ESTABLISH THE BAR DATE FOR FILING PROOFS OF CLAIMS.

PURSUANT TO THE MASSACHUSETTS LOCAL BANKRUPTCY RULES, YOU HAVE UNTIL THIRTY (30) DAYS AFTER THE SECTION 341 MEETING TO FILE AN OBJECTION TO CONFIRMATION OF THE CHAPTER 13 PLAN, WHICH OBJECTION MUST BE SERVED ON THE DEBTOR, DEBTOR'S COUNSEL AND THE CHAPTER 13 TRUSTEE.

UNITED STATES BANKRUPTCY COURT
DISTRICT OF MASSACHUSETTS

OFFICIAL LOCAL FORM 3

PRE–CONFIRMATION CHAPTER 13 PLAN

Docket No.: _____

DEBTORS: (H) _____   SS#: _____

(W) _____   SS#: _____

I. PLAN PAYMENT AND TERM:

Debtor(s) shall pay monthly to the Trustee the sum of $ _____ for the term of:

☐ 36 Months. 11 U.S.C. § 1325(b)(4)(A)(i);

450

☐ 60 Months. 11 U.S.C. § 1325(b)(4)(A)(ii);

☐ 60 Months. 11 U.S.C. § 1322(d)(2). Debtor avers the following cause:

_____

_____

_____; or

☐ __ Months. The Debtor states as reasons therefore: _____

_____

_____

II. SECURED CLAIMS:

A. Claims to be paid through the plan (including arrears):

Creditor   Description of Claim (pre-petition   Amount of Claim
                        arrears, purchase money, etc.)
_____   _____ $ _____

_____   _____ $ _____

_____   _____ $ _____

Total of secured claims to be paid through the Plan: $ _____

B. Claims to be paid directly by debtor to creditors (Not through Plan):

Creditor   Description of Claim

_____   _____

_____   _____

_____   _____

C. Modification of Secured Claims:

Creditor   Details of Modification   Amt. of Claim to Be
                        (Additional Details   Paid Through Plan
                        May Be Attached)

_____   _____   _____

_____   _____   _____

D.   Leases:

    i.   The Debtor(s) intend(s) to reject the residential/personal property lease claims of _____; or

    ii.   The Debtor(s) intend(s) to assume the residential/personal property lease claims of _____.

    iii.   The arrears under the lease to be paid under the plan are _____.

III.   PRIORITY CLAIMS:

A.   Domestic Support Obligations:

Creditor	Description of Claim	Amount of Claim
_____	_____	$ _____

B.   Other:

Creditor	Description of Claim	Amount of Claim
_____	_____	$ _____
_____	_____	$ _____
_____	_____	$ _____
_____	_____	$ _____

Total of Priority Claims to Be Paid Through the Plan: $_____

IV.   ADMINISTRATIVE CLAIMS:

A.   Attorneys Fees (to be paid through the plan): $ _____

B.   Miscellaneous Fees:

Creditor	Description of Claim	Amount of Claim
_____	_____	$ _____
_____	_____	$ _____
_____	_____	$ _____

C.   The Chapter 13 Trustee's fee is determined by Order of the United States Attorney General. The calculation of the Plan payment set forth utilizes a 10% Trustee's commission.

V.   UNSECURED CLAIMS:

The general unsecured creditors shall receive a dividend of ___ % of their claims.

A.   General unsecured claims $ _____

B.   Undersecured claims arising after lien avoidance/cramdown:

Creditor   Description of Claim   Amount of Claim

_____   _____ $ _____

_____   _____ $ _____

_____   _____ $ _____

C.   Non–Dischargeable Unsecured Claims:

Creditor   Description of Claim   Amount of Claim

_____   _____ $ _____

_____   _____ $ _____

_____   _____ $ _____

Total of Unsecured Claims (A + B + C): $ _____

D.   Multiply total by percentage: $ _____
(Example: Total of $38,500.00 × .22 dividend = $8,470.00)

E.   Separately classified unsecured claims (co-borrower, etc.):

Creditor   Description of Claim   Amount of Claim

_____   _____ $ _____

_____   _____ $ _____

_____   _____ $ _____

Total amount of separately classified claims payable at ___%: $ _____

VI.   OTHER PROVISIONS:

A.   Liquidation of assets to be used to fund plan: _____.

_____

B.   Miscellaneous Provisions: _____.

_____

_____

VII.   CALCULATION OF PLAN PAYMENT:

a) Secured claims (Section I–A Total): $ _____

b) Priority claims (Section II–A & B Total): $ _____

c) Administrative claims (Section III–A&B Total): $ _____

d) Regular unsecured claims (Section IV–D Total): + $ _____

e) Separately classified unsecured claims: $ _____

f) Total of a + b + c + d + e above: = $ _____

g) Divide (f) by .90 for total including Trustee's fee:
                    Cost of Plan   = $ _____

(This represents the total amount to be paid into the Chapter 13 Plan.)

h) Divide (g), Cost of Plan, by Term of Plan, _____ months

i) Round up to nearest dollar for Monthly Plan Payment: $ _____
(Enter this amount on page 1)

Pursuant to 11 U.S.C. § 1326(a)(1) unless the Court orders otherwise, debtor shall commence making the payments proposed by a plan within thirty (30) days after the petition is filed. Pursuant to 11 U.S.C. § 1326(a)(1)(C), the debtor shall make preconfirmation adequate protection payments directly to the secured creditor.

VIII.   LIQUIDATION ANALYSIS

A.   Real Estate:

Address	Fair Market Value	Total Amount of Recorded Liens (Schedule D)
_____	$ _____	$ _____
_____	$ _____	$ _____
_____	$ _____	$ _____

Total Net Equity for Real Property: $ _____

Less Total Exemptions (Schedule C): $ _____

Available Chapter 7: $ _____

B.   Automobile (Describe year, make, model):

_____ Value $ _____ Lien $ _____ Exemption $ _____

_____ Value $ _____ Lien $ _____ Exemption $ _____

Total Net Equity: $ _____

Less Total Exemptions (Schedule C) $ _____

Available Chapter 7: $ _____

C.   All other Assets: (All remaining items on schedule B): (Itemize as necessary)

_____

_____

Total Net Value: $ _____

Less Exemptions (Schedule C): $ _____

Available Chapter 7: $ _____

D.   Summary of Liquidation Analysis (total amount available under Chapter 7):

Net Equity (A and B) plus Other Assets (C) less all claimed exemptions: $ _____

E.   Additional Comments regarding Liquidation Analysis: _____

IX.   SIGNATURES.

Pursuant to the Chapter 13 rules, the debtor or his or her attorney is required to serve a copy of the Plan upon the Chapter 13 Trustee, all creditors and interested parties, and to file a Certificate of Service accordingly.

_____   _____
Debtor's Attorney   Date

Attorney's Address: _____

                      _____

                      _____

                Tel. # (   ) _____—_____

                Email Address: _____

I/WE DECLARE UNDER THE PENALTIES OF PERJURY THAT THE FORE-GOING REPRESENTATIONS OF FACT ARE TRUE AND CORRECT TO THE BEST OF OUR KNOWLEDGE AND BELIEF.

_____   _____
Debtor   Date

_____   _____
Debtor   Date

[Effective August 1, 1997. Amended December 8, 2003; January 2006; May 1, 2008.]

OFFICIAL LOCAL FORM 3A. POST–CONFIRMATION AMENDED CHAPTER 13 PLAN

UNITED STATES BANKRUPTCY COURT
DISTRICT OF MASSACHUSETTS

DATED: _____

POST–CONFIRMATION _____ AMENDED CHAPTER 13 PLAN

(Insert First, Second etc.)

Docket No.: _____

DEBTOR(S): (H) _____   SS#: _____

(W) _____   SS#: _____

I. AMENDED PLAN PAYMENT AND TERM:

TERM OF THE PLAN: _____ Months (Total length of Plan—not no. of months remaining.) If the plan is longer than thirty-six (36) months, a statement of cause under 11 U.S.C. § 1322(d) must be attached hereto.

AMENDED PLAN PAYMENT: Debtor(s) to pay monthly: $ _____

EFFECTIVE: ___ / ___ / ___ (Insert new payment beginning date.)

The claims listed below must include amounts previously disbursed by the Trustee on all claims which have subsequently been withdrawn or disallowed.

II. SECURED CLAIMS:

A. Claims to be paid through the plan (including arrears):

Creditor	Description of Claim (pre-petition arrears, purchase money, etc.)	Amount of Claim
_____	_____	$ _____
_____	_____	$ _____
_____	_____	$ _____

Total of secured claims to be paid through the Plan: $ _____

B. Claims to be paid directly by debtor to creditors (Not through Plan):

Creditor	Description of Claim
_____	_____
_____	_____
_____	_____

C. Modification of Secured Claims:

Creditor	Details of Modification (Additional Details May Be Attached)	Amt. of Claim to Be Paid Through Plan
_____	_____	_____
_____	_____	_____
_____	_____	_____

D. Leases:

    i.   The Debtor(s) intend(s) to reject the residential/personal property lease claims of _____; or

    ii. The Debtor(s) intend(s) to assume the residential/personal property lease claims of _____.

    iii. The arrears under the lease to be paid under the plan are _____.

III. PRIORITY CLAIMS:

A. Domestic Support Obligations:

Creditor	Description of Claim	Amount of Claim
_____	_____	$ _____

B. Other:

Creditor	Description of Claim	Amount of Claim
_____	_____	$ _____
_____	_____	$ _____
_____	_____	$ _____
_____	_____	$ _____

Total of Priority Claims to Be Paid Through the Plan: $ _____

IV. ADMINISTRATIVE CLAIMS:

A. Attorneys Fees (to be paid through the plan): $ _____

B. Miscellaneous Fees:

Creditor	Description of Claim	Amount of Claim
_____	_____	$ _____
_____	_____	$ _____
_____	_____	$ _____

C. The Chapter 13 Trustee's fee is determined by Order of the United States Attorney General. The calculation of the Plan payment set forth utilizes a 10% Trustee's commission.

V. UNSECURED CLAIMS: The general unsecured creditors shall receive a dividend of ___ % of their claims.

A. General unsecured claims: $ _____

B. Undersecured claims arising after lien avoidance/cramdown:

Creditor   Description of Claim   Amount of Claim

_____   _____ $ _____

_____   _____ $ _____

_____   _____ $ _____

C. Non–Dischargeable Unsecured Claims:

Creditor   Description of Claim   Amount of Claim

_____   _____ $ _____

_____   _____ $ _____

_____   _____ $ _____

Total of Unsecured Claims (A + B + C): $ _____

D. Multiply total by percentage: $ _____
(Example: Total of $38,500.00 × .22 dividend = $8,470.00)

E. Separately classified unsecured claims (co-borrower, etc.):

Creditor   Description of Claim   Amount of Claim

_____   _____ $ _____

_____   _____ $ _____

_____   _____ $ _____

Total amount of separately classified claims payable at ___%: $ _____

VI. OTHER PROVISIONS:

A. Liquidation of assets to be used to fund plan: _____.

_____

B. Miscellaneous Provisions:

_____

C. Set forth below, all changes from the previously Confirmed Plan:

Secured: _____.

Priority: _____.

Unsecured: _____.

Term: _____.

Plan Payment: _____.

VII. CALCULATION OF AMENDED PLAN PAYMENT:

a) Secured claims (Section II–A Total): $ _____
b) Priority claims (Section III–A & B Total): $ _____
c) Administrative claims (Section IV–A&B Total): $ _____
d) Regular unsecured claims (Section V–D Total): + $ _____
e) Separately classified unsecured claims: $ _____

f) Total of a + b + c + d + e above: = $ _____
g) Divide (f) by .90 for total including Trustee's fee:
                                    Cost of Plan   = $ _____
(This represents the total amount to be paid into the Chapter 13 Plan.)
h) Subtract the total amount of payment the Debtor has
      paid to the Trustee to date: $ _____
i) Total amount left to be paid (g minus h) $ _____
j) Divide (i) by # of months remaining: _____
k) Round up to nearest dollar: Amended Monthly Plan
      Payment $ _____

                    Date Amended Payment to begin: ____/____/_____

VIII. LIQUIDATION ANALYSIS.

☐ The Debtor avers that there have been no material changes to the total amount set forth in the Summary of the Liquidation Analysis of the Debtor's previously Confirmed Plan.

A. Real Estate:

List Each Address	Fair Market Value	Total Amt. of Recorded Liens (Schedule D)
_____	$ _____	$ _____
_____	$ _____	$ _____
_____	$ _____	$ _____
Total Net Equity for Real Property:		$ _____
Less Total Exemptions (Schedule C):		$ _____
Available Chapter 7:		$ _____

B.   Automobile (Describe year, make, model):

_____ Value $ _____ Lien $ _____ Exemption $ _____

_____ Value $ _____ Lien $ _____ Exemption $ _____

Total Net Equity: $ _____

Less Total Exemptions (Schedule C) $ _____

Available Chapter 7: $ _____

C.   All other Assets: (All remaining items on schedule B): (Itemize as necessary)

_____

Total Net Value: $ _____

Less Exemptions (Schedule C): $ _____

Available Chapter 7: $ _____

D.   Liquidation Summary (Total amount available under Chapter 7):

Net Equity (A and B) plus Other Assets (C) less all claimed exemptions: $ _____

Additional Comments regarding Liquidation Analysis:

_____

_____

IX.   Signatures.

Pursuant to the Chapter 13 rules, the debtor(s) or his or her counsel will serve a copy of the Plan upon the Chapter 13 Trustee, all creditors and interested parties, and file a Certificate of Service accordingly.

_____   _____

Debtor's Counsel   Date

Counsel's Address: _____

_____

_____

Tel. # (   ) _____—_____

Email Address: _____

I/WE DECLARE UNDER THE PENALTIES OF PERJURY THAT THE FORE-GOING REPRESENTATIONS OF FACT ARE TRUE AND CORRECT TO THE BEST OF OUR KNOWLEDGE AND BELIEF.

_____   _____

Debtor   Date

_____   _____
Debtor   Date

[Effective May 1, 2008.]

OFFICIAL LOCAL FORM 4.   ORDER CONFIRMING
CHAPTER 13 PLAN

UNITED STATES BANKRUPTCY COURT DISTRICT OF MASSACHUSETTS

UNITED STATES BANKRUPTCY COURT
DISTRICT OF MASSACHUSETTS

In re   Case No.

                             ,   Chapter

                    Debtor

ORDER CONFIRMING CHAPTER 13 PLAN

The debtor(s) filed a First Amended Chapter 13 Plan (the "Plan") on _____. The debtor(s) filed a Certificate of Service on _____, reflecting that the Plan was served on all creditors and parties in interest. No objections to the confirmation of the Plan were filed, or all objections were overruled by the Court or resolved by the parties. Upon consideration of the foregoing, the Court hereby orders the following:

1.   The Plan is confirmed. The term of the Plan ____ months.

2.   The debtor(s) shall pay to the chapter 13 trustee the sum of $_____ per month commencing _____ which payments shall continue through completion of the Plan and shall be made on the first day of each month unless otherwise ordered by the Court. Payments shall be made by Money Order or Bank Treasurer's check (personal checks will not be accepted) and shall be made payable to and forwarded to; Chapter 13 Trustee, P.O. Box 8250, Boston, MA 02114 or, if applicable, Chapter 13 Trustee, P.O. Box 16607, Worcester, MA 01601.

3.   The effective date of confirmation of the Plan is _____. The disbursements to be made by the chapter 13 trustee pursuant to the confirmed plan are set forth on the attached summary which is incorporated by reference. Interested parties should consult the detailed provisions of the Plan for treatment of their particular claims and other significant provisions of the Plan. Unless otherwise ordered by the court, all property of the estate as defined in 11 U.S.C. §§ 541 and 1306, including, but not limited to, any appreciation in the value of real property owned by the debtor as of the commencement of the case, shall remain property of the estate during the term of the plan and shall vest in the debtor(s) only upon discharge. All property of the estate shall remain within the exclusive jurisdiction of the bankruptcy court. The debtor(s) shall not transfer, sell or otherwise alienate property of the estate other than in accordance with the confirmed plan or other order of the bankruptcy court. The debtor shall be responsible for, preserving and protecting property of the estate.

Dated: _____, 20__

_____
United States Bankruptcy Judge

SUMMARY OF DISBURSEMENTS TO BE MADE UNDER THE PLAN

A.   SECURED CLAIMS
1.   Modified Secured Claims

The secured claim of (Creditor) is being modified as follows: (describe modified treatment). The secured creditor is retaining its lien on (describe property) to the following extent: _____. The balance of the claim will be treated as an unsecured claim in the sum of $_____ as set forth below.

2.   Unmodified Secured Claims

(Creditor) is retaining its lien on (describe property). The debtor(s) shall continue to make regular monthly payments in accordance with the contract with (creditor). (Creditor) will be paid its prepetition arrearage in the sum of $_____ over _____ months in the sum of $_____ per month.

3.   Administrative Claims

(Creditor) will be paid $_____ over _____ months.

4.   Priority Claims

   a) Tax Claims

   b) Other

5.   Unsecured Claims

6.   Other Pertinent Provisions

[Effective August 1, 1997. Amended effective September 1, 1999.]

OFFICIAL LOCAL FORM 5. ORDER AND NOTICE FIXING DEADLINE FOR FILING PROOFS OF CLAIM IN CHAPTER 11 CASES

UNITED STATES BANKRUPTCY COURT
DISTRICT OF MASSACHUSETTS

In re   Case No.

                      ,   Chapter

                    Debtor

ORDER AND NOTICE FIXING DEADLINE
FOR FILING PROOFS OF CLAIM IN CHAPTER 11 CASES

This matter having come before the Court on the Motion for an Order Fixing Deadline for Filing Proofs of Claim (the "Motion"), and good cause having been shown, it is hereby

ORDERED, ADJUDGED AND DECREED:

1. Except as provided in paragraphs 2 or 3 below, any individual or entity asserting a claim against the estate of the Debtor must file a proof of claim with the Clerk's Office, United States Bankruptcy Court for the District of Massachusetts, _____—_____ (address) _____, on or before 4:00 p.m. on _____, 20 ___ (the "Bar Date"). A proof of claim shall not be deemed filed until it is actually received and time stamped by the Clerk of the United States Bankruptcy Court at the above address.

2. No proof of claim shall be required with respect to any claim listed as liquidated, undisputed and not contingent in the Debtor's Schedules of Liabilities filed with this Court on _____, 20 ___, provided, however, that no such claim may be allowed in an amount exceeding the amount as listed unless a proof of claim for a higher amount is filed.

3. Any individual or entity asserting a claim of the type described in 11 U.S.C. § 502(g), (h) or (i) shall file a proof of claim with the Clerk's Office, United States Bankruptcy Court for the District of Massachusetts, at the address specified above by the Bar Date or, if later, the 30th day after (a) in the case of the claim of the type described in 11 U.S.C. § 502(g), entry of an Order of this Court approving the rejection of the executory contract or unexpired lease giving rise to such claim; (b) in the case of a claim of a type described in 11 U.S.C. § 502(h), entry of an Order or Judgment avoiding such transfer; or (c) in the case of a claim of the type described in 11 U.S.C. § 502(i), the date such type of claim arises.

4. Any claim against the Debtor for which a proof of claim is required, but is not timely filed under the terms of this Order, shall be forever disallowed and barred as a claim against the Debtor whether for purposes of voting, sharing in any distribution, or in any other way participating as a party in interest in this proceeding.

5. The Debtor shall serve a copy of this Order upon all creditors listed in the Schedules, and all parties who filed or entered their appearance in this case, within fourteen (14) days after the entry of this Order. Service of this Order shall constitute effective notice of the Bar Date. The Debtor shall promptly file a certificate of service with this Court.

Entered at Boston, Massachusetts, this ___ day of _____, 20 ___.

_____
United States Bankruptcy Judge

[Effective August 1, 1997.   Amended December 8, 2003; December 1, 2009.]

OFFICIAL LOCAL FORM 6. REAFFIRMATION AGREEMENT

UNITED STATES BANKRUPTCY COURT
DISTRICT OF MASSACHUSETTS

**UNITED STATES BANKRUPTCY COURTS
DISTRICT OF MASSACHUSETTS**

In re   Case No.

                    ,   Chapter

             Debtor

REAFFIRMATION AGREEMENT COVER SHEET

This form must be completed in its entirety and filed, with the reaffirmation agreement attached, within the time set under Rule 4008. It may be filed by any party to the reaffirmation agreement.

1. Creditor's Name: _____

2. Amount of the debt subject to this reaffirmation agreement:

   $ ___ on the date of bankruptcy

   $ ___ to be paid under reaffirmation agreement

3. Annual percentage rate of interest: ___% prior to bankruptcy ___% under reaffirmation agreement (___ Fixed Rate ___ Adjustable Rate)

4. Repayment terms (if fixed rate): $ _____ per month for ___ months

5. Collateral, if any, securing the debt: Current market value: $ _____ Description: _____

6. Does the creditor assert that the debt is nondischargeable? ___ Yes ___ No (If yes, attach a declaration setting forth the nature of the debt and basis for the contention that the debt is nondischargeable.)

Debtor's Schedule I and J Entries	**Debtor's Income and Expenses as Stated on Reaffirmation Agreement**
7A. Total monthly income from Schedule I, line 16 $___	7B. Monthly income from all sources after payroll deductions $___
8A. Total monthly expenses from Schedule J, line 16 $___	8B. Monthly expenses $___
9A. Total monthly payment on reaffirmed debts not listed on Schedule J $___	9B. Total monthly payments on reaffirmed debts not included in monthly expenses $___
	10B. Net monthly income (Subtract sum of lines 8B and 9B from line 7B. If total is less than zero, put the number in brackets.) $___

11. Explain with specificity any difference between the income amounts (7A and 7B): _____

12. Explain with specificity any difference between the expense amounts (8A and 8B): _____

If line 11 or 12 is completed, the undersigned debtor, and joint debtor if applicable, certifies that any explanation contained on those lines is true and correct.

_____   _____
Signature of Debtor (only required   Signature of Joint Debtor (if applicable,
if line 11 or 12 is completed.)   and line 11 or 12 is completed)

Other Information

( ) Check this box if the total on line 10B is less than zero. If that number is less than zero, a presumption of undue hardship arises (unless the creditor is a credit union) and you must explain with specificity the sources of funds available to the Debtor to make the monthly payments on the reaffirmed debt: _____
_____

Was debtor represented by counsel during the course of negotiating this reaffirmation agreement?

___ Yes ___ No

If debtor was represented by counsel during the course of negotiating this reaffirmation agreement, has counsel executed a certification (affidavit or declaration) in support of the reaffirmation agreement?

___ Yes ___ No

FILER'S CERTIFICATION

I hereby certify that the attached agreement is a true and correct copy of the reaffirmation agreement between the parties identified on this Reaffirmation Agreement Cover Sheet.

_____
Signature

_____
Print/Type Name & Signer's Relation to Case

_____

UNITED STATES BANKRUPTCY COURT
DISTRICT OF MASSACHUSETTS

☐ Presumption of Undue Hardship
☐ No Presumption of Undue Hardship
(Check box as directed in Part D: Debtor's Statement In Support of Reaffirmation
Agreement.)

In re   Case No.

                                             Chapter

            Debtor(s)

REAFFIRMATION AGREEMENT

[Indicate all documents included in this filing by checking each applicable box.]
☐   Part A: Disclosures, Instructions,   ☐   Part D: Debtor's Statement in

and Notice to Debtor (Pages 1–5)   Support of Reaffirmation Agreement

☐   Part B: Reaffirmation Agreement   ☐   Part E: Motion for Court Approval

☐   Part C: Certification by Debtor's Attorney   ☐   Proposed Order Approving Reaffirmation Agreement

Name of Creditor: _____

☐   [Check this box if] Creditor is a Credit Union as defined in § 19(b)(1)(a)(iv) of the Federal Reserve Act.

PART A: DISCLOSURE STATEMENT, INSTRUCTIONS AND NOTICE TO DEBTOR

1. **DISCLOSURE STATEMENT**—*Before Agreeing to Reaffirm a Debt, Review These Important Disclosures:*

SUMMARY OF REAFFIRMATION AGREEMENT

This Summary is made pursuant to the requirements of the Bankruptcy Code.

AMOUNT REAFFIRMED

The amount of debt you have agreed to reaffirm: $ _____

The amount of debt you have agreed to reaffirm includes all fees and costs (if any) that have accrued as of the date of this disclosure. Your credit agreement may obligate you to pay additional amounts which may come due after the date of this disclosure. Consult your credit agreement.

ANNUAL PERCENTAGE RATE

[The annual percentage rate can be disclosed in different ways, depending on the type of debt.]

a. If the debt is an extension of "credit" under an "open end credit plan," as those terms are defined in § 103 of the Truth in Lending Act, such as a credit card, the creditor may disclose the annual percentage rate shown in (i) below or, to the extent this rate is not readily available or not applicable, the simple interest rate shown in (ii) below, or both.

   (i) The Annual Percentage Rate disclosed, or that would have been disclosed, to the debtor in the most recent periodic statement prior to entering into the reaffirmation agreement described in Part B below or, if no such periodic statement was given to the debtor during the prior six months, the annual percentage rate as it would have been so disclosed at the time of the disclosure statement: ___ %.

— **And/Or** —

   (ii) The simple interest rate applicable to the amount reaffirmed as of the date his disclosure statement is given to the debtor: _____ %. If different simple interest

rates apply to different balances included in the amount reaffirmed, the amount of each balance and the rate applicable to it are:

    $ _____ @ _____ %;

    $ _____ @ _____ %;

    $ _____ @ _____ %.

b. If the debt is an extension of credit other than under than an open end credit plan, the creditor may disclose the annual percentage rate shown in (i) below, or, to the extent this rate is not readily available or not applicable, the simple interest rate shown in (ii) below, or both.

(i) The Annual Percentage Rate under § 128(a)(4) of the Truth in Lending Act, as disclosed to the debtor in the most recent disclosure statement given to the debtor prior to entering into the reaffirmation agreement with respect to the debt or, if no such disclosure statement was given to the debtor, the annual percentage rate as it would have been so disclosed: _____ %.

--- **And/Or** ---

(ii) The simple interest rate applicable to the amount reaffirmed as of the date this disclosure statement is given to the debtor: _____ %. If different simple interest rates apply to different balances included in the amount reaffirmed, the amount of each balance and the rate applicable to it are:

$ _____ @ _____ %;

$ _____ @ _____ %;

$ _____ @ _____ %.

c. If the underlying debt transaction was disclosed as a variable rate transaction on the most recent disclosure given under the Truth in Lending Act: The interest rate on your loan may be a variable interest rate which changes from time to time, so that the annual percentage rate disclosed here may be higher or lower.

d. If the reaffirmed debt is secured by a security interest or lien, which has not been waived or determined to be void by a final order of the court, the following items or types of items of the debtor's goods or property remain subject to such security interest or lien in connection with the debt or debts being reaffirmed in the reaffirmation agreement described in Part B.

Item or Type of Item   Original Purchase Price or Original Amount of Loan

Optional --- At the election of the creditor, a repayment schedule using one or a combination of the following may be provided:

Repayment Schedule:

Your first payment in the amount of $ _____ is due on _____ (date), but the future payment amount may be different. Consult your reaffirmation agreement or credit agreement, as applicable.

--- **Or** ---

Your payment schedule will be: _____ (number) payments in the amount of $ _____ each, payable (monthly, annually, weekly, etc.) on the _____ (day) of each _____ (week, month, etc.), unless altered later by mutual agreement in writing.

--- **Or** ---

A reasonably specific description of the debtor's repayment obligations to the extent known by the creditor or creditor's representative.

2. **INSTRUCTIONS AND NOTICE TO DEBTOR**

Reaffirming a debt is a serious financial decision. The law requires you to take certain steps to make sure the decision is in your best interest. If these steps are not completed, the reaffirmation agreement is not effective, even though you have signed it.

a. Read the disclosures in this Part A carefully. Consider the decision to reaffirm carefully. Then, if you want to reaffirm, sign the reaffirmation agreement in Part B (or you may use a separate agreement you and your creditor agree on).

b. Complete and sign Part D and be sure you can afford to make the payments you are agreeing to make and have received a copy of the disclosure statement and a completed and signed reaffirmation agreement.

c. If you were represented by an attorney during the negotiation of your reaffirmation agreement, the attorney must have signed the certification in Part C.

d. If you were not represented by an attorney during the negotiation of your reaffirmation agreement, you must have completed and signed Part E.

e. The original of this disclosure must be filed with the court by you or your creditor. If a separate reaffirmation agreement (other than the one in Part B) has been signed, it must be attached.

f. If the creditor is not a Credit Union and you were represented by an attorney during the negotiation of your reaffirmation agreement, your reaffirmation agreement becomes effective upon filing with the court unless the reaffirmation is presumed to be an undue hardship as explained in Part D. If the creditor is a Credit Union and you were represented by an attorney during the negotiation of your reaffirmation agreement, your reaffirmation agreement becomes effective upon filing with the court.

g. If you were not represented by an attorney during the negotiation of your reaffirmation agreement, it will not be effective unless the court approves it. The court will notify you and the creditor of the hearing on your reaffirmation agreement.

You must attend this hearing in bankruptcy court where the judge will review your reaffirmation agreement. The bankruptcy court must approve your reaffirmation agreement as consistent with your best interests, except that no court approval is required if your reaffirmation agreement is for a consumer debt secured by a mortgage, deed of trust, security deed, or other lien on your real property, like your home.

YOUR RIGHT TO RESCIND (CANCEL) YOUR REAFFIRMATION AGREEMENT

You may rescind (cancel) your reaffirmation agreement at any time before the bankruptcy court enters a discharge order, or before the expiration of the 60–day period that begins on the date your reaffirmation agreement is filed with the court, whichever occurs later. To rescind (cancel) your reaffirmation agreement, you must notify the creditor that your reaffirmation agreement is rescinded (or canceled).

Frequently Asked Questions:

What are your obligations if you reaffirm the debt?

A reaffirmed debt remains your personal legal obligation. It is not discharged in your bankruptcy case. That means that if you default on your reaffirmed debt after your bankruptcy case is over, your creditor may be able to take your property or your wages. Otherwise, your obligations will be determined by the reaffirmation agreement which may have changed the terms of the original agreement. For example, if you are reaffirming an open end credit agreement, the creditor may be permitted by that agreement or applicable law to change the terms of that agreement in the future under certain conditions.

Are you required to enter into a reaffirmation agreement by any law?

No, you are not required to reaffirm a debt by any law. Only agree to reaffirm a debt if it is in your best interest. Be sure you can afford the payments you agree to make.

What if your creditor has a security interest or lien?

Your bankruptcy discharge does not eliminate any lien on your property. A "lien" is often referred to as a security interest, deed of trust, mortgage or security deed. Even if you do not reaffirm and your personal liability on the debt is discharged, because of the lien your creditor may still have the right to take the security property if you do not pay the debt or default on it. If the lien is on an item of personal property that is exempt under your State's law or that the trustee has abandoned, you may be able to redeem the item rather than reaffirm the debt. To redeem, you make a single payment to the creditor equal to the current value of the security property, as agreed by the parties or determined by the court.

NOTE: When this disclosure refers to what a creditor "may" do, it does not use the word "may" to give the creditor specific permission. The word "may" is used to tell you what might occur if the law permits the creditor to take the action. If you have questions about your reaffirming a debt or what the law requires, consult with the attorney who helped you negotiate this agreement reaffirming a debt. If you don't have an attorney helping you, the judge will explain the effect of your reaffirming a debt when the hearing on the reaffirmation agreement is held.

PART B: REAFFIRMATION AGREEMENT.

I (we) agree to reaffirm the debts arising under the credit agreement described below.

    1.   Brief description of credit agreement:

    2.   Description of any changes to the credit agreement made as part of this reaffirmation agreement:

SIGNATURE(S):

Borrower: Accepted by creditor:

_____   _____
(Print Name of Borrower)   (Printed Name of Creditor)

_____   _____
(Signature)   (Address of Creditor)

Date: _____   _____
                                                          (Signature)

Co-borrower, if also reaffirming these   _____
debts   (Printed Name and Title of Individual Signing for Creditor)

_____   _____
(Print Name of Co-borrower)   Date of creditor acceptance:

_____   _____
(Signature)

Date: _____

PART C: CERTIFICATION BY DEBTOR'S ATTORNEY (IF ANY).
[Check each applicable box.]

    ☐ *[Check box, if applicable]* I hereby certify that, based on information provided by the debtor, (1) this agreement represents a fully informed and voluntary agreement by the debtor; (2) based upon information provided, this agreement does not impose an undue hardship on the debtor or any dependent of the debtor; and (3) I have fully advised the debtor of the legal effect and consequences of this agreement and any default under this agreement.

     ☐ *[Check box, if applicable and the creditor is not a Credit Union.]* A presumption of undue hardship has been established with respect to this agreement. In my opinion, however, the debtor is able to make the required payment. Notwithstanding the foregoing, I do not warrant the ability of the debtor to perform the terms of this reaffirmation agreement, and the execution of this declaration by me shall in no way be construed as a guaranty by me of the debtor's obligations under this reaffirmation agreement.

Printed Name of Debtor's Attorney: _____

Signature of Debtor's Attorney: _____

Date: _____

PART D: DEBTOR'S STATEMENT IN SUPPORT OF REAFFIRMATION AGREEMENT

     [Read and complete numbered paragraphs 1 and 2, **OR**, if the creditor is a Credit Union and the debtor is represented by an attorney, read the unnumbered paragraph below. Sign the appropriate signature line(s) and date your signature. If you complete paragraphs 1 and 2 and your income less monthly expenses does not leave enough to make the payments under this reaffirmation agreement, check the box at the top of page 1 indicating "Presumption of Undue Hardship." Otherwise, check the box at the top of page 1 indicating "No Presumption of Undue Hardship"]

1.   I believe this reaffirmation agreement will not impose an undue hardship on my dependents or me. I can afford to make the payments on the reaffirmed debt because my monthly income (take home pay plus any other income received) is $ ..., and my actual current monthly expenses including monthly payments on post-bankruptcy debt and other reaffirmation agreements total $ ..., leaving $ ... to make the required payments on this reaffirmed debt.

     I understand that if my income less my monthly expenses does not leave enough to make the payments, this reaffirmation agreement is presumed to be an undue hardship on me and must be reviewed by the court. However, this presumption may be overcome if I explain to the satisfaction of the court how I can afford to make the payments here: _____.

2.   I received a copy of the Reaffirmation Disclosure Statement in Part A and a completed and signed reaffirmation agreement.

Signed: _____ Date: _____
           (Debtor)

Signed: _____ Date: _____
           (Joint Debtor, if any)

— Or—

[If the creditor is a Credit Union and the debtor is represented by an attorney]

     I believe this reaffirmation agreement is in my financial interest. I can afford to make the payments on the reaffirmed debt. I received a copy of the Reaffirmation Disclosure Statement in Part A and a completed and signed reaffirmation agreement.

Signed: _____ Date: _____
           (Debtor)

Signed: _____ Date: _____
           (Joint Debtor, if any)

PART E: MOTION FOR COURT APPROVAL

[To be completed and filed only if the debtor is not represented by an attorney in negotiating the reaffirmation agreement.]

Motion for Court Approval of Reaffirmation Agreement

I (we), the debtor(s), affirm the following to be true and correct:

I am not represented by an attorney in connection with this reaffirmation agreement.

I believe this reaffirmation agreement is in my best interest based on the income and expenses I have disclosed in my Statement in Support of this reaffirmation agreement, and because (provide any additional relevant reasons the court should consider):

Therefore, I ask the court for an order approving this reaffirmation agreement.

Signed: _____ Date: _____
           (Debtor)

Signed: _____ Date: _____
           (Joint Debtor, if any)

United States Bankruptcy Court
District of Massachusetts

In re   Case No.

          ,   Chapter

      Debtor

ORDER APPROVING REAFFIRMATION AGREEMENT

The debtor(s) _____ have filed a motion for approval of the
      (Name(s) of Debtor(s))

reaffirmation agreement dated _____ made between the debtor(s) and
           (Date of Agreement)

_____. The court held the hearing required by 11 U.S.C. § 524(d)
(Name of Creditor)

on notice to the debtor(s) and the creditor on _____
                             (Date).

COURT ORDER: The court grants the debtor's motion and approves the reaffirmation agreement described above.

BY THE COURT

Date: _____   _____
                               United States Bankruptcy Judge

[Effective September 1, 1999; Amended effective October 1, 2006; December 1, 2009.]

OFFICIAL LOCAL FORM 7. DECLARATION RE: ELECTRONIC FILING
UNITED STATES BANKRUPTCY COURT
DISTRICT OF MASSACHUSETTS

In re	)	Chapter
	)	Case No.
	)	
	)	
	)	
Debtor	)	
	)	

DECLARATION RE: ELECTRONIC FILING

PART I—DECLARATION

I[We] _____ and _____, *hereby declare(s) under penalty of perjury* that all of the information contained in my _____ (singly or jointly the "Document"), filed electronically, is true and correct. I understand that this *DECLARATION* is to be filed with the Clerk of Court electronically concurrently with the electronic filing of the Document. I understand that failure to file this *DECLARATION* may cause the Document to be struck and any request contained or relying thereon to be denied, without further notice.

I further understand that, pursuant to the Massachusetts Electronic Filing Local Rule (MEFR) 7(b), all paper documents containing original signatures executed under the penalties of perjury and filed electronically with the Court are the property of the bankruptcy estate and shall be maintained by the authorized CM/ECF Registered User for a period of five (5) years after the closing of this case.

Dated:

_____
(Affiant)

_____
(Joint Affiant)

PART II—DECLARATION OF ATTORNEY (IF AFFIANT IS REPRESENTED BY COUNSEL)

I certify that the affiant(s) signed this form before I submitted the Document, I gave the affiant(s) a copy of the Document and this *DECLARATION*, and I have followed all other electronic filing requirements currently established by local rule and standing order. This *DECLARATION* is based on all information of which I have knowledge and my signature below constitutes my certification of the foregoing under Fed.R.Bankr.P. 9011. I have reviewed and will comply with the provisions of MEFR 7.

Dated:

Signed: _____
            Attorney for Affiant

[Effective March 1, 2003. Amended effective January 1, 2005.]

OFFICIAL LOCAL FORM 8.   CHAPTER 13 AGREEMENT BETWEEN DEBTOR AND COUNSEL—RIGHTS AND RESPONSIBILITIES OF CHAPTER 13 DEBTORS AND THEIR ATTORNEYS

UNITED STATES BANKRUPTCY COURT
DISTRICT OF MASSACHUSETTS

In re	)	Chapter
	)	Case No.
	)	
	)	
	)	
Debtor	)	
	)	

CHAPTER 13 AGREEMENT BETWEEN DEBTOR AND COUNSEL
RIGHTS AND RESPONSIBILITIES OF CHAPTER 13 DEBTORS
AND THEIR ATTORNEYS

It is important for debtors who file bankruptcy cases under Chapter 13 to understand their rights and responsibilities. It is also useful for debtors to know what their attorney's responsibilities are, and understand the importance of communicating with their attorney to make the case successful. Debtors should also know that they may expect certain services to be performed by their attorney. To encourage that debtors and their attorneys understand their rights and responsibilities in the bankruptcy process, the following terms are agreed to by the debtors and their attorneys.

BEFORE THE CASE IS FILED:

The DEBTOR agrees to:

1.   Provide the attorney with accurate financial information; and

2.   Discuss with the attorney the debtor's objectives in filing the case.

The ATTORNEY agrees to:

1.   Meet with the debtor to review the debtor's debts, assets, income and expenses;

2.   Counsel the debtor regarding the advisability of filing either a Chapter 7 or Chapter 13 case, discuss both procedures with the debtor, and answer the debtor's questions;

3.   Explain what payments will be made through the plan, and what payments will be made directly by the debtor for mortgage and vehicle loan payments, as well as which claims accrue interest;

4.   Explain to the debtor how, when, and where to make the Chapter 13 plan payments, as well as the debtor's obligation to continue making mortgage payments, without interruption, and the likely consequences for failure to do so;

5.   Explain to the debtor how the attorney's fees and trustee's fees are paid, and provide an executed copy of this document to the debtor;

6.   Explain to the debtor that the first plan payment must be made to the Trustee within 30 days of the date the plan is filed;

7.   Advise the debtor of the requirement to attend the 341 Meeting of Creditors, and instruct debtor as to the date, time and place of the meeting;

8.   Advise the debtor of the necessity of maintaining appropriate insurance on all real estate, motor vehicles and business assets; and

9.   Timely prepare and file the debtor's petition, plan and schedules.

AFTER THE CASE IS FILED:

The DEBTOR agrees to:

Keep the Trustee and attorney informed for the debtor's address and telephone number;

1.   Inform the attorney of any wage garnishments or attachments of assets which occur or continue after the filing of the case;

2.   Contact the attorney if the debtor loses his/her job or has other financial problems (the attorney may be able to have the Chapter 13 plan payments reduced or suspended in those circumstances), or alternatively obtains a material increase in income or assets;

3.   Advise counsel if the debtor is sued during the case;

4.   Inform the attorney if tax refunds to which the debtor is entitled are seized or not received;

Advise counsel and the Trustee before buying or selling property or before entering into any long-term loan agreements, to determine what approvals are required;

Provide the Trustee and the attorney, prior to the Section 341 meeting of creditors, with documentary evidence as to debtor's income from all sources and the value of any asset in which the debtor has an interest, together with a copy of any declaration of homestead covering the debtor's real estate, proof of insurance on any real property or automobiles in which the debtor has an interest, and any other documents which the Trustee might reasonably request in order to assess whether the debtor's proposed plan should be confirmed.

The ATTORNEY agrees to provide the following legal services in consideration of the compensation further described below:

1.   Appear at the 341 Meeting of Creditors with the debtor;

2.   Respond to objections to plan confirmation, and where necessary, prepare an amended plan;

3.   Prepare, file and serve one necessary modification to the plan which may include suspending, lowering, or increasing plan payments;

4.   Prepare, file and serve necessary amended schedules in accordance with information provided by the debtor;

5.   Prepare, file and serve necessary motions to buy, sell or refinance real property;

6.   Object to improper or invalid claims, if necessary, based upon documentation provided by the debtor;

7.   Represent the debtor in motions for relief from stay;

8.   Where appropriate, prepare, file and serve necessary motions to avoid liens on real or personal property; and

9.   Provide such other legal services as necessary for the administration of the case.

The initial fees charged in this case are $_____.   Any and all additional terms of compensation and additional services agreed to be rendered, if any, are set forth in writing and annexed hereto.   If the initial fees are not sufficient to compensate the attorney for the legal services rendered in this case, the attorney further agrees to apply to the court for additional fees.   If the debtor disputes the legal services provided or the fees charged by the attorney, an objection may be filed with the court and the matter set for hearing.

Debtor signature: _____ Dated:_____

Co–debtor signature: _____ Dated:_____

Attorney for the debt-   _____ Dated:_____
or(s) signature:

[Effective March 1, 2003.]

OFFICIAL LOCAL FORM 9. REQUEST FOR EXTENSION TO FILE CREDIT COUNSELING CERTIFICATE

In re   Chapter
                                             Bankruptcy No.

             ,
        Debtor(s)

MOTION PURSUANT TO 11 U.S.C. § 109(h)(3) FOR EXTENSION OF TIME TO FILE CREDIT COUNSELING CERTIFICATE

Pursuant to 11 U.S.C. § 109(h)(3), the Debtor(s) certify(ies) that he/she/they did not obtain the credit counseling briefing pursuant to 11 U.S.C. § 109(h)(1) and moves that the Court extend the time to file and/or obtain a credit counseling certificate, based upon the following grounds:

1) The following exigent circumstances exist preventing compliance (for example, foreclosure, eviction, incarceration, medical or other problems):

   _____

2) I/We (**Check whichever applies**)

   ____ did request credit counseling services from an approved agency but was/were unable to obtain said services during the 5–day period following the request.

   ____ did not request credit counseling services.

3) I/We request an extension of time to a date no longer than 45 days after the date of the filing of the bankruptcy petition because:

   _____

Signed under the pains and penalties of perjury on this ____ day of _____ ,
____.

_____   _____
Debtor   Joint Debtor

ORDER

☐ The Motion is denied.

☐ The Motion is approved. The time for filing the certificate is extended to ___.

_____
Dated: United States Bankruptcy Judge

[Effective October 1, 2006. Amended effective May 1, 2008.]

OFFICIAL LOCAL FORM 10. MOTION BROUGHT
UNDER 11 U.S.C. § 521(f)

UNITED STATES BANKRUPTCY COURT
DISTRICT OF MASSACHUSETTS

In re   Case No.
                                         Chapter

        Debtor

REQUEST FOR DEBTOR TO FILE FEDERAL
TAX INFORMATION WITH THE COURT

I, _____, am a party in interest in the above captioned case, and qualify as such for the following reasons:

_____

_____

The tax information designated below cannot be obtained from any other source, and is necessary for the following reasons: _____

Accordingly, pursuant to 11 U.S.C. § 521(f)(1–4), I hereby request that the Debtor file the following tax information with the Court:

_____

_____

I hereby declare under penalty of perjury that the foregoing is true and correct.

Dated:

Signed: _____ Print Name: _____

Address: _____

                                 Telephone Number: _____

Certificate of Service

I hereby certify that on _____ I mailed, by United States Postal Service, postage pre-paid, the Request for Debtor to File Tax Information With the Court on the following non CM/ECF participants:

ORDER

By the Court

____ The Motion is Denied

____ The Motion is Granted.

Dated: _____   _____
                                        United States Bankruptcy Judge

[Effective October 1, 2006.]

OFFICIAL LOCAL FORM 11. MOTION BROUGHT
UNDER 11 U.S.C. § 521(G)
UNITED STATES BANKRUPTCY COURT
DISTRICT OF MASSACHUSETTS

In re   Case No.
                                               Chapter

        Debtor

MOTION BY PARTY IN INTEREST FOR ACCESS TO
DEBTOR'S FEDERAL TAX INFORMATION

I, _____ am a party in interest in the above captioned case, and qualify as such for the following reasons:

_____

The tax information designated below cannot be obtained from any other source, and is necessary for the following reasons:

_____

I attempted, but failed, to resolve the dispute over access to the tax information prior to the filing of this motion.

Accordingly, pursuant to 11 U.S.C. § 521(g)(2), I hereby request access to the Debtor's tax information on file with the Court for the years: _____.

I hereby declare under penalty of perjury that the foregoing is true and correct.

Dated: _____

Signed: _____ Print Name: _____

Address: _____

Telephone Number: _____

Certificate of Service

I hereby certify that on _____ I mailed, by United States Postal Service, postage pre-paid, the Request for Debtor to File Tax Information With the Court on the following non CM/ECF participants:

ORDER

____ The Motion is Denied.

____ The Motion is Granted. The Clerk shall print a copy of the requested documents and mail the documents to the Movant. The Movant shall maintain the confidentiality of the documents. Sanctions may be imposed for the improper uses, disclosure, or dissemination or the information contained in the documents.

Dated: _____
                                          United States Bankruptcy Judge

[Effective October 1, 2006.]

OFFICIAL LOCAL FORM 12.   MOTION FOR ENTRY OF DISCHARGE

UNITED STATES BANKRUPTCY COURT
DISTRICT OF MASSACHUSETTS

In re   Case No.
                                     Chapter

         Debtor

MOTION FOR ENTRY OF DISCHARGE

I, _____, hereby move for an entry of a Chapter 13 discharge and certify as follows:

1. I have paid all domestic support obligations payable under any judicial or administrative order, or required by statute including:

   a. child support and spousal maintenance and alimony, that were due on or before the date of the motion, including all payments due under the plan for amounts due before the petition was filed; and

   b. any domestic support obligations that arose after the filing of the petition;

2. I have completed a financial management course pursuant to 11 U.S.C. § 1328(g)(1) and filed a certification of completion with the Court; and

3. I have:

   a. not claimed a homestead exemption in excess of the $125,000 cap described in § 522(q)(1), or

   b. claimed a homestead exemption in excess of $125,000 but there is no proceeding pending in which the debtor may be found guilty of a felony of the kind described in § 522(q)(1)(A) or liable for a debt of the kind described in § 522(q)(1)(B).

I hereby declare under the penalty of perjury that the foregoing is true and correct.

Dated: _____

Signed: _____   Print Name: _____

Address: _____

Telephone Number: _____

[Effective October 1, 2006.]

OFFICIAL LOCAL FORM 13.   MOTION FOR RELIEF FROM STAY—REAL ESTATE WORKSHEET

UNITED STATES BANKRUPTCY COURT
DISTRICT OF MASSACHUSETTS

In re   Case No.

                                                         Chapter

Debtor
MOTION FOR RELIEF FROM STAY—REAL ESTATE WORKSHEET
(To be attached to Motion for Relief from Stay)

I _____ of _____
(Name and Title)   (Name of Organization/Corporation/Moving Party)

(hereinafter, "Movant") hereby declare (or certify, verify, or state):

BACKGROUND INFORMATION

1. (a). Date chapter 13 petition was filed (if case has been converted from Chapter 7 to Chapter 13, provide date of petition and date of conversion):

(b). Address of real property which is the subject of this motion: _____
   _____.

2. (a). Original Mortgagee's Name and Address: _____
   _____.

   (b). Name and Address of Current Mortgage Holder: _____
   _____.

   (c). Name of Note Holder, if different than Mortgage Holder: _____
   _____.

3. Date of Mortgage: _____.

4. Post–Petition payment address, if different than above: _____
   _____.

5. The manner in which the Movant perfected its interest in the property: _____
   _____.

6. Other collateral securing the note: _____
   _____.

7. Other liens and encumbrances affecting the property in the order of their priority:

Names of Senior Lien holder	Amount Due	Source of Information (e.g., Schedules filed by Debtor(s), public records)

Movant's Lien		
Names of Junior Lien holders	Amount Due	Source of Information

8. Existence and Date of Recorded Homestead (if known): _____ .

DEBT/VALUE REPRESENTATIONS

9. Total pre-petition and post-petition indebtedness of Debtor(s) to Movant at the time of filing the motion: $ _____ .

(Note: this amount may not be relied on as a "payoff" quotation.)

10. (a). Movant's estimated fair market value of the real property: $ _____ .

    (b). Source of estimated fair market valuation: _____ .

    (c). Liquidation value of the real property: _____ .

STATUS OF DEBT AS OF THE PETITION DATE

11. (a). Total pre-petition indebtedness of Debtor(s) to Movant as of petition filing date: $ _____ .

    (b). Amount of principal: $ _____ .

    (c). Amount of interest: $ _____ .

    (d). Amount of escrow (taxes and insurance): $ _____ .

    (e). Amount of forced placed insurance expended by Movant: $ _____ .

    (f). Amount of Attorney's fees billed to Debtor(s) pre-petition: $ _____ .

    (g). Amount of pre-petition late fees, if any, billed to Debtor(s): $ _____ .

12. Contractual interest rate: ___ (If interest rate is (or was) adjustable, please list the rate(s) and dates(s) the rate(s) was/were in effect on a separate sheet and attach the sheet as an exhibit to this form; please list the exhibit number here: ___ .)

13. Explain any additional pre-petition fees, charges or amounts charged to the account of the Debtor(s) and not listed above: _____

(If additional space is needed, list the amounts on a separate sheet and attach the sheet as an exhibit to this form; list the exhibit number here: ___ .)

AMOUNT OF ALLEGED POST–PETITION DEFAULT
(AS OF _____ MM/DD/YYYY)

14. Date last payment was received: _____ (mm/dd/yyyy)

15. Total number of post-petition payments due from the date of the filing of petition through the date of this Motion or (mm/dd/yyyy): _____ .

SCHEDULE OF POST–PETITION PAYMENTS IN DEFAULT

(Do not substitute computer generated internal accountings):

Paym't Due Date	Amt. of Paym't Due	Amt. of Paym't Rec'd	Date Paym't Rec'd	Amt. Applied to Principal	Amt. Applied to Interest	Amt. Applied to Escrow	Late Fee Charged if any	Amt. Not Applied

Paym't Due Date	Amt. of Paym't Due	Amt. of Paym't Rec'd	Date Paym't Rec'd	Amt. Applied to Principal	Amt. Applied to Interest	Amt. Applied to Escrow	Late Fee Charged if any	Amt. Not Applied
Totals	$	$		$	$	$		$

16. Amount of Movant's Attorneys' fees charged to Debtor to date for the preparation and filing of this Motion: $ ___.

17. Other Attorneys' fees charged to Debtor post-petition: $ ___.

18. Amount of Movant's post-petition inspection fees: $ ___.

19. Amount of Movant's post-petition appraisal/broker's price opinion: $ ___.

20. Amount of forced placed insurance or insurance provided by the Movant post-petition: $ _____.

21. Sum held in suspense by Movant in connection with this contract, if applicable: $ _____.

22. Amount of other post-petition advances or charges (e.g. real estate taxes, insurance): $ _____.

23. Total amount of postpetition default, including all payments, fees, and charges: $ _____.

24. Amount and date of post-petition payments offered by the Debtor(s) and refused by the Movant: Amount(s) $ _____;

   Date(s): _____.

REQUIRED ATTACHMENTS TO MOTION

Attach the following documents to this motion and indicate the exhibit number associated with the documents:

(1) Copies of documents that indicate Movant's interest in the subject property. For purposes of example only, a complete and legible copy of the promissory note or other debt instrument together with a complete and legible copy of the mortgage and any assignments in the chain from the original mortgagee to the current moving party. (Exhibits ___.)

(2) Copies of documents establishing proof of standing to bring this motion if different from the above. (Exhibits ___.)

(3) Copies of documents establishing that Movant's interest in the real property is perfected. For the purposes of example only, a complete and legible copy of the Financing Statement (UCC–1) filed with either the Clerk's Office or the Register of the county the property is located in. (Exhibits ___.)

CERTIFICATION AND DECLARATION FOR BUSINESS RECORDS

The undersigned certifies that the information provided in this worksheet and any exhibits attached to this worksheet (other than transactional documents attached as required in paragraphs (1) through (3) above) are derived from records that (a) were made at or near the time of the occurrence of the matters set forth by, or from information transmitted by a person with knowledge of those matters; and (b) were prepared and kept in the regular course of business.

In the event the Worksheet is not fully completed, Movant shall explain the reasons therefor and the reasonable efforts made to obtain the information. _____

The undersigned further certifies that copies of any transactional documents attached to this worksheet as required by paragraphs 1, 2, or 3, immediately above, are true and accurate copies of the original documents. The undersigned further certifies that the original documents are in Movant's possession, except as follows: _____.

I/WE DECLARE UNDER THE PENALTY OF PERJURY THAT THE FORE-GOING REPRESENTATIONS OF FACT ARE TRUE AND CORRECT TO THE BEST OF MY/OUR KNOWLEDGE AND BELIEF.

_____   _____

Signature   Date

_____

Printed Name

_____

Title and Organization

[Effective December 1. 2009.]

OFFICIAL LOCAL FORM 14.   DEBTOR(S)' SCHEDULE OF DISPUTED PAYMENTS IN OPPOSITION TO MOTION FOR RELIEF FROM STAY—POSTPETITION TRANSACTION HISTORY

UNITED STATES BANKRUPTCY COURT
DISTRICT OF MASSACHUSETTS

In re   Chapter 13

                                                       Case No.

                    ,

            Debtor

DEBTOR(S)' SCHEDULE OF DISPUTED PAYMENTS IN OPPOSITION TO MOTION FOR RELIEF FROM STAY—POSTPETITION TRANSACTION HISTORY

Amount Paid	Date	Money Order/Check No./ or Other Form of Payment

In the event the Worksheet is not fully completed, the Debtor(s) shall explain the reasons therefor and the reasonable efforts made to obtain the information. _____

I/WE DECLARE UNDER THE PENALTY OF PERJURY THAT THE FOREGOING REPRESENTATIONS OF FACT ARE TRUE AND CORRECT TO THE BEST OF MY/OUR KNOWLEDGE AND BELIEF.

_____   _____
Signature   Date

_____
Printed Name

[Effective December 1. 2009.]

OFFICIAL LOCAL FORM 15.   COMBINED PLAN OF REORGANIZATION AND DISCLOSURE STATE-MENT FOR SMALL BUSINESS DEBTOR

UNITED STATES BANKRUPTCY COURT
DISTRICT OF MASSACHUSETTS

In re   Chapter

                                                                     Case No.

                         Debtor

COMBINED PLAN OF REORGANIZATION AND DISCLOSURE STATEMENT FOR SMALL BUSINESS DEBTOR DATED _____

I. INTRODUCTION

A. General

This is the Combined Plan of Reorganization and Disclosure Statement for a Small Business Debtor (the "Plan and Disclosure Statement") for _____ _____ (the "Debtor").   Portions of the Plan and Disclosure Statement which refer solely to the Plan of reorganization will be referred to as the "Plan".   This Plan and Disclosure Statement contains a description of (1) the Debtor, (2) the operation of its business, and (3) its expectations for future operations.   It also discusses the valuation of the Debtor's assets and alternatives to the Plan.   Also included is the Debtor's Plan.

On _____, (the "Petition Date")the Debtor filed a voluntary petition for relief under Title 11, United States Code, known as the Bankruptcy Code (the "Code"). The Chapter 11 case is pending in the United States Bankruptcy Court for the District of Massachusetts in (Boston)(Worcester)(Springfield), Massachusetts (the "Court").   During the case, the Debtor has maintained its _____ business as a Debtor–in–Possession under Sections 1107 and 1108 of the Code.

Pursuant to Section 1125 of the Code, this Plan and Disclosure Statement is being sent to all holders of claims against the Debtor so that the Debtor may solicit votes for the Plan and creditors may be provided with information concerning the Plan, the Debtor and the prospect of future operations.   All references herein to the Plan and the Disclosure Statement are as it may be amended from time to time.

[A summary description of the Plan should be stated here.]

THE PLAN IS A LEGALLY BINDING ARRANGEMENT AND SHOULD BE READ IN ITS ENTIRETY.   ACCORDINGLY, SOLICITED PARTIES MAY WISH TO CONSULT WITH THEIR ATTORNEYS REGARDING THE CONTENTS OF THE PLAN AND DISCLOSURE STATEMENT.

B. Attachments.

Accompanying this Disclosure Statement is a copy of a financial forecast for the Debtor, annexed as Exhibit A.

[Addition attachments, if any, should be described here.]

II. THE PLAN

A. Payment of Administrative Claims.

Administrative Claims will be paid in cash, in full, on the later of the Effective Date or the date they are allowed by an Order of the Bankruptcy Court. Ordinary trade debt incurred by the Debtor in the course of the Chapter 11 case will be paid on an ongoing basis in accordance with the ordinary business practices and terms between the Debtor and its trade creditors. The payments contemplated by the Plan will be conclusively deemed to constitute full satisfaction of Allowed Administrative Claims.

Administrative Claims include any post-petition fees and expenses allowed to professionals employed upon Court authority to render services to the Debtor during the course of the Chapter 11 cases.

B. Payment of Tax Claims.

Priority Claims, as scheduled or as filed and allowed by the Court, of whatever kind or nature will be paid in monthly installments with interest over a _____ year period from the Petition Date. As of the Petition Date, the Massachusetts Department of Revenue ("DOR") was owed approximately $ _____ and the Internal Revenue Service was owed approximately $ _____.

[Additional priority claims and their treatment should be described here. For example, claim of the Department of Unemployment Assistance.]

C. Designation and Payment of Classes of Claims.

[A list of classes and their treatment should be stated here.]

D. Treatment of Executory Contracts and Unexpired Leases.

Please check one:

[ ] The Plan does not propose to reject any executor agreements.

[ ] The executory contracts shown on Exhibit B are hereby rejected.

The Debtor may file a motion or amend this Plan to reject other executory contracts and leases prior to Confirmation. Subject to the requirements of Section 365 of the Bankruptcy Code, all executory contracts or unexpired leases of the Debtor that are not rejected, have not been rejected by order of the Bankruptcy Court or are not the subject of a motion to reject pending 90 days after the Confirmation Date will be deemed assumed. If any party to an executory contract or unexpired lease which is deemed assumed pursuant to the Plan objects to such assumption, the Bankruptcy

Court may conduct a hearing on such objections on any date which is either mutually agreeable to the parties or fixed by the Bankruptcy Court. All payments to cure defaults that may be required by Section 365(b)(1) of the Bankruptcy Code will be made by the Debtor. In the event of a dispute regarding the amount of any such payments or the ability of the Debtor to provide for adequate assurance of future performance, the Debtor will make any payments required by Section 365(b)(1) of the Bankruptcy Code after the entry of a Final Order resolving such dispute.

All proofs of Claim with respect to Claims arising from the rejection of executory contracts or unexpired leases must be filed with the Bankruptcy Court within thirty (30) days from and after the date of entry of an order of the Bankruptcy Court approving such rejection or such Claims will be barred. A creditor whose claims arise from rejection of executory contracts and unexpired leases will be treated as an unsecured creditor.

E.   Means for Implementation of the Plan

On Confirmation, all property of Debtor, tangible and intangible, including, without limitation, licenses, furniture, fixtures and equipment, will revert, free and clear of all claims and interests except as provided herein, to the Debtor. The Debtor will pay the claims described above from its operations post-Confirmation. The Debtor estimates that on the Effective Date the funds to be distributed are approximate $ _____ to administrative claimants. The Debtor expects to have sufficient cash on hand to make the payments required on the Effective Date.

All quarterly disbursement fees, arising under 23 U.S.C. § 1930 ("Quarterly Fees"), accrued prior to confirmation shall be paid in full, on or before the date of confirmation of the Debtor's plan, by the Debtor or any successor to the Debtor. All Quarterly Fees which accrue post-confirmation shall be paid in full on a timely basis by the Debtor or any successor to the Debtor prior to the Debtor's case being closed, converted or dismissed.

[Additional provisions, if any, for implementing the plan can be inserted here.]

F.   Provision for Disputed Claims:

The Debtor may object to the allowance of any Claims within 90 days of the Effective Date by filing an objection with the Bankruptcy Court and serving a copy thereof on the holder of the Claim in which event the Claim objected to will be treated as a Disputed Claim under the Plan. If and when a Disputed Claim is finally resolved by allowance of the Claim in whole or in part, the Debtor will make any payments in respect of such Allowed Claim in accordance with the Plan.

III.   INFORMATION PERTAINING TO THE DEBTOR

A.   Description of the Debtor's Business.

[Describe the Debtor's business here.]

B.   Background Regarding the Debtor.

[The Debtor's background can be stated here.]

C.   General Information Regarding The Debtor's Market and Sales.

[The Debtor's market and sales should be described here.]

D.   Officers, Directors and Shareholders.

[You must describe the officers, directors and shareholders here together with their salaries going forward.]

E.   Problems and Corrections.

[You should describe what problems compelled the filing of the Chapter 11 and how the Debtor has cured those problems for its successful rehabilitation.]

F.   Other Issues and Matters.

[Other issues and matters can be described here.]

G.   Risks.

[What are the risks to completion of the Plan? Describe them here.]

IV. VOTING AND CONFIRMATION

A. General Requirements

In order to confirm a Plan, the Code requires that the Bankruptcy Court make a series of determinations concerning the Plan, including that: (1) the Plan has classified Claims in a permissible manner; (2) the Plan complies with the technical requirements of Chapter 11 of the Code; (3) the proponent of the Plan has proposed the Plan in good faith; (4) the disclosures concerning the Plan as required by

Chapter 11 of the Code have been adequate and have included information concerning all payments made or promised by the Debtor in connection with the Plan; (5) the Plan has been accepted by the requisite vote of creditors, except, as explained below, to the extent that "cramdown" is available under Section 1129(b) of the Code; (6) the Plan is "feasible" (that is, there is a reasonable prospect that the Debtor will be able to perform its obligations under the Plan and continue to operate its business without further financial reorganization, except if the Plan contemplates a liquidation of the Debtor's assets); and (7) the Plan is in the "best interests" of all creditors (that is, that creditors will receive at least as much under the Plan as they would receive in a Chapter 7 liquidation). To confirm the Plan, the Bankruptcy Court must find that all of these conditions are met. Thus, even if the creditors of the Debtor accept the Plan by the requisite number of votes, the Bankruptcy Court must make independent findings respecting the Plan's feasibility and whether it is in the best interests of the Debtor's creditors before it may confirm the Plan. The Debtor believes that the Plan fulfills all of the statutory conditions of Section 1129 of the Code. The statutory conditions to confirmation are more fully discussed immediately below.

B. Classification of Claims and Interests

The Code requires that a plan of reorganization place each creditor's claim in a class with other claims which are "substantially similar." The Debtor believes that the Plan meets the classification requirements of the Code.

C. Voting

As a condition to Confirmation, the Code requires that each impaired class of claims accept the Plan. The Code defines acceptance of a Plan by a class of claims as acceptance by holders of two-thirds in dollar amount and a majority in number of claims of that class, but for that purpose the only ballots counted are those of the creditors who are allowed to vote and who actually vote to accept or to reject the Plan. Persons who are considered "insiders," as that term is defined in Section 101 of the Code, may vote, but its vote is not counted in determining acceptance of the Plan. Classes of claims that are not "impaired" under the Plan are deemed to have accepted the Plan. Acceptances of the Plan are being solicited only from those persons who hold Allowed Secured and Unsecured Claims that are impaired under the Plan. An Allowed Claim is "impaired" if the legal, equitable, or contractual rights attaching to the Allowed Claims of the class are modified, other than by curing defaults and reinstating maturity or by payment in full in cash. A claim to which an objection is filed is not an Allowed Claim. However, the Court may allow such a claim for purposes of voting on the Plan. If you have not received an objection to your claim prior to Confirmation of the Plan and you have received a ballot for purposes of voting on the Plan, then most likely your claim is an Allowed Claim. If you have a question, you should consult your own attorney.

D. Best Interests of Creditors

Notwithstanding acceptance of the Plan by creditors of each class, in order to confirm the Plan the Bankruptcy Court must independently determine that the Plan is in the best interests of all classes of creditors impaired by the Plan. The "best interests" test requires that the Bankruptcy Court find that the Plan provides to each member of each impaired class of claims a recovery which has a value at least equal to the value of the distribution which each such creditor would receive if the Debtor was liquidated under Chapter 7 of the Code. Please see the discussion of liquidation value below.

1. Confirmation Without Acceptance by All Impaired Classes

Even if a plan is not accepted by all impaired classes, it may still be confirmed. The Code contains provisions for confirmation of a plan where at least one impaired class of claims has accepted it. These "cramdown" provisions are set forth in Section 1129(b) of the Code.

492

A plan of reorganization may be confirmed under the cram-down provisions if, in addition to satisfying the usual requirements of Section 1129 of the Code, it (i) "does not discriminate unfairly" and (ii) "is fair and equitable," with respect to each class of claims that is impaired under, and has not accepted, the plan. As used by the Code, the phrases "discriminate unfairly" and "fair and equitable" have narrow and specific meanings unique to bankruptcy law.

The requirement that a plan of reorganization not "discriminate unfairly" means that a dissenting class must be treated equally with respect to other classes of equal rank. The Debtor believes that its Plan does not "discriminate unfairly" with respect to any class of Claims.

The "fair and equitable" standard differs according to the type of claim to which it is applied. In the case of secured creditors, the standard is met if the secured creditor retains its lien and is paid the present value of its interest in the property which secures the secured creditor's claim. With respect to unsecured creditors, the standard is met if the unsecured creditor receives payment in the full amount of its claim or, in the event that it receives less than the full amount of its claim, no junior class receives or retains any interest in property of the debtor. The standard as applicable to unsecured creditors is also known as the "absolute priority rule."

V. LIQUIDATION VALUATION

To calculate what creditors would receive if the Debtor was to be liquidated, the Bankruptcy Court must first determine the aggregate dollar amount that would be generated from the Debtor's assets if the Chapter 11 case were converted to a Chapter 7 case under the Code and the assets were liquidated by a trustee in bankruptcy (the "Liquidation Value"). The Liquidation Value would consist of the net proceeds from the disposition of the assets of the Debtor augmented by the cash held by the Debtor.

The Liquidation Value available to general creditors would be reduced by (a) the claims of secured creditors to the extent of the value of its collateral, and (b) by the costs and expenses of the liquidation, as well as other administrative expenses of the Debtor's estates. The Debtor's costs of liquidation under Chapter 7 would include the compensation of trustees, as well as of counsel and of other professionals retained by the trustees; disposition expenses; all unpaid expenses incurred by Debtor during the Chapter 11 case (such as compensation for attorneys) which are allowed in the Chapter 7 proceeding; litigation costs; and claims arising from the operation of the Debtor's business during the pendency of the Chapter 11 reorganization and Chapter 7 liquidation cases. Once the percentage recoveries in liquidation of secured creditors, priority claimants, general creditors and equity security holders are ascertained, the value of the distribution available out of the Liquidation Value is compared with the value of the property offered to each of the classes of Claims under the Plan to determine if the Plan is in the best interests of each creditor and equity security holder.

The liquidation valuation of a business is often a contested issue in a Chapter 11 case. Two methods of valuation widely used are the so-called "auction" method and the "going concern" method. Using the auction approach, assets tend to be valued as though they were sold at a public auction and not in use at the time of the sale. The auction method is widely used with tangible personal property such as trucks, trailers and tractors, assets which you can touch and feel and which are easily valued as a function of the initial purchase price and subsequent depreciation from use. The latter approach, the going concern method, tends to value assets based upon its contribution to earnings. The going concern method tends to be used with assets that tend not to suffer a decline from use such as accounts of a utility, maintenance contracts and the like.

[Other information regarding liquidation can be described here.]

The following table of estimated amounts suggests a likely liquidation scenario for the Debtor.

Source and Application of Funds	Amount	Assumptions
Proceeds from collection of accounts receivable and cash on hand		
Proceeds from liquidation of inventory and furniture, fixtures and equipment on cessation of business		
Proceeds from other assets		
Total		
Payment of Secured Creditors		
Chapter 7 Trustee fees and expenses		Estimated costs of trustee commission and counsel fees.
Chapter 11 expenses		Includes unpaid monthly operating expenses and professional fees and expenses.
Priority debt		
Net available for unsecured creditors		

The Debtor estimates that its unsecured creditors would receive a dividend of ___ % in liquidation. The Plan provides a dividend of at least ___ %. The Debtor believes that the Plan is in the best interests of all creditors. Thus, a conversion to Chapter 7 with the additional costs noted above would provide less of a return to the creditors.

VI.   FEDERAL INCOME TAX CONSEQUENCES

Implementation of the Plan may result in federal income tax consequences to holders of Allowed Claims. Tax consequences to a particular creditor may depend on the particular circumstances or facts regarding the claim of the creditor. No tax opinion has been sought or will be obtained with respect to any tax consequences of the Plan, and the following disclosure (the "Tax Disclosure") does not constitute and is not intended to constitute either a tax opinion or tax advice to any Person. Rather, the Tax Disclosure is provided for informational purposes only.

Because the Debtor intends to continue its existence and business operations, it will receive a discharge with respect to its outstanding indebtedness. Actual debt cancellation in excess of the fair market value of the consideration—stock, cash or other property—paid in respect of such debt will hereinafter be referred to as a "Debt Discharge Amount."

In general, the IRC provides that a taxpayer who realizes a cancellation or discharge of indebtedness must include the Debt Discharge Amount in its gross income in the taxable year of discharge. The Debt Discharge Amounts may arise with respect to Creditors who will receive, in partial satisfaction of their Claims, including any accrued interest, consideration consisting of or including cash. The Debtor's Debt Discharge Amount may be increased to the extent that unsecured Creditors holding unscheduled claims fail to timely file a Proof of Claim and have their Claims discharged on the Confirmation Date pursuant to section 1141 of the Bankruptcy Code. No income from the discharge of indebtedness is realized to the extent that payment of the liability being discharged would have given rise to a deduction.

If a taxpayer is in a case under the Bankruptcy Code and a cancellation of indebtedness occurs pursuant to a confirmed plan, however, such Debt Discharge Amount is specifically excluded from gross income (the "Bankruptcy Exception"). The Debtor intends to take the position that the Bankruptcy Exception applies to it. Accordingly, the Debtor believes it will not be required to include in income any Debt Discharge Amount as a result of Plan transactions.

Section 108(b) of the IRC, however, requires certain tax attributes of the Debtor to be reduced by the Debt Discharge Amount excluded from income. Tax attributes are reduced in the following order of priority: net operating losses and net operating loss carry-overs; general business credits; minimum tax credits; capital loss carry-overs; basis of property of the taxpayer; passive activity loss or credit carry-overs; and foreign tax credit carry-overs. Tax attributes are generally reduced by one dollar for each dollar excluded from gross income, except that general tax credits, minimum tax credits, and foreign tax credits are reduced by 33.3 cents for each dollar excluded from gross income. An election can be made to alter the order of priority of attribute reduction by first applying the reduction against depreciable property held by the taxpayer in an amount not to exceed the aggregate adjusted basis of such property. The Debtor does not presently intend to make such election. If this decision were to change, the deadline for making such election is the due date (including extensions) of the Debtor's federal income tax return for the taxable year in which such debt is discharged pursuant to the Plan.

The federal tax consequences of the plan to a hypothetical investor typical of the holders of claims or interests in this case depend to a large degree on the accounting method adopted by that hypothetical investor. A "hypothetical investor" in this case is defined as a general unsecured creditor. In accordance with federal tax law, a holder of such a claim that uses the accrual method and who has posted its original sale to the Debtor as income at the time of the product sold or the service provided hypothetically should adjust any net operating loss to reflect the dividend paid by the Debtor under the Plan provided that holder previously deducted the liability to the Debtor as a "bad debt" for federal income tax purposes. Should that holder lack a net operating loss, then in accordance with federal income tax provisions, the holder should treat the dividend paid as ordinary income, again provided the holder previously deducted the liability to the debtor as a "bad debt" for federal income tax purposes. If the accrual basis holder of the claim did not deduct the liability as a "bad debt" for federal income tax purposes, then the dividend paid by the Debtor has no current income tax implication. A holder of a claim that uses a cash method of accounting would, in accordance with federal income tax laws, treat the dividend as income at the time of receipt.

THE DEBTOR MAKES NO REPRESENTATIONS REGARDING THE PARTICULAR TAX CONSEQUENCES OF CONFIRMATION AND CONSUMMATION OF THE PLAN AS TO ANY CREDITOR. EACH PARTY AFFECTED BY THE PLAN SHOULD CONSULT HER, HIS OR ITS OWN TAX ADVISORS REGARDING THE SPECIFIC TAX CONSEQUENCES OF THE PLAN WITH RESPECT TO A CLAIM.

VII. FEASIBILITY

The Bankruptcy Code requires as a condition to Confirmation that the Bankruptcy Court find that liquidation of the Debtor or the need for further reorganization is not likely to follow after Confirmation. The Debtor depends on recurring monthly revenue from its business and it has prepared financial projections and related schedules which are attached hereto as Exhibit A. Those projections show that the Debtor is capable of operating well into the future and generating sufficient funds to perform its obligations in the Plan and continuing without the need for further financial reorganization.

VIII. DISCLAIMERS

THE CONTENT OF THIS DISCLOSURE STATEMENT HAS BEEN APPROVED BY THE BANKRUPTCY COURT AS PROVIDING ADEQUATE INFORMATION TO CREDITORS SO THAT THEY MAY HAVE SUFFICIENT INFORMATION TO VOTE ON THE PLAN. NO REPRESENTATIONS CONCERNING THE DEBTOR, INCLUDING THOSE RELATING TO ITS FUTURE BUSINESS OPERATIONS, OR THE VALUE OF ITS ASSETS, ANY PROPERTY, AND CREDITORS' CLAIMS, INCONSISTENT WITH ANYTHING CONTAINED HEREIN HAVE BEEN AUTHORIZED. THE DEBTOR DOES NOT WARRANT OR REPRESENT THAT THE INFORMATION CONTAINED HEREIN IS COMPLETE OR WITHOUT OMISSIONS. THE BANKRUPTCY COURT'S APPROVAL OF THIS PLAN OF REORGANIZATION AND DISCLOSURE STATEMENT DOES NOT CONSTITUTE A RECOMMENDATION FOR OR AGAINST THE PLAN.

THIS DISCLOSURE STATEMENT MAY NOT BE RELIED UPON FOR ANY PURPOSE OTHER THAN TO DETERMINE HOW TO VOTE ON THE PLAN, AND NOTHING CONTAINED IN IT WILL CONSTITUTE AN ADMISSION OF ANY FACT OR LIABILITY BY ANY PARTY, OR BE ADMISSIBLE IN ANY PROCEEDING INVOLVING THE DEBTOR OR ANY OTHER PARTY, OR BE DEEMED CONCLUSIVE ADVICE ON THE TAX OR OTHER LEGAL EFFECTS OF THE REORGANIZATION ON HOLDERS OF CLAIMS.

THE STATEMENTS CONTAINED IN THIS DISCLOSURE STATEMENT ARE MADE AS OF THIS DATE UNLESS ANOTHER TIME IS SPECIFIED, AND NEITHER DELIVERY OF THIS DISCLOSURE STATEMENT NOR ANY EXCHANGE OF RIGHTS MADE IN CONNECTION WITH THIS DISCLOSURE STATEMENT WILL, UNDER ANY CIRCUMSTANCES, CREATE AN IMPLICATION THAT THERE HAS BEEN NO CHANGE IN THE FACTS SINCE THE DATE OF THE DISCLOSURE STATEMENT AND THE MATERIALS RELIED UPON IN PREPARATION OF THIS DISCLOSURE STATEMENT WAS COMPILED.

IX. EFFECT OF THE ORDER CONFIRMING THE PLAN

To understand the full effect of an order confirming the Plan you should read Section 1141 of the Code. The following is a summary of that section.

A. The provisions of the confirmed Plan bind the Debtor, any entity issuing securities under the plan, any entity acquiring property under the Plan, and any creditor, equity security holder, or general partner in the debtor, whether or not the claim or interest of such creditor, equity security holder, or general partner is impaired under the Plan and whether or not such creditor, equity security holder, or general partner has accepted the Plan.

B. Except as otherwise provided in the Plan or the order confirming the Plan, the confirmation of the Plan vests all of the property of the estate in the Debtor.

C. Except as otherwise provided in the Plan or in the order confirming the Plan, after confirmation of the Plan, the property dealt with by the Plan is free and clear of all claims and interests of creditors, equity security holders, and of general partners in the Debtor.

D. Except as otherwise provided in the Plan, or in the order confirming the plan, the confirmation of the Plan discharges the debtor from any debt that arose before the date of such confirmation. There may be other exceptions set forth in Section 1141.

E.   The confirmation of the Plan does not discharge a debtor if the Plan provides for the liquidation of all or substantially all of the property of the estate, the Debtor does not engage in business after consummation of the plan; and the Debtor would be denied a discharge if the case were a case under chapter 7.

X. CONCLUSION

The Bankruptcy Court has determined that this Plan and Disclosure Statement contains information sufficient for holders of Claims to make an informed judgment in exercising their right to vote on the Plan. The Plan is the result of an effort by the Debtor to provide creditors with a meaningful dividend. An alternative to the Plan is liquidation which will, in all likelihood, reduce significantly the return to creditors on its Allowed Claims. The Debtor believes that the Plan is clearly preferable to liquidation.

A BALLOT IS ENCLOSED WITH THIS DISCLOSURE STATEMENT. YOU SHOULD VOTE TO ACCEPT OR REJECT THE PLAN ON THAT BALLOT AND RETURN IT AS FOLLOWS: BALLOTS SHOULD BE SENT TO:

[Fill in here information as to who gets the ballots.]

By

/s/ _____
Attorney
Address
BBO #
Telephone
Email

UNITED STATES BANKRUPTCY COURT
DISTRICT OF MASSACHUSETTS

In re   Chapter

                                                           Case No.

            Debtor

MOTION TO COMBINE THE HEARING
ON THE DEBTOR'S SMALL BUSINESS PLAN OF REORGANIZATION
AND DISCLOSURE STATEMENT FOR SMALL BUSINESS DEBTOR
WITH THE HEARING ON CONFIRMATION

To the Honorable _____, Bankruptcy Judge:

Debtor Corporation, Debtor-in-Possession (the "Debtor") in the above-named case moves the Court to combine the hearing on the Debtor's Combined Plan of Reorganization and Disclosure Statement for Small Business Debtor and in support hereof respectfully represents:

1. On, _____, the Debtor filed its Chapter 11 petition herein.

2. On, _____, the Debtor filed its Combined Plan of Reorganization and Disclosure Statement for Small Business Debtor.

3. The Debtor has attached hereto as Exhibit A the proposed form of Notice and as Exhibit B the proposed form of Ballot for Creditor Claims.

WHEREFORE, the Debtor prays that the Court (i) schedule a combined hearing on the Combined Plan of Reorganization and Disclosure Statement for Small Business Debtor, (ii) approve the form of notice and form of ballot appended hereto, (iii) otherwise approve the balloting procedures described above, and (iv) grant them such other and further relief as this Court deems just and proper.

By

/s/ _____

Attorney
Address
BBO #
Telephone
Email

UNITED STATES BANKRUPTCY COURT
DISTRICT OF MASSACHUSETTS

In re   Chapter

                                             Case No.

                   Debtor

BALLOT FOR ACCEPTING OR REJECTING
THE COMBINED PLAN OF REORGANIZATION AND DISCLOSURE
STATEMENT FOR SMALL BUSINESS DEBTOR PROPOSED BY THE DEBTOR

The Debtor, _____, has filed a **COMBINED PLAN OF REORGANIZATION AND DISCLOSURE STATEMENT FOR SMALL BUSINESS DEBTOR PROPOSED BY THE DEBTOR** dated _____ (the "Plan and Disclosure Statement") The Disclosure Statement is intended to provide you with information to assist you in deciding how to vote your ballot.

This Ballot is being sent to holders of all claims in all Classes asserted against the Debtor, which claims are classified in the Plan and Disclosure Statement. The holders of such claims are entitled to vote to accept or reject the Plan. The Plan is described in the **COMBINED PLAN OF REORGANIZATION AND DISCLOSURE STATEMENT FOR SMALL BUSINESS DEBTOR PROPOSED BY THE DEBTOR** distributed with this Ballot. The Plan can be confirmed by the Bankruptcy Court and thereby made binding on creditors if accepted by the holders of at least two-thirds in dollar amount and more than one-half in number of the allowed claims in at least one class of unsecured claims voting on the Plan. In the event the requisite acceptances are not obtained, the Bankruptcy Court may nevertheless confirm the Plan if it determines that the Plan accords fair and equitable treatment to rejecting classes and otherwise satisfies the requirements of 11 U.S.C. § 1129(b).

To have your vote count, you must complete and return this Ballot prior to the voting deadline set forth below.

PLEASE READ AND FOLLOW THE ENCLOSED INSTRUCTIONS CARE-
FULLY. COMPLETE, SIGN, AND DATE THIS BALLOT AND RETURN IT
BY MAIL OR OVERNIGHT DELIVERY SO THAT IT IS RECEIVED BY 4:30
P.M. (EASTERN) ON _____, AT THE FOLLOWING ADDRESS:

[Fill in here information as to who gets the ballots.]

Item 1. Vote on Plan. (Please check one.) The undersigned, the holder of a claim
in Class ___ in the unpaid amount of $ _____

    [ ] ACCEPTS   [ ] REJECTS
    (Votes FOR) the Plan   (Votes AGAINST) the Plan

Item 2. Authorization. By return of this Ballot, the undersigned certifies that it is
the holder of a claim in Class ___ to which this Ballot pertains (or an authorized
signatory therefor) and has full power and authority to vote to accept or reject the
Plan. The undersigned further certifies that it has received a copy of the Disclosure
Statement (including the appendices and exhibits thereto) and understands that the
solicitation of votes for the Plan is subject to all the terms and conditions set forth in
the Disclosure Statement. No fees, commissions, or other remuneration will be
payable to any person for soliciting votes on the Plan. If your address or contact
information has changed, please note the new information below.

Name of Creditor: _____
               (Print or Type)

Social Security
or Federal Tax I.D. No.: _____
                  (Required)

Name of Person signing below: _____

Title/Affiliation with Creditor: _____

Telephone: _____

Signature: _____

Date Completed: ___ / ___ / ___

VOTING DEADLINE: YOUR VOTE MUST BE RECEIVED AT THE AD-
DRESS ON THE FRONT OF THIS BALLOT, PRIOR TO THE VOTING
DEADLINE, WHICH IS 4:30 P.M. (EASTERN) ON _____ OR YOUR
VOTE WILL NOT BE COUNTED.

UNITED STATES BANKRUPTCY COURT
DISTRICT OF MASSACHUSETTS

In re   Chapter

                                             Case No.

        Debtor

ORDER AND NOTICE CONDITIONALLY DETERMINING THAT "SMALL BUSINESS PLAN OF REORGANIZATION AND DISCLOSURE STATEMENT" PROVIDES ADEQUATE INFORMATION AND THAT A SEPARATE DISCLOSURE STATEMENT IS NOT NECESSARY, AND SETTING HEARING ON CONFIRMATION AND RELATED MATTERS

1. On _____ 20 ___ the Debtor filed "Small Business Plan of Reorganization and disclosure Statement" (docket #__ which appears to contain adequate information.

2. Section 1125(f) of the Bankruptcy Code allows This Court to "determine that the plan itself provides adequate information and that a separate disclosure statement is not necessary." The Court has conditionally made such a determination in this case.

3. Within 5 days of the entry of this Order the Debtor shall mail the "Small Business Plan of Reorganization and Disclosure Statement," the ballot, and this Order to the United States trustee, creditors, equity holders, and other parties in interest pursuant to Fed. R. Bankr. P. 3017(d) and file a certificate of service. At the earliest time possible, the Debtor shall provide, as appropriate, to a single creditor or all creditors additional information which is reasonably requested.

4. Please take note that the Court will hold a hearing on, _____. 20____ at ___ am/pm, on the final approval of the Court's determination that a separate disclosure statement is not necessary and on confirmation of the Plan.

5. Objections to (1) the Court's determination that a separate disclosure statement is not required, and (2) confirmation of the plan and other related matters are due not later than _____, 20 ___ at 4:30 p.m.

6. Ballots must be submitted to counsel for the debtor as set forth in the Plan so as to be received by _____, 20 ___ at 4:30 p.m.

7. Motions for valuation, termination of the automatic stay, dismissal or conversion to another chapter which are now pending or subsequently filed will be heard at the same time as the combined disclosure and confirmation hearing unless otherwise expressly scheduled by the Court.

Dated: _____, 20 _____

_____
United States Bankruptcy Judge

FOR SERVICE ON THE UNITED STATES TRUSTEE, ALL CREDITORS, EQUITY HOLDERS, AND PARTIES IN INTEREST.

[Effective December 1. 2009.]

OFFICIAL LOCAL FORM 16. REPORT OF MEDIATION
UNITED STATES BANKRUPTCY COURT
FOR THE DISTRICT OF MASSACHUSETTS

_____ Division

```
                                    )
        In re                       )        Chapter
                                    )        Case No.
                                    )
                                    )
                                    )
        Debtor(s)                   )
                                    )
```

REPORT OF MEDIATION

The undersigned Mediator hereby reports to the Court that the parties in the above-captioned matter [have been unable to reach settlement, and that further resort to mediation would be unavailing at this time] *or* [have reached a settlement which will shortly be filed with the Court by one or more of the parties within a reasonable time].

DATED:

_____
Mediator
[Address and Telephone]

[To be served on all parties to the dispute and the U.S. Trustee]

[Effective November 3, 2009.]

SELECTED ORDERS

STANDING ORDER 09–01. LIMITED APPEARANCE ON BEHALF OF PRO SE DEBTORS

Notwithstanding the provisions of Massachusetts Local Bankruptcy Rules 9010–1 and 9010–3, an attorney representing, without compensation, an otherwise pro se debtor may file a notice of limited appearance setting forth the specific contested matter or adversary proceeding in which the attorney appears and may decline representation of that debtor in other matters or proceedings, but may not withdraw without leave of court from the matter or proceeding in which the attorney has chosen to appear until the final disposition thereof.

[Dated April 7, 2009.]

STANDING ORDER 09–02. CERTAIN STATEMENTS IN STIPULATIONS TO BE EXPRESSED CONSPICUOUSLY

Any provision of a stipulation or agreement filed with the Court, by which it is stipulated or agreed in a chapter 7 or 13 case that the case shall be dismissed, or relief from the automatic stay under 11 U.S.C. § 362(a) shall be granted, upon the failure of the debtor to make payments beyond those necessary to cure a prior postpetition default, shall be conspicuously set forth in capital letters and bold type.

[Dated April 7, 2009.]

AMENDED STANDING ORDER 09–04. MEDIATION LIST

This Court encourages alternative dispute resolution whenever feasible. In furtherance of that goal,

501

the Clerk of this Court will maintain a list of those persons who have advised the Clerk that they are available to serve as mediators in disputes that arise in bankruptcy cases in contested matters or adversary proceedings and have qualified for inclusion (the "Mediation List")[1] The Mediation List itself shall include only the names of individuals and not the organizations to which they might belong.[2] In order to qualify for inclusion in the Mediation List, the applicant (hereafter the "Mediator") shall represent to the Clerk in writing that:

1. the Mediator (i) is qualified as a mediator, as defined by Massachusetts General Laws ch. 233, § 23C;[3] and (ii) shall accept no mediation assignment unless the Mediator has knowledge and experience in the subject matter in dispute and in relevant provisions of the Bankruptcy Code, the Federal Rules of Bankruptcy Procedure (the "Federal Rules") and the Local Rules of the United States Bankruptcy Court for the District of Massachusetts (the "Local Rules"); and (iii) shall accept no mediation assignment which would represent a conflict of interest for the Mediator of any kind;

2. the Mediator shall be available to accept no less than three (3) mediations on a pro bono basis[4] in any calendar year, commencing on the date on which the Mediator has been included on the Mediation List. Notwithstanding this requirement, a Mediator may qualify for inclusion on the Mediation List in the event that fewer than three pro bono mediation assignments are offered to the Mediator during the said calendar year; and

3. the Mediator shall accept no assignment relative to disputes in bankruptcy cases absent a written agreement between the proposed Mediator and the mediation participants (the "Party"; "Parties"), which agreement shall (i) disclose the compensation agreement between the Parties and the Mediator and (ii) contain terms substantially as follows:

a) In the event that one of the Parties is an estate representative, the estate representative shall seek leave from the Court, in advance, to submit the dispute to mediation and to retain and compensate the Mediator pursuant to the provisions of 11 U.S.C. § 327 and Federal Rule 2014 and Local Rule 2014–1; and the Mediator submits to the jurisdiction of the Court and agrees that his/her compensation shall be determined on proper application, pursuant to Federal Rule 2016 and Local Rule 2016–1; provided, however, that while the Mediator's application shall set forth the hours spent on the mediation, it shall not divulge the content of the mediation.

b) The Mediator and the Parties are prohibited from divulging outside of the mediation, any oral or written information disclosed by the Parties or by witnesses in the course of the mediation. No person may rely on or introduce as evidence in any arbitral,

judicial, or other proceedings, evidence pertaining to any aspect of the mediation effort, whether occurring before, during or subsequent to the mediation session, including but not limited to: (a) views expressed or suggestions made by a Party with respect to a possible settlement of the dispute; (b) the fact that another Party had or had not indicated willingness to accept a proposal for settlement made by the Mediator; (c) proposals made or views expressed by the Mediator; (d) statements or admissions made by a Party in the course of the mediation; (e) documents prepared for the purpose of, in the course of, or pursuant to the mediation; (f) statements or actions which may otherwise constitute a waiver of a legally protected privilege; and (g) documents prepared subsequent to the mediation which refer to any of the foregoing. In addition, without limiting the foregoing, Rule 408 of the Federal Rules of Evidence and any applicable federal or state statute, rule, common law or judicial precedent relating to the privileged nature of settlement discussions, mediation or other alternative dispute resolution procedure shall apply. Parties and their counsel may disclose information obtained at the mediation session to members of their respective organizations who shall also be bound by the confidentiality provisions of this agreement. Information otherwise discoverable or admissible in evidence, however, does not become exempt from discovery, or inadmissible in evidence, merely by being used by a Party in or relating to a mediation session. These provisions shall not preclude a Party, its counsel or the Mediator from responding in confidence to appropriately conducted inquiries or surveys concerning the use of mediation generally.

c) The disclosure by a Party of privileged information to the Mediator shall not waive or otherwise adversely affect the privileged nature of the information.

d) The Mediator shall not be compelled to disclose to the Court or to any person outside the mediation conference any of the records, reports, summaries, notes, communication, or other documents received or made by a Mediator while serving in such capacity. The Mediator shall not testify or be compelled to testify in regard to the mediation in connection with any arbitral, judicial, or other proceeding. The Mediator shall not be a necessary party in any proceedings relating to the mediation. Aside from proof of actual fraud or unethical conduct, there shall be no liability on the part of, and no cause of action shall arise against, any person who serves as a Mediator hereunder on account of any act or omission in the course and scope of such person's duties as a Mediator.

e) Prior to entering upon the mediation, the Parties shall notify the Court that they have submitted a matter to mediation and shall seek any necessary or appropriate orders of continuance. Following the mediation, the Mediator will notify the Court if the matter has been settled, and the parties shall then file the appropriate motions for approval of the settlement as may be required or appropriate under the Bankruptcy Code or Federal or Local Rules. In the event that settlement has not been reached and further mediation is believed to be unwarranted, the Mediator shall so notify the Court.[5] No other information concerning the mediation may be given to the Court by the Mediator or any Party.

f) No subpoena, summons, citation, or other process shall be served at or near the location of any mediation session, upon any person entering, leaving or attending any mediation session.

[Dated: November 3, 2009. Amended effective November 2, 2010.]

[1] Inclusion in the Court's Mediation List shall not expressly or impliedly represent any finding by the Court that the person listed is qualified by education or experience to mediate any particular dispute. In addition, notwithstanding the provisions of Massachusetts Local Bankruptcy Rule 7016–1, the Court may order the parties to mediation in an appropriate case, and should the parties be unable to agree upon the selection of a mediator, the Court shall appoint a mediator from the Mediation List. However, the parties may select a mediator of their choosing whether or not the mediator is on the Mediation List.

[2] On request of an individual on the Mediation List, the Clerk shall also maintain a copy of that person's professional biography of not more than three (3) pages.

[3] In an appropriate case and at the sole discretion of the Chief Judge, the requirement of thirty (30) hours of mediation training may be waived where the applicant demonstrates an equivalence of ability and experience obtained as a mediator appointed by a judicial or governmental body.

[4] If the Mediator concludes that the mediation should be conducted on a pro bono basis on account of the financial need of any party, the Mediator shall not accept compensation from any other party to the mediation.

[5] Attached hereto is a form of Report of Mediation to be used by Mediators for the applicable notification to the Court.

EMERGENCY STANDING ORDER 10–2. LOAN MODIFICATION AND FORBEARANCE AGREEMENTS

Unless conspicuously identified and specifically approved by the court in advance, any provision in a loan modification agreement, forbearance agreement, stipulation relating to a motion for relief from the automatic stay under 11 U.S.C. § 362(a) or similar agreement, which provides that, upon default by the debtor, the benefits of the automatic stay will be waived shall be deemed unenforceable and void.

[Dated: March 2, 2010.]

STANDING ORDER 10–03. ATTACHMENTS OR EXHIBITS TO PROOFS OF CLAIM

Pursuant to Massachusetts Local Rule 9018–1(f), the Clerk of this Court or his delegate(s) may, sua sponte and without the necessity of any separate order, cause the attachment or exhibit to a proof of claim or to any other document filed with this Court to be imaged as a "private event" under the Court's electronic filing system in the event that the attachment or exhibit contains medical information with respect to any person or otherwise contains information whose unrestricted disclosure may not be appropriate. Nothing herein shall constitute an affirmative obligation by the Court to locate or identify such information in any attachment or exhibit or preclude any party in interest from requesting that the Court terminate the "private event" status of the attachment or exhibit and make the information public.

[Dated: July 1, 2010.]

RULES OF PROCEDURE OF THE
JUDICIAL PANEL ON
MULTIDISTRICT LITIGATION

Renumbered and Amended Effective November 2, 1998

Including Amendments Effective July 6, 2011

I. RULES FOR MULTIDISTRICT LITIGATION
UNDER 28 U.S.C. § 1407

RULE 1.1. DEFINITIONS

(a) "Panel" means the members of the United States Judicial Panel on Multidistrict Litigation appointed by the Chief Justice of the United States pursuant to 28 U.S.C. § 1407.

(b) "Chair" means the Chair of the Panel appointed by the Chief Justice of the United States pursuant to Section 1407, or the member of the Panel properly designated to act as Chair.

(c) "Clerk of the Panel" means the official that the Panel appoints to that position. The Clerk of the Panel shall perform such duties that the Panel or the Panel Executive delegates.

(d) "Electronic Case Filing (ECF)" refers to the Panel's automated system that receives and stores documents filed in electronic form. All attorneys filing pleadings with the Panel must do so using ECF. All pro se individuals are non-ECF users, unless the Panel orders otherwise.

(e) "MDL" means a multidistrict litigation docket which the Panel is either considering or has created

by transferring cases to a transferee district for coordinated or consolidated pretrial proceedings pursuant to Section 1407.

(f) "Panel Executive" means the official appointed to act as the Panel's Chief Executive and Legal Officer. The Panel Executive may appoint, with the approval of the Panel, necessary deputies, clerical assistants and other employees to perform or assist in the performance of the duties of the Panel Executive. The Panel Executive, with the approval of the Panel, may make such delegations of authority as are necessary for the Panel's efficient operation.

(g) "Pleadings" means all papers, motions, responses, or replies of any kind filed with the Panel, including exhibits attached thereto, as well as all orders and notices that the Panel issues.

(h) "Tag-along action" refers to a civil action pending in a district court which involves common questions of fact with either (1) actions on a pending motion to transfer to create an MDL or (2) actions previously transferred to an existing MDL, and which the Panel would consider transferring under Section 1407.

(i) "Transferee district" is the federal district court to which the Panel transfers an action pursuant to Section 1407, for inclusion in an MDL.

(j) "Transferor district" is the federal district court where an action was pending prior to its transfer pursuant to Section 1407, for inclusion in an MDL, and where the Panel may remand that action at or before the conclusion of pretrial proceedings.

[Former Rule 1 adopted May 3, 1993, effective July 1, 1993. Renumbered Rule 1.1 September 1, 1998, effective November 2, 1998. Amended September 8, 2010, effective October 4, 2010.]

RULE 2.1. RULES AND PRACTICE

(a) Customary Practice. The Panel's customary practice shall govern, unless otherwise fixed by statute or these Rules.

(b) Failure to Comply With Rules. When a pleading does not comply with these Rules, the Clerk of the Panel may advise counsel of the deficiencies and set a date for full compliance. If counsel does not fully comply within the established time, the Clerk of the Panel shall file the non-complying pleading, but the Chair may thereafter order it stricken.

(c) Admission to Practice Before the Panel. Every member in good standing of the Bar of any district court of the United States is entitled to practice before the Panel, provided, however, that he or she has established and maintains a CM/ECF account with any United States federal court. Any attorney of record in any action transferred under Section 1407 may continue to represent his or her client in any district court of the United States to which such action is transferred. Parties are not required to obtain local counsel.

(d) Pendency of Motion or Conditional Order. The pendency of a motion, order to show cause, conditional transfer order or conditional remand order before the Panel pursuant to 28 U.S.C. § 1407 does not affect or suspend orders and pretrial proceedings in any pending federal district court action and does not limit the pretrial jurisdiction of that court. An order to transfer or remand pursuant to 28 U.S.C. § 1407 shall be effective only upon its filing with the clerk of the transferee district court.

(e) Reassignment. If for any reason the transferee judge is unable to continue those responsibilities, the Panel shall make the reassignment of a new transferee judge.

[Former Rule 5 adopted May 3, 1993, effective July 1, 1993. Renumbered Rule 1.2 September 1, 1998, effective November 2, 1998. Former Rule 4 adopted May 3, 1993, effective July 1, 1993. Renumbered Rule 1.3 and amended September 1, 1998, effective November 2, 1998. Former Rule 6 adopted

May 3, 1993, effective July 1, 1993. Renumbered Rule 1.4 September 1, 1998, effective November 2, 1998. Former Rule 18 adopted May 3, 1993, effective July 1, 1993. Renumbered Rule 1.5 September 1, 1998, effective November 2, 1998. Former Rules 1.2, 1.3, 1.4, and 1.5 redesignated and amended September 8, 2010, effective October 4, 2010.]

RULE 3.1. ELECTRONIC RECORDS AND FILES; COPY FEES

(a) Electronic Record. Effective October 4, 2010, the official Panel record shall be the electronic file maintained on the Panel's servers. This record includes, but is not limited to, Panel pleadings, documents filed in paper and then scanned and made part of the electronic record, and Panel orders and notices filed. The official record also includes any documents or exhibits that may be impractical to scan. These documents and exhibits shall be kept in the Panel offices.

(b) Maintaining Records. Records and files generated prior to October 4, 2010, may be (i) maintained at the Panel offices, (ii) temporarily or permanently removed to such places at such times as the Clerk of the Panel or the Chair shall direct, or (iii) transferred whenever appropriate to the Federal Records Center.

(c) Fees. The Clerk of the Panel may charge fees for duplicating records and files, as prescribed by the Judicial Conference of the United States.

[Former Rule 2 adopted May 3, 1993, effective July 1, 1993. Renumbered Rule 5.1 and amended September 1, 1998, effective November 2, 1998. Former Rule 5.1 redesignated and amended September 8, 2010, effective October 4, 2010.]

RULE 3.2. ECF USERS: FILING REQUIREMENTS

(a) Form of Pleadings. This Rule applies to pleadings that ECF users file with the Panel.

(i) Each pleading shall bear the heading "Before the United States Judicial Panel on Multidistrict Litigation," the identification "MDL No. ___" and the descriptive title designated by the Panel. If the Panel has not yet designated a title, counsel shall use an appropriate description.

(ii) The final page of each pleading shall contain the name, address, telephone number, fax number and email address of the attorney or party designated to receive service of pleadings in the case, and the name of each party represented.

(iii) Each brief submitted with a motion and any response to it shall not exceed 20 pages, exclusive of exhibits. Each reply shall not exceed 10 pages and shall address arguments raised in the response(s). Absent exceptional circumstances and those set forth in Rule 6.1(d), the Panel will not grant motions to exceed page limits.

(iv) Each pleading shall be typed in size 12 point font (for both text and footnotes), double spaced (text only), in a letter size document (8 ½ × 11 inch) with sequentially numbered pages.

(v) Each exhibit shall be separately numbered and clearly identified.

(vi) Proposed Panel orders shall not be submitted.

(b) Place of Filing. Counsel shall sign and verify all pleadings electronically in accordance with these Rules and the Panel's Administrative Policies and Procedures for Electronic Case Filing found at www. jpml.uscourts.gov. A pleading filed electronically constitutes a written document for the purpose of these Rules and the Federal Rules of Civil Procedure and is deemed the electronically signed original thereof. All pleadings, except by pro se litigants, shall conform with this Rule beginning on October 4, 2010.

(i)* Pleadings shall not be transmitted directly to any Panel member.

(c) Attorney Registration. Only attorneys identified, or to be identified, pursuant to Rule 4.1, shall file pleadings. Each of these attorneys must register as a Panel CM/ECF user through www.jpml.uscourts.gov. Registration/possession of a CM/ECF account with any United States federal court shall be deemed consent to receive electronic service of all Panel orders and notices as well as electronic service of pleadings from other parties before the Panel.

(d) Courtesy Copy of Specified Pleadings. Counsel shall serve the Clerk of the Panel, for delivery within 1 business day of filing, with a courtesy paper copy of any of the following pleadings: (i) a motion to transfer and its supporting brief; (ii) a response to a show cause order; (iii) a motion to vacate a conditional transfer order or a conditional remand order; (iv) any response, reply, supplemental information or interested party response related to the pleadings listed in (i), (ii) and (iii); and (v) a corporate disclosure statement. No courtesy copies of any other pleadings are required. Courtesy copies of pleadings totaling 10 pages or less (including any attachments) may be faxed to the Panel. The courtesy copy shall include all exhibits, shall be clearly marked "Courtesy Copy— Do Not File," shall contain the CM/ECF pleading number (if known), and shall be mailed or delivered to:

Clerk of the Panel
United States Judicial Panel on Multidistrict
  Litigation
Thurgood Marshall Federal Judiciary Building
One Columbus Circle, NE,
Room G–255, North Lobby
Washington, DC 20002–8041

(e) Privacy Protections. The privacy protections contained in Rule 5.2 of the Federal Rules of Civil Procedure shall apply to all Panel filings.

[Former Rule 3 adopted May 3, 1993, effective July 1, 1993. Renumbered Rule 5.11 and amended September 1, 1998, effective November 2, 1998; renumbered Rule 5.1.1 and amended March 25, 2010, effective April 1, 2010. Former Rule 7 adopted May 3, 1993, effective July 1, 1993. Renumbered Rule 5.12 and amended September 1, 1998, effective November 2, 1998. Amended April 2, 2001, effective April 2, 2001; paragraph (a) suspended in part by Order filed April 19, 2005; renumbered Rule 5.1.2 and amended March 25, 2010, effective April 1, 2010. Former Rule 9 adopted May 3, 1993, effective July 1, 1993. Renumbered Rule 7.1 and amended September 1, 1998, effective November 2, 1998. Amended April 2, 2001, effective April 2, 2001. Former Rules 5.1.1, 5.1.2, and 7.1 redesignated in part and amended September 8, 2010, effective October 4, 2010. Amended effective July 6, 2011.]

* So in original. No subdivision (ii) promulgated.

RULE 3.3. NON–ECF USERS: FILING REQUIREMENTS

(a) Definition of Non–ECF Users. Non–ECF users are all pro se individuals, unless the Panel orders otherwise. This Rule shall apply to all motions, responses and replies that non-ECF users file with the Panel.

(b) Form of Pleadings. Unless otherwise set forth in this Rule, the provisions of Rule 3.2 shall apply to non-ECF users.

(i) Each pleading shall be flat and unfolded; plainly written or typed in size 12 point font (for both text and footnotes), double spaced (text only), and printed single-sided on letter size (8 ½ × 11 inch) white paper with sequentially numbered pages; and fastened at the top-left corner without side binding or front or back covers.

(ii) Each exhibit shall be separately numbered and clearly identified. Any exhibits exceeding a cumulative total of 50 pages shall be bound separately.

(c) Place of Filing. File an original and one copy of all pleadings with the Clerk of the Panel by mailing or delivering to:

Clerk of the Panel
United States Judicial Panel on Multidistrict
  Litigation
Thurgood Marshall Federal Judiciary Building
One Columbus Circle, NE,
Room G–255, North Lobby
Washington, DC 20002–8041

(i) Pleadings not exceeding a total of 10 pages, including exhibits, may be faxed to the Panel office.

(ii) The Clerk of the Panel shall endorse the date for filing on all pleadings submitted for filing.

[Former Rule 3 adopted May 3, 1993, effective July 1, 1993. Renumbered Rule 5.11 and amended September 1, 1998, effective November 2, 1998; renumbered Rule 5.1.1 and amended March 25, 2010, effective April 1, 2010. Former Rule 7 adopted May 3, 1993, effective July 1, 1993. Renumbered Rule 5.12 and amended September 1, 1998, effective November 2, 1998. Amended April 2, 2001, effective April 2, 2001; paragraph (a) suspended in part by Order filed April 19, 2005; renumbered Rule 5.1.2 and amended March 25, 2010, effective April 1, 2010. Former Rule 9 adopted May 3, 1993, effective July 1, 1993. Renumbered Rule 7.1 and amended September 1, 1998, effective November 2, 1998. Amended April 2, 2001, effective April 2, 2001. Former Rules 5.1.1, 5.1.2, and 7.1 redesignated in part and amended September 8, 2010, effective October 4, 2010.]

RULE 4.1. SERVICE OF PLEADINGS

(a) Proof of Service. The Panel's notice of electronic filing shall constitute service of pleadings. Registration/possession by counsel of a CM/ECF account with any United States federal court shall be deemed consent to receive electronic service of all pleadings. All pleadings shall contain a proof of service on all other parties in all involved actions. The proof of service shall indicate the name and manner of service. If a party is not represented by counsel, the proof of service shall indicate the name of the party and the party's last known address. The proof of service shall indicate why any person named as a party in a constituent complaint was not served with the Section 1407 pleading.

(b) Service Upon Transferor Court. The proof of service pertaining to motions for a transfer or remand pursuant to 28 U.S.C. § 1407 shall certify that counsel has transmitted a copy of the motion for filing to the clerk of each district court where an affected action is pending.

(c) Notice of Appearance. Within 14 days after the issuance of a (i) notice of filing of a motion to initiate transfer under Rule 6.2, (ii) notice of filed opposition to a CTO under Rule 7.1, (iii) a show cause order under Rules* 8.1, (iv) notice of filed opposition to a CRO under Rule 10.2, or (v) notice of filing of a motion to remand under Rule 10.3, each party or designated attorney as required hereinafter shall file a Notice of Appearance notifying the Clerk of the Panel of the name, address and email address of the attorney designated to file and receive service of all pleadings. Each party shall designate only one attorney. Any party not represented by counsel shall be served by mailing such pleadings to the party's last known address. Except in extraordinary circumstances, the Panel will not grant requests for an extension of time to file the Notice of Appearance.

(d) Liaison Counsel. If the transferee district court appoints liaison counsel, this Rule shall be satis-

fied by serving each party in each affected action and all liaison counsel. Liaison counsel shall receive copies of all Panel orders concerning their particular litigation and shall be responsible for distribution to the parties for whom he or she serves as liaison counsel.

[Former Rule 8 adopted May 3, 1993, effective July 1, 1993. Renumbered Rule 5.2 and amended September 1, 1998, effective November 2, 1998; March 26, 2009, effective December 1, 2009. Former Rule 5.2 redesignated and amended September 8, 2010, effective October 4, 2010. Technical revisions effective July 6, 2011.]

* So in original.

RULE 5.1. CORPORATE DISCLOSURE STATEMENT

(a) Requirements. A nongovernmental corporate party must file a disclosure statement that: (1) identifies any parent corporation and any publicly held corporation owning 10% or more of its stock; or (2) states that there is no such corporation.

(b) Deadline. A party shall file the corporate disclosure statement within 14 days after issuance of a notice of the filing of a motion to transfer or remand, an order to show cause, or a motion to vacate a conditional transfer order or a conditional remand order.

(c) Updating. Each party must update its corporate disclosure statement to reflect any change in the information therein (i) until the matter before the Panel is decided, and (ii) within 14 days after issuance of a notice of the filing of any subsequent motion to transfer or remand, order to show cause, or motion to vacate a conditional transfer order or a conditional remand order in that docket.

[Former Rule 2 adopted May 3, 1993, effective July 1, 1993. Renumbered Rule 5.1 and amended September 1, 1998, effective November 2, 1998. Former Rule 5.3 redesignated and amended September 8, 2010, effective October 4, 2010. Amended effective July 6, 2011.]

RULE 5.1.3. FILING OF PAPERS: COMPUTER GENERATED DISK REQUIRED [DELETED SEPT. 8, 2010, EFF. OCT. 4, 2010

[Added May 22, 2000, effective June 1, 2000. And amended July 30, 2007, effective July 30, 2007; renumbered Rule 5.1.3 and amended March 25, 2010, effective April 1, 2010. Deleted September 8, 2010, effective October 4, 2010.]

RULE 6.1. MOTION PRACTICE

(a) Application. This Rule governs all motions requesting Panel action generally. More specific provisions may apply to motions to transfer (Rule 6.2), miscellaneous motions (Rule 6.3), conditional transfer orders (Rule 7.1), show cause orders (Rule 8.1), conditional remand orders (Rule 10.2) and motions to remand (Rule 10.3).

(b) Form of Motions. All motions shall briefly describe the action or relief sought and shall include:

(i) a brief which concisely states the background of the litigation and movant's factual and legal contentions;

(ii) a numbered schedule providing

(A) the complete name of each action involved, listing the full name of each party included as such on the district court's docket sheet, not shortened by the use of references such as "et al." or "etc.";

(B) the district court and division where each action is pending;

(C) the civil action number of each action; and

(D) the name of the judge assigned each action, if known;

(iii) a proof of service providing

(A) a service list listing the full name of each party included on the district court's docket sheet and the complaint, including opt-in plaintiffs not listed on the docket sheet; and

(B) in actions where there are 25 or more plaintiffs listed on the docket sheet, list the first named plaintiff with the reference "et al." if all the plaintiffs are represented by the same attorney(s);

(iv) a copy of all complaints and docket sheets for all actions listed on the Schedule; and

(v) exhibits, if any, identified by number or letter and a descriptive title.

(c) Responses and Joinders. Any other party may file a response within 21 days after filing of a motion. Failure to respond to a motion shall be treated as that party's acquiescence to it. A joinder in a motion shall not add any action to that motion.

(d) Replies. The movant may file a reply within 7 days after the lapse of the time period for filing a response. Where a movant is replying to more than one response in opposition, the movant may file a consolidated reply with a limit of 20 pages.

(e) Alteration of Time Periods. The Clerk of the Panel has the discretion to shorten or enlarge the time periods set forth in this Rule as necessary.

(f) Notification of Developments. Counsel shall promptly notify the Clerk of the Panel of any development that would partially or completely moot any Panel matter.

[Former Rule 10 adopted May 3, 1993, effective July 1, 1993. Renumbered Rule 7.2 and amended September 1, 1998, effective November 2, 1998. Amended April 2, 2001, effective April 2, 2001; March 26, 2009, December 1, 2009.

Former Rule 7.2 redesignated in part and amended September 8, 2010, effective October 4, 2010.]

RULE 6.2. MOTIONS TO TRANSFER FOR COORDINATED OR CONSOLIDATED PRETRIAL PROCEEDINGS

(a) Initiation of Transfer. A party to an action may initiate proceedings to transfer under Section 1407 by filing a motion in accordance with these Rules. A copy of the motion shall be filed in each district court where the motion affects a pending action.

(b) Notice of Filing of Motion to Transfer. Upon receipt of a motion, the Clerk of the Panel shall issue a "Notice of Filing of Motion to Transfer" to the service list recipients. The Notice shall contain the following: the filing date of the motion, caption, MDL docket number, briefing schedule and pertinent Panel policies. After a motion is filed, the Clerk of the Panel shall consider any other pleading to be a response unless the pleading adds an action. The Clerk of the Panel may designate such a pleading as a motion, and distribute a briefing schedule applicable to all or some of the parties, as appropriate.

(c) Notice of Appearance. Within 14 days of issuance of a "Notice of the Filing of a Motion to Transfer," each party or designated attorney shall file a Notice of Appearance in accordance with Rule 4.1(c).

(d) Notice of Potential Tag-along Actions. Any party or counsel in a new group of actions under consideration for transfer under Section 1407 shall promptly notify the Clerk of the Panel of any potential tag-along actions in which that party is also named or in which that counsel appears.

(e) Interested Party Responses. Any party or counsel in one or more potential tag-along actions as well as amicus curiae may file a response to a pending motion to transfer. Such a pleading shall be deemed an Interested Party Response.

(f) Amendment to a Motion. Before amending a motion to transfer, a party shall first contact the Clerk of the Panel to ascertain whether such amendment is feasible and permissible considering the Panel's hearing schedule. Any such amendment shall be entitled "Amendment to Motion for Transfer," and shall clearly and specifically identify and describe the nature of the amendment.

(i) Where the amended motion includes new civil actions, the amending party shall file a "Schedule of Additional Actions" and a revised Proof of Service.

(ii) The Proof of Service shall state (A) that all new counsel have been served with a copy of the amendment and all previously-filed motion papers, and (B) that all counsel previously served with the original motion have been served with a copy of the amendment.

(iii) The Clerk of the Panel may designate the amendment with a different denomination (*e.g.*, a notice of potential tag-along action(s)) and treatment.

(h) Oral Argument.* The Panel shall schedule oral arguments as needed and as set forth in Rule 11.1.

[Former Rule 10 adopted May 3, 1993, effective July 1, 1993. Renumbered Rule 7.2 and amended September 1, 1998, effective November 2, 1998. Amended April 2, 2001, effective April 2, 2001; March 26, 2009, December 1, 2009. Former Rule 15 adopted May 3, 1993, effective July 1, 1993. Renumbered Rule 6.2 and amended September 1, 1998, effective November 2, 1998. Former Rule 7.2 redesignated in part and amended September 8, 2010, effective October 4, 2010. Technical revisions effective July 6, 2011.]

* So in original.

RULE 6.3. MOTIONS FOR MISCELLANEOUS RELIEF

(a) Definition. Motions for miscellaneous relief include, but are not limited to, requests for extensions of time, exemption from ECF requirements, page limit extensions, or expedited consideration of any motion.

(b) Panel Action. The Panel, through the Clerk, may act upon any motion for miscellaneous relief, at any time, without waiting for a response. A motion for extension of time to file a pleading or perform an act under these Rules must state specifically the revised date sought and must be filed before the deadline for filing the pleading or performing the act. Any party aggrieved by the Clerk of the Panel's action may file objections for consideration. Absent exceptional circumstances, the Panel will not grant any extensions of time to file a notice of opposition to either a conditional transfer order or a conditional remand order.

[Former Rule 15 adopted May 3, 1993, effective July 1, 1993. Renumbered Rule 6.2 and amended September 1, 1998, effective November 2, 1998. Former Rule 6.2 redesignated and amended September 8, 2010, effective October 4, 2010.]

RULE 7.1. CONDITIONAL TRANSFER ORDERS (CTO) FOR TAG–ALONG ACTIONS

(a) Notice of Potential Tag-along Actions. Any party or counsel in actions previously transferred under Section 1407 shall promptly notify the Clerk of the Panel of any potential tag-along actions in which that party is also named or in which that counsel appears. The Panel has several options: (i) filing a CTO under Rule 7.1, (ii) filing a show cause order under Rule 8.1, or (iii) declining to act (Rule 7.1(b)(i)).

(b) Initiation of CTO. Upon learning of the pendency of a potential tag-along action, the Clerk of the Panel may enter a conditional order transferring that action to the previously designated transferee district court for the reasons expressed in the Panel's previous opinions and orders. The Clerk of the Panel shall serve this order on each party to the litigation but shall not send the order to the clerk of the transferee district court until 7 days after its entry.

(i)* If the Clerk of the Panel determines that a potential tag-along action is not appropriate for inclusion in an MDL proceeding and does not enter a CTO, an involved party may move for its transfer pursuant to Rule 6.1.

(c) Notice of Opposition to CTO. Any party opposing the transfer shall file a notice of opposition with the Clerk of the Panel within the 7–day period. In such event, the Clerk of the Panel shall not transmit the transfer order to the clerk of the transferee district court, but shall notify the parties of the briefing schedule.

(d) Failure to Respond. Failure to respond to a CTO shall be treated as that party's acquiescence to it.

(e) Notice of Appearance. Within 14 days after the issuance of a "Notice of Filed Opposition" to a CTO, each opposing party or designated attorney shall file a Notice of Appearance in accordance with Rule 4.1(c).

(f) Motion to Vacate CTO. Within 14 days of the filing of its notice of opposition, the party opposing transfer shall file a motion to vacate the CTO and brief in support thereof. The Clerk of the Panel shall set the motion for the next appropriate hearing session. Failure to file and serve a motion and brief shall be treated as withdrawal of the opposition and the Clerk of the Panel shall forthwith transmit the order to the clerk of the transferee district court.

(g) Notification of Developments. Parties to an action subject to a CTO shall notify the Clerk of the Panel if that action is no longer pending in its transferor district court.

(h) Effective Date of CTO. CTOs are effective when filed with the clerk of the transferee district court.

[Former Rule 12 adopted May 3, 1993, effective July 1, 1993. Renumbered Rule 7.4 and amended September 1, 1998, effective November 2, 1998. Amended April 2, 2001, effective April 2, 2001; March 26, 2009, December 1, 2009. Former Rule 7.4 redesignated and amended September 8, 2010, effective October 4, 2010. Technical revisions effective July 6, 2011.]

* So in original. No subdivision (ii) promulgated.

RULE 7.2. MISCELLANEOUS PROVISIONS CONCERNING TAG–ALONG ACTIONS

(a) Potential Tag-alongs in Transferee Court. Potential tag-along actions filed in the transferee district do not require Panel action. A party should request assignment of such actions to the Section 1407 transferee judge in accordance with applicable local rules.

(b) Failure to Serve. Failure to serve one or more of the defendants in a potential tag-along action with the complaint and summons as required by Rule 4 of the Federal Rules of Civil Procedure does not preclude transfer of such action under Section 1407. Such failure, however, may constitute grounds for denying the proposed transfer where prejudice can be shown. The failure of the Clerk of the Panel to serve a CTO on all plaintiffs or defendants or their counsel may constitute grounds for the Clerk to reinstate the CTO or for the aggrieved party to seek § 1407(c) remand.

[Former Rule 13 adopted May 3, 1993, effective July 1, 1993. Renumbered Rule 7.5 and amended September 1, 1998, effective November 2, 1998. Amended April 2, 2001, effective April 2, 2001. Former Rule 7.5 redesignated and amended September 8, 2010, effective October 4, 2010. Amended effective July 6, 2011.]

RULE 8.1. SHOW CAUSE ORDERS

(a) Entry of Show Cause Order. When transfer of multidistrict litigation is being considered on the initiative of the Panel pursuant to 28 U.S.C. § 1407(c)(i), the Clerk of the Panel may enter an order directing the parties to show cause why a certain civil action or actions should not be transferred for coordinated or consolidated pretrial proceedings. Any party shall also promptly notify the Clerk of the Panel whenever they learn of any other federal district court actions which are similar to those which the show cause order encompasses.

(b) Notice of Appearance. Within 14 days of the issuance of an order to show cause, each party or designated attorney shall file a Notice of Appearance in accordance with Rule 4.1(c).

(c) Responses. Unless otherwise provided by order, any party may file a response within 21 days of the filing of the show cause order. Failure to respond to a show cause order shall be treated as that party's acquiescence to the Panel action.

(d) Replies. Within 7 days after the lapse of the time period for filing a response, any party may file a reply.

(e) Notification of Developments. Counsel shall promptly notify the Clerk of the Panel of any develop-ment that would partially or completely moot any matter subject to a show cause order.

[Former Rule 7.3 adopted May 3, 1993, effective July 1, 1993. Renumbered Rule 7.3 and amended September 1, 1998, effective November 2, 1998; March 26, 2009, effective December 1, 2009. Former Rule 7.3 redesignated and amended September 8, 2010, effective October 4, 2010.]

RULE 9.1. TRANSFER OF FILES; NOTIFICATION REQUIREMENTS

(a) Notice to Transferee Court Clerk. The Clerk of the Panel, via a notice of electronic filing, will notify the clerk of the transferee district whenever a Panel transfer order should be filed in the transferee district court. Upon receipt of an electronically certified copy of a Panel transfer order from the clerk of the transferee district, the clerk of the transferor district shall transmit the record of each transferred action to the transferee district and then, unless Rule 9.1(b) applies, close the transferred action in the transferor district.

(b) Retention of Claims. If the transfer order provides for the separation and simultaneous remand of any claim, cross-claim, counterclaim, or third-party claim, the clerk of the transferor district shall retain jurisdiction over any such claim and shall not close the action.

(c) Notice to Clerk of Panel. The clerk of the transferee district shall promptly provide the Clerk of the Panel with the civil action numbers assigned to all transferred actions and the identity of liaison counsel, if or when designated. The clerk of the transferee district shall also promptly notify the Clerk of the Panel of any dispositive ruling that terminates a transferred action.

[Former Rule 19 adopted May 3, 1993, effective July 1, 1993. Renumbered Rule 1.6 and amended September 1, 1998, effective November 2, 1998. Former Rule 1.6 redesignated in part and amended September 8, 2010, effective October 4, 2010.]

RULE 10.1. TERMINATION AND REMAND

(a) Termination. Where the transferee district court terminates an action by valid order, including but not limited to summary judgment, judgment of dismissal and judgment upon stipulation, the transferee district court clerk shall transmit a copy of that order to the Clerk of the Panel. The terminated action shall not be remanded to the transferor court and the transferee court shall retain the original files and records unless the transferee judge or the Panel directs otherwise.

(b) Initiation of Remand. Typically, the transferee judge recommends remand of an action, or a part of it, to the transferor court at any time by filing a suggestion of remand with the Panel. However, the

Panel may remand an action or any separable claim, cross-claim, counterclaim or third-party claim within it, upon

    (i) the transferee court's suggestion of remand,

    (ii) the Panel's own initiative by entry of an order to show cause, a conditional remand order or other appropriate order, or

    (iii) motion of any party.

[Former Rule 14 adopted May 3, 1993, effective July 1, 1993. Renumbered Rule 7.6 and amended September 1, 1998, effective November 2, 1998. Amended April 2, 2001, effective April 2, 2001; March 26, 2009, effective December 1, 2009. Former Rule 7.6 redesignated in part and amended September 8, 2010, effective October 4, 2010.]

RULE 10.2. CONDITIONAL REMAND ORDERS (CRO)

(a) Entering a CRO. Upon the suggestion of the transferee judge or the Panel's own initiative, the Clerk of the Panel shall enter a conditional order remanding the action or actions to the transferor district court. The Clerk of the Panel shall serve this order on each party to the litigation but shall not send the order to the clerk of the transferee district court for 7 days from the entry thereof.

    (i)* The Panel may, on its own initiative, also enter an order that the parties show cause why a matter should not be remanded. Rule 8.1 applies to responses and replies with respect to such a show cause order.

(b) Notice of Opposition. Any party opposing the CRO shall file a notice of opposition with the Clerk of the Panel within the 7–day period. In such event, the Clerk of the Panel shall not transmit the remand order to the clerk of the transferee district court and shall notify the parties of the briefing schedule.

(c) Failure to Respond. Failure to respond to a CRO shall be treated as that party's acquiescence to it.

(d) Notice of Appearance. Within 14 days after the issuance of a "Notice of Filed Opposition" to a CRO, each opposing party or designated attorney shall file a Notice of Appearance in accordance with Rule 4.1(c).

(e) Motion to Vacate CRO. Within 14 days of the filing of its notice of opposition, the party opposing remand shall file a motion to vacate the CRO and brief in support thereof. The Clerk of the Panel shall set the motion for the next appropriate Panel hearing session. Failure to file and serve a motion and brief shall be treated as a withdrawal of the opposition and the Clerk of the Panel shall forthwith transmit the order to the clerk of the transferee district court.

(f) Effective Date of CRO. CROs are not effective until filed with the clerk of the transferee district court.

[Former Rule 14 adopted May 3, 1993, effective July 1, 1993. Renumbered Rule 7.6 and amended September 1, 1998, effective November 2, 1998. Amended April 2, 2001, effective April 2, 2001; March 26, 2009, effective December 1, 2009. Former Rule 7.6 redesignated in part and amended September 8, 2010, effective October 4, 2010. Technical revisions effective July 6, 2011.]

* So in original. No subdivision (ii) promulgated.

RULE 10.3. MOTION TO REMAND

(a) Requirements of the Motion. If the Clerk of the Panel does not enter a CRO, a party may file a motion to remand to the transferor court pursuant to these Rules. Because the Panel is reluctant to order a remand absent the suggestion of the transferee judge, the motion must include:

    (i) An affidavit reciting whether the movant has requested a suggestion of remand and the judge's response, whether the parties have completed common discovery and other pretrial proceedings, and whether the parties have complied with all transferee court orders.

    (ii) A copy of the transferee district court's final pretrial order, if entered.

(b) Filing Copy of Motion. Counsel shall file a copy of the motion to remand in the affected transferee district court.

(c) Notice of Appearance. Within 14 days of the issuance of a "Notice of Filing" of a motion to remand, each party or designated attorney shall file a Notice of Appearance in accordance with Rule 4.1(c).

[Former Rule 14 adopted May 3, 1993, effective July 1, 1993. Renumbered Rule 7.6 and amended September 1, 1998, effective November 2, 1998. Amended April 2, 2001, effective April 2, 2001; March 26, 2009, effective December 1, 2009. Former Rule 7.6 redesignated in part and amended September 8, 2010, effective October 4, 2010. Technical revisions effective July 6, 2011.]

RULE 10.4. TRANSFER OF FILES ON REMAND

(a) Designating the Record. Upon receipt of an order to remand from the Clerk of the Panel, the parties shall furnish forthwith to the transferee district clerk a stipulation or designation of the contents of the record or part thereof to be remanded.

(b) Transfer of Files. Upon receipt of an order to remand from the Clerk of the Panel, the transferee district shall transmit to the clerk of the transferor district the following concerning each remanded action:

    (i) a copy of the individual docket sheet for each action remanded;

(ii) a copy of the master docket sheet, if applicable;

(iii) the entire file for each action remanded, as originally received from the transferor district and augmented as set out in this Rule;

(iv) a copy of the final pretrial order, if applicable; and

(v) a "record on remand" as designated by the parties in accordance with 10.4(a).

[Former Rule 19 adopted May 3, 1993, effective July 1, 1993. Renumbered Rule 1.6 and amended September 1, 1998, effective November 2, 1998. Former Rule 1.6 redesignated in part and amended September 8, 2010, effective October 4, 2010.]

RULE 11.1. HEARING SESSIONS AND ORAL ARGUMENT

(a) Schedule. The Panel shall schedule sessions for oral argument and consideration of other matters as desirable or necessary. The Chair shall determine the time, place and agenda for each hearing session. The Clerk of the Panel shall give appropriate notice to counsel for all parties. The Panel may continue its consideration of any scheduled matters.

(b) Oral Argument Statement. Any party affected by a motion may file a separate statement setting forth reasons why oral argument should, or need not, be heard. Such statements shall be captioned "Reasons Why Oral Argument Should [Need Not] Be Heard" and shall be limited to 2 pages.

(i)* The parties affected by a motion to transfer may agree to waive oral argument. The Panel will take this into consideration in determining the need for oral argument.

(c) Hearing Session. The Panel shall not consider transfer or remand of any action pending in a federal district court when any party timely opposes such transfer or remand without first holding a hearing session for the presentation of oral argument. The Panel may dispense with oral argument if it determines that:

(i) the dispositive issue(s) have been authoritatively decided; or

(ii) the facts and legal arguments are adequately presented and oral argument would not significantly aid the decisional process.

Unless otherwise ordered, the Panel shall consider all other matters, such as a motion for reconsideration, upon the basis of the pleadings.

(d) Notification of Oral Argument. The Panel shall promptly notify counsel of those matters in which oral argument is scheduled, as well as those matters that the Panel will consider on the pleadings. The Clerk of the Panel shall require counsel to file and serve notice of their intent to either make or waive oral argument. Failure to do so shall be deemed a waiver of oral argument. If counsel does not attend oral argument, the matter shall not be rescheduled and that party's position shall be treated as submitted for decision on the basis of the pleadings filed.

(i) Absent Panel approval and for good cause shown, only those parties to actions who have filed a motion or written response to a motion or order shall be permitted to present oral argument.

(ii) The Panel will not receive oral testimony except upon notice, motion and an order expressly providing for it.

(e) Duty to Confer. Counsel in an action set for oral argument shall confer separately prior to that argument for the purpose of organizing their arguments and selecting representatives to present all views without duplication. Oral argument is a means for counsel to emphasize the key points of their arguments, and to update the Panel on any events since the conclusion of briefing.

(f) Time Limit for Oral Argument. Barring exceptional circumstances, the Panel shall allot a maximum of 20 minutes for oral argument in each matter. The time shall be divided among those with varying viewpoints. Counsel for the moving party or parties shall generally be heard first.

[Former Rule 16 adopted May 3, 1998, effective July 1, 1993. Renumbered Rule 16.1 and amended September 1, 1998, effective November 2, 1998. Amended April 2, 2001, effective April 2, 2001. Former Rule 16.1 redesignated and amended September 8, 2010, effective October 4, 2010.]

* So in original. No subdivision (ii) promulgated.

RULE 12 TO 15. [RESERVED]

II. RULES FOR MULTICIRCUIT PETITIONS FOR REVIEW UNDER 28 U.S.C. § 2112(a)(3)

RULE 25.1. DEFINITIONS

The Panel promulgates these Rules pursuant to its authority under 28 U.S.C. § 2112(a)(3) to provide a means for the random selection of one circuit court of

appeals to hear consolidated petitions for review of agency decisions.

An "Agency" means an agency, board, commission or officer of the United States government, that has received two or more petitions for review in a circuit court of appeals to enjoin, set aside, suspend, modify or otherwise review or enforce an action.

[Former Rule 20 adopted May 3, 1993, effective July 1, 1993. Renumbered Rule 25.1 and amended September 1, 1998, effective November 2, 1998. Amended September 8, 2010, effective October 4, 2010.]

RULE 25.2.   FILING OF NOTICES

(a) Submitting Notice. An affected agency shall submit a notice of multicircuit petitions for review pursuant to 28 U.S.C. § 2112(a)(3) to the Clerk of the Panel by electronic means in the manner these Rules require and in accordance with the Panel's Administrative Policies and Procedures for Electronic Case Filing, except that the portion of Rule 3.2(d) requiring a courtesy copy is suspended in its entirety.

(b) Accompaniments to Notices. All notices of multicircuit petitions for review shall include:

(i) a copy of each involved petition for review as the petition for review is defined in 28 U.S.C. § 2112(a)(2);

(ii) a schedule giving

(A) the date of the relevant agency order;

(B) the case name of each petition for review involved;

(C) the circuit court of appeals in which each petition for review is pending;

(D) the appellate docket number of each petition for review;

(E) the date of filing by the court of appeals of each petition for review; and

(F) the date of receipt by the agency of each petition for review; and

(iii) proof of service (*see* Rule 25.3).

(c) Scope of Notice. All notices of multicircuit petitions for review shall embrace exclusively petitions for review filed in the courts of appeals within 10 days after issuance of an agency order and received by the affected agency from the petitioners within that 10–day period.

(d) Filing at the Panel. The Clerk of the Panel shall file the notice of multicircuit petitions for review and endorse thereon the date of filing.

(e) Filing With Each Circuit Clerk. The affected agency shall file copies of notices of multicircuit petitions for review with the clerk of each circuit court of appeals in which a petition for review is pending.

[Former Rule 21 adopted May 3, 1993, effective July 1, 1993. Renumbered Rule 25.2 and amended September 1, 1998, effective November 2, 1998. Amended September 8, 2010, effective October 4, 2010. Technical revisions effective July 6, 2011.]

RULE 25.3.   SERVICE OF NOTICES

(a) Proof of Service. Notices of multicircuit petitions for review shall include proof of service on all other parties in the petitions for review included in the notice. Rule 25 of the Federal Rules of Appellate Procedure governs service and proof of service. The proof of service shall state the name, address and email address of each person served and shall indicate the party represented by each and the manner in which service was accomplished on each party. If a party is not represented by counsel, the proof of service shall indicate the name of the party and his or her last known address. The affected party shall submit proof of service for filing with the Clerk of the Panel and shall send copies thereof to each person included within the proof of service.

(b) Service on Clerk of Circuit. The proof of service pertaining to notices of multicircuit petitions for review shall certify the affected party has mailed or delivered copies of the notices to the clerk of each circuit court of appeals in which a petition for review is pending that is included in the notice. The Clerk shall file the notice with the circuit court.

[Former Rule 22 adopted May 3, 1993, effective July 1, 1993. Renumbered Rule 25.3 September 1, 1998, effective November 2, 1998. Amended September 8, 2010, effective October 4, 2010.]

RULE 25.4.   FORM OF NOTICES;
PLACE OF FILING

(a) Unless otherwise provided here, Rule 3.2 governs the form of a notice of multicircuit petitions for review. Each notice shall bear the heading Notice to the United States Judicial Panel on Multidistrict Litigation of Multicircuit Petitions for Review," followed by a brief caption identifying the involved agency, the relevant agency order, and the date of the order.

(b) Rule 3.2(b) and (c) govern the manner of filing a notice of multicircuit petitions for review.

[Former Rule 23 adopted May 3, 1993, effective July 1, 1993. Renumbered Rule 25.4 and amended September 1, 1998, effective November 2, 1998. Amended September 8, 2010, effective October 4, 2010.]

RULE 25.5.   RANDOM SELECTION

(a) Selection Process. Upon filing a notice of multicircuit petitions for review, the Clerk of the Panel shall randomly select a circuit court of appeals from a drum containing an entry for each circuit wherein a constituent petition for review is pending. Multiple petitions for review pending in a single circuit shall be allotted only a single entry in the drum. A designated deputy other than the random selector shall witness the random selection. Thereafter, an order on behalf of the Panel shall be issued, signed by the random selector and the witness,

(i) consolidating the petitions for review in the court of appeals for the circuit that was randomly selected; and

(ii) designating that circuit as the one in which the record is to be filed pursuant to Rules 16 and 17 of the Federal Rules of Appellate Procedure.

(b) Effective Date. A consolidation of petitions for review shall be effective when the Clerk of the Panel enters the consolidation order.

[Former Rule 24 adopted May 3, 1993, effective July 1, 1993. Renumbered Rule 17.1 September 1, 1998, effective November 2, 1998. Former Rule 17.1 redesignated and amended September 8, 2010, effective October 4, 2010.]

RULE 25.6. SERVICE OF PANEL CONSOLIDATION ORDER

(a) The Clerk of the Panel shall serve the Panel's consolidation order on the affected agency through the individual or individuals, as identified in Rule 25.2(a), who submitted the notice of multicircuit petitions for review on behalf of the agency.

(b) That individual or individuals, or anyone else designated by the agency, shall promptly serve the Panel's consolidation order on all other parties in all petitions for review included in the Panel's consolidation order, and shall promptly submit a proof of that service to the Clerk of the Panel. Rule 25.3 governs service.

(c) The Clerk of the Panel shall serve the Panel's consolidation order on the clerks of all circuit courts of appeals that were among the candidates for the Panel's random selection.

[Former Rule 25 adopted May 3, 1993, effective July 1, 1993. Renumbered Rule 25.5 and amended September 1, 1998, effective November 2, 1998. Former Rule 25.5 redesignated and amended September 8, 2010, effective October 4, 2010.]

III. CONVERSION TABLE

New to Old:

New Rule	Previous Rule		New Rule	Previous Rule
1.1	1.1		9.1	1.6
2.1	1.2, 1.3, 1.4, 1.5		10.1	7.6
3.1	5.1		10.2	7.6
3.2	5.1.1, 5.1.2, 7.1		10.3	7.6
3.3	5.1.1, 5.1.2, 7.1		10.4	1.6
4.1	5.2		11.1	16.1
5.1	5.3		25.1	25.1
6.1	7.2		25.2	25.1, 25.2
6.2	7.2		25.3	25.3
6.3	6.2		25.4	25.1, 25.4
7.1	7.4		25.5	17.1
7.2	7.5		25.6	25.5
8.1	7.3			

Old to New:

Previous Rule	New Rule		Previous Rule	New Rule
1.1	1.1		7.1	3.2, 3.3
1.2	2.1		7.2	6.1
1.3	2.1		7.3	8.1
1.4	2.1		7.4	7.1
1.5	2.1		7.5	7.2
1.6	10.4		7.6	10.1
5.1	3.1		16.1	11.1
5.1.1	3.2, 3.3		17.1	25.5
5.1.2	3.2, 3.3		25.1	25.1, 25.2, 25.4
5.1.3	-		25.2	25.2
5.2	4.1		25.3	25.3
5.3	5.1		25.4	25.4
6.2	6.3		25.5	25.6

[October 2010.]

FEDERAL COURTS MISCELLANEOUS FEE SCHEDULES

COURT OF APPEALS FEE SCHEDULE

(Issued in accordance with 28 U.S.C. § 1913)

(Effective November 1, 2011)

The fees included in the Court of Appeals Miscellaneous Fee Schedule are to be charged for services provided by the courts of appeals.

- The United States should not be charged fees under this schedule, except as prescribed in Items 2, 4, and 5 when the information requested is available through remote electronic access.

- Federal agencies or programs that are funded from judiciary appropriations (agencies, organizations, and individuals providing services authorized by the Criminal Justice Act, 18 U.S.C. § 3006A, and bankruptcy administrators) should not be charged any fees under this schedule.

(1) For docketing a case on appeal or review, or docketing any other proceeding, $450.

- Each party filing a notice of appeal pays a separate fee to the district court, but parties filing a joint notice of appeal pay only one fee.

- There is no docketing fee for an application for an interlocutory appeal under 28 U.S.C. § 1292(b) or other petition for permission to appeal under Fed. R. App. P. 5, unless the appeal is allowed.

- There is no docketing fee for a direct bankruptcy appeal or a direct bankruptcy cross appeal, when the fee has been collected by the bankruptcy court in accordance with item 14 of the Bankruptcy Court Miscellaneous Fee Schedule.

(2) For conducting a search of the court of appeals records, $30 per name or item searched. This fee applies to services rendered on behalf of the United States if the information requested is available through remote electronic access.

(3) For certification of any document, $11.

(4) For reproducing any document, $.50 per page. This fee applies to services rendered on behalf of the United States if the document requested is available through remote electronic access.

(5) For reproducing recordings of proceedings, regardless of the medium, $30, including the cost of materials. This fee applies to services rendered on behalf of the United States if the recording is available through remote electronic access.

(6) For reproducing the record in any appeal in which the court of appeals does not require an appendix pursuant to Fed. R. App. P.30(f), $83.

(7) For retrieving a record from a Federal Records Center, National Archives, or other storage location removed from the place of business of the court, $53.

(8) For a check paid into the court which is returned for lack of funds, $53.

(9) For copies of opinions, a fee commensurate with the cost of printing, as fixed by each court.

(10) For copies of the local rules of court, a fee commensurate with the cost of distributing the copies. The court may also distribute copies of the local rules without charge.

(11) For filing:

- Any separate or joint notice of appeal or application for appeal from the Bankruptcy Appellate Panel, $5.

- A notice of the allowance of an appeal from the Bankruptcy Appellate Panel, $5.

(12) For counsel's requested use of the court's videoconferencing equipment in connection with each oral argument, the court may charge and collect a fee of $200 per remote location.

(13) For original admission of an attorney to practice, including a certificate of admission, $176. For a duplicate certificate of admission or certificate of good standing, $18.

DISTRICT COURT MISCELLANEOUS FEE SCHEDULE[1]

(Effective November 1, 2011)

The fees included in the District Court Miscellaneous Fee Schedule are to be charged for services provided by the district courts.

• The United States should not be charged fees under this schedule, with the exception of those specifically prescribed in Items 2, 4 and 5, when the information requested is available through remote electronic access.

• Federal agencies or programs that are funded from judiciary appropriations (agencies, organizations, and individuals providing services authorized by the Criminal Justice Act, 18 U.S.C. § 3006 and bankruptcy administrators) should not be charged any fees under this schedule.

1. For filing any document that is not related to a pending case or proceeding, $46.

2. For conducting a search of the district court records, $30 per name or item searched. This fee applies to services rendered on behalf of the United States if the information requested is available through electronic access.

3. For certification of any document, $11. For exemplification of any document, $18.

4. For reproducing any record or paper, $.50 per page. This fee shall apply to paper copies made from either: (1) original documents; or (2) microfiche or microfilm reproductions of the original records. This fee shall apply to services rendered on behalf of the United States if the record or paper requested is available through electronic access.

5. For reproduction of an audio recording of a court proceeding, $30. This fee applies to services rendered on behalf of the United States, if the recording is available electronically.

6. For each microfiche sheet of film or microfilm jacket copy of any court record, where available, $6.

7. For retrieval of a record from a Federal Records Center, National Archives, or other storage location removed from the place of business of the court, $53.

8. For a check paid into the court which is returned for lack of funds, $53.

9. For an appeal to a district judge from a judgment of conviction by a magistrate judge in a misdemeanor case, $37.

10. For original admission of attorneys to practice, $176 each, including a certificate of admission. For a duplicate certificate of admission or certificate of good standing, $18.

11. The court may charge and collect fees commensurate with the cost of providing copies of the local rules of court. The court may also distribute copies of the local rules without charge.

12. The clerk shall assess a charge for the handling of registry funds deposited with the court, to be assessed from interest earnings and in accordance with the detailed fee schedule issued by the Director of the Administrative Office of the United States Courts.
    For management of registry funds invested through the Court Registry Investment System, a fee at a rate of 2.5 basis points shall be assessed from interest earnings.

13. For filing an action brought under Title III of the Cuban Liberty and Democratic Solidarity (LIBERTAD) Act of 1996, P.L. 104-114, 110 Stat. § 785 (1996), $6,355. (This fee is in addition to the filing fee prescribed in 28 U.S.C. § 1914(a) for instituting any civil action other than a writ of habeas corpus.)

[1] Issued in accordance with 28 U.S.C. § 1914.

BANKRUPTCY COURT MISCELLANEOUS FEE SCHEDULE
(28 U.S.C. § 1930)

(Effective November 1, 2011)

The fees included in the Bankruptcy Court Miscellaneous Fee Schedule are to be charged for services provided by the bankruptcy courts.

- The United States should not be charged fees under this schedule, with the exception of those specifically prescribed in Items 1, 3 and 5 when the information requested is available through remote electronic access.

- Federal agencies or programs that are funded from judiciary appropriations (agencies, organizations, and individuals providing services authorized by the Criminal Justice Act, 18 U.S.C. § 3006A, and bankruptcy administrators) should not be charged any fees under this schedule.

(1) For reproducing any document, $.50 per page. This fee applies to services rendered on behalf of the United States if the document requested is available through electronic access.

(2) For certification of any document, $11.

For exemplification of any document, $21.

(3) For reproduction of an audio recording of a court proceeding, $30. This fee applies to services rendered on behalf of the United States if the recording is available electronically.

(4) For filing an amendment to the debtor's schedules of creditors, lists of creditors, or mailing list, $30, except:

- The bankruptcy judge may, for good cause, waive the charge in any case.
- This fee must not be charged if -
  - the amendment is to change the address of a creditor or an attorney for a creditor listed on the schedules; or
  - the amendment is to add the name and address of an attorney for a creditor listed on the schedules.

(5) For conducting a search of the bankruptcy court records, $30 per name or item searched. This fee applies to services rendered on behalf of the United States if the information requested is available through electronic access.

(6) For filing a complaint, $293, except:

- If the trustee or debtor-in-possession files the complaint, the fee must be paid only by the estate, to the extent there is an estate.
- This fee must not be charged if -
  - the debtor is the plaintiff; or

- a child support creditor or representative files the complaint and submits the form required by § 304(g) of the Bankruptcy Reform Act of 1994.

(7) For filing any document that is not related to a pending case or proceeding, $46.

(8) Administrative fee for filing a case under Title 11 or when a motion to divide a joint case under Title 11 is filed, $46.

(9) For payment to trustees pursuant to 11 U.S.C. § 330(b)(2), a $15 fee applies in the following circumstances:

- For filing a petition under Chapter 7.
- For filing a motion to reopen a Chapter 7 case.
- For filing a motion to divide a joint Chapter 7 case.
- For filing a motion to convert a case to a Chapter 7 case.
- For filing a notice of conversion to a Chapter 7 case.

(10) In addition to any fees imposed under Item 9, above, the following fees must be collected:

- For filing a motion to convert a Chapter 12 case to a Chapter 7 case or a notice of conversion pursuant to 11 U.S.C. § 1208(a), $45.
- For filing a motion to convert a Chapter 13 case to a Chapter 7 case or a notice of conversion pursuant to 11 U.S.C. § 1307(a), $10.

The fee amounts in this item are derived from the fees prescribed in 28 U.S.C. § 1930(a).

If the trustee files the motion to convert, the fee is payable only from the estate that exists prior to conversion.

If the filing fee for the chapter to which the case is requested to be converted is less than the fee paid at the commencement of the case, no refund may be provided.

(11) For filing a motion to reopen, the following fees apply:

- For filing a motion to reopen a Chapter 7 case, $245.
- For filing a motion to reopen a Chapter 9 case, $1000.
- For filing a motion to reopen a Chapter 11 case, $1000.
- For filing a motion to reopen a Chapter 12 case, $200.

- For filing a motion to reopen a Chapter 13 case, $235.
- For filing a motion to reopen a Chapter 15 case, $1000.

The fee amounts in this item are derived from the fees prescribed in 28 U.S.C. § 1930(a).

The reopening fee must be charged when a case has been closed without a discharge being entered.

The court may waive this fee under appropriate circumstances or may defer payment of the fee from trustees pending discovery of additional assets. If payment is deferred, the fee should be waived if no additional assets are discovered.

The reopening fee must not be charged in the following situations:

- to permit a party to file a complaint to obtain a determination under Rule 4007(b); or
- when a debtor files a motion to reopen a case based upon an alleged violation of the terms of the discharge under 11 U.S.C. § 524; or
- when the reopening is to correct an administrative error.

(12) For retrieval of a record from a Federal Records Center, National Archives, or other storage location removed from the place of business of the court, $53.

(13) For a check paid into the court which is returned for lack of funds, $53.

(14) For filing an appeal or cross appeal from a judgment, order, or decree, $293.

This fee is collected in addition to the statutory fee of $5 that is collected under 28 U.S.C. § 1930(c) when a notice of appeal is filed.

Parties filing a joint notice of appeal should pay only one fee.

If a trustee or debtor-in-possession is the appellant, the fee must be paid only by the estate, to the extent there is an estate.

Upon notice from the court of appeals that a direct appeal or direct cross-appeal has been authorized, an additional fee of $157* must be collected.

(15) For filing a case under Chapter 15 of the Bankruptcy Code, $1000.

This fee is derived from and equal to the fee prescribed in 28 U.S.C. § 1930(a)(3) for filing a case commenced under Chapter 11 of Title 11.

(16) The court may charge and collect fees commensurate with the cost of providing copies of the local rules of court. The court may also distribute copies of the local rules without charge.

(17) The clerk shall assess a charge for the handling of registry funds deposited with the court, to be assessed from interest earnings and in accordance with the detailed fee schedule issued by the Director of the Administrative office of the United States Courts.

For management of registry funds invested through the Court Registry Investment System, a fee at a rate of 2.5 basis points shall be assessed from interest earnings.

(18) For a motion filed by the debtor to divide a joint case filed under 11 U.S.C. § 302, the following fees apply:

- For filing a motion to divide a joint Chapter 7 case, $245.
- For filing a motion to divide a joint Chapter 11 case, $1000.
- For filing a motion to divide a joint Chapter 12 case, $200.
- For filing a motion to divide a joint Chapter 13 case, $235.

These fees are derived from and equal to the filing fees prescribed in 28 U.S.C. § 1930(a).

(19) For filing the following motions, $176:

- To terminate, annul, modify or condition the automatic stay;
- To compel abandonment of property of the estate pursuant to Rule 6007(b) of the Federal Rules of Bankruptcy Procedure; or
- To withdraw the reference of a case or proceeding under 28 U.S.C. § 157(d).

This fee must not be collected in the following situations:

- For a motion for relief from the co-debtor stay;
- For a stipulation for court approval of an agreement for relief from a stay; or
- For a motion filed by a child support creditor or its representative, if the form required by § 304(g) of the Bankruptcy Reform Act of 1994 is filed.

* The approved increase in the notice of appeal fee necessitates that the supplemental direct appeal fee be reduced to ensure that the total fee for filing a direct appeal does not exceed the established appellate filing fee of $450.

JUDICIAL PANEL ON MULTIDISTRICT LITIGATION FEE SCHEDULE

(Effective November 1, 2011)

Following are fees to be charged for services provided by the Judicial Panel on Multidistrict Litigation. No fees are to be charged for services rendered on behalf of the United States, with the exception of those specifically prescribed in items 1 and 3. No fees under this schedule shall be charged to federal agencies or programs which are funded from judiciary appropriations, including, but not limited to, agencies, organizations, and individuals providing services authorized by the Criminal Justice Act, 18 U.S.C. § 3006A.

(1) For every search of the records of the court conducted by the clerk of the court or a deputy clerk, $30 per name or item searched. This fee shall apply to services rendered on behalf of the United States if the information requested is available through electronic access.

(2) For certification of any document or paper, whether the certification is made directly on the document or by separate instrument, $11.

(3) For reproducing any record or paper, $.50 per page. This fee shall apply to paper copies made from either: (1) original documents; or (2) microfiche or microfilm reproductions of the original records. This fee shall apply to services rendered on behalf of the United States if the record or paper requested is available through electronic access.

(4) For retrieval of a record from a Federal Records Center, National Archives, or other storage location removed from the place of business of the court, $53.

(5) For a check paid into the Panel which is returned for lack of funds, $53.

ELECTRONIC PUBLIC ACCESS FEE SCHEDULE

(Effective September 7, 2011)

(Issued in Accordance with 28 U.S.C. §§ 1913, 1914, 1926, 1930, 1932)

As directed by Congress, the Judicial Conference has determined that the following fees are necessary to reimburse expenses incurred by the judiciary in providing electronic public access to court records. These fees shall apply to the United States unless otherwise stated. No fees under this schedule shall be charged to federal agencies or programs which are funded from judiciary appropriations, including, but not limited to, agencies, organizations, and individuals providing services authorized by the Criminal Justice Act, 18 U.S.C. § 3006A, and bankruptcy administrator programs.

I. For electronic access to court data via a federal judiciary Internet site: eight cents per page, with the total for any document, docket sheet, or case-specific report not to exceed the fee for thirty pages—provided however that transcripts of federal court proceedings shall not be subject to the thirty-page fee limit. For electronic access to an audio file of a court hearing via a federal judiciary Internet site: $2.40 per audio file. Attorneys of record and parties in a case (including *pro se* litigants) receive one free electronic copy of all documents filed electronically, if receipt is required by law or directed by the filer. No fee is owed under this provision until an account holder accrues charges of more than $10 in a quarterly billing cycle. Consistent with Judicial Conference policy, courts may, upon a showing of cause, exempt indigents, bankruptcy case trustees, individual researchers associated with educational institutions, courts, section 501(c)(3) not-for-profit organizations, court appointed pro bono attorneys, and pro bono ADR neutrals from payment of these fees. Courts must find that parties from the classes of persons or entities listed above seeking exemption have demonstrated that an exemption is necessary in order to avoid unreasonable burdens and to promote public access to information. For individual researchers, courts must also find that the defined research project is intended for academic research, and not for commercial purposes or internet redistribution. Any user granted an exemption agrees not to sell for profit the data obtained as a result. Any transfer of data obtained as the result of a fee exemption is prohibited unless expressly authorized by the court. Exemptions may be granted for a definite period of time and may be revoked at the discretion of the court granting the exemption.

II. For printing copies of any record or document accessed electronically at a public terminal in the courthouse: ten cents per page. This fee shall apply to services rendered on behalf of the United States if the record requested is remotely available through electronic access.

III. For every search of court records conducted by the PACER Service Center, $26 per name or item searched.

IV. For the PACER Service Center to reproduce on paper any record pertaining to a PACER account, if this information is remotely available through electronic access, 50 cents per page.

V. For a check paid to the PACER Service Center which is returned for lack of funds, $45.

JUDICIAL CONFERENCE POLICY NOTES

Courts should not exempt local, state or federal government agencies, members of the media, attorneys or others not members of one of the groups listed above. Exemptions should be granted as the exception, not the rule. A court may not use this exemption language to exempt all users. An exemption applies only to access related to the case or purpose for which it was given. The prohibition on transfer of information received without fee is not intended to bar a quote or reference to information received as a result of a fee exemption in a scholarly or other similar work.

The electronic public access fee applies to electronic court data viewed remotely from the public records of individual cases in the court, including filed documents and the docket sheet. Audio files of court hearings do not include naturalization ceremonies or appellate oral arguments. Electronic court data may be viewed free at public terminals at the courthouse and courts may provide other local court information at no cost. Examples of information that can be provided at no cost include: local rules, court forms, news items, court calendars, opinions, and other information—such as court hours, court location, telephone listings—determined locally to benefit the public and the court.

PUBLISHER'S APPENDIX—FEDERAL RULES OF EVIDENCE COMPARISON CHART

The following table sets forth a side-by-side comparison of the Federal Rules of Evidence in effect until December 1, 2011 and the revised Federal Rules of Evidence that became effective December 1, 2011. The side-by-side format offers a concise tool for counsel's reference in examining the revised text of a given rule.

Text Effective Until 12/1/11	Text Effective 12/1/11
ARTICLE I. GENERAL PROVISIONS **Rule 101. Scope**	**ARTICLE I. GENERAL PROVISIONS** **Rule 101. Scope; Definitions**
These rules govern proceedings in the courts of the United States and before the United States bankruptcy judges and United States magistrate judges, to the extent and with the exceptions stated in rule 1101.	**(a) Scope.** These rules apply to proceedings in United States courts. The specific courts and proceedings to which the rules apply, along with exceptions, are set out in Rule 1101. **(b) Definitions.** In these rules: (1) "civil case" means a civil action or proceeding; (2) "criminal case" includes a criminal proceeding; (3) "public office" includes a public agency; (4) "record" includes a memorandum, report, or data compilation; (5) a "rule prescribed by the Supreme Court" means a rule adopted by the Supreme Court under statutory authority; and (6) a reference to any kind of written material or any other medium includes electronically stored information.

Text Effective Until 12/1/11	Text Effective 12/1/11
Rule 102. Purpose and Construction	**Rule 102. Purpose**
These rules shall be construed to secure fairness in administration, elimination of unjustifiable expense and delay, and promotion of growth and development of the law of evidence to the end that the truth may be ascertained and proceedings justly determined.	These rules should be construed so as to administer every proceeding fairly, eliminate unjustifiable expense and delay, and promote the development of evidence law, to the end of ascertaining the truth and securing a just determination.
Rule 103. Rulings on Evidence	**Rule 103. Rulings on Evidence**
(a) **Effect of erroneous ruling.** Error may not be predicated upon a ruling which admits or excludes evidence unless a substantial right of the party is affected, and	(a) **Preserving a Claim of Error.** A party may claim error in a ruling to admit or exclude evidence only if the error affects a substantial right of the party and:

(1) **Objection.** In case the ruling is one admitting evidence, a timely objection or motion to strike appears of record, stating the specific ground of objection, if the specific ground was not apparent from the context; or	(1) if the ruling admits evidence, a party, on the record:
	
	     (A) timely objects or moves to strike; and
	
	     (B) states the specific ground, unless it was apparent from the context; or

(2) **Offer of proof.** In case the ruling is one excluding evidence, the substance of the evidence was made known to the court by offer or was apparent from the context within which questions were asked.	(2) if the ruling excludes evidence, a party informs the court of its substance by an offer of proof, unless the substance was apparent from the context.
Once the court makes a definitive ruling on the record admitting or excluding evidence, either at or before trial, a party need not renew an objection or offer of proof to preserve a claim of error for appeal.	(b) **Not Needing to Renew an Objection or Offer of Proof.** Once the court rules definitively on the record—either before or at trial—a party need not renew an objection or offer of proof to preserve a claim of error for appeal.
(b) **Record of offer and ruling.** The court may add any other or further statement which shows the	(c) **Court's Statement About the Ruling; Directing an Offer of Proof.** The court may make any

Text Effective Until 12/1/11	Text Effective 12/1/11
character of the evidence, the form in which it was offered, the objection made, and the ruling thereon. It may direct the making of an offer in question and answer form.	statement about the character or form of the evidence, the objection made, and the ruling. The court may direct that an offer of proof be made in question-and-answer form.
(c) **Hearing of jury.** In jury cases, proceedings shall be conducted, to the extent practicable, so as to prevent inadmissible evidence from being suggested to the jury by any means, such as making statements or offers of proof or asking questions in the hearing of the jury.	(d) **Preventing the Jury from Hearing Inadmissible Evidence.** To the extent practicable, the court must conduct a jury trial so that inadmissible evidence is not suggested to the jury by any means.
(d) **Plain error.** Nothing in this rule precludes taking notice of plain errors affecting substantial rights although they were not brought to the attention of the court.	(e) **Taking Notice of Plain Error.** A court may take notice of a plain error affecting a substantial right, even if the claim of error was not properly preserved.
Rule 104. Preliminary Questions	**Rule 104. Preliminary Questions**
(a) **Questions of admissibility generally.** Preliminary questions concerning the qualification of a person to be a witness, the existence of a privilege, or the admissibility of evidence shall be determined by the court, subject to the provisions of subdivision (b). In making its determination it is not bound by the rules of evidence except those with respect to privileges.	(a) **In General.** The court must decide any preliminary question about whether a witness is qualified, a privilege exists, or evidence is admissible. In so deciding, the court is not bound by evidence rules, except those on privilege.
(b) **Relevancy conditioned on fact.** When the relevancy of evidence depends upon the fulfillment of a condition of fact, the court shall admit it upon, or subject to, the introduction of evidence sufficient to support a finding of the fulfillment of the condition.	(b) **Relevance That Depends on a Fact.** When the relevance of evidence depends on whether a fact exists, proof must be introduced sufficient to support a finding that the fact does exist. The court may admit the proposed evidence on the condition that the proof be introduced later.

Text Effective Until 12/1/11	Text Effective 12/1/11
(c) **Hearing of jury.** Hearings on the admissibility of confessions shall in all cases be conducted out of the hearing of the jury. Hearings on other preliminary matters shall be so conducted when the interests of justice require, or when an accused is a witness and so requests.	**(c)** **Conducting a Hearing So That the Jury Cannot Hear It.** The court must conduct any hearing on a preliminary question so that the jury cannot hear it if: **(1)** the hearing involves the admissibility of a confession; **(2)** a defendant in a criminal case is a witness and so requests; or **(3)** justice so requires.
(d) **Testimony by accused.** The accused does not, by testifying upon a preliminary matter, become subject to cross-examination as to other issues in the case.	**(d)** **Cross–Examining a Defendant in a Criminal Case.** By testifying on a preliminary question, a defendant in a criminal case does not become subject to cross-examination on other issues in the case.
(e) **Weight and credibility.** This rule does not limit the right of a party to introduce before the jury evidence relevant to weight or credibility.	**(e)** **Evidence Relevant to Weight and Credibility.** This rule does not limit a party's right to introduce before the jury evidence that is relevant to the weight or credibility of other evidence.
Rule 105. Limited Admissibility	**Rule 105. Limiting Evidence That Is Not Admissible Against Other Parties or for Other Purposes**
When evidence which is admissible as to one party or for one purpose but not admissible as to another party or for another purpose is admitted, the court, upon request, shall restrict the evidence to its proper scope and instruct the jury accordingly.	If the court admits evidence that is admissible against a party or for a purpose—but not against another party or for another purpose—the court, on timely request, must restrict the evidence to its proper scope and instruct the jury accordingly.

Text Effective Until 12/1/11	Text Effective 12/1/11
Rule 106. Remainder of or Related Writings or Recorded Statements	**Rule 106. Remainder of or Related Writings or Recorded Statements**
When a writing or recorded statement or part thereof is introduced by a party, an adverse party may require the introduction at that time of any other part or any other writing or recorded statement which ought in fairness to be considered contemporaneously with it.	If a party introduces all or part of a writing or recorded statement, an adverse party may require the introduction, at that time, of any other part—or any other writing or recorded statement—that in fairness ought to be considered at the same time.

Text Effective Until 12/1/11	Text Effective 12/1/11
ARTICLE II.　JUDICIAL NOTICE **Rule 201.　Judicial Notice of Adjudicative Facts**	**ARTICLE II.　JUDICIAL NOTICE** **Rule 201.　Judicial Notice of Adjudicative Facts**
(a)　**Scope of rule.**　This rule governs only judicial notice of adjudicative facts.	(a)　**Scope.**　This rule governs judicial notice of an adjudicative fact only, not a legislative fact.
(b)　**Kinds of facts.**　A judicially noticed fact must be one not subject to reasonable dispute in that it is either (1) generally known within the territorial jurisdiction of the trial court or (2) capable of accurate and ready determination by resort to sources whose accuracy cannot reasonably be questioned.	(b)　**Kinds of Facts That May Be Judicially Noticed.**　The court may judicially notice a fact that is not subject to reasonable dispute because it: (1)　is generally known within the trial court's territorial jurisdiction; or (2)　can be accurately and readily determined from sources whose accuracy cannot reasonably be questioned.
(c)　**When discretionary.**　A court may take judicial notice, whether requested or not. (d)　**When mandatory.**　A court shall take judicial notice if requested by a party and supplied with the necessary information.	(c)　**Taking Notice.**　The court: (1)　may take judicial notice on its own; or (2)　must take judicial notice if a party requests it and the court is supplied with the necessary information.
(e)　**Opportunity to be heard.**　A party is entitled upon timely request to an opportunity to be heard as to the propriety of taking judicial notice and the tenor of the matter noticed.　In the absence of prior notification, the request may be made after judicial notice has been taken.	(d)　**Timing.**　The court may take judicial notice at any stage of the proceeding.
(f)　**Time of taking notice.**　Judicial notice may be taken at any stage of the proceeding.	(e)　**Opportunity to Be Heard.**　On timely request, a party is entitled to be heard on the propriety of taking judicial notice and the na-

Text Effective Until 12/1/11	Text Effective 12/1/11
	ture of the fact to be noticed. If the court takes judicial notice before notifying a party, the party, on request, is still entitled to be heard.
(g) Instructing jury. In a civil action or proceeding, the court shall instruct the jury to accept as conclusive any fact judicially noticed. In a criminal case, the court shall instruct the jury that it may, but is not required to, accept as conclusive any fact judicially noticed.	**(f) Instructing the Jury.** In a civil case, the court must instruct the jury to accept the noticed fact as conclusive. In a criminal case, the court must instruct the jury that it may or may not accept the noticed fact as conclusive.

Text Effective Until 12/1/11	Text Effective 12/1/11
ARTICLE III.　PRESUMPTIONS IN CIVIL ACTIONS AND PROCEEDINGS	**ARTICLE III.　PRESUMPTIONS IN CIVIL CASES**
Rule 301.　Presumptions in General in Civil Actions and Proceedings	**Rule 301.　Presumptions in Civil Cases Generally**
In all civil actions and proceedings not otherwise provided for by Act of Congress or by these rules, a presumption imposes on the party against whom it is directed the burden of going forward with evidence to rebut or meet the presumption, but does not shift to such party the burden of proof in the sense of the risk of nonpersuasion, which remains throughout the trial upon the party on whom it was originally cast.	In a civil case, unless a federal statute or these rules provide otherwise, the party against whom a presumption is directed has the burden of producing evidence to rebut the presumption. But this rule does not shift the burden of persuasion, which remains on the party who had it originally.
Rule 302.　Applicability of State Law in Civil Actions and Proceedings	**Rule 302.　Applying State Law to Presumptions in Civil Cases**
In civil actions and proceedings, the effect of a presumption respecting a fact which is an element of a claim or defense as to which State law supplies the rule of decision is determined in accordance with State law.	In a civil case, state law governs the effect of a presumption regarding a claim or defense for which state law supplies the rule of decision.

Text Effective Until 12/1/11	Text Effective 12/1/11
ARTICLE IV. RELEVANCY AND ITS LIMITS **Rule 401. Definition of "Relevant Evidence"**	**ARTICLE IV. RELEVANCE AND ITS LIMITS** **Rule 401. Test for Relevant Evidence**
"Relevant evidence" means evidence having any tendency to make the existence of any fact that is of consequence to the determination of the action more probable or less probable than it would be without the evidence.	Evidence is relevant if: **(a)** it has any tendency to make a fact more or less probable than it would be without the evidence; and **(b)** the fact is of consequence in determining the action.
Rule 402. Relevant Evidence Generally Admissible; Irrelevant Evidence Inadmissible	**Rule 402. General Admissibility of Relevant Evidence**
All relevant evidence is admissible, except as otherwise provided by the Constitution of the United States, by Act of Congress, by these rules, or by other rules prescribed by the Supreme Court pursuant to statutory authority. Evidence which is not relevant is not admissible.	Relevant evidence is admissible unless any of the following provides otherwise: • the United States Constitution; • a federal statute; • these rules; or • other rules prescribed by the Supreme Court. Irrelevant evidence is not admissible.
Rule 403. Exclusion of Relevant Evidence on Grounds of Prejudice, Confusion, or Waste of Time	**Rule 403. Excluding Relevant Evidence for Prejudice, Confusion, Waste of Time, or Other Reasons**
Although relevant, evidence may be excluded if its probative value is substantially outweighed by the danger of unfair prejudice, confusion of the issues, or misleading the jury, or by considerations of undue delay, waste of time, or needless presentation of cumulative evidence.	The court may exclude relevant evidence if its probative value is substantially outweighed by a danger of one or more of the following: unfair prejudice, confusing the issues, misleading the jury, undue delay, wasting time, or needlessly presenting cumulative evidence.

Text Effective Until 12/1/11	Text Effective 12/1/11
Rule 404. Character Evidence Not Admissible to Prove Conduct; Exceptions; Other Crimes	**Rule 404. Character Evidence; Crimes or Other Acts**

(a) **Character evidence generally.** Evidence of a person's character or a trait of character is not admissible for the purpose of proving action in conformity therewith on a particular occasion, except:

   (1) **Character of accused.** In a criminal case, evidence of a pertinent trait of character offered by an accused, or by the prosecution to rebut the same, or if evidence of a trait of character of the alleged victim of the crime is offered by an accused and admitted under Rule 404(a)(2), evidence of the same trait of character of the accused offered by the prosecution;

   (2) **Character of alleged victim.** In a criminal case, and subject to the limitations imposed by Rule 412, evidence of a pertinent trait of character of the alleged victim of the crime offered by an accused, or by the prosecution to rebut the same, or evidence of a character trait of peacefulness of the alleged victim offered by the prosecution in a homicide case to rebut evidence that the alleged victim was the first aggressor;

   (3) **Character of witness.** Evidence of the character of a witness, as provided in Rules 607, 608, and 609.

(a) **Character Evidence.**

   (1) *Prohibited Uses.* Evidence of a person's character or character trait is not admissible to prove that on a particular occasion the person acted in accordance with the character or trait.

   (2) *Exceptions for a Defendant or Victim in a Criminal Case.* The following exceptions apply in a criminal case:

      (A) a defendant may offer evidence of the defendant's pertinent trait, and if the evidence is admitted, the prosecutor may offer evidence to rebut it;

      (B) subject to the limitations in Rule 412, a defendant may offer evidence of an alleged victim's pertinent trait, and if the evidence is admitted, the prosecutor may:

         (i) offer evidence to rebut it; and

         (ii) offer evidence of the defendant's same trait; and

      (C) in a homicide case, the prosecutor may offer evidence of the alleged victim's trait of peacefulness to rebut evidence that the victim was the first aggressor.

   (3) **Exceptions for a Witness.** Evidence of a witness's char-

Text Effective Until 12/1/11	Text Effective 12/1/11
	acter may be admitted under Rules 607, 608, and 609.

(b) **Other crimes, wrongs, or acts.** Evidence of other crimes, wrongs, or acts is not admissible to prove the character of a person in order to show action in conformity therewith. It may, however, be admissible for other purposes, such as proof of motive, opportunity, intent, preparation, plan, knowledge, identity, or absence of mistake or accident, provided that upon request by the accused, the prosecution in a criminal case shall provide reasonable notice in advance of trial, or during trial if the court excuses pretrial notice on good cause shown, of the general nature of any such evidence it intends to introduce at trial.	**(b)** **Crimes, Wrongs, or Other Acts.**
	
	 (1) *Prohibited Uses.* Evidence of a crime, wrong, or other act is not admissible to prove a person's character in order to show that on a particular occasion the person acted in accordance with the character.
	
	 (2) *Permitted Uses; Notice in a Criminal Case.* This evidence may be admissible for another purpose, such as proving motive, opportunity, intent, preparation, plan, knowledge, identity, absence of mistake, or lack of accident. On request by a defendant in a criminal case, the prosecutor must:
	
	    (A) provide reasonable notice of the general nature of any such evidence that the prosecutor intends to offer at trial; and
	
	    (B) do so before trial—or during trial if the court, for good cause, excuses lack of pretrial notice.

Rule 405. Methods of Proving Character	**Rule 405. Methods of Proving Character**
(a) **Reputation or opinion.** In all cases in which evidence of character or a trait of character of a person is admissible, proof may be made by testimony as to reputation or by testimony in the form of an opinion. On cross-examination, inquiry is allowable into relevant specific instances of conduct.	**(a)** **By Reputation or Opinion.** When evidence of a person's character or character trait is admissible, it may be proved by testimony about the person's reputation or by testimony in the form of an opinion. On cross-examination of the character witness, the court may allow an inquiry into relevant

Text Effective Until 12/1/11	Text Effective 12/1/11
	specific instances of the person's conduct.
(b) Specific instances of conduct. In cases in which character or a trait of character of a person is an essential element of a charge, claim, or defense, proof may also be made of specific instances of that person's conduct.	**(b) By Specific Instances of Conduct.** When a person's character or character trait is an essential element of a charge, claim, or defense, the character or trait may also be proved by relevant specific instances of the person's conduct.
Rule 406. Habit; Routine Practice	**Rule 406. Habit; Routine Practice**
Evidence of the habit of a person or of the routine practice of an organization, whether corroborated or not and regardless of the presence of eyewitnesses, is relevant to prove that the conduct of the person or organization on a particular occasion was in conformity with the habit or routine practice.	Evidence of a person's habit or an organization's routine practice may be admitted to prove that on a particular occasion the person or organization acted in accordance with the habit or routine practice. The court may admit this evidence regardless of whether it is corroborated or whether there was an eyewitness.
Rule 407. Subsequent Remedial Measures	**Rule 407. Subsequent Remedial Measures**
When, after an injury or harm allegedly caused by an event, measures are taken that, if taken previously, would have made the injury or harm less likely to occur, evidence of the subsequent measures is not admissible to prove negligence, culpable conduct, a defect in a product, a defect in a product's design, or a need for a warning or instruction. This rule does not require the exclusion of evidence of subsequent measures when offered for another purpose, such as proving ownership, control, or feasibility of precautionary measures, if controverted, or impeachment.	When measures are taken that would have made an earlier injury or harm less likely to occur, evidence of the subsequent measures is not admissible to prove: • negligence; • culpable conduct; • a defect in a product or its design; or • a need for a warning or instruction. But the court may admit this evidence for another purpose, such as impeachment or—if disputed—proving ownership, control, or the feasibility of precautionary measures.

Text Effective Until 12/1/11	Text Effective 12/1/11
Rule 408. Compromise and Offers to Compromise	**Rule 408. Compromise Offers and Negotiations**
(a) **Prohibited uses.** Evidence of the following is not admissible on behalf of any party, when offered to prove liability for, invalidity of, or amount of a claim that was disputed as to validity or amount, or to impeach through a prior inconsistent statement or contradiction:	(a) **Prohibited Uses.** Evidence of the following is not admissible—on behalf of any party—either to prove or disprove the validity or amount of a disputed claim or to impeach by a prior inconsistent statement or a contradiction:
(1) furnishing or offering or promising to furnish—or accepting or offering or promising to accept—a valuable consideration in compromising or attempting to compromise the claim; and	(1) furnishing, promising, or offering—or accepting, promising to accept, or offering to accept—a valuable consideration in compromising or attempting to compromise the claim; and
(2) conduct or statements made in compromise negotiations regarding the claim, except when offered in a criminal case and the negotiations related to a claim by a public office or agency in the exercise of regulatory, investigative, or enforcement authority.	(2) conduct or a statement made during compromise negotiations about the claim—except when offered in a criminal case and when the negotiations related to a claim by a public office in the exercise of its regulatory, investigative, or enforcement authority.
(b) **Permitted uses.** This rule does not require exclusion if the evidence is offered for purposes not prohibited by subdivision (a). Examples of permissible purposes include proving a witness's bias or prejudice; negating a contention of undue delay; and proving an effort to obstruct a criminal investigation or prosecution.	(b) **Exceptions.** The court may admit this evidence for another purpose, such as proving a witness's bias or prejudice, negating a contention of undue delay, or proving an effort to obstruct a criminal investigation or prosecution.

Text Effective Until 12/1/11	Text Effective 12/1/11
Rule 409. Payment of Medical and Similar Expenses	**Rule 409. Offers to Pay Medical and Similar Expenses**
Evidence of furnishing or offering or promising to pay medical, hospital, or similar expenses occasioned by an injury is not admissible to prove liability for the injury.	Evidence of furnishing, promising to pay, or offering to pay medical, hospital, or similar expenses resulting from an injury is not admissible to prove liability for the injury.
Rule 410. Inadmissibility of Pleas, Plea Discussions, and Related Statements	**Rule 410. Pleas, Plea Discussions, and Related Statements**
Except as otherwise provided in this rule, evidence of the following is not, in any civil or criminal proceeding, admissible against the defendant who made the plea or was a participant in the plea discussions: (1) a plea of guilty which was later withdrawn; (2) a plea of nolo contendere; (3) any statement made in the course of any proceedings under Rule 11 of the Federal Rules of Criminal Procedure or comparable state procedure regarding either of the foregoing pleas; or (4) any statement made in the course of plea discussions with an attorney for the prosecuting authority which do not result in a plea of guilty or which result in a plea of guilty later withdrawn. However, such a statement is admissible (i) in any proceeding wherein another statement made in the course of the same plea or plea discussions has been introduced and the statement ought in fairness be considered contemporaneously with it, or (ii) in a criminal proceeding for perjury or false statement	**(a) Prohibited Uses.** In a civil or criminal case, evidence of the following is not admissible against the defendant who made the plea or participated in the plea discussions: (1) a guilty plea that was later withdrawn; (2) a nolo contendere plea; (3) a statement made during a proceeding on either of those pleas under Federal Rule of Criminal Procedure 11 or a comparable state procedure; or (4) a statement made during plea discussions with an attorney for the prosecuting authority if the discussions did not result in a guilty plea or they resulted in a later-withdrawn guilty plea. **(b) Exceptions.** The court may admit a statement described in Rule 410(a)(3) or (4): (1) in any proceeding in which another statement made during the same plea or plea discussions has been introduced, if in fairness the statements ought to be con-

Text Effective Until 12/1/11	Text Effective 12/1/11
if the statement was made by the defendant under oath, on the record and in the presence of counsel.	sidered together; or (2) in a criminal proceeding for perjury or false statement, if the defendant made the statement under oath, on the record, and with counsel present.

Rule 411. Liability Insurance	**Rule 411. Liability Insurance**
Evidence that a person was or was not insured against liability is not admissible upon the issue whether the person acted negligently or otherwise wrongfully. This rule does not require the exclusion of evidence of insurance against liability when offered for another purpose, such as proof of agency, ownership, or control, or bias or prejudice of a witness.	Evidence that a person was or was not insured against liability is not admissible to prove whether the person acted negligently or otherwise wrongfully. But the court may admit this evidence for another purpose, such as proving a witness's bias or prejudice or proving agency, ownership, or control.

Rule 412. Sex Offense Cases; Relevance of Alleged Victim's Past Sexual Behavior or Alleged Sexual Predisposition	**Rule 412. Sex–Offense Cases: The Victim's Sexual Behavior or Predisposition**
(a) Evidence Generally Inadmissible. The following evidence is not admissible in any civil or criminal proceeding involving alleged sexual misconduct except as provided in subdivisions (b) and (c): (1) Evidence offered to prove that any alleged victim engaged in other sexual behavior. (2) Evidence offered to prove any alleged victim's sexual predisposition.	**(a) Prohibited Uses.** The following evidence is not admissible in a civil or criminal proceeding involving alleged sexual misconduct: (1) evidence offered to prove that a victim engaged in other sexual behavior; or (2) evidence offered to prove a victim's sexual predisposition.
(b) Exceptions. (1) In a criminal case, the following evidence is admissible, if otherwise admissible under these rules:	**(b) Exceptions.** (1) *Criminal Cases.* The court may admit the following evidence in a criminal case:

Text Effective Until 12/1/11	Text Effective 12/1/11
(A) evidence of specific instances of sexual behavior by the alleged victim offered to prove that a person other than the accused was the source of semen, injury or other physical evidence;	**(A)** evidence of specific instances of a victim's sexual behavior, if offered to prove that someone other than the defendant was the source of semen, injury, or other physical evidence;
(B) evidence of specific instances of sexual behavior by the alleged victim with respect to the person accused of the sexual misconduct offered by the accused to prove consent or by the prosecution; and	**(B)** evidence of specific instances of a victim's sexual behavior with respect to the person accused of the sexual misconduct, if offered by the defendant to prove consent or if offered by the prosecutor; and
(C) evidence the exclusion of which would violate the constitutional rights of the defendant.	**(C)** evidence whose exclusion would violate the defendant's constitutional rights.
(2) In a civil case, evidence offered to prove the sexual behavior or sexual predisposition of any alleged victim is admissible if it is otherwise admissible under these rules and its probative value substantially outweighs the danger of harm to any victim and of unfair prejudice to any party. Evidence of an alleged victim's reputation is admissible only if it has been placed in controversy by the alleged victim.	**(2)** *Civil Cases.* In a civil case, the court may admit evidence offered to prove a victim's sexual behavior or sexual predisposition if its probative value substantially outweighs the danger of harm to any victim and of unfair prejudice to any party. The court may admit evidence of a victim's reputation only if the victim has placed it in controversy.
(c) Procedure To Determine Admissibility.	**(c) Procedure to Determine Admissibility.**
(1) A party intending to offer evidence under subdivision (b) must—	**(1)** *Motion.* If a party intends to offer evidence under Rule 412(b), the party must:
(A) file a written motion at least 14 days before trial specifically describing the evidence	**(A)** file a motion that specifically describes the evidence and states the purpose for which it is

Text Effective Until 12/1/11	Text Effective 12/1/11
and stating the purpose for which it is offered unless the court, for good cause requires a different time for filing or permits filing during trial; and	to be offered;
(B) serve the motion on all parties and notify the alleged victim or, when appropriate, the alleged victim's guardian or representative.	**(B)** do so at least 14 days before trial unless the court, for good cause, sets a different time;
	(C) serve the motion on all parties; and
	(D) notify the victim or, when appropriate, the victim's guardian or representative.
(2) Before admitting evidence under this rule the court must conduct a hearing in camera and afford the victim and parties a right to attend and be heard. The motion, related papers, and the record of the hearing must be sealed and remain under seal unless the court orders otherwise.	**(2)** *Hearing.* Before admitting evidence under this rule, the court must conduct an in camera hearing and give the victim and parties a right to attend and be heard. Unless the court orders otherwise, the motion, related materials, and the record of the hearing must be and remain sealed.
	(d) **Definition of "Victim."** In this rule, "victim" includes an alleged victim.
Rule 413. Evidence of Similar Crimes in Sexual Assault Cases	**Rule 413. Similar Crimes in Sexual–Assault Cases**
(a) In a criminal case in which the defendant is accused of an offense of sexual assault, evidence of the defendant's commission of another offense or offenses of sexual assault is admissible, and may be considered for its bearing on any matter to which it is relevant.	**(a)** **Permitted Uses.** In a criminal case in which a defendant is accused of a sexual assault, the court may admit evidence that the defendant committed any other sexual assault. The evidence may be considered on any matter to which it is relevant.
(b) In a case in which the Government intends to offer evidence under this rule, the attorney for the Government shall disclose the evidence to the defendant, including statements of witnesses or a summary of the substance of any testi-	**(b)** **Disclosure to the Defendant.** If the prosecutor intends to offer this evidence, the prosecutor must disclose it to the defendant, including witnesses' statements or a summary of the expected testimony. The prosecutor must do so at

Text Effective Until 12/1/11	Text Effective 12/1/11
mony that is expected to be offered, at least fifteen days before the scheduled date of trial or at such later time as the court may allow for good cause.	least 15 days before trial or at a later time that the court allows for good cause.
(c) This rule shall not be construed to limit the admission or consideration of evidence under any other rule.	**(c)** **Effect on Other Rules.** This rule does not limit the admission or consideration of evidence under any other rule.
(d) For purposes of this rule and Rule 415, "offense of sexual assault" means a crime under Federal law or the law of a State (as defined in section 513 of title 18, United States Code) that involved—	**(d)** **Definition of "Sexual Assault."** In this rule and Rule 415, "sexual assault" means a crime under federal law or under state law (as "state" is defined in 18 U.S.C. § 513) involving:
(1) any conduct proscribed by chapter 109A of title 18, United States Code;	**(1)** any conduct prohibited by 18 U.S.C. chapter 109A;
(2) contact, without consent, between any part of the defendant's body or an object and the genitals or anus of another person;	**(2)** contact, without consent, between any part of the defendant's body—or an object—and another person's genitals or anus;
(3) contact, without consent, between the genitals or anus of the defendant and any part of another person's body;	**(3)** contact, without consent, between the defendant's genitals or anus and any part of another person's body;
(4) deriving sexual pleasure or gratification from the infliction of death, bodily injury, or physical pain on another person; or	**(4)** deriving sexual pleasure or gratification from inflicting death, bodily injury, or physical pain on another person; or
(5) an attempt or conspiracy to engage in conduct described in paragraphs (1)–(4).	**(5)** an attempt or conspiracy to engage in conduct described in subparagraphs (1)–(4).
Rule 414. Evidence of Similar Crimes in Child Molestation Cases	**Rule 414. Similar Crimes in Child–Molestation Cases**
(a) In a criminal case in which the defendant is accused of an offense of child molestation, evidence of the defendant's commission of another offense or offenses of child	**(a)** **Permitted Uses.** In a criminal case in which a defendant is accused of child molestation, the court may admit evidence that the defendant committed any other

Text Effective Until 12/1/11	Text Effective 12/1/11
molestation is admissible, and may be considered for its bearing on any matter to which it is relevant.	child molestation. The evidence may be considered on any matter to which it is relevant.
(b) In a case in which the Government intends to offer evidence under this rule, the attorney for the Government shall disclose the evidence to the defendant, including statements of witnesses or a summary of the substance of any testimony that is expected to be offered, at least fifteen days before the scheduled date of trial or at such later time as the court may allow for good cause.	**(b) Disclosure to the Defendant.** If the prosecutor intends to offer this evidence, the prosecutor must disclose it to the defendant, including witnesses' statements or a summary of the expected testimony. The prosecutor must do so at least 15 days before trial or at a later time that the court allows for good cause.
(c) This rule shall not be construed to limit the admission or consideration of evidence under any other rule.	**(c) Effect on Other Rules.** This rule does not limit the admission or consideration of evidence under any other rule.
(d) For purposes of this rule and Rule 415, "child" means a person below the age of fourteen, and "offense of child molestation" means a crime under Federal law or the law of a State (as defined in section 513 of title 18, United States Code) that involved—	**(d) Definition of "Child" and "Child Molestation."** In this rule and Rule 415:
(1) any conduct proscribed by chapter 109A of title 18, United States Code, that was committed in relation to a child;	**(1)** "child" means a person below the age of 14; and
(2) any conduct proscribed by chapter 110 of title 18, United States Code;	**(2)** "child molestation" means a crime under federal law or under state law (as "state" is defined in 18 U.S.C. § 513) involving:
(3) contact between any part of the defendant's body or an object and the genitals or anus of a child;	**(A)** any conduct prohibited by 18 U.S.C. chapter 109A and committed with a child;
(4) contact between the genitals or anus of the defendant and any part of the body of a child;	**(B)** any conduct prohibited by 18 U.S.C. chapter 110;
	(C) contact between any part of the defendant's body—or an object—and a child's genitals or anus;

Text Effective Until 12/1/11	Text Effective 12/1/11
(5) deriving sexual pleasure or gratification from the infliction of death, bodily injury, or physical pain on a child; or	**(D)** contact between the defendant's genitals or anus and any part of a child's body;
(6) an attempt or conspiracy to engage in conduct described in paragraphs (1)–(5).	**(E)** deriving sexual pleasure or gratification from inflicting death, bodily injury, or physical pain on a child; or
	(F) an attempt or conspiracy to engage in conduct described in subparagraphs (A)–(E).
Rule 415. Evidence of Similar Acts in Civil Cases Concerning Sexual Assault or Child Molestation	**Rule 415. Similar Acts in Civil Cases Involving Sexual Assault or Child Molestation**
(a) In a civil case in which a claim for damages or other relief is predicated on a party's alleged commission of conduct constituting an offense of sexual assault or child molestation, evidence of that party's commission of another offense or offenses of sexual assault or child molestation is admissible and may be considered as provided in Rule 413 and Rule 414 of these rules.	**(a)** **Permitted Uses.** In a civil case involving a claim for relief based on a party's alleged sexual assault or child molestation, the court may admit evidence that the party committed any other sexual assault or child molestation. The evidence may be considered as provided in Rules 413 and 414.
(b) A party who intends to offer evidence under this Rule shall disclose the evidence to the party against whom it will be offered, including statements of witnesses or a summary of the substance of any testimony that is expected to be offered, at least fifteen days before the scheduled date of trial or at such later time as the court may allow for good cause.	**(b)** **Disclosure to the Opponent.** If a party intends to offer this evidence, the party must disclose it to the party against whom it will be offered, including witnesses' statements or a summary of the expected testimony. The party must do so at least 15 days before trial or at a later time that the court allows for good cause.
(c) This rule shall not be construed to limit the admission or consideration of evidence under any other rule.	**(c)** **Effect on Other Rules.** This rule does not limit the admission or consideration of evidence under any other rule.

Text Effective Until 12/1/11	Text Effective 12/1/11
ARTICLE V. PRIVILEGES **Rule 501. General Rule**	**ARTICLE V. PRIVILEGES** **Rule 501. Privilege in General**
Except as otherwise required by the Constitution of the United States or provided by Act of Congress or in rules prescribed by the Supreme Court pursuant to statutory authority, the privilege of a witness, person, government, State, or political subdivision thereof shall be governed by the principles of the common law as they may be interpreted by the courts of the United States in the light of reason and experience. However, in civil actions and proceedings, with respect to an element of a claim or defense as to which State law supplies the rule of decision, the privilege of a witness, person, government, State, or political subdivision thereof shall be determined in accordance with State law.	The common law—as interpreted by United States courts in the light of reason and experience—governs a claim of privilege unless any of the following provides otherwise: • the United States Constitution; • a federal statute; or • rules prescribed by the Supreme Court. But in a civil case, state law governs privilege regarding a claim or defense for which state law supplies the rule of decision.
Rule 502. Attorney–Client Privilege and Work Product; Limitations on Waiver	**Rule 502. Attorney–Client Privilege and Work Product; Limitations on Waiver**
The following provisions apply, in the circumstances set out, to disclosure of a communication or information covered by the attorney-client privilege or work-product protection.	The following provisions apply, in the circumstances set out, to disclosure of a communication or information covered by the attorney-client privilege or work-product protection.
(a) **Disclosure made in a Federal proceeding or to a Federal office or agency; scope of a waiver.** When the disclosure is made in a Federal proceeding or to a Federal office or agency and waives the attorney-client privilege or work-product protection, the waiver extends to an undisclosed communication or information in a Federal or State proceeding only if: (1) the waiver is intentional; (2) the disclosed and undisclosed	(a) **Disclosure Made in a Federal Proceeding or to a Federal Office or Agency; Scope of a Waiver.** When the disclosure is made in a federal proceeding or to a federal office or agency and waives the attorney-client privilege or work-product protection, the waiver extends to an undisclosed communication or information in a federal or state proceeding only if: (1) the waiver is intentional;

Text Effective Until 12/1/11	Text Effective 12/1/11
communications or information concern the same subject matter; and **(3)** they ought in fairness to be considered together.	**(2)** the disclosed and undisclosed communications or information concern the same subject matter; and **(3)** they ought in fairness to be considered together.
(b) **Inadvertent disclosure.** When made in a Federal proceeding or to a Federal office or agency, the disclosure does not operate as a waiver in a Federal or State proceeding if: **(1)** the disclosure is inadvertent; **(2)** the holder of the privilege or protection took reasonable steps to prevent disclosure; and **(3)** the holder promptly took reasonable steps to rectify the error, including (if applicable) following Federal Rule of Civil Procedure 26(b)(5)(B).	**(b)** **Inadvertent Disclosure.** When made in a federal proceeding or to a federal office or agency, the disclosure does not operate as a waiver in a federal or state proceeding if: **(1)** the disclosure is inadvertent; **(2)** the holder of the privilege or protection took reasonable steps to prevent disclosure; and **(3)** the holder promptly took reasonable steps to rectify the error, including (if applicable) following Federal Rule of Civil Procedure 26(b)(5)(B).
(c) **Disclosure made in a State proceeding.** When the disclosure is made in a State proceeding and is not the subject of a State-court order concerning waiver, the disclosure does not operate as a waiver in a Federal proceeding if the disclosure: **(1)** would not be a waiver under this rule if it had been made in a Federal proceeding; or **(2)** is not a waiver under the law of the State where the disclosure occurred.	**(c)** **Disclosure Made in a State Proceeding.** When the disclosure is made in a state proceeding and is not the subject of a state-court order concerning waiver, the disclosure does not operate as a waiver in a federal proceeding if the disclosure: **(1)** would not be a waiver under this rule if it had been made in a federal proceeding; or **(2)** is not a waiver under the law of the state where the disclosure occurred.
(d) **Controlling effect of a court order.** A Federal court may order that the privilege or protection is not waived by disclosure connected with the litigation pending before the court—in which event the	**(d)** **Controlling Effect of a Court Order.** A federal court may order that the privilege or protection is not waived by disclosure connected with the litigation pending before the court—in which event the

Text Effective Until 12/1/11	Text Effective 12/1/11
disclosure is also not a waiver in any other Federal or State proceeding.	disclosure is also not a waiver in any other federal or state proceeding.
(e) Controlling effect of a party agreement. An agreement on the effect of disclosure in a Federal proceeding is binding only on the parties to the agreement, unless it is incorporated into a court order.	**(e) Controlling Effect of a Party Agreement.** An agreement on the effect of disclosure in a federal proceeding is binding only on the parties to the agreement, unless it is incorporated into a court order.
(f) Controlling effect of this rule. Notwithstanding Rules 101 and 1101, this rule applies to State proceedings and to Federal court-annexed and Federal court-mandated arbitration proceedings, in the circumstances set out in the rule. And notwithstanding Rule 501, this rule applies even if State law provides the rule of decision.	**(f) Controlling Effect of this Rule.** Notwithstanding Rules 101 and 1101, this rule applies to state proceedings and to federal court-annexed and federal court-mandated arbitration proceedings, in the circumstances set out in the rule. And notwithstanding Rule 501, this rule applies even if state law provides the rule of decision.
(g) Definitions. In this rule: (1) "attorney-client privilege" means the protection that applicable law provides for confidential attorney-client communications; and (2) "work-product protection" means the protection that applicable law provides for tangible material (or its intangible equivalent) prepared in anticipation of litigation or for trial.	**(g) Definitions.** In this rule: (1) "attorney-client privilege" means the protection that applicable law provides for confidential attorney-client communications; and (2) "work-product protection" means the protection that applicable law provides for tangible material (or its intangible equivalent) prepared in anticipation of litigation or for trial.

Text Effective Until 12/1/11	Text Effective 12/1/11
ARTICLE VI. WITNESSES **Rule 601. General Rule of Competency**	**ARTICLE VI. WITNESSES** **Rule 601. Competency to Testify in General**
Every person is competent to be a witness except as otherwise provided in these rules. However, in civil actions and proceedings, with respect to an element of a claim or defense as to which State law supplies the rule of decision, the competency of a witness shall be determined in accordance with State law.	Every person is competent to be a witness unless these rules provide otherwise. But in a civil case, state law governs the witness's competency regarding a claim or defense for which state law supplies the rule of decision.
Rule 602. Lack of Personal Knowledge	**Rule 602. Need for Personal Knowledge**
A witness may not testify to a matter unless evidence is introduced sufficient to support a finding that the witness has personal knowledge of the matter. Evidence to prove personal knowledge may, but need not, consist of the witness' own testimony. This rule is subject to the provisions of rule 703, relating to opinion testimony by expert witnesses.	A witness may testify to a matter only if evidence is introduced sufficient to support a finding that the witness has personal knowledge of the matter. Evidence to prove personal knowledge may consist of the witness's own testimony. This rule does not apply to a witness's expert testimony under Rule 703.
Rule 603. Oath or Affirmation	**Rule 603. Oath or Affirmation to Testify Truthfully**
Before testifying, every witness shall be required to declare that the witness will testify truthfully, by oath or affirmation administered in a form calculated to awaken the witness' conscience and impress the witness' mind with the duty to do so.	Before testifying, a witness must give an oath or affirmation to testify truthfully. It must be in a form designed to impress that duty on the witness's conscience.
Rule 604. Interpreters	**Rule 604. Interpreter**
An interpreter is subject to the provisions of these rules relating to qualification as an expert and the administra-	An interpreter must be qualified and must give an oath or affirmation to make a true translation.

Text Effective Until 12/1/11	Text Effective 12/1/11
tion of an oath or affirmation to make a true translation.	

Rule 605. Competency of Judge as Witness	Rule 605. Judge's Competency as a Witness
The judge presiding at the trial may not testify in that trial as a witness. No objection need be made in order to preserve the point.	The presiding judge may not testify as a witness at the trial. A party need not object to preserve the issue.

Rule 606. Competency of Juror as Witness	Rule 606. Juror's Competency as a Witness
(a) **At the trial.** A member of the jury may not testify as a witness before that jury in the trial of the case in which the juror is sitting. If the juror is called so to testify, the opposing party shall be afforded an opportunity to object out of the presence of the jury.	(a) **At the Trial.** A juror may not testify as a witness before the other jurors at the trial. If a juror is called to testify, the court must give a party an opportunity to object outside the jury's presence.
(b) **Inquiry into validity of verdict or indictment.** Upon an inquiry into the validity of a verdict or indictment, a juror may not testify as to any matter or statement occurring during the course of the jury's deliberations or to the effect of anything upon that or any other juror's mind or emotions as influencing the juror to assent to or dissent from the verdict or indictment or concerning the juror's mental processes in connection therewith. But a juror may testify about (1) whether extraneous prejudicial information was improperly brought to the jury's attention, (2) whether any outside influence was improperly brought to bear upon any juror, or (3) whether there was a mistake in entering the verdict onto the verdict form. A juror's affidavit or evidence of any statement by the juror may not be received on a	(b) **During an Inquiry Into the Validity of a Verdict or Indictment.** (1) *Prohibited Testimony or Other Evidence.* During an inquiry into the validity of a verdict or indictment, a juror may not testify about any statement made or incident that occurred during the jury's deliberations; the effect of anything on that juror's or another juror's vote; or any juror's mental processes concerning the verdict or indictment. The court may not receive a juror's affidavit or evidence of a juror's statement on these matters. (2) *Exceptions.* A juror may testify about whether:

Text Effective Until 12/1/11	Text Effective 12/1/11
matter about which the juror would be precluded from testifying.	**(A)** extraneous prejudicial information was improperly brought to the jury's attention; **(B)** an outside influence was improperly brought to bear on any juror; or **(C)** a mistake was made in entering the verdict on the verdict form.
Rule 607. Who May Impeach	**Rule 607. Who May Impeach a Witness**
The credibility of a witness may be attacked by any party, including the party calling the witness.	Any party, including the party that called the witness, may attack the witness's credibility.
Rule 608. Evidence of Character and Conduct of Witness	**Rule 608. A Witness's Character for Truthfulness or Untruthfulness**
(a) Opinion and reputation evidence of character. The credibility of a witness may be attacked or supported by evidence in the form of opinion or reputation, but subject to these limitations: (1) the evidence may refer only to character for truthfulness or untruthfulness, and (2) evidence of truthful character is admissible only after the character of the witness for truthfulness has been attacked by opinion or reputation evidence or otherwise.	**(a) Reputation or Opinion Evidence.** A witness's credibility may be attacked or supported by testimony about the witness's reputation for having a character for truthfulness or untruthfulness, or by testimony in the form of an opinion about that character. But evidence of truthful character is admissible only after the witness's character for truthfulness has been attacked.
(b) Specific instances of conduct. Specific instances of the conduct of a witness, for the purpose of attacking or supporting the witness' character for truthfulness, other than conviction of crime as provided in rule 609, may not be proved by extrinsic evidence. They may, however, in the discretion of the court, if probative of	**(b) Specific Instances of Conduct.** Except for a criminal conviction under Rule 609, extrinsic evidence is not admissible to prove specific instances of a witness's conduct in order to attack or support the witness's character for truthfulness. But the court may, on cross-examination, allow them to be inquired into if they are probative of the

Text Effective Until 12/1/11	Text Effective 12/1/11
truthfulness or untruthfulness, be inquired into on cross-examination of the witness (1) concerning the witness' character for truthfulness or untruthfulness, or (2) concerning the character for truthfulness or untruthfulness of another witness as to which character the witness being cross-examined has testified. The giving of testimony, whether by an accused or by any other witness, does not operate as a waiver of the accused's or the witness' privilege against self-incrimination when examined with respect to matters that relate only to character for truthfulness.	character for truthfulness or untruthfulness of: (1) the witness; or (2) another witness whose character the witness being cross-examined has testified about. By testifying on another matter, a witness does not waive any privilege against self-incrimination for testimony that relates only to the witness's character for truthfulness.
Rule 609. Impeachment by Evidence of Conviction of Crime	**Rule 609. Impeachment by Evidence of a Criminal Conviction**
(a) **General rule.** For the purpose of attacking the character for truthfulness of a witness, (1) evidence that a witness other than an accused has been convicted of a crime shall be admitted, subject to Rule 403, if the crime was punishable by death or imprisonment in excess of one year under the law under which the witness was convicted, and evidence that an accused has been convicted of such a crime shall be admitted if the court determines that the probative value of admitting this evidence outweighs its prejudicial effect to the accused; and (2) evidence that any witness has been convicted of a crime shall be admitted regardless of the punishment, if it readily can be determined that establishing the elements of the crime required proof or admission of an act of dishonesty or false statement by the witness.	(a) **In General.** The following rules apply to attacking a witness's character for truthfulness by evidence of a criminal conviction: (1) for a crime that, in the convicting jurisdiction, was punishable by death or by imprisonment for more than one year, the evidence: (A) must be admitted, subject to Rule 403, in a civil case or in a criminal case in which the witness is not a defendant; and (B) must be admitted in a criminal case in which the witness is a defendant, if the probative value of the evidence outweighs its prejudicial effect to that defendant; and (2) for any crime regardless of the punishment, the evidence must be admitted if the court can readily determine that establishing the elements of

Text Effective Until 12/1/11	Text Effective 12/1/11
	the crime required proving—or the witness's admitting—a dishonest act or false statement.
(b) Time limit. Evidence of a conviction under this rule is not admissible if a period of more than ten years has elapsed since the date of the conviction or of the release of the witness from the confinement imposed for that conviction, whichever is the later date, unless the court determines, in the interests of justice, that the probative value of the conviction supported by specific facts and circumstances substantially outweighs its prejudicial effect. However, evidence of a conviction more than 10 years old as calculated herein, is not admissible unless the proponent gives to the adverse party sufficient advance written notice of intent to use such evidence to provide the adverse party with a fair opportunity to contest the use of such evidence.	**(b) Limit on Using the Evidence After 10 Years.** This subdivision (b) applies if more than 10 years have passed since the witness's conviction or release from confinement for it, whichever is later. Evidence of the conviction is admissible only if: (1) its probative value, supported by specific facts and circumstances, substantially outweighs its prejudicial effect; and (2) the proponent gives an adverse party reasonable written notice of the intent to use it so that the party has a fair opportunity to contest its use.
(c) Effect of pardon, annulment, or certificate of rehabilitation. Evidence of a conviction is not admissible under this rule if (1) the conviction has been the subject of a pardon, annulment, certificate of rehabilitation, or other equivalent procedure based on a finding of the rehabilitation of the person convicted, and that person has not been convicted of a subsequent crime that was punishable by death or imprisonment in excess of one year, or (2) the conviction has been the subject of a pardon, annulment, or other equivalent procedure based on a finding of innocence.	**(c) Effect of a Pardon, Annulment, or Certificate of Rehabilitation.** Evidence of a conviction is not admissible if: (1) the conviction has been the subject of a pardon, annulment, certificate of rehabilitation, or other equivalent procedure based on a finding that the person has been rehabilitated, and the person has not been convicted of a later crime punishable by death or by imprisonment for more than one year; or (2) the conviction has been the subject of a pardon, annulment, or other equivalent procedure based on a finding of innocence.

Text Effective Until 12/1/11	Text Effective 12/1/11
(d) **Juvenile adjudications.** Evidence of juvenile adjudications is generally not admissible under this rule. The court may, however, in a criminal case allow evidence of a juvenile adjudication of a witness other than the accused if conviction of the offense would be admissible to attack the credibility of an adult and the court is satisfied that admission in evidence is necessary for a fair determination of the issue of guilt or innocence.	**(d)** **Juvenile Adjudications.** Evidence of a juvenile adjudication is admissible under this rule only if: **(1)** it is offered in a criminal case; **(2)** the adjudication was of a witness other than the defendant; **(3)** an adult's conviction for that offense would be admissible to attack the adult's credibility; and **(4)** admitting the evidence is necessary to fairly determine guilt or innocence.
(e) **Pendency of appeal.** The pendency of an appeal therefrom does not render evidence of a conviction inadmissible. Evidence of the pendency of an appeal is admissible.	**(e)** **Pendency of an Appeal.** A conviction that satisfies this rule is admissible even if an appeal is pending. Evidence of the pendency is also admissible.
Rule 610. Religious Beliefs or Opinions	**Rule 610. Religious Beliefs or Opinions**
Evidence of the beliefs or opinions of a witness on matters of religion is not admissible for the purpose of showing that by reason of their nature the witness' credibility is impaired or enhanced.	Evidence of a witness's religious beliefs or opinions is not admissible to attack or support the witness's credibility.
Rule 611. Mode and Order of Interrogation and Presentation	**Rule 611. Mode and Order of Examining Witnesses and Presenting Evidence**
(a) **Control by court.** The court shall exercise reasonable control over the mode and order of interrogating witnesses and presenting evidence so as to (1) make the interrogation and presentation effective for the ascertainment of the truth, (2) avoid needless con-	**(a)** **Control by the Court; Purposes.** The court should exercise reasonable control over the mode and order of examining witnesses and presenting evidence so as to: **(1)** make those procedures effective for determining the

Text Effective Until 12/1/11	Text Effective 12/1/11
sumption of time, and (3) protect witnesses from harassment or undue embarrassment.	truth; (2) avoid wasting time; and (3) protect witnesses from harassment or undue embarrassment.
(b) **Scope of cross-examination.** Cross-examination should be limited to the subject matter of the direct examination and matters affecting the credibility of the witness. The court may, in the exercise of discretion, permit inquiry into additional matters as if on direct examination.	(b) **Scope of Cross–Examination.** Cross-examination should not go beyond the subject matter of the direct examination and matters affecting the witness's credibility. The court may allow inquiry into additional matters as if on direct examination.
(c) **Leading questions.** Leading questions should not be used on the direct examination of a witness except as may be necessary to develop the witness' testimony. Ordinarily leading questions should be permitted on cross-examination. When a party calls a hostile witness, an adverse party, or a witness identified with an adverse party, interrogation may be by leading questions.	(c) **Leading Questions.** Leading questions should not be used on direct examination except as necessary to develop the witness's testimony. Ordinarily, the court should allow leading questions: (1) on cross-examination; and (2) when a party calls a hostile witness, an adverse party, or a witness identified with an adverse party.
Rule 612. Writing Used To Refresh Memory	**Rule 612. Writing Used to Refresh a Witness's Memory**
Except as otherwise provided in criminal proceedings by section 3500 of title 18, United States Code, if a witness uses a writing to refresh memory for the purpose of testifying, either— (1) while testifying, or (2) before testifying, if the court in its discretion determines it is necessary in the interests of justice, an adverse party is entitled to have the writing produced at the hearing, to inspect it, to cross-examine the witness	(a) **Scope.** This rule gives an adverse party certain options when a witness uses a writing to refresh memory: (1) while testifying; or (2) before testifying, if the court decides that justice requires the party to have those options. (b) **Adverse Party's Options; Deleting Unrelated Matter.** Unless 18 U.S.C. § 3500 provides otherwise in a criminal case, an adverse par-

Text Effective Until 12/1/11	Text Effective 12/1/11
thereon, and to introduce in evidence those portions which relate to the testimony of the witness. If it is claimed that the writing contains matters not related to the subject matter of the testimony the court shall examine the writing in camera, excise any portions not so related, and order delivery of the remainder to the party entitled thereto. Any portion withheld over objections shall be preserved and made available to the appellate court in the event of an appeal. If a writing is not produced or delivered pursuant to order under this rule, the court shall make any order justice requires, except that in criminal cases when the prosecution elects not to comply, the order shall be one striking the testimony or, if the court in its discretion determines that the interests of justice so require, declaring a mistrial.	ty is entitled to have the writing produced at the hearing, to inspect it, to cross-examine the witness about it, and to introduce in evidence any portion that relates to the witness's testimony. If the producing party claims that the writing includes unrelated matter, the court must examine the writing in camera, delete any unrelated portion, and order that the rest be delivered to the adverse party. Any portion deleted over objection must be preserved for the record. **(c)** **Failure to Produce or Deliver the Writing.** If a writing is not produced or is not delivered as ordered, the court may issue any appropriate order. But if the prosecution does not comply in a criminal case, the court must strike the witness's testimony or—if justice so requires—declare a mistrial.
Rule 613. Prior Statements of Witnesses	**Rule 613. Witness's Prior Statement**
(a) **Examining witness concerning prior statement.** In examining a witness concerning a prior statement made by the witness, whether written or not, the statement need not be shown nor its contents disclosed to the witness at that time, but on request the same shall be shown or disclosed to opposing counsel.	**(a)** **Showing or Disclosing the Statement During Examination.** When examining a witness about the witness's prior statement, a party need not show it or disclose its contents to the witness. But the party must, on request, show it or disclose its contents to an adverse party's attorney.
(b) **Extrinsic evidence of prior inconsistent statement of witness.** Extrinsic evidence of a prior inconsistent statement by a witness is not admissible unless the witness is afforded an opportunity to explain or deny the same and the opposite party is afforded an opportunity to interrogate the witness thereon, or the interests of justice otherwise require. This provision does not apply to admis-	**(b)** **Extrinsic Evidence of a Prior Inconsistent Statement.** Extrinsic evidence of a witness's prior inconsistent statement is admissible only if the witness is given an opportunity to explain or deny the statement and an adverse party is given an opportunity to examine the witness about it, or if justice so requires. This subdivision (b) does not apply to an opposing party's statement under Rule

Text Effective Until 12/1/11	Text Effective 12/1/11
sions of a party-opponent as defined in rule 801(d)(2).	801(d)(2).

Rule 614. Calling and Interrogation of Witnesses by Court	Rule 614. Court's Calling or Examining a Witness
(a) Calling by court. The court may, on its own motion or at the suggestion of a party, call witnesses, and all parties are entitled to cross-examine witnesses thus called.	**(a) Calling.** The court may call a witness on its own or at a party's request. Each party is entitled to cross-examine the witness.
(b) Interrogation by court. The court may interrogate witnesses, whether called by itself or by a party.	**(b) Examining.** The court may examine a witness regardless of who calls the witness.
(c) Objections. Objections to the calling of witnesses by the court or to interrogation by it may be made at the time or at the next available opportunity when the jury is not present.	**(c) Objections.** A party may object to the court's calling or examining a witness either at that time or at the next opportunity when the jury is not present.

Rule 615. Exclusion of Witnesses	Rule 615. Excluding Witnesses
At the request of a party the court shall order witnesses excluded so that they cannot hear the testimony of other witnesses, and it may make the order of its own motion. This rule does not authorize exclusion of (1) a party who is a natural person, or (2) an officer or employee of a party which is not a natural person designated as its representative by its attorney, or (3) a person whose presence is shown by a party to be essential to the presentation of the party's cause, or (4) a person authorized by statute to be present.	At a party's request, the court must order witnesses excluded so that they cannot hear other witnesses' testimony. Or the court may do so on its own. But this rule does not authorize excluding: **(a)** a party who is a natural person; **(b)** an officer or employee of a party that is not a natural person, after being designated as the party's representative by its attorney; **(c)** a person whose presence a party shows to be essential to presenting the party's claim or defense; or **(d)** a person authorized by statute to be present.

Text Effective Until 12/1/11	Text Effective 12/1/11
ARTICLE VII. OPINIONS AND EXPERT TESTIMONY **Rule 701. Opinion Testimony by Lay Witnesses**	**ARTICLE VII. OPINIONS AND EXPERT TESTIMONY** **Rule 701. Opinion Testimony by Lay Witnesses**
If the witness is not testifying as an expert, the witness' testimony in the form of opinions or inferences is limited to those opinions or inferences which are (a) rationally based on the perception of the witness, and (b) helpful to a clear understanding of the witness' testimony or the determination of a fact in issue, and (c) not based on scientific, technical, or other specialized knowledge within the scope of Rule 702.	If a witness is not testifying as an expert, testimony in the form of an opinion is limited to one that is: **(a)** rationally based on the witness's perception; **(b)** helpful to clearly understanding the witness's testimony or to determining a fact in issue; and **(c)** not based on scientific, technical, or other specialized knowledge within the scope of Rule 702.
Rule 702. Testimony by Experts	**Rule 702. Testimony by Expert Witnesses**
If scientific, technical, or other specialized knowledge will assist the trier of fact to understand the evidence or to determine a fact in issue, a witness qualified as an expert by knowledge, skill, experience, training, or education, may testify thereto in the form of an opinion or otherwise, if (1) the testimony is based upon sufficient facts or data, (2) the testimony is the product of reliable principles and methods, and (3) the witness has applied the principles and methods reliably to the facts of the case.	A witness who is qualified as an expert by knowledge, skill, experience, training, or education may testify in the form of an opinion or otherwise if: **(a)** the expert's scientific, technical, or other specialized knowledge will help the trier of fact to understand the evidence or to determine a fact in issue; **(b)** the testimony is based on sufficient facts or data; **(c)** the testimony is the product of reliable principles and methods; and **(d)** the expert has reliably applied the principles and methods to the facts of the case.

Text Effective Until 12/1/11	Text Effective 12/1/11
Rule 703. Bases of Opinion Testimony by Experts	**Rule 703. Bases of an Expert's Opinion Testimony**
The facts or data in the particular case upon which an expert bases an opinion or inference may be those perceived by or made known to the expert at or before the hearing. If of a type reasonably relied upon by experts in the particular field in forming opinions or inferences upon the subject, the facts or data need not be admissible in evidence in order for the opinion or inference to be admitted. Facts or data that are otherwise inadmissible shall not be disclosed to the jury by the proponent of the opinion or inference unless the court determines that their probative value in assisting the jury to evaluate the expert's opinion substantially outweighs their prejudicial effect.	An expert may base an opinion on facts or data in the case that the expert has been made aware of or personally observed. If experts in the particular field would reasonably rely on those kinds of facts or data in forming an opinion on the subject, they need not be admissible for the opinion to be admitted. But if the facts or data would otherwise be inadmissible, the proponent of the opinion may disclose them to the jury only if their probative value in helping the jury evaluate the opinion substantially outweighs their prejudicial effect.
Rule 704. Opinion on Ultimate Issue	**Rule 704. Opinion on an Ultimate Issue**
(a) Except as provided in subdivision (b), testimony in the form of an opinion or inference otherwise admissible is not objectionable because it embraces an ultimate issue to be decided by the trier of fact.	**(a)** **In General—Not Automatically Objectionable.** An opinion is not objectionable just because it embraces an ultimate issue.
(b) No expert witness testifying with respect to the mental state or condition of a defendant in a criminal case may state an opinion or inference as to whether the defendant did or did not have the mental state or condition constituting an element of the crime charged or of a defense thereto. Such ultimate issues are matters for the trier of fact alone.	**(b)** **Exception.** In a criminal case, an expert witness must not state an opinion about whether the defendant did or did not have a mental state or condition that constitutes an element of the crime charged or of a defense. Those matters are for the trier of fact alone.

Text Effective Until 12/1/11	Text Effective 12/1/11
Rule 705. Disclosure of Facts or Data Underlying Expert Opinion	**Rule 705. Disclosing the Facts or Data Underlying an Expert's Opinion**
The expert may testify in terms of opinion or inference and give reasons therefor without first testifying to the underlying facts or data, unless the court requires otherwise. The expert may in any event be required to disclose the underlying facts or data on cross-examination.	Unless the court orders otherwise, an expert may state an opinion—and give the reasons for it—without first testifying to the underlying facts or data. But the expert may be required to disclose those facts or data on cross-examination.
Rule 706. Court Appointed Experts	**Rule 706. Court–Appointed Expert Witnesses**
(a) Appointment. The court may on its own motion or on the motion of any party enter an order to show cause why expert witnesses should not be appointed, and may request the parties to submit nominations. The court may appoint any expert witnesses agreed upon by the parties, and may appoint expert witnesses of its own selection. An expert witness shall not be appointed by the court unless the witness consents to act. A witness so appointed shall be informed of the witness' duties by the court in writing, a copy of which shall be filed with the clerk, or at a conference in which the parties shall have opportunity to participate. A witness so appointed shall advise the parties of the witness' findings, if any; the witness' deposition may be taken by any party; and the witness may be called to testify by the court or any party. The witness shall be subject to cross-examination by each party, including a party calling the witness.	**(a) Appointment Process.** On a party's motion or on its own, the court may order the parties to show cause why expert witnesses should not be appointed and may ask the parties to submit nominations. The court may appoint any expert that the parties agree on and any of its own choosing. But the court may only appoint someone who consents to act. **(b) Expert's Role.** The court must inform the expert of the expert's duties. The court may do so in writing and have a copy filed with the clerk or may do so orally at a conference in which the parties have an opportunity to participate. The expert: **(1)** must advise the parties of any findings the expert makes; **(2)** may be deposed by any party; **(3)** may be called to testify by the court or any party; and **(4)** may be cross-examined by any party, including the party that called the expert.

Text Effective Until 12/1/11	Text Effective 12/1/11
(b) **Compensation.** Expert witnesses so appointed are entitled to reasonable compensation in whatever sum the court may allow. The compensation thus fixed is payable from funds which may be provided by law in criminal cases and civil actions and proceedings involving just compensation under the fifth amendment. In other civil actions and proceedings the compensation shall be paid by the parties in such proportion and at such time as the court directs, and thereafter charged in like manner as other costs.	**(c)** **Compensation.** The expert is entitled to a reasonable compensation, as set by the court. The compensation is payable as follows: **(1)** in a criminal case or in a civil case involving just compensation under the Fifth Amendment, from any funds that are provided by law; and **(2)** in any other civil case, by the parties in the proportion and at the time that the court directs—and the compensation is then charged like other costs.
(c) **Disclosure of appointment.** In the exercise of its discretion, the court may authorize disclosure to the jury of the fact that the court appointed the expert witness.	**(d)** **Disclosing the Appointment to the Jury.** The court may authorize disclosure to the jury that the court appointed the expert.
(d) **Parties' experts of own selection.** Nothing in this rule limits the parties in calling expert witnesses of their own selection.	**(e)** **Parties' Choice of Their Own Experts.** This rule does not limit a party in calling its own experts.

Text Effective Until 12/1/11	Text Effective 12/1/11
ARTICLE VIII. HEARSAY Rule 801. Definitions	**ARTICLE VIII. HEARSAY** Rule 801. Definitions That Apply to This Article; Exclusions From Hearsay
The following definitions apply under this article: (a) **Statement.** A "statement" is (1) an oral or written assertion or (2) nonverbal conduct of a person, if it is intended by the person as an assertion.	(a) **Statement.** "Statement" means a person's oral assertion, written assertion, or nonverbal conduct, if the person intended it as an assertion.
(b) **Declarant.** A "declarant" is a person who makes a statement.	(b) **Declarant.** "Declarant" means the person who made the statement.
(c) **Hearsay.** "Hearsay" is a statement, other than one made by the declarant while testifying at the trial or hearing, offered in evidence to prove the truth of the matter asserted.	(c) **Hearsay.** "Hearsay" means a statement that: (1) the declarant does not make while testifying at the current trial or hearing; and (2) a party offers in evidence to prove the truth of the matter asserted in the statement.
(d) **Statements which are not hearsay.** A statement is not hearsay if— (1) **Prior statement by witness.** The declarant testifies at the trial or hearing and is subject to cross-examination concerning the statement, and the statement is (A) inconsistent with the declarant's testimony, and was given under oath subject to the penalty of perjury at a trial, hearing, or other proceeding, or in a deposition, or (B) consistent with the declarant's testimony and is of-	(d) **Statements That Are Not Hearsay.** A statement that meets the following conditions is not hearsay: (1) *A Declarant–Witness's Prior Statement.* The declarant testifies and is subject to cross-examination about a prior statement, and the statement: (A) is inconsistent with the declarant's testimony and was given under penalty of perjury at a trial, hearing, or other proceeding or in a de-

Text Effective Until 12/1/11	Text Effective 12/1/11
fered to rebut an express or implied charge against the declarant of recent fabrication or improper influence or motive, or (C) one of identification of a person made after perceiving the person; or	position; **(B)** is consistent with the declarant's testimony and is offered to rebut an express or implied charge that the declarant recently fabricated it or acted from a recent improper influence or motive in so testifying; or **(C)** identifies a person as someone the declarant perceived earlier.
(2) Admission by party-opponent. The statement is offered against a party and is (A) the party's own statement, in either an individual or a representative capacity or (B) a statement of which the party has manifested an adoption or belief in its truth, or (C) a statement by a person authorized by the party to make a statement concerning the subject, or (D) a statement by the party's agent or servant concerning a matter within the scope of the agency or employment, made during the existence of the relationship, or (E) a statement by a coconspirator of a party during the course and in furtherance of the conspiracy. The contents of the statement shall be considered but are not alone sufficient to establish the declarant's authority under subdivision (C), the agency or employment relationship and scope thereof under subdivision (D), or the existence of the conspiracy and the participation therein of the declarant and the party against whom the statement is offered under subdivision (E).	**(2) *An Opposing Party's Statement.*** The statement is offered against an opposing party and: **(A)** was made by the party in an individual or representative capacity; **(B)** is one the party manifested that it adopted or believed to be true; **(C)** was made by a person whom the party authorized to make a statement on the subject; **(D)** was made by the party's agent or employee on a matter within the scope of that relationship and while it existed; or **(E)** was made by the party's coconspirator during and in furtherance of the conspiracy. The statement must be considered but does not by itself establish the declarant's authority under (C); the existence or scope of the relationship under (D); or the

Text Effective Until 12/1/11	Text Effective 12/1/11
	existence of the conspiracy or participation in it under (E).
Rule 802. Hearsay Rule	**Rule 802. The Rule Against Hearsay**
Hearsay is not admissible except as provided by these rules or by other rules prescribed by the Supreme Court pursuant to statutory authority or by Act of Congress.	Hearsay is not admissible unless any of the following provides otherwise: • a federal statute; • these rules; or • other rules prescribed by the Supreme Court.
Rule 803. Hearsay Exceptions; Availability of Declarant Immaterial	**Rule 803. Exceptions to the Rule Against Hearsay—Regardless of Whether the Declarant Is Available as a Witness**
The following are not excluded by the hearsay rule, even though the declarant is available as a witness: (1) **Present sense impression.** A statement describing or explaining an event or condition made while the declarant was perceiving the event or condition, or immediately thereafter.	The following are not excluded by the rule against hearsay, regardless of whether the declarant is available as a witness: (1) ***Present Sense Impression.*** A statement describing or explaining an event or condition, made while or immediately after the declarant perceived it.
(2) **Excited utterance.** A statement relating to a startling event or condition made while the declarant was under the stress of excitement caused by the event or condition.	(2) ***Excited Utterance.*** A statement relating to a startling event or condition, made while the declarant was under the stress of excitement that it caused.
(3) **Then existing mental, emotional, or physical condition.** A statement of the declarant's then existing state of mind, emotion, sensation, or physical condition (such as intent, plan, motive, design, mental feeling, pain, and bodily health), but	(3) ***Then–Existing Mental, Emotional, or Physical Condition.*** A statement of the declarant's then-existing state of mind (such as motive, intent, or plan) or emotional, sensory, or physical condition (such as mental feeling, pain, or bodily

Text Effective Until 12/1/11	Text Effective 12/1/11
not including a statement of memory or belief to prove the fact remembered or believed unless it relates to the execution, revocation, identification, or terms of declarant's will.	health), but not including a statement of memory or belief to prove the fact remembered or believed unless it relates to the validity or terms of the declarant's will.
(4) Statements for purposes of medical diagnosis or treatment. Statements made for purposes of medical diagnosis or treatment and describing medical history, or past or present symptoms, pain, or sensations, or the inception or general character of the cause or external source thereof insofar as reasonably pertinent to diagnosis or treatment.	**(4) *Statement Made for Medical Diagnosis or Treatment.*** A statement that: **(A)** is made for—and is reasonably pertinent to—medical diagnosis or treatment; and **(B)** describes medical history; past or present symptoms or sensations; their inception; or their general cause.
(5) Recorded recollection. A memorandum or record concerning a matter about which a witness once had knowledge but now has insufficient recollection to enable the witness to testify fully and accurately, shown to have been made or adopted by the witness when the matter was fresh in the witness' memory and to reflect that knowledge correctly. If admitted, the memorandum or record may be read into evidence but may not itself be received as an exhibit unless offered by an adverse party.	**(5) *Recorded Recollection.*** A record that: **(A)** is on a matter the witness once knew about but now cannot recall well enough to testify fully and accurately; **(B)** was made or adopted by the witness when the matter was fresh in the witness's memory; and **(C)** accurately reflects the witness's knowledge. If admitted, the record may be read into evidence but may be received as an exhibit only if offered by an adverse party.
(6) Records of regularly conducted activity. A memorandum, report, record, or data compilation, in any	**(6) *Records of a Regularly Conducted Activity.*** A record of an act, event, condition, opinion, or diagnosis

Text Effective Until 12/1/11	Text Effective 12/1/11
form, of acts, events, conditions, opinions, or diagnoses, made at or near the time by, or from information transmitted by, a person with knowledge, if kept in the course of a regularly conducted business activity, and if it was the regular practice of that business activity to make the memorandum, report, record or data compilation, all as shown by the testimony of the custodian or other qualified witness, or by certification that complies with Rule 902(11), Rule 902(12), or a statute permitting certification, unless the source of information or the method or circumstances of preparation indicate lack of trustworthiness. The term "business" as used in this paragraph includes business, institution, association, profession, occupation, and calling of every kind, whether or not conducted for profit.	if: **(A)** the record was made at or near the time by—or from information transmitted by—someone with knowledge; **(B)** the record was kept in the course of a regularly conducted activity of a business, organization, occupation, or calling, whether or not for profit; **(C)** making the record was a regular practice of that activity; **(D)** all these conditions are shown by the testimony of the custodian or another qualified witness, or by a certification that complies with Rule 902(11) or (12) or with a statute permitting certification; and **(E)** neither the source of information nor the method or circumstances of preparation indicate a lack of trustworthiness.
(7) Absence of entry in records kept in accordance with the provisions of paragraph (6). Evidence that a matter is not included in the memoranda reports, records, or data compilations, in any form, kept in accordance with the provisions of paragraph (6), to prove the nonoccurrence or nonexistence of the matter, if the matter was of a kind of which a memoran-	**(7)** *Absence of a Record of a Regularly Conducted Activity.* Evidence that a matter is not included in a record described in paragraph (6) if: **(A)** the evidence is admitted to prove that the matter did not occur or exist; **(B)** a record was regularly kept for a matter of

Text Effective Until 12/1/11	Text Effective 12/1/11
dum, report, record, or data compilation was regularly made and preserved, unless the sources of information or other circumstances indicate lack of trustworthiness.	that kind; and **(C)** neither the possible source of the information nor other circumstances indicate a lack of trustworthiness.

(8) **Public records and reports.** Records, reports, statements, or data compilations, in any form, of public offices or agencies, setting forth (A) the activities of the office or agency, or (B) matters observed pursuant to duty imposed by law as to which matters there was a duty to report, excluding, however, in criminal cases matters observed by police officers and other law enforcement personnel, or (C) in civil actions and proceedings and against the Government in criminal cases, factual findings resulting from an investigation made pursuant to authority granted by law, unless the sources of information or other circumstances indicate lack of trustworthiness.	**(8)** *Public Records.* A record or statement of a public office if:
	
	(A) it sets out:
	
	    (i) the office's activities;
	
	    (ii) a matter observed while under a legal duty to report, but not including, in a criminal case, a matter observed by law-enforcement personnel; or
	
	    (iii) in a civil case or against the government in a criminal case, factual findings from a legally authorized investigation; and
	
	(B) neither the source of information nor other circumstances indicate a lack of trustworthiness.

(9) **Records of vital statistics.** Records or data compilations, in any form, of births, fetal deaths, deaths, or marriages, if the report thereof was made to a public office pursuant to requirements of law.	**(9)** *Public Records of Vital Statistics.* A record of a birth, death, or marriage, if reported to a public office in accordance with a legal duty.

Text Effective Until 12/1/11	Text Effective 12/1/11
(10) **Absence of public record or entry.** To prove the absence of a record, report, statement, or data compilation, in any form, or the nonoccurrence or nonexistence of a matter of which a record, report, statement, or data compilation, in any form, was regularly made and preserved by a public office or agency, evidence in the form of a certification in accordance with rule 902, or testimony, that diligent search failed to disclose the record, report, statement, or data compilation, or entry.	**(10)** ***Absence of a Public Record.*** Testimony—or a certification under Rule 902—that a diligent search failed to disclose a public record or statement if the testimony or certification is admitted to prove that: **(A)** the record or statement does not exist; or **(B)** a matter did not occur or exist, if a public office regularly kept a record or statement for a matter of that kind.
(11) **Records of religious organizations.** Statements of births, marriages, divorces, deaths, legitimacy, ancestry, relationship by blood or marriage, or other similar facts of personal or family history, contained in a regularly kept record of a religious organization.	**(11)** ***Records of Religious Organizations Concerning Personal or Family History.*** A statement of birth, legitimacy, ancestry, marriage, divorce, death, relationship by blood or marriage, or similar facts of personal or family history, contained in a regularly kept record of a religious organization.
(12) **Marriage, baptismal, and similar certificates.** Statements of fact contained in a certificate that the maker performed a marriage or other ceremony or administered a sacrament, made by a clergyman, public official, or other person authorized by the rules or practices of a religious organization or by law to perform the act certified, and purporting to have been issued at the time of the act or within a reasonable time thereafter.	**(12)** ***Certificates of Marriage, Baptism, and Similar Ceremonies.*** A statement of fact contained in a certificate: **(A)** made by a person who is authorized by a religious organization or by law to perform the act certified; **(B)** attesting that the person performed a marriage or similar ceremony or administered a sacrament; and

Text Effective Until 12/1/11	Text Effective 12/1/11
	(C) purporting to have been issued at the time of the act or within a reasonable time after it.
(13) **Family records.** Statements of fact concerning personal or family history contained in family Bibles, genealogies, charts, engravings on rings, inscriptions on family portraits, engravings on urns, crypts, or tombstones, or the like.	**(13)** ***Family Records.*** A statement of fact about personal or family history contained in a family record, such as a Bible, genealogy, chart, engraving on a ring, inscription on a portrait, or engraving on an urn or burial marker.
(14) **Records of documents affecting an interest in property.** The record of a document purporting to establish or affect an interest in property, as proof of the content of the original recorded document and its execution and delivery by each person by whom it purports to have been executed, if the record is a record of a public office and an applicable statute authorizes the recording of documents of that kind in that office.	**(14)** ***Records of Documents That Affect an Interest in Property.*** The record of a document that purports to establish or affect an interest in property if: **(A)** the record is admitted to prove the content of the original recorded document, along with its signing and its delivery by each person who purports to have signed it; **(B)** the record is kept in a public office; and **(C)** a statute authorizes recording documents of that kind in that office.
(15) **Statements in documents affecting an interest in property.** A statement contained in a document purporting to establish or affect an interest in property if the matter stated was relevant to the purpose of the document, unless dealings with the property since the document was made have been inconsistent with the	**(15)** ***Statements in Documents That Affect an Interest in Property.*** A statement contained in a document that purports to establish or affect an interest in property if the matter stated was relevant to the document's purpose—unless later dealings with the property are inconsistent with the truth of the statement or the pur-

Text Effective Until 12/1/11	Text Effective 12/1/11
truth of the statement or the purport of the document.	port of the document.
(16) **Statements in ancient documents.** Statements in a document in existence twenty years or more the authenticity of which is established.	(16) ***Statements in Ancient Documents.*** A statement in a document that is at least 20 years old and whose authenticity is established.
(17) **Market reports, commercial publications.** Market quotations, tabulations, lists, directories, or other published compilations, generally used and relied upon by the public or by persons in particular occupations.	(17) ***Market Reports and Similar Commercial Publications.*** Market quotations, lists, directories, or other compilations that are generally relied on by the public or by persons in particular occupations.
(18) **Learned treatises.** To the extent called to the attention of an expert witness upon cross-examination or relied upon by the expert witness in direct examination, statements contained in published treatises, periodicals, or pamphlets on a subject of history, medicine, or other science or art, established as a reliable authority by the testimony or admission of the witness or by other expert testimony or by judicial notice. If admitted, the statements may be read into evidence but may not be received as exhibits.	(18) ***Statements in Learned Treatises, Periodicals, or Pamphlets.*** A statement contained in a treatise, periodical, or pamphlet if: **(A)** the statement is called to the attention of an expert witness on cross-examination or relied on by the expert on direct examination; and **(B)** the publication is established as a reliable authority by the expert's admission or testimony, by another expert's testimony, or by judicial notice. If admitted, the statement may be read into evidence but not received as an exhibit.
(19) **Reputation concerning personal or family history.** Reputation among members of a person's family by	(19) ***Reputation Concerning Personal or Family History.*** A reputation among a person's family by blood,

Text Effective Until 12/1/11	Text Effective 12/1/11
blood, adoption, or marriage, or among a person's associates, or in the community, concerning a person's birth, adoption, marriage, divorce, death, legitimacy, relationship by blood, adoption, or marriage, ancestry, or other similar fact of personal or family history.	adoption, or marriage—or among a person's associates or in the community—concerning the person's birth, adoption, legitimacy, ancestry, marriage, divorce, death, relationship by blood, adoption, or marriage, or similar facts of personal or family history.
(20) **Reputation concerning boundaries or general history.** Reputation in a community, arising before the controversy, as to boundaries of or customs affecting lands in the community, and reputation as to events of general history important to the community or State or nation in which located.	(20) *Reputation Concerning Boundaries or General History.* A reputation in a community—arising before the controversy—concerning boundaries of land in the community or customs that affect the land, or concerning general historical events important to that community, state, or nation.
(21) **Reputation as to character.** Reputation of a person's character among associates or in the community.	(21) *Reputation Concerning Character.* A reputation among a person's associates or in the community concerning the person's character.
(22) **Judgment of previous conviction.** Evidence of a final judgment, entered after a trial or upon a plea of guilty (but not upon a plea of nolo contendere), adjudging a person guilty of a crime punishable by death or imprisonment in excess of one year, to prove any fact essential to sustain the judgment, but not including, when offered by the Government in a criminal prosecution for purposes other than impeachment, judgments against persons other than the accused. The pendency of an appeal may be shown but does not affect admissibility.	(22) *Judgment of a Previous Conviction.* Evidence of a final judgment of conviction if: (A) the judgment was entered after a trial or guilty plea, but not a nolo contendere plea; (B) the conviction was for a crime punishable by death or by imprisonment for more than a year; (C) the evidence is admitted to prove any fact essential to the judgment; and

Text Effective Until 12/1/11	Text Effective 12/1/11
	(D) when offered by the prosecutor in a criminal case for a purpose other than impeachment, the judgment was against the defendant. The pendency of an appeal may be shown but does not affect admissibility.
(23) Judgment as to personal, family, or general history, or boundaries. Judgments as proof of matters of personal, family or general history, or boundaries, essential to the judgment, if the same would be provable by evidence of reputation.	**(23) *Judgments Involving Personal, Family, or General History, or a Boundary.*** A judgment that is admitted to prove a matter of personal, family, or general history, or boundaries, if the matter: **(A)** was essential to the judgment; and **(B)** could be proved by evidence of reputation.
(24) [Other exceptions.] [Transferred to Rule 807.]	**(24) [*Other Exceptions.*]** [Transferred to Rule 807.]
Rule 804. Hearsay Exceptions; Declarant Unavailable	**Rule 804. Exceptions to the Rule Against Hearsay—When the Declarant Is Unavailable as a Witness**
(a) Definition of unavailability. "Unavailability as a witness" includes situations in which the declarant—	**(a) Criteria for Being Unavailable.** A declarant is considered to be unavailable as a witness if the declarant:
(1) is exempted by ruling of the court on the ground of privilege from testifying concerning the subject matter of the declarant's statement; or	**(1)** is exempted from testifying about the subject matter of the declarant's statement because the court rules that a privilege applies;
(2) persists in refusing to testify concerning the subject matter of the declarant's statement despite an order of the	**(2)** refuses to testify about the subject matter despite a court order to do so;

Text Effective Until 12/1/11	Text Effective 12/1/11
court to do so; or	
(3) testifies to a lack of memory of the subject matter of the declarant's statement; or	(3) testifies to not remembering the subject matter;
(4) is unable to be present or to testify at the hearing because of death or then existing physical or mental illness or infirmity; or	(4) cannot be present or testify at the trial or hearing because of death or a then-existing infirmity, physical illness, or mental illness; or
(5) is absent from the hearing and the proponent of a statement has been unable to procure the declarant's attendance (or in the case of a hearsay exception under subdivision (b)(2), (3), or (4), the declarant's attendance or testimony) by process or other reasonable means.	(5) is absent from the trial or hearing and the statement's proponent has not been able, by process or other reasonable means, to procure:
	(A) the declarant's attendance, in the case of a hearsay exception under Rule 804(b)(1) or (6); or
A declarant is not unavailable as a witness if exemption, refusal, claim of lack of memory, inability, or absence is due to the procurement or wrongdoing of the proponent of a statement for the purpose of preventing the witness from attending or testifying.	(B) the declarant's attendance or testimony, in the case of a hearsay exception under Rule 804(b)(2), (3), or (4).
	But this subdivision (a) does not apply if the statement's proponent procured or wrongfully caused the declarant's unavailability as a witness in order to prevent the declarant from attending or testifying.
(b) **Hearsay exceptions.** The following are not excluded by the hearsay rule if the declarant is unavailable as a witness:	(b) **The Exceptions.** The following are not excluded by the rule against hearsay if the declarant is unavailable as a witness:
(1) **Former testimony.** Testimony given as a witness at another hearing of the same or a different proceeding, or in a deposition taken in compliance with law in the course of the same or another proceeding, if the party against whom the testimony is now offered, or, in a civil	(1) *Former Testimony.* Testimony that:
	(A) was given as a witness at a trial, hearing, or lawful deposition, whether given during the current proceeding or a different one; and

Text Effective Until 12/1/11	Text Effective 12/1/11
action or proceeding, a predecessor in interest, had an opportunity and similar motive to develop the testimony by direct, cross, or redirect examination.	**(B)** is now offered against a party who had—or, in a civil case, whose predecessor in interest had—an opportunity and similar motive to develop it by direct, cross-, or redirect examination.
(2) Statement under belief of impending death. In a prosecution for homicide or in a civil action or proceeding, a statement made by a declarant while believing that the declarant's death was imminent, concerning the cause or circumstances of what the declarant believed to be impending death.	**(2) _Statement Under the Belief of Imminent Death._** In a prosecution for homicide or in a civil case, a statement that the declarant, while believing the declarant's death to be imminent, made about its cause or circumstances.
(3) Statement against interest. A statement that:	**(3) _Statement Against Interest._** A statement that:
(A) a reasonable person in the declarant's position would have made only if the person believed it to be true because, when made, it was so contrary to the declarant's proprietary or pecuniary interest or had so great a tendency to invalidate the declarant's claim against someone else or to expose the declarant to civil or criminal liability; and	**(A)** a reasonable person in the declarant's position would have made only if the person believed it to be true because, when made, it was so contrary to the declarant's proprietary or pecuniary interest or had so great a tendency to invalidate the declarant's claim against someone else or to expose the declarant to civil or criminal liability; and
(B) is supported by corroborating circumstances that clearly indicate its trustworthiness, if it is offered in a criminal case as one that tends to expose the declarant to criminal liability.	**(B)** is supported by corroborating circumstances that clearly indicate its trustworthiness, if it is offered in a criminal case as one that tends to expose the declarant to criminal liability.

Text Effective Until 12/1/11	Text Effective 12/1/11
(4) Statement of personal or family history. (A) A statement concerning the declarant's own birth, adoption, marriage, divorce, legitimacy, relationship by blood, adoption, or marriage, ancestry, or other similar fact of personal or family history, even though declarant had no means of acquiring personal knowledge of the matter stated; or (B) a statement concerning the foregoing matters, and death also, of another person, if the declarant was related to the other by blood, adoption, or marriage or was so intimately associated with the other's family as to be likely to have accurate information concerning the matter declared.	**(4) *Statement of Personal or Family History.*** A statement about: **(A)** the declarant's own birth, adoption, legitimacy, ancestry, marriage, divorce, relationship by blood, adoption, or marriage, or similar facts of personal or family history, even though the declarant had no way of acquiring personal knowledge about that fact; or **(B)** another person concerning any of these facts, as well as death, if the declarant was related to the person by blood, adoption, or marriage or was so intimately associated with the person's family that the declarant's information is likely to be accurate.
(5) [Other exceptions.] [Transferred to Rule 807.]	**(5)** [*Other Exceptions.*] [Transferred to Rule 807.]
(6) Forfeiture by wrongdoing. A statement offered against a party that has engaged or acquiesced in wrongdoing that was intended to, and did, procure the unavailability of the declarant as a witness.	**(6) *Statement Offered Against a Party That Wrongfully Caused the Declarant's Unavailability.*** A statement offered against a party that wrongfully caused—or acquiesced in wrongfully causing—the declarant's unavailability as a witness, and did so intending that result.

Text Effective Until 12/1/11	Text Effective 12/1/11
Rule 805. Hearsay Within Hearsay	**Rule 805. Hearsay Within Hearsay**
Hearsay included within hearsay is not excluded under the hearsay rule if each part of the combined statements conforms with an exception to the hearsay rule provided in these rules.	Hearsay within hearsay is not excluded by the rule against hearsay if each part of the combined statements conforms with an exception to the rule.
Rule 806. Attacking and Supporting Credibility of Declarant	**Rule 806. Attacking and Supporting the Declarant's Credibility**
When a hearsay statement, or a statement defined in Rule 801(d)(2)(C), (D), or (E), has been admitted in evidence, the credibility of the declarant may be attacked, and if attacked may be supported, by any evidence which would be admissible for those purposes if declarant had testified as a witness. Evidence of a statement or conduct by the declarant at any time, inconsistent with the declarant's hearsay statement, is not subject to any requirement that the declarant may have been afforded an opportunity to deny or explain. If the party against whom a hearsay statement has been admitted calls the declarant as a witness, the party is entitled to examine the declarant on the statement as if under cross-examination.	When a hearsay statement—or a statement described in Rule 801(d)(2)(C), (D), or (E)—has been admitted in evidence, the declarant's credibility may be attacked, and then supported, by any evidence that would be admissible for those purposes if the declarant had testified as a witness. The court may admit evidence of the declarant's inconsistent statement or conduct, regardless of when it occurred or whether the declarant had an opportunity to explain or deny it. If the party against whom the statement was admitted calls the declarant as a witness, the party may examine the declarant on the statement as if on cross-examination.
Rule 807. Residual Exception	**Rule 807. Residual Exception**
A statement not specifically covered by Rule 803 or 804 but having equivalent circumstantial guarantees of trustworthiness, is not excluded by the hearsay rule, if the court determines that (A) the statement is offered as evidence of a material fact; (B) the statement is more probative on the point for which it is offered than any other evidence which the proponent can procure through reasonable efforts; and (C) the general purposes of these rules and the	**(a) In General.** Under the following circumstances, a hearsay statement is not excluded by the rule against hearsay even if the statement is not specifically covered by a hearsay exception in Rule 803 or 804: **(1)** the statement has equivalent circumstantial guarantees of trustworthiness;

Text Effective Until 12/1/11	Text Effective 12/1/11
interests of justice will best be served by admission of the statement into evidence. However, a statement may not be admitted under this exception unless the proponent of it makes known to the adverse party sufficiently in advance of the trial or hearing to provide the adverse party with a fair opportunity to prepare to meet it, the proponent's intention to offer the statement and the particulars of it, including the name and address of the declarant.	**(2)** it is offered as evidence of a material fact; **(3)** it is more probative on the point for which it is offered than any other evidence that the proponent can obtain through reasonable efforts; and **(4)** admitting it will best serve the purposes of these rules and the interests of justice. **(b)** **Notice.** The statement is admissible only if, before the trial or hearing, the proponent gives an adverse party reasonable notice of the intent to offer the statement and its particulars, including the declarant's name and address, so that the party has a fair opportunity to meet it.

Text Effective Until 12/1/11	Text Effective 12/1/11
ARTICLE IX. AUTHENTICATION AND IDENTIFICATION **Rule 901. Requirement of Authentication or Identification**	**ARTICLE IX. AUTHENTICATION AND IDENTIFICATION** **Rule 901. Authenticating or Identifying Evidence**
(a) **General provision.** The requirement of authentication or identification as a condition precedent to admissibility is satisfied by evidence sufficient to support a finding that the matter in question is what its proponent claims.	(a) **In General.** To satisfy the requirement of authenticating or identifying an item of evidence, the proponent must produce evidence sufficient to support a finding that the item is what the proponent claims it is.
(b) **Illustrations.** By way of illustration only, and not by way of limitation, the following are examples of authentication or identification conforming with the requirements of this rule:	(b) **Examples.** The following are examples only—not a complete list—of evidence that satisfies the requirement:
(1) **Testimony of witness with knowledge.** Testimony that a matter is what it is claimed to be.	(1) ***Testimony of a Witness with Knowledge.*** Testimony that an item is what it is claimed to be.
(2) **Nonexpert opinion on handwriting.** Nonexpert opinion as to the genuineness of handwriting, based upon familiarity not acquired for purposes of the litigation.	(2) ***Nonexpert Opinion About Handwriting.*** A nonexpert's opinion that handwriting is genuine, based on a familiarity with it that was not acquired for the current litigation.
(3) **Comparison by trier or expert witness.** Comparison by the trier of fact or by expert witnesses with specimens which have been authenticated.	(3) ***Comparison by an Expert Witness or the Trier of Fact.*** A comparison with an authenticated specimen by an expert witness or the trier of fact.
(4) **Distinctive characteristics and the like.** Appearance, contents, substance, internal patterns, or other distinctive characteristics, taken in con-	(4) ***Distinctive Characteristics and the Like.*** The appearance, contents, substance, internal patterns, or other distinctive characteristics of the

Text Effective Until 12/1/11	Text Effective 12/1/11
junction with circumstances.	item, taken together with all the circumstances.
(5) **Voice identification.** Identification of a voice, whether heard firsthand or through mechanical or electronic transmission or recording, by opinion based upon hearing the voice at any time under circumstances connecting it with the alleged speaker.	(5) *Opinion About a Voice.* An opinion identifying a person's voice—whether heard firsthand or through mechanical or electronic transmission or recording—based on hearing the voice at any time under circumstances that connect it with the alleged speaker.
(6) **Telephone conversations.** Telephone conversations, by evidence that a call was made to the number assigned at the time by the telephone company to a particular person or business, if (A) in the case of a person, circumstances, including self-identification, show the person answering to be the one called, or (B) in the case of a business, the call was made to a place of business and the conversation related to business reasonably transacted over the telephone.	(6) *Evidence About a Telephone Conversation.* For a telephone conversation, evidence that a call was made to the number assigned at the time to: (A) a particular person, if circumstances, including self-identification, show that the person answering was the one called; or (B) a particular business, if the call was made to a business and the call related to business reasonably transacted over the telephone.
(7) **Public records or reports.** Evidence that a writing authorized by law to be recorded or filed and in fact recorded or filed in a public office, or a purported public record, report, statement, or data compilation, in any form, is from the public office where items of this nature are kept.	(7) *Evidence About Public Records.* Evidence that: (A) a document was recorded or filed in a public office as authorized by law; or (B) a purported public record or statement is from the office where items of this kind are kept.
(8) **Ancient documents or data compilation.** Evidence that	(8) *Evidence About Ancient Documents or Data Compi-*

Text Effective Until 12/1/11	Text Effective 12/1/11
a document or data compilation, in any form, (A) is in such condition as to create no suspicion concerning its authenticity, (B) was in a place where it, if authentic, would likely be, and (C) has been in existence 20 years or more at the time it is offered.	*lations.* For a document or data compilation, evidence that it: (A) is in a condition that creates no suspicion about its authenticity; (B) was in a place where, if authentic, it would likely be; and (C) is at least 20 years old when offered.
(9) **Process or system.** Evidence describing a process or system used to produce a result and showing that the process or system produces an accurate result.	(9) *Evidence About a Process or System.* Evidence describing a process or system and showing that it produces an accurate result.
(10) **Methods provided by statute or rule.** Any method of authentication or identification provided by Act of Congress or by other rules prescribed by the Supreme Court pursuant to statutory authority.	(10) *Methods Provided by a Statute or Rule.* Any method of authentication or identification allowed by a federal statute or a rule prescribed by the Supreme Court.
Rule 902. Self-authentication	**Rule 902. Evidence That Is Self–Authenticating**
Extrinsic evidence of authenticity as a condition precedent to admissibility is not required with respect to the following:	The following items of evidence are self-authenticating; they require no extrinsic evidence of authenticity in order to be admitted:
(1) **Domestic public documents under seal.** A document bearing a seal purporting to be that of the United States, or of any State, district, Commonwealth, territory, or insular possession thereof, or the Panama Canal Zone, or the Trust Territory of the Pacific Islands, or of a political subdivision, department, officer, or agency thereof,	(1) *Domestic Public Documents That Are Sealed and Signed.* A document that bears: (A) a seal purporting to be that of the United States; any state, district, commonwealth, territory, or insular possession of the United States; the former

Text Effective Until 12/1/11	Text Effective 12/1/11
and a signature purporting to be an attestation or execution.	Panama Canal Zone; the Trust Territory of the Pacific Islands; a political subdivision of any of these entities; or a department, agency, or officer of any entity named above; and **(B)** a signature purporting to be an execution or attestation.
(2) Domestic public documents not under seal. A document purporting to bear the signature in the official capacity of an officer or employee of any entity included in paragraph (1) hereof, having no seal, if a public officer having a seal and having official duties in the district or political subdivision of the officer or employee certifies under seal that the signer has the official capacity and that the signature is genuine.	**(2) *Domestic Public Documents That Are Not Sealed but Are Signed and Certified.*** A document that bears no seal if: **(A)** it bears the signature of an officer or employee of an entity named in Rule 902(1)(A); and **(B)** another public officer who has a seal and official duties within that same entity certifies under seal—or its equivalent—that the signer has the official capacity and that the signature is genuine.
(3) Foreign public documents. A document purporting to be executed or attested in an official capacity by a person authorized by the laws of a foreign country to make the execution or attestation, and accompanied by a final certification as to the genuineness of the signature and official position (A) of the executing or attesting person, or (B) of any foreign official whose certificate of genuineness of signature and official position relates to the execution or attestation or is in a chain of certificates of genuineness of signature and	**(3) *Foreign Public Documents.*** A document that purports to be signed or attested by a person who is authorized by a foreign country's law to do so. The document must be accompanied by a final certification that certifies the genuineness of the signature and official position of the signer or attester—or of any foreign official whose certificate of genuineness relates to the signature or attestation or is in a chain of certificates of genuineness relating to the signature or attestation. The certification may be made by a secretary of a

Text Effective Until 12/1/11	Text Effective 12/1/11
official position relating to the execution or attestation. A final certification may be made by a secretary of an embassy or legation, consul general, consul, vice consul, or consular agent of the United States, or a diplomatic or consular official of the foreign country assigned or accredited to the United States. If reasonable opportunity has been given to all parties to investigate the authenticity and accuracy of official documents, the court may, for good cause shown, order that they be treated as presumptively authentic without final certification or permit them to be evidenced by an attested summary with or without final certification.	United States embassy or legation; by a consul general, vice consul, or consular agent of the United States; or by a diplomatic or consular official of the foreign country assigned or accredited to the United States. If all parties have been given a reasonable opportunity to investigate the document's authenticity and accuracy, the court may, for good cause, either: (A) order that it be treated as presumptively authentic without final certification; or (B) allow it to be evidenced by an attested summary with or without final certification.
(4) **Certified copies of public records.** A copy of an official record or report or entry therein, or of a document authorized by law to be recorded or filed and actually recorded or filed in a public office, including data compilations in any form, certified as correct by the custodian or other person authorized to make the certification, by certificate complying with paragraph (1), (2), or (3) of this rule or complying with any Act of Congress or rule prescribed by the Supreme Court pursuant to statutory authority.	(4) ***Certified Copies of Public Records.*** A copy of an official record—or a copy of a document that was recorded or filed in a public office as authorized by law—if the copy is certified as correct by: (A) the custodian or another person authorized to make the certification; or (B) a certificate that complies with Rule 902(1), (2), or (3), a federal statute, or a rule prescribed by the Supreme Court.
(5) **Official publications.** Books, pamphlets, or other publications purporting to be issued by public authority.	(5) ***Official Publications.*** A book, pamphlet, or other publication purporting to be issued by a public authority.
(6) **Newspapers and periodicals.** Printed materials pur-	(6) ***Newspapers and Periodicals.*** Printed material pur-

Text Effective Until 12/1/11	Text Effective 12/1/11
porting to be newspapers or periodicals.	porting to be a newspaper or periodical.
(7) Trade inscriptions and the like. Inscriptions, signs, tags, or labels purporting to have been affixed in the course of business and indicating ownership, control, or origin.	**(7) *Trade Inscriptions and the Like.*** An inscription, sign, tag, or label purporting to have been affixed in the course of business and indicating origin, ownership, or control.
(8) Acknowledged documents. Documents accompanied by a certificate of acknowledgment executed in the manner provided by law by a notary public or other officer authorized by law to take acknowledgments.	**(8) *Acknowledged Documents.*** A document accompanied by a certificate of acknowledgment that is lawfully executed by a notary public or another officer who is authorized to take acknowledgments.
(9) Commercial paper and related documents. Commercial paper, signatures thereon, and documents relating thereto to the extent provided by general commercial law.	**(9) *Commercial Paper and Related Documents.*** Commercial paper, a signature on it, and related documents, to the extent allowed by general commercial law.
(10) Presumptions under Acts of Congress. Any signature, document, or other matter declared by Act of Congress to be presumptively or prima facie genuine or authentic.	**(10) *Presumptions Under a Federal Statute.*** A signature, document, or anything else that a federal statute declares to be presumptively or prima facie genuine or authentic.
(11) Certified domestic records of regularly conducted activity. The original or a duplicate of a domestic record of regularly conducted activity that would be admissible under Rule 803(6) if accompanied by a written declaration of its custodian or other qualified person, in a manner complying with any Act of Congress or rule prescribed by the Supreme Court pursuant to statutory authority,	**(11) *Certified Domestic Records of a Regularly Conducted Activity.*** The original or a copy of a domestic record that meets the requirements of Rule 803(6)(A)–(C), as shown by a certification of the custodian or another qualified person that complies with a federal statute or a rule prescribed by the Supreme Court. Before the trial or hearing, the proponent must give an adverse

Text Effective Until 12/1/11	Text Effective 12/1/11
certifying that the record—	party reasonable written notice of the intent to offer the record—and must make the record and certification available for inspection—so that the party has a fair opportunity to challenge them.
(A) was made at or near the time of the occurrence of the matters set forth by, or from information transmitted by, a person with knowledge of those matters;	
(B) was kept in the course of the regularly conducted activity; and	
(C) was made by the regularly conducted activity as a regular practice.	
A party intending to offer a record into evidence under this paragraph must provide written notice of that intention to all adverse parties, and must make the record and declaration available for inspection sufficiently in advance of their offer into evidence to provide an adverse party with a fair opportunity to challenge them.	
(12) Certified foreign records of regularly conducted activity. In a civil case, the original or a duplicate of a foreign record of regularly conducted activity that would be admissible under Rule 803(6) if accompanied by a written declaration by its custodian or other qualified person certifying that the record—	**(12) *Certified Foreign Records of a Regularly Conducted Activity.*** In a civil case, the original or a copy of a foreign record that meets the requirements of Rule 902(11), modified as follows: the certification, rather than complying with a federal statute or Supreme Court rule, must be signed in a manner that, if falsely made, would subject the maker to a criminal penalty in the country where the certification is signed. The proponent must also meet the notice requirements of Rule 902(11).
(A) was made at or near the time of the occurrence of the matters set forth by, or from information transmitted by, a person with knowledge of those matters;	

Text Effective Until 12/1/11	Text Effective 12/1/11
(B) was kept in the course of the regularly conducted activity; and **(C)** was made by the regularly conducted activity as a regular practice. The declaration must be signed in a manner that, if falsely made, would subject the maker to criminal penalty under the laws of the country where the declaration is signed. A party intending to offer a record into evidence under this paragraph must provide written notice of that intention to all adverse parties, and must make the record and declaration available for inspection sufficiently in advance of their offer into evidence to provide an adverse party with a fair opportunity to challenge them.	
Rule 903. Subscribing Witness' Testimony Unnecessary	**Rule 903. Subscribing Witness's Testimony**
The testimony of a subscribing witness is not necessary to authenticate a writing unless required by the laws of the jurisdiction whose laws govern the validity of the writing.	A subscribing witness's testimony is necessary to authenticate a writing only if required by the law of the jurisdiction that governs its validity.

Text Effective Until 12/1/11	Text Effective 12/1/11
ARTICLE X. CONTENTS OF WRITINGS, RECORDINGS, AND PHOTOGRAPHS **Rule 1001. Definitions**	**ARTICLE X. CONTENTS OF WRITINGS, RECORDINGS, AND PHOTOGRAPHS** **Rule 1001. Definitions That Apply to This Article**
For purposes of this article the following definitions are applicable:	In this article:
(1) **Writings and recordings.** "Writings" and "recordings" consist of letters, words, or numbers, or their equivalent, set down by handwriting, typewriting, printing, photostating, photographing, magnetic impulse, mechanical or electronic recording, or other form of data compilation.	**(a)** A "writing" consists of letters, words, numbers, or their equivalent set down in any form. **(b)** A "recording" consists of letters, words, numbers, or their equivalent recorded in any manner.
(2) **Photographs.** "Photographs" include still photographs, X-ray films, video tapes, and motion pictures.	**(c)** A "photograph" means a photographic image or its equivalent stored in any form.
(3) **Original.** An "original" of a writing or recording is the writing or recording itself or any counterpart intended to have the same effect by a person executing or issuing it. An "original" of a photograph includes the negative or any print therefrom. If data are stored in a computer or similar device, any printout or other output readable by sight, shown to reflect the data accurately, is an "original".	**(d)** An "original" of a writing or recording means the writing or recording itself or any counterpart intended to have the same effect by the person who executed or issued it. For electronically stored information, "original" means any printout—or other output readable by sight—if it accurately reflects the information. An "original" of a photograph includes the negative or a print from it.
(4) **Duplicate.** A "duplicate" is a counterpart produced by the same impression as the original, or from the same matrix, or by means of photography, including enlargements and miniatures, or by mechanical or electronic re-recording, or by chemical reproduction, or by other	**(e)** A "duplicate" means a counterpart produced by a mechanical, photographic, chemical, electronic, or other equivalent process or technique that accurately reproduces the original.

Text Effective Until 12/1/11	Text Effective 12/1/11
equivalent techniques which accurately reproduces the original.	
Rule 1002. Requirement of Original	**Rule 1002. Requirement of the Original**
To prove the content of a writing, recording, or photograph, the original writing, recording, or photograph is required, except as otherwise provided in these rules or by Act of Congress.	An original writing, recording, or photograph is required in order to prove its content unless these rules or a federal statute provides otherwise.
Rule 1003. Admissibility of Duplicates	**Rule 1003. Admissibility of Duplicates**
A duplicate is admissible to the same extent as an original unless (1) a genuine question is raised as to the authenticity of the original or (2) in the circumstances it would be unfair to admit the duplicate in lieu of the original.	A duplicate is admissible to the same extent as the original unless a genuine question is raised about the original's authenticity or the circumstances make it unfair to admit the duplicate.
Rule 1004. Admissibility of Other Evidence of Contents	**Rule 1004. Admissibility of Other Evidence of Content**
The original is not required, and other evidence of the contents of a writing, recording, or photograph is admissible if—	An original is not required and other evidence of the content of a writing, recording, or photograph is admissible if:
(1) **Originals lost or destroyed.** All originals are lost or have been destroyed, unless the proponent lost or destroyed them in bad faith; or	(a) all the originals are lost or destroyed, and not by the proponent acting in bad faith;
(2) **Original not obtainable.** No original can be obtained by any available judicial process or procedure; or	(b) an original cannot be obtained by any available judicial process;
(3) **Original in possession of opponent.** At a time when an original was under the control of the party against whom offered, that party was put on notice, by the	(c) the party against whom the original would be offered had control of the original; was at that time put on notice, by pleadings or otherwise, that the original would be a subject of proof at the trial or

Text Effective Until 12/1/11	Text Effective 12/1/11
pleadings or otherwise, that the contents would be a subject of proof at the hearing, and that party does not produce the original at the hearing; or	hearing; and fails to produce it at the trial or hearing; or
(4) Collateral matters. The writing, recording, or photograph is not closely related to a controlling issue.	**(d)** the writing, recording, or photograph is not closely related to a controlling issue.

Rule 1005. Public Records	**Rule 1005. Copies of Public Records to Prove Content**
The contents of an official record, or of a document authorized to be recorded or filed and actually recorded or filed, including data compilations in any form, if otherwise admissible, may be proved by copy, certified as correct in accordance with rule 902 or testified to be correct by a witness who has compared it with the original. If a copy which complies with the foregoing cannot be obtained by the exercise of reasonable diligence, then other evidence of the contents may be given.	The proponent may use a copy to prove the content of an official record—or of a document that was recorded or filed in a public office as authorized by law—if these conditions are met: the record or document is otherwise admissible; and the copy is certified as correct in accordance with Rule 902(4) or is testified to be correct by a witness who has compared it with the original. If no such copy can be obtained by reasonable diligence, then the proponent may use other evidence to prove the content.

Rule 1006. Summaries	**Rule 1006. Summaries to Prove Content**
The contents of voluminous writings, recordings, or photographs which cannot conveniently be examined in court may be presented in the form of a chart, summary, or calculation. The originals, or duplicates, shall be made available for examination or copying, or both, by other parties at reasonable time and place. The court may order that they be produced in court.	The proponent may use a summary, chart, or calculation to prove the content of voluminous writings, recordings, or photographs that cannot be conveniently examined in court. The proponent must make the originals or duplicates available for examination or copying, or both, by other parties at a reasonable time and place. And the court may order the proponent to produce them in court.

Text Effective Until 12/1/11	Text Effective 12/1/11
Rule 1007. Testimony or Written Admission of Party	**Rule 1007. Testimony or Statement of a Party to Prove Content**
Contents of writings, recordings, or photographs may be proved by the testimony or deposition of the party against whom offered or by that party's written admission, without accounting for the nonproduction of the original.	The proponent may prove the content of a writing, recording, or photograph by the testimony, deposition, or written statement of the party against whom the evidence is offered. The proponent need not account for the original.
Rule 1008. Functions of Court and Jury	**Rule 1008. Functions of the Court and Jury**
When the admissibility of other evidence of contents of writings, recordings, or photographs under these rules depends upon the fulfillment of a condition of fact, the question whether the condition has been fulfilled is ordinarily for the court to determine in accordance with the provisions of rule 104. However, when an issue is raised (a) whether the asserted writing ever existed, or (b) whether another writing, recording, or photograph produced at the trial is the original, or (c) whether other evidence of contents correctly reflects the contents, the issue is for the trier of fact to determine as in the case of other issues of fact.	Ordinarily, the court determines whether the proponent has fulfilled the factual conditions for admitting other evidence of the content of a writing, recording, or photograph under Rule 1004 or 1005. But in a jury trial, the jury determines—in accordance with Rule 104(b)—any issue about whether: **(a)** an asserted writing, recording, or photograph ever existed; **(b)** another one produced at the trial or hearing is the original; or **(c)** other evidence of content accurately reflects the content.

Text Effective Until 12/1/11	Text Effective 12/1/11
ARTICLE XI. MISCELLANEOUS RULES **Rule 1101. Applicability of Rules**	**ARTICLE XI. MISCELLANEOUS RULES** **Rule 1101. Applicability of the Rules**
(a) **Courts and judges.** These rules apply to the United States district courts, the District Court of Guam, the District Court of the Virgin Islands, the District Court for the Northern Mariana Islands, the United States courts of appeals, the United States Claims Court, and to United States bankruptcy judges and United States magistrate judges, in the actions, cases, and proceedings and to the extent hereinafter set forth. The terms "judge" and "court" in these rules include United States bankruptcy judges and United States magistrate judges.	(a) **To Courts and Judges.** These rules apply to proceedings before: • United States district courts; • United States bankruptcy and magistrate judges; • United States courts of appeals; • the United States Court of Federal Claims; and • the district courts of Guam, the Virgin Islands, and the Northern Mariana Islands.
(b) **Proceedings generally.** These rules apply generally to civil actions and proceedings, including admiralty and maritime cases, to criminal cases and proceedings, to contempt proceedings except those in which the court may act summarily, and to proceedings and cases under title 11, United States Code.	(b) **To Cases and Proceedings.** These rules apply in: • civil cases and proceedings, including bankruptcy, admiralty, and maritime cases; • criminal cases and proceedings; and • contempt proceedings, except those in which the court may act summarily.
(c) **Rule of privilege.** The rule with respect to privileges applies at all stages of all actions, cases, and proceedings.	(c) **Rules on Privilege.** The rules on privilege apply to all stages of a case or proceeding.
(d) **Rules inapplicable.** The rules (other than with respect to privileges) do not apply in the following situations: (1) **Preliminary questions of fact.** The determination of questions of fact preliminary	(d) **Exceptions.** These rules—except for those on privilege—do not apply to the following: (1) the court's determination, under Rule 104(a), on a preliminary question of fact gov-

Text Effective Until 12/1/11	Text Effective 12/1/11
to admissibility of evidence when the issue is to be determined by the court under rule 104.	erning admissibility;
(2) Grand jury. Proceedings before grand juries.	(2) grand-jury proceedings; and
(3) Miscellaneous proceedings. Proceedings for extradition or rendition; preliminary examinations in criminal cases; sentencing, or granting or revoking probation; issuance of warrants for arrest, criminal summonses, and search warrants; and proceedings with respect to release on bail or otherwise.	(3) miscellaneous proceedings such as: • extradition or rendition; • issuing an arrest warrant, criminal summons, or search warrant; • a preliminary examination in a criminal case; • sentencing; • granting or revoking probation or supervised release; and • considering whether to release on bail or otherwise.
(e) Rules applicable in part. In the following proceedings these rules apply to the extent that matters of evidence are not provided for in the statutes which govern procedure therein or in other rules prescribed by the Supreme Court pursuant to statutory authority: the trial of misdemeanors and other petty offenses before United States magistrate judges; review of agency actions when the facts are subject to trial de novo under section 706(2)(F) of title 5, United States Code; review of orders of the Secretary of Agriculture under section 2 of the Act entitled "An Act to authorize association of producers of agricultural products" approved February 18, 1922 (7 U.S.C. 292), and under sections 6 and 7(c) of the Perishable Agricultural Commodities Act, 1930 (7 U.S.C. 499f, 499g(c)); naturalization and revocation of naturalization under sections 310–318 of the Immigration and Nationality Act (8 U.S.C. 1421–1429); prize pro-	**(e) Other Statutes and Rules.** A federal statute or a rule prescribed by the Supreme Court may provide for admitting or excluding evidence independently from these rules.

Text Effective Until 12/1/11	Text Effective 12/1/11
ceedings in admiralty under sections 7651–7681 of title 10, United States Code; review of orders of the Secretary of the Interior under section 2 of the Act entitled "An Act authorizing associations of producers of aquatic products" approved June 25, 1934 (15 U.S.C. 522); review of orders of petroleum control boards under section 5 of the Act entitled "An Act to regulate interstate and foreign commerce in petroleum and its products by prohibiting the shipment in such commerce of petroleum and its products produced in violation of State law, and for other purposes", approved February 22, 1935 (15 U.S.C. 715d); actions for fines, penalties, or forfeitures under part V of title IV of the Tariff Act of 1930 (19 U.S.C. 1581–1624), or under the Anti–Smuggling Act (19 U.S.C. 1701–1711); criminal libel for condemnation, exclusion of imports, or other proceedings under the Federal Food, Drug, and Cosmetic Act (21 U.S.C. 301–392); disputes between seamen under sections 4079, 4080, and 4081 of the Revised Statutes (22 U.S.C. 256–258); habeas corpus under sections 2241–2254 of title 28, United States Code; motions to vacate, set aside or correct sentence under section 2255 of title 28, United States Code; actions for penalties for refusal to transport destitute seamen under section 4578 of the Revised Statutes (46 U.S.C. 679); actions against the United States under the Act entitled "An Act authorizing suits against the United States in admiralty for damage caused by and salvage service rendered to public vessels belonging to the United States, and for other purposes", approved March 3, 1925 (46 U.S.C. 781–790), as implemented by section 7730 of title 10, United States Code.	

Text Effective Until 12/1/11	Text Effective 12/1/11
Rule 1102. Amendments	**Rule 1102. Amendments**
Amendments to the Federal Rules of Evidence may be made as provided in section 2072 of title 28 of the United States Code.	These rules may be amended as provided in 28 U.S.C. § 2072.
Rule 1103. Title	**Rule 1103. Title**
These rules may be known and cited as the Federal Rules of Evidence.	These rules may be cited as the Federal Rules of Evidence.

†